Arms and Armour

review

The Dollar conversions have been made at the rate of exchange prevailing at the date of the sale.

SBN 0-86248-003-5

Glenmayne, Galashiels, Scotland.

ISBN 0-8256-9687-9
Order Number 450022
Quick Fox,
33 West 60th Street,
New York, N.Y. 10023.

Printed by Apollo Press, Worthing, Sussex, England.
Bound by R. J. Acford, Chichester, Sussex, England.

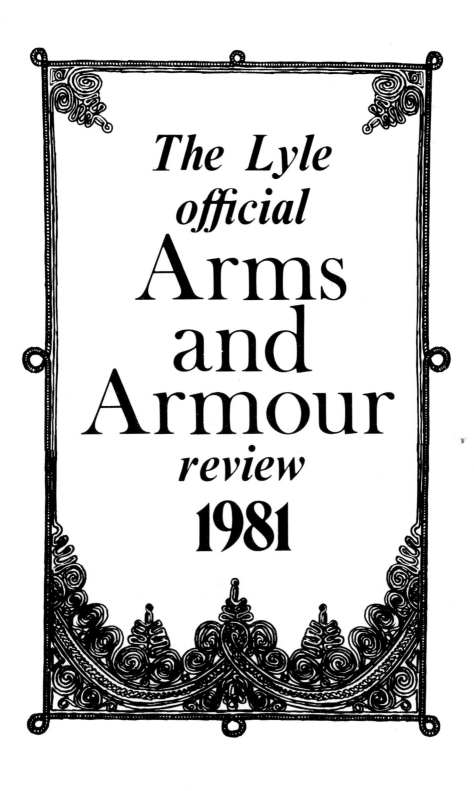

The Lyle official
Arms and Armour
review
1981

Acknowledgements

EDITED BY TONY CURTIS
COMPILED BY MARGARET ANDERSON

JANICE MONCRIEFF
SUSAN LOWER
BRIAN HOLTON
NICOLA PARK
CARMEN MILIVOYEVICH
ELAINE HARLAND
MAY MUTCH
ROBERT SUTHERLAND

All photographs and text throughout this book relate to recent sales at the Lewes Auction Room of Messrs. WALLIS & WALLIS to whom the publishers are deeply indebted.

INTRODUCTION

As the interest in all things antique widens steadily from year to year, the tendency towards specialisation becomes ever more marked. This is a tendency which has been fostered by a wealth of beautifully produced highly informative books published at very reasonable prices.

No longer has the would-be specialist to spend long periods tracking down obscure out-of-print volumes in search of information fundamental to the pursuit of his interest; a few pounds wisely spent will equip him with works of considerable scholarship on any chosen subject.

But scholarship is rarely at ease in the market place, and there are relatively few publications available whose sole, or even primary, aim is to accurately indicate the current values of the objects they describe. This is a task not to be undertaken lightly, for it is one that requires encyclopedic knowledge coupled with a ready understanding of market trends. In achieving this rare blend, the publishers are deeply indebted to Messrs. Wallis and Wallis of Lewes, possibly the world's leading specialist auctioneers of all things military.

This, the Lyle Official Arms & Armour Review 1981, is the sixth edition of an annual review of current values in a field which is gaining a steadily widening circle of devotees.

TONY CURTIS

Contents

Arms and Armour *review*

'Going great guns' would be a good way to describe the arms and armour market this year.

The phrase has a double meaning because not only has the arms and armour collectors' world received very little setback from the current international recession but also 'great guns' are coming into their own as collectors' items.

Wallis and Wallis, the world famous saleroom for arms and armour in Lewes in Sussex, have discovered an excellent way of selling cannon which up till now have been something of a very heavy drag on the market.

Mr. Butler of Wallis and Wallis hit on the notion of selling them 'in situ' and he catalogues items but leaves them where they have been sitting for perhaps a century or more. They are auctioned in his saleroom in Sussex and the buyer collects from the place they are with the original owners. This method has been very successful because not only does it remove the sellers' need to encur heavy freight charges but it also removes the trouble of having to return them if they are unsold.

Failing to sell is not however a problem that cannons have come up against and Mr. Butler is amazed at the very keen interest they arouse whenever one comes up for sale. He has been selling cannons to stately homes and tourist sites and can find a new home for every 32 pounder or 24 pounder in either iron or bronze that comes his way. Most sought after are cannons dating from the Georgian period and they make prices of around £1,000. The most enthusiastic buyers of cannons recently have been the Australian government who have recently built and equipped a tourist complex out of an old gunpowder factory. They have furnished it with five cannons bought from Wallis and Wallis – all at prices of around £1,000 each.

The most interesting cannon to come Mr. Butler's way in the past year was a fine bronze one that was brought up from the sea off the South of Ireland. It was sent by the finder to Sussex and authenticated by specialists from the Tower of London as dating from between 1540 and 1550, in the reign of Henry VIII. They think it might have been on one of the ships that sank during the time of the Spanish Armada in the reign of Henry's daughter Elizabeth. Mr. Butler included the cannon in a special sale held in the Directors' Club in London in September and it shot its way well past the £1,000 estimate. Cannons are the collectibles of the future – if you have room for them – and Mr. Butler thinks that anyone with a cannon in the garden has something very valuable, worth far more than its scrap price.

Another interesting development in the past year is the emergence on the collecting scene of autographs and documents in a much more significant way than they have been in the past.

This is perhaps due to the simple passage of time because many of the items now appearing are World War II documents which would have been collected by a generation of people who are now beginning to die off and their collections are being disposed of by their descendants. These World War II papers have made a big impact at Wallis and Wallis and all have exceeded their estimates in a big way. Two fairly large collections have been sold during the past year and as one would expect any papers with the signature of Adolf Hitler have fetched high prices. Two typed promotion orders signed by him and dated 1945 made £300.

Other Nazi items included a birthday card written in holograph by Reinhard Heydrich to a colonel friend which made £270. Another typed letter from the prisoner of Spandau, Rudolf Hess, dated 1937 before his fortunes took their downward turn, made £40.

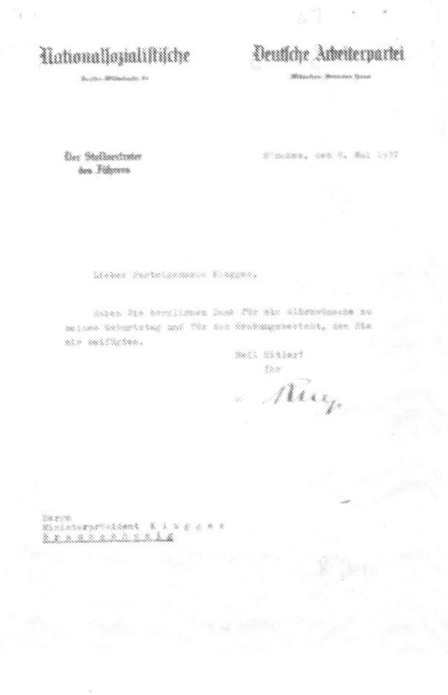
Nationalsozialistische Deutsche Arbeiterpartei

Der Stellvertreter des Führers

Typed letter signed by Rudolf Hess, £40.

A very interesting Nazi visitors' book from the Panzertruppen-Schule Wunsdorf made a very reputable £510. It contained hundreds of ink signatures and watercolour illustrations and also had an interesting historical footnote because the fly leaf was inscribed with 'This book was found in the Officers' Mess, Belsen, April 1945.'

Visitor's Book from the Panzertruppen-Schule Wunsdorf, £510.

To fetch prices like these however, documents have either to have very good historical associations or to be written by hand by a famous character from the past. Historical associations are all important.

The same holds good for pictures which every now and again make their appearances at arms and armour sales. Portraits of military men are much sought after if they depict a well known sitter. For example a pair of oil portraits of Lord Cochrane in full dress Infantry uniform and dating from around 1850, made £260 this year at Lewes.

Pair of oil paintings of Lord Cochrane, £260.

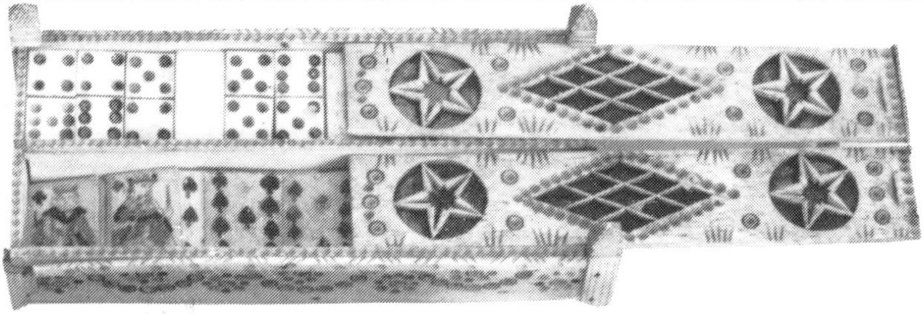

French Napoleonic prisoner-of-war domino set, £175

Other interesting relics of long past conflicts which made a strong impact on the market this year were relics from French prisoners of war who were brought to this country to be interned during the Napoleonic Wars. These men were very often treated in a cruel and callous manner and hundreds of them died of starvation and neglect. To augment their money and food supplies some of the prisoners spent their time making toys and gewgaws to sell to the people who looked after their camps or who lived nearby. Since they had no raw materials to hand and were unable to buy them they had to use their ingenuity and made things from old bits of wood, straw and even meat bones left over from their meals. The articles they made are so charming that many of them have survived as family treasures to the present day.

Several British museums have examples of ships made by French prisoners from bits of bone and these can be extremely valuable. Other things they made include toys – many of them moveable – like the two figures of women spinning which were sold for £120 this year at Wallis and Wallis. They also made domino and cribbage sets, beautifully carved and decorated. Prices for good examples of these range from £75 to over £200.

The work put into these little things records the long hours of hungry idleness spent by the prisoners who also turned out religious shrines, ships in bottles, models of buildings, mirror frames and boxes decorated with straw marquetry. A lovely French marquetry wooden box with sliding drawers and a straw marquetry town scene on its underlid made £50 this year.

The Lewes saleroom was lucky enough to secure the collection of an owner of a considerable number of French prisoner of war items but he did not want his collection sold all at once so it was fed through several sales. The appearance of these pieces and the interesting prices they made sparked off the interest of other collectors and what was previously a trickle of French things has since grown to a steady stream of them coming up for sale – all at good prices.

France figured too when another interesting thing came up for sale this year. It was a Napoleonic sword inscribed with the name of an eminent politician during the revolutionary period. Though the sword was not in mint condition, the associations with the name were sufficiently strong for it to arouse lively interest among French collectors who pushed the price up to an unprecedented £7,000. As in the Napoleonic Wars however, the French were not successful and the sword went to a Belgian collector.

Swords are still very popular with collectors and among the British military swords anything from the Napoleonic time fetches very good money. A good sword however is usually so highly prized by its owner that it only comes on the market rarely when the owner is forced to sell. Among interesting swords that came up for auction this year were an English 18th century silver hilted hunting sword, hallmarked London 1735, which made £575.

There were also several Nazi officers' swords which made prices ranging from £60 to over £200. A fine Scottish Georgian basket hilted broadsword dated 1823 by Macleod of Edinburgh sold for £625. This sword made such an excellent price because, while pistols are often marked with the maker's name, it is more rare for this to occur on a sword. From time to time makers' initials can be found engraved beneath the guards but often these are forged. Forgeries however are relatively few because if they are to be successful and deceive the experts, they have to be done on very high quality blades.

It is interesting how national sentiment can play a large part in determining the price of certain weapons . . especially swords. For several years now Japanese collectors have made a point of buying back into Japan all the very good examples of their weapons and armour that have come up for sale in Britain and on the Continent. Britain is especially rich in Japanese weapons because of our participation in the last war. In September Wallis and Wallis' special sale included a very fine Japanese blade made in 1390 and inscribed with the name of the swordsmith. It too went back to Japan for well over £500 which was its pre-sale estimate.

Up to the last couple of years there has been very little interest in Spanish weapons but recently perhaps because of the new regime in Spain or

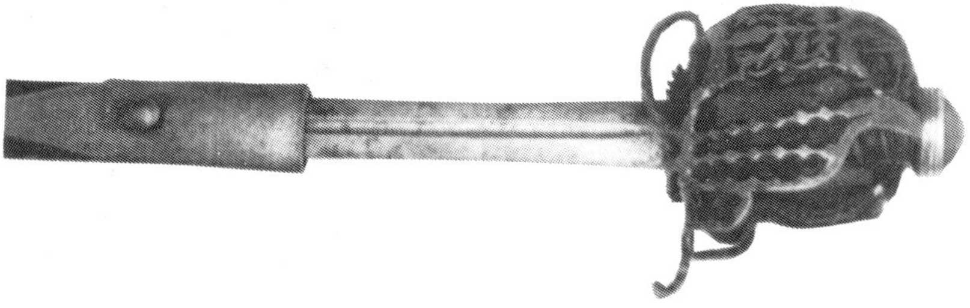

Georgian Scottish basket hilted broadsword, £625.

Middle Eastern weapons, like this Turkish blunderbuss pistol at £220, may be a growing market.

because of the increased prosperity of the country, Spanish weapons too have been demanding higher and higher prices from Spanish buyers.

'Inject some money into a nation and they want to buy back their heritage,' said Mr. Butler who has seen it happen many times. He sold a pair of 16 bore silver mounted Spanish miquelet flintlock belt pistols for £2,000 to a Spanish customer this year whereas a couple of years ago they would have been lucky to make a fraction of that price.

One exception to the rule about increased wealth making nations go 'nationalistic' are the Middle Eastern states who have still not come into the arms and armour market as strongly as they plunged into rugs, pictures and

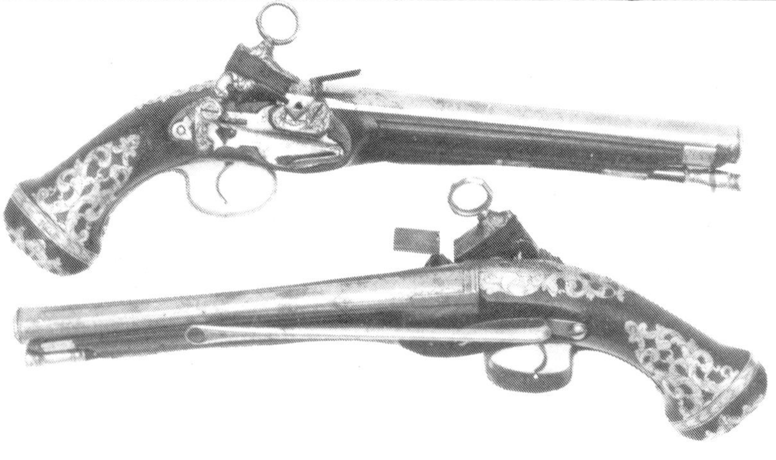

Pair of Spanish miquelet flintlock belt pistols, £2,000.

manuscripts a few years ago. They make what has been called 'patchy' appearances at weapons sales but do not seem yet to have made up their minds to emerge strongly into the Eastern weapons market. Yet there are many fine examples of these types of arms about and specialists feel that this is a good area for collectors to concentrate on if they are buying with investment in mind.

As everyone interested in antiques knows, the American market is currently in recession. Where they dominated all areas of the trade a few years ago, American buyers have fallen off markedly. As far as arms and armour is concerned they have been replaced by Continentals – first by Germans and more recently by the Belgians who in the past year have emerged as a very potent buying force indeed. In spite of the recession however Americans still continue to buy the very best examples of American weapons that come up for sale in Britain – but only the very best. Middle market pieces which used to go back over the Atlantic as well are now being snapped up by Continental buyers. Americans were great collectors of guns and perhaps because of the dwindling of their spending power, the gun market is static at the moment. It is one of the few areas of the trade where prices do not show an increase over those of last year. 'Very crisp' guns of course will always find buyers – and at good prices – but they are appearing more rarely for sale than in the past and people who own them are generally hanging onto them. It appears that no matter how bad the recession collectors still have money for the finest items and they are still reluctant to put their own collections on the market.

'A man has to have his back to the wall before he sells his collection,' said Mr. Butler.

If guns are generally marking time however there has been a very pronounced increase in prices raised for uniforms recently. Two or three years ago a good tunic could be picked up for only a couple of pounds – today it can run into hundreds. Anyone with ceremonial uniform dating back before 1914 has a very valuable item on their hands especially if there is a headdress with it. For example, a Lieutenant's uniform of the Royal Horse Guards (The Blues) from 1902, with the headdress, cuirass, shoulder belt and white buckskin breeches made £1,550 recently.

Lieutenant's uniform of The Royal Horse Guards, £1,550.

Officer's full dress uniform of the Black Watch, £1,050.

Another more recent uniform only dating from 1931 – an officer's complete fulldress uniform of the Black Watch made £1,050.

Romance is never very far from the saleroom when arms and armour is being sold. Every item on sale has been treasured because of the part it played in some man's life. Many vendors bring in things for sale and say 'My grandfather told me that this . . . .' However unless grandfather's story is fully documented – which it unfortunately rarely is – no value can be legally attached to it. Wallis and Wallis, who cherish the old stories because of their romantic attachment to the items on sale, usually add a little piece to the catalogue entry stating 'vendors says . . .'. This way the old stories can be passed on to the new buyers. History is ineradicably associated with many items – for example this year a set of French percussion duelling pistols made by Verney of Lyon came up for sale. They sold for £2,000 partly because Verney is famous as having been the man who made arms for Napoleon.

The fascination goes on without slackening. Every year brings more interesting pieces for the collector to thrill over. While other sections of the antique market can shiver in recession, arms and armour presses ahead . . . going great guns, in fact.

LIZ TAYLOR

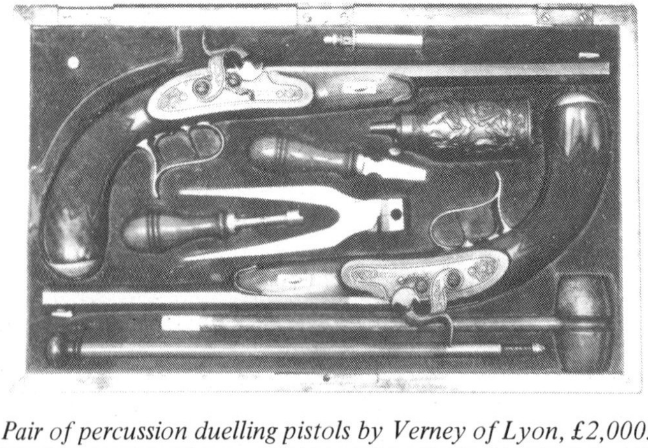

Pair of percussion duelling pistols by Verney of Lyon, £2,000.

EDGED WEAPONS

BAYONETS

An 1887 Mark III sword bayonet for the Martini Henry rifle, plain blade 18in., by 'Wilkinson Sword, London', stamped with crown, 'WD' ordnance stamps etc., issue stamp for 1893, steel mounts, diced leather grips, in scarce brass mounted brown leather scabbard. $66 £30

A scarce mid 19th century Hirschfanger sword bayonet of one of the German States, straight, double edged blade 17½in., small crosspiece with rounded quillons, ribbed solid brass hilt, with spring catch lug. $88 £40

An E.I.C. Sapper's and Miner's sword bayonet, circa 1845, single edged blade, 22in., with central fuller, steel socket and knucklebow. $87 £40

A 1st Model 1836 pattern brass hilted Brunswick bayonet, spatulate blade 17in. $119 £55

A brass hilted Remington M.63 sword bayonet, slightly recurving blade 20in., stamped 'U.S.' at forte, ribbed hilt, in its brass mounted leather scabbard. $119 £55

A scarce Danish Krag Jorgensen Model 1889 bayonet, blade 17¾in., of 'T' section, small crosspiece, walnut grips to hilt, in its steel mounted leather scabbard. $130 £60

A late 17th century plug bayonet, slightly curved blade 8in., with incised back edge, reversed brass quillons, plain brass mounts, in its brass mounted leather sheath. $148 £65

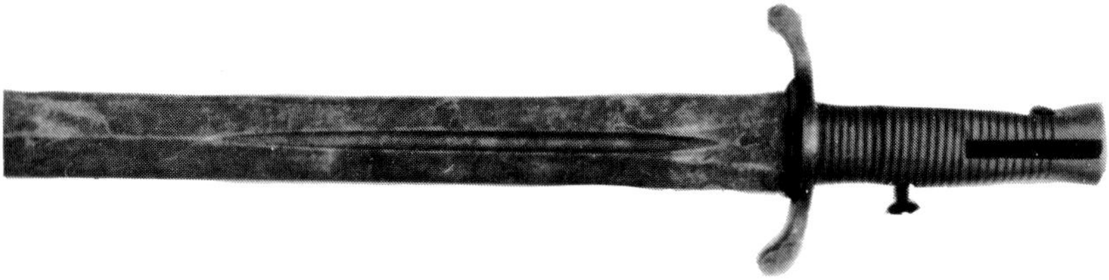

A rare 1838 brass hilted Brunswick sword bayonet, double edged, spatulate blade 22in., with short fuller, also stamped with crown, 'VR', 'Enfield'. $174 £80

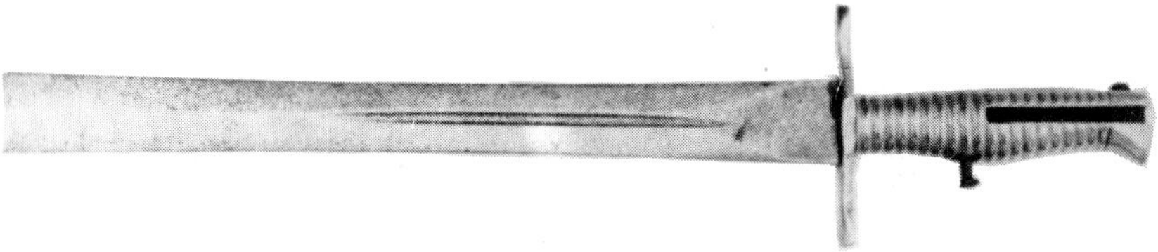

A scarce 1st Model 1836 pattern brass hilted Brunswick bayonet, spatulate blade 17in., straight crosspiece, round slot. $174 £80

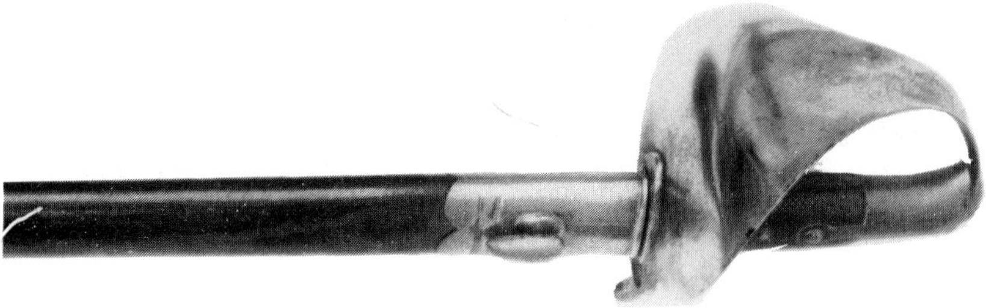

An 1858 pattern Naval cutlass bayonet, slightly curved blade 25¾in., 'knight's head' mark and ordnance stamp at forte, steel sheet guard, diced leather grips, in its steel mounted leather scabbard. $174 £80

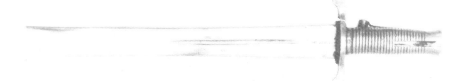

A brass hilted 1848 pattern Brunswick bayonet, straight, double edged, slightly spatulate blade 22in., with ordnance stamp at forte, also stamped 'Enfield 1849'. $242 £110

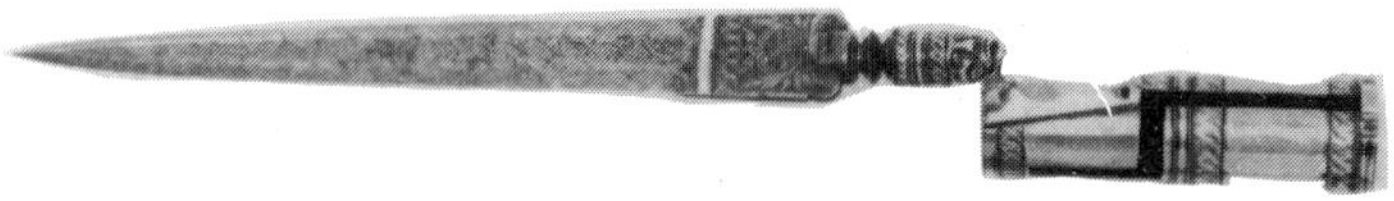

A very fine mid 18th century French Fusilier's socket bayonet, spear point, double edged blade 8in., the facetted socket of solid silver, the blade mount in the form of a 'Turk's head' wearing turban, in patent leather scabbard. $315 £145

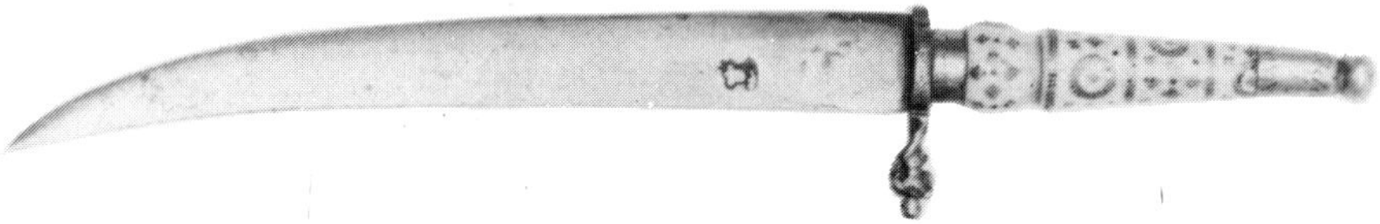

A late 17th century English plug bayonet, curved single edged blade 10½in., brass crosspiece with quillon in the form of a standing female figure, ivory grip with silver piquet stud inlaid patterns of circles, etc., brass mounts. $434 £200

An English late 17th century plug bayonet, double edged, tapering blade 8¼in., reversed gilt bronze crossguard with chiselled hounds' head terminals, ivory hilt with swelling base and inlaid with silver pique stud patterns. $651 £300

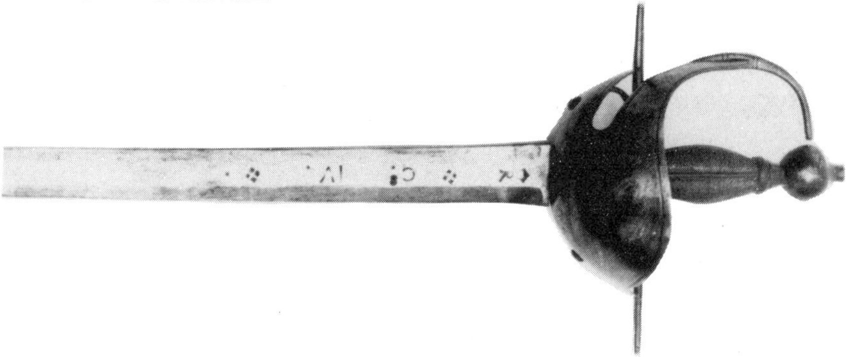

A Spanish 18th century Bilbo broadsword, double edged blade 31in., marked at forte with crown above 'R', 'Cs. IV' (for Charles IV) and '1801', steel bowl guard, rounded, straight quillons, copper wirebound grip, ovoid pommel.
$296 £130

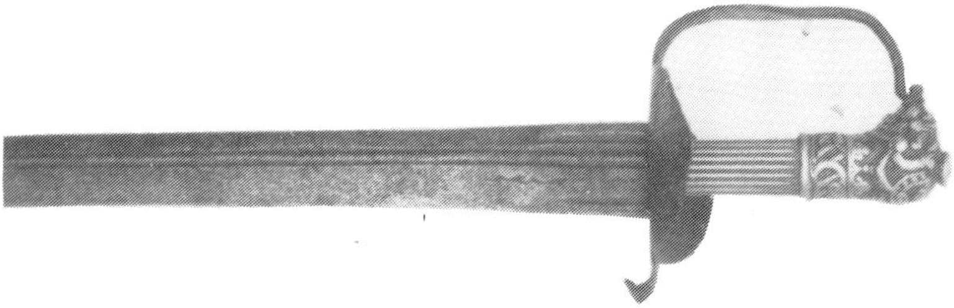

A 17th century Cromwellian broadsword, straight, double edged, tapering blade 31½in., with narrow double fullers for entire length and signed 'Saraval', iron double shell guard with simple line pattern, gargoyle head pommel. $330 £150

An early 18th century Cavalry broadsword, single edged, tapering blade 30in., with narrow back fuller, basket iron guard, with rectangular panels, ovoid pommel, wood grip. $412 £190

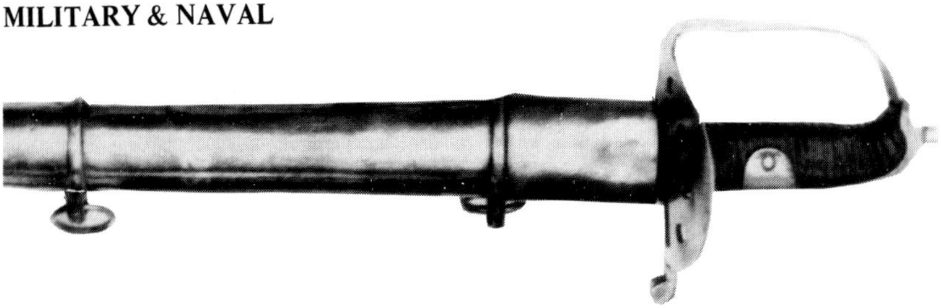

An Austrian 1803 model Cavalry trooper's heavy broadsword, straight, single edged blade, 34in., with spear point, engraved on back-strap 'Fischer' and engraved with Austrian Eagle, pierced, circular steel guard, plain steel knuckle-bow stamped '1865' and mounts, ribbed leather covered grip, in its heavy iron scabbard with wooden liner. $477 £220

A Prussian 1732 Model Cuirassier broadsword, double edged, tapering blade 36½in., cast brass semi-basket guard, with pommel, wirebound, leather covered grip, thumb ring. $572 £260

A Prussian 1732 Cuirassier broadsword, broad, double edged blade 36in., cast brass basket guard, brass thumb ring and ovoid pommel, brass wirebound grip. $673 £310

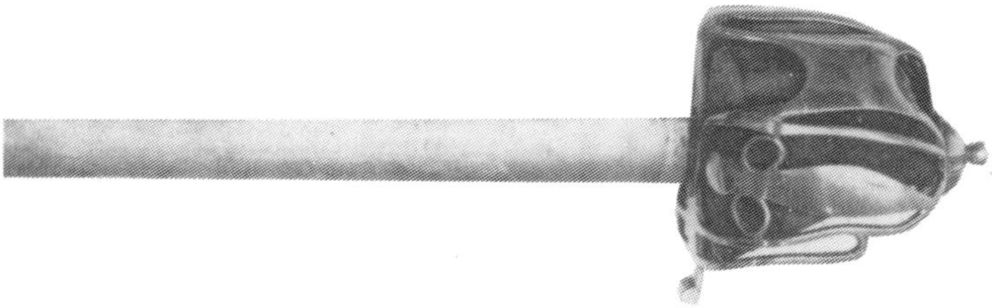

An early Victorian Scottish officer's broadsword, plain double edged blade 32in., copper guard of traditional form, red liner, flattened pommel, wirebound, leather covered grip. $140 £60

A Scottish broadsword, made for a boy, double edged, tapering blade 16½in., of flattened diamond section, etched with crossed standards and thistles and foliate scrolls, plated guard of traditional basket form, oval flattened pommel, in its blue velvet covered scabbard with three mounts of German silver. $195 £90

A Scottish officer's late Victorian Military broadsword, narrow, double edged blade 32½in., with short fuller engraved 'Donald Curry, London, Warranted', steel basket hilt of traditional pattern, wirebound, fishskin covered grip, in its leather scabbard with plated mounts. $275 £125

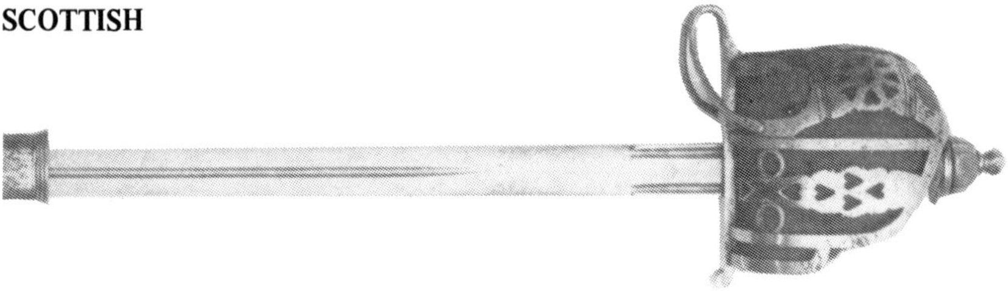

An Edward VII Scottish Infantry officer's 1865 pattern military broadsword, blade 32in., with central fuller, by 'Henry Wilkinson, Pall Mall', etched with royal cypher, crown, thistles, the Regt. 'Royal Scots', in its plated steel scabbard. $275 £125

A Victorian Scottish officer's broadsword, circa 1865, of the Black Watch, straight, double edged blade 31½in., with part double fullers, steel basket guard of traditional pattern, wirebound, fishskin covered grip, original crimson tassel and red liner, in its steel mounted leather scabbard. $315 £145

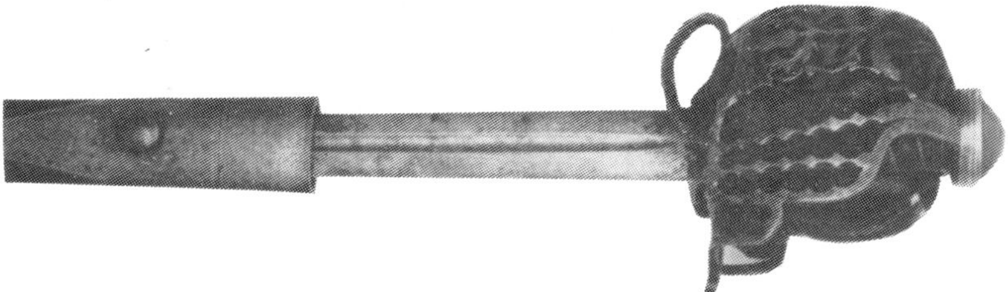

A fine Georgian Scottish basket hilted broadsword by Macleod of Edinburgh, dated 1823, double edged, straight blade 33½in., with single broad fullers etched 'Andrea Ferrara'. Finely wrought, filed, pierced, facetted and engraved steel basket guard pierced with 'St. Andrew and cross' surrounded by thistles. $1,625 £625

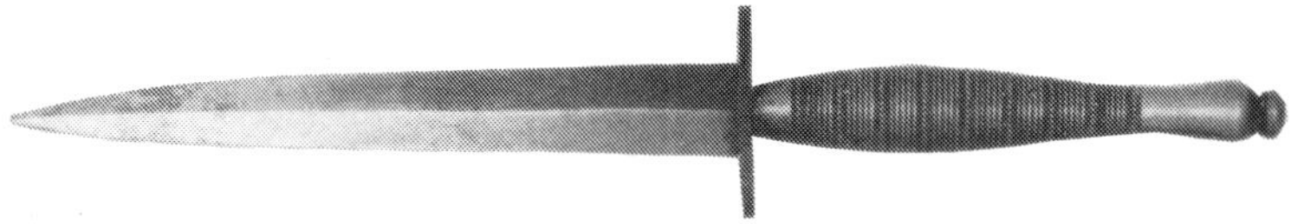

A World War II Commando dagger, blade 6¾in., oval steel crosspiece, ribbed and beaded brass hilt, the base with W.D. arrow, in its leather sheath with blackened brass tip, leather tongue. $208 £80

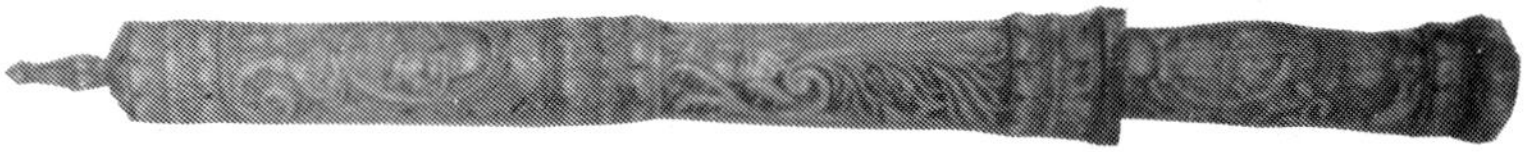

A 19th century carved Romantic 'Dieppe' bone dagger in the form of a Polish dagger basselard, hollow ground quatrefoil sectioned tapered steel blade 11in. Hilt and sheath carved en suite with four portraits of Polish kings. $265 £115

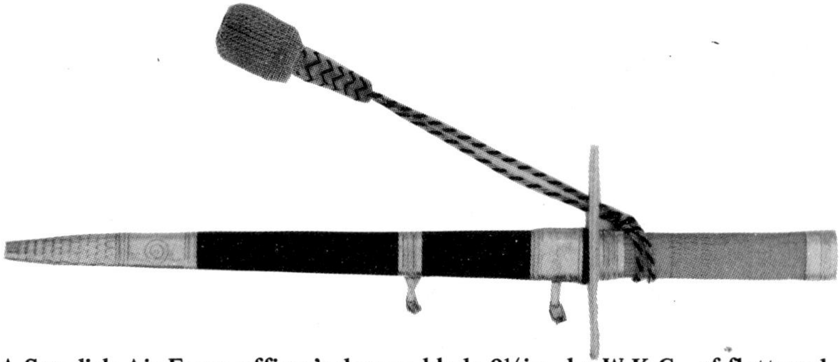

A Swedish Air Force officer's dagger, blade 9¼in., by W.K.C., of flattened diamond section, gilt hilt, with rectangular crosspiece, Swedish crowns to pommel, gilt wirebound grip, bullion dress knot, in its patent black leather sheath. $260 £120

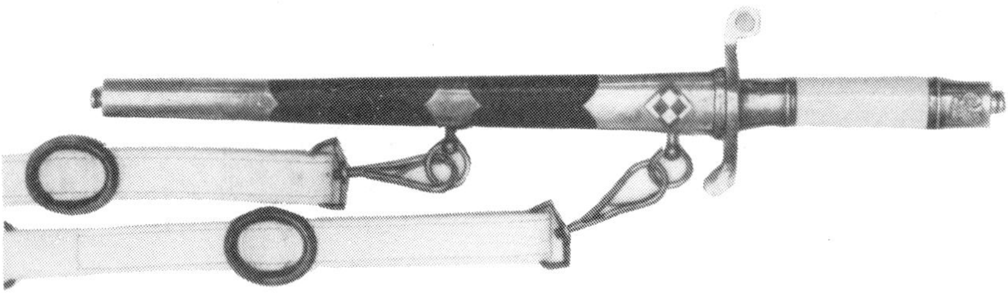

An Albanian Air Force officer's dagger, plated blade 9in., plain, plated reversed crosspiece, plated mounts, the pommel with Albanian Eagle ivorine grip, spring catch, in its leather covered metal sheath. $341 £155

A Polish pre-World War II Air Force honour dagger, plated blade 9¼in., etched with Polish Eagle, scrolls and honour inscription in Polish, plated, squared crosspiece and mounts, yellow grip, mounts decorated in laurel sprays. $396 £180

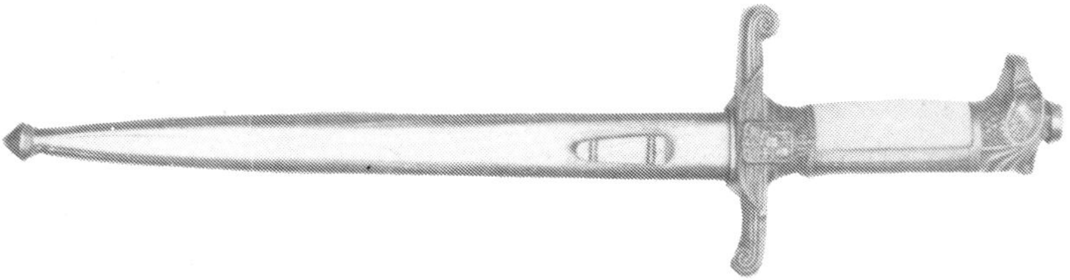

A Rumanian Air Force officer's dress dagger, straight, tapering, double edged blade 6in., by 'F. W. Holler', white metal hilt, reversed crosspiece, 'eagle's head' pommel, white ivorine grips, in its plated metal sheath. $506 £230

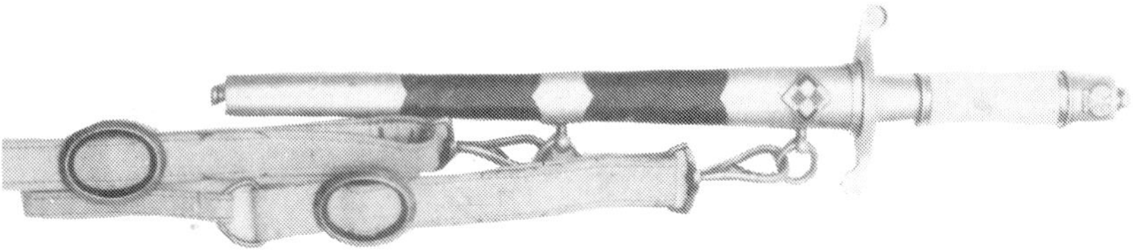

A Polish Air Force officer's dagger, plain, plated blade 9in., reversed crosspiece with spring catch, white grip, plated pommel with Polish Eagle on the side, in its leather covered metal sheath with three plain plated mounts. $572 £260

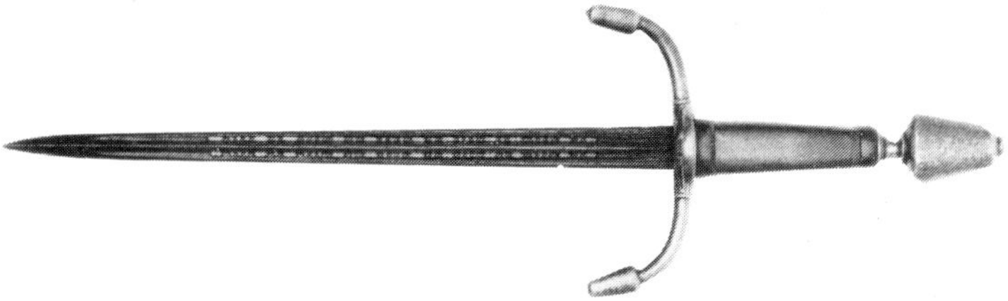

An early 17th century left-hand dagger, the 9in. blade of diamond section, deeply fullered and pierced almost to the tip, the crosspiece with large thumb ring and down drooping quillons, plain wooden grip. $1,140 £500

A silver mounted dagger, bichaq, blade 5¼in., eared hilt covered in Eastern silver, in its sheath of solid Eastern silver with 'monster head' terminal. $98 £45

A silver mounted dagger, bichaq, blade 7in., with inscription, the hilt covered in Eastern silver, eared pommel, in its wooden lined sheath of Eastern silver, terminating in 'monster head'. $110 £50

CHILANUM

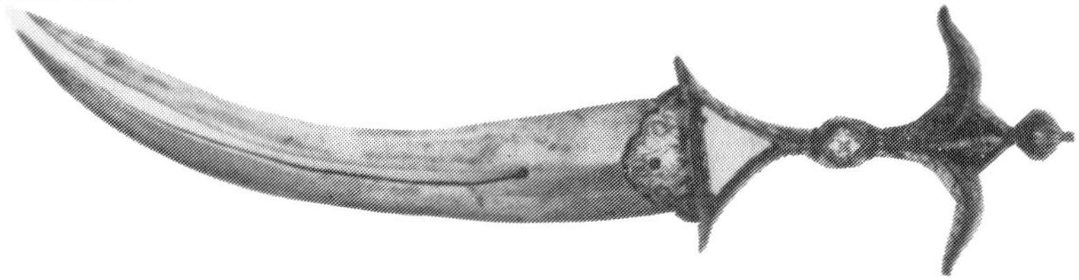

An Indian dagger chilanum, curved, bifurcated blade 8½in., iron hilt with triangle openwork base and overlaid in gold damascene patterns. $130 £60

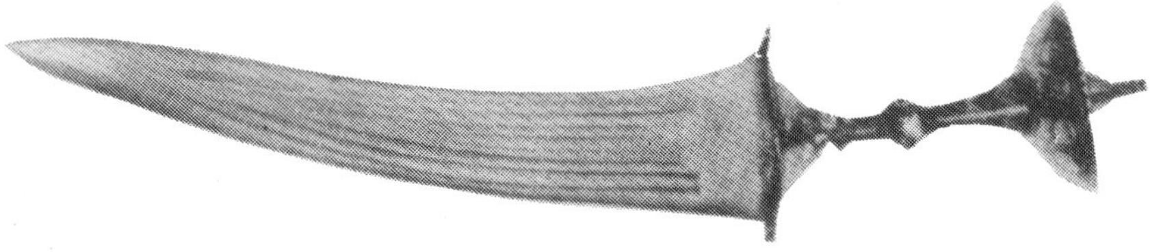

An Indian dagger chilanum, recurving multi-fullered blade 10in., integral with baluster grip, hilt inlaid with stylised brass flowers. $175 £75

DAGGERS
DHA

A large dha dagger, broad, single edged blade 10in., with three marks at base, solid ivory hilt, in its leather covered wooden sheath. $83 £36

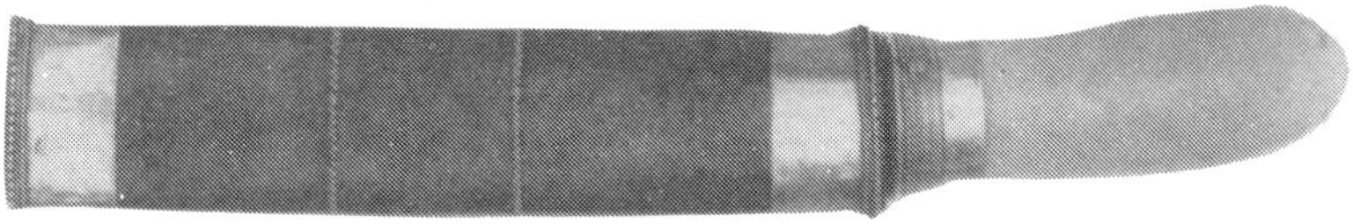

A Burmese silver mounted dha dagger, slightly curved blade 8in., ivory hilt with Eastern sheet silver base mount, in its wooden sheath, with two Eastern sheet silver bands and wire mounts. $161 £70

A Burmese dha, slightly curved blade 24in., inlaid on both sides for entire length with figures and foliage etc., in Eastern silver, the hilt covered in Eastern sheet silver with copper bands etc., in its wooden scabbard, partly covered in leather. $198 £90

EASTERN

An all steel 19th century Indian dagger, highly polished curved single edged bi-furcated blade 10in. Silver damascened with birds, flowers and foliage at forte en suite with steel hilt. In its tooled leather sheath. $138 £60

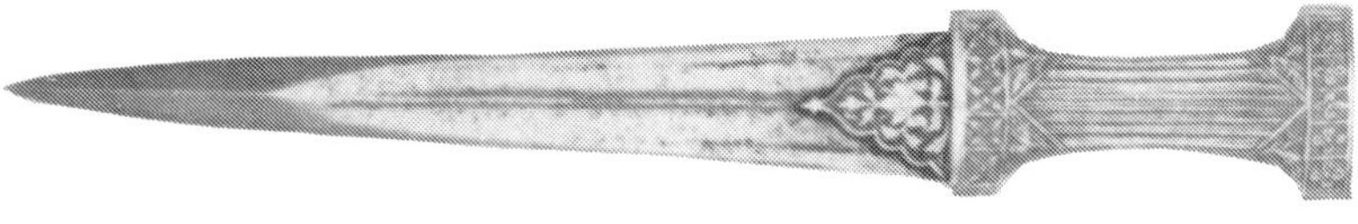

An Indo-Persian silver hilted dagger, double edged, tapering blade 10¼in., with reinforced point and with central rib, iron mount at forte chiselled with gold damascene foliate pattern, the hilt of solid Eastern silver. $195 £90

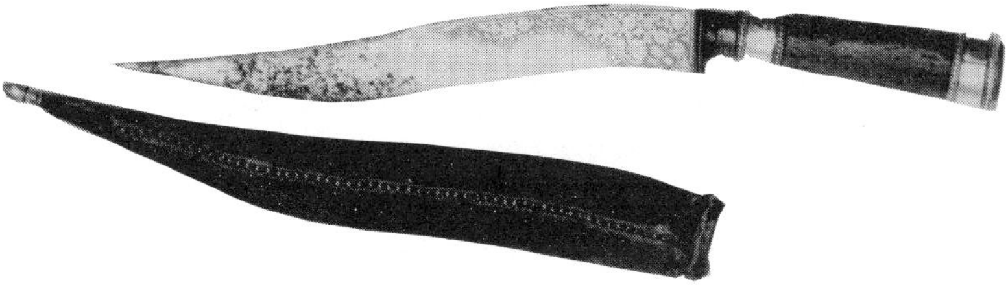

An unusual Indo-Persian dagger, circa 1780, recurved swollen single edged blade 9½in., with swollen tip and false edge, silver mounted stag horn hilt, red agate pommel, in its green leather covered sheath with silver chape. $198 £95

An old Indian triple bladed dagger, brass knuckleduster grip with short and long curved blades, 2in. and 5½in., knuckleduster with double crested blade 4in., brass grip, overall length 13in. $546 £210

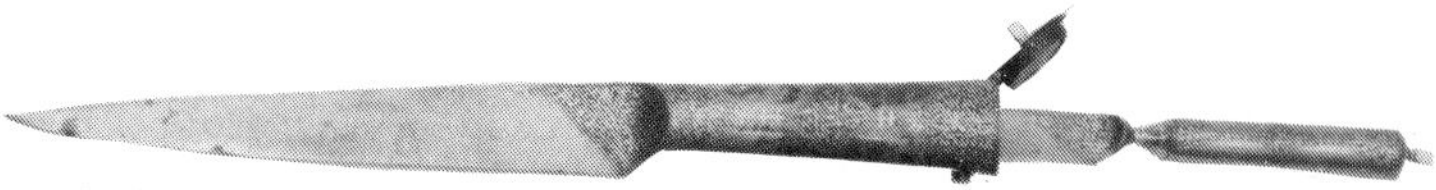

An Indian all steel dagger, kard, watered steel, single edged blade 9in., all steel hollow hilt, hinged pommel cap, gold damascened opening to reveal a smaller all steel kard, watered steel blade 7¼in., in green velvet covered, wooden sheath. $542 £250

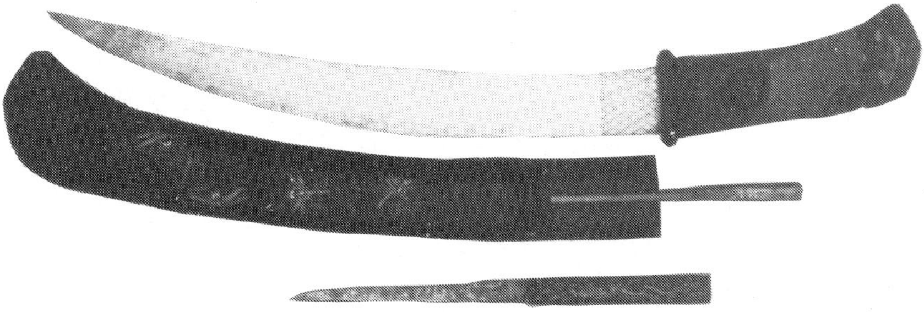

An unusual Japanese dagger kubikiri, sharply curved blade 29¼cm. mumei, two mekugi ana, itame hada, gunome hamon, o-kissaki. Cord bound tsuka, ribbed lacquered saya. $754 £290

A Nazi Army officer's dagger by Eickhorn, plated mounts, orange grip, in its plated sheath. $119 £55

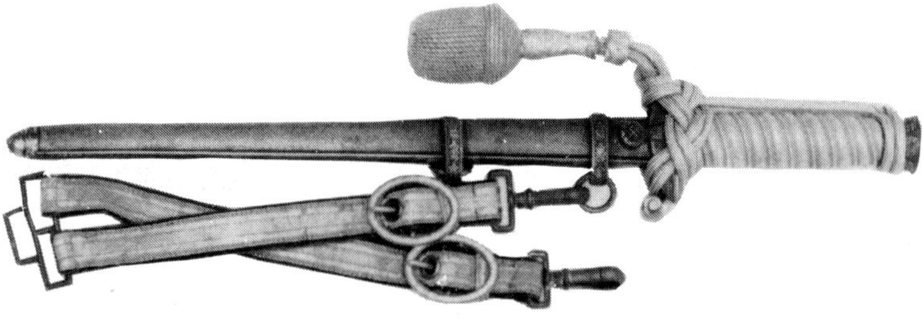

A Nazi Army officer's dagger, by W.K.C., plated mounts, orange grip, in its plated sheath with original hanging straps and belt lug with bullion dress knot. $119 £55

A Nazi Luftwaffe officer's 2nd pattern dagger, by W.K.C., grey metal mounts, silver wirebound yellow ivorine grip, in its metal sheath. $130 £60

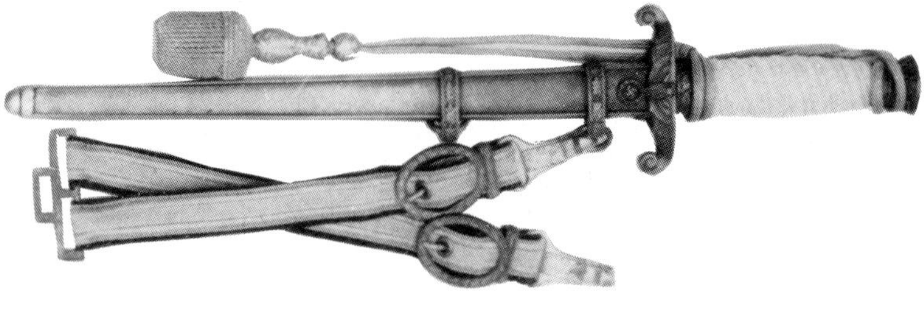

A Nazi Army officer's dagger, by W.K.C., grey metal mounts, white grip, in its grey metal sheath with hanging straps and belt clip. $130 £60

A Nazi Luftwaffe officer's 1st pattern dagger, plated blade by Siegfried, grey metal mounts, wirebound, blue leather covered grip, in its blue leather covered metal sheath with original hanging chains and belt clip. $152 £70

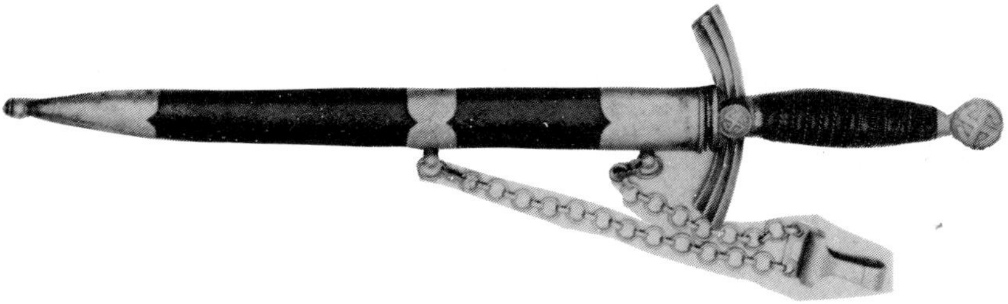

A Nazi 1st pattern Luftwaffe officer's dagger, German silver crosspiece and mounts, wirebound, leather covered grip, in its leather covered metal sheath with plated mounts, hanging chains and belt clip. $187 £90

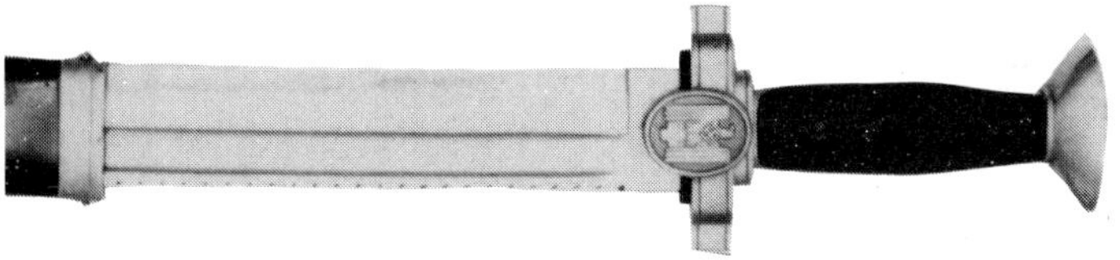

A Nazi Red Cross man's dagger, plated mounts, in its metal sheath with plated mounts. $198 £95

A Nazi 1st pattern Luftwaffe officer's dagger, by E. & F. Horster, aluminium mounts, wirebound, blue leather covered grip, in its leather covered steel sheath with aluminium mounts, hanging chains and belt clip. $229 £110

A Nazi 1st pattern Luftwaffe officer's dagger, plated blade 12in., by Paul Weyersberg, with small inspection stamp, plated mounts, blue leather covered, wirebound grip, in its blue leather covered metal sheath. $250 £115

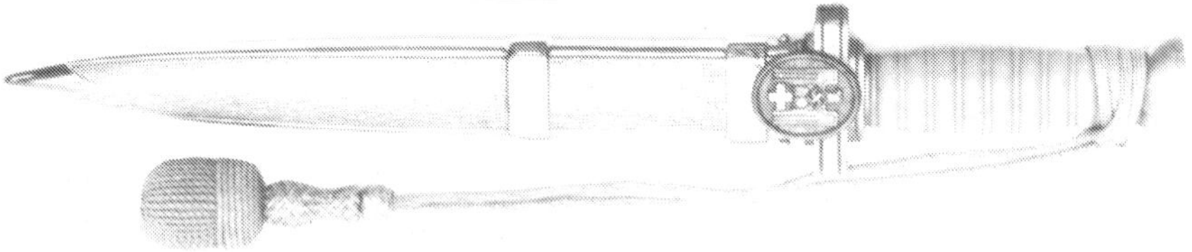

A Nazi Red Cross officer's dagger, plated mounts, orange grip, in its chrome plated sheath, with bullion dress knot. $264 £120

A Nazi Waterways Protection Police officer's dagger, by Eickhorn, police emblem to wirebound, blue leather covered grip, in its gilt sheath. $315 £150

A Nazi 2nd Model R.L.B. officer's dagger, plated mounts, leather bound grip with enamelled emblem, in its leather covered sheath with plated mounts.
$368 £175

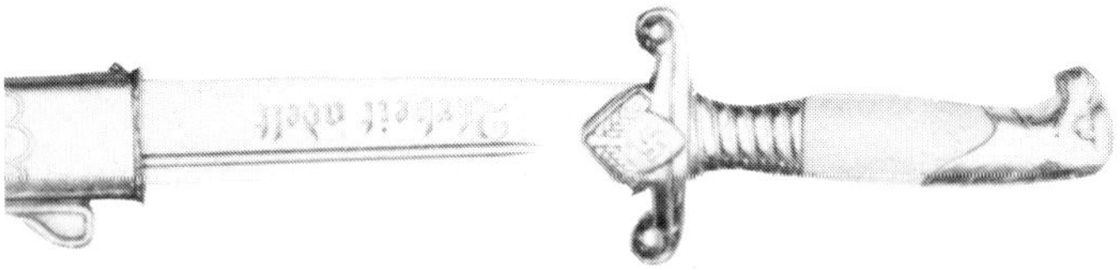

A Nazi R.A.D. officer's dagger by Krebs, plated mounts, in its plated sheath.
$449 £180

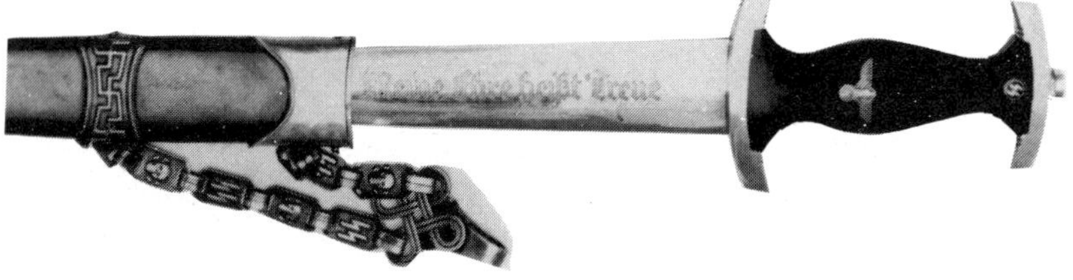

A Nazi S.S. officer's 1936 model dagger, by Rich. Abr. Herder, plated mounts, in its sheath with plated mounts, hanging chains and belt clip. $645 £310

An Arab large silver hilted jambiya, curved blade 15in., with raised central rib, the hilt covered in Eastern silver, the front with intricate filigree pattern with beaded mounts. $104 £48

An Indian silver dagger jambiya, double edged blade with raised rib 7in., silver hilt engraved and chased with flowers and foliage, in its velvet covered sheath with pierced silver mounts of foliate and floral design, large locket. $140 £60

A silver mounted Balkan jambiya, curved, fullered blade 11in. of watered steel, the hilt covered in Eastern sheet silver embossed with foliate patterns, in its sheath of Eastern silver. $182 £80

A silver mounted Arab jambiya, curved blade 6in., horn hilt, partly overlaid with plain and foliate chiselled Eastern sheet silver, in its wooden lined sheath. $187 £85

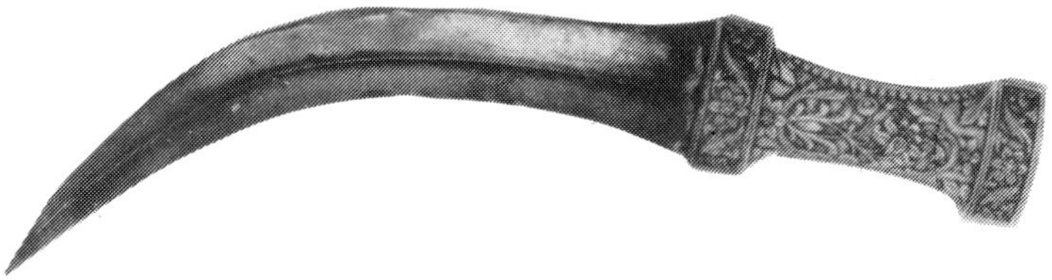

An Indo-Persian jambiya, ribbed, curved blade 10in. of watered steel, ivory hilt, elaborately chiselled with floral and foliate patterns. $310 £135

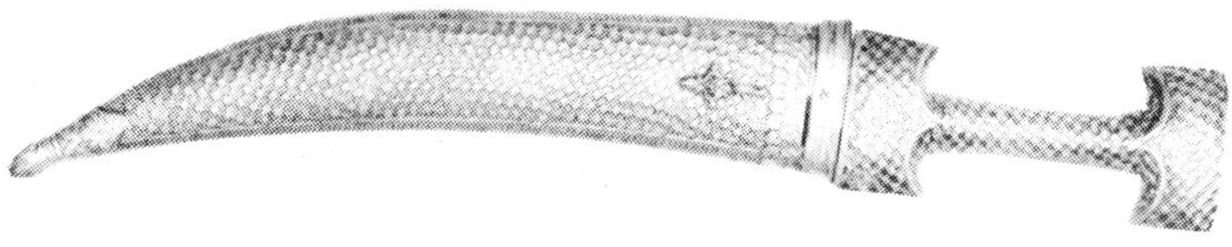

A Balkan silver mounted jambiya, curved blade 11½in., with central rib, with gold damascened foliate decoration at forte with inscriptions, the hilt covered with Eastern silver decorated with 'link' patterns, in its sheath of solid Eastern silver. $400 £180

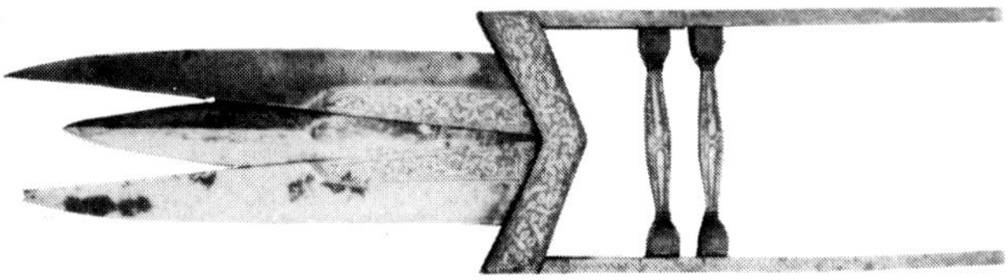

An Indian scissors katar, divided blade cover 8in., concealed blade 7in., iron hilt and twin grips with damascene decoration. $137 £60

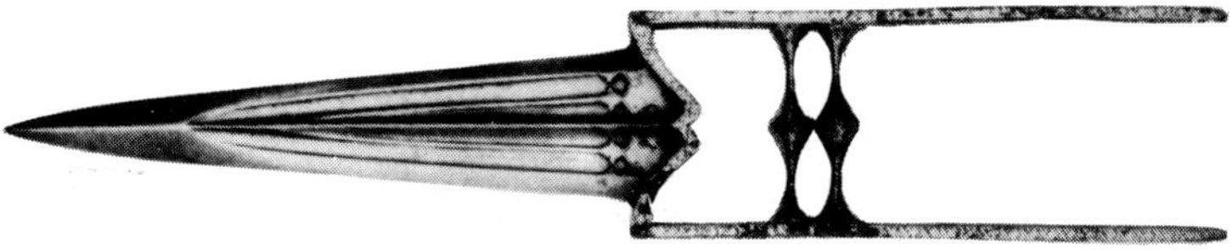

An Indian all steel katar, fluted, multi-fullered blade 10½in., with reinforced point, double baluster grips, the hilt covered with gold foliate damascene decoration. $146 £70

An Indian all steel scissors katar, hinged blade 7½in., folding to reveal 6½in. inner blade. Steel hilt foliate silver damascened overall, in its velvet covered sheath. $154 £70

An Indian large all steel katar, broad blade 15in., with reinforced tip (width at forte 3in.), hand guard loop and grip extension chiselled with foliate patterns, twin baluster grips. $165 £75

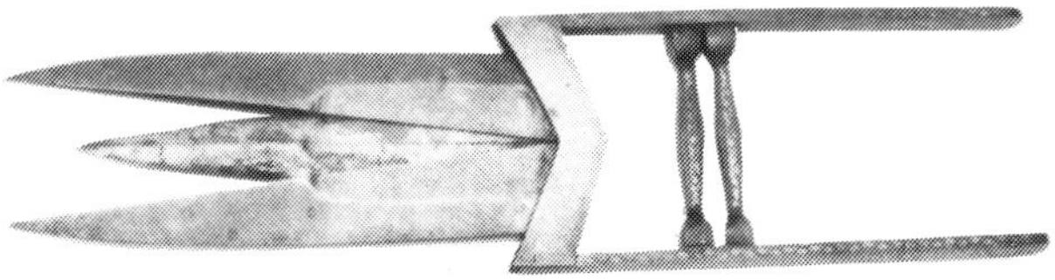

An Indian scissors katar, blade 8in., divided and with central blade 6½in., with reinforced point, twin pillar grips, steel guard. $200 £85

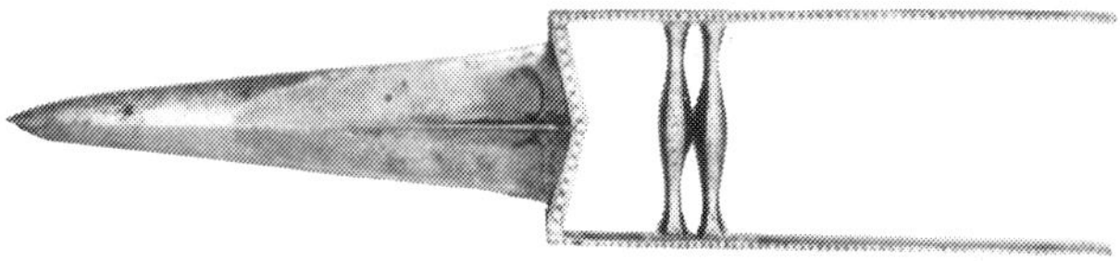

A late 18th century watered steel gold damascened Indian thrusting dagger, katar, 15in., triangular shaped watered blade 8in., with central rib and armour piercing swollen tip. Watered steel hilt. $242 £110

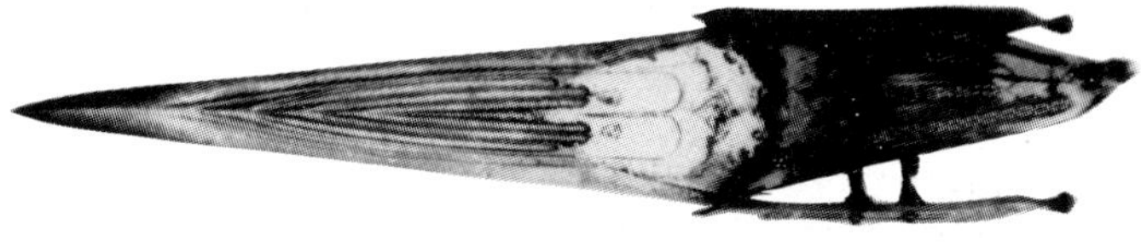

An Indian Tanjoori thrusting dagger, katar, circa 1700, double edged blade 12in., with deep chevron fullers, steel fist guard, grip formed of two hollowed balls. $251 £110

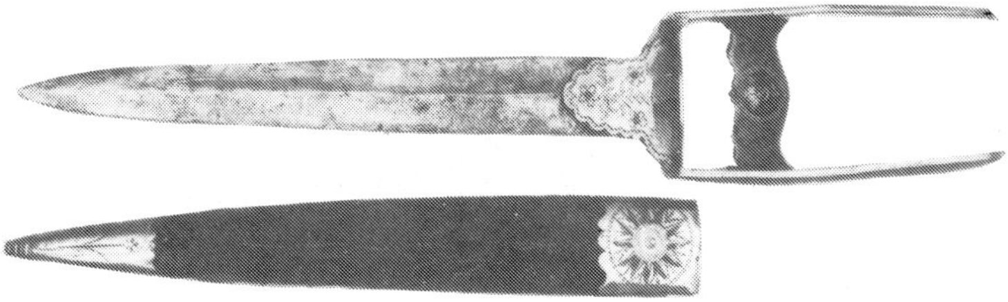

A 19th century Indian dagger, katar, double edged blade 12in. Copper gilt hilt border engraved with floral engraved blade mount. Hilt with four enamelled silver plates in its foliate engraved copper gilt mounted sheath. $704 £320

KATTI

A Coorg Ayda katti, broad blade 15½in., the hilt of horn, finely diced and with horn pommel decorated with circular patterns. $141 £65

KILIJ

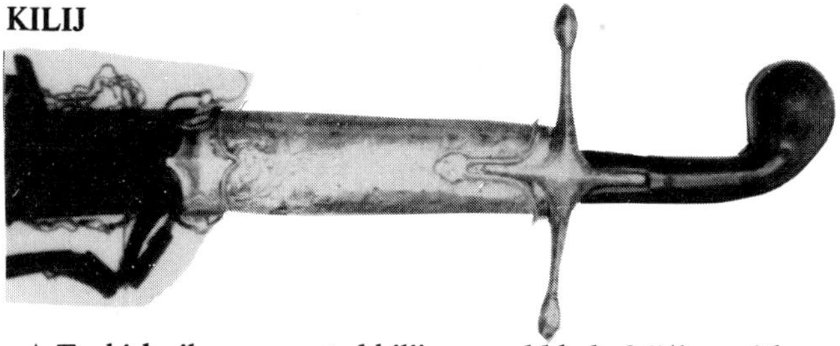

A Turkish silver mounted kilij, curved blade 26½in., with pronounced clipped-back tip, the crosspiece of Eastern silver, silver straps, eared rhino horn grips, in its leather covered wooden scabbard with two large Eastern silver mounts. $304 £140

KINDJAL

A Russian Military kindjal (possibly World War I), with heavy double edged blade 17¼in., with raised central rib, plain wooden grips with small control stamp '59' within circle, iron plain mounts, in its leather covered wooden sheath with similar stamp, iron ring mount and chape. $91 £40

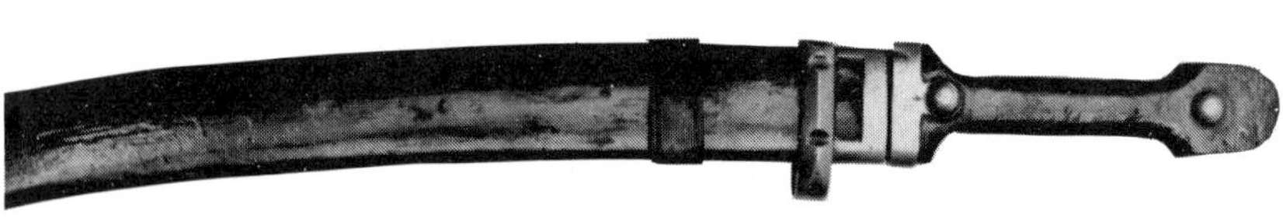

A 19th century Russian Artillery kindjal, curved, double-fullered blade 17in., brass mounted black grips, in its brass mounted, black painted, wooden sheath, the blade and some mounts with bow and arrow arsenal mark with a leather frog. $103 £45

A Caucasian large kindjal, single edged, straight blade 25in., curved at tip, multi-fullered, some gold inlaid foliate patterns to tip and forte, horn grips, three iron mounts with pierced, Eastern silver floral base mounts, the back grip mounted with three Turkish silver coins. $108 £50

A Caucasian long kindjal, single edged, multi-fullered blade 24½in., struck at forte with two armourer's marks, horn grips and silver straps, mounted with two Eastern silver domed mounts and six Imperial Russian silver coins. $163 £75

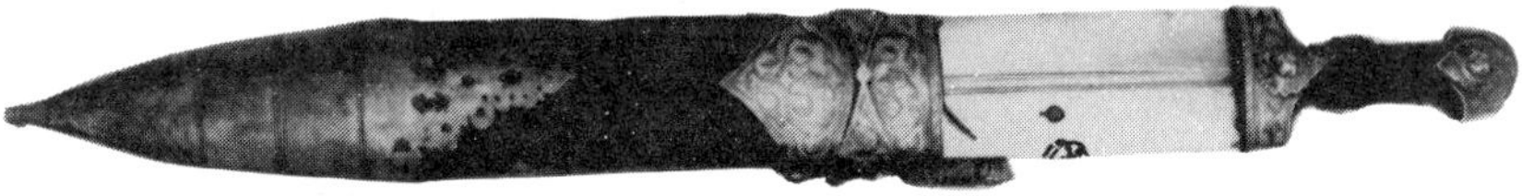

A Caucasian (Georgian) silver mounted kindjal, broad, double edged blade 16¼in., with central fuller, horn hilt partly overlaid with Eastern silver decorated with nielloed foliate pattern, wirebound grip, in its velvet covered wooden sheath with Eastern silver locket, large iron lower chape pierced at top. $174 £80

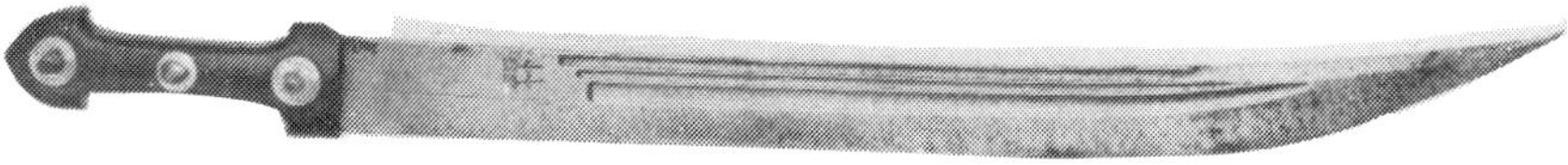

A large Persian dagger kindjal, slightly curved, tri-fullered, single edged blade 23½in., struck with double armourer's mark, two-piece horn grips, silver coins used as rivet heads, in its leather covered sheath with steel mounts. $174 £80

DAGGERS
KINDJAL

A Caucasian kindjal, double edged, multi-fullered, tapering blade 13in., etched at forte with dated '1910' and cyrillic script, horn grips with white metal mounts, in its leather covered wooden sheath with white metal mounts. $205 £90

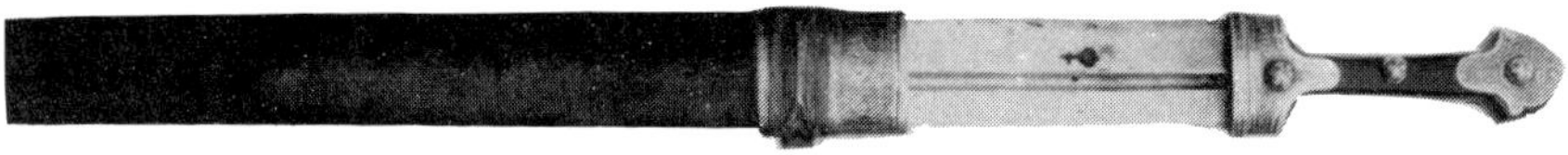

A large Caucasian kindjal, broad, double edged blade 20½in., with deep central fuller, struck with armourer's mark at forte, horn grips with white metal niello decorated mounts, in its leather covered wooden sheath. $217 £100

A good Caucasian kindjal, double edged blade 14in., with tapering point and deep central fuller, the hilt and sheath covered in white metal and nielloed with foliate and other embossed patterns, the back plain, two domed mounts to hilt. $239 £110

A silver mounted Caucasian kindjal, double edged, multi-fullered blade 15in., horn grips mounted with Eastern silver, in its leather covered wooden sheath, with two large Eastern silver mounts, beaded, wirebound tip. $282 £130

A vast Caucasian ceremonial kindjal, long, broad blade 35in., width 3¼in., broad central fuller, plain horn grips, with fluted grip, conical mounts, in its leather covered wooden sheath with iron ring mount chiselled with foliate pattern and with companion knife in compartment, blade 6¼in., segment horn hilt. $429 £165

A Java kris, straight, watered steel blade 14in., wooden hilt carved in the form of a standing demon, gilt, beaded cup base mount, in its white metal sheet covered wooden sheath. $119 £55

An old Javanese dagger kris, watered, double edged, tapered blade 13¼in., struck with armourer's mark, well carved solid ivory garuda hilt, in its hardwood scabbard with typical boat-shaped top section. $169 £65

A Moro kris, straight blade 20½in., with toothed extension, wooden hilt cord and rattan bound, roped silver wire binding below wooden pommel, in its wooden sheath, part rattan bound. $135 £65

A large Bali kris, wavy, watered steel blade 17in., white metal hilt in the form of Raksha, set with coloured stones, figure height 6in., in its wooden sheath. $160 £70

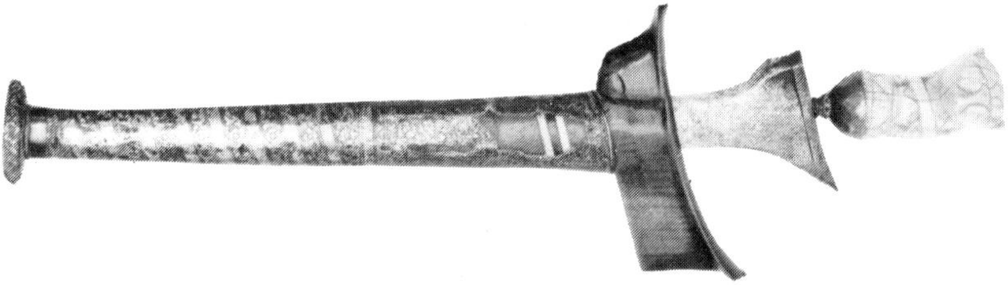

A good Sumatran dagger kris, slightly waved, watered blade 13½in., large ivory garuda hilt on silver cup, in its polished wooden sheath covered in foliate and floral embossed silver designs. $156 £75

A Sumatran kris, double edged, straight, watered steel blade 14½in., inlaid on both sides with silver inscriptions in Arabic, being the start of the 26th Chapter of the Koran, stylised wooden garuda hilt, in its wooden sheath. $174 £80

A Sumatran kris, wavy, watered steel blade 14in., the ivory stylised garuda hilt with Eastern silver foliate cup base mount, in its wooden sheath covered in Eastern sheet silver. $217 £100

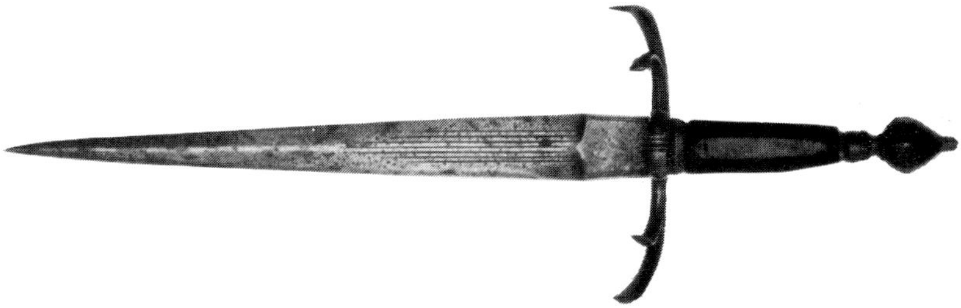

A 17th century main gauche dagger, shallow diamond sectioned swollen, tapering blade 11½in., with seven fullers each side. Steel crosspiece integral with thumb ring and twin curved quillons. $1,061 £510

PHURBU

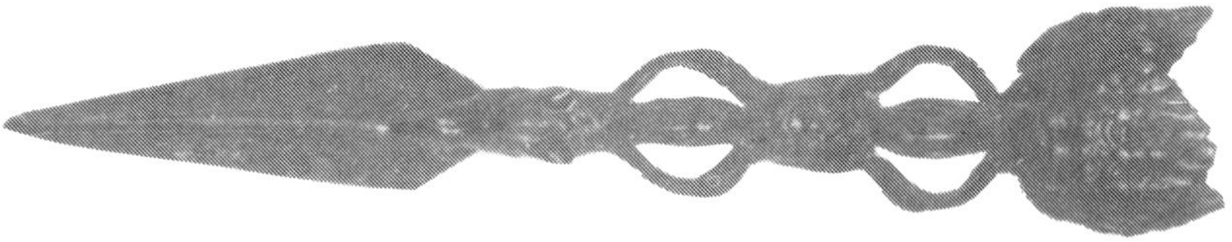

An old Tibetan bronzed exorcising dagger phurbu, triangular blade 3½in., issuing from monster's mouth, surmounted by thunderbolt symbol, with centre of double demon masks, the pommel in the form of three grotesque masks, overall 9½in. $104 £40

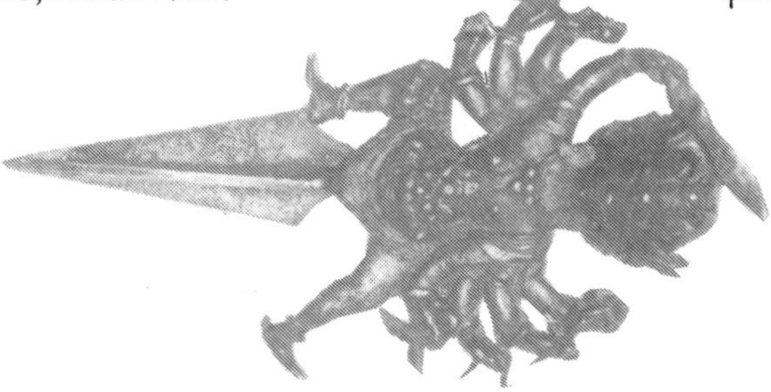

An ornate old Tibetan bronzed exorcising dagger phurbu, triangular blade 3½in., issuing from eight armed standing demon waving sword, skirt with demon mask and with three demon heads to pommel, overall 7½in. $141 £65

A Georgian Naval officer's dirk, circa 1800, straight, double edged blade 10½in., with central fuller, plain, reversed copper crosspiece, octagonal bone grip with vertical flutes and copper mounts, in its leather sheath.
$78 £36

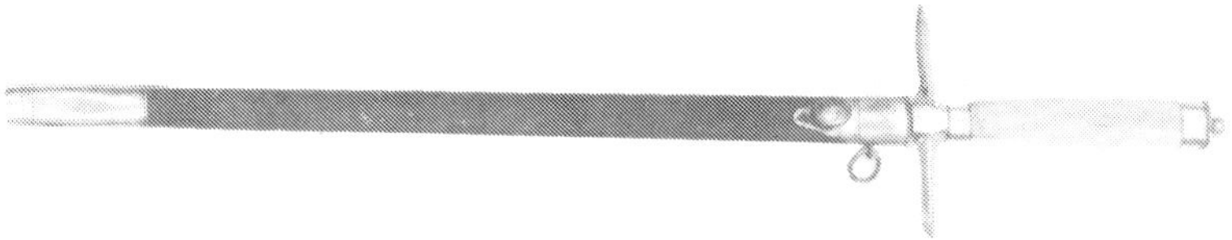

A Georgian Naval officer's dirk, circa 1800, slim, straight, tapering, transitional rapier blade 12in. with central fuller, copper gilt propellor type crosspiece, octagonal ivory grip with plain copper gilt octagonal mounts, in its leather sheath.
$88 £40

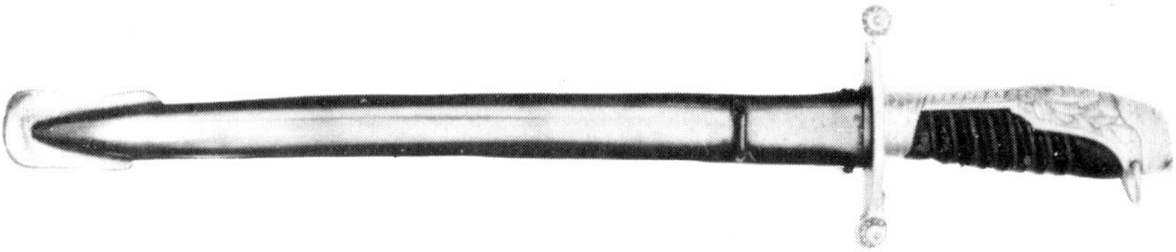

A Uruguayan officer's dress dirk, plated, straight blade 12in., gilt crosspiece with beaded terminals, gilt metal Cap-of-Liberty pommel, the back-strap decorated with arms of Uruguay, wirebound, black leather covered grip, in its black steel sheath. $146 £70

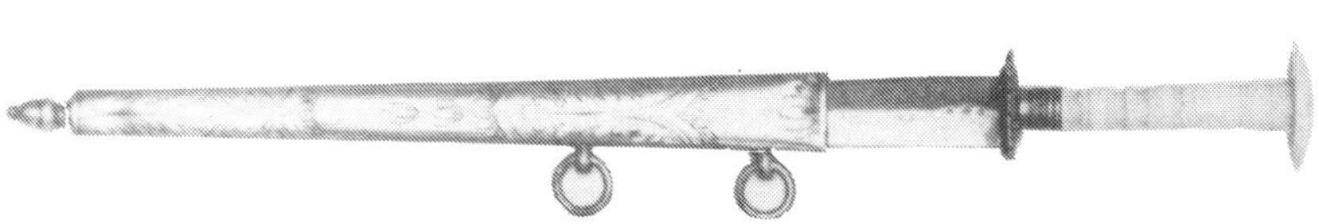

A Georgian Naval officer's dirk, plain, double edged, tapering blade 7in., small copper gilt rectangular guard with scaled pattern, turned ivory hilt with 'mushroom' pommel, in its copper sheath and with acorn finial.
$163 £75

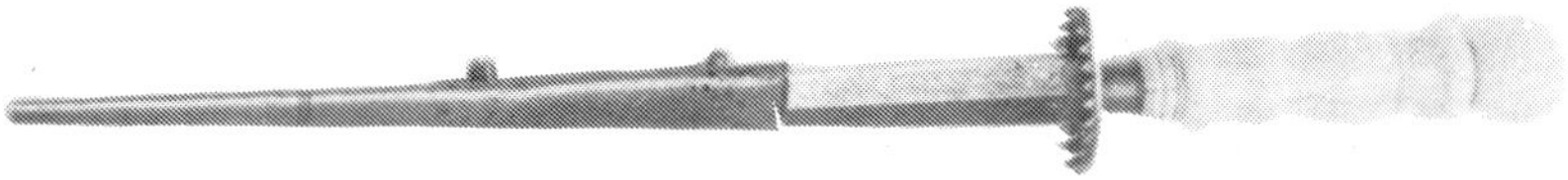

An unusual Georgian silver mounted midshipman's dirk, shallow diamond sectioned blade 4¾in., oval silver guard with down-turned foliate engraved toothed border. Silver ferrule, baluster turned ivory grip with spherical integral pommel, in its silver sheath. $165 £75

A Georgian Naval officer's dirk, circa 1800, double edged, plain, tapering blade 12½in., copper gilt, curved crosspiece with openwork side loops inset with diamond section, spadroon hilt with copper gilt straps and pommel, stained green fluted ivory grip, in its leather sheath. $163 £75

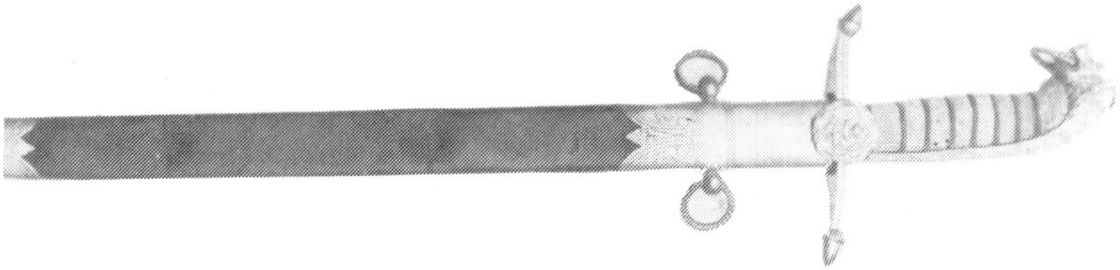

A Victorian Naval officer's dirk, straight, single edged blade 17½in., reversed gilt crosspiece with central spring catch release button, gilt mounts, 'lion's head' pommel with roped ring in mouth, gilt wirebound, white fishskin covered grip, in its leather scabbard. $180 £77

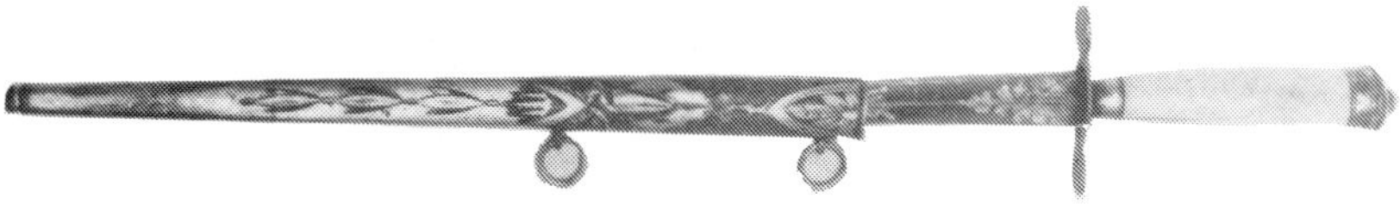

A Georgian Naval officer's blued and gilt dirk, shallow diamond sectioned, hollow ground blade 8in. Copper gilt crosspiece with chiselled 'lion's head' terminals, copper gilt mounted turned ivory grip with bun pommel. $242 £110

DIRKS
MILITARY & NAVAL

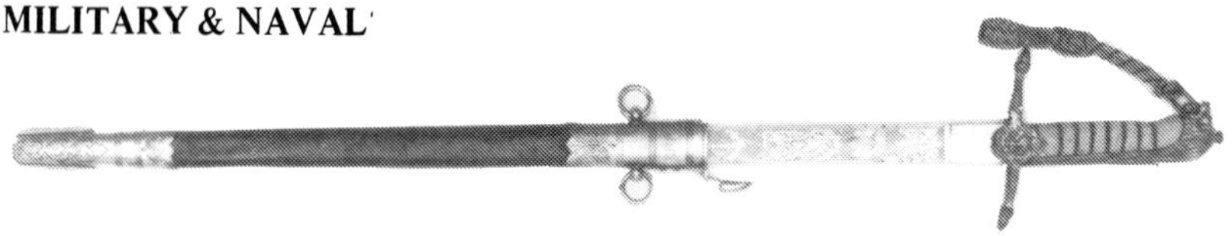

A George VI Naval officer's dirk, blade 17½in., copper gilt mounts, 'lion's head' pommel, wirebound white fishskin covered grip, spring catch, in its copper mounted leather sheath. $299 £115

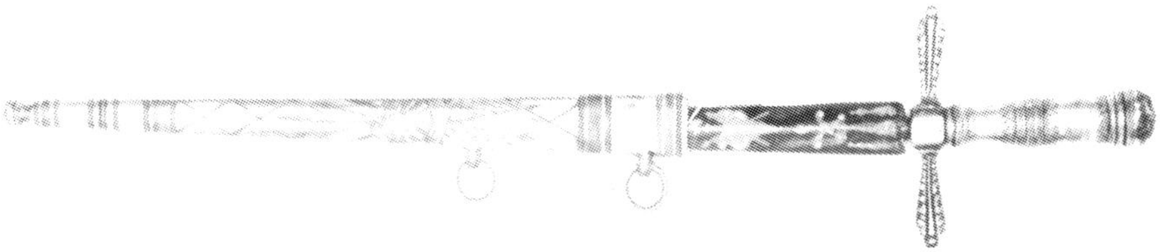

A Georgian Naval officer's dirk, double edged, tapering blade 8½in., solid copper gilt hilt, straight quillons of flattened form, turned grip and 'lion's head' pommel, in its copper gilt sheath. $264 £120

SCOTTISH

A late 18th century Scottish dirk, plain, single edged blade 12in., with single narrow back fullers, corded wood hilt, plain brass base mounts and pommel cap, in its leather sheath. Provision for companion knife and fork. $208 £80

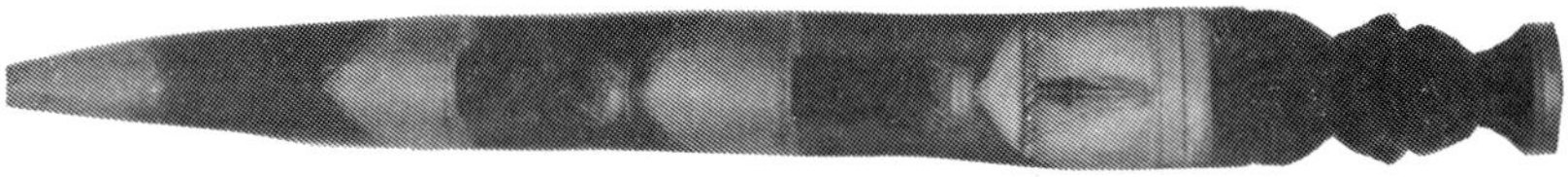

A late 19th century Scottish dirk, single edged fullered blade 13½in., with scalloped back. Strapwork carved hilt, engraved ferrule and pommel cap. In its engraved white metal mounted brown leather sheath with companion knife and fork en suite. $253 £110

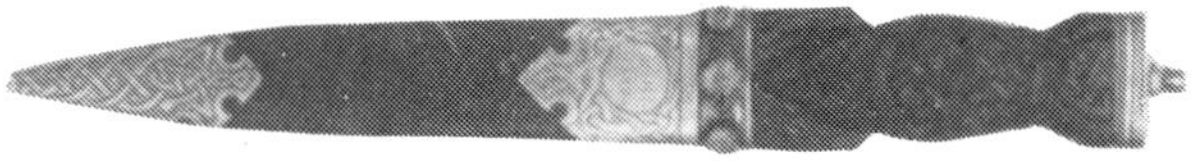

A silver mounted Scottish dirk, scallop back edge blade 6¼in., silver mounted corded wood flattened hilt with faceted yellow glass mounts to base mount, in its leather covered wooden sheath with silver chape and locket. $345 £150

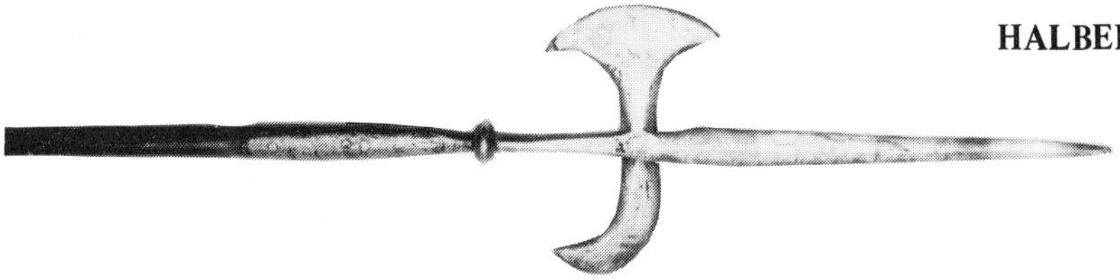

An 18th century American style halberd, flattened, tapering, double edged spike 17in., axe blade 6½in., curved beak, the centre engraved with crown above traces of Coat-of-Arms, on a round wooden haft. $177 £85

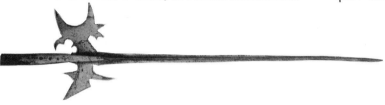

A good 16th century halberd, long spike 30in. of diamond section, crescent blade 4½in., flattened beak, with curved and spiked extensions, on a wooden haft. $354 £170

A German polearm halberd, circa 1550, steel head 20in., with top spike of squared section. Blades both pierced with clover shapes, scalloped edges and deeply struck with a crisp armourer's mark of a cross with splayed foot upon semi circle. Integral haft spurs, on its wooden haft. $456 £200

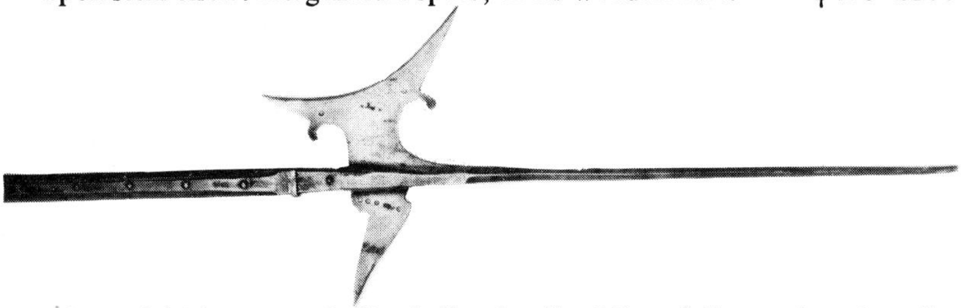

A good 16th century Italian halberd, spike 23in. of diamond section, flattened blade 10in., pierced with two holes with crescent cutting edge, long flattened beak pierced at base and struck with an armourer's mark, long straps on octagonal wooden haft, overall length 8ft. $562 £270

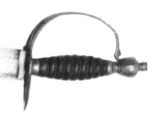

A Georgian Naval hanger, circa 1780, plain, curved, single edged blade 29in., brass slotted guard, fluted knucklebow, ovoid pommel engraved with fouled anchor, spiral wood grip. $99 £45

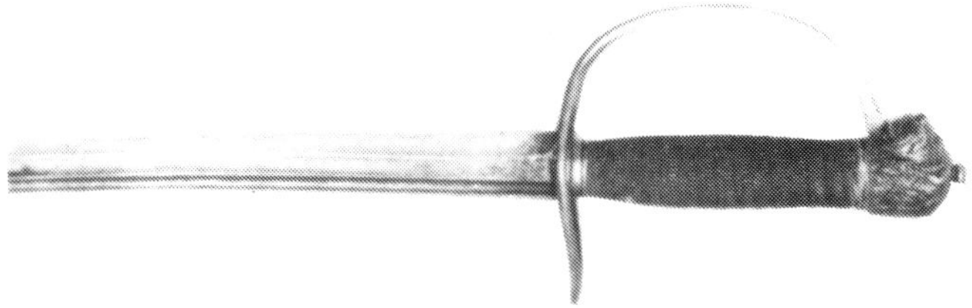

A good late 18th century hanger of the type favoured by Naval officers, plain, curved, single edged, double fullered blade 24½in., with clipped-back point, copper gilt hilt with slotted guard, fluted knucklebow and 'lion's head' pommel. $114 £52

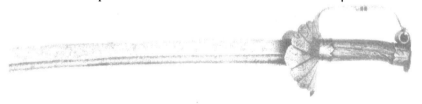

A good English late 17th century hanger, slightly curved, single edged blade 24½in., with single back fuller, 'Running Wolf' mark, spurious date '1531', large iron shell guard, single iron knucklebow, iron mounts, stag horn grip. $132 £60

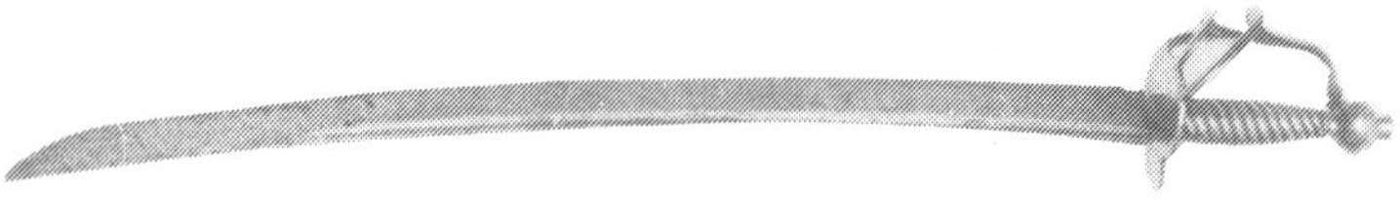

A mid 18th century brass hilted Militia hanger, slightly curved, single edged blade 24½in., with narrow back fuller, heart-shaped guard engraved '1st E.S.L.M.' (East Sussex Local Militia), brass knucklebow with double side loop, twist spiral grip, ovoid pommel. $176 £80

A late 17th century English brass hilted hanger, curved blade 20in., brass, small double shell guard, single knucklebow, gargoyle pommel, foliate scroll grip. $174 £80

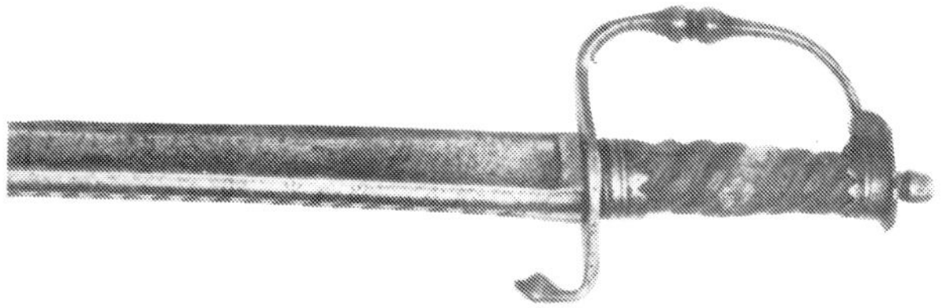

An English late 18th century hanger, slightly curved, single edged blade 21in., with saw-backed edge, single back fuller, iron single knucklebow incorporating baluster insert, iron mounts, spiral wood grip. $198 £90

A hallmarked silver mounted English hunting hanger by J. P. of London, year letter for 1763, part-fullered, single edged, straight blade 21½in., , silver mounted hilt, ribbed crosspiece with swollen whorled quillon terminals, ribbed chape mouth. $228 £100

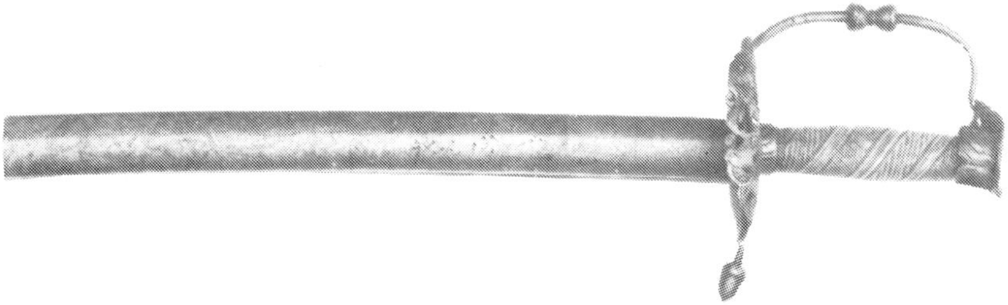

An English late 17th century hanger, single edged, curved blade 24½in., iron shell guard, up-turned small shell guard, iron mounts, twist bone grip. $242 £110

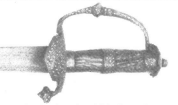

A late 17th century English hanger, slightly curved, single edged blade 27in., narrow back fuller, leaf-shaped iron shell guard, single iron knucklebow, iron pommel and mounts, decorated overall with silver piquet studded pattern.
$264 £120

A Georgian hanger, circa 1780, plain, curved blade 29in., double fullered, and with pronounced, clipped-back tip, fluted steel knucklebow with slotted guard, chiselled 'leopard's head' pommel, spiral fluted ivory grip.
$260 £120

A Georgian hanger, circa 1780, curved blade 29in., with narrow back fuller and etched with dragon etc., semi-basket steel guard with slotted base and two side loop scrolls, fluted ivory grip. $325 £150

A Georgian hallmarked silver mounted hanger, slightly curved, bi-fullered, single edged blade 26¾in., hallmarked silver guard (I.R. London 1739-40). Fenestrated guard and shell shaped thumb piece. In its silver mounted leather sheath. $495 £225

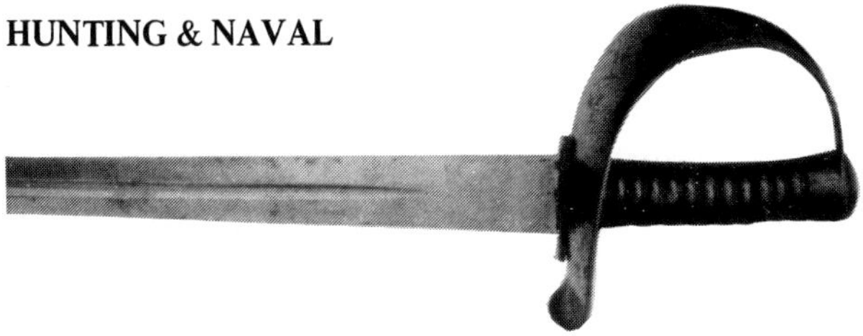

A late 19th century continental Naval cutlass, straight, single edged blade 30in., with short central fuller, sheet steel bowl guard, ribbed steel grip.
$54 £25

A late pattern Naval cutlass, single edged, straight blade 28in., with clipped-back tip, etched within panel 'Manufactured by the Wilkinson Sd Coy, London', steel bowl guard with turned down edges, ribbed brass grips, spring catch. $65 £30

A Victorian Naval cutlass, slightly curved blade 29in., double edged at tip, sheet brass guard, ribbed iron grip, in its leather scabbard. $65 £30

An early 19th century continental 'figure-of-eight' Naval cutlass, curved blade 24½in., with back fuller, thin sheet steel guard, ribbed iron grip.
$76 £35

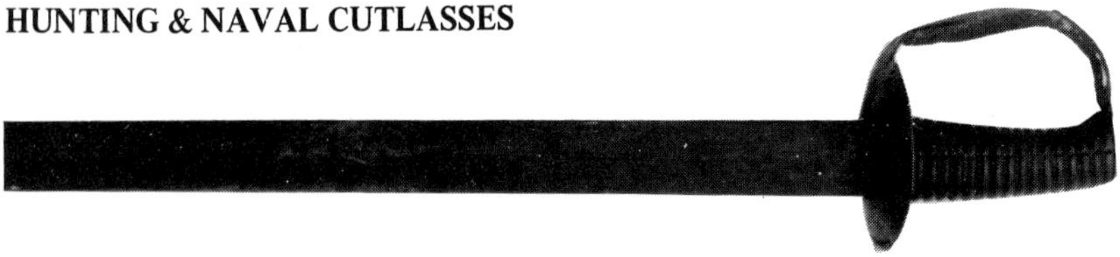

An early 19th century 'figure-of-eight' Naval boarding cutlass, plain, single edged blade 28½in., iron sheet guard and ribbed iron grip. $82 £38

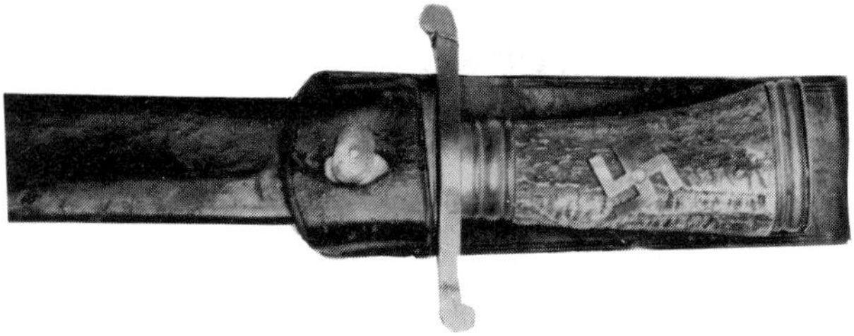

A Nazi era hunting cutlass, broad, single edged blade 14¼in., heavy hilt with plain brass crosspiece and mounts, stag horn grip mounted with large brass swastika, in its brass mounted leather sheath. $100 £44

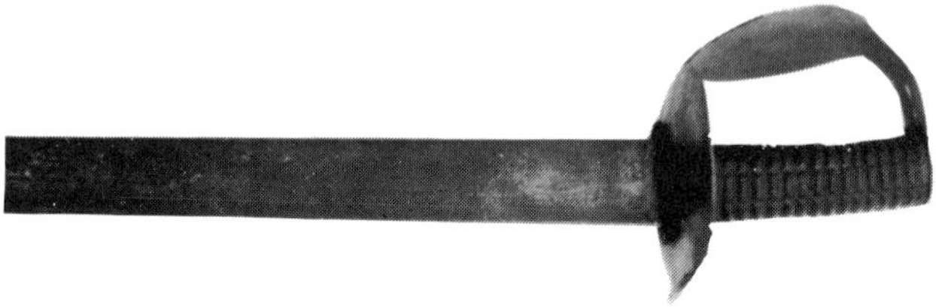

An early 19th century 'figure-of-eight' Naval cutlass, single edged blade 25½in., with clipped-back point, iron guard, ribbed iron grip. $100 £46

A late Victorian Naval cutlass, curved blade 26½in., stamped at forte 'Mole B'ham', sheet steel guard, ribbed iron hilt, in its steel mounted leather scabbard. $108 £50

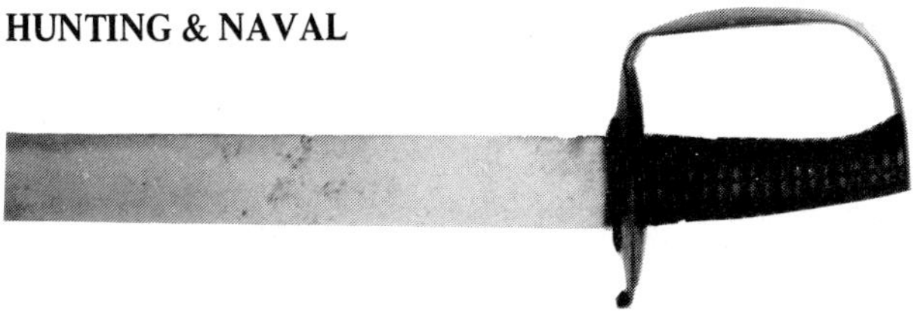

An early 19th century 'figure-of-eight' Naval cutlass, straight, single edged blade 29in., iron sheet guard and ribbed grip. $119 £55

A late 18th century Georgian Naval 'figure-of-eight' cutlass, single edged, straight blade 28in., with back fuller, sheet iron guard, round sheet iron grip. $152 £70

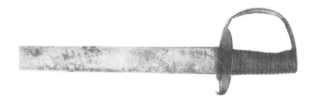

A Georgian 'figure-of-eight' cutlass, plain blade 29in., iron guard, ribbed iron grip. $165 £70

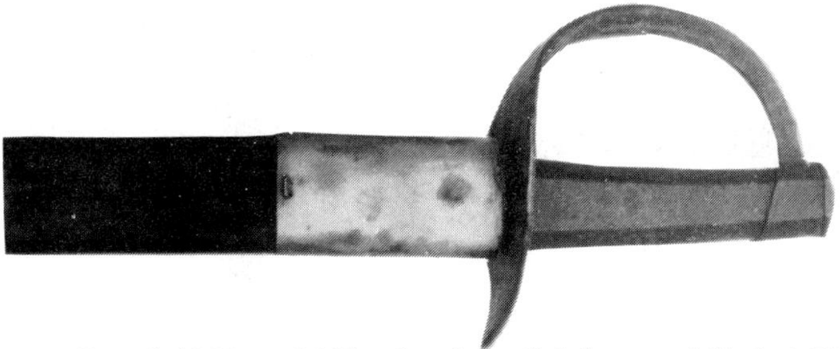

A French 1833 model Naval cutlass, slightly curved blade 26½in., iron hilt with flattened knucklebow and octagonal grip, in its brass mounted leather scabbard. $174 £80

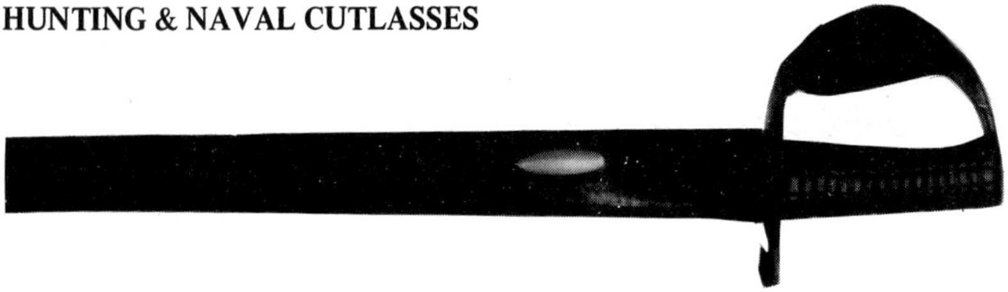

An early 19th century Georgian Naval 'figure-of-eight' cutlass, single edged blade 28in., stamped with crown, 'GR', iron sheet guard and ribbed grip, in its leather scabbard with brass frog lug. $195 £90

A Prussian Naval boarding cutlass, circa 1860, straight blade 23in., with spear point and recurving cutting edge, by 'A.C.', with scales mark, iron half-basket solid guard, iron mounts, brass wirebound leather covered grip. $239 £110

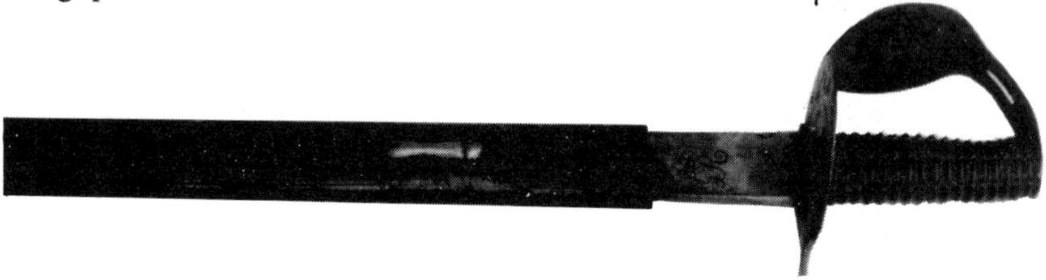

An early 19th century Georgian Naval 'figure-of-eight' cutlass, straight, single edged blade 29in., with spear point, iron guard and ribbed grip, in its leather scabbard with brass belt lug. $250 £115

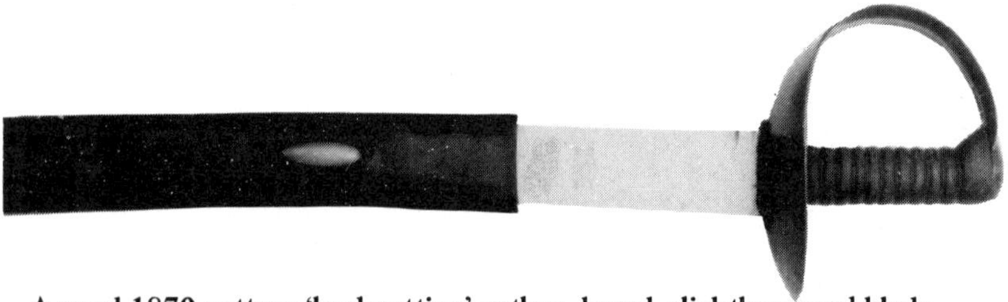

A good 1870 pattern 'lead cutting' cutlass, broad, slightly curved blade 28½in., double edged at tip, and etched 'Lead Cutter' within foliate scroll and 'Wilkinson, Pall Mall, London', sheet steel bowl guard, ribbed grip, in its leather scabbard with brass lug and chape. $336 £155

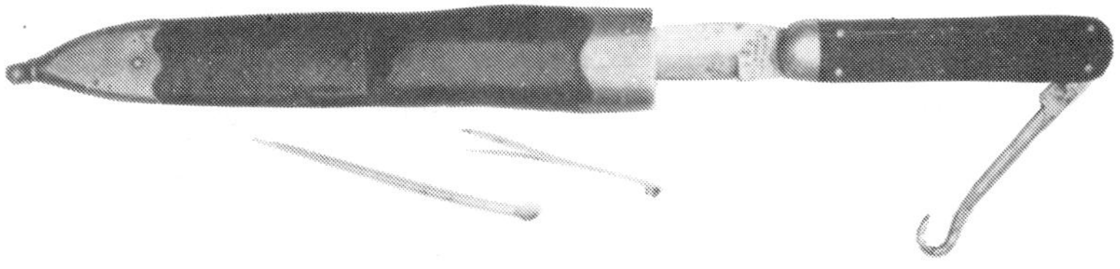

A Victorian huntsman's knife, by Thornhill in hallmarked silver mounted sheath, clipped-back blade 2¾in., white metal mounted chequered two-piece horn grip with hinged button hook, grip contains concealed sewing spike and tweezers, in its hallmarked silver mounted leather sheath. $64 £29

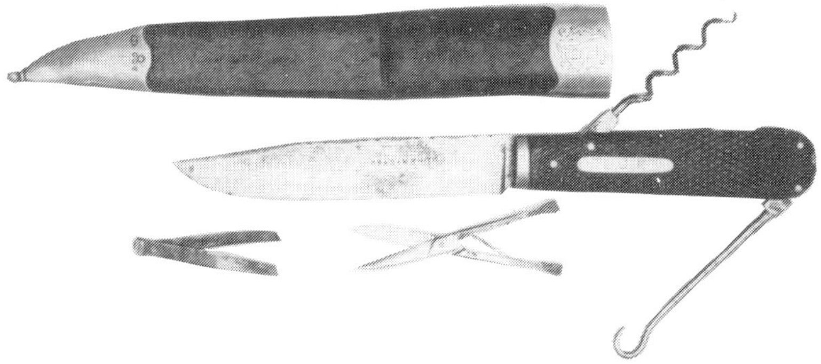

A Victorian hunting knife, single edged blade 5in. stamped 'Thornhill, 144 New Bond Str., Graham Knife', scalloped edge. Chequered horn grips with hinged corkscrew and button hook with slide-in tweezers, spike and scissors. $84 £38

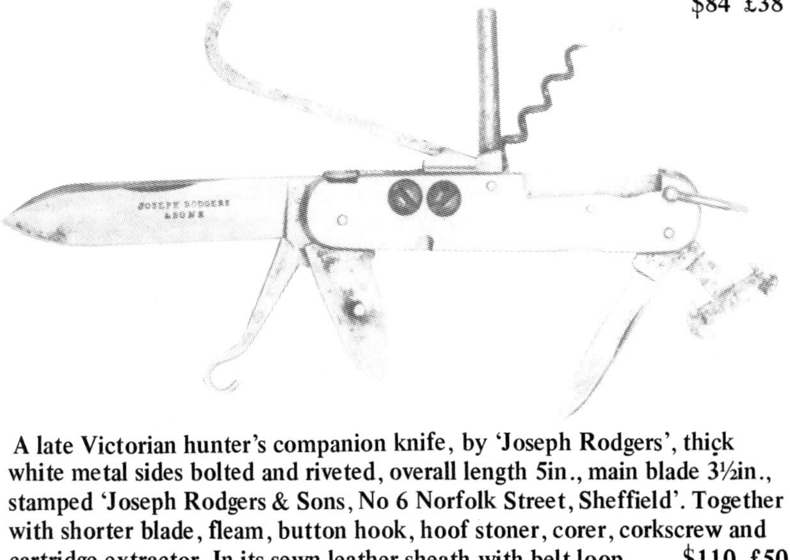

A late Victorian hunter's companion knife, by 'Joseph Rodgers', thick white metal sides bolted and riveted, overall length 5in., main blade 3½in., stamped 'Joseph Rodgers & Sons, No 6 Norfolk Street, Sheffield'. Together with shorter blade, fleam, button hook, hoof stoner, corer, corkscrew and cartridge extractor. In its sewn leather sheath with belt loop. $110 £50

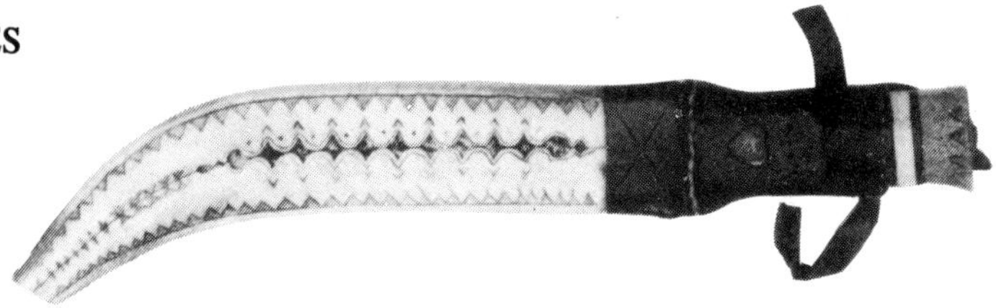

An unusually large and heavy Laplander's knife, single edged, straight blade 8½in. Bone and leather segmented grip with engraved tooth decoration to pommel. In its geometrically carved and pierced two-piece bone sheath with leather top. $135 £65

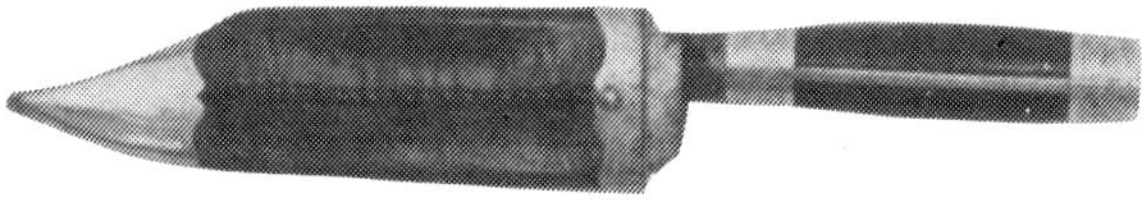

A 19th century Spanish gold mounted knife, broad single edged, slight clipped back blade 5¾in. Cylindrical horn grip with foliate engraved gold ferrule, pommel and ribs. In its foliate engraved gold mounted leather sheath. $216 £94

A scarce Canadian Army issue parachutist's fighting knife, double edged blade of flattened diamond section, 7in., small crossguard and green painted ribbed copper hilt, in its well made leather arm scabbard stamped 'Knife Parachutist Sleeve-Scabbard Mk. 1 H. Sheffield M.45'. $290 £126

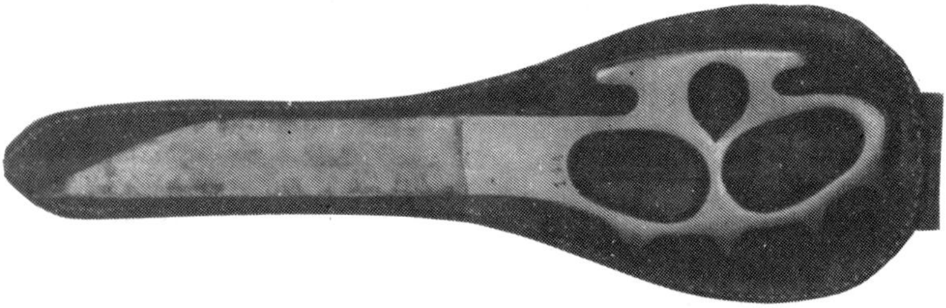

A rare Middle East Commando knuckle-knife of World War II period, steel Bowie type blade with spear point, 5¾in., brass heavily knuckled hilt stamped '144', in its original leather sheath with securing strap and brass eye. $338 £130

A silver mounted bade bade, slim blade 8½in., tulip hilt covered in Eastern sheet silver embossed with foliate patterns, in its Eastern sheet silver sheath, pierced horn foliate throat mounts. $141 £65

A silver mounted bade bade, blade 7½in., horn tulip hilt, in its wooden sheath with Eastern sheet silver top and bottom mounts embossed with floral and foliate patterns and bound with silver bands. $152 £70

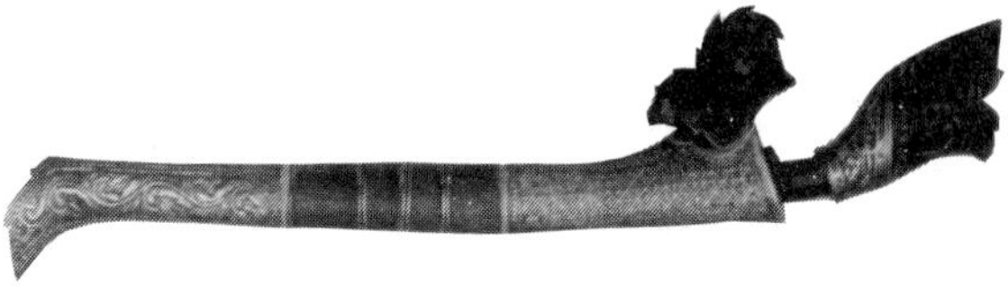

A silver mounted bade bade, slim blade 7½in., tulip horn hilt with carved decoration and Eastern silver base mount embossed with foliate pattern, in its wooden sheath with silver bands and long Eastern sheet silver mounts, bone foliate throat mount. $152 £70

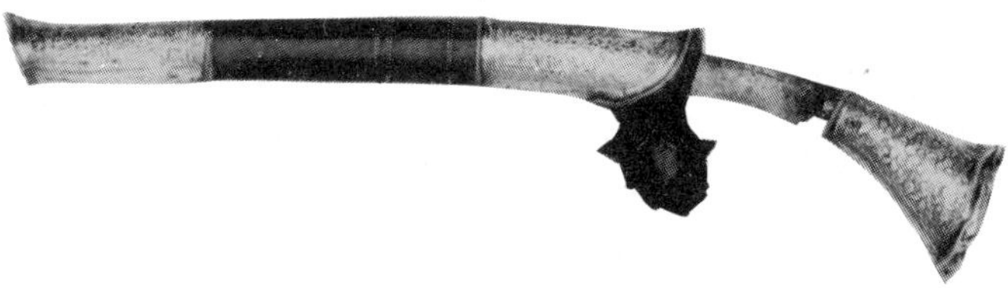

A silver mounted bade bade, slightly recurving blade 8¼in., tulip type hilt overlaid with Eastern sheet silver embossed with foliate patterns, in its wooden sheath with two Eastern sheet silver mounts. $150 £72

A silver mounted bade bade, iron, spear blade 7in., tulip carved horn hilt, with base band of Eastern silver embossed with foliate patterns, in its wooden sheath with two long mounts of Eastern silver embossed with foliate and floral patterns. $176 £80

A silver mounted bade bade, slightly recurving blade 8in., tulip hilt overlaid with Eastern sheet silver, in its wooden sheath with two Eastern sheet silver mounts. $176 £80

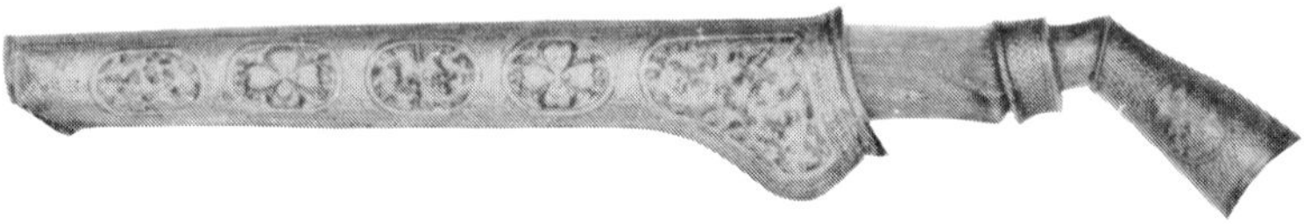

A silver mounted Malayan knife bade bade, straight, laminated, single edged blade 8½in., Eastern silver covered hilt and sheath well embossed with foliate vignettes. $177 £85

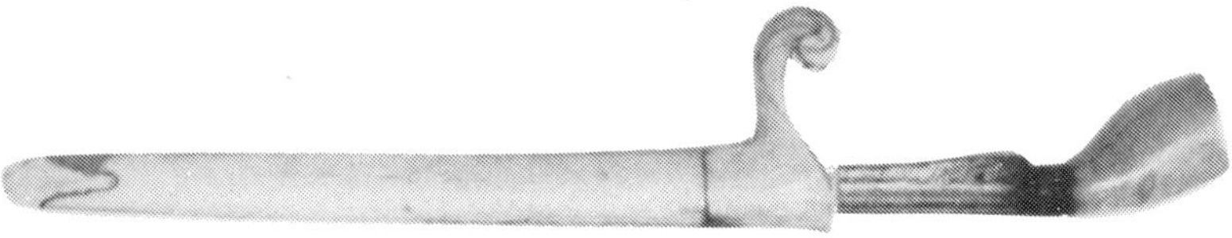

An ivory mounted bade bade, straight, single edged blade 11¼in., tulip hilt of plain ivory, in its solid ivory sheath with scrolled throat extension. $219 £95

A Victorian folding bowie type dagger, double edged blade 4in., by 'Moore', German silver foliate embossed crosspiece, stag horn grips, with spring thumb release catch. $39 £18

A Victorian Bowie type knife, shallow diamond sectioned blade 5in. Gilt iron crosspiece with ball finials, ribbed gilt, white metal ferrule, rounded polished ebony handle, in its gilt, white metal mounted velvet covered sheath. $48 £22

A Victorian folding bowie knife, single edged, spatulate blade 5in., by 'Allender, Sheffield', white metal embossed crosspiece, stag horn grips inset with white metal rectangular panel, spring thumb release. $54 £25

A bowie knife, double edged blade 6in., with spear point, cockerel stamp at forte, white metal sheet crosspiece and pommel, tortoiseshell mounted grips, in its leather sheath with plain white metal sheet mounts. $74 £34

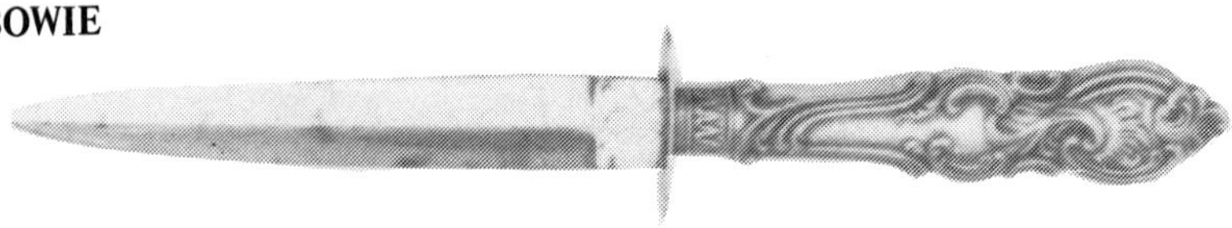

A Victorian Bowie knife, double edged blade 5½in., of flattened diamond section, by "R. Lingard, Blacroft, Sheffield", lightly etched: "Never Draw Me Without Reason Nor Sheath Me Without Honour". $76 £35

A South American folding bowie type knife, double edged blade 4¾in., of flattened diamond section, white metal crosspiece with 'monster head' quillons and mask to central panel, white metal pommel. $76 £35

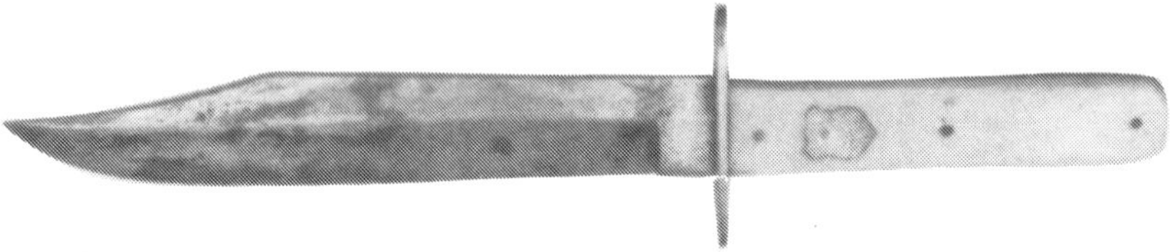

A Victorian bowie knife, double edged blade 5½in., of flattened diamond section, by 'R. Lingard, Blacroft, Sheffield', lightly etched 'Never Draw Me Without Reason Nor Sheath Me Without Honour', white metal plain oval crossguard. $76 £35

A folding bowie knife, clipped-back, single edged blade 7¾in., marked 'Juan Canedo, Buenos Aires', white metal small crosspiece, stag horn grips inset with spring release button, thumb release spring catch. $104 £40

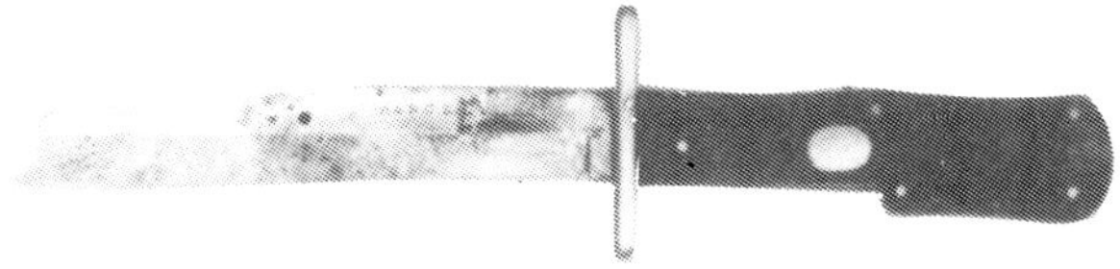

A folding bowie knife, clipped-back blade 7¼in., by 'A. & N. C.S.L.', white metal crosspiece, diced black wooden grips, with spring release button. $100 £45

A good Victorian bowie type knife, polished shallow diamond sectioned, double edged blade 5in., stamped 'Rodgers Cutlers to Her Majesty'. Ball finialled, white metal crosspiece, in its white metal mounted gilt tooled red Morocco leather sheath. $117 £45

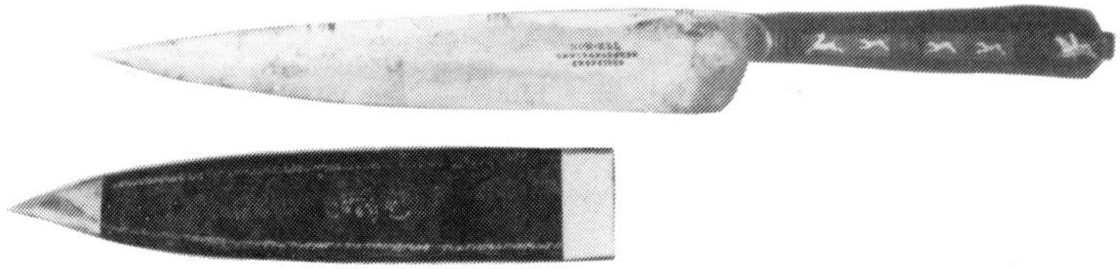

An unusual 19th century bowie type hunting knife by 'Unwin & Rodgers', blade 9½in. of gaucho form, with scalloped back. Heat moulded horn grip of octagonal form, in its white metal mounted gilt tooled Morocco sheath. $130 £50

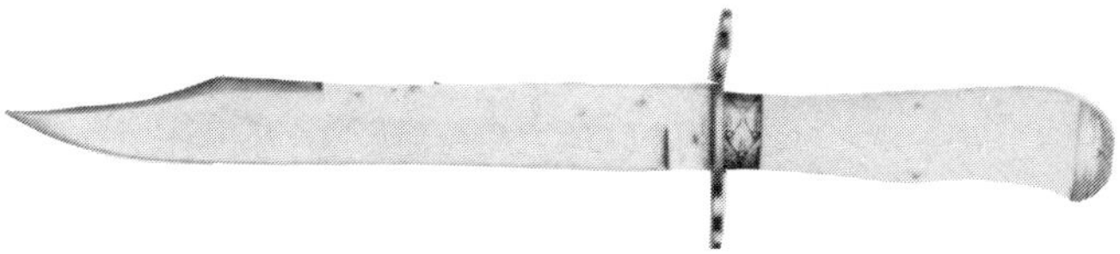

A good Victorian bowie knife, clipped-back blade 7½in., stamped 'George Butler & Co., Trinity Works, Sheffield, England', small white metal crossguard, white metal mounted hilt with ivory grips. $119 £55

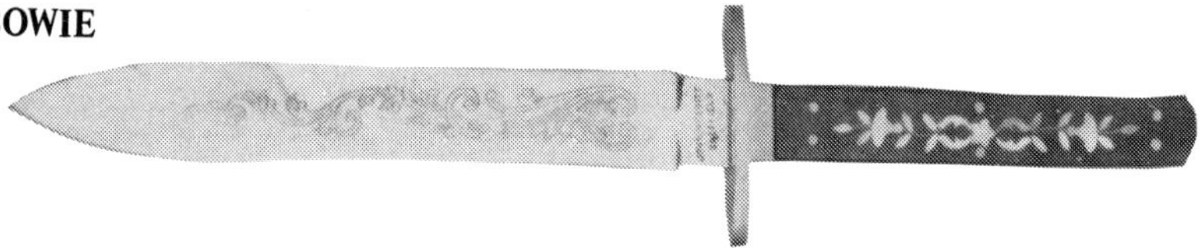

A Victorian Bowie type knife, broad, slightly waisted, shallow diamond sectioned blade 6¼in., stamped 'John Nesbitt, Sheffield' at forte, solid white metal crosspiece, two-piece polished horn grips inlaid with mother-of-pearl sections of foliage. $121 £55

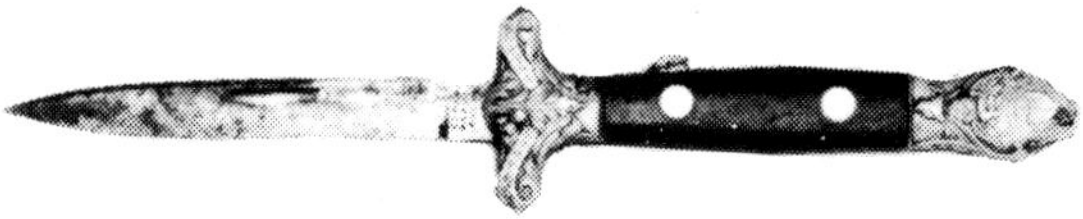

A Victorian folding Bowie type knife, single edged blade 4½in., stamped 'Edward Barnes & Sons', white metal mounted hilt embossed 'Liberty & Union' with foliage, pommel with U.S. Eagle, eight stars, shield, laurel, Phrigian cap, scales of justice, two-piece polished bone grip, sprung securing catch. $145 £65

A Victorian Bowie knife, slightly curved, clipped-back blade 7in., well etched with foliage and 'Draw Me Not Without A Cause, Nor Sheath Me With Dishonour', white metal crosspiece, ferrule and grip strap, two-piece rounded ivory grips, 'pistol' shaped hilt. $143 £65

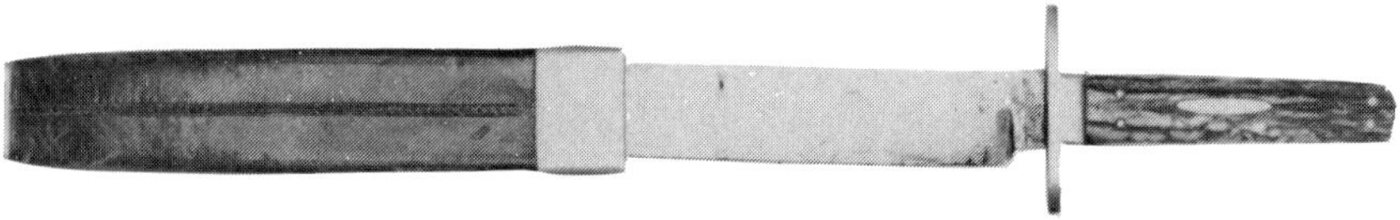

A good Victorian bowie knife, single edged blade 8½in., marked at forte 'Joseph Rodgers & Sons, 6 Norfolk Street, Sheffield,' plain German silver crosspiece, stag horn grips, in its leather sheath. $152 £70

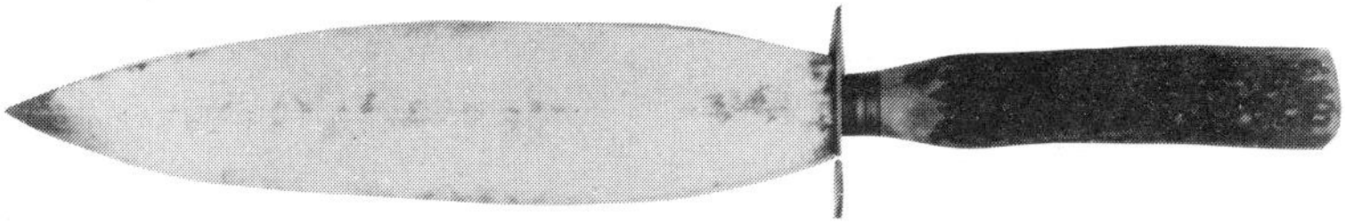

An unusual old bowie knife, broad, double edged, spear shaped blade 9in., faintly etched 'California Bowie', white metal oval crosspiece, stag horn hilt with white metal mounts, in its red cloth re-covered sheath. $163 £75

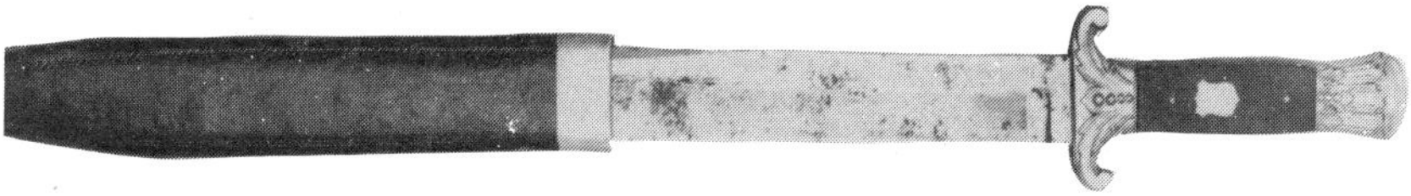

A good late 19th century continental bowie knife, clipped-back blade 8½in., frost etched on one side with scrolling foliage, white metal mounted ebony gripped hilt, in its white metal mounted embossed leather sheath. $174 £80

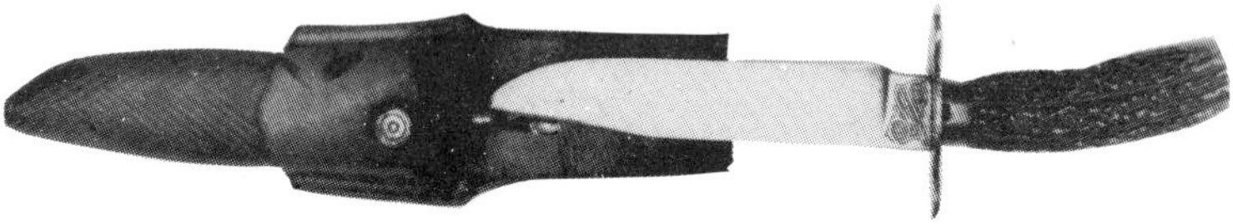

A bowie knife, clipped-back blade 7in., by 'Wilkinson, Pall Mall, London', etched 'R.B.D. Hunting Knife No 1', steel crosspiece, stag horn hilt, in its diced leather covered, wooden sheath, with leather frog and spring catch. $182 £80

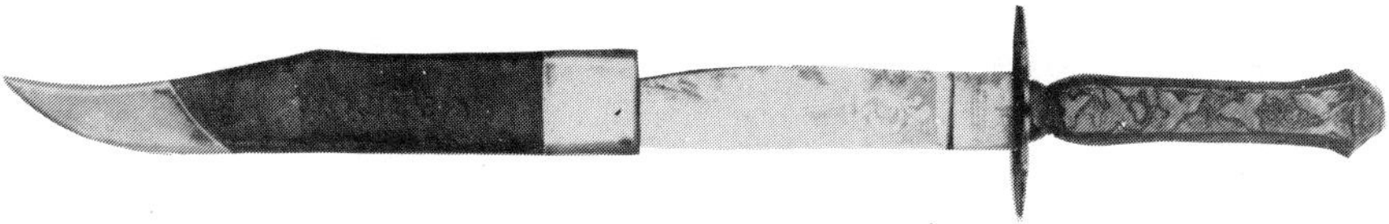

A good Victorian bowie knife, single edged, pronounced clipped-back blade 8in., by 'Joseph Gill, Parliament St., Sheffield', and etched within scroll 'The Gold Finder', pewter hilt, diamond style crosspiece. $434 £200

A good silver mounted Sumatran knife sekin, double edged, fullered, incurved blade 7½in., foliate embossed silver ferrule to carved rootwood hilt, in its foliate carved rootwood sheath. $171 £75

A moplah , broad blade 12in., with incised decoration at edge, sexagonal ivory hilt with Eastern silver base mount with three bands and geometric pattern decoration. $187 £82

FOLDING CLASP

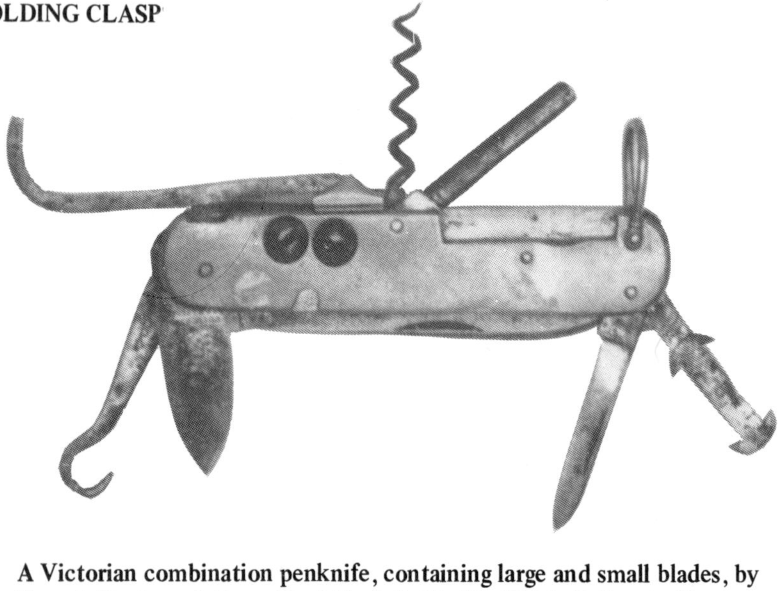

A Victorian combination penknife, containing large and small blades, by 'Joseph Rodgers & Sons, No 6 Norfolk St., Sheffield, Cutlers to Her Majesty', button hook, hoof stone remover, corkscrew, bleeding cutter, fleam, scoop and corkscrew. $57 £26

A good Spanish clasp knife, heavy blade 9in., bearing cutler's mark of a 'Clay Pipe', with clipped-back tip, horn side panels, steel frame. $80 £35

A large Spanish folding clasp knife Navaja, single edged blade 14in., with part scallop back edge and pronounced clipped-back tip, brass and bone panel mounted grip. $76 £35

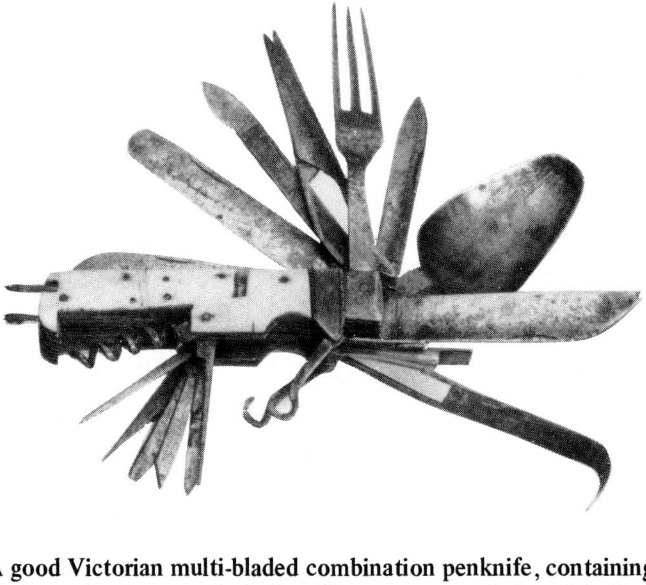

A good Victorian multi-bladed combination penknife, containing twenty blades or implements, including file, saw, spoon, fork and knife, brass whistle, corkscrew, two button hooks, bone sided plates with two prickers inset. $93 £45

A South American silver mounted gaucho knife, blade 4¾in., stamped 'M. Mailhos, Montevideo', silver hilt and sheath with silver bands, sheath with belt hook engraved 'P.G.' $44 £20

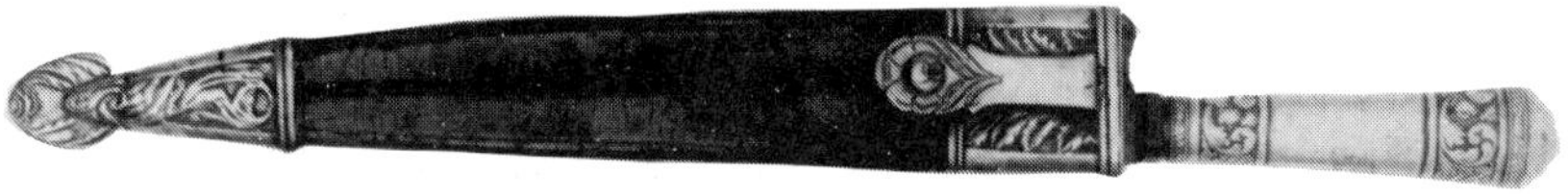

A large silver mounted South American gaucho knife, single edged, spear blade 13in., hilt of South American silver decorated with foliate scrolls, in its leather sheath with two silver mounts, belt lug stamped 'L. Toma'. $83 £36

PIA KAETTA

A Singalese dagger pia kaetta, blade 7in., elaborately carved bone grips with foliate decorated Eastern silver mounts, in its wooden sheath. $141 £65

A Singalese dagger pia kaetta, iron blade 7in., partly sheathed in brass, bone carved hilt with brass scroll decorated base, silver sheet embossed pommel cap. $166 £80

A Victorian Gothic stiletto, diamond section blade 5¾in., gilt hilt with urn quillons, floral and fluted baluster grip, in its velvet covered sheath with gilt metal mounts decorated with foliate patterns. $76 £35

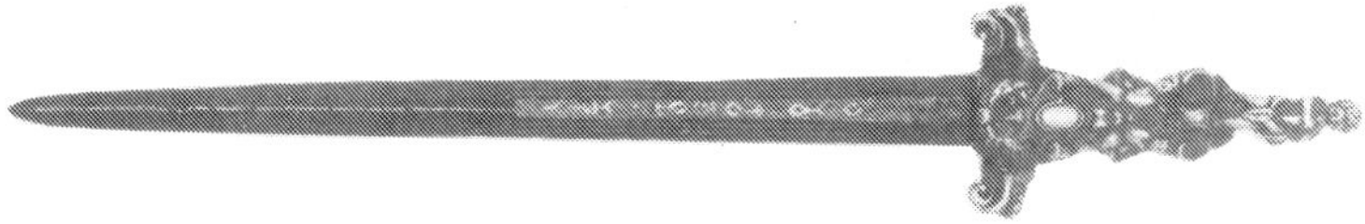

A late 17th century French stiletto, double edged blade 9¼in., brass inlaid at stepped, ribbed forte, shallow diamond section tip. Brass hilt chiselled with three cherubs amidst scrolls, quillons formed by dogs on scrolls with foliate swag as ricasso block. $520 £200

TROUSSE

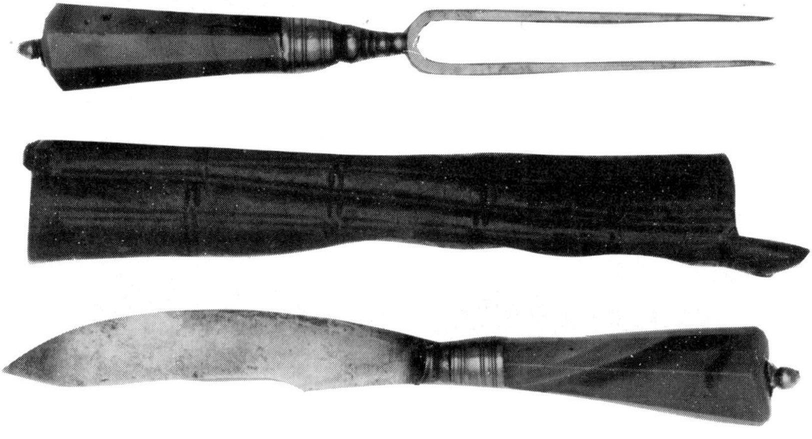

A good German 18th century trousse, consisting of knife, with curved, clipped-back blade 4¾in., and double prong fork, both with facetted agate handles, with silver gilt plain mounts, in their blind tooled decorated leather covered wooden sheath. $208 £100

A silver mounted Nepalese kukri, curved blade 17in., wooden hilt with part carved decoration, in its leather covered wooden sheath with large bottom mount and chape of Indian silver. $104 £50

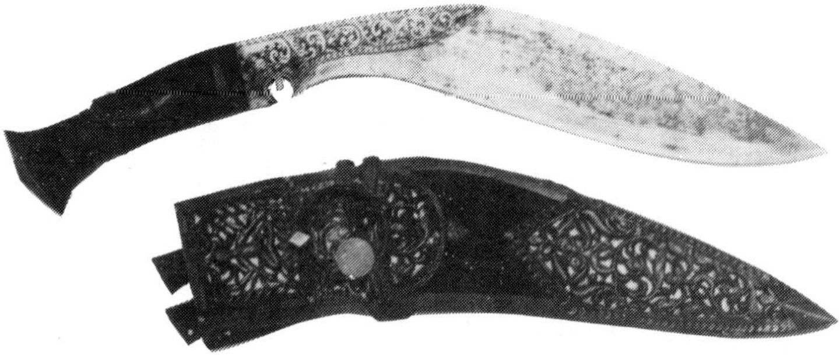

A silver mounted Nepalese kukri, curved blade 12½in., foliate decoration at forte, horn hilt with brass mounts, in its black velvet covered sheath with large Eastern silver mounts with openwork patterns of floral sprays, a God, etc., with foil backing, silver carrying ring, Indian coin, silver band. $207 £90

A silver mounted presentation quality kukri of the 4th Gurkhas, curved blade 11in., etched with regimental badge, horn hilt with plain Indian silver mounts, in its green velvet covered wooden sheath with two large Indian silver mounts. $286 £130

PARTISAN

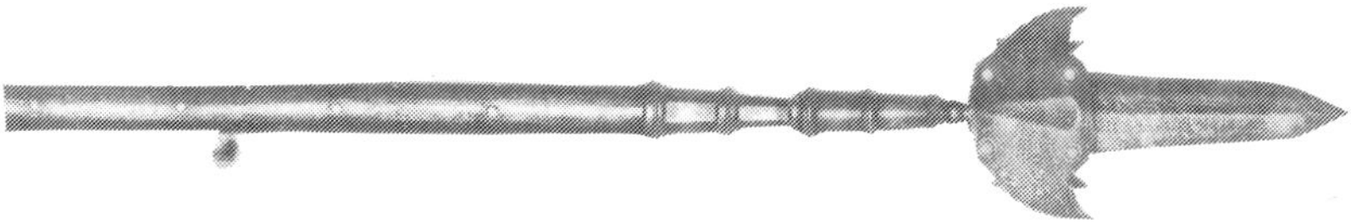

A 17th century European ceremonial partisan, steel head 11½in., etched with trophies of Arms, scrolls, hearts etc., and imitation watered steel pattern, pierced with four holes, turned haft mount, mounted on associated wooden haft with long iron straps, overall 7ft.6in. $198 £90

POLEARMS

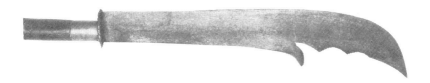

A 19th century Chinese polearm of glaive form, broad steel blade 22½in., with hooked back. Pierced brass guard of tsuba form with bamboo shaped rim and punched decoration, on its original brass mounted pole. $132 £60

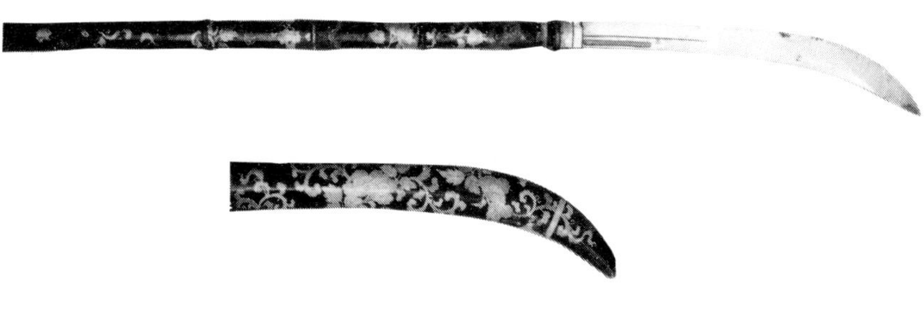

A good Japanese polearm Naginata, blade 39½cm., signed 'Iwami Nokami Fujiwara Masanao', broad gunome hamon, twin red lacquered hi. Black lacquered pole and cover, silvered copper mounts. $520 £250

A 17th century transitional rapier, slim, straight, tapering, double edged blade 27in., with short fullers, iron pierced shell guard, crosspiece with looped terminals, fluted ovoid iron pommel, copper wirebound grip. $94 £45

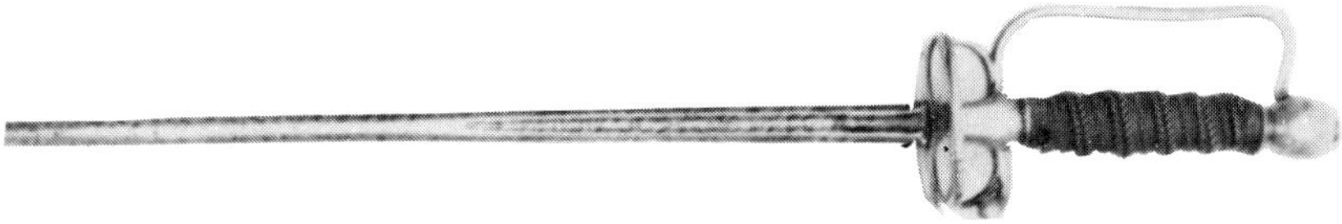

An early 18th century transitional smallsword rapier, slim rapier blade 31in. of flattened diamond section, short fuller with inscription 'May Sinal Sandissmo', brass hilt with plain, double shell guard, plain slim, rounded knucklebow, ovoid pommel, copper wirebound grip. $228 £105

A 17th century European transitional rapier, tapering, double edged blade 29½in., multi-fullered at forte, iron hilt, with double shell guard, baluster mounts to edges, fluted pommel and wirebound grip with 'Turk's head' terminals. $542 £250

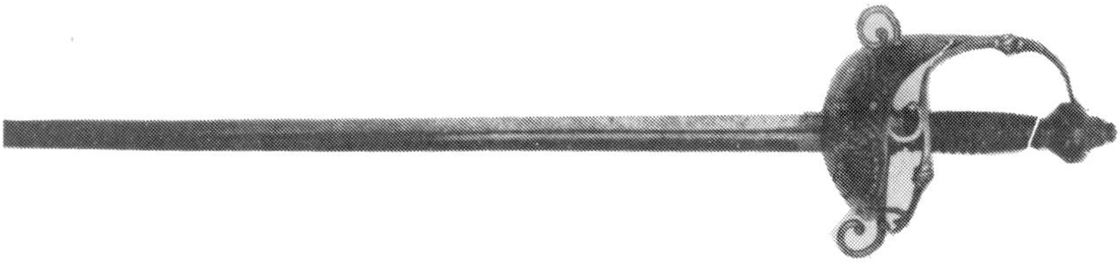

An English rapier, circa 1625, of the type used during the Civil War, flattened diamond section, double edged blade 37in., short fullers, pierced steel guard, integral scroll finialled quillons, raised side bar and knucklebow. Foliate chiselled pommel, steel wirebound grip. $780 £300

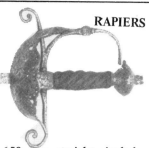

A 17th century transitional cup-hilted rapier, circa 1650, slim, straight, singled edged, tapering blade 37½in., iron hilt, with mortuary style cup guard, pierced overall and with circular panels chiselled with linear designs. $1,000 £425

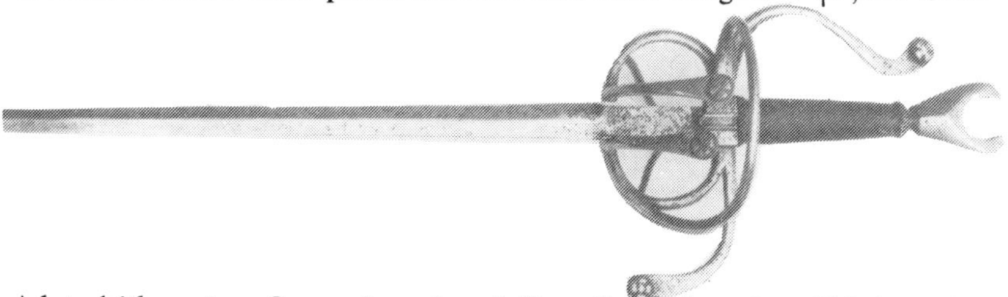

A late 16th century Germanic rapier, shallow diamond sectioned blade 42½in., including rectangular ricasso. Steel swept hilt and quillon terminals. Leather covered grip with brass Turks' heads. $1,245 £525

SABRES

An Arab sabre nimcha, sharply curved, single edged blade 15in., steel recurved crosspiece with swollen terminals, brass mounted wooden hilt of octagonal cross-section and terminating in stylised horse's head, the hilt decorated with inlaid white metal scroll plates and red inlays in geometric patterns. $100 £45

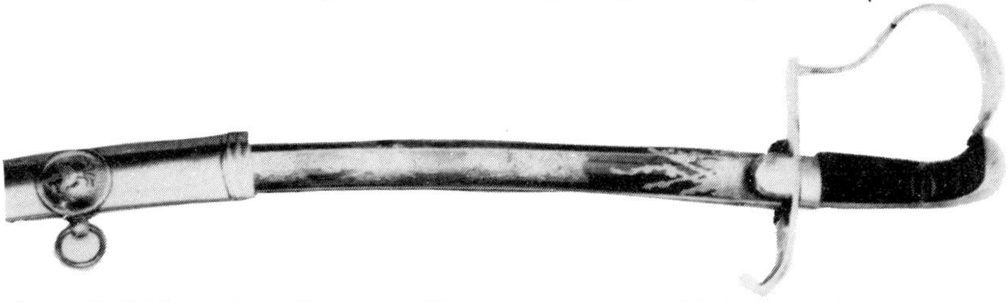

An early 19th century German officer's sabre, curved blade 33in., by 'Gebr. Weyersberg in Solingen', with clipped-back tip, plain steel hilt with stirrup guard, ribbed leather covered grip, in its steel scabbard. $141 £65

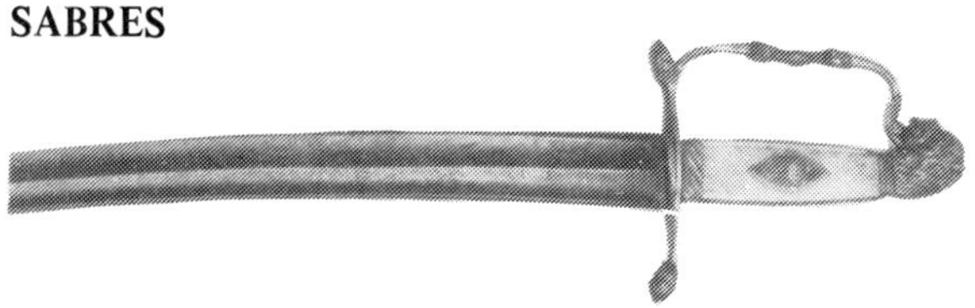

A Napoleonic era continental officer's sabre, curved, double fullered blade 32½in., copper gilt hilt with single knucklebow, 'lion's head' pommel, diced ivory grips. $155 £65

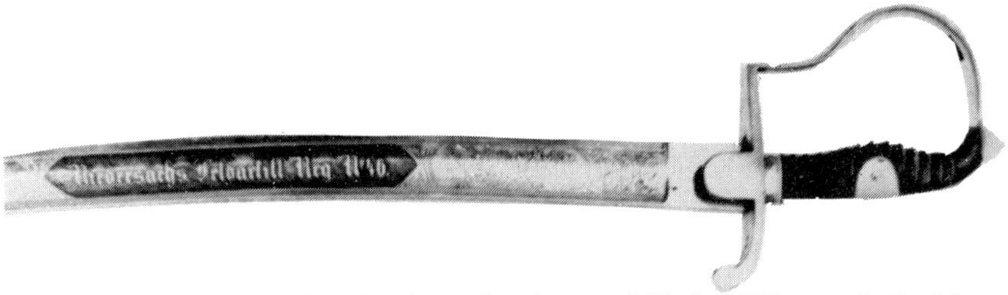

A Prussian Artillery officer's sabre, plated, curved blade 29½in., etched with Regiment 'Niedersachs Feldartill Reg. No 46' on blued panel, also with Prussian Eagle and foliate scrolls and military trophies, plated guard with plain stirrup guard, leather covered ribbed grip. $171 £75

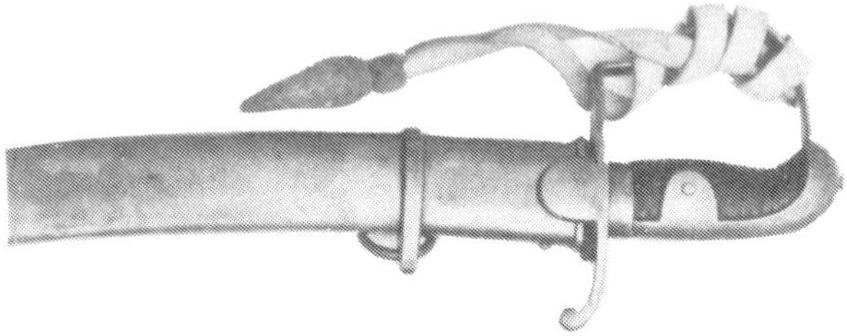

A Prussian Mounted Artillery trooper's sabre, circa 1830, plain, curved blade 32½in., heavy plain steel hilt with stirrup guard, leather covered ribbed grip, in its heavy steel scabbard. $190 £80

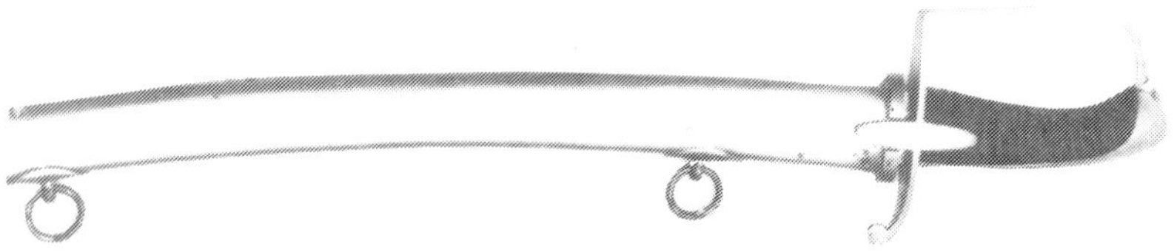

A 1788 Cavalry trooper's sabre, plain, curved blade 35½in., with narrow back fuller, with traces of maker on back-strap 'Woolley & Co', plain steel hilt with single knucklebow, ribbed leather covered grip, in its steel scabbard. $198 £90

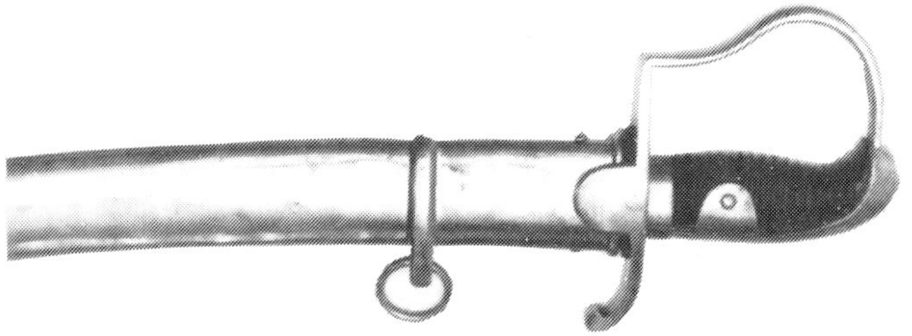

A Prussian Mounted Artillery trooper's sabre, circa 1830, plain, curved blade 33in., heavy steel hilt with stirrup guard and plain mounts, the crosspiece stamped 'A.M.V.3.90', ribbed leather covered grip, in its heavy steel scabbard. $198 £90

A Georgian officer's mameluke sabre, curved blade 33½in., with blued and gilt panels etched with crown, 'GR' and 1801-16 Royal Arms, plain steel crosspiece, plain ivory grip. $215 £90

A Georgian Volunteer Cavalry officer's sabre, curved, fullered blued and gilt blade 29½in., copper gilt stirrup hilt, pierced knucklebow, chiselled 'lion's head' pommel with mane on back-strap. Silver wire covered shark-skin grip. $220 £100

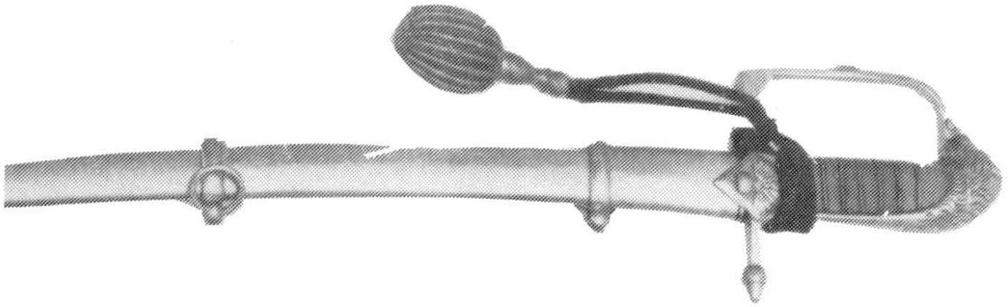

A Victorian 1897 pattern Infantry officer's sword, blade 32in., by 'Hobson, Lexington St.', etched with '1st Vol. Batt. Royal Lancaster Regt.', foliage, steel hilt, wirebound fishskin covered grip, in its plated scabbard. $250 £105

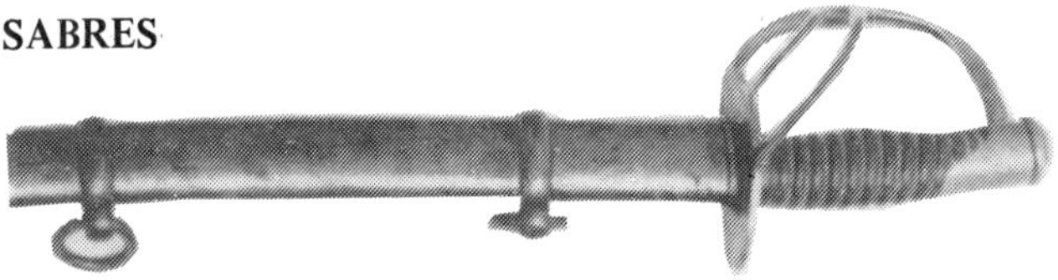

A U.S. Civil War period Cavalry trooper's sabre, curved blade 35in., by 'Crosby W. Chelmsford Mass.' and 'U.S. 1864 A.G.M.', triple bar brass guard, brass mounts, ribbed, leather covered grip, in its steel scabbard. $250 £105

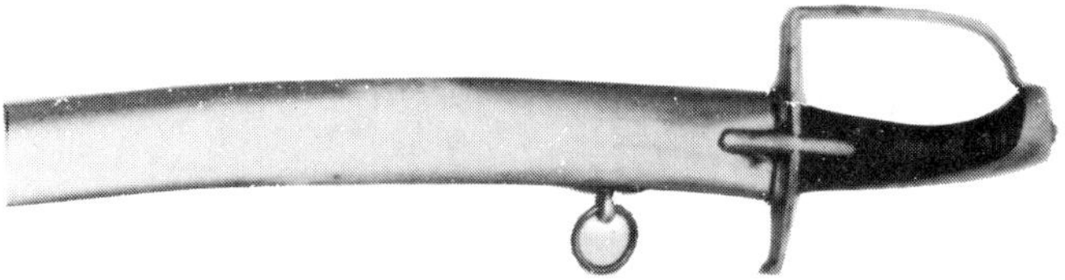

A scarce 1788 pattern Light Cavalry trooper's sabre, plain, curved blade 33½in., iron hilt with plain knucklebow and mounts, ribbed leather grips, in its iron scabbard. $282 £130

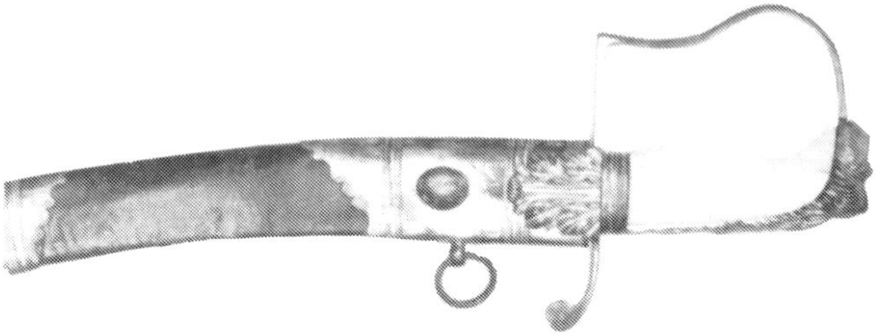

A Georgian officer's sabre, circa 1800, curved blade 28½in., copper gilt hilt, plain stirrup guard, langets chiselled with foliate pattern, 'lion's head' pommel, diced ivory grip, in its leather scabbard with three copper gilt mounts. $308 £140

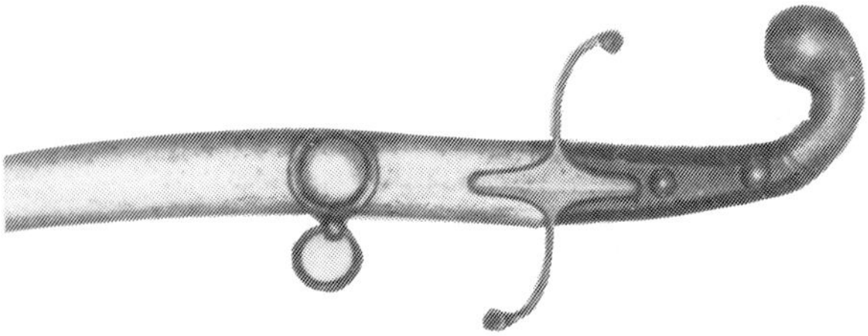

A Napoleonic era continental officer's mameluke sabre, plain, single edged, curved blade 32½in., plain reversed steel crossguard, curved bulbous steel pommel, wooden grips with two bulbous steel rivets, in its steel scabbard. $403 £155

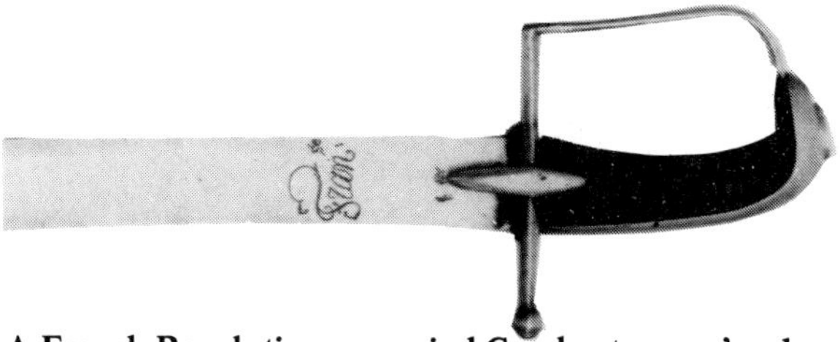

A French Revolutionary period Cavalry trooper's sabre, circa 1790, curved blade 32½in., engraved 'Klingenthal' on back-strap and with Cap-of-Liberty stamp at forte, brass, plain hilt with plain, single knucklebow, ribbed leather covered grip. $343 £158

A Napoleonic era continental officer's sabre, curved blade 34in., maker 'E.W.K.' at forte, plain steel hilt with single knucklebow, rectangular langets, copper wirebound, ribbed leather grip, in its steel scabbard. $358 £165

A good Georgian 1803 pattern general officers sabre. Curved blade 28½in., retaining approximately 70 per cent original blue and gilt etched decoration. $391 £180

An English Cavalry trooper's sabre, circa 1750, curved, double fullered blade 29in., three-quarter basket iron guard, flattened circular pommel, wood grip. $412 £190

An Edward VII Lord Lieutenant's mameluke dress sabre, curved, clipped-back blade 32½in., by 'Anderson & Son, St. James St.', plated crosspiece chiselled with crown within wreath and scrolls, horn grips, in its steel scabbard. $433 £190

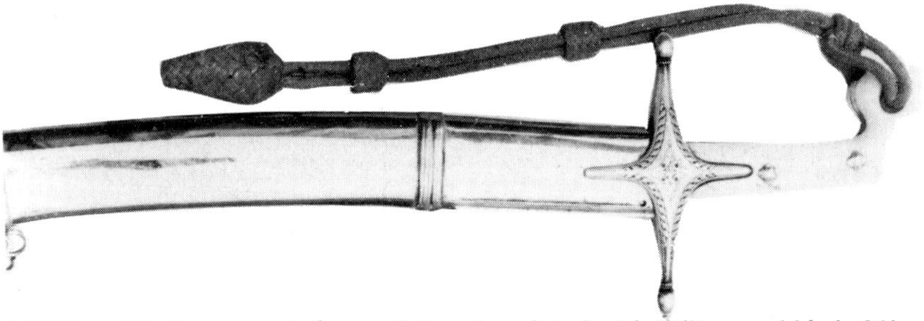

A William IV silver mounted mameluke sabre, fitted with Kilij curved blade 31in., with pronounced clipped-back tip, the crosspiece, straps and mounts of silver, the back-strap engraved with presentation inscription 'J.J.B. From Sir H.D. 1836', ivory grips with two silver rosettes, in chrome plated scabbard. $434 £200

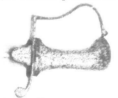

A Georgian sabre, of an officer serving in India, Eastern curved single edged blade 30½in., the back-strap with inscription in gold in Eastern lettering, iron solid hilt, with stirrup knucklebow, in its leather covered wooden scabbard with four Eastern silver gilt mounts. $440 £200

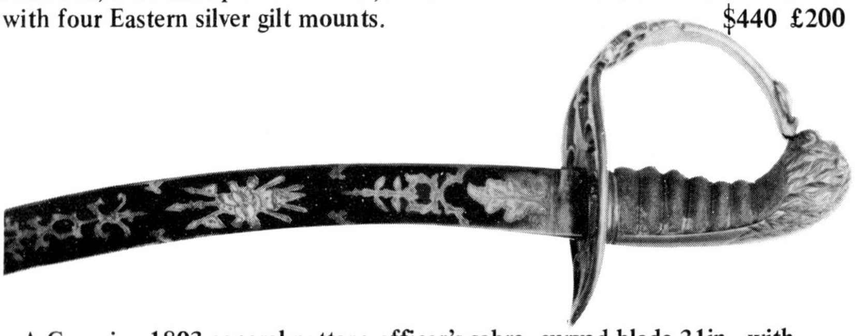

A Georgian 1803 general pattern officer's sabre, curved blade 31in., with clipped-back point, copper hilt with slotted guard and 'lion's head' pommel, wirebound, fishskin, covered grip, in its leather scabbard. $466 £215

A silver mounted Georgian officer's sabre, 1806, curved blade 33in., plain hilt of silver, with stirrup knucklebow, diced ivory grip, in its leather scabbard with three silver mounts (2 hallmarked). $550 £250

A Napoleonic era continental Cavalry officer's sabre, curved blade 31½in., signed at forte 'P. Knecht a Solingen', triple bar gilt brass guard, lozenge shaped langets and plain mounts, brass wirebound ribbed leather covered grip, in its steel scabbard with brass carrying rings. $594 £270

A French Napoleonic era officer's sabre, curved blade 32in., gilt hilt with fluted knucklebow, shield langets engraved with frond, 'lion's head' pommel with fluted strap, finely diced black wood flattened grip, in its gilt metal scabbard. $1,100 £500

A Victorian Volunteer Cavalry officer's presentation mameluke sabre, curved blade 31in., with clipped-back tip, by 'Hawkes & Co., London, manufacturers to the Queen', ornate copper gilt crosspiece, pierced quillons, copper gilt mounts with two rosettes to ivory grips, in its copper gilt scabbard. $1,324 £610

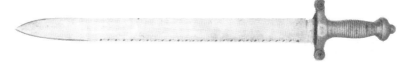

A mid 19th century continental brass hilted 'Roman' type sidearm, straight, saw-backed blade 20in., by 'F. Horster, Solingen', also stamped at forte with shield mark containing 'F', ribbed grip. $44 £20

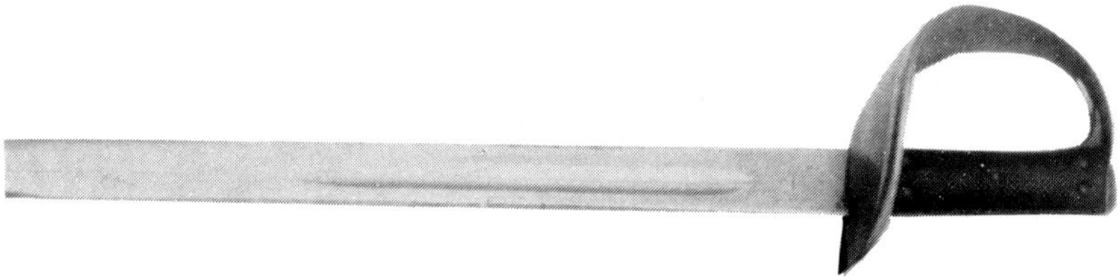

An 1855 Cavalry trooper's pattern sidearm, probably issued and adapted for naval use, straight, single edged blade 28in., with short fuller, steel bowl guard without Maltese Cross, diced leather grips. $43 £20

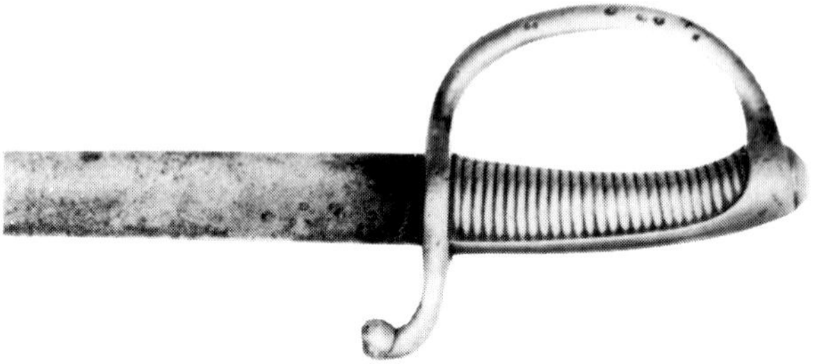

A French brass hilted model of AN IX Infantry sidearm, curved blade 23in., with inspector's stamps at forte and engraved on back-strap 'Manufre Roy de Klingenthal, Octobre 1814', brass grip and knucklebow with stamps. $65 £30

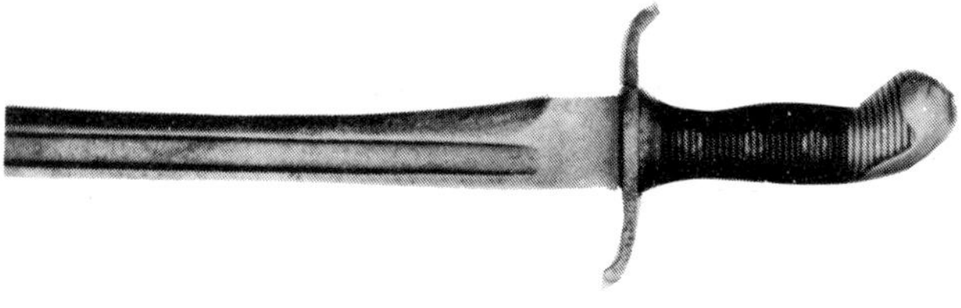

A Saxony Artillery sidearm, long, straight blade 24½in., with single edged in-curved cutting edge and spatulate tip, back-strap with traces of 'A' above '80', steel crosspiece, ribbed composition grip secured with three brass rivets, brass pommel. $75 £32

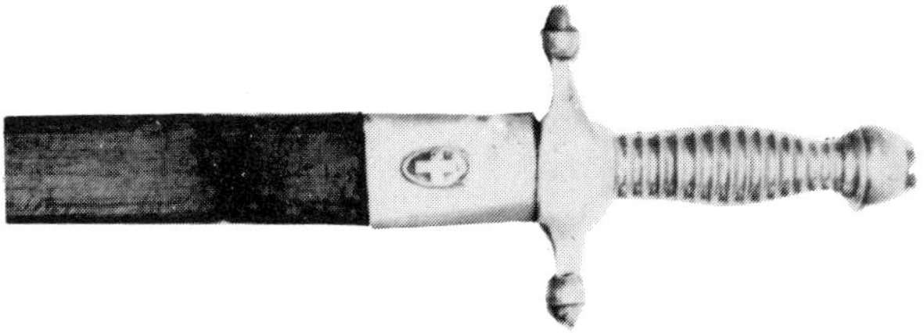

An early 19th century Italian brass hilted sidearm, straight, double fullered blade 18in., brass crosspiece with the Cross of Savoy, ribbed grip, in its brass mounted leather scabbard. $80 £35

An early 19th century brass hilted sidearm, possibly U.S., straight, double edged, fullered blade 17¼in., elaborate brass hilt, with scroll decorated cross-piece, the grip with Masonic reversed triangle device and star pattern. $100 £45

An unusual mid 19th century Constabulary sidearm, fitted with spatulate Brunswick type blade 22½in., plain, single, brass knucklebow and mounted spiral, fishskin covered grip, spring catch, in its brass mounted leather scabbard. $98 £45

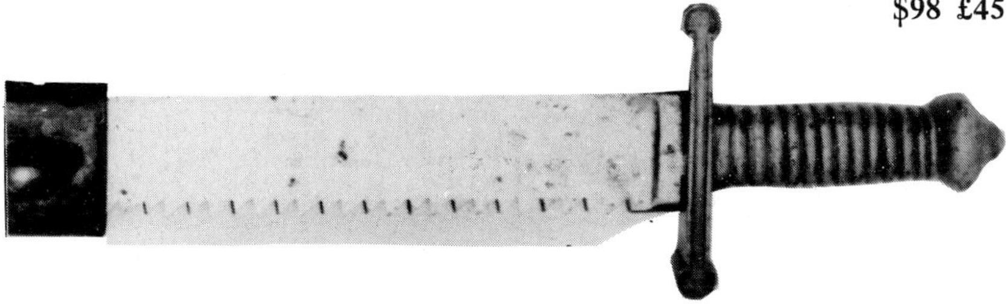

An early 19th century continental brass hilted pioneer sidearm, broad saw-backed blade 19½in., straight crosspiece, ribbed grip, skull cracker pommel, in its brass mounted leather sheath. $108 £50

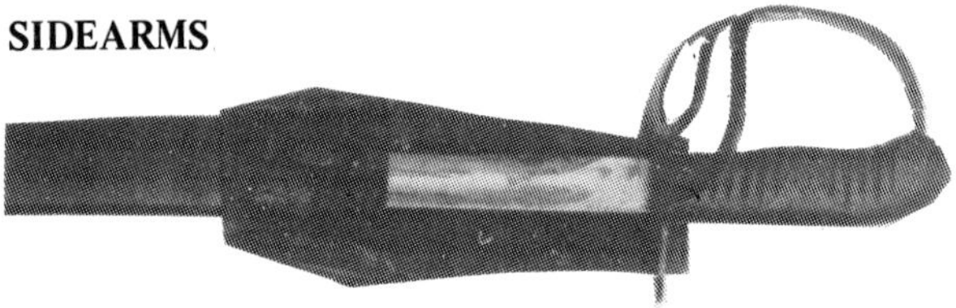

A German World War II period Naval short sidearm, 'Butcher' style, single edged blade 16½in., by 'Simson & Co. Suhl', steel triple bar hilt, ribbed wooden grip, small quillon stamped 'I.T.D. 1843', in its steel 'Butcher' bayonet style scabbard. $155 £65

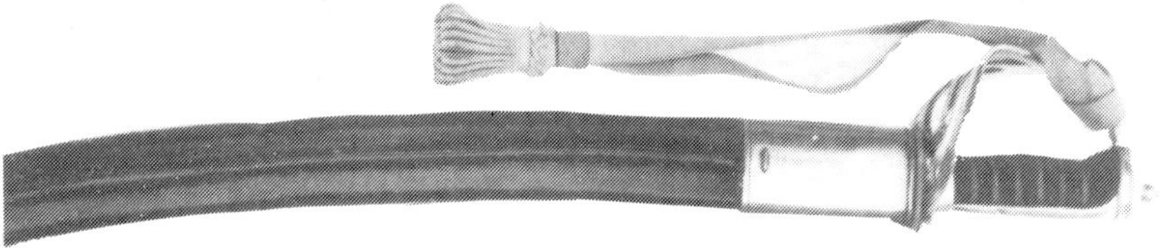

An 1896 pattern Mountain Artillery sidearm, slightly curved blade 30in., by 'John Round, Sheffield' with Indian Govt. Inspector's stamp at forte, officially fitted with a non-standard Cavalry officer's three bar plated guard. $154 £70

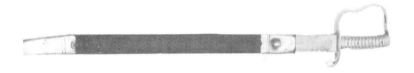

An 1856 pattern brass hilted pioneer sidearm, saw-backed blade 22½in., by 'A. & E. H.', ordnance stamps at forte, stirrup guard, ribbed grip, in its brass mounted leather scabbard. $154 £70

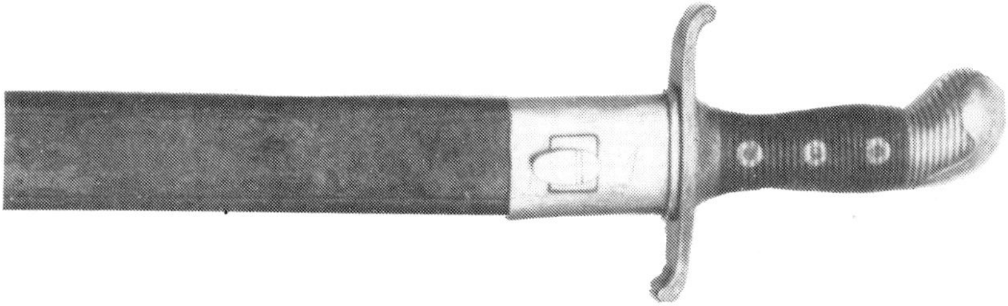

A late 19th century Saxony Artillery sidearm, spatulate blade 24½in., with incised cutting edge, by 'Gebr. Weyersberg', steel crossguard, ribbed composition grip, brass pommel, in its brass mounted leather scabbard. $190 £80

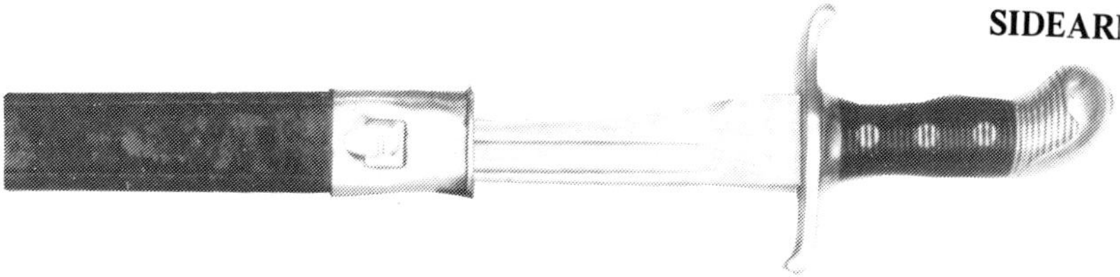

A 19th century Saxony Artillery sidearm, spatulate, point blade 24½in., with recessed cutting edge, stamped on back-strap with crowned 'A' above '80', steel reversed crosspiece, brass pommel, ribbed composition grip. $176 £80

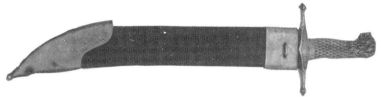

An early 19th century continental brass hilted sidearm, plain, broad, slightly curving, single edged blade 15¾in., straight, brass crosspiece, 'lion's head' pommel, scale grip, in its leather scabbard with two large brass mounts.
$198 £90

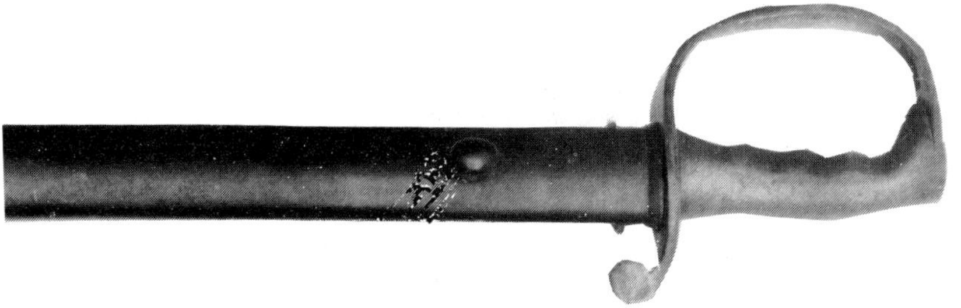

A Dundas pattern Artillery sidearm (1842-1855), slightly curved, single edged blade 28½in., ordnance stamps at forte, back-strap stamped 'Harvey', solid brass hilt with single knucklebow and shaped grip, in its steel scabbard.
$380 £175

An English Grenadier sidearm, circa 1750, slightly curved blade 30½in., with narrow back fuller and marked 'S. Harvey', steel three-quarter basket guard, with diamond openwork panels, flattened circular pommel. $542 £250

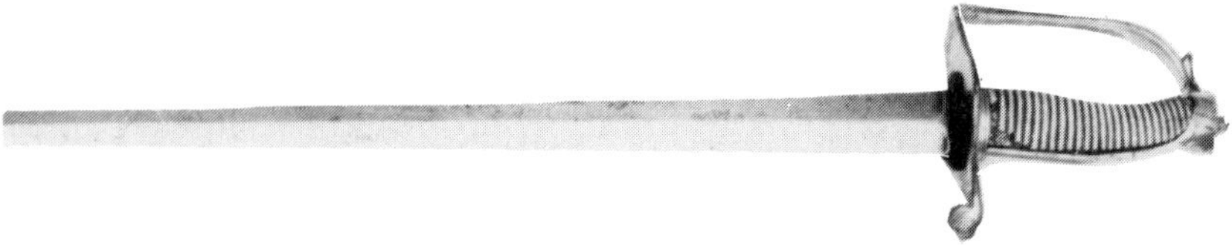

A late 18th century Georgian officer's spadroon, plain, straight, double edged blade 30½in., of flattened diamond section, plain copper, fighting hilt with single guard and solid side loop, ribbed ivory grip. $108 £50

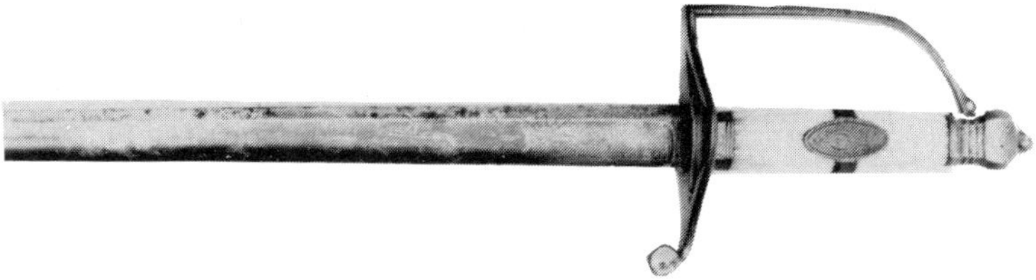

A 1786 pattern Georgian Infantry officer's spadroon, single edged blade 32in., engraved on back-strap 'J. J. Runkel, Solingen', and etched with pre-1801 Royal Arms crown, 'GR', military trophies and foliage, fluted ivory grip. $262 £115

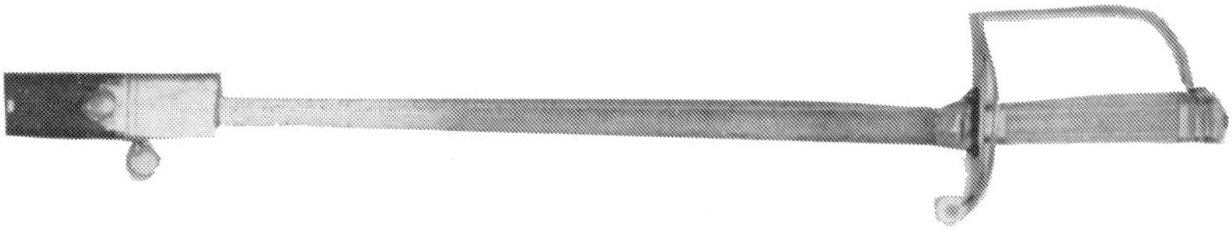

A late 18th century silver hilted spadroon, straight, single edged blade 32in., the hilt of silver, with traces of gilt, plain, single knucklebow and side loop (hallmarked below guard, London, 1791, maker 'F.T.'), fluted ivory grip. $440 £200

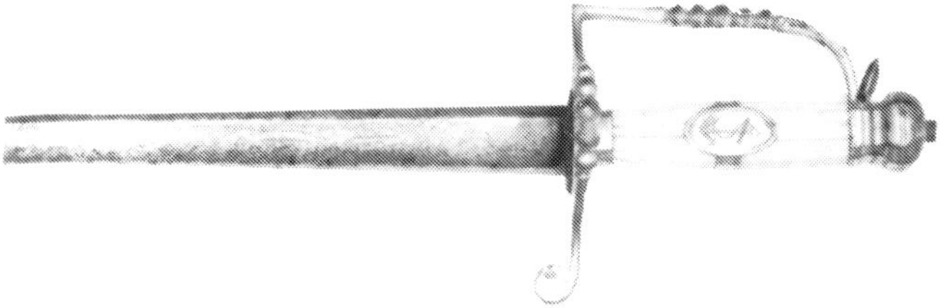

A Georgian Senior Naval officer's spadroon 1789/03, straight, single edged blade 32in., and with contemporary engraving on back-strap 'Courtney, Boston 1789', copper gilt hilt, fluted ivory grip. $506 £230

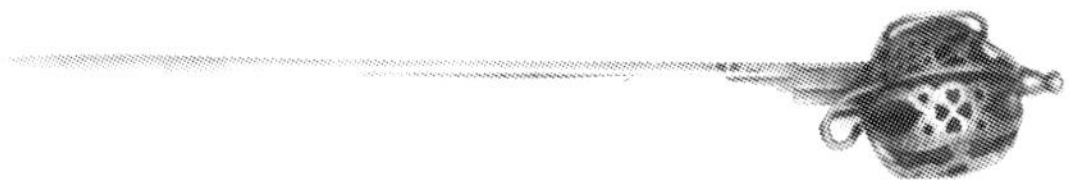

An attractive silver miniature Scottish broadsword, blade 8in. (hallmarked Birmingham 1910), the basket guard pierced and engraved, wooden grip, red liner. $165 £75

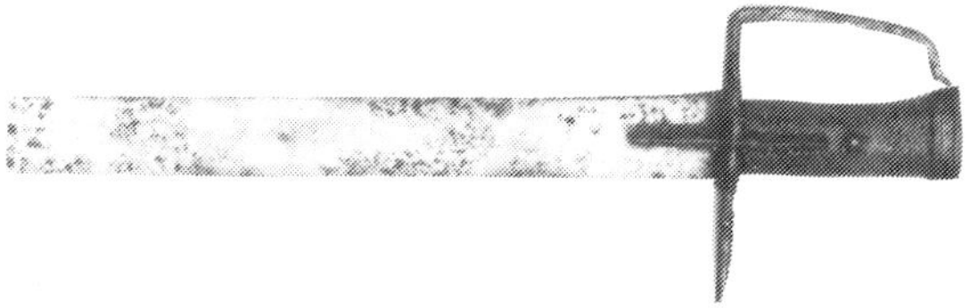

A Central European sword, straight, double edged, tapering blade 31in., iron, plain hilt with single flattened knucklebow, plain mounts, straight, long back quillon, slim, long langets, shagreen covered grip. $238 £108

A Georgian Tower warder's sword, double edged, tapering blade 31½in., of flattened diamond section, copper gilt hilt with large shell guard chiselled with House of Hanover, flattened knucklebow with side loop. $369 £170

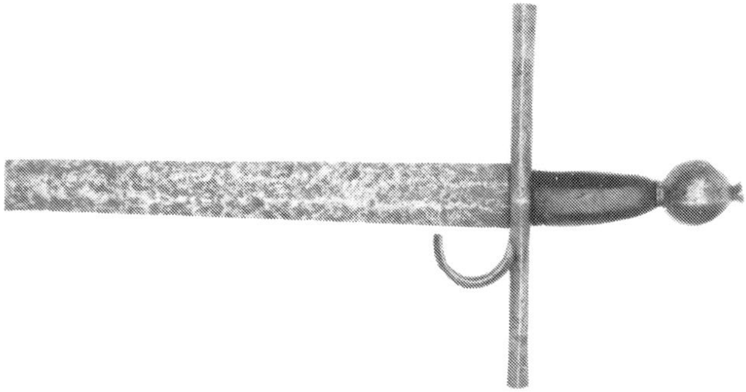

An old sword, with double edged, straight, 14th century, blade 35in., straight iron crosspiece of diamond form, one down-curved loop ring, ovoid iron octagonal pommel, leather bound grip. $440 £200

A Venetian sword schiavona, circa 1580, straight, single edged, fullered blade 40in., multi bar swept hilt wrought from one piece, incorporating large thumb ring, integral square section quillon with swollen finial. Brass pommel of eared form, wirebound grip with brass ferrules. $755 £290

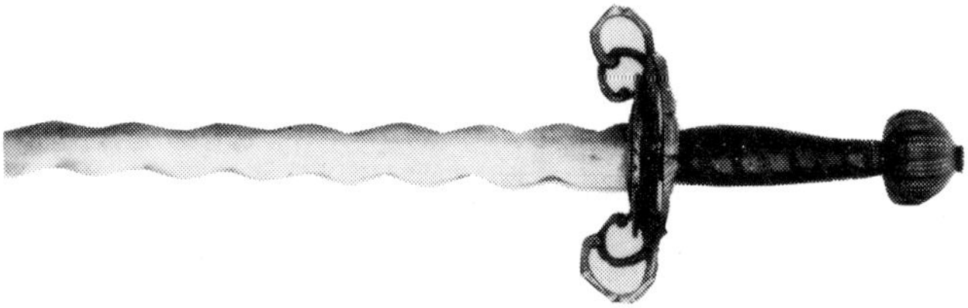

A 17th century Italian sword, flamberge blade 32in., iron 'crab-claw' type quillons, fluted iron shell guard with three iron side loops, heavy fluted iron melon-shaped pommel, spiral, wirebound leather covered grip. $650 £300

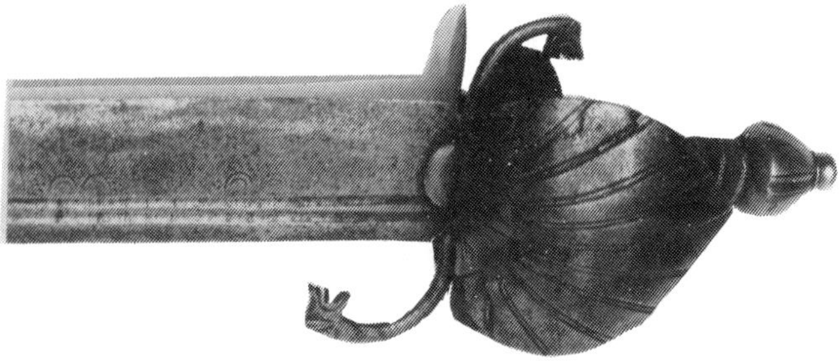

A late 16th century German falchion, 2¼in., broad blade 26in. long, slightly curved with twin fullers, stamped twice 'Sebastiani Hermander'. Broad steel shell-shaped guard, counter guard with thumb ring, steel pommel and wire-bound skin covered grips. $806 £310

A 1796 pattern, Cavalry officer's sword, plain blade 35½in., with hatchet point, 'ladder' pattern steel basket hilt, wirebound, fishskin covered grip. $88 £40

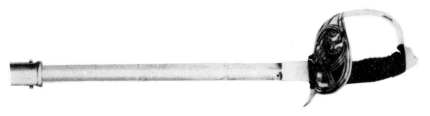

An 1889 pattern Prussian Cavalry officer's sword, plated blade 32½in., etched with Regt. 'Jager Zu Pferde XI A.K.', plated guard, ribbed black grips, in its plated scabbard. $163 £75

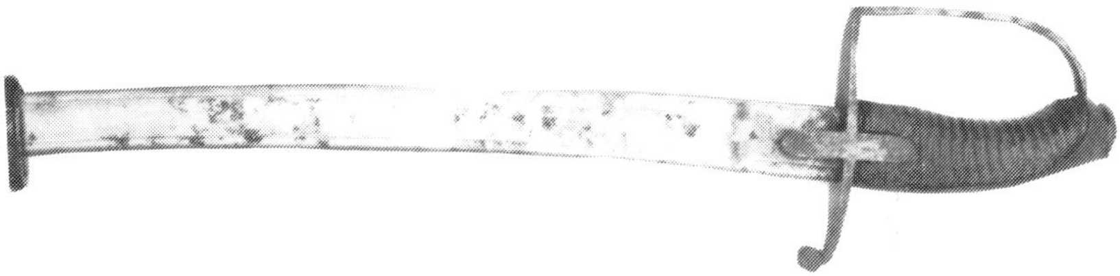

A 1788 pattern Light Cavalry trooper's sword, plain, single edged, curved blade 35in., with narrow back fuller, plain steel hilt with plain knucklebow, engraved 'D.48', langets and mounts, ribbed, fishskin covered grip. $176 £80

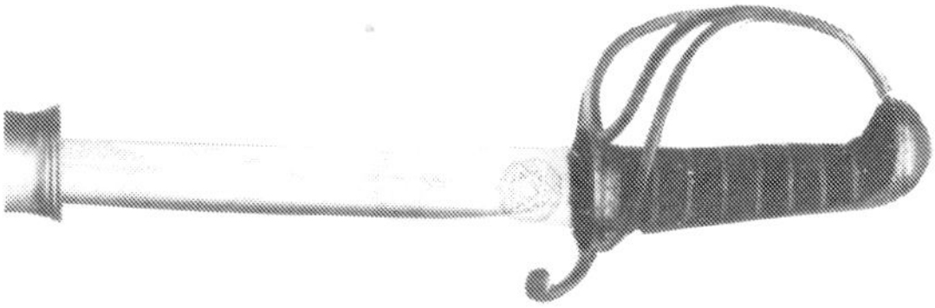

A Victorian 1821 pattern Light Cavalry officer's sword, straight fullered blade 36in., by 'Wilkinson', triple bar steel guard, wirebound, diced leather covered grip, in its steel scabbard. $209 £95

A Cavalry troopers's sword, circa 1780, straight, single edged blade 35½in., with broad and narrow back fullers, spear point, semi-basket steel hilt with slotted guard and double loop side scrolls, brass, wirebound, leather covered grip, ovoid pommel. $212 £96

An 1889 pattern Imperial German Cavalry officer's sword, plated blade 31½in., etched with regiment on blued panel 'Husaren Regt Landgraf Friedrich II Von Hessen Homburg (2 Kurhess) No 14', white metal hilt with folding guard, ribbed composition grips. $228 £105

A Nazi Cavalry officer's sword, curved, plated blade 31½in., by 'Eickhorn', gilt hilt, with stirrup knucklebow and mounts, wirebound, black ribbed grip, in its black painted scabbard. $228 £105

An 1803 pattern Georgian Light Cavalry officer's sword, curved blade 31in., by 'Gibson Thomson Craig's Warranted', copper gilt hilt, 'lion's head' pommel, wirebound, horn grip, in its leather scabbard with three large copper gilt mounts. $253 £115

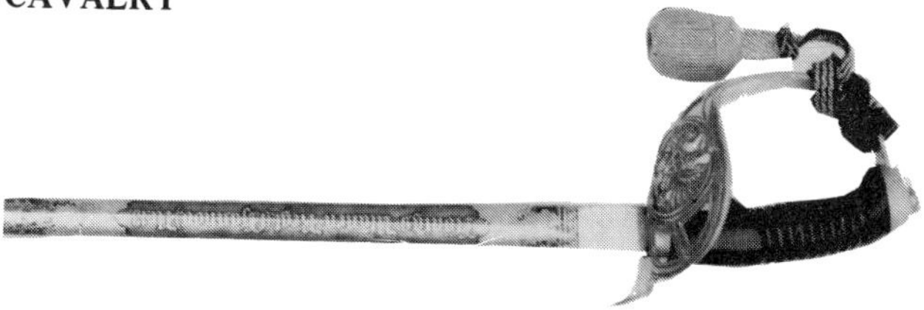

An 1889 pattern Prussian Cavalry officer's sword, plated blade 32½in., etched with Regt. 'Konigs Ulanen Regt. (I. Hannou) NR 13', plated white metal hilt, composition ribbed grip with dress knot, in its black painted steel scabbard. $260 £125

An Edward VII 1897 pattern infantry officer's sword, blade 32½in., by "Flight, Winchester", etched with Royal Arms and Royal Cypher within panels. $282 £130

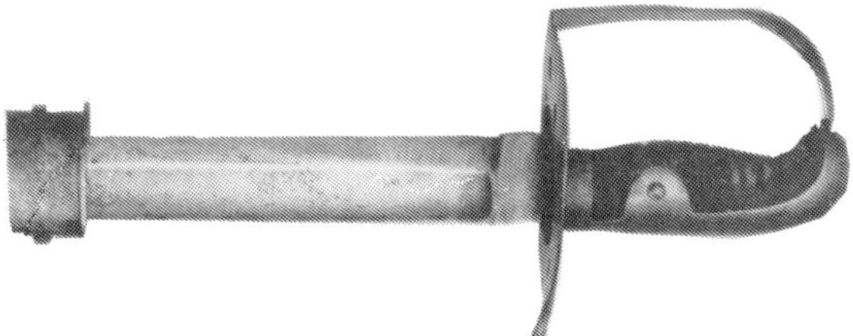

A 1796 pattern Heavy Cavalry trooper's sword, straight, single edged blade 34in., with spear point, ordnance stamp at forte, steel hilt with pierced guard, leather covered ribbed grip, in its steel scabbard, stamped at top 'Osborn & Gunby, Birmm'. $297 £135

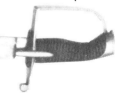

A 1788 Light Cavalry trooper's sword, curved blade 35in., etched at forte 'Gill's Warranted', thick, plain steel guard, plain steel lozenge langets and mounts, ribbed fishskin covered grip, in its steel scabbard with leather inserts. $330 £150

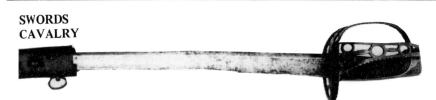

A French revolutionary period Cavalry officer's sword, slightly curved blade 29in. etched with 'Pour Le Salut De Ma Patrie Vivre Libre Ou Mourir', brass slotted hilt with additional fold-out side guard, retained with spring catch, brass mounts, copper wirebound grip. $434 £200

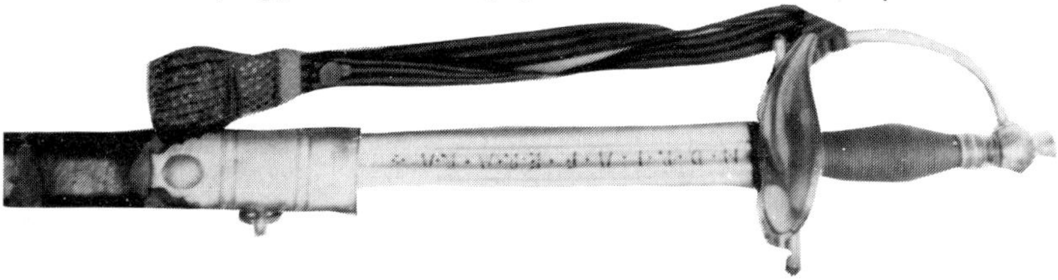

A 1796 pattern, Heavy Cavalry officer's un-dress sword, double edged, tapering blade 32in., with 'Running Wolf' mark and multi-fullered at forte, signed 'Andrea Ferrara', copper gilt boat guard, knucklebow and mounts, simulated silver wirebound grip, original crimson and bullion wire dress knot. $553 £255

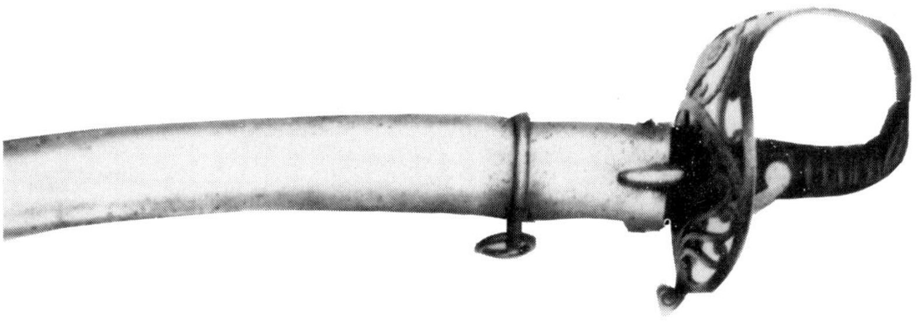

A 1796 pattern, Cavalry officer's sword, curved, pipe-backed blade 33½in., clipped-back tip, pierced steel guard, steel mounts, wirebound, ribbed covered grip, in its heavy steel scabbard. $629 £290

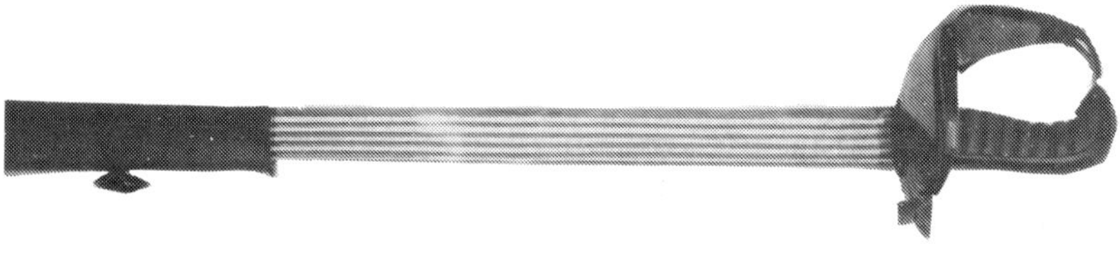

A Volunteer Cavalry officer's sword, circa 1796, broad, multi-fullered, single edged, straight blade 36in., with Bowie type clipped-back point, steel, semi-basket guard, wirebound, fishskin covered grip, in its steel scabbard. $884 £340

A Victorian dress courtsword, slender, etched, double edged blade 31½in., copper gilt hilt with beaded edges, in its engraved copper gilt mounted black patent leather scabbard with bullion dress knot. $114 £50

An Early Victorian courtsword, circa 1840, straight, tapering blade 30in. of flattened diamond section, by 'Buckmaster, 3 New Burlington Street', copper gilt hilt with shell guard with applied crown 'VR', single knucklebow, crown pommel, copper wirebound grip, in its leather scabbard. $121 £55

A 19th century papal dress courtsword, slim, straight, single edged blade 31in., of flattened diamond section, gilt hilt, 'lion's head' terminal, shell guard with papal device, mother-of-pearl grips, in its leather scabbard. $124 £57

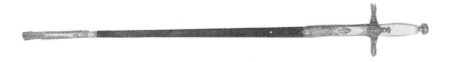

A 19th century continental court dress sword (possibly one of the Italian States), plain, straight, double edged blade 31in., Gothic style cruciform hilt with gilt chiselled crosspiece, small urn pommel, mother-of-pearl panel grips, in its leather scabbard. $156 £60

A late 19th century Victorian courtsword, slim, straight blade 31½in., by 'Humphreys, Haymarket, London', copper gilt hilt, the shell guard chiselled with two dragons and foliage, plumed helmet pommel, copper wirebound grip, in its patent leather scabbard. $198 £90

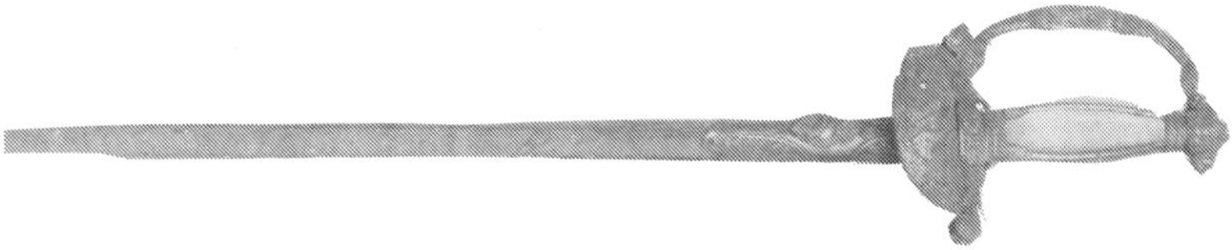

A French dress courtsword, circa 1820, plain, straight, tapering, triangular blade 33in., fine copper gilt chiselled hilt, the shell guard chiselled with winged Figure of Victory, mother-of-pearl grips, in its vellum covered wooden scabbard. $220 £100

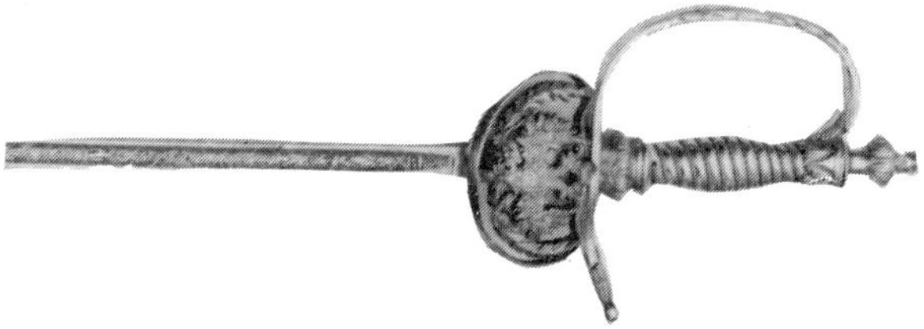

An Imperial Russian courtsword, plated blade 30in., half fullered, half diamond section, gilt metal hilt with partly pierced shell guard with Imperial Eagle, single knucklebow, spiral grip, chiselled urn pommel, in its leather scabbard. $239 £110

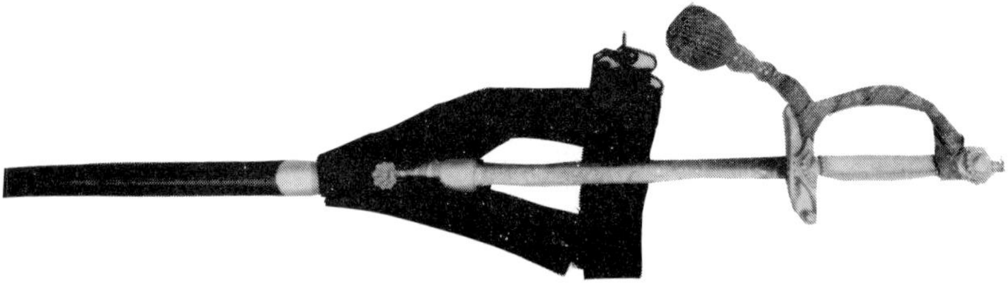

A late Victorian courtsword, slim blade 30½in., by 'Firmin & Sons, 153 Strand, London', gilt hilt with beaded decoration to shell guard, urn pommel grip and knucklebow, original bullion dress knot, in its patent scabbard. $245 £118

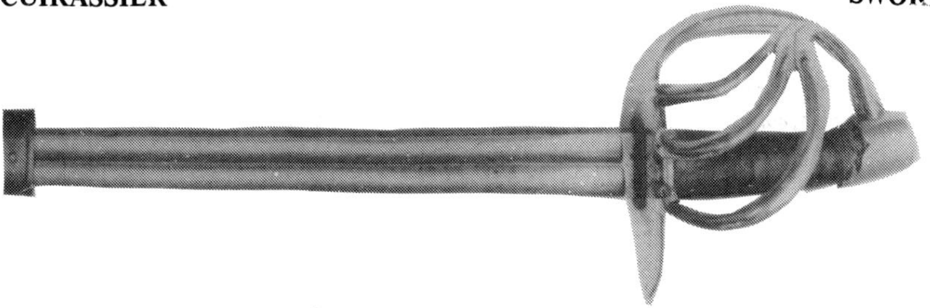

A French AN XI Cuirassier trooper's sword, straight, single edged, double fullered blade 37½in., brass hilt, leather covered grip, in its steel scabbard. $217 £100

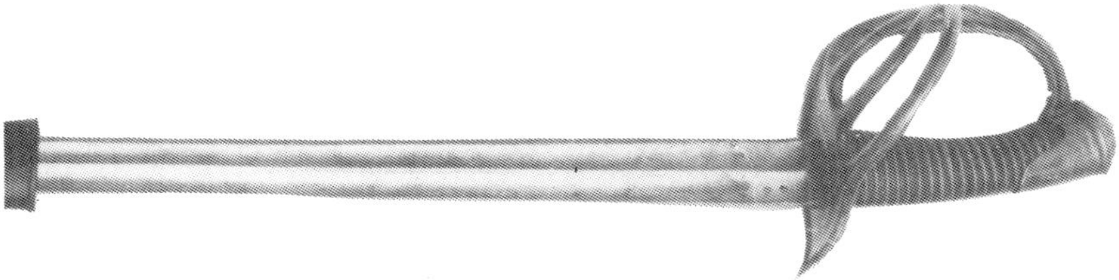

A French AN XI Cuirassier trooper's sword, straight, double fullered blade 36in., with spear point, brass hilt with triple bar guard, rounded pommel, wirebound brass grip, in its steel scabbard. $285 £125

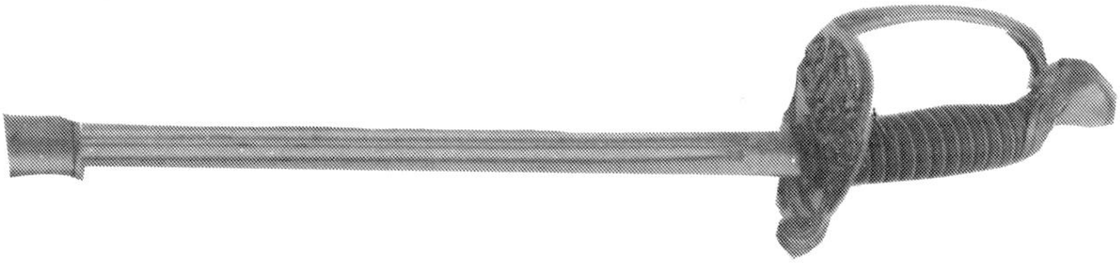

A Saxony Cuirassier officer's sword, multi-fullered, double edged blade 29in., with spear point, etched at forte with crowned 'A.R.' cypher, gilt hilt with side loop panel, fluted knucklebow, gilt wirebound fishskin covered grip, in its plated scabbard. $347 £160

A French AN XI Cuirassier trooper's sword, straight, single edged blade 37½in., with double fullers, ordnance stamps at forte, triple bar brass hilt, brass mounts, brass wirebound leather covered grip, in its steel scabbard. $333 £160

SWORDS
CUIRASSIER

A French AN XI Cuirassier trooper's sword, single edged, double fullered blade 37in., with spear point, back-strap engraved 'Manufre Rle Du Klingenthal, Obre 1814', triple bar brass guard, brass mounts, brass wirebound leather grip, in its steel scabbard. $401 £185

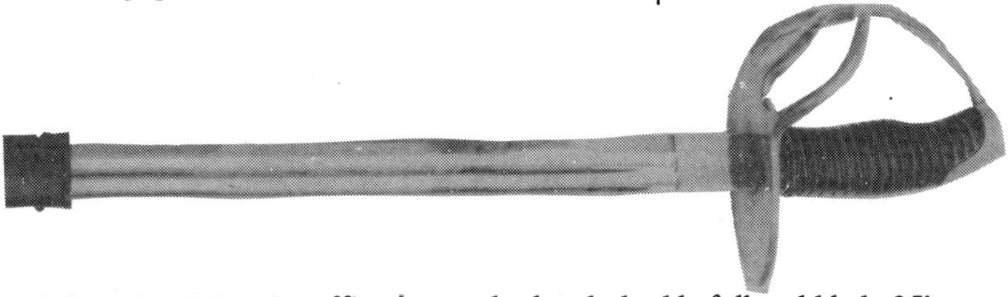

A Bavarian Cuirassier officer's sword, plated, double fullered blade 35in., etched with Bavarian motto in scroll, upon laurel spray, gilt triple bar guard, plain mounts, copper wirebound black grip, in its black painted scabbard. $412 £190

DRESS

A U.S. Military Academy cadet's dress sword, straight blade 30in., cast crosspiece with 'eagle's head' terminals, quillon block marked 'M.A.', cast ribbed hilt, urn pommel, in its plated metal scabbard with brass mounts. $65 £30

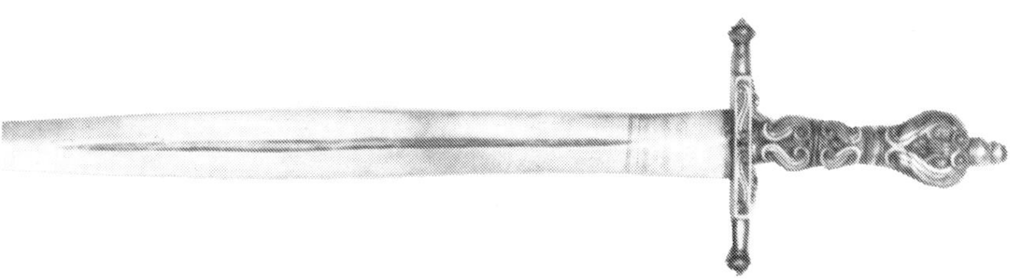

A Victorian dress sword of the Queen's Bodyguard for Scotland, The Royal Company of Archers, spatulate blade with single central fuller, 19¼in., etched at forte 'Holbeck & Sons, 4 New Bond St, London', gilt brass crossguard. $99 £45

An officer's dress sword of the 62nd (Wiltshire) Regt., circa 1830, plain, straight, tapering, double edged blade 32in., copper gilt hilt with shell guard with beaded rim decoration and with Badge of the 62nd Regt. affixed. $130 £50

A late 19th century U.S. Army officer's dress sword, slim, straight blade 31in., of flattened diamond section, gilt hilt with double shell guard (one folding), wirebound, fishskin covered grip with bullion dress knot, in its plated scabbard. $114 £50

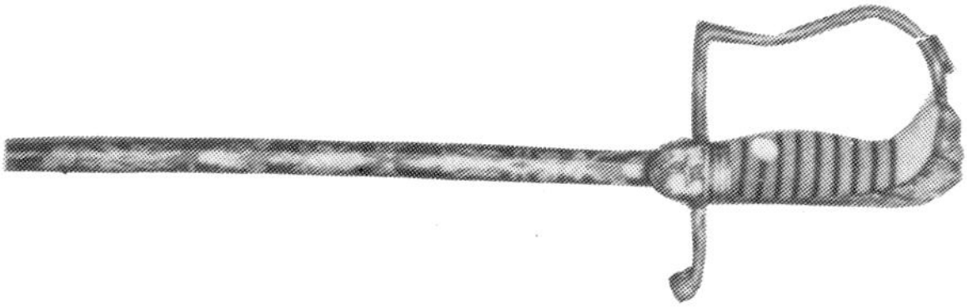

A Georgian Naval officer's dress sword as carried circa 1812-25, straight, slim, single edged blade 27in., copper gilt hilt with rounded stirrup guard, 'lion's head' pommel, copper wirebound diced ivory grip. $215 £90

A Georgian Heavy Cavalry officer's 1796 pattern dress sword, double edged blade 32in., with part central fuller, copper gilt hilt with boat guard, plain knucklebow and ovoid pommel, silver, simulated wirebound grip. $198 £90

An Imperial Austrian Naval officer's dress sword, straight, plated blade 28in., gilt brass hilt with partly pierced shell guard, knucklebow in form of serpent and oak leaves, 'lion's head' pommel, fluted mother-of-pearl grips. $440 £200

A Royal Horse Guards officer's dress sword, circa 1832, long, single edged blade 39in., with hatchet point, brass hilt, crown to back of shell, Tudor Rose to pommel, triple bar feathered guard, ribbed, fishskin covered grip. $651 £300

A Victorian 2nd Life Guards officer's dress sword, circa 1865, plain, straight, single edged blade 35in., steel guard, brass diced pommel, wirebound, fishskin covered grip, original red cloth front white wash leather liner, in its plated scabbard with three brass mounts. $673 £310

A 2nd Life Guards officer's dress sword, dated 1832, single edged blade 33in., with hatchet point by 'Prosser, Manufacturer to the King, London 1832', with 'P' proof stamp, brass hilt, flaming grenade to back of shell and pommel strap, brass wirebound, spiral, fishskin covered grip. $1035 £450

An Assam Naga sword dao, heavy, chisel edged, watered steel blade 19in., with squared end and narrowing towards hilt, brass mounted, red lacquered wooden hilt, brass mounted ivory rectangular pommel, in its red lacquered, rattan bound, open-sided wooden scabbard. $108 £50

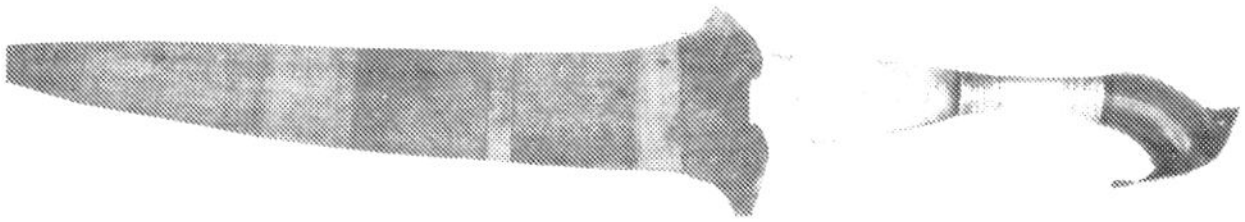

A silver mounted moro sword barong, single edged, heavy blade 19in., of watered steel, large ribbed silver hilt mount and well carved wooden pommel terminating in a stylised 'bird's head' with small scrolls. $176 £80

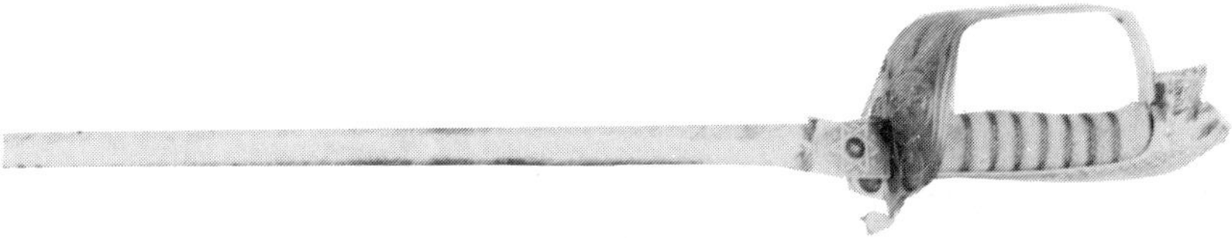

An Imperial Chinese Naval officer's sword, single edged blade 31½in., by 'Pascallatkey & Sons, Cowes', gilt semi-solid basket guard of English type, Chinese dragon head pommel, wirebound, white fishskin covered grip, folding side guard. $195 £90

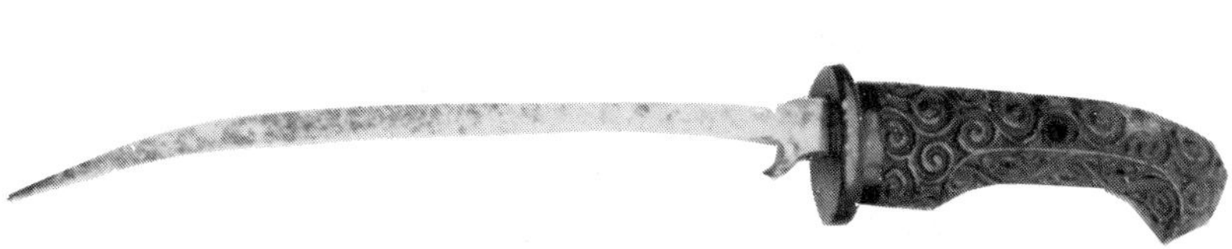

A Japanese sword breaker jitte, blade of square section 30½cm., mumei, blade with faint characters inscribed above hook. Hilt and sheath carved with red and black lacquer overall in clouded formations. $293 £135

An early 18th century European hunting sword, single edged, slightly curved blade 19¼in., with clipped-back point, brass shell guard, masks to small back quillon, knucklebow with central design of figures, stag horn grip. $82 £36

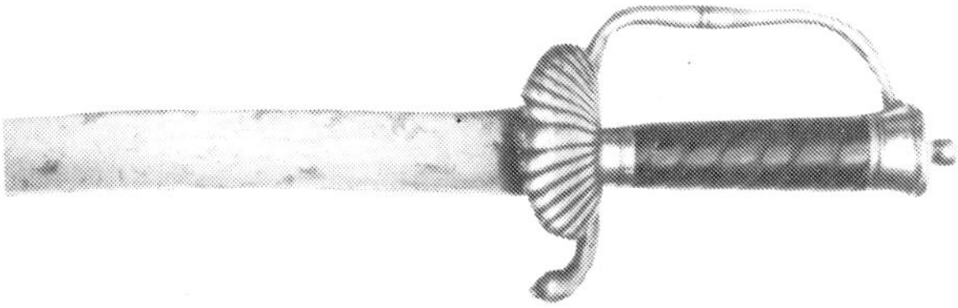

A mid 18th century hunting sword, single edged, slightly curved blade 18in., with long, clipped-back edge, fluted brass shell guard, plain brass knucklebow and mounts, twist spiral horn grip. $110 £50

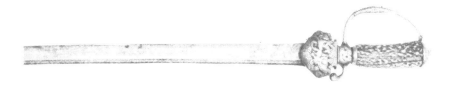

A mid 18th century European hunting sword, single edged, curved blade 17½in., deeply struck at Forte with Carolean Crown over Tudor Rose mark, single iron knucklebow, iron mounts and stag horn grip. $132 £60

A mid 18th century hunting sword, curved, double fullered blade 25½in., brass reversed crosspiece with 'monster's head' terminals with central panel with bears, spiral green stained ivory grip, brass pommel cap. $137 £60

A mid 18th century European hunting sword, plain curved blade 23½., brass shellguard with relief design of Orpheus and stags etc, brass knucklebow with central standing figure playing a flute. $150 £65

A mid 19th century German dress hunting sword, single edged blade 16½in., German silver shell guard, reversed hoof quillons, fluted pommel and mounts, stag horn grip, in its leather sheath the top mount of German silver.$152 £70

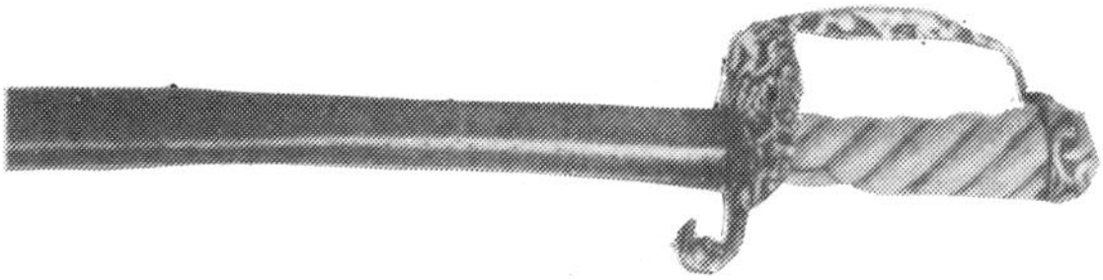

An early 18th century European hunting sword, slightly curved, single edged blade 25in., with back fuller, with 'Running Wolf' mark, brass shell guard, foliate decorated pommel, twist ivory grip. $225 £95

A mid 18th century European hunting sword, double edged, straight, tapering blade 25in., of flattened diamond section, brass hilt, with flattened single knucklebow, 'monster head' back quillon, 'lion's head' pommel, copper wire-bound grip. $220 £100

An early 17th century European hunting sword, plain, straight, single edged blade 26in., with single back fuller and clipped-back point, fluted iron shell guard, plain iron knucklebow of flattened form, with similar back quillon, stag horn grips. $330 £150

A Russian mid 18th century dress hunting sword, single edged, clipped-back blade 17½in. of watered steel, narrow double back fullers, etched at forte and silver overlaid with Imperial crowned Eagle and crowned cypher of Empress Elizabeth 1st (1741-62), octagonal agate hilt with white metal and silver mounts, in its leather covered wooden sheath with plain silver mounts. $434 £200

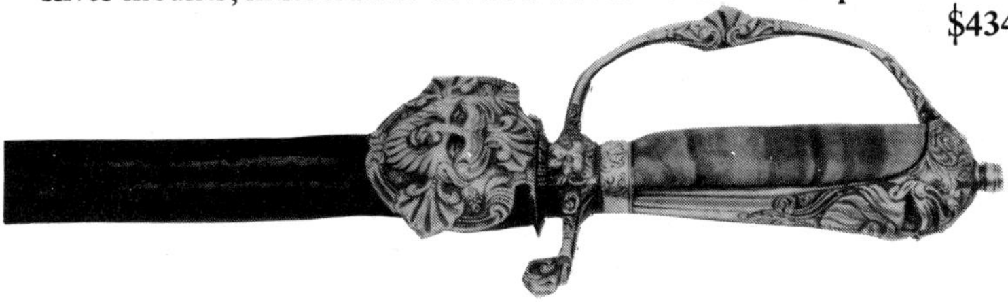

An English mid 18th century silver hilted hunting sword, signed 'Sahagun', slightly curved, multi-fullered, saw-backed blade 21½in., silver shell guard, tiger stripe horn grips, the pommel chased and chiselled with scallop and foliate sprays, bearded human mask to back-strap. $603 £290

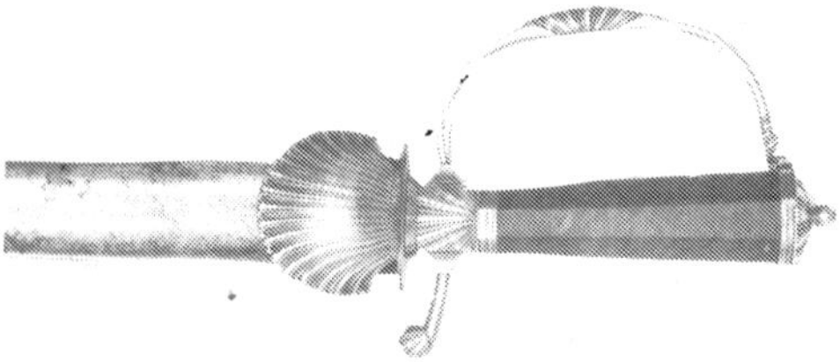

An English early 18th century silver hilted hunting sword, plain, slightly curved, single edged blade 21in., finely fluted, silver shell guard, silver knucklebow and mounts, the top of knucklebow with hallmark (London 1735), octagonal agate grip. $1,265 £575

A Nazi Army officer's sword, plated, slightly curved blade 33in., by 'E. Pack', brass hilt, with stirrup guard and mounts chiselled with oak leaves etc., army eagle on langet, wirebound, black ribbed grip, in its black painted metal scabbard with original dress knot. $141 £65

A Nazi Army officer's sword of Eickhorn Special pattern series 'Roon', plated, curved blade 31½in., gilt hilt, with army eagle engraved on langet, stirrup knucklebow and mounts, wirebound, black ribbed grip, in its black painted metal scabbard. $150 £66

A Nazi Army officer's sword, plated, slightly curved blade 34½in., by 'Alcosa', gilt hilt, stirrup guard and mounts decorated with oak leaves, Nazi Eagle on langet, 'lion's head' pommel inset with red glass eyes, wirebound, black ribbed grip, in its black painted metal scabbard. $152 £70

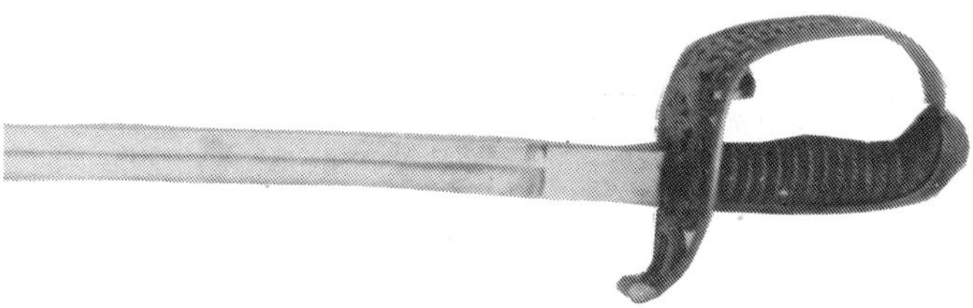

An Imperial German officer's sword of the State of Hesse, slightly curved blade 32½in., brass guard, wirebound, fishskin covered grip, in its plated scabbard. $176 £80

An Imperial German Bergbau officer's sword, slightly curved blade 32in., by 'Mohr & Speyer, Berlin', plain, brass hilt with stirrup guard, Bergbau emblems to langet, wirebound, ribbed fishskin covered grip, in its brass mounted leather scabbard. $228 £105

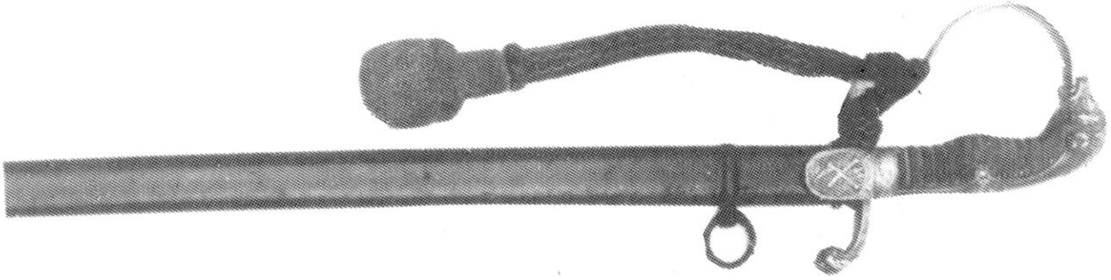

An Imperial German Artillery officer's sword, plain, slightly curved blade 31½in., by 'W. K. C.', brass hilt with stirrup guard decorated with Iron Cross etc., 'lion's head' pommel, crossed cannon on langet, the other langet with officer's initials, wirebound, ribbed fishskin covered grip, in its black painted metal scabbard. $231 £105

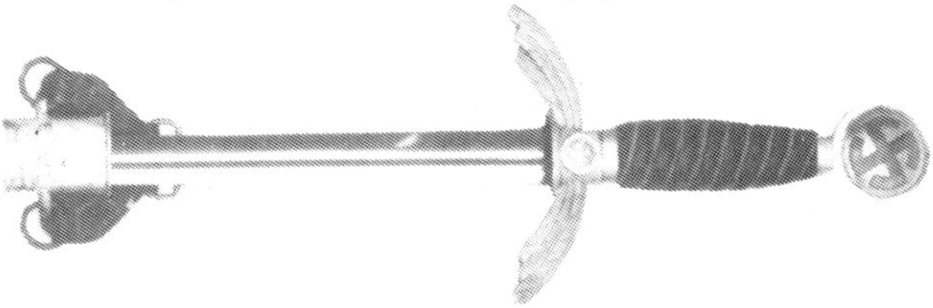

A Nazi Luftwaffe officer's sword, plated blade 28½in., by 'Alcosa', plated mounts, wirebound, blue leather covered grip, in its blue leather covered steel scabbard with two plated mounts and leather belt clip frog. $231 £105

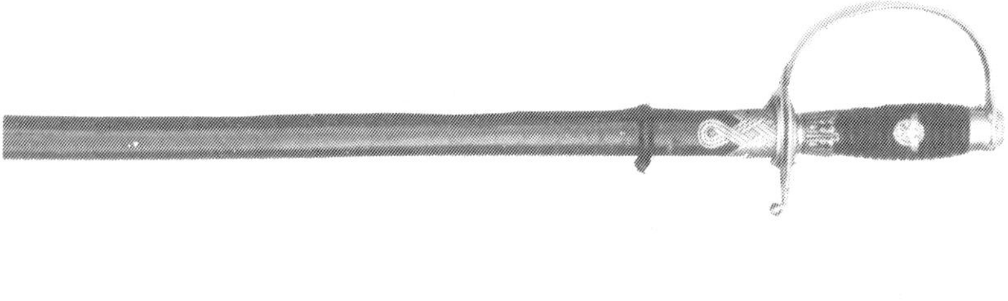

A Nazi Police NCO's sword, blade 32½in., by 'W. K. C.', also stamped with S.S. runes, plated hilt, Police badge inset in black, ribbed grip, in its black painted metal scabbard with plated top mount. $231 £105

A Nazi Water Customs officer's sword, plated, curved blade 33in., by 'Eickhorn', gilt hilt, stirrup knucklebow, Nazi Eagle on langet, 'lion's head' pommel, backstrap and ring mount decorated with oak leaves, wirebound, black ribbed grip, in its black painted metal scabbard. $250 £120

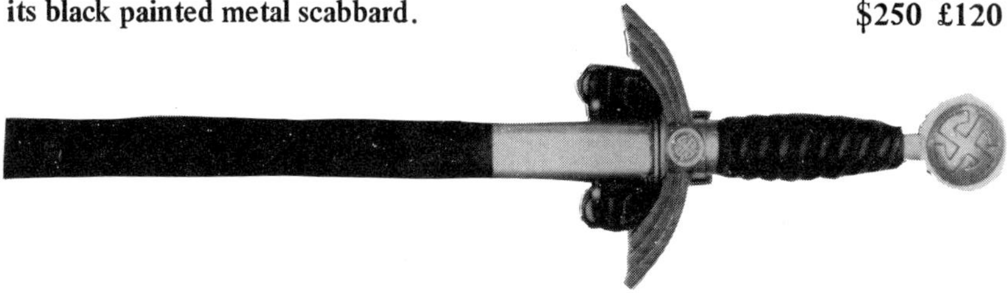

A Nazi Luftwaffe officer's sword, plated blade 28½in., by 'Paul Weyersberg', with small inspection stamp, plated mounts, wirebound, blue leather covered grip, in its blue leather covered metal scabbard with plated mounts and integral frog. $260 £120

A Nazi Luftwaffe officer's sword, plated blade 28½in., by 'S.M.F.', grey metal mounts, wirebound, blue leather covered grip, in its grey metal mounted, leather covered scabbard with integral frog and clip. $304 £140

A Nazi S.S. officer's sword, by Pet Dan Krebs, blade 33in., plated knucklebow and mounts, S.S. runes inset in wirebound grip, in its black painted metal scabbard with plated mounts. $330 £150

SWORDS
IMPERIAL GERMAN & NAZI

An Imperial German 1889 pattern Infantry officer's sword as worn by Colonial troops, straight, plated, double fullered blade 30½in., brass guard crown to pommel, wirebound, fishskin covered grip, in its black painted metal scabbard. $347 £160

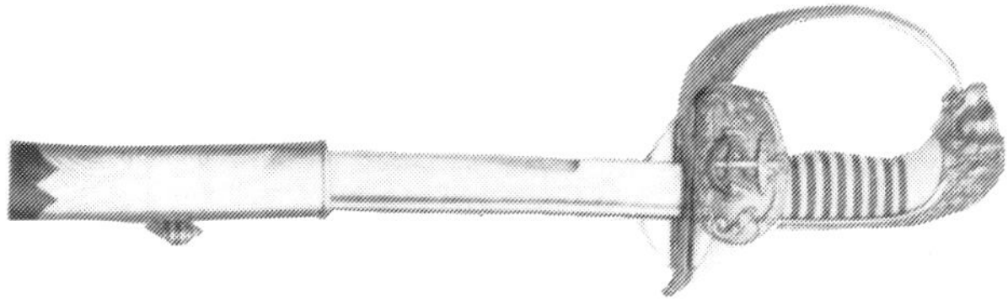

A Nazi Naval officer's sword, slightly curved, pipe-backed, clipped-back blade 31½in., by 'A.C.S.', gilt hilt with large and small folding guards, 'lion's head' pommel, gilt wirebound, white ivorine grip, in its gilt metal mounted leather scabbard. $495 £210

KHANDA

An Indian sword khanda style blade 26in., with spatulate point and toothed back edge mount, brass hilt with down-drooping 'monster head' quillons, 'leopard's head' pommel, curved knucklebow. $195 £75

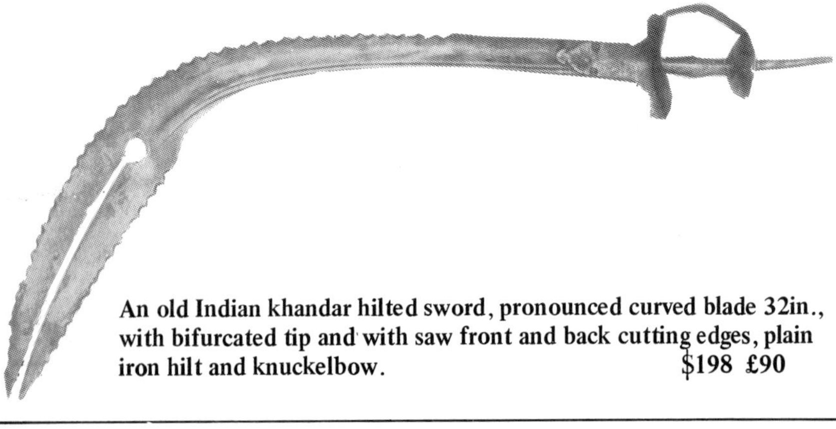

An old Indian khandar hilted sword, pronounced curved blade 32in., with bifurcated tip and with saw front and back cutting edges, plain iron hilt and knuckelbow. $198 £90

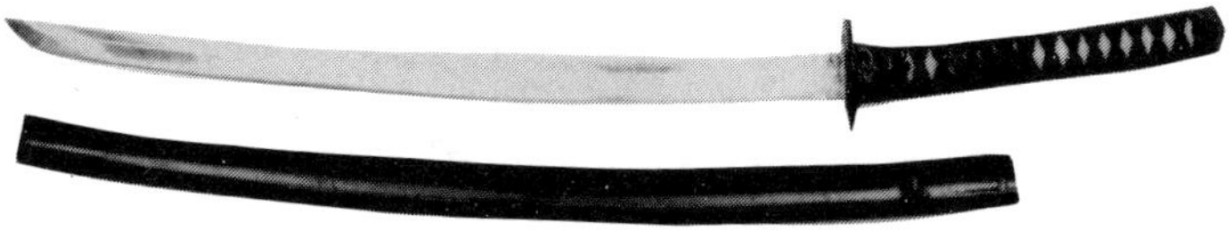

A Japanese sword katana, blade 56cm., mumei, two mekugi ana, ito suguha hamon. Iron tape bound same tsuka, menuki, as dragon with ken, iron tsuba and whirled rim, in its black lacquered saya. $434 £200

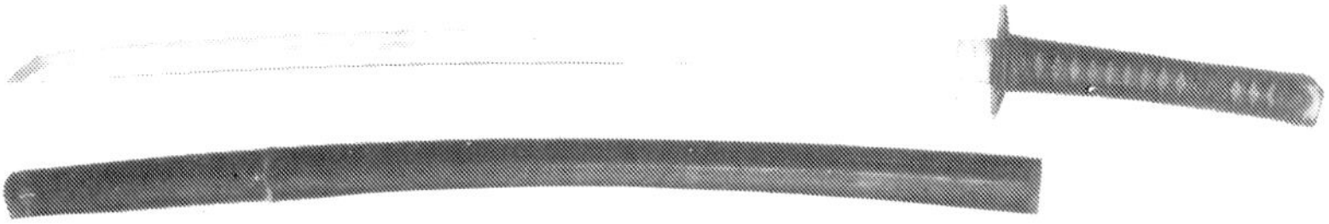

A Japanese sword katana, blade 68cm., mumei, shin-shinto, one mekugi ana. Broad gunome hamon, itane hada. Leather bound tsuka, iron fuchi kashira and tsuba, shakudo menuki, in its iron mounted black leather saya. $902 £410

A Japanese sword katana, blade 69½cm., mumei with two mekugi ana, bo-hi kaki-toshi, Chu suguha hamon, itane hada. Iron mokume hada tsuba, tape bound same tsuka with shakudo fuchi kashira carved as waves with gilt shells and spray, in its black lacquered saya with iron kojiri. $911 £420

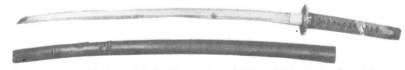

A Japanese sword katana, blade 61cm., signed 'Bizen Nokuni Osofune Munemitsu', dated Eisho 2nd year (1505), one mekugi ana. Ito suguha hamon. Tape bound black tsuka with gilt dragon menuki, shakudo koshira. Gilt rimmed shakudo nanako tsuba, mother-of-pearl fleck lacquered saya. $1,170 £450

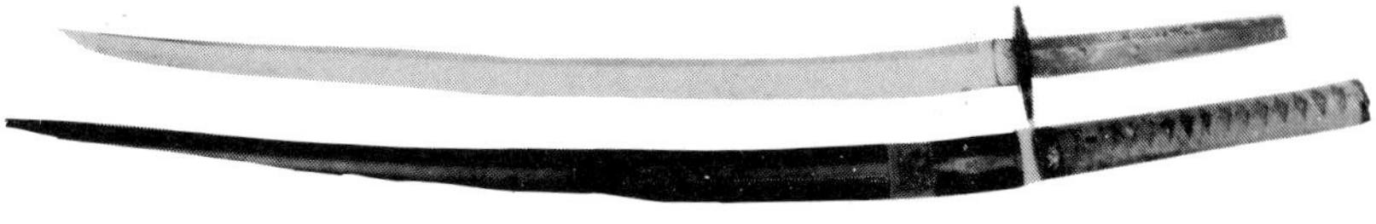

A Japanese heavy sword katana, blade 65cm., signed 'Hizen Nokuni Minamoto Munetsugu with two mekugi ana. Broad gunome hamon, straight itame hada, broad nie clouds. $2,495 £1,150

MAMELUKE

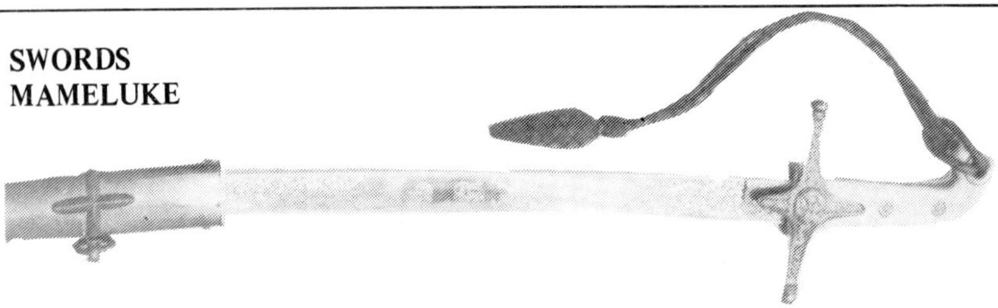

A George V 1831 pattern general officer's mameluke sword, curved blade 32½in., by 'Edward Thurkle, Soho, London', gilt crosspiece and mounts, ivory grips, in its plated scabbard. $330 £139

A Hussar officer's mameluke Levee sword, circa 1830, mounted with good curved Eastern blade, 31in., with long and short fullers, pronounced, clipped-back tip, copper gilt crosspiece, ivory grips, in its copper gilt scabbard. $835 £385

MANDAU

An old Dyak mandau, curved blade 21½in., horn hilt with carved top with some hair tufts, in its rattan band bound wooden sheath with stylised carved decoration and hair tuft mount. $61 £28

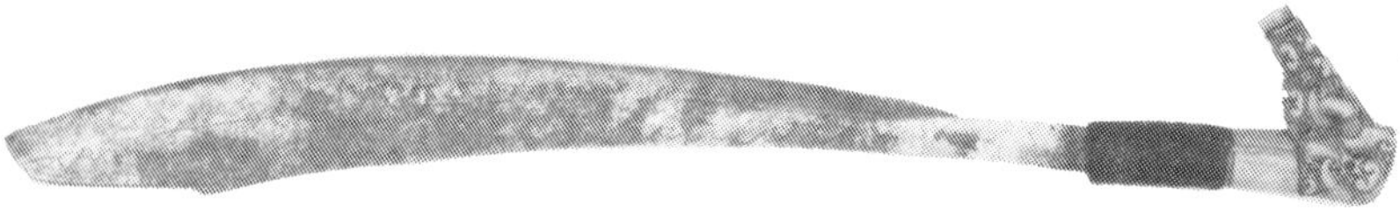

A well carved 18th century Dyak head hunter's sword mandau, curved, single edged, engraved blade 16½in., broadening towards the point, cord bound carved bone hilt finely worked with figures, geometrical patterns and scrolls. $110 £50

A World War II Italian Air Force officer's sword, slim blade 29in., gilt guard in the form of a wing, 'eagle's head' pommel and feathered back-strap, black ribbed, wooden grip, small side clip of propellor form, in its leather covered metal scabbard. $76 £35

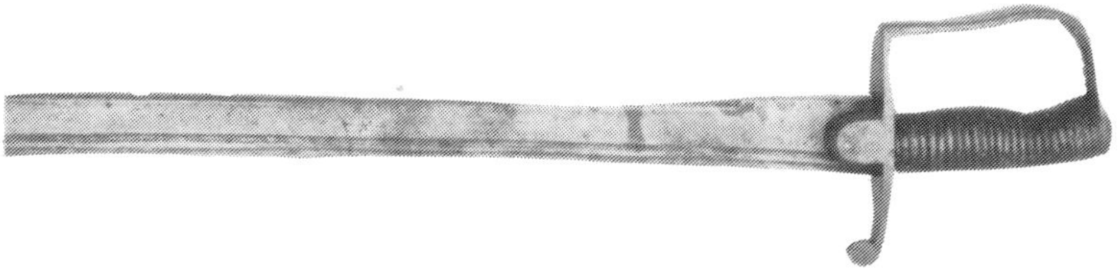

A late 18th century continental trooper's sword, slightly curved blade 33in., struck with three star marks, with long double back fullers and clipped-back point, iron heavy knuckebow and mounts, ribbed iron grip. $95 £40

A Georgian Naval officer's sword of 1822 Infantry pattern, flat, slightly curved blade 29in., with clipped-back tip, pierced brass 1822 pattern hilt, with oval panel inset with crowned fouled anchor, 'lion's head' pommel, ribbed leather covered grip, in a leather scabbard. $98 £45

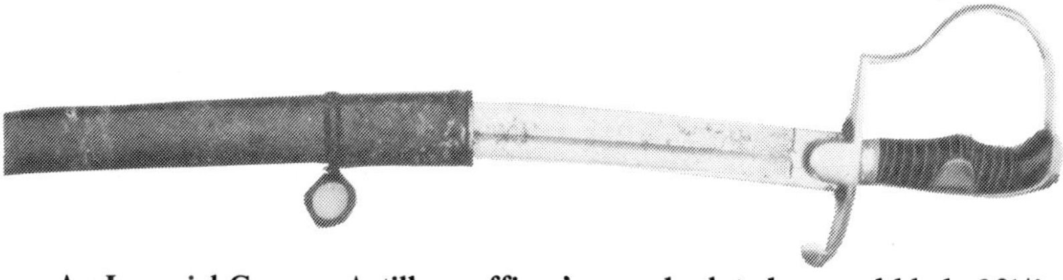

An Imperial German Artillery officer's sword, plated, curved blade 30½in., by 'W. K. C.', well etched with Regt. 'Feld-Art Regt V. Scharnhorst (I. Hannou) No. 10' and Battle Honours within scrolls bordered with oak leaves, 'Peninsula; Waterloo; Gohrde', in its black painted steel scabbard. $100 £45

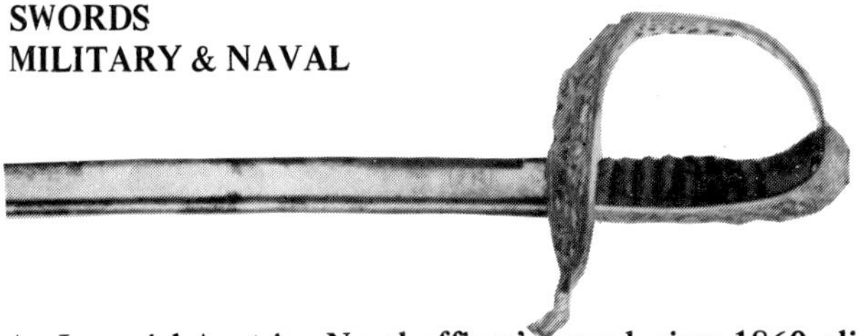

An Imperial Austrian Naval officer's sword, circa 1860, slightly curved, pipe-backed, clipped-back blade 29in., by 'Ohligs Husmann in Wien', stippled background gilt hilt with elaborately pierced and chiselled bowl guard, 'eagle's head' back quillon. $108 £50

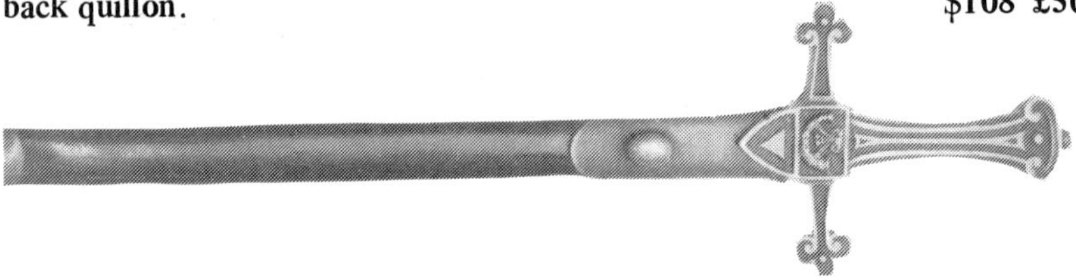

A Victorian Gothic brass hilted drummer's Mark I sword of a Light Infantry Regt., straight, double edged blade 18in., by 'Firmin & Sons, Strand, London', brass hilt with strung bugle device to centre panel, in its brass mounted leather scabbard. $120 £50

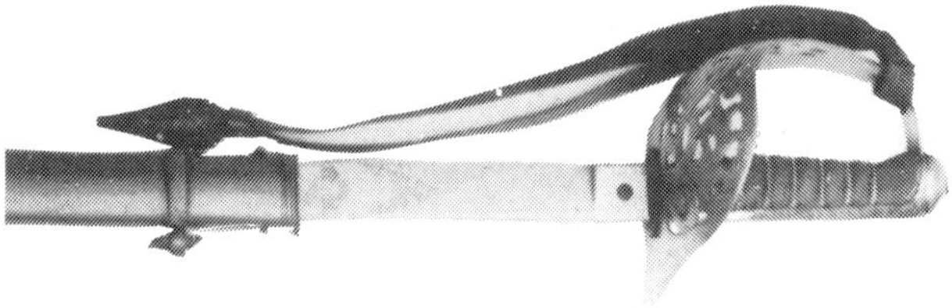

A Victorian 1895 pattern Infantry officer's sword, long, custom-made blade 33½in., No. 22466, by 'Henry Wilkinson, Pall Mall', etched with battle honours 'Tel-El-Mahouta, Masameh, Kassassin, Tel-El-Kebir', steel hilt, wirebound, fish-skin covered grip, leather dress knot, in its steel scabbard. $120 £50

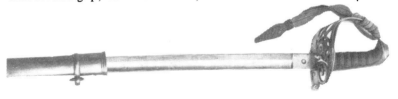

A Victorian 1854 pattern Coldstream Guards officer's sword, slightly curved blade 32½in., steel hilt, copper wirebound, fishskin covered grip, with Infantry bullion dress acorn knot, in its steel scabbard. $125 £54

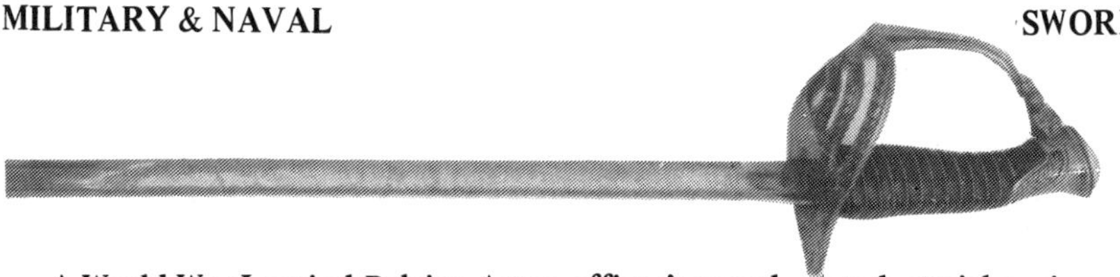

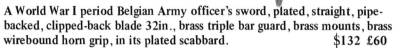

A World War I period Belgian Army officer's sword, plated, straight, pipe-backed, clipped-back blade 32in., brass triple bar guard, brass mounts, brass wirebound horn grip, in its plated scabbard. $132 £60

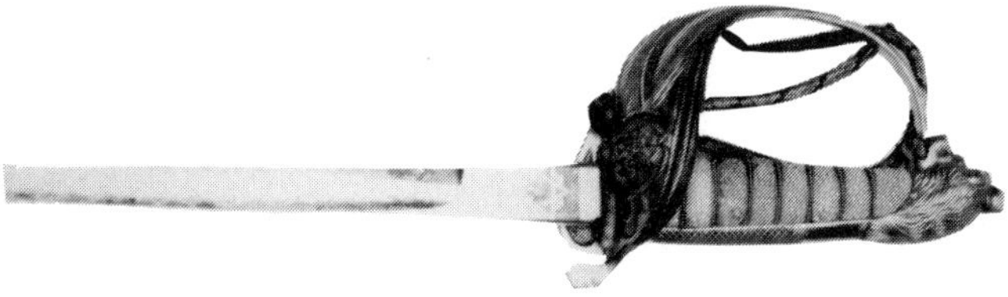

A post-1902 Naval officer's sword, blade 31¾in., by 'Clement Gray, Sheffield', gilt hilt with 'lion's head' pommel and folding side guard, gilt, wirebound, white fishskin covered grip, in its brass mounted leather scabbard. $148 £65

A Victorian Naval officer's sword, circa 1860, of an officer of flag rank, slightly curved blade 31½in., by 'Henry Wilkinson, Pall Mall', gilt guard, 'lion's head' pommel, gilt wirebound, white fishskin covered grip, in its leather scabbard with three gilt mounts with oak leaf chiselled pattern. $141 £65

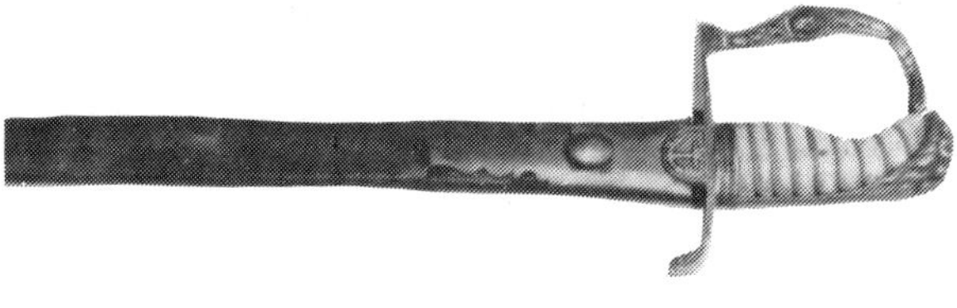

An early 19th century continental Naval officer's sword, plain, straight, single edged blade 31in., brass hilt with flattened knucklebow with central device of lion mask, small langets with fouled anchor, 'lion's head' pommel, wirebound, ivory grip, in its brass mounted leather scabbard. $155 £65

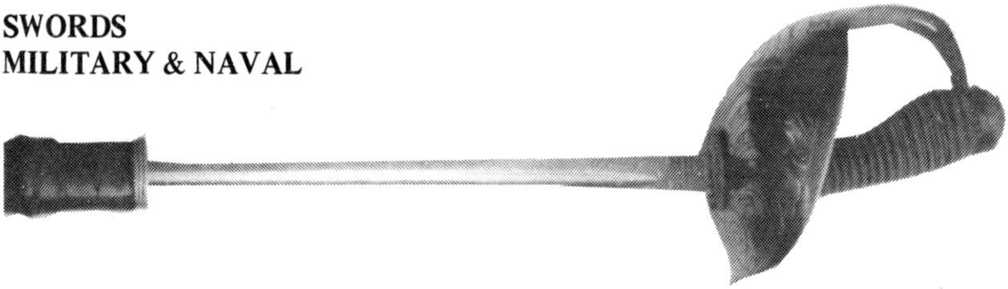

A George V 1912 pattern Cavalry officer's sword, straight, slim blade 34½in., by 'Henry Wilkinson, Pall Mall', No. 44306, bowl guard, silver wirebound, fishskin covered grip, in its leather covered field service scabbard. $155 £65

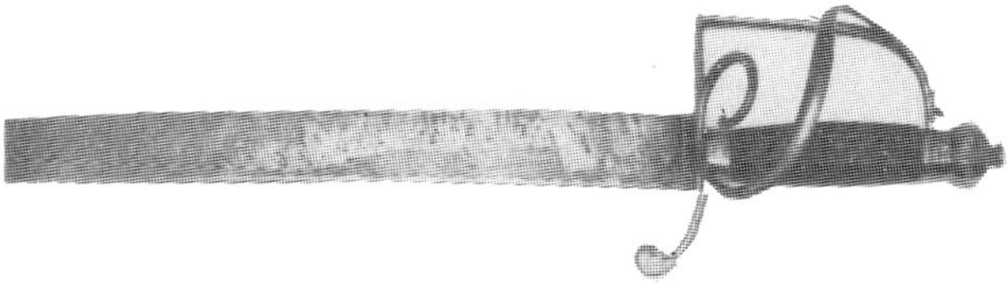

A late 18th century Georgian officer's sword, slightly curved, single edged blade 33½in., with inventory stamp of cannon, dated '1889' and 'M.A.', with wavy, watered steel finish, steel hilt with plain knucklebow and side loop, plain steel mounts, fluted wooden grip. $182 £70

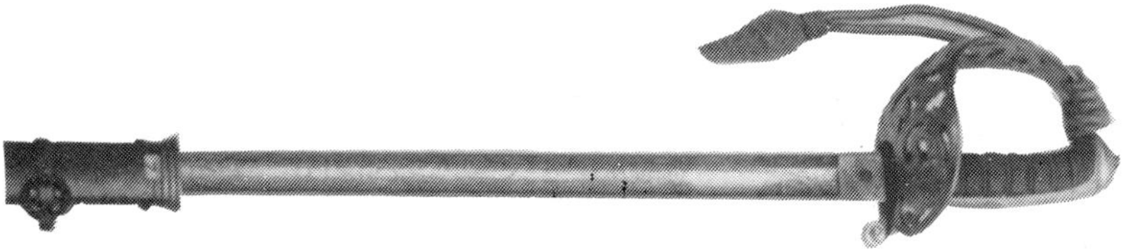

A Victorian 1857 pattern Royal Engineers officer's sword, blade 32½in., by 'T. McBride, St. James', London', copper gilt hilt, gilt wirebound, fishskin covered grip, bullion acorn dress knot, in its steel scabbard. $165 £70

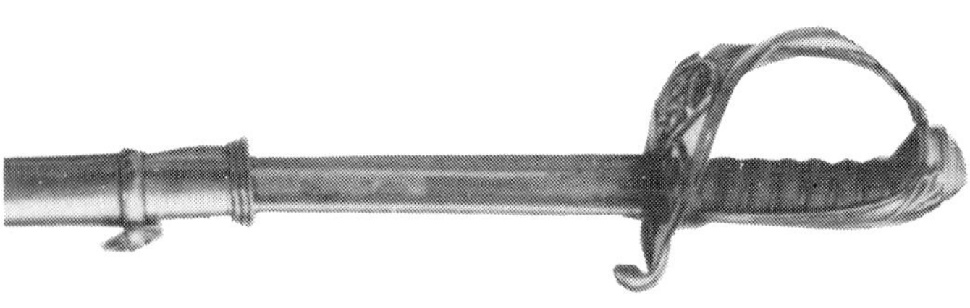

A George IV Field Infantry officer's sword, slightly curved, pipe-backed, clipped-back blade 32½in., copper hilt, folding side guard, wirebound, fishskin covered grip, in its brass scabbard. $165 £70

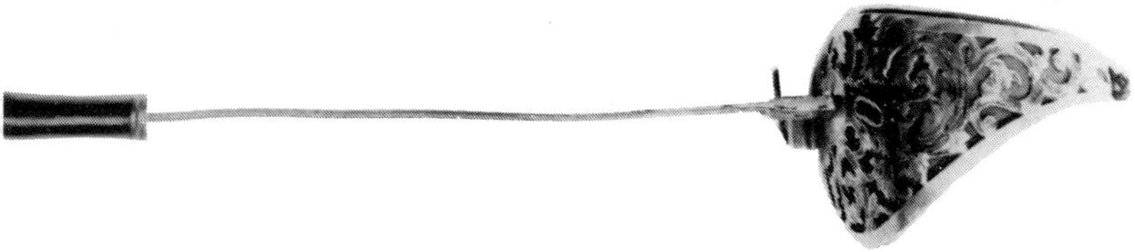

An Edward VII Highland Regiment field officer's sword, slender, fullered, double edged claymore blade 32½in., regulation pierced engraved foliate guard, wirebound, skin covered grip with original chamois and red felt liner. $171 £75

An unusual Georgian short boarding sword, probably specially made for a Naval officer, circa 1785, plain, broad, double edged blade 17½in., with spear point, steel openwork guard with rippled edges, ovoid pommel, in its original plain steel mounted scabbard with leather frog. $174 £80

A post-1902 Naval officer's sword, straight blade 31½in., gilt brass hilt, with 'lion's head' pommel, folding small side guard, gilt wirebound, white fishskin covered grip, bullion dress knot, in its gilt brass mounted leather scabbard. $217 £80

A Georgian Naval officer's sword, circa 1805, for ranks of commanders and above, straight, fullered blade 32¼in., copper gilt stirrup hilt, 'lion's head' pommel, copper wirebound, ivory grip. $184 £85

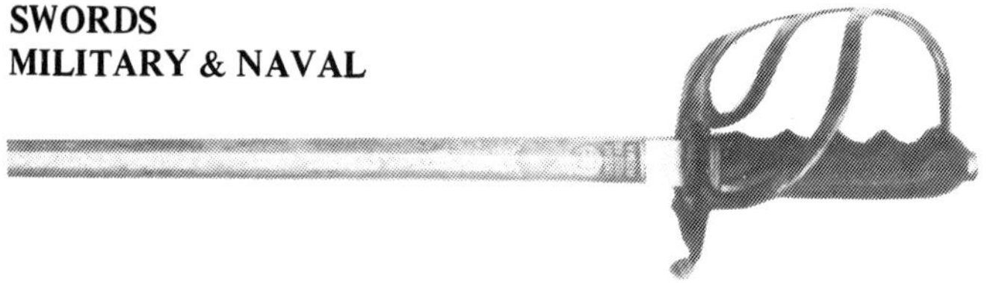

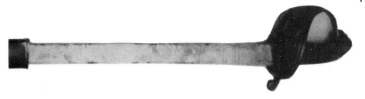

An Italian World War II Army officer's sword, straight blade 33½in., by 'Horster', plated triple bar steel hilt, plain plated mounts, shaped black grip, in its metal scabbard and with original belt with bullion cloth facing and chain. $187 £85

A Georgian 1827 pattern naval officer's sword, single edged flat slightly curved blade 29½in., etched with Royal arms, cown, fouled anchor, coronet officer's initials "H.N." $187 £85

An Edward VII 1821 pattern Heavy Cavalry officer's sword of the XIVth King's Hussars, blade 35in., by 'Henry Wilkinson, Pall Mall', fitted with 'Wilkinson's patent solid hilt', steel guard, hatched composition wirebound grip, in its leather scabbard with plated mounts. $215 £90

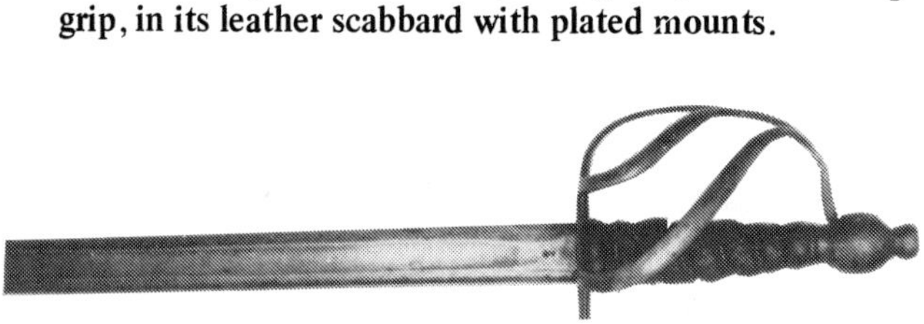

A Dragoon trooper's sword, circa 1780, straight, single edged blade 30½in., steel half-basket hilt with slotted base and double side loop, ovoid pommel, fishskin covered, wirebound grip. $247 £95

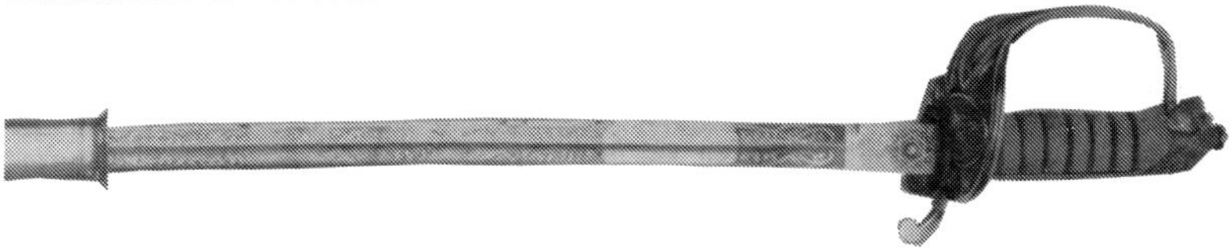

A post-1902 Naval officer's sword, blade 31½in., by 'Stumbles & Son, Ore Street, Devonport', gilt brass hilt, folding side guard, wirebound, white fish-skin covered grip, 'lion's head' pommel, in its brass mounted leather scabbard. $209 £95

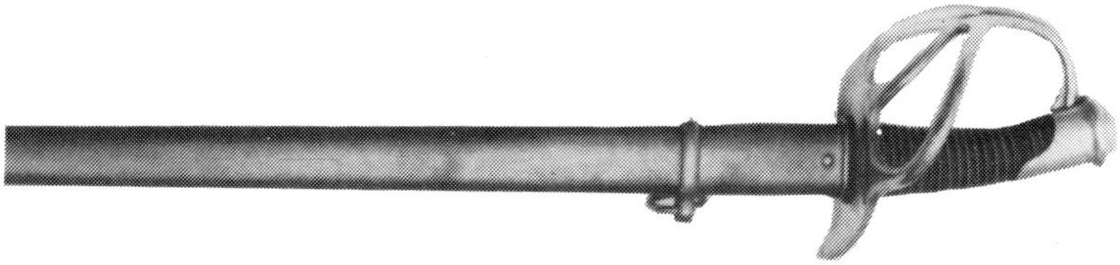

A French Light Cavalry trooper's 1882 model sword, blade 34in., engraved on back-strap 'Mre d'Armes de Chatt, Mars 1886 Cavrie. Legere Mle. 1882', triple bar brass hilt, brass wirebound, ribbed leather grip, in its steel scabbard. $225 £95

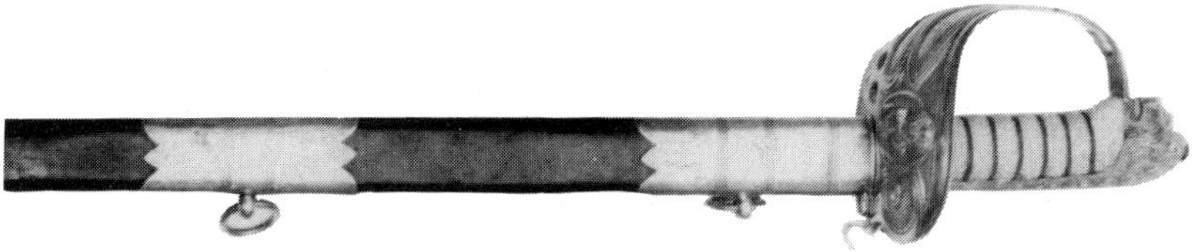

A late Victorian Naval officer's sword, blade 31½in., by 'Henry Wilkinson, Pall Mall', brass hilt, 'lion's head' pommel, copper wirebound, white fishskin covered grip, in its brass mounted leather scabbard. $217 £100

An 1879 pattern Saxony Garde Reiter Regiment trooper's sword, slightly curved blade 34in., by 'P. D. Luneschloss', brass semi-basket hilt, original dress knot, ribbed, leather covered grip, in its steel scabbard. $240 £100

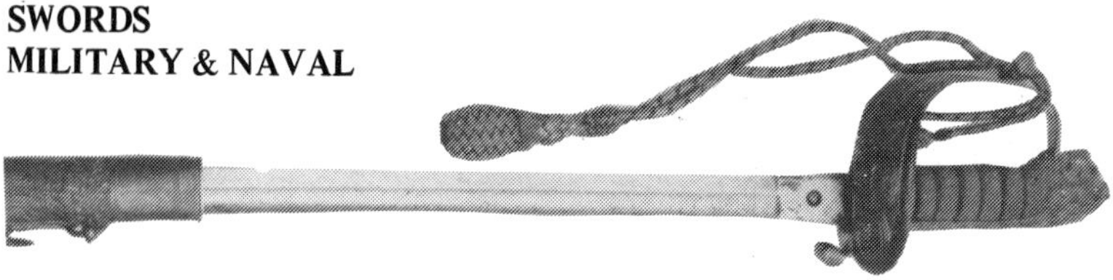

A post-1902 Naval flag officer's sword, blade 31½in., by 'Henry Wilkinson, Pall Mall', gilt hilt, 'lion's head' pommel, wirebound, white fishskin covered grip, bullion dress knot, in its leather scabbard with three gilt mounts.
$235 £100

A post-1902 Naval warrant officer's sword, blade 31in., brass guard and mounts folding side guard, ribbed fishskin covered grip, bullion dress knot, in its brass mounted leather scabbard with black patent leather un-dress sword belt.
$231 £105

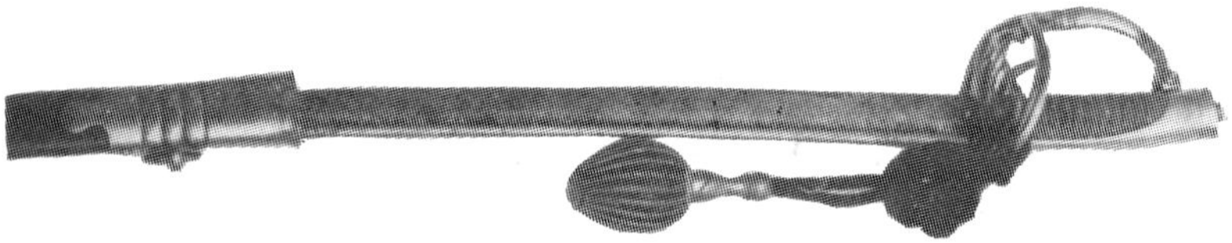

A Dutch 19th century Naval officer's sword, curved, pipe-backed, clipped-back blade 34½in., by 'H. Hollenkamp Amsterdam', gilt brass hilt, side loop inset with openwork fouled anchor, single knucklebow, plain mounts, wire-bound, fishskin covered grip, in its leather scabbard. $250 £105

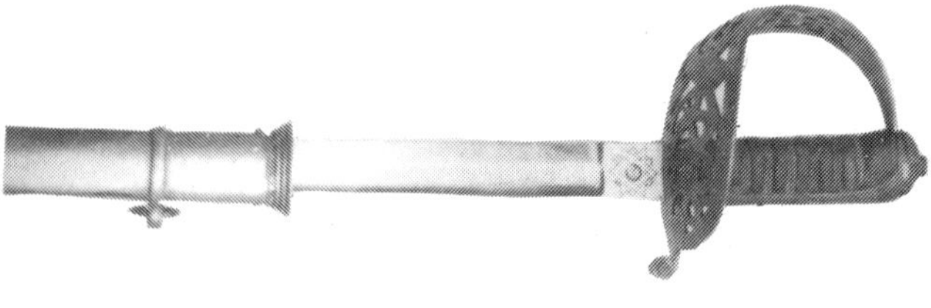

A Victorian Heavy Cavalry officer's 1821 pattern un-dress sword, blade 34½in., by 'Henry Wilkinson, Pall Mall', No. 27935, plated hilt, wirebound, fishskin covered grip, in its plated scabbard. $250 £105

A 19th century Dutch Naval officer's sword, slightly curved, pipe-backed, clipped-back blade 27½in., marked at forte 'Fr. Busch, Klingenthal', gilt hilt with pierced guard, single knucklebow, ribbed ivory grip, in its gilt mounted leather scabbard. $250 £105

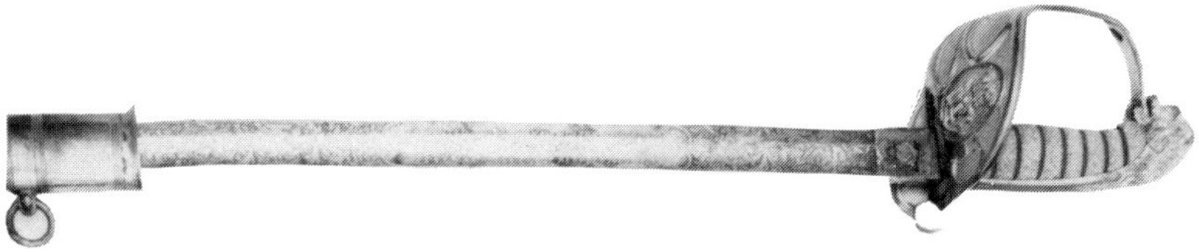

A Victorian Naval officer's sword, slightly curved blade 32½in., by 'Warren, Cursitor St., London', copper gilt hilt, 'lion's head' pommel, wirebound, white fishskin covered grip, folding side guard, in its leather scabbard. $239 £110

A Prussian 1889 pattern Infantry officer's sword, straight, multi-fullered blade 31½in., etched 'Eisenhauer Garantiert', and with crowned cypher 'F.A.R.' (For Saxony) at forte, gilt hilt with folding side guard, wirebound, fishskin covered grip, original bullion dress knot, in its black painted metal scabbard. $285 £120

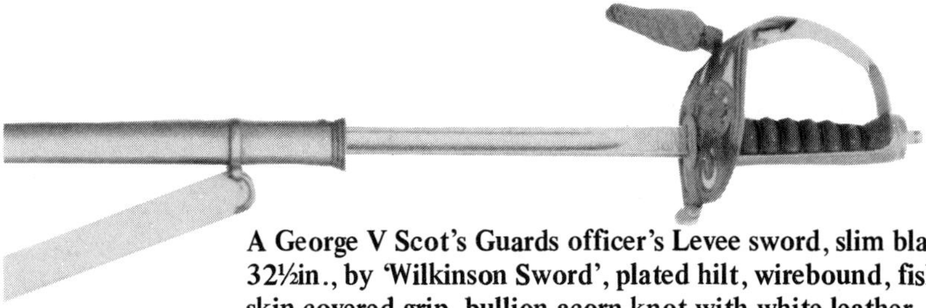

A George V Scot's Guards officer's Levee sword, slim blade 32½in., by 'Wilkinson Sword', plated hilt, wirebound, fish-skin covered grip, bullion acorn knot with white leather strap, in its plated scabbard with web sword belt and white leather slings. $282 £130

A George VI R.A.F. officer's sword, blade 32in., gilt brass hilt with Royal cypher, R.A.F. badge, 'eagle's head' pommel, brass wirebound, fishskin covered grip, in its patent leather scabbard with gilt brass mounts. $308 £140

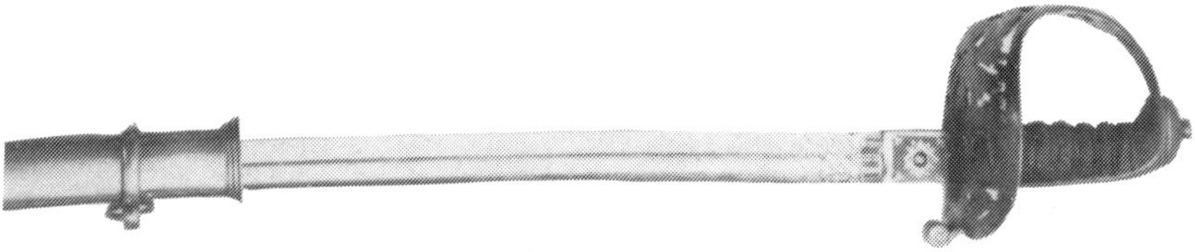

A Victorian Royal Engineers officer's 1857 pattern sword, slightly curved blade 34½in., etched at forte with 'Lanarkshire Engineers', gilt brass hilt, wirebound, fishskin covered grip, in its steel scabbard. $330 £140

A Prussian Garde Infantry 1889 pattern officer's sword, straight, plated, fullered blade 33in., by 'Weyersberg & Co.', gilt hilt with extra chiselled decoration of fronds, laurel sprays and foliate patterns, lion mask on knucklebow, wirebound, fishskin covered grip, in its black painted metal scabbard. $355 £150

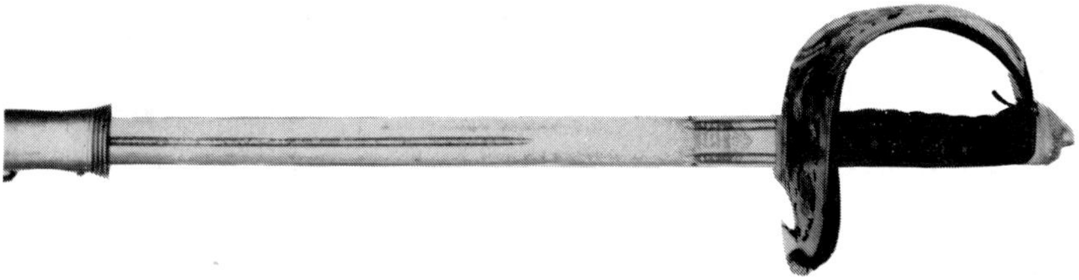

A post-1902 Scottish field officer's sword of the Royal Scots Fusiliers, straight, double edged blade 32in., by 'Henry Wilkinson, Pall Mall', etched with Royal Scots Fusiliers, plated guard, red liner, plated mounts, wirebound, fishskin covered grip, in its plated scabbard. $312 £150

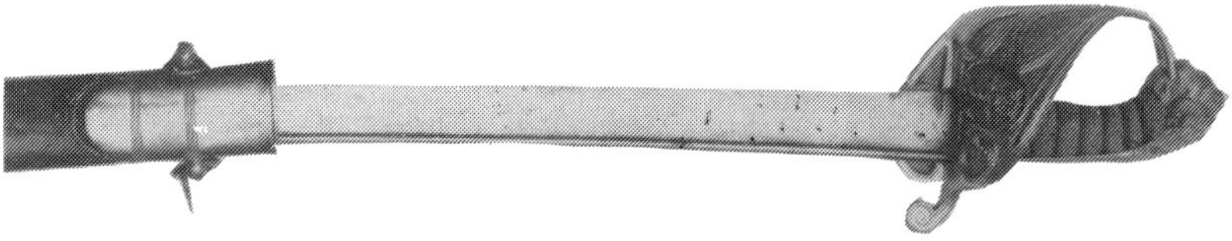

A Georgian 1827 pattern Naval officer's sword, slightly curved, pipe-backed blade 30in., pronounced clipped-back point, etched maker at forte 'Prosser, Maker to the King', copper gilt hilt with folding side guard, chiselled 'lion's head' pommel, copper wirebound, fishskin covered grip, in its leather scabbard with locket and chape of copper. $355 £150

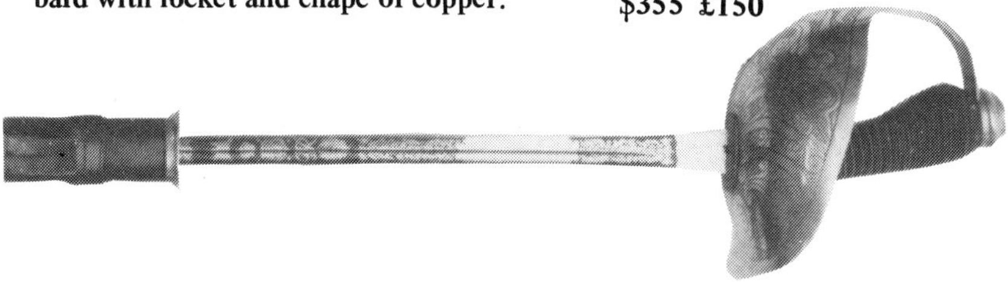

A George VI 1912 pattern Cavalry officer's sword, slim, straight blade 33½in., plated bowl guard, wirebound, fishskin covered grip, in its leather covered field service scabbard. $390 £165

A French Revolutionary period officer's sword, slightly curved blade 30½in., etched 'Pour La Nation La Loi Le (Roi)' (last word obliterated at the Revolution), by 'Liger, Rue Coquillere A Paris'. Brass hilt with fluted knucklebow and gilt plumed helmet pommel, wirebound grip. $434 £200

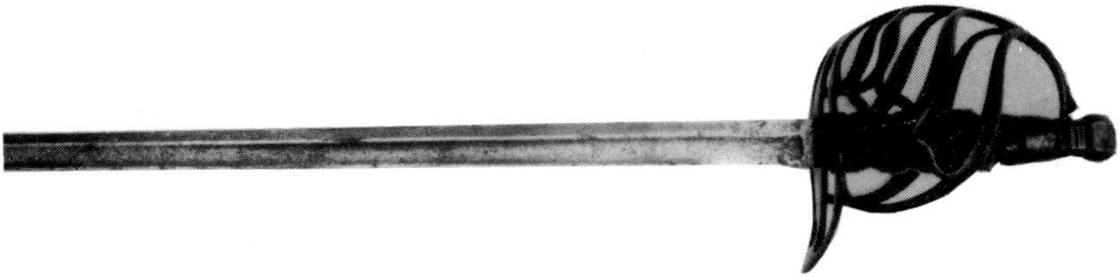

An English Dragoon trooper's sword, circa 1770, plain, straight, single edged blade 32in., looped and slotted basket guard, octagonal pommel, wirebound, leather covered grip. $437 £210

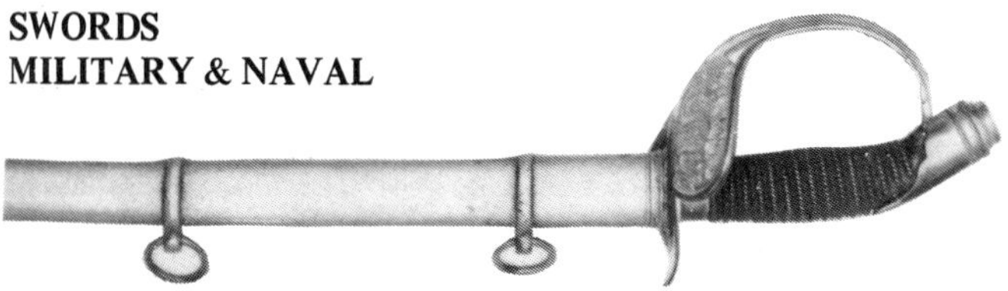

An 1889 pattern Prussian Infantry officer's sword, as carried by officers stationed in China, plated, multi-fullered blade 33in., gilt hilt, the Prussian Eagle replaced by a Chinese Dragon, brass wirebound, fishskin covered grip, in its plated scabbard. $437 £210

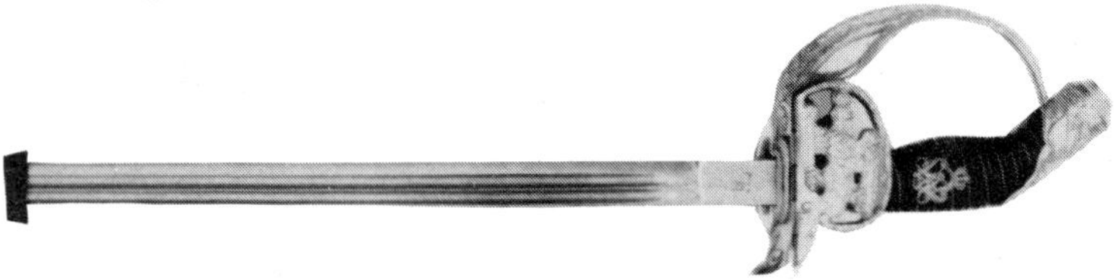

An 1889 pattern Prussian Infantry officer's sword, straight, double fullered blade 31in., by 'W. K. & C.', of watered steel, gilt hilt with folding guard pierced with the Prussian Eagle, knucklebow chiselled with laurel leaves, wirebound, black ribbed grip, in its metal scabbard. $500 £230

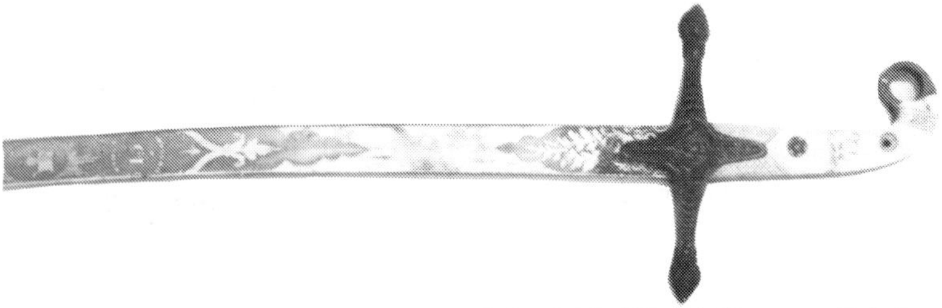

A Victorian officer's Levee sword of the 15th (Kings) Hussars, slightly curved, single edged, clipped-back blade 32in., by 'Hawkes & Co. London'. copper gilt crosspiece, two-piece part chequered case in grips, in its copper gilt mounted fishskin covered scabbard with two hanging rings. $704 £320

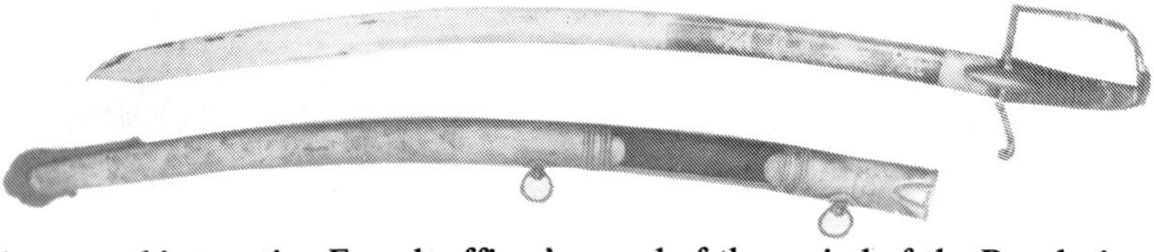

A rare and interesting French officer's sword of the period of the Revolution, circa 1790, slightly curved blade 32½in., with pronounced clipped back tip, retaining much original blued and gilt etched decoration of military trophies and foliage, the locket with original presentation inscription :"Le Directoire Executif au Cen (I.E. for "Citoyen"), Calandre Lieutenant" $16,000 £7,000

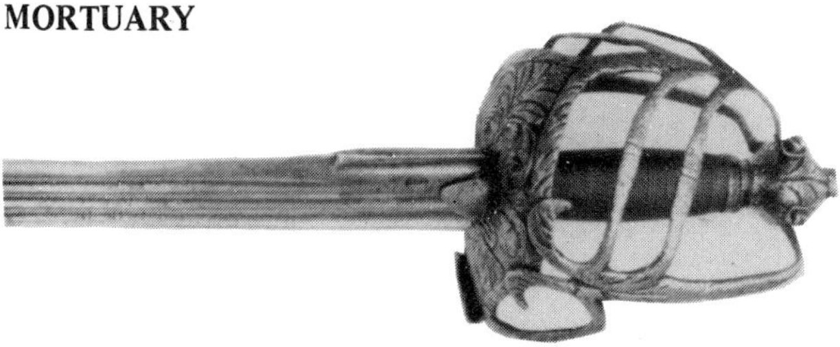

A 17th century mortuary sword, multi-fullered blade 31in., with clipped-back point, struck at forte with traces of inscription in fullers 'Anno Fara Isis', iron basket hilt, the bowl guard chiselled with masks and foliate patterns, ovoid conical pommel, wirebound grip. $499 £230

PATTERN

An 1860 pattern American Staff and Field officer's sword, shallow diamond sectioned blade 29¼in., etched with 'Lilley & Co. Columbus', copper gilt hilt with folding shell guard, wirebound, sharkskin grip. $88 £40

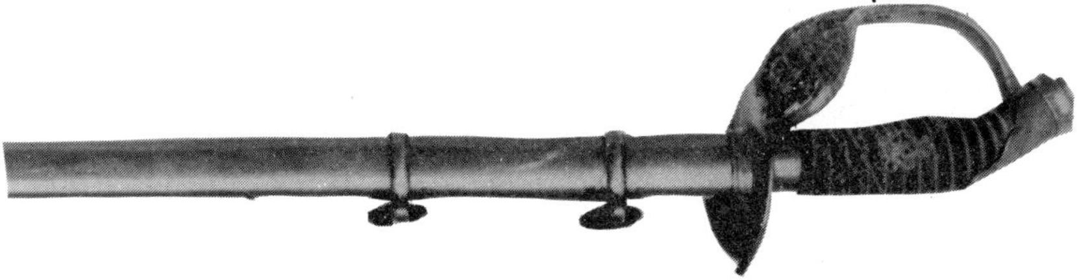

A Prussian 1889 pattern Infantry officer's sword, plated, double fullered blade 32in., by 'W. K. C.', brass guard, brass wirebound, fishskin covered grip, mounted with 'WRII' cypher, in its plated metal scabbard. $108 £50

A Victorian 1827 pattern Light Rifle Volunteer officer's sword, slim blade 32in., by 'Thurkle, High Holborn', etched with crown, 'VR', regiment '2nd London Rifle Volunteers', etc., plated hilt, black leather dress knot, in its plated scabbard. $130 £60

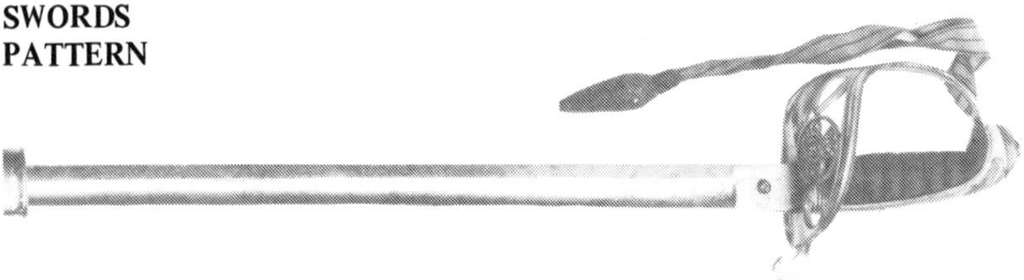

A Victorian 1822 pattern Infantry officer's sword, slightly curved blade 32½in., by 'Noel Edwards & Sons, London', etched with 'Kilkenny Militia', copper gilt hilt with folding side guard, wirebound, fishkin covered grip, with crimson and gilt sword knot. $143 £65

An 1889 pattern Prussian Infantry officer's sword, plated, straight, plated multi-fullered blade 32in., with early Eickhorn mark, copper gilt hilt with folding side guard pierced with Prussian Eagle, the knucklebow, pommel and mounts with additional chiselled decoration of oak leaves and scrolls, wirebound, black ribbed grip. $154 £70

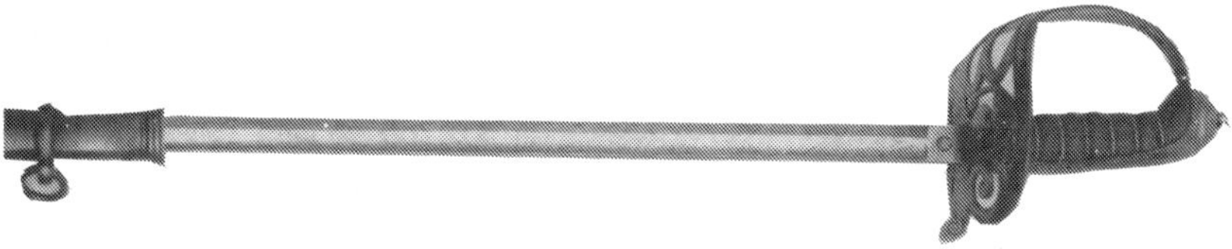

A Victorian 1854 Levee pattern Grenadier Guards officer's sword, slim, straight blade 32in., by 'Cater, Pall Mall', etched with Battle Honours to the Crimea, steel guard, wirebound, fishskin covered grip, in its steel scabbard. $184 £85

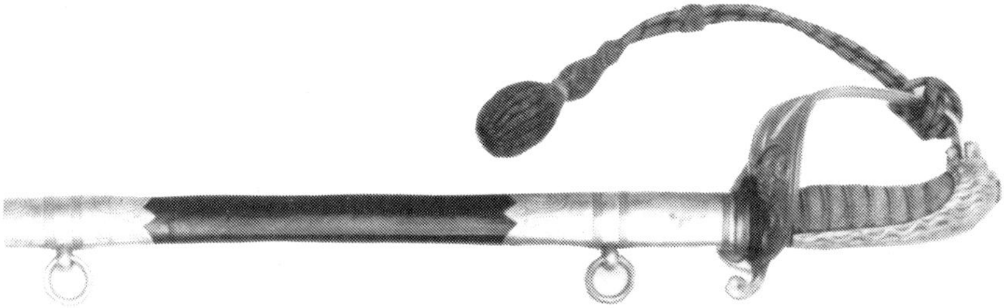

A Victorian light pattern Naval officer's sword, narrow, straight, plain blade 29½in., by 'Fraser & Davis, Portsmouth', copper gilt hilt with folding side guard, 'lion's head' pommel, gilt wirebound, white fishskin covered grip, in its copper gilt metal mounted leather scabbard. $189 £86

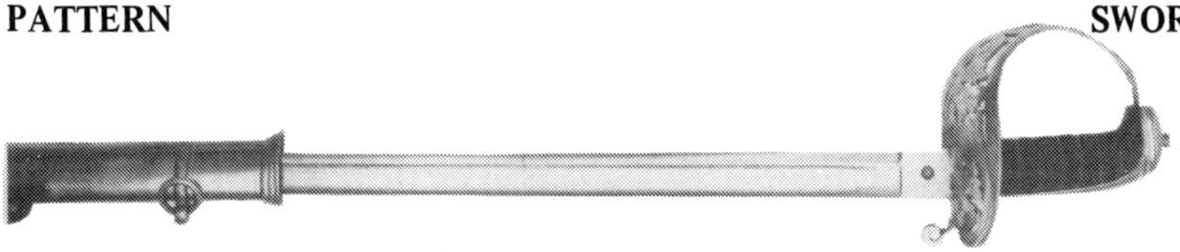

A Victorian 1857 pattern Royal Engineers officer's sword, blade 32½in., by 'E. Thurkle, Soho, London', brass hilt, copper wirebound black fishskin covered grip, in its steel scabbard. $204 £90

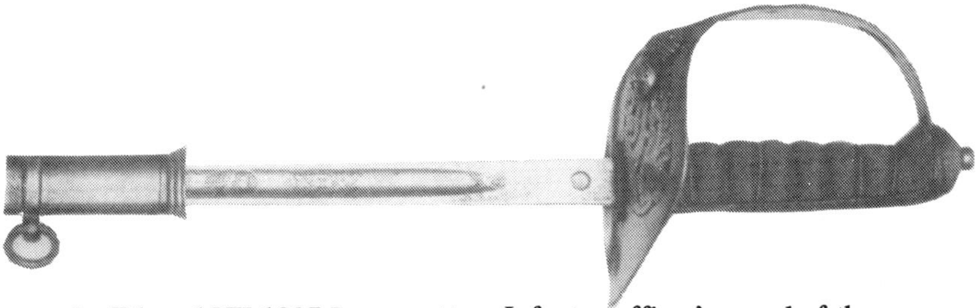

An Edward VII 1897 Levee pattern Infantry officer's sword of the Northumberland Fusiliers, slim, plated blade 32in., by 'Jones', etched with 'V. Northumberland Fusiliers', grenade badge and scrolls, steel hilt with addition of white metal grenade badge, wirebound, fishskin covered grip, in its steel scabbard. $209 £95

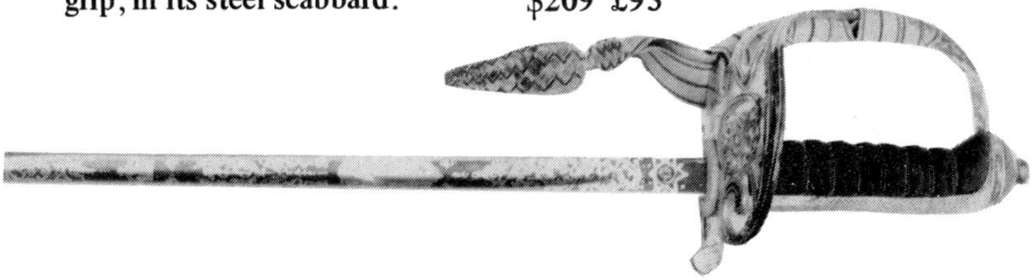

An Edward VII Royal Army Medical Corps light pattern officer's sword, slim blade 32½in., by 'J. R. Gaunt, 53 Conduit St., London', gilt hilt, wirebound, black fishskin covered grip, original bullion dress knot, in its plated scabbard. $285 £125

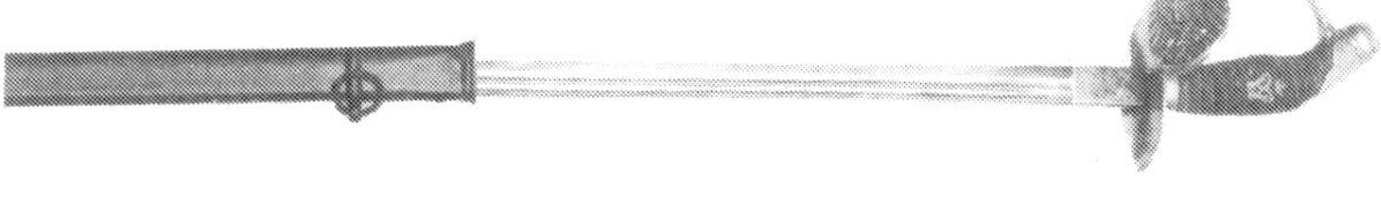

A Prussian 1889 pattern Infantry officer's sword as carried by Colonial troops, straight, double fullered blade 32in., brass hilt, wirebound, fishskin covered grip with crowned 'WII' cypher, in its black painted metal scabbard. $275 £125

An Austrian Cavalry officer's 1904 pattern sword, plated, slightly curved pipe-backed, clipped-back blade 30in., plated hilt and mounts, pierced honeysuckle guard, brass wirebound, fishskin covered grip, in its plated scabbard with original dress knot with 'K' cypher (of the Emperor Karl). $304 £140

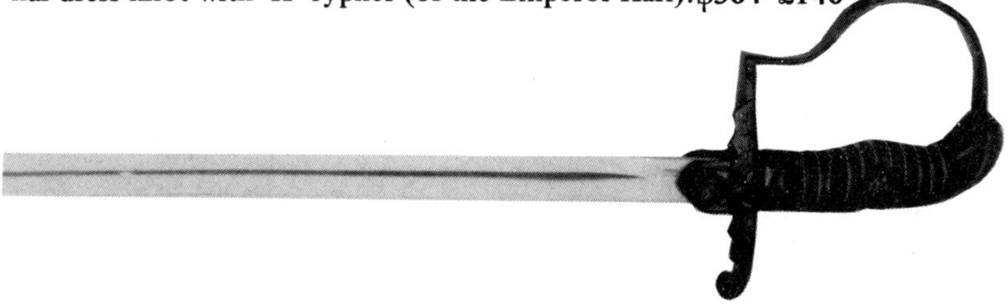

A Nazi Army officer's 'Prinz Eugen' pattern sword, plated, curved blade 31½in., by 'Eickhorn', bronzed stirrup guard and mounts, Nazi Eagle to langet and pommel, wirebound, black ribbed grip, in its black painted metal scabbard. $304 £140

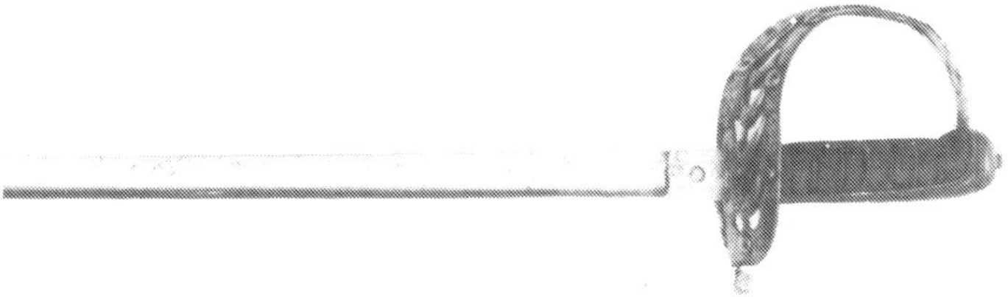

An officer's sword of the 2nd Life Guards, straight, plated blade 37in., by 'Hawkes', etched with Battle Honours to Tel-El-Kebir in scrolled panels, plated hilt, wirebound, fishskin covered grip. $396 £180

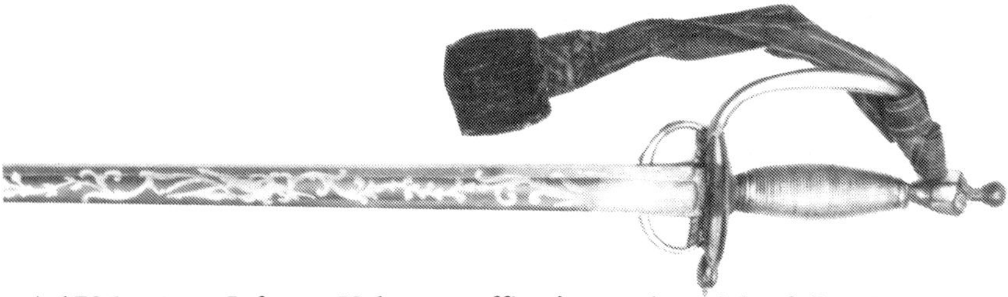

A 1796 pattern Infantry Volunteer officer's sword, straight, fullered, single edged blade 32¼in., etched with 'J. Speet froudrisseur F.W.S.' at forte, regulation copper gilt hilt with folding shell guard, sheet silver covered grip, silver bullion dress knot. $418 £190

An 1827 pattern Rifle Volunteer officer's sword of Lieutenant Colonel Mellor of the Ashton-under-Lyne Volunteers, blade 32½in., heavily plated silver hilt, wirebound, fishskin covered grip, in its silvered steel scabbard. Together with a well executed oil painting of Colonel Mellor.

$726 £330

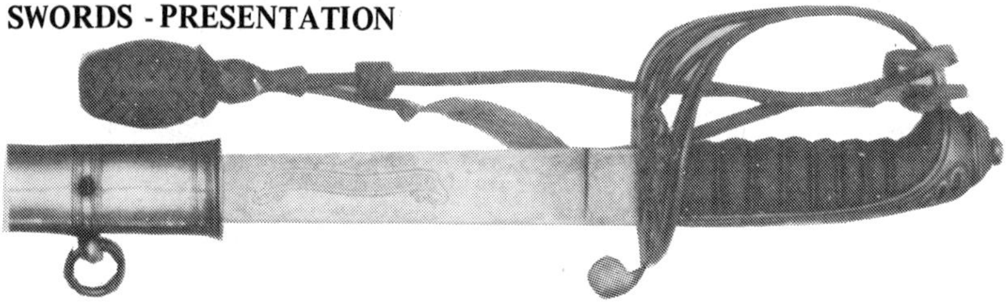

A Victorian 1822 pattern NCO's presentation sword, plain, single edged blade 32in., by 'Thurkle, Soho, London', copper guard, copper, wire-bound, fishskin covered grip, spring catch, in its black patent leather scabbard, with three silver gilt mounts. $132 £60

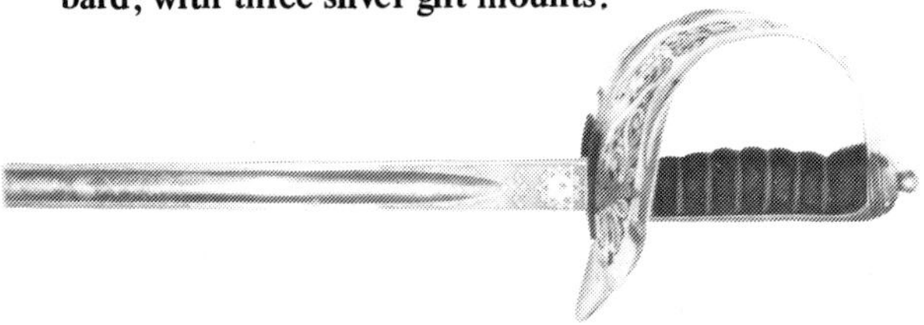

A George V 1897 pattern Infantry officer's presentation sword, blade 32½in., by 'Sanderson Bros & Newbould, Sheffield', silver plated hilt, wirebound, fishskin covered grip, in its leather field service scabbard with frog. $176 £80

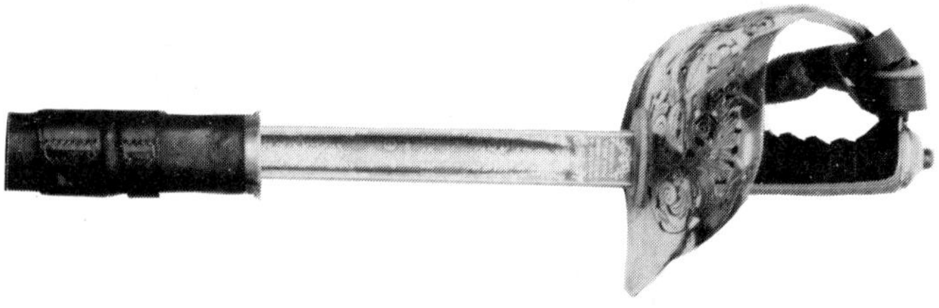

A World War I period 1897 pattern Infantry officer's presentation sword, blade 32½in., by 'Wilkinson', etched with inscription 'To J. G. from H. B. F. 1917', plated guard, wirebound, fishskin grip, in its leather curved field service scabbard with leather dress knot. $217 £100

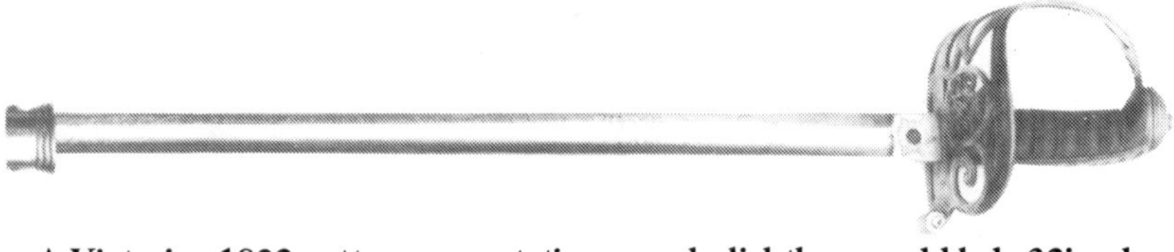

A Victorian 1822 pattern presentation sword, slightly curved blade 32in., by 'Henry Wilkinson, Pall Mall,' etched with inscription '. . . to V. Skipton Gouldsbury M.D., For His Gallant Services During the Ashantee War of 1873', steel hilt, copper wirebound, fishskin covered grip, in its steel scabbard. $220 £100

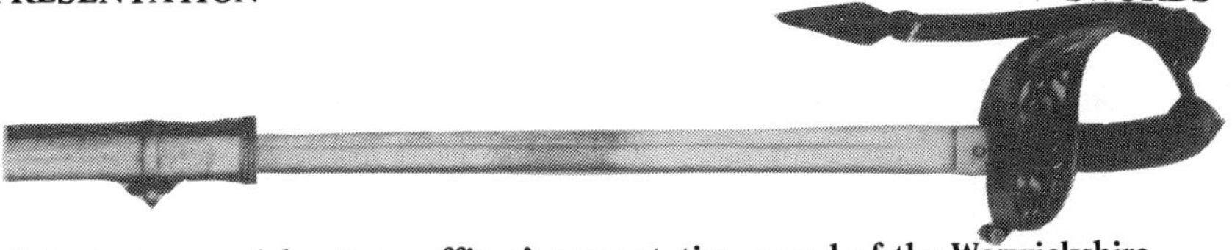

A Victorian special pattern officer's presentation sword of the Warwickshire Rifle Vols., blade 32in., by 'Reeves', etched with crown, 'VR', strung bugle, 'Warwickshire Rifle Volunteers', steel bowl guard pierced with scrolls and oak leaf sprays, silver wire, bound fishskin covered grip, steel fluted pommel, black leather dress knot, in its steel scabbard, together with black patent leather dress belt with double silver bullion stripe and slings. $483 £210

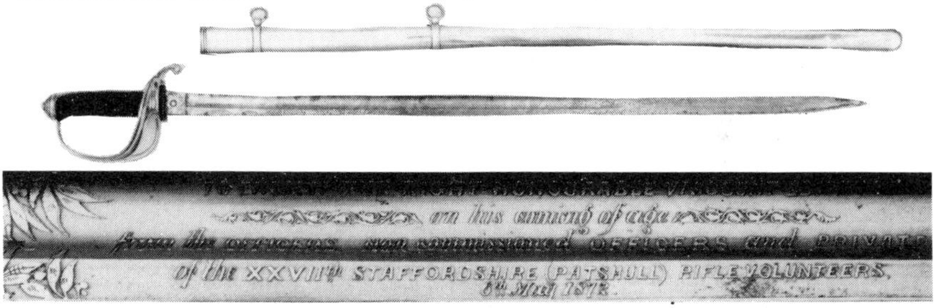

A Victorian 1821 pattern Artillery Volunteer officer's hallmarked silver mounted presentation sword, blade 33in., by 'Lawson & Ward, 5 Hatton Garden, London', etched with 'Presented to G. W. Wilkinson Esq., upon the occasion of his being raised to the rank of Major in the 1st Monmouthshire Artillery Volunteers Risca, February 10th 1894', triple bar guard and mounts of solid silver (HM London 1893), wirebound, fishskin covered grip, in its scabbard of solid silver. $694 £320

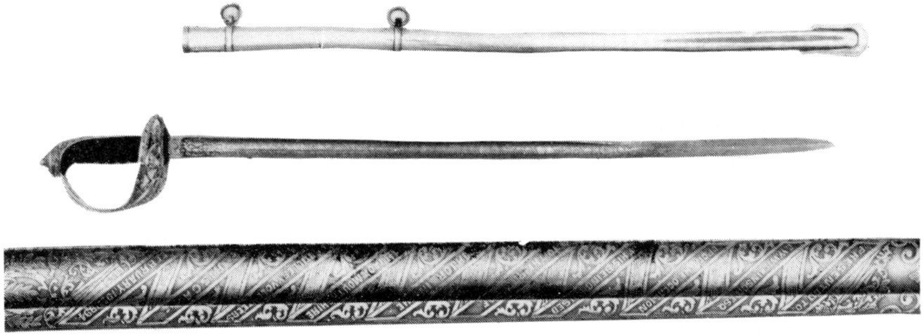

A Victorian 1827 pattern hallmarked silver hilted officer's presentation sword, slightly curved blade 32½in., by 'Robt. Mole & Sons, manufacturers Birmingham', etched inscription 'To Ensign The Right Honourable Viscount Lewisham on His coming of age, from the non-commissioned officers and privates of XXVIIth, Staffordshire (Patshull) Rifle Volunteers, 6th May 1872, hilt of solid hallmarked silver. $1,302 £600

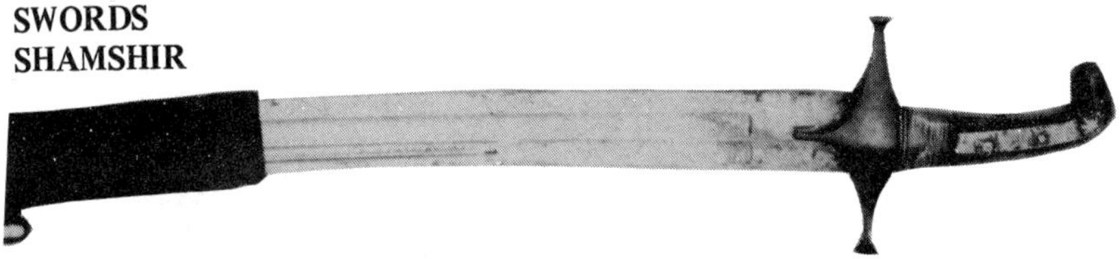

A Turkish shamshir, curved, single edged, multi-fullered blade 34in., by 'Nikittits Constantinople', etched with crescent moon, military trophies and foliage, steel crosspiece, horn grips, in its tooled leather covered wooden scabbard with two iron ring mounts. $166 £80

An Indo-Persian sword shamsir, watered blade 33in., with Qum or gravel-meander, pattern gold inlaid with maker's cartouche 'Assad Ullah, the servant of Shah Abbas', iron hilt, two-piece rounded bone grips, in its black leather covered scabbard. $228 £100

An Indo-Persian shamshir, curved blade 33½in. of watered steel, crosspiece, straps and pommel mount of Eastern silver decorated with foliate nielloed pattern, ivory grips, in its snake skin covered wooden scabbard. $388 £170

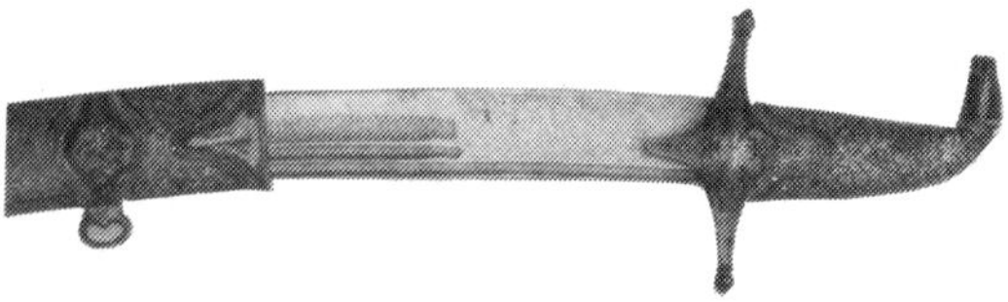

A silver mounted Caucasian shamshir, curved blade 30½in., with broad central fuller and narrow back double fullers, with watered steel pattern, the hilt and crossguard embossed with foliate sprays, in its leather covered wooden scabbard with three large Eastern silver mounts. $924 £420

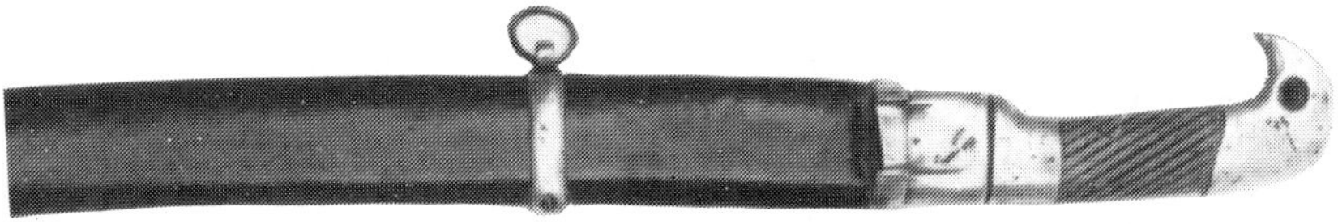

An Imperial Russian 1881 pattern Military shasqua, slightly curved, single edged blade 34in., brass mounts, spiral, fluted wood grip, in its brass mounted, leather covered wooden scabbard. $264 £120

SMALLSWORDS

A late Victorian cut-steel hilted smallsword, straight, slim, triangular blade 31in., etched with crossed lances and foliage, bright steel hilt with shell guard with star patterns, urn pommel, in its patent leather scabbard with steel mounts. $80 £35

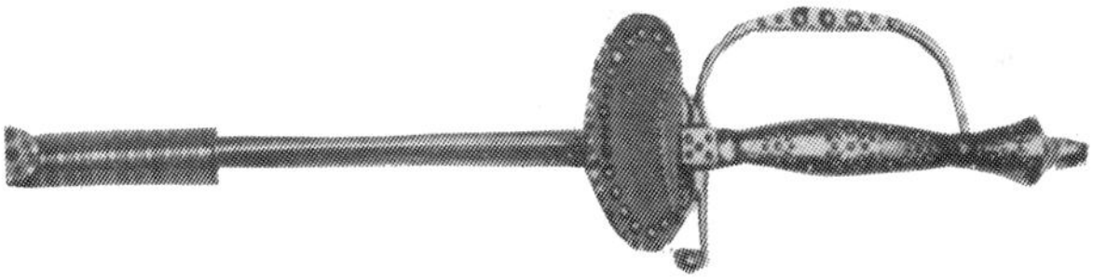

A late Victorian cut-steel hilted smallsword, straight, tapering, triangular blade 31in., by 'D. Dote, Conduit Street', etched with crossed axes and foliage, shell guard and hilt decorated with faceted studs, urn pommel, in its patent leather scabbard with steel mounts. $92 £40

A mid 18th century smallsword, colichmarde blade 30in., etched at forte with Cavalier head and foliate scrolls, iron hilt with double shell guard, knucklebow with some scrolled pattern, pierced ovoid pommel, wirebound grip. $126 £55

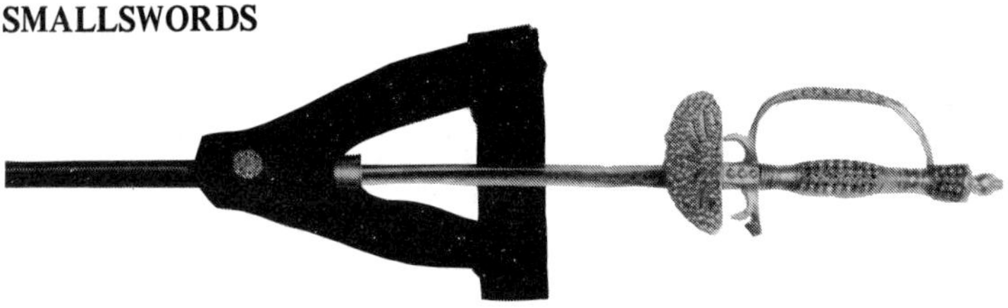

A late Victorian cut-steel hilted smallsword, slim tapering, triangular blade 29½in., openwork fretted shell guard, the hilt and urn pommel decorated with facetted studs, in its black patent leather scabbard. $146 £70

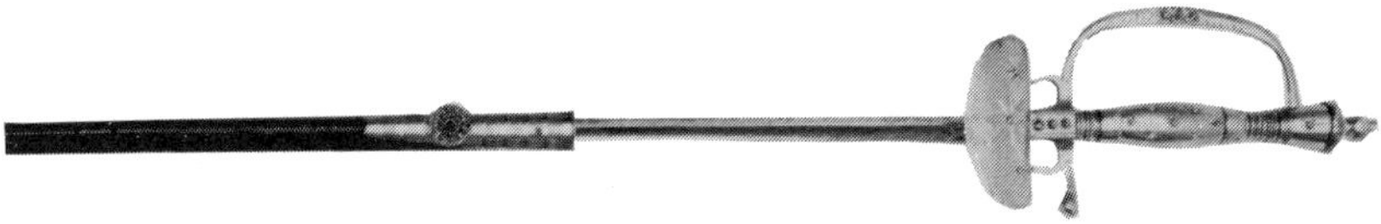

A cut-steel hilted smallsword, slim, tapering, triangular blade 31in., shell guard with star patterns, the knucklebow, grip and urn pommel with some facetted studded decoration, in its black patent leather scabbard. $156 £75

A late 18th century smallsword, colichmarde blade 31in., oval steel shell guard with toothed rim, steel knucklebow and mounts, ovoid pommel, silver band and wirebound grip, in its vellum covered wooden scabbard. $341 £155

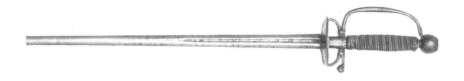

An English 17th century transitional smallsword, the 38in. rapier blade of flattened diamond section with short, deep fullers signed 'Tomas (Ail(a)', steel hilt with double shell guard, large pas d'ane rings and spherical pommel, original brass wirebound grip. $352 £160

A French mid 18th century cut silver hilted smallsword, fitted with slim 17th century transitional rapier blade, 30in. of flattened diamond section, signed in short fuller 'Arnoldt Bavffert Sole Deo Gloria', oval dish guard, the pommel and grip of openwork pattern, silver pod chain knucklebow.
$434 £200

An hallmarked silver hilted smallsword, circa 1710, slender, hollow ground blade 28in., etched with 'A La Teste Noire, Sur Le Pont, St. Michel, a Paris', with gilt infill. Silver hilt of swollen form, silver wirebound grip.
$663 £255

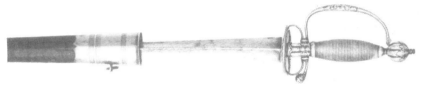

A silver hilted smallsword, circa 1770, tapering, triangular blade 25in., the double shell guard partly chiselled with foliate patterns and two masks, the knucklebow, quillon block, back quillon and fluted pommel similarly decorated, silver wirebound grip, in its leather covered wooden scabbard.
$660 £300

A russet gilt hilted smallsword, circa 1740, colichmarde blade 33¼in., steel hilt , silver wirebound grip with 'Turks' heads', in its russet gilt mounted leather scabbard with two hanging rings. $1,235 £475

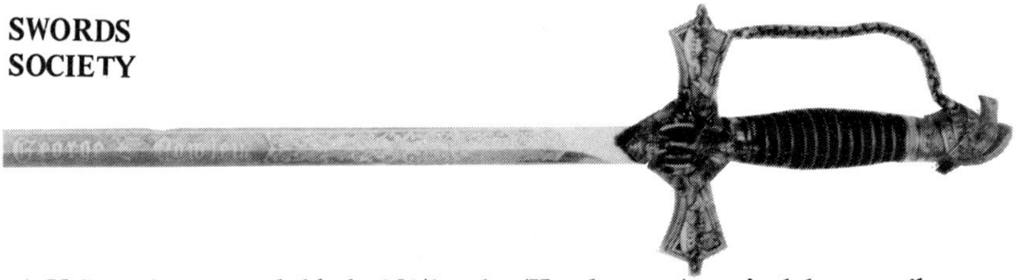

A U.S. society sword, blade 28½in., by 'Henderson Ames', elaborate gilt cast crossguard with standing knight, chain knucklebow, wirebound, leather covered grip, in its plated scabbard with brass mounts. $108 £50

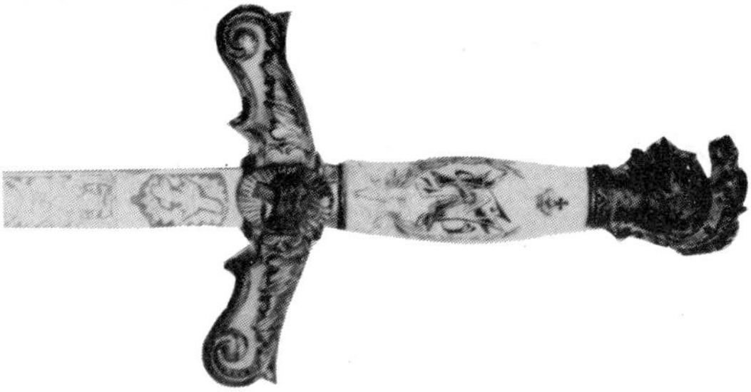

A U.S. society sword, blade 28½in., by 'M. C. Lilley, Columbus', gold washed, elaborate Gothic hilt with plated, pierced crossguard and plumed helmet pommel, ivory grip, in its plated scabbard. $108 £50

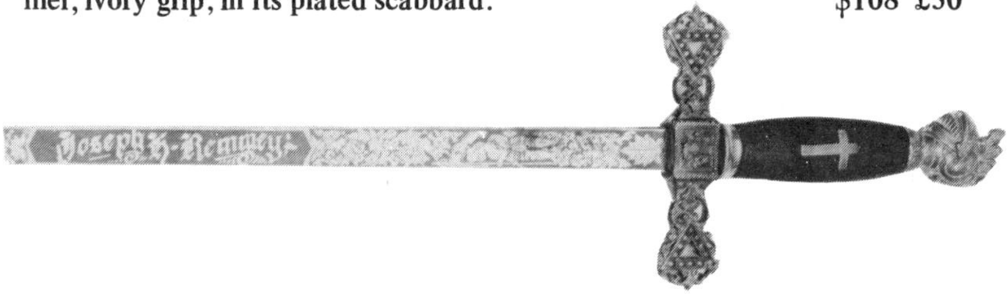

A U.S. society sword, plated blade 28½in., by 'Henderson Ames, Michigan', pierced, plated crosspiece, 'knight's helmet' pommel, black grip inset with cross, in its plated scabbard. $108 £50

A U.S. society sword, blade 30in., by 'M. C. Lilley, Columbus', gold wash background, elaborate plated Gothic hilt, with enamelled masonic emblem, plumed helmet pommel, chain guard, ivorine grip, in its plated scabbard. $108 £50

A U.S. society sword, plated blade 27½in., by 'Brockway, Middletown', gold wash background, plated cruciform crosspiece, chain guard, 'knight's helmet' pommel, black grips mounted with plated cross, in its plated scabbard. $119 £55

A U.S. society sword, blade 31in., by 'Henderson Ames Co., Michigan', gold wash finish, elaborate Gothic hilt with cast pierced crosspiece with enamelled masonic symbols, ivory grip, in its plated scabbard. $130 £60

A U.S. society sword, plated blade 29in., by 'Armstrong, Detroit', gold wash background, plated Gothic crosspiece, 'knight's helmet' pommel, chain knucklebow, bone grip, in its plated scabbard with three Gothic mounts. $152 £70

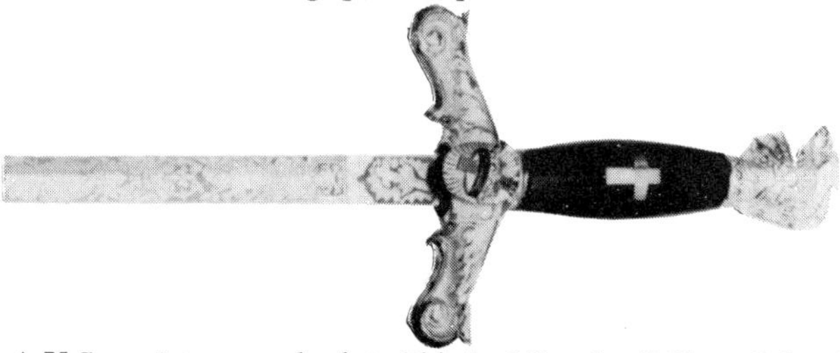

A U.S. society sword, plated blade 26in., by 'Lilley, Columbus', gold wash background, plated Gothic crosspiece and 'knight's helmet' pommel, cross inset in black grip, in its plated scabbard. $163 £75

A 19th century continental swordstick, straight, slim blade 26in. of flattened diamond section, blackened bamboo hilt with horn top, in its blackened bamboo scabbard with metal, bullet shaped ferrule. $108 £50

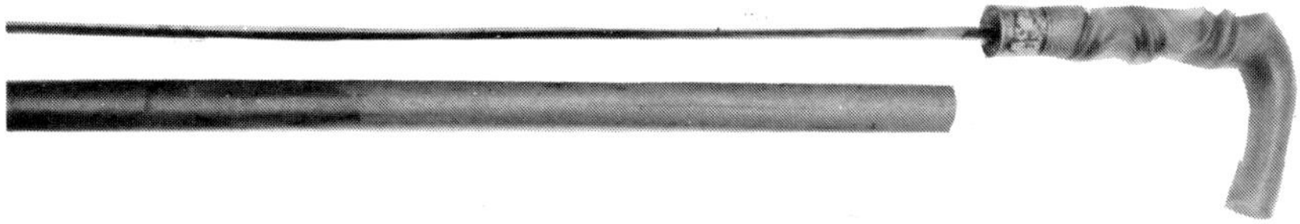

A late Georgian swordstick, slim, straight blade 27in., of flattened diamond section, twist handle of rhino horn, with white metal ferrule with hound's head, twisting to lock the blade in malacca scabbard. $152 £70

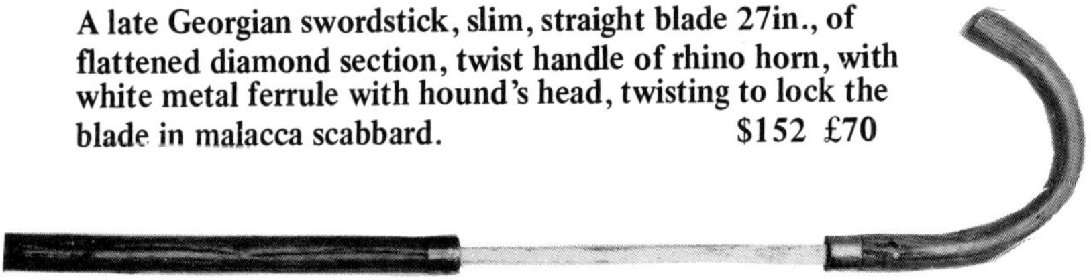

A Victorian swordstick of the type favoured by customs officers, square sectioned blade 30in., stamped 'Mole Birm', brass mounted with wooden handle and stick. $228 £100

A Victorian sword cane, double edged, shallow flattened diamond sectioned blade 28in., etched with 'Artilleria Fabrica De Toledo' at forte, hallmarked silver top (Birmingham 1887), silver ferrule, male malacca cane. $342 £150

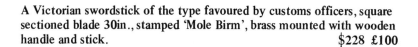

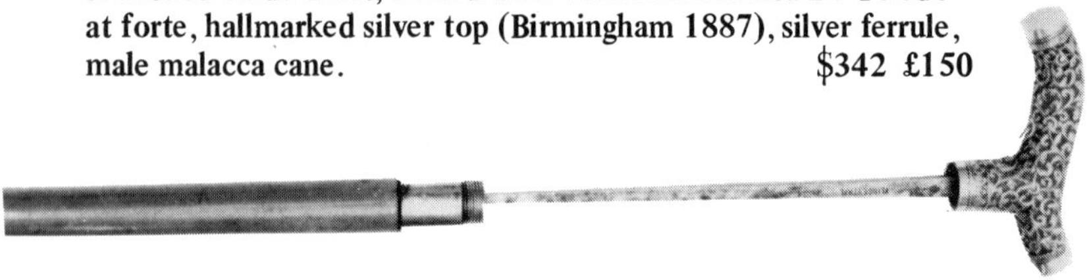

A French silver handled swordstick, tapered, square sectioned blade 27½in., stamped 'Klingenthal, Coulaux & C', silver T-shaped handle, chiselled with scrolling foliage in low relief against a punctuate ground, Screw fitting with malacca cane. $365 £160

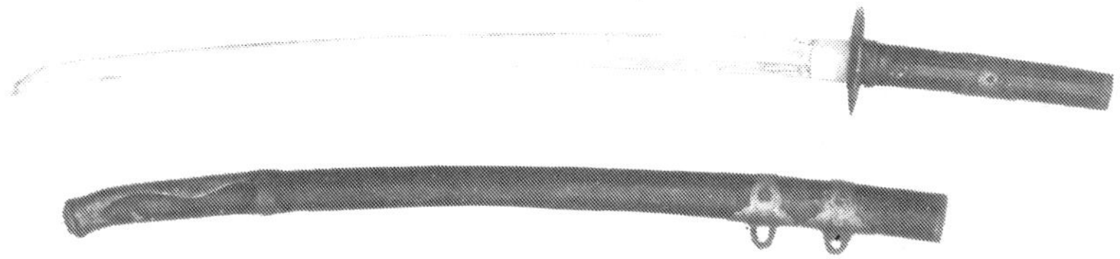

A Japanese sword tachi, blade 68cm., signed and dated, shin-shinto, two mekugi ana, gunome hamon. Foliate engraved brass mounts, Aoi tsuba, two ashi, wooden tsuka, lacquered saya. $990 £450

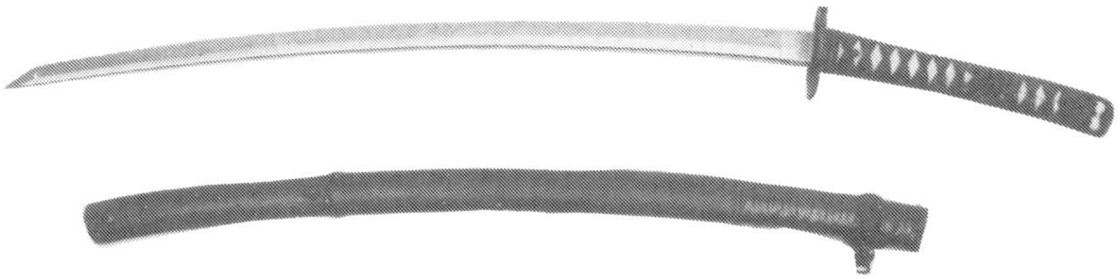

A Japanese sword tachi, blade 65cm. signed 'Bizen Osafune Sukesada', dated Tensho 3rd year (1575), katana-mei, gunome hamon. Tachi koshirae, tape bound same tsuka, single ashi with kojiri, green lacquered saya. $2,366 £910

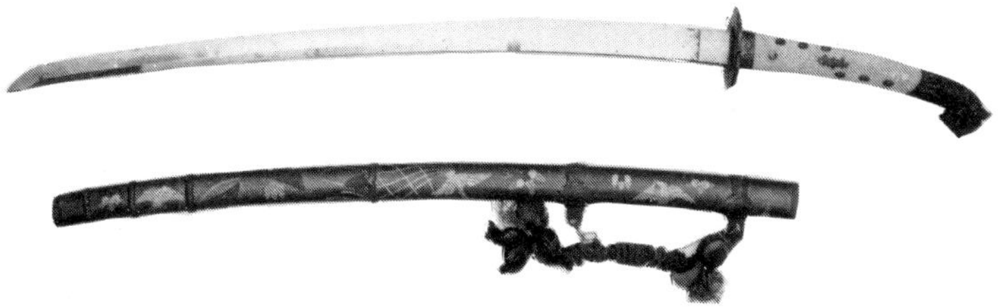

A Japanese sword tachi, blade 74½cm. signed 'Ushu Yajima-shin Fujiwara Kunishige saku kore' and dated Keio 2nd year (1866), Gyaku choji hamon, extensive nie lines, muji or very tight masame hada. $2,912 £1,400

TULWAR

An Indian tulwar, made for a boy, single edged, curved blade 16in., plain iron hilt with wheel pommel, overlaid with silver floral and foliate damascene patterns, in its green vellum covered wooden scabbard with Eastern silver strap and partly pierced silver locket and chape. $152 £70

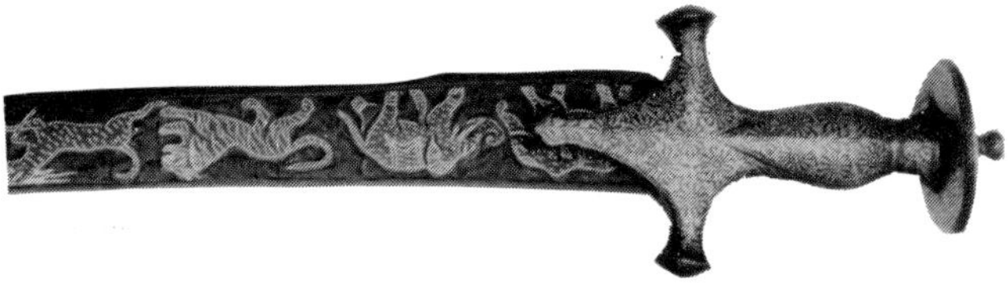

An Indian tulwar, curved blade 31in., chiselled for entire length with animals, heightened in gold, iron hilt covered in gold damascene foliate patterns. $238 £110

WAKIZASHI

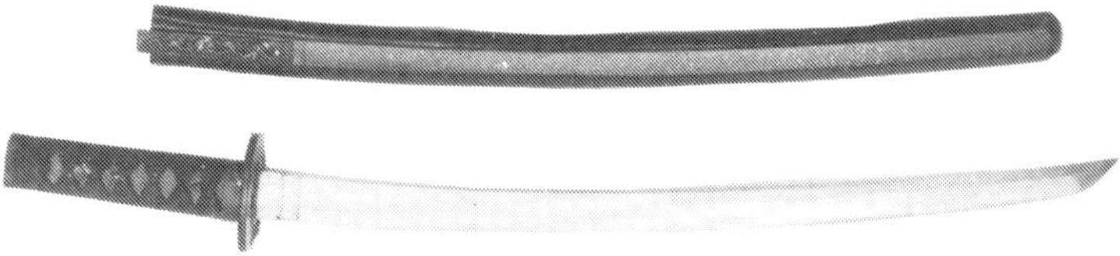

A Japanese shortsword wakizashi, blade 52¼cm. signed Fujiwara Moriyuki, three mekugi ana, chusuguha hamon, heavy iron tsuba inlaid with silver and gilt peonies and gambolling lion, shakudo nanako fuchi kashira, gilt lion menuki, tape bound same tsuka, in its black lacquered saya. $855 £360

YATAGHAN

A gold damascened Turkish sword yataghan, slightly curved, single edged blade 23in., with small back fullers, signed by the makers in gold damascened cartouche with long inscription and foliate borders. Two-piece walrus ivory grips. In its leather covered scabbard with large engraved Eastern silver chape and locket. $354 £170

FLINTLOCK & MATCHLOCK WEAPONS

BLUNDERBUSS

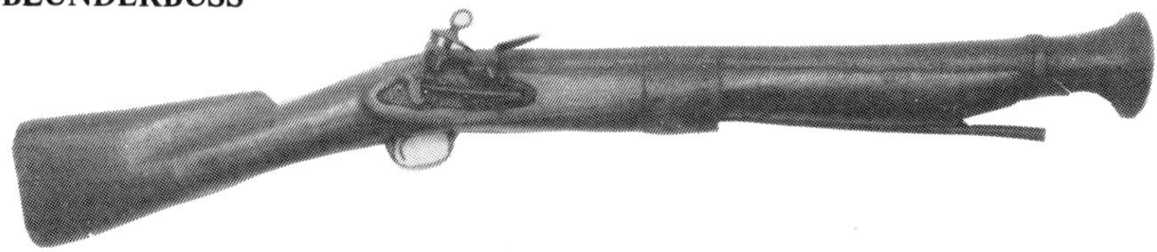

A Spanish miquelet flintlock, bell mouthed blunderbuss, circa 1765, probably made in Ripoll, 44in., half octagonal, stepped barrel 26in., deeply engraved 'IINA' at breech. Bell muzzle and chevron engraved reinforcing band. Full-stocked, bridled striated frizzen, ring top jaw screw, bridled cock with stepped neck, iron furniture, regulation trigger guard, wooden ramrod. $586 £270

A Turkish flintlock blunderbuss pistol fitted with spring bayonet, 19½in., swamped steel barrel 10in., turned breech reinforces, breech chiselled with foliate upon a gold ground with three maker's poincons, sliding top thumb catch releases sprung triangular bayonet with sprung securing catch. Full-stocked, foliate engraved, slightly rounded lock of French type with bridled frizzen. $660 £300

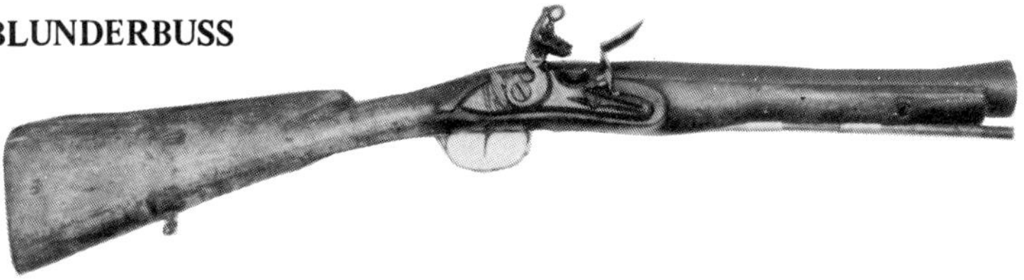

A Russian Military doglock flintlock blunderbuss, circa 1770, 30¼in., barrel 14¼in., swollen muzzle, struck with military proofs at ‘bottleneck’ breech. Full-stocked, stepped lock with swivel dog catch, unbridled squared frizzen, throathole cock with ring top jaw screw. Wooden ramrod with steel worm.
$707 £310

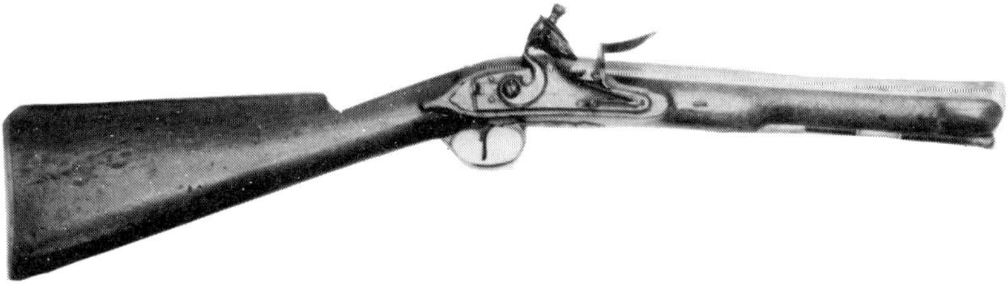

A brass barrelled flintlock blunderbuss by ‘H. W. Mortimer’, circa 1790, 30in., flared barrel 14in., London proved, engraved ‘H. W. Mortimer-London-Gun-Maker to His Majesty’ within teardrop. Full-stocked, stepped bolted lock. Brass mounts of military type, horn tipped ebony ramrod with steel worm. $825 £380

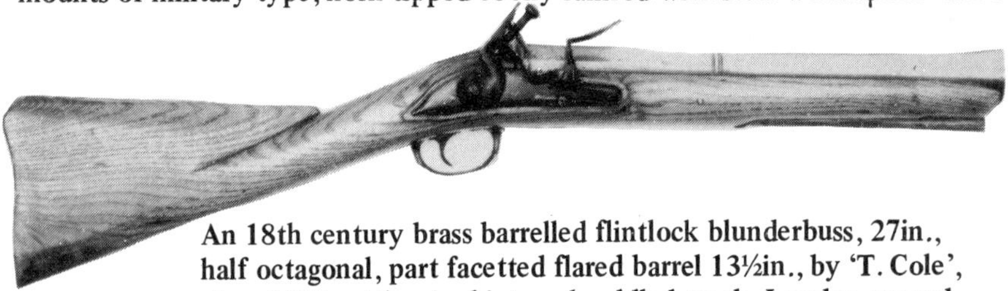

An 18th century brass barrelled flintlock blunderbuss, 27in., half octagonal, part facetted flared barrel 13½in., by ‘T. Cole’, circa 1685, with raised integral saddle breech, London proved. Full-stocked, banana shaped lock. $868 £400

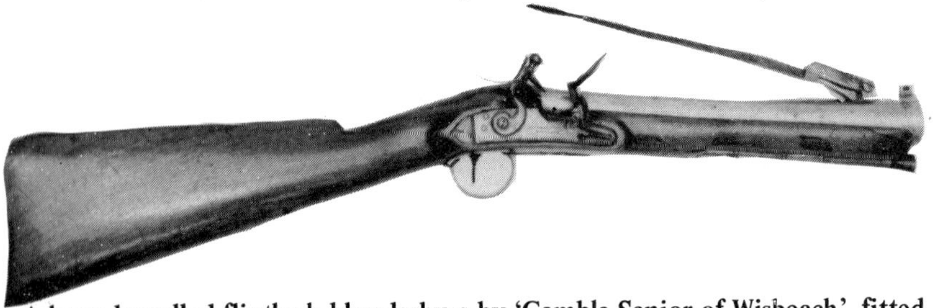

A brass barrelled flintlock blunderbuss by ‘Gamble Senior of Wisbeach’, fitted with spring bayonet, 28in., flared barrel 12in., Tower proved, 9in. roller bearing sprung triangular sectioned bayonet released by sliding thumb catch on barrel tang. Full-stocked, stepped line border engraved lock, roller bearing frizzen spring. Acorn finialled trigger guard, horn tipped wooden ramrod. $977 £450

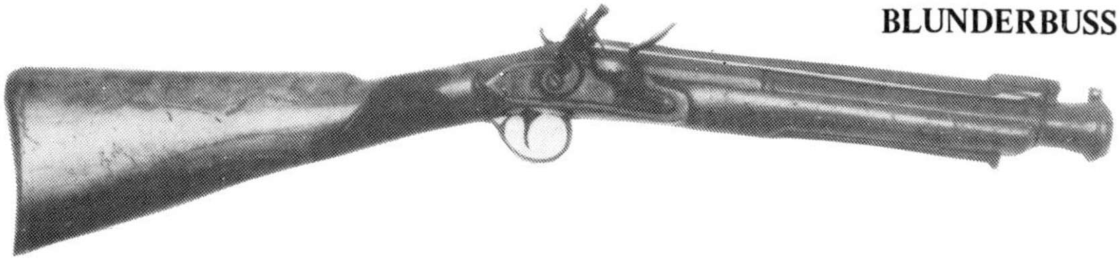

A brass barrelled flintlock blunderbuss by 'J. R. Evans', circa 1790, fitted with spring bayonet, 30½in., half octagonal barrel 14½in., Tower proved, engraved 'London' on top flat, bell mouth muzzle. Sprung triangular top bayonet 12½in. released by sliding top thumb catch. Full-stocked, stepped border engraved lock with maker's name, roller bearing frizzen spring. $1,042 £480

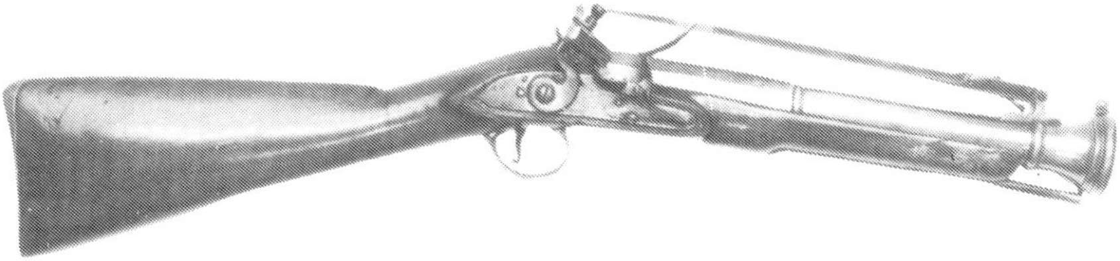

A brass barrelled Volunteer type flintlock blunderbuss, by 'Tomlinson', circa 1780, 31½in., half octagonal barrel, 14½in., with two London proof marks and maker's mark 'R.T.', engraved 'Dublin', reinforced bell mouth. Fitted with 12in. spring bayonet released by sliding catch on barrel tang, full-stocked, plain brass mounts of regulation type. $1,056 £480

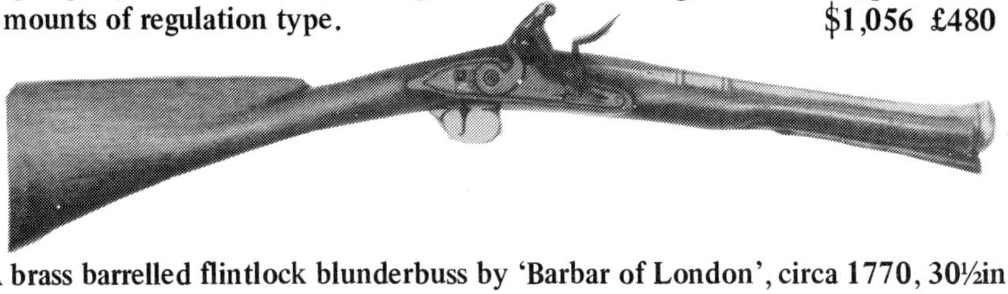

A brass barrelled flintlock blunderbuss by 'Barbar of London', circa 1770, 30½in., half octagonal, stepped, bell mouthed barrel 14in., Tower proved, engraved 'London' in script. Full-stocked, stepped bolted lock with dog tooth border engraved 'Barbar'. Brass mounts, swollen trigger guard finial. Horn tipped wooden ramrod with steel worm. $1,237 £570

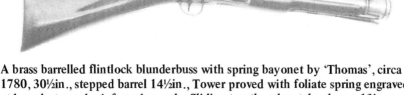

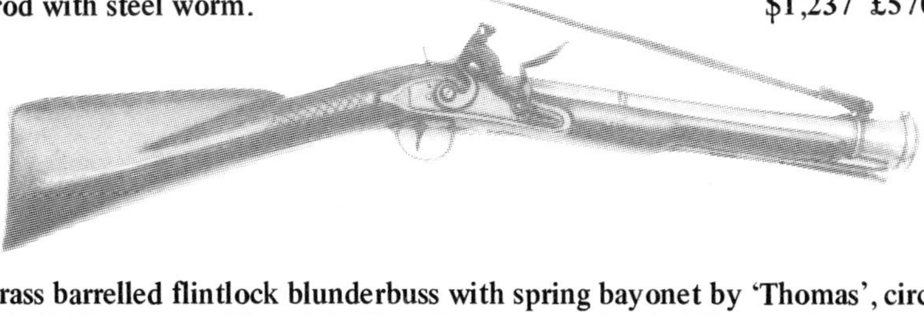

A brass barrelled flintlock blunderbuss with spring bayonet by 'Thomas', circa 1780, 30½in., stepped barrel 14½in., Tower proved with foliate spring engraved at breech, turned reinforced muzzle. Sliding top thumb catch releases 13in. triangular sectioned bayonet. Full-stocked, stepped border engraved lock with 'Thomas' within flourish, roller bearing frizzen spring. $1,892 £860

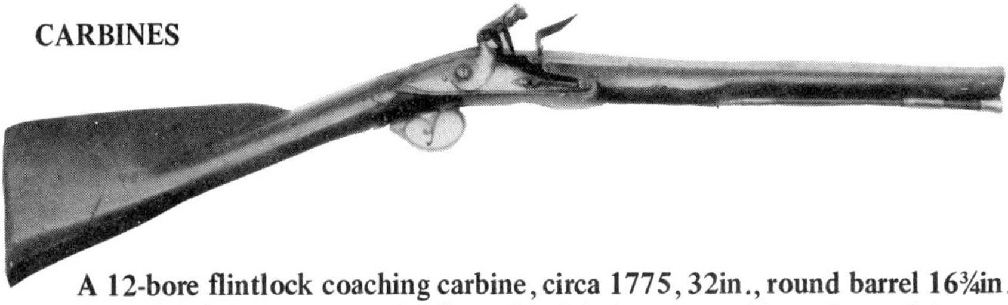

A 12-bore flintlock coaching carbine, circa 1775, 32in., round barrel 16¾in., plain walnut iron mounted full-stock, plain long tanged buttplate, plain trigger guard with husk finial, plain steel sideplate and ramrod pipes, the stock with teardrop lock surround. $424 £200

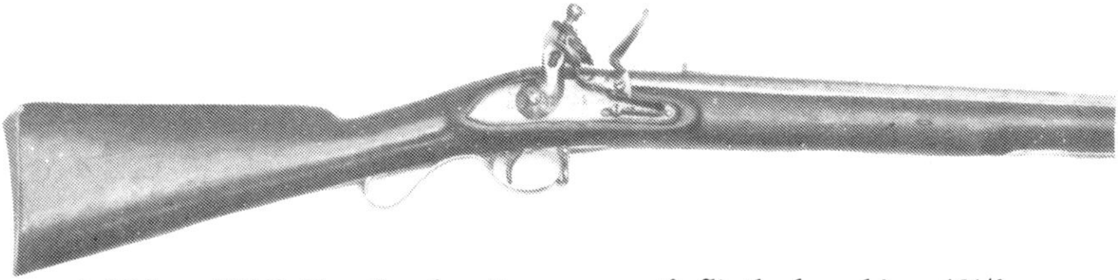

A 10-bore E.I.C. New Land pattern sergeant's flintlock carbine, 49½in., barrel 33in., London proved, fixed rearsight. Full-stocked, regulation lock and brass mounts, scrolled finger rest behind trigger guard, steel sling swivels and original ramrod. $616 £280

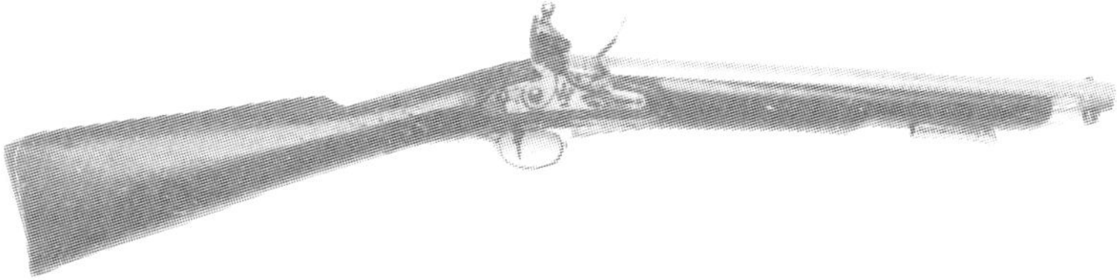

A 16-bore British military flintlock Paget carbine, 32in., barrel 16in., Tower proved, full-stocked, stepped bolted lock engraved 'Tower' with crowned 'GR', fixed rearsight. Regulation brass mounts, steel saddle bar with lanyard ring. $968 £440

A 16-bore breech loading Sartorius military flintlock carbine, 37in., barrel 18¼in. to interrupted thread breech, turned with use of sprung hinged lever. Half-stocked, stepped bolted lock with roller bearing frizzen spring. Hinge up breech with interrupted thread, butterfly rearsight. $1,302 £600

An old 12-bore decorative wheelock carbine, 37½in., barrel 25½in.. Full-stocked, lock with external wheel and mainspring, swollen ribbed wheel and cock bridles, pellet and foliate chiselled cock on baluster stem, sliding pan cover, steel trigger guard, ivory fish-tail buttplate. $1,660 £700

CANNON IGNITER

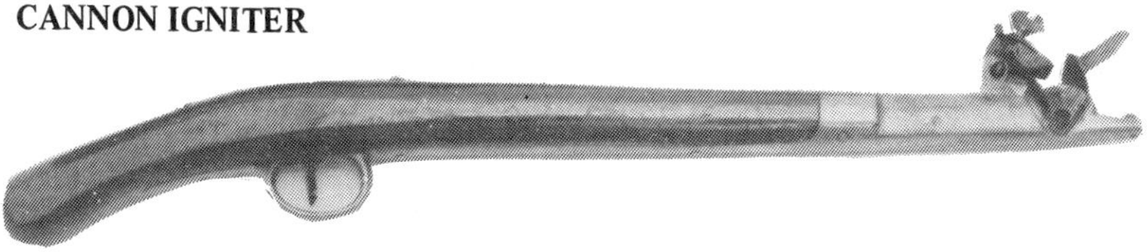

A British Military brass framed flintlock, 'arm's length', cannon igniter, 22¼in., boxlock construction, removable sideplate. Throathole cock with slotted wing nut top jaw screw, frizzen spring sunk in frame terminal. Pan pierced to fire vent. Long integral brass bottom strap terminating in trigger guard. Rounded wooden stock with flattened grip. $1,060 £450

EPROUVETTE

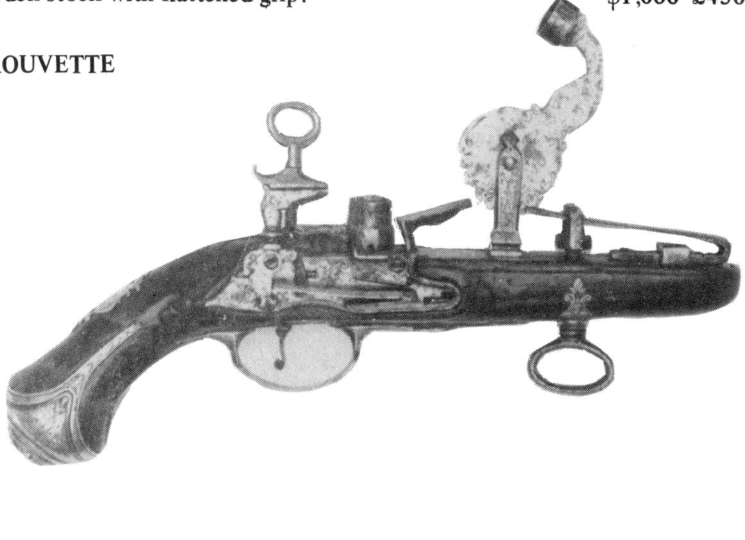

A Spanish miquelet flintlock powder tester eprouvette, dated 1789, 10½in., overall, foliate engraved lock, striated frizzen, foliate engraved steel wheel with graduations 1-12 and ring screw puller for slackening spring tension. $1,085 £500

A massive detached flintlock lock presumably from a rampart gun, plate 8½in., engraved 'Barnett'. Lock well made and of good military style. $260 £120

A detached Italian wheellock lock with two cocks, circa 1630-50, plate 23.5cm. stamped on the inside with maker's mark 'G.Z.', within ring of pellets, foliate finial to lockplate. Bridled external wheel, hinged pan cover, twin cocks foliate chiselled at necks. $890 £410

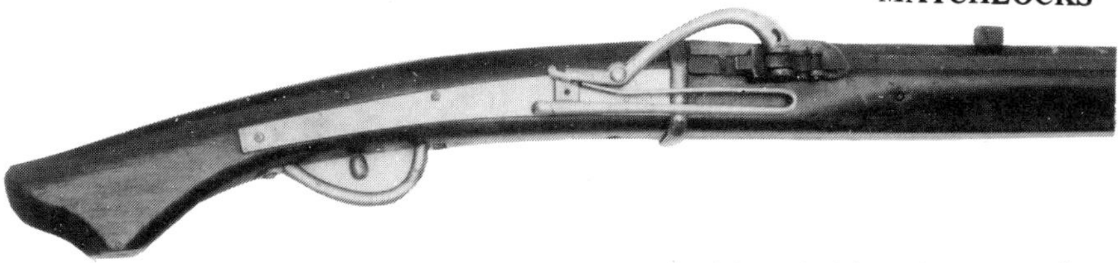

A 20-bore Japanese matchlock gun, 45in., octagonal barrel. Silver damascened for its entire length with Buddhistic emblems, chidori and flags. Full-stocked in cherrywood, back-action brass lock with external mainspring, brass trigger guard, button trigger and sheet buttcap. $412 £190

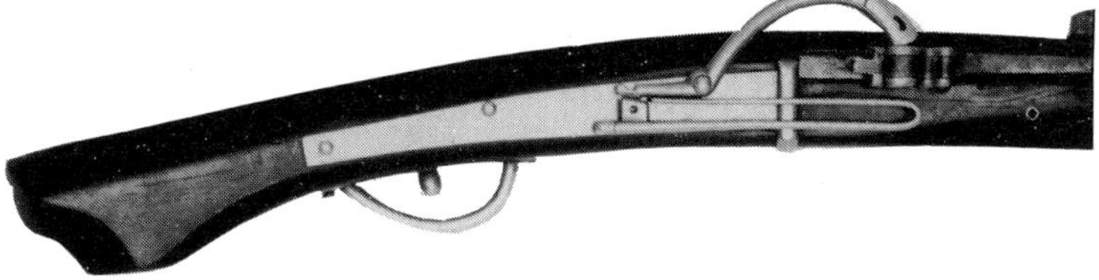

A 24-bore Japanese matchlock gun, 36½in., octagonal barrel 23¾in., signed Funiu Chogen Suiju Saku. Block sights with swollen muzzle. Full-stocked in cherrywood. Brass back-action lock with external mainspring. Plain brass furniture and pin plates, carved butt, wooden ramrod. $760 £350

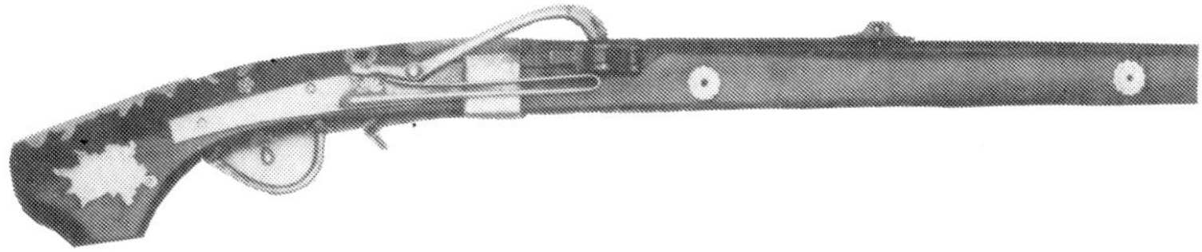

A 26-bore Japanese matchlock gun, 51½in., octagonal barrel 39½in., signed Banshu Noju Igawa Terunaga Koresaku, block rearsight, raised ribs to barrel flats, swollen muzzle. Full-stocked in magnolia wood. Brass back-action lock with brass serpent and mainspring. Brass trigger guard and pan cover. $1,100 £500

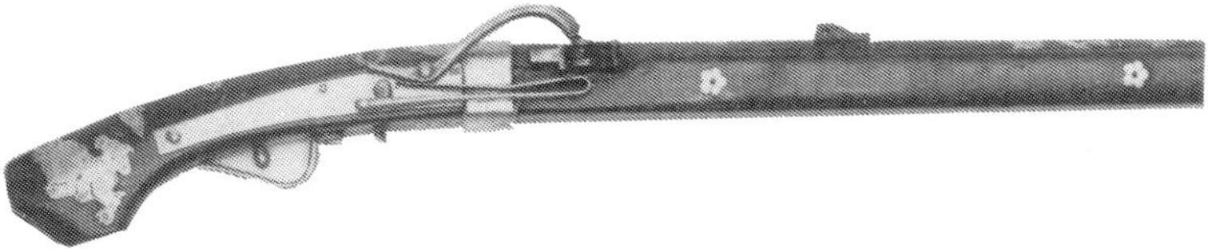

A 32-bore Japanese matchlock gun, 51½in., octagonal barrel 39in., signed Goshu Nokuni Yukiu Noja? Tomoyama?. Block rearsight. Full-stocked in magnolia wood. Brass back-action lock with brass serpent and external brass mainspring. Brass trigger guard and pan cover. $1,122 £510

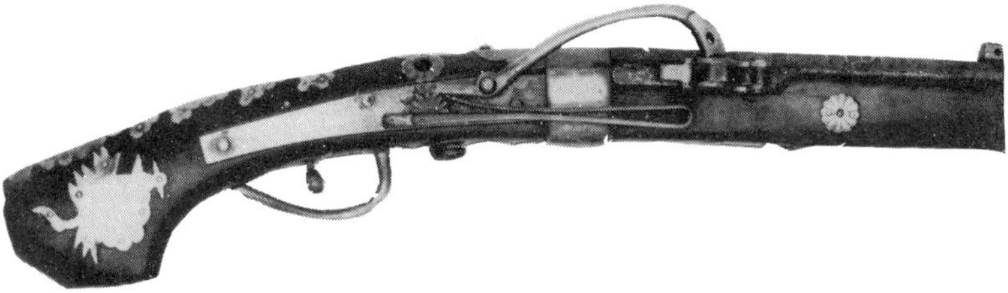

A 20-bore Japanese matchlock gun, circa 1750, by 'Goshaku', 51in., tapered octagonal barrel 39½in., with pierced block sights. Breech inlaid with brass and copper with deer beneath tree, hinged brass pan cover. Breech signed Shuchokunin Goshaku Tetsuan. Full-stocked in cherrywood with carved butt. Back-action brass lock, external mainspring. Inlaid and engraved brass furniture, button trigger, rounded trigger guard. $1,107 £510

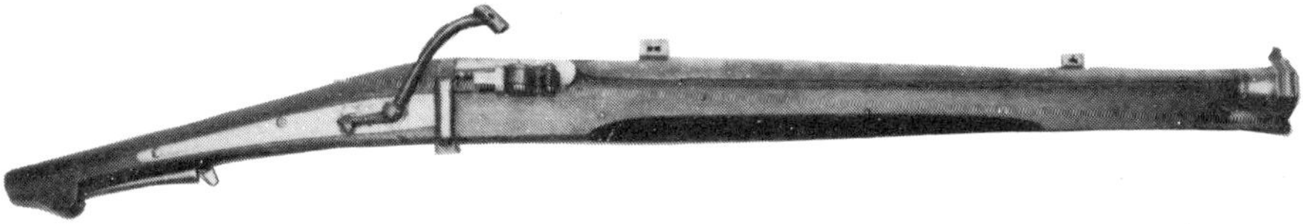

A Japanese matchlock gun, 43in. heavy barrel 28in., signed Shibatsugi Chosaemono Kunitaka Saku Kore Wo of tapered form, block sights, octagonal stepped muzzle inlaid with silver two comma mon. Full-stocked in magnolia wood, back-action brass lock with steel serpent. Hinged pan cover, brass mounts, wooden ramrod. $1,300 £625

A 22-bore Japanese matchlock rifle, 35½in., five-groove rifled barrel 23½in., silver damascened with butterflies, flowers and Buddhistic emblems, sighted flattened barrel top. Full-stocked in cherrywood, back-action iron lock and serpent with brass head. Brass pan cover and silver flash guard. Brass furniture and pin plates, engraved throatguard. $1,848 £840

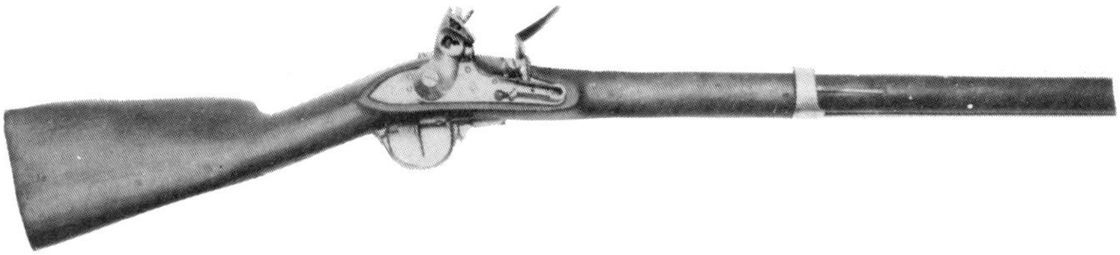

A 12-bore Turkish or Egyptian contract military flintlock musket (of French 1822 model design), 57¼in., barrel 42½in., with Turkish inspector's stamps at breech. Full-stocked, plain steel trigger guard and mounts, three barrel bands secured with spring catches, lockplate struck with Turkish script mark, brass pan. $353 £155

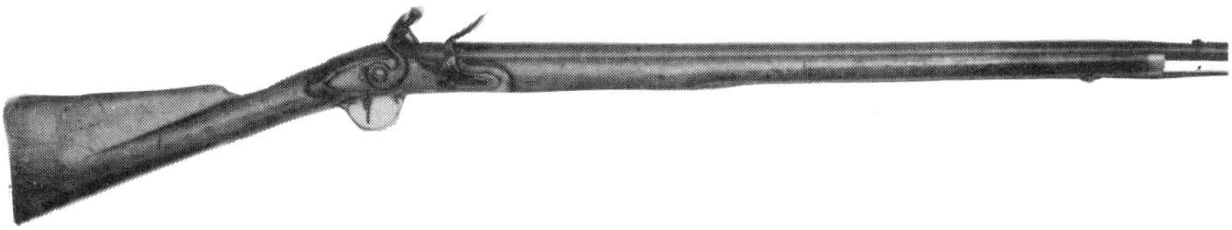

A 22-bore cadet's Volunteer flintlock musket by 'Parr', circa 1780, 42in., barrel 27½in., Tower proved. Full-stocked, border engraved lock, unbridled frizzen, regulation type brass mounts including sheet sideplate and acorn finialled trigger guard. Steel ramrod. $651 £300

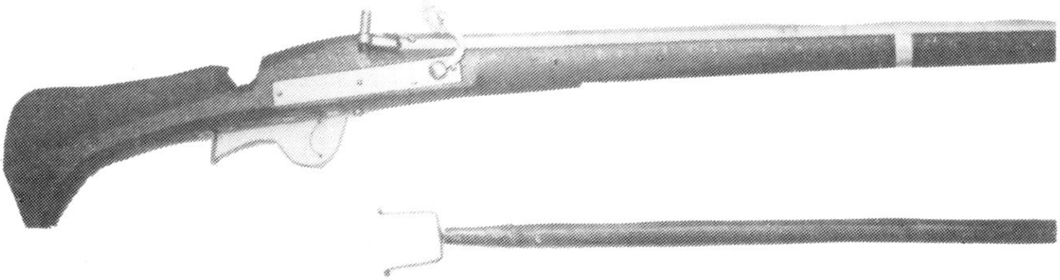

A 14-bore German Military matchlock musket, circa 1580, 57¾in., overall length. Half octagonal barrel 43¼in., with ribbed step, rearsight with hemi-spherical depression on mount for extinguishing match. Rectangular pan with chiselled floor and hinged pan cover, tall fence behind pan. Rectangular lock-plate, steel serpent with foliate engraved wing nut tightened match holder. $2,250 £950

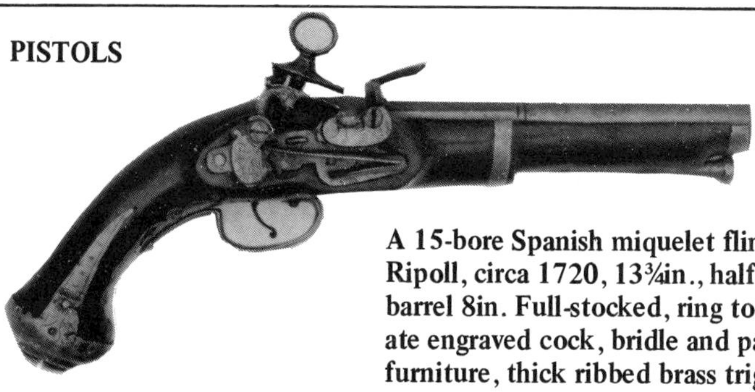

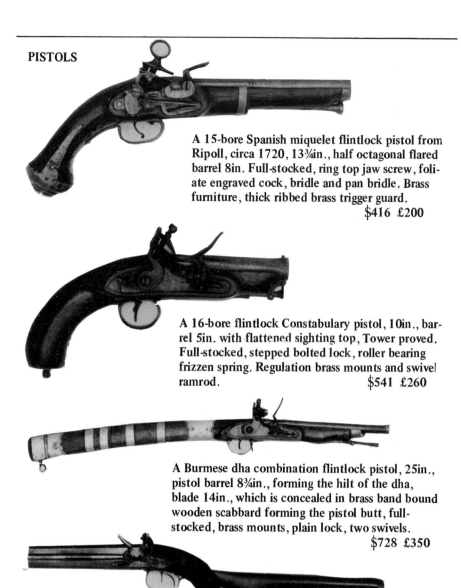

A 15-bore Spanish miquelet flintlock pistol from Ripoll, circa 1720, 13¾in., half octagonal flared barrel 8in. Full-stocked, ring top jaw screw, foliate engraved cock, bridle and pan bridle. Brass furniture, thick ribbed brass trigger guard. $416 £200

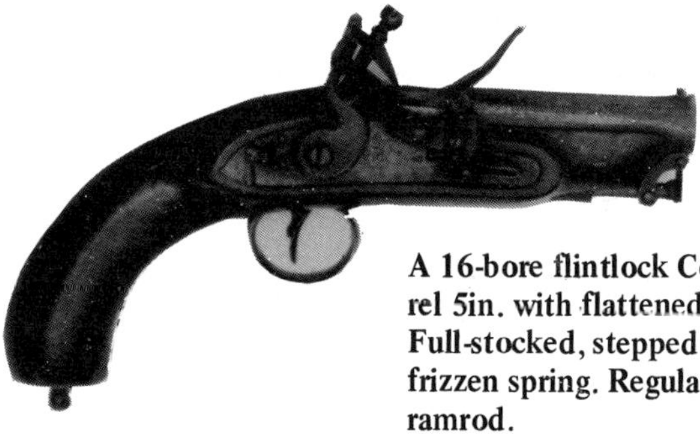

A 16-bore flintlock Constabulary pistol, 10in., barrel 5in. with flattened sighting top, Tower proved. Full-stocked, stepped bolted lock, roller bearing frizzen spring. Regulation brass mounts and swivel ramrod. $541 £260

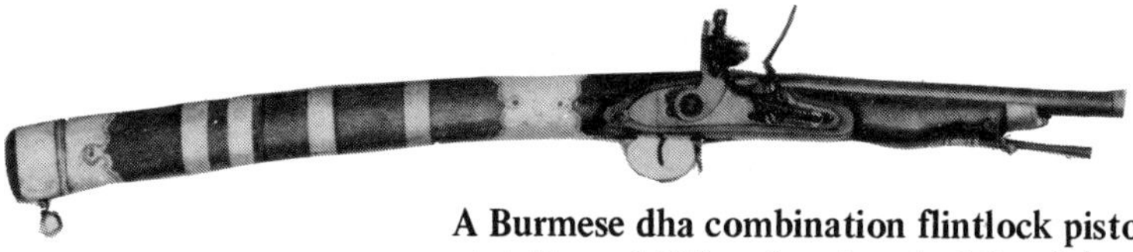

A Burmese dha combination flintlock pistol, 25in., pistol barrel 8¾in., forming the hilt of the dha, blade 14in., which is concealed in brass band bound wooden scabbard forming the pistol butt, full-stocked, brass mounts, plain lock, two swivels. $728 £350

A double barrelled 20-bore over and under sidelock flintlock carbine pistol with detachable shoulder stock by 'Tatham & Egg', circa 1810, 24in. overall, octagonal browned twist barrels 7¾in. inlaid with twin silver breech lines. Rifled top barrel, smooth-bore lower. $4,557 £2,100

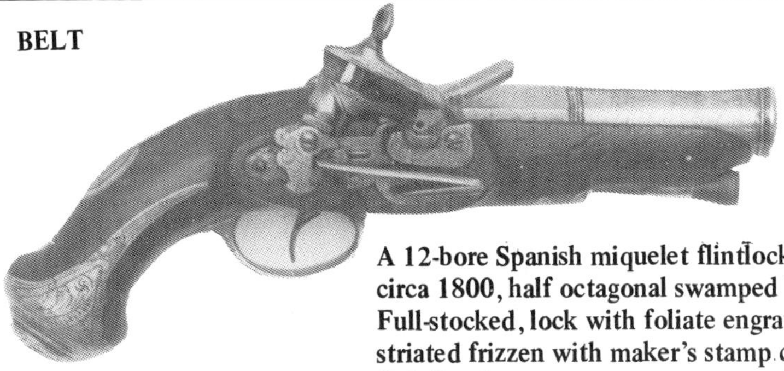

A 12-bore Spanish miquelet flintlock belt pistol, circa 1800, half octagonal swamped barrel 5¼in. Full-stocked, lock with foliate engraved bridles, striated frizzen with maker's stamp crowned 'Jph Dop'. $394 £270

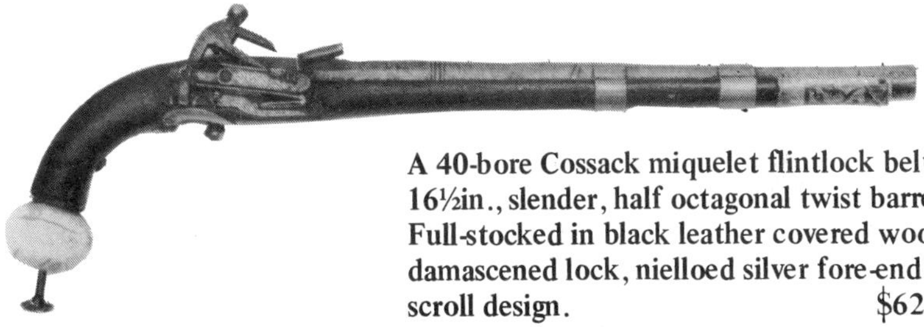

A 40-bore Cossack miquelet flintlock belt pistol, 16½in., slender, half octagonal twist barrel 12in. Full-stocked in black leather covered wood, gold damascened lock, nielloed silver fore-end in scroll design. $629 £290

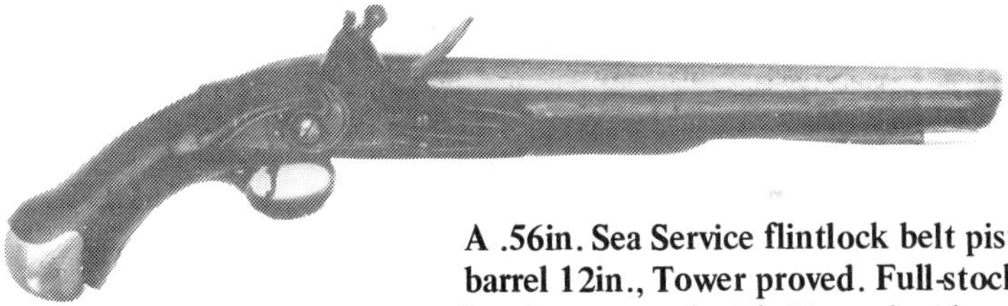

A .56in. Sea Service flintlock belt pistol, 19in., barrel 12in., Tower proved. Full-stocked, lock border engraved with 'Tower' and crowned 'GR'. Regulation brass mounts, buttcap engraved '35'. Sprung steel belt hook. $836 £380

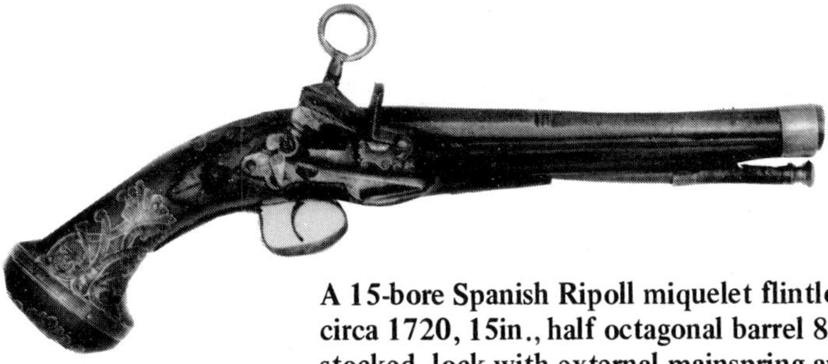

A 15-bore Spanish Ripoll miquelet flintlock belt pistol, circa 1720, 15in., half octagonal barrel 8¾in. Full-stocked, lock with external mainspring and frizzen spring, striated frizzen stamped with maker's mark of 'Vasy' within heart shape. Rare ovoid butt barrel tang, steel trigger guard. $1,193 £550

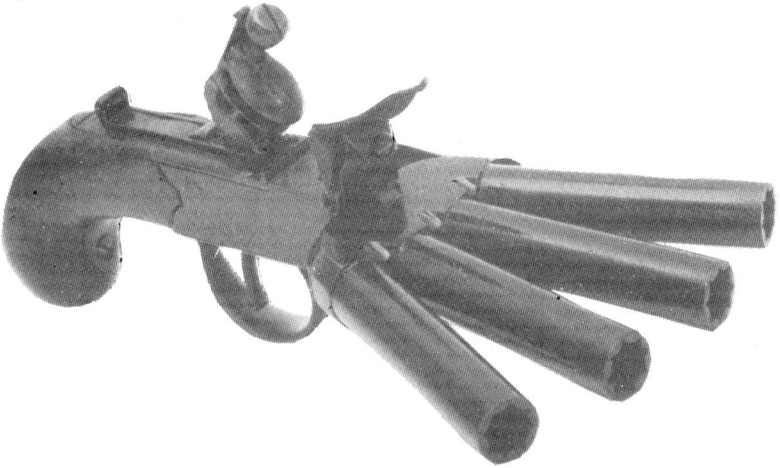

A four-barrelled 50-bore boxlock flintlock 'duck's foot' belt pistol, by 'H. Nock', circa 1800, 9in., turn-off barrels 3in., Tower proved, muzzles slotted for turning keys, sprung steel belt hook, sliding top thumb safety through throathole cock locking variable tension sprung teardrop frizzen to fence, round walnut butt with chamfered silver escutcheon. $4,740 £2,000

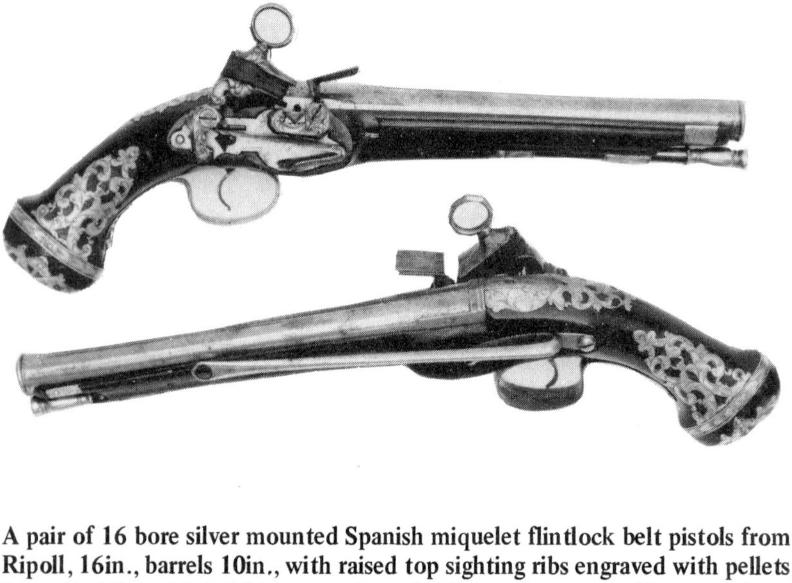

A pair of 16 bore silver mounted Spanish miquelet flintlock belt pistols from Ripoll, 16in., barrels 10in., with raised top sighting ribs engraved with pellets, turned bridles, striated frizzens and pan bridles with serpents. Facetted ring top jaw screws. Thick ribbed silver trigger guards, barrel tang surrounds incorporating dolphins and crowns. $4,160 £2,000

A silver inlaid Turkish flintlock blunderbuss pistol, 18in., flared barrel 10in., inlaid with silver beading and flourishing geometric designs overall. Full-stocked, stepped lock with bridled frizzen. Brass furniture, spear finialled trigger guard. $315 £145

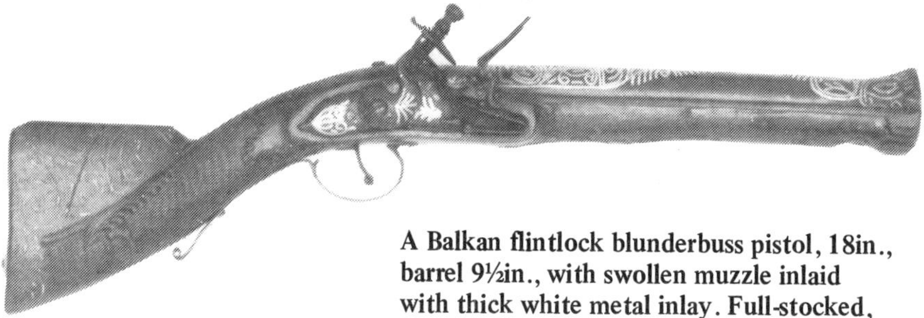

A Balkan flintlock blunderbuss pistol, 18in., barrel 9½in., with swollen muzzle inlaid with thick white metal inlay. Full-stocked, lock inlaid en suite with barrels. $418 £190

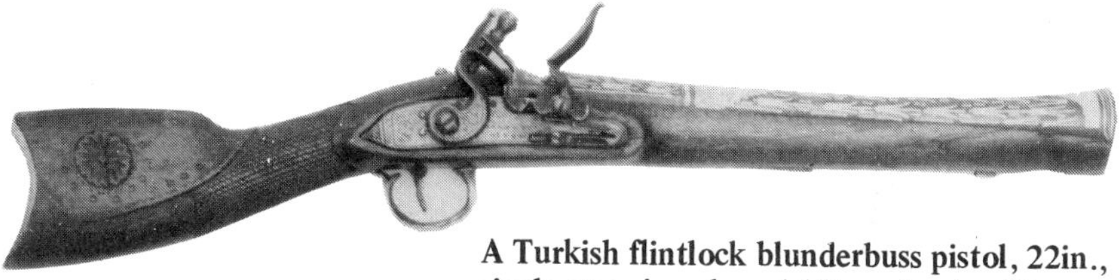

A Turkish flintlock blunderbuss pistol, 22in., single stage iron barrel 12in., struck with maker's mark and overlaid with small strips of silver in geometric patterns, chequered walnut full-stock with brass mounts, including trigger guard and ramrod pipes. $458 £210

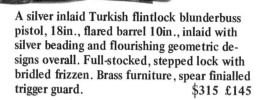

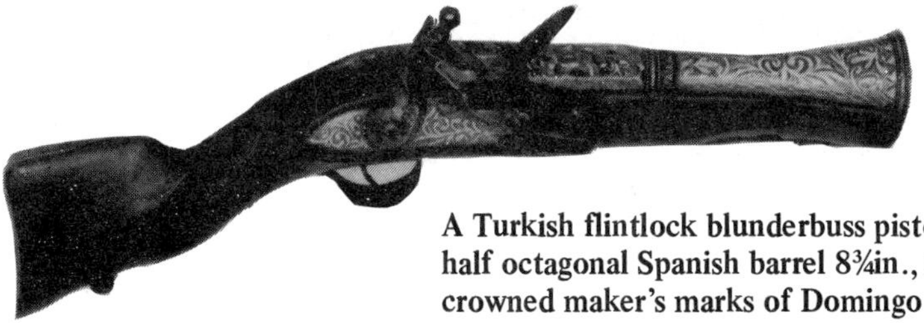

A Turkish flintlock blunderbuss pistol, 17½in., half octagonal Spanish barrel 8¾in., struck with crowned maker's marks of Domingo Mas (Ripoll, circa 1715) and fleur-de-lys. Full-stocked, military type lock with brass pan. Brass furniture. $477 £220

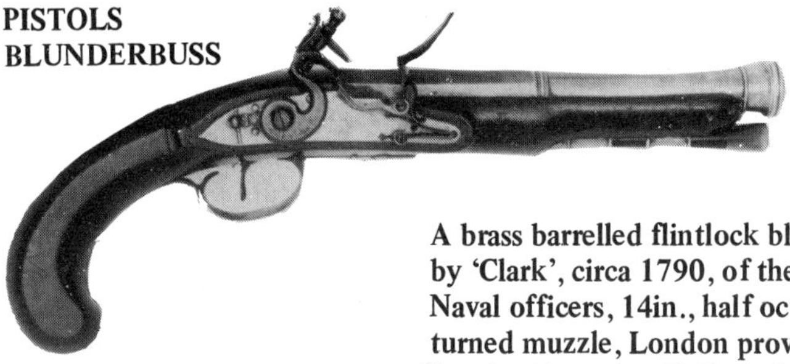

A brass barrelled flintlock blunderbuss pistol by 'Clark', circa 1790, of the type favoured by Naval officers, 14in., half octagonal barrel 8in., turned muzzle, London proved, engraved 'London' in script. Full-stocked, brass lock with stepped bolted tail engraved 'Clark'. $597 £275

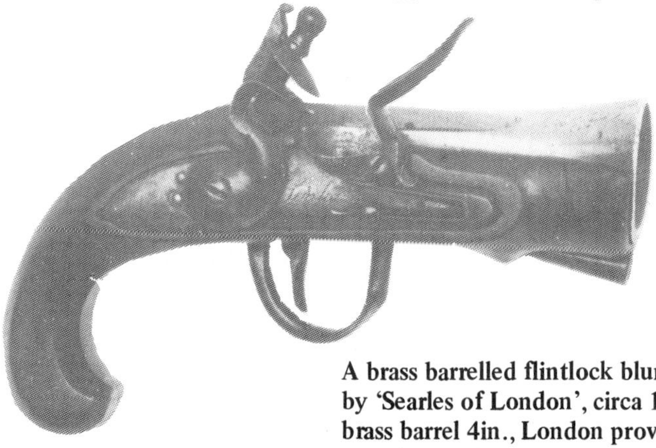

A brass barrelled flintlock blunderbuss pistol, by 'Searles of London', circa 1775, 7½in., brass barrel 4in., London proved, wide bell mouth muzzle engraved 'Happy Is He That Escapes Me'. Full-stocked, steel trigger guard with off-set 'feet' screwed to stock. $1,045 £475

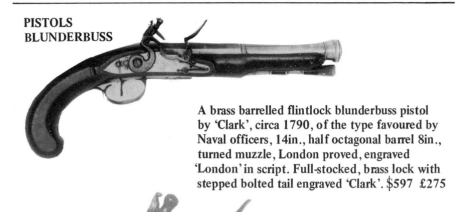

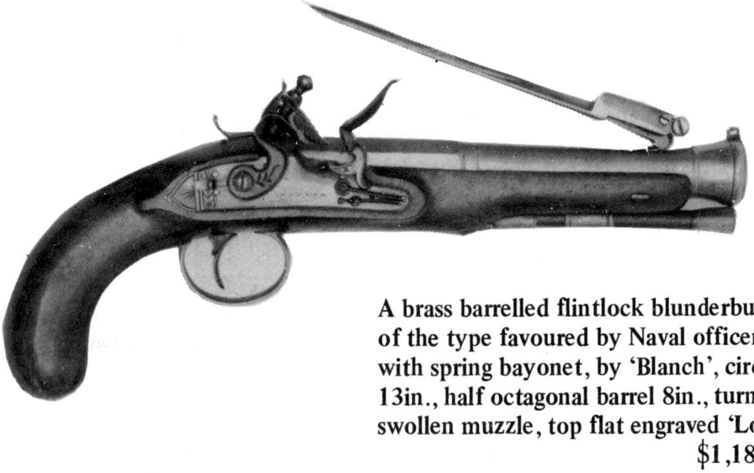

A brass barrelled flintlock blunderbuss pistol of the type favoured by Naval officers, fitted with spring bayonet, by 'Blanch', circa 1780, 13in., half octagonal barrel 8in., turned swollen muzzle, top flat engraved 'London'.
$1,186 £570

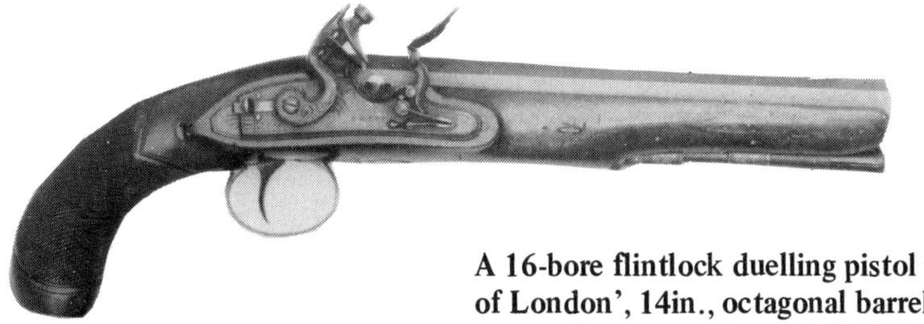

A 16-bore flintlock duelling pistol by 'Bratt of London', 14in., octagonal barrel 9in., Birmingham proved, gold inlaid 'London', with breech line and vent. Full-stocked, stepped bolted lock. Roller bearing frizzen spring, rainproof pan. Chequered butt.
$347 £160

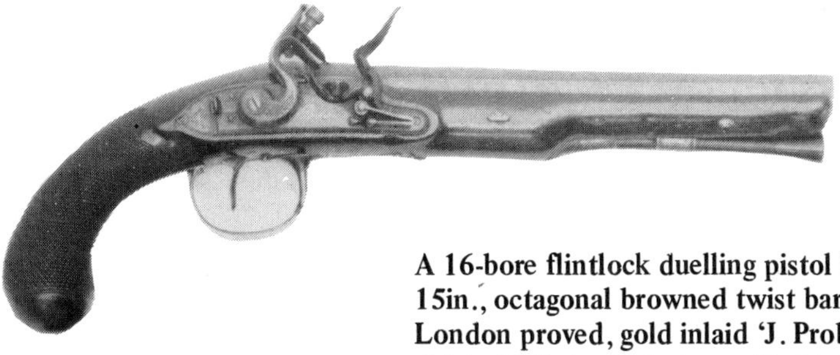

A 16-bore flintlock duelling pistol by Probin, 15in., octagonal browned twist barrel 9½in., London proved, gold inlaid 'J. Probin', fixed sights. Full-stocked, stepped bolted lock. Roller bearing frizzen spring, capstan screw set trigger, gold lined vent.Foliate finialled trigger guard with floral urn engraved on bow.
$890 £410

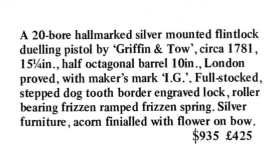

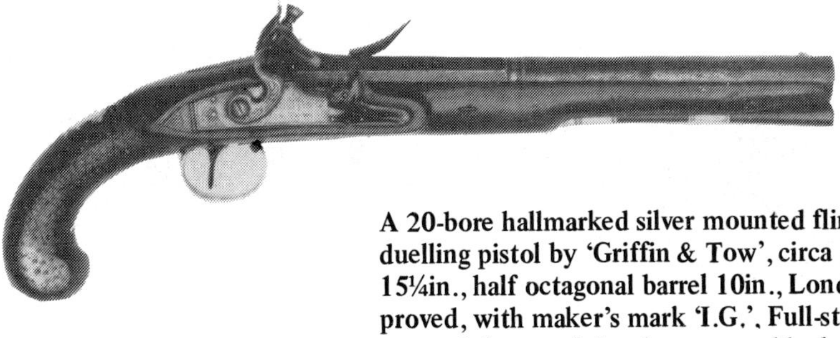

A 20-bore hallmarked silver mounted flintlock duelling pistol by 'Griffin & Tow', circa 1781, 15¼in., half octagonal barrel 10in., London proved, with maker's mark 'I.G.'. Full-stocked, stepped dog tooth border engraved lock, roller bearing frizzen ramped frizzen spring. Silver furniture, acorn finialled with flower on bow.
$935 £425

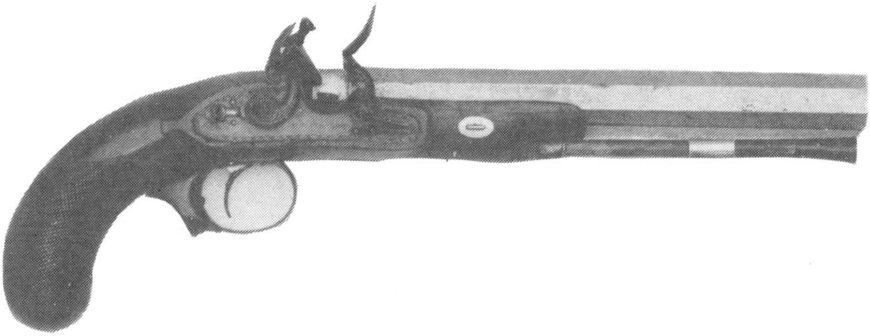

A 36-bore flintlock duelling pistol, by 'John Manton', No. 6034, circa 1813, 15½in., heavy octagonal barrel 10in., engraved 'Dover St., London'. Half-stocked in field maple, bolted cock, roller bearing frizzen spring, rainproof pan. Engraved pineapple finialled steel detented lock, frond tip border engraved with 'Jno. Manton & Son'. French style trigger guard with trophy on bow, with horn steadying block at rear of trigger guard bow for centre finger. Silver barrel wedge plates and escutcheon, rounded chequered grip.
$1,265 £575

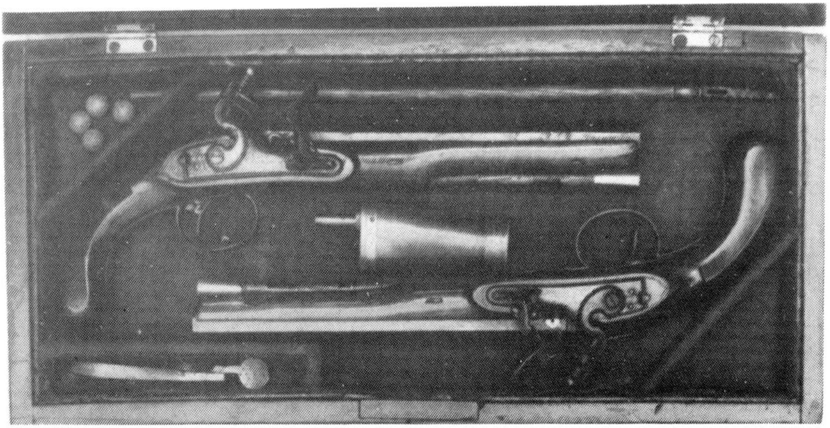

A pair of 25-bore flintlock duelling pistols by 'Hodgson & Co.', circa 1800, 14½in., octagonal twist barrels 9in., gold line inlaid at breeches, gold lined vents and pans. Full-stocked, stepped bolted detented locks, single set triggers, roller bearing frizzen springs, rainproof pans. Engraved steel furniture, pineapple finialled trigger guards. In a green beize lined mahogany case. $1,844 £850

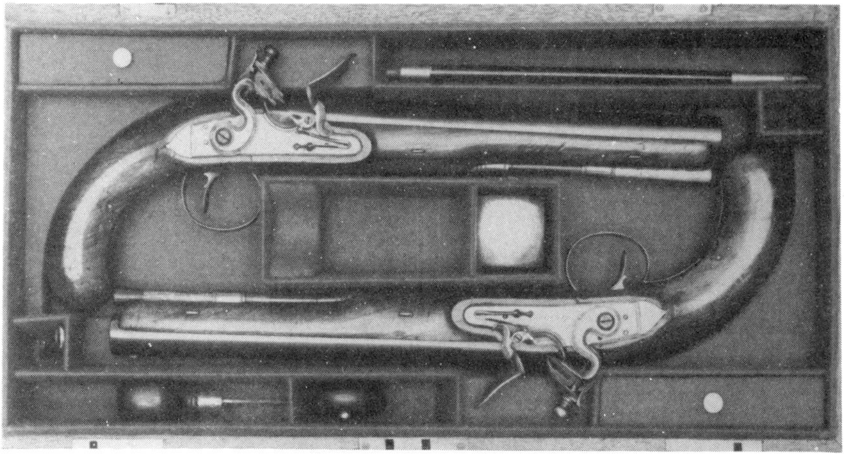

A pair of 16-bore flintlock duelling pistols by 'Barton of London', circa 1790, 15in., round barrels 10in., engraved on top flat 'Barton London', silver foresights. Full-stocked, stepped lockplates. Pineapple finialled trigger guards, wooden ramrods, one horn tipped, one with reversible 'powder measure' top and steel worm. Contained in a blue beize lined and fitted mahogany case.
$2,280 £1,000

A pair of 16-bore flintlock duelling pistols by 'John Manton', No. 1217 (for 1790), 15in., octagonal twist barrels 10in., engraved 'Manton London', gold lined vents, silver foresights. Half-stocked, stepped bolted locks, roller bearing frizzens, ramp frizzen springs, rainproof pans. Trophy engraved pineapple finialled trigger guards. Horn forecaps, brass tipped wooden ramrods with brass capped worms. In a green beize lined fitted mahogany case.$3,255 £1,500

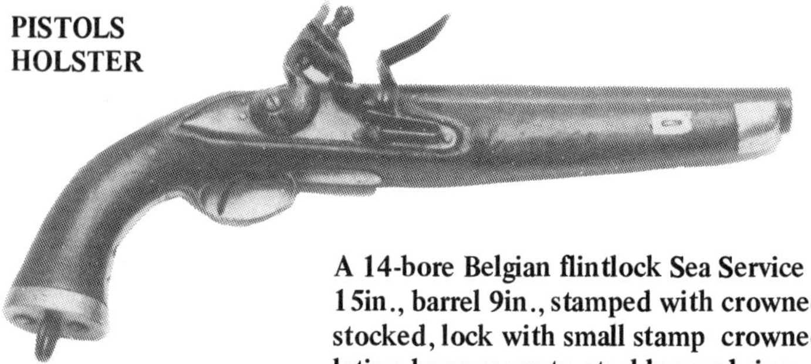

A 14-bore Belgian flintlock Sea Service holster pistol, 15in., barrel 9in., stamped with crowned 'B'. Full-stocked, lock with small stamp crowned 'D.N.', regulation brass mounts, steel lanyard ring. $295 £125

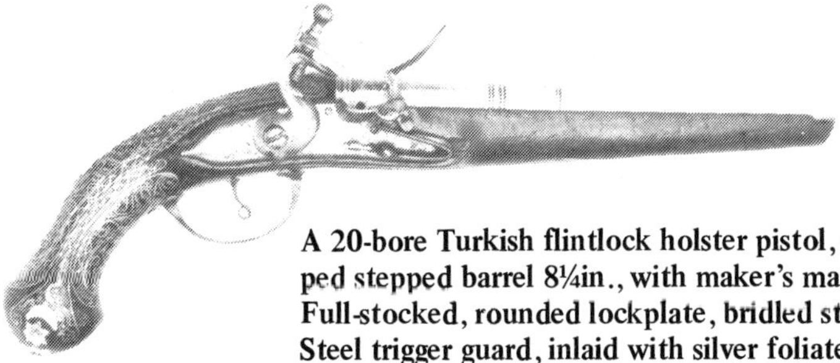

A 20-bore Turkish flintlock holster pistol, round swamped stepped barrel 8¼in., with maker's mark at breech. Full-stocked, rounded lockplate, bridled striated frizzen. Steel trigger guard, inlaid with silver foliate device. $330 £150

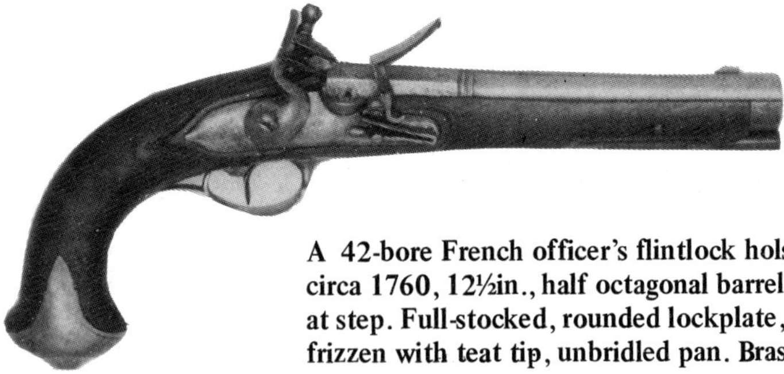

A 42-bore French officer's flintlock holster pistol, circa 1760, 12½in., half octagonal barrel 7½in., ribbed at step. Full-stocked, rounded lockplate, cock and frizzen with teat tip, unbridled pan. Brass furniture. $347 £160

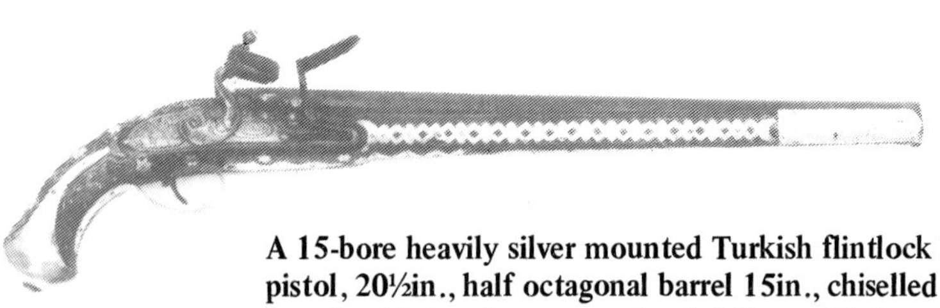

A 15-bore heavily silver mounted Turkish flintlock holster pistol, 20½in., half octagonal barrel 15in., chiselled at breech with trophy, crescent and foliage with traces of gilt ground. Full-stocked, roller bearing frizzen spring. Solid silver furniture. $374 £170

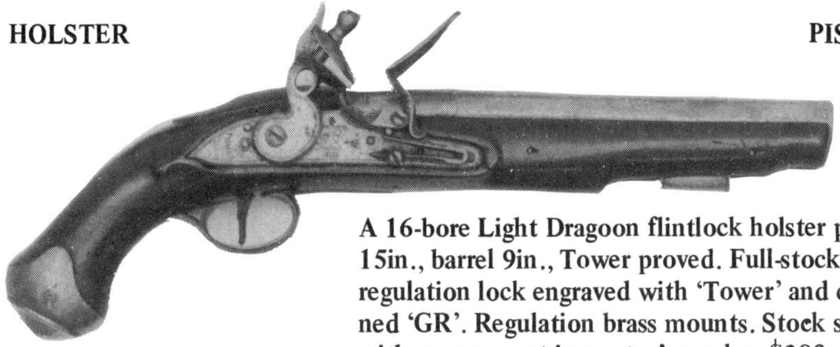

A 16-bore Light Dragoon flintlock holster pistol, 15in., barrel 9in., Tower proved. Full-stocked, regulation lock engraved with 'Tower' and crowned 'GR'. Regulation brass mounts. Stock struck with government inspector's marks. $380 £175

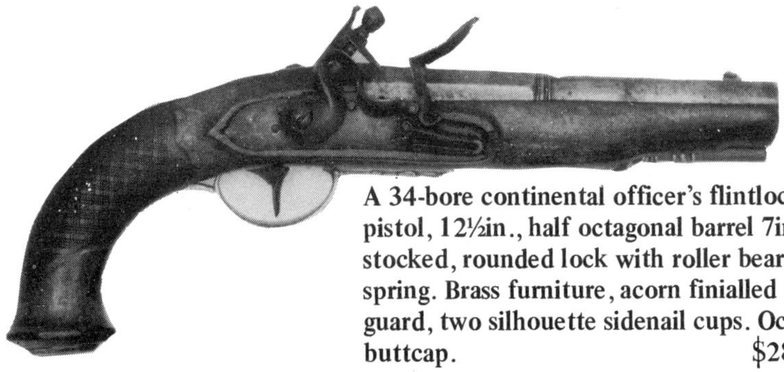

A 34-bore continental officer's flintlock holster pistol, 12½in., half octagonal barrel 7in. Full-stocked, rounded lock with roller bearing frizzen spring. Brass furniture, acorn finialled trigger guard, two silhouette sidenail cups. Octagonal buttcap. $280 £175

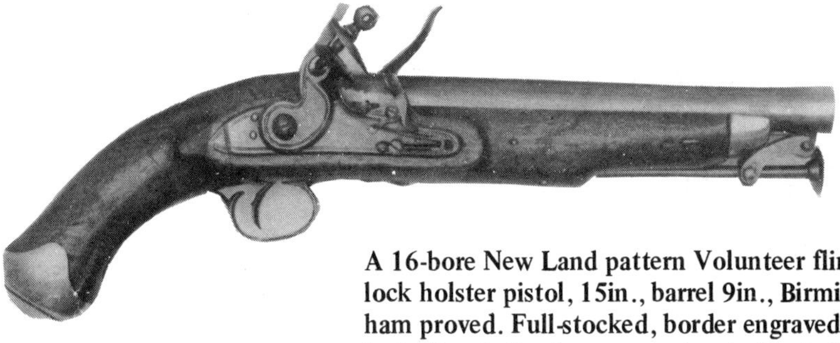

A 16-bore New Land pattern Volunteer flintlock holster pistol, 15in., barrel 9in., Birmingham proved. Full-stocked, border engraved lock. Regulation brass mounts, steel swivel ramrod. $391 £180

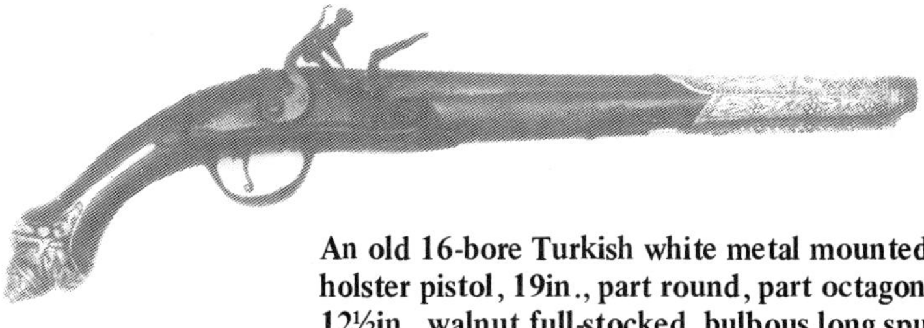

An old 16-bore Turkish white metal mounted flintlock holster pistol, 19in., part round, part octagonal barrel 12½in., walnut full-stocked, bulbous long spurred buttcap and pommel, iron trigger guard. $418 £190

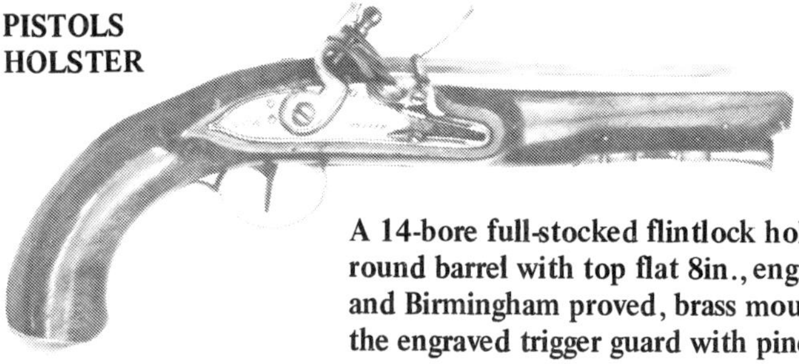

A 14-bore full-stocked flintlock holster pistol, 13½in., round barrel with top flat 8in., engraved 'Kingston' and Birmingham proved, brass mounted walnut stock, the engraved trigger guard with pineapple finial. $418 £190

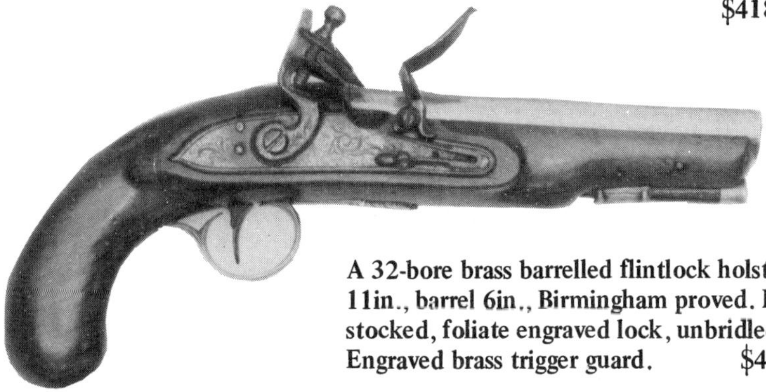

A 32-bore brass barrelled flintlock holster pistol, 11in., barrel 6in., Birmingham proved. Full-stocked, foliate engraved lock, unbridled frizzen. Engraved brass trigger guard. $412 £190

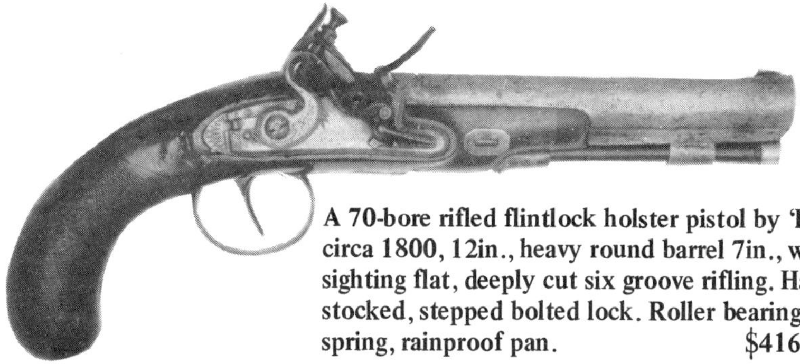

A 70-bore rifled flintlock holster pistol by 'Patrick', circa 1800, 12in., heavy round barrel 7in., with top sighting flat, deeply cut six groove rifling. Half-stocked, stepped bolted lock. Roller bearing frizzen spring, rainproof pan. $416 £200

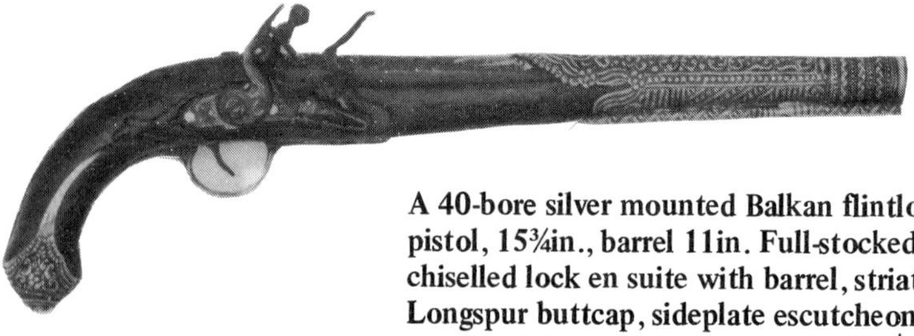

A 40-bore silver mounted Balkan flintlock holster pistol, 15¾in., barrel 11in. Full-stocked, scroll chiselled lock en suite with barrel, striated frizzen. Longspur buttcap, sideplate escutcheon, trigger guard and large heavy muzzle sheath. $434 £200

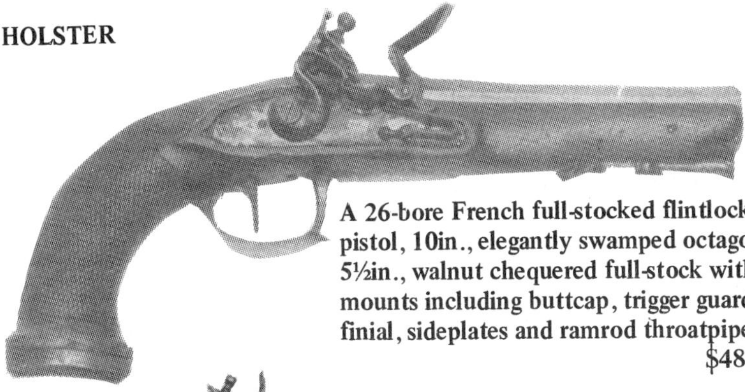

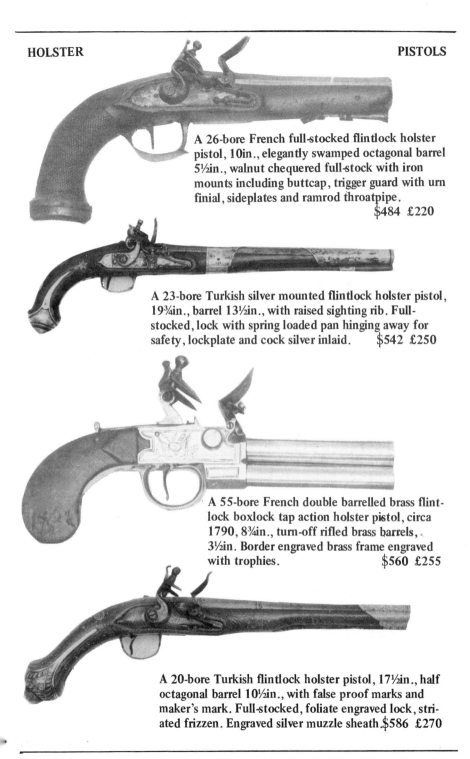

A 26-bore French full-stocked flintlock holster pistol, 10in., elegantly swamped octagonal barrel 5½in., walnut chequered full-stock with iron mounts including buttcap, trigger guard with urn finial, sideplates and ramrod throatpipe. $484 £220

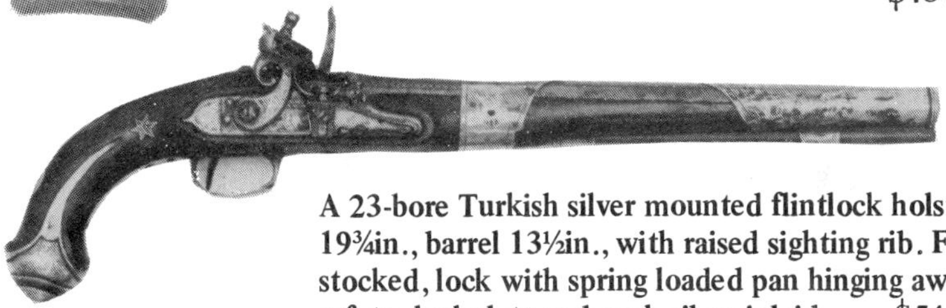

A 23-bore Turkish silver mounted flintlock holster pistol, 19¾in., barrel 13½in., with raised sighting rib. Full-stocked, lock with spring loaded pan hinging away for safety, lockplate and cock silver inlaid. $542 £250

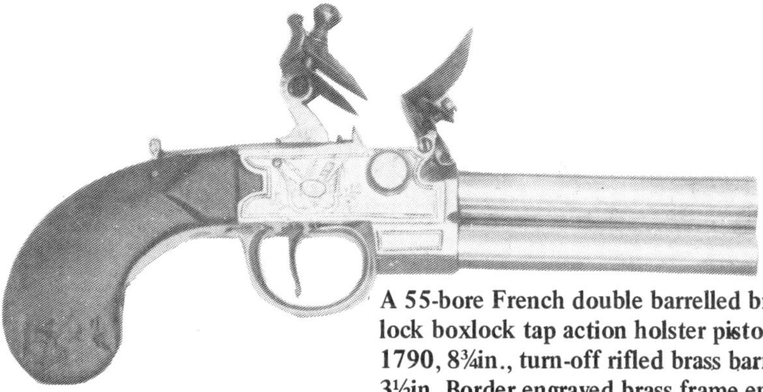

A 55-bore French double barrelled brass flintlock boxlock tap action holster pistol, circa 1790, 8¾in., turn-off rifled brass barrels, 3½in. Border engraved brass frame engraved with trophies. $560 £255

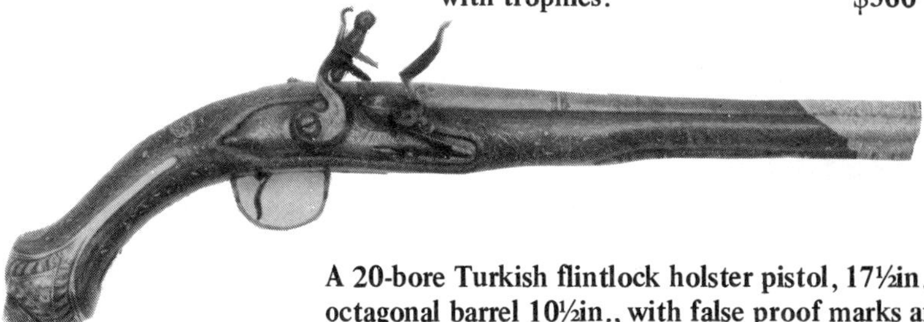

A 20-bore Turkish flintlock holster pistol, 17½in., half octagonal barrel 10½in., with false proof marks and maker's mark. Full-stocked, foliate engraved lock, striated frizzen. Engraved silver muzzle sheath. $586 £270

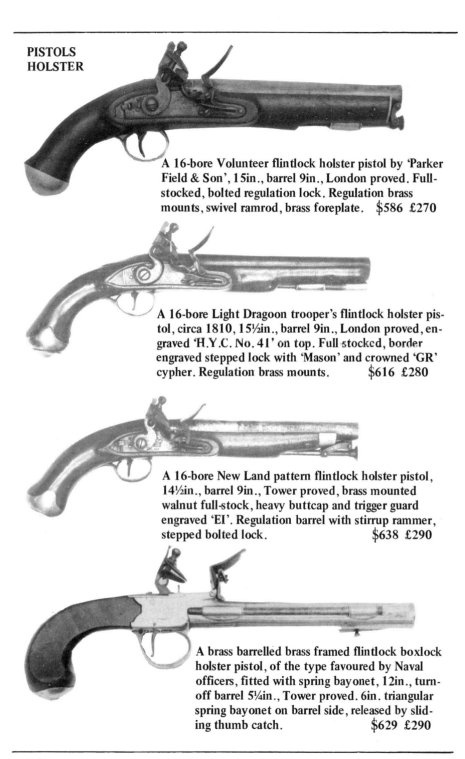

A 16-bore Volunteer flintlock holster pistol by 'Parker Field & Son', 15in., barrel 9in., London proved. Full-stocked, bolted regulation lock. Regulation brass mounts, swivel ramrod, brass foreplate. $586 £270

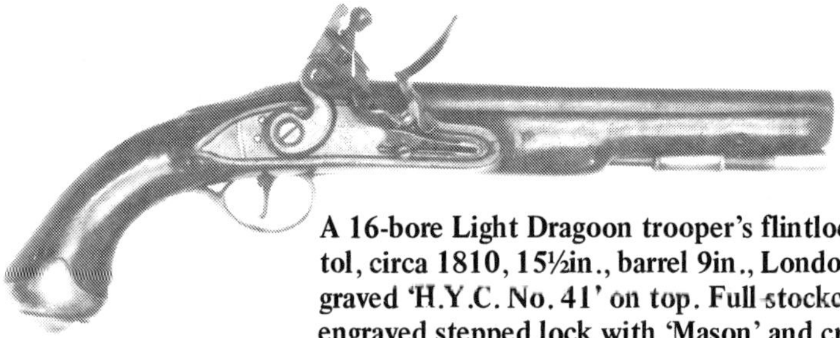

A 16-bore Light Dragoon trooper's flintlock holster pistol, circa 1810, 15½in., barrel 9in., London proved, engraved 'H.Y.C. No. 41' on top. Full-stocked, border engraved stepped lock with 'Mason' and crowned 'GR' cypher. Regulation brass mounts. $616 £280

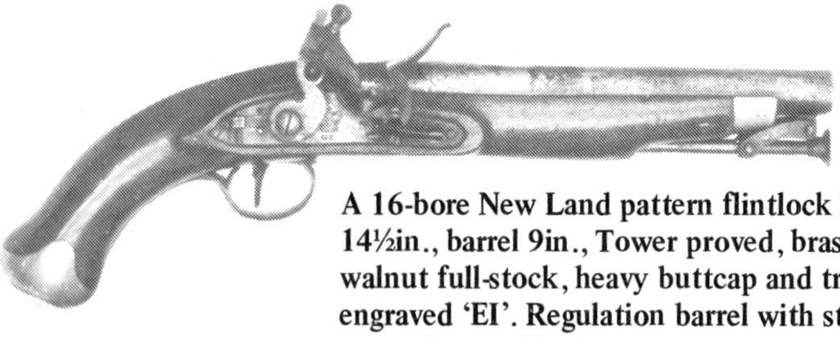

A 16-bore New Land pattern flintlock holster pistol, 14½in., barrel 9in., Tower proved, brass mounted walnut full-stock, heavy buttcap and trigger guard engraved 'EI'. Regulation barrel with stirrup rammer, stepped bolted lock. $638 £290

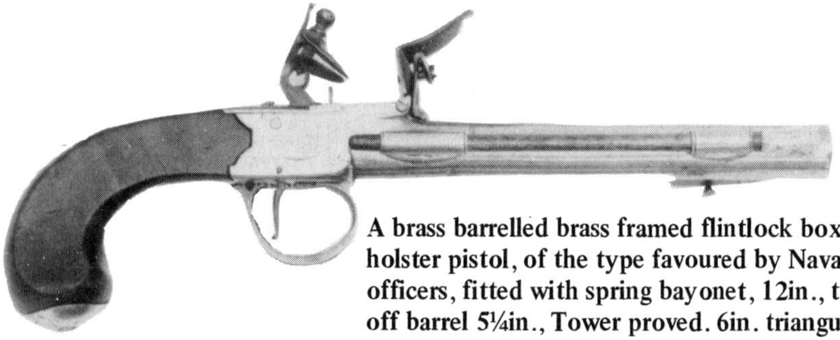

A brass barrelled brass framed flintlock boxlock holster pistol, of the type favoured by Naval officers, fitted with spring bayonet, 12in., turn-off barrel 5¼in., Tower proved. 6in. triangular spring bayonet on barrel side, released by sliding thumb catch. $629 £290

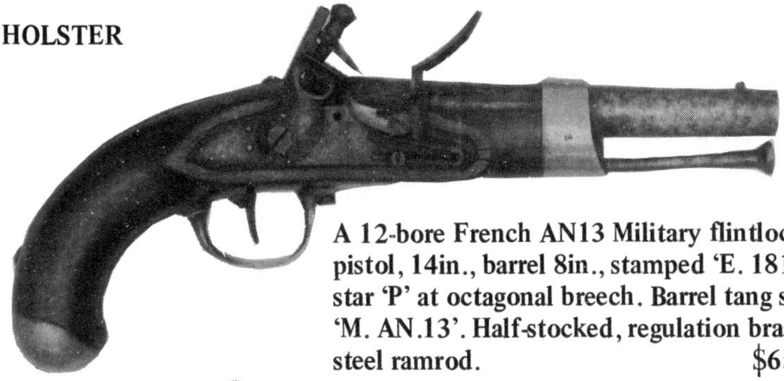

A 12-bore French AN13 Military flintlock holster pistol, 14in., barrel 8in., stamped 'E. 1815', 'C' star 'P' at octagonal breech. Barrel tang stamped 'M. AN.13'. Half-stocked, regulation brass mounts, steel ramrod. $651 £300

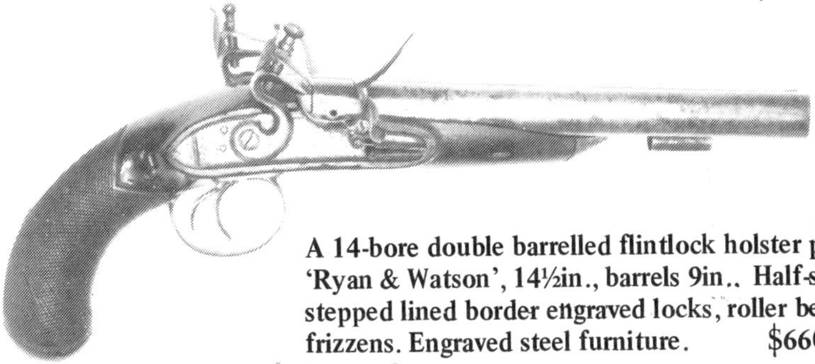

A 14-bore double barrelled flintlock holster pistol by 'Ryan & Watson', 14½in., barrels 9in.. Half-stocked, stepped lined border engraved locks, roller bearing frizzens. Engraved steel furniture. $660 £300

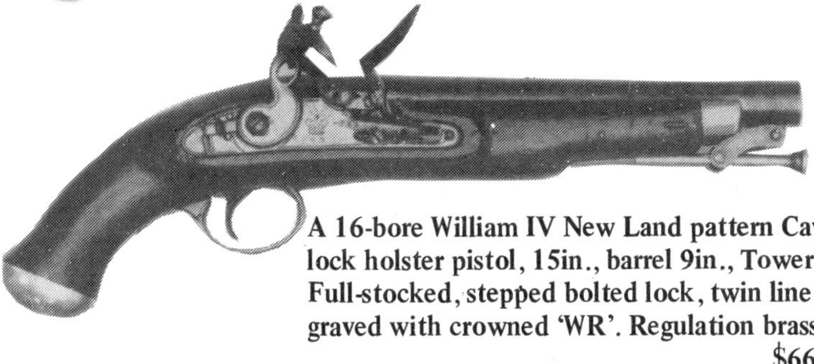

A 16-bore William IV New Land pattern Cavalry flintlock holster pistol, 15in., barrel 9in., Tower proved. Full-stocked, stepped bolted lock, twin line border engraved with crowned 'WR'. Regulation brass mounts. $660 £300

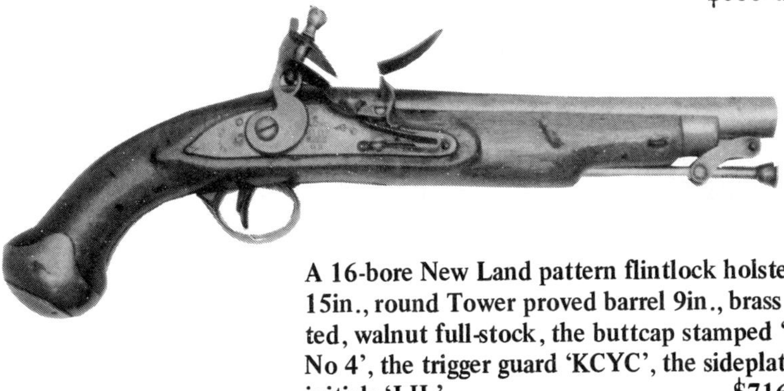

A 16-bore New Land pattern flintlock holster pistol, 15in., round Tower proved barrel 9in., brass mounted, walnut full-stock, the buttcap stamped 'TN*T No 4', the trigger guard 'KCYC', the sideplate with initials 'J.H.'. $716 £330

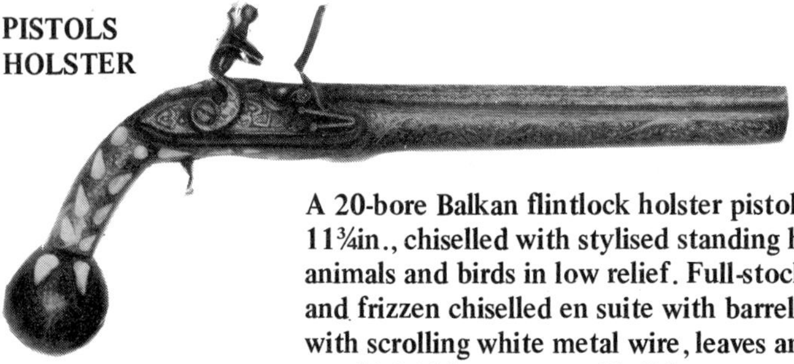

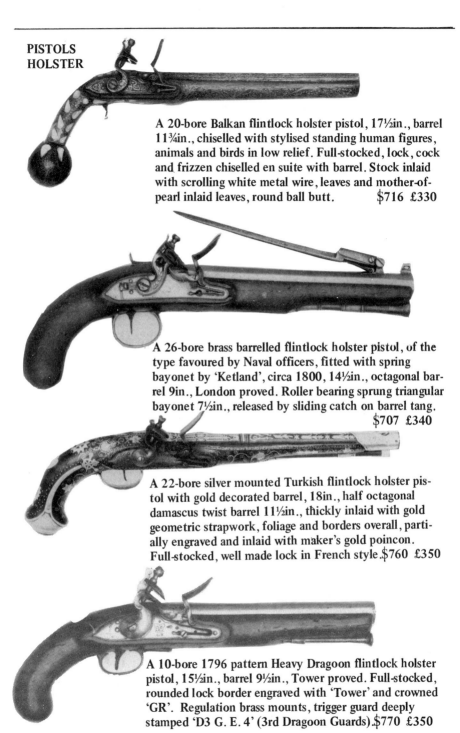

A 20-bore Balkan flintlock holster pistol, 17½in., barrel 11¾in., chiselled with stylised standing human figures, animals and birds in low relief. Full-stocked, lock, cock and frizzen chiselled en suite with barrel. Stock inlaid with scrolling white metal wire, leaves and mother-of-pearl inlaid leaves, round ball butt. $716 £330

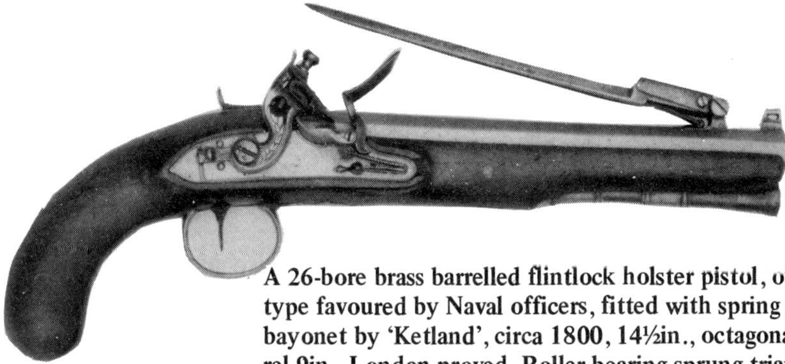

A 26-bore brass barrelled flintlock holster pistol, of the type favoured by Naval officers, fitted with spring bayonet by 'Ketland', circa 1800, 14½in., octagonal barrel 9in., London proved. Roller bearing sprung triangular bayonet 7½in., released by sliding catch on barrel tang. $707 £340

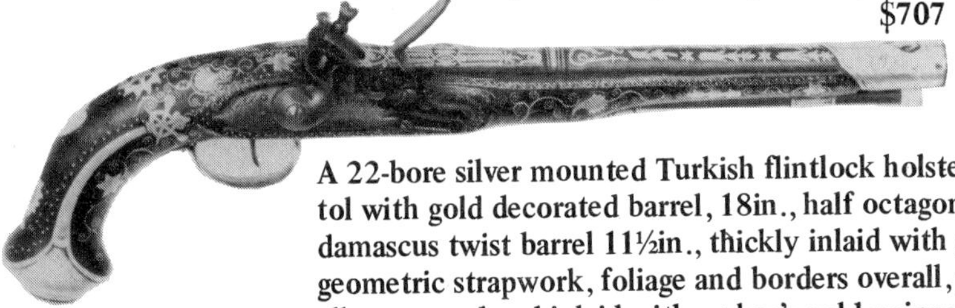

A 22-bore silver mounted Turkish flintlock holster pistol with gold decorated barrel, 18in., half octagonal damascus twist barrel 11½in., thickly inlaid with gold geometric strapwork, foliage and borders overall, partially engraved and inlaid with maker's gold poincon. Full-stocked, well made lock in French style. $760 £350

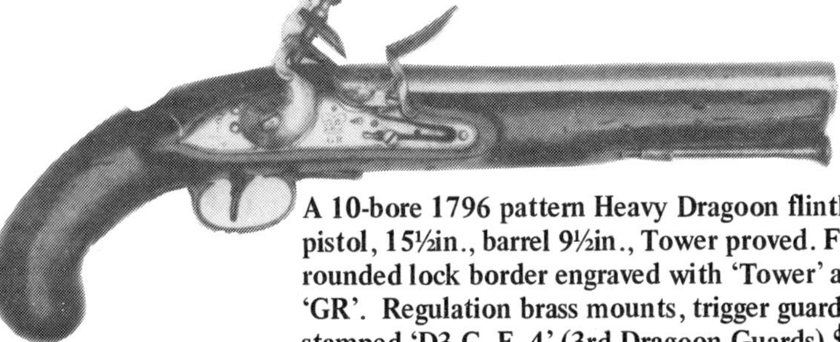

A 10-bore 1796 pattern Heavy Dragoon flintlock holster pistol, 15½in., barrel 9½in., Tower proved. Full-stocked, rounded lock border engraved with 'Tower' and crowned 'GR'. Regulation brass mounts, trigger guard deeply stamped 'D3 G. E. 4' (3rd Dragoon Guards). $770 £350

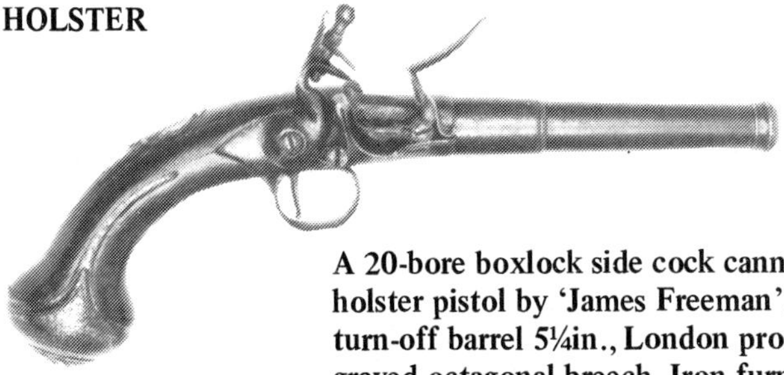

A 20-bore boxlock side cock cannon barrelled flintlock holster pistol by 'James Freeman', circa 1725, 12½in., turn-off barrel 5¼in., London proved. Facetted engraved octagonal breech. Iron furniture, longspur butt-cap with grotesque mask boss. $792 £360

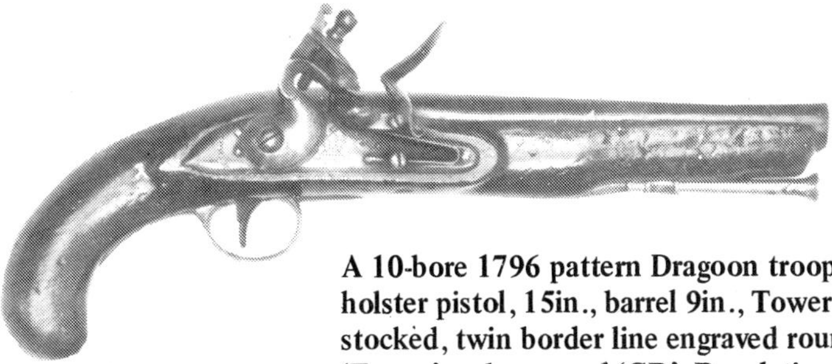

A 10-bore 1796 pattern Dragoon trooper's flintlock holster pistol, 15in., barrel 9in., Tower proved. Full-stocked, twin border line engraved rounded lock with 'Tower' and crowned 'GR'. Regulation brass mounts, steel ramrod. $792 £360

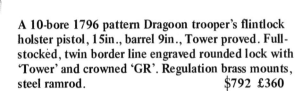

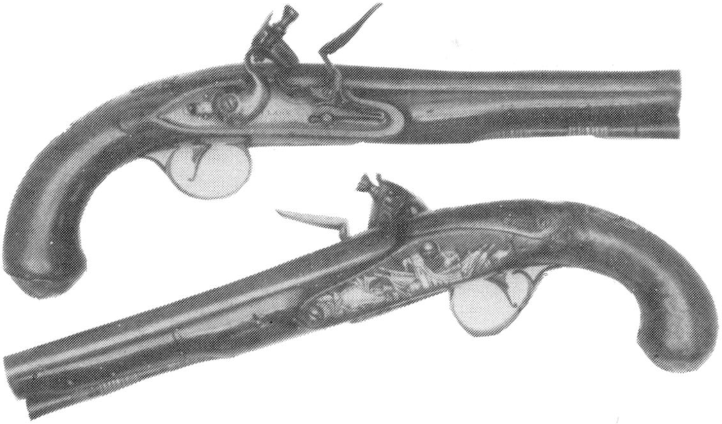

A pair of 16-bore brass mounted flintlock holster pistols, circa 1770, 13¾in., swamped browned barrels, London proved with maker's marks 'W.S.' beneath star, engraved 'London' within teardrops. Full-stocked, slightly rounded border engraved bolted locks with relieved pans and close fitting frizzens. Brass furniture, acorn finialled trigger guards. $1,100 £500

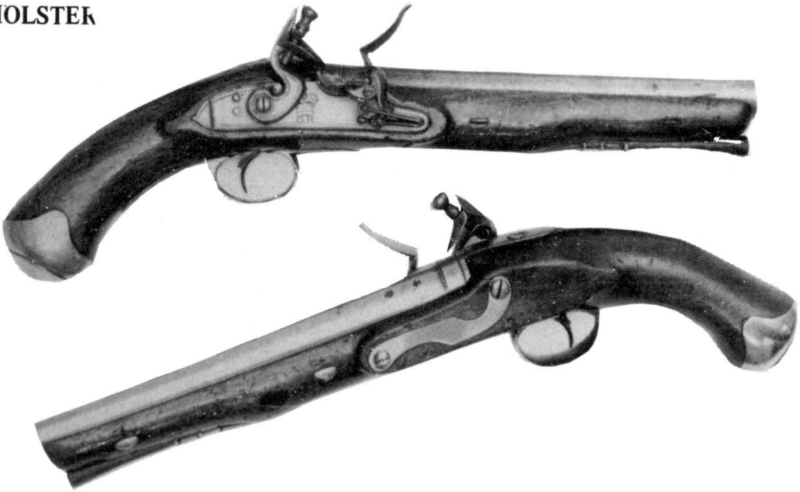

A brace of 16-bore Volunteer flintlock holster pistols, 15½in., barrels 9in., Birmingham proved. Full-stocked, border engraved locks with crowned 'GR' cyphers, roller bearing frizzen springs. Regulation brass mounts, stocks stamped with stockmaker's name 'R. Hollis'. $1,088 £500

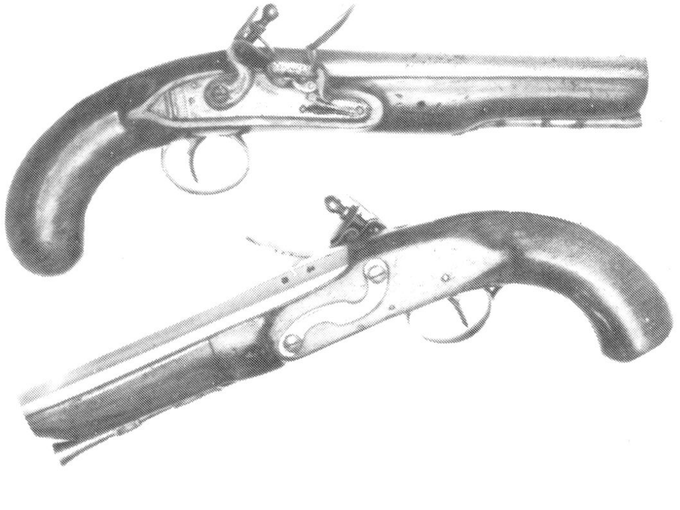

A pair of 17-bore brass barrelled flintlock holster pistols, 13in., octagonal barrels 7¼in., Birmingham proved, stamped 'London' at breeches. Full-stocked, line border engraved locks with 'Sharpe'. Brass furniture, engraved trigger guard bows. Rounded grips and steel ramrods. $1,155 £525

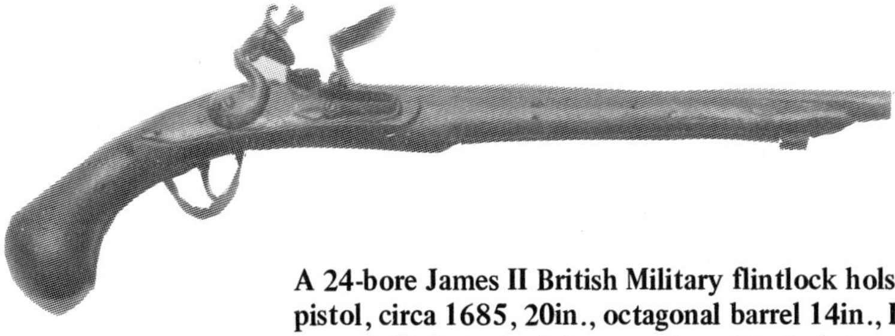

A 24-bore James II British Military flintlock holster pistol, circa 1685, 20in., octagonal barrel 14in., London proved. Full-stocked, banana-shaped lockplate, spear finialled frizzen spring, unbridled frizzen, lock secured by three sidenails, barrel tang secured by one bolt rising upwards through spear finial of trigger guard.
$1,280 £540

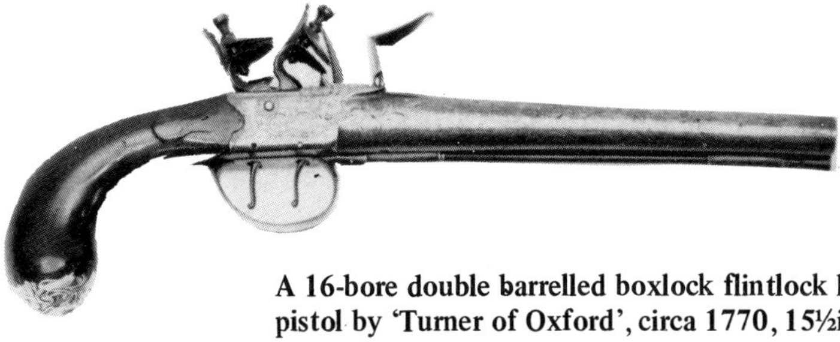

A 16-bore double barrelled boxlock flintlock holster pistol by 'Turner of Oxford', circa 1770, 15½in., barrels 9in., forged integrally with each other. Frizzen springs sunk in breech tops, dog tooth engraved frizzens and cocks. Front trigger fires left barrel and conversely.
$1,193 £550

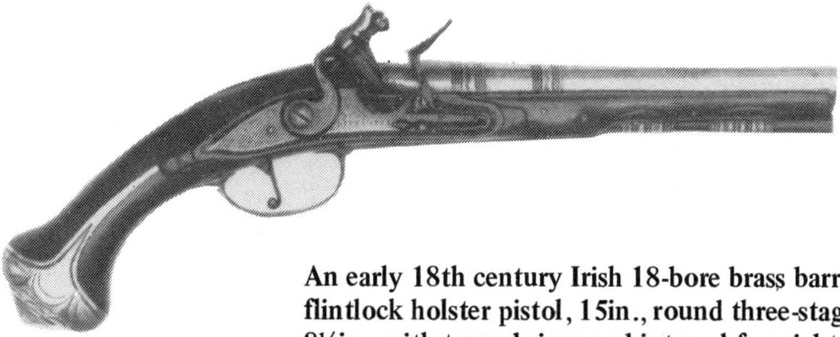

An early 18th century Irish 18-bore brass barrelled flintlock holster pistol, 15in., round three-stage barrel 8½in., with turned rings and integral foresight, flat banana-shaped lock with foliated decoration and signed 'Fitz Patrick', engraved cock, the top jaw and screw, frizzen and pan of angular design. $1,210 £550

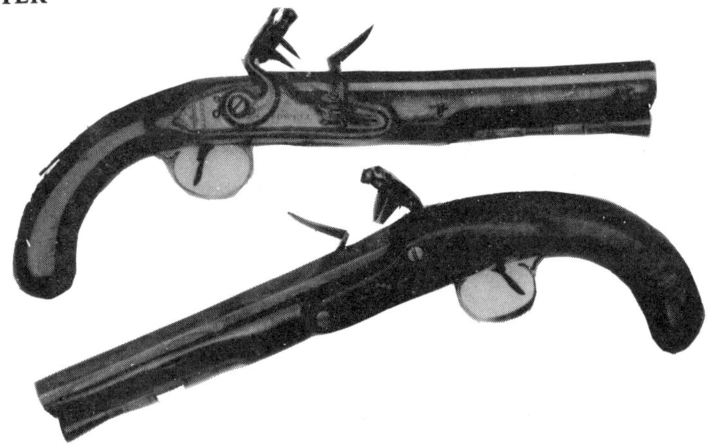

A pair of 24-bore flintlock holster pistols by 'Powell of Dublin', circa 1780, 12½in., octagonal browned barrels 7in., engraved 'Dublin' with foliate breeches. Full-stocked, stepped lockplates, roller bearing frizzen springs. Brass furniture.
$1,193 £550

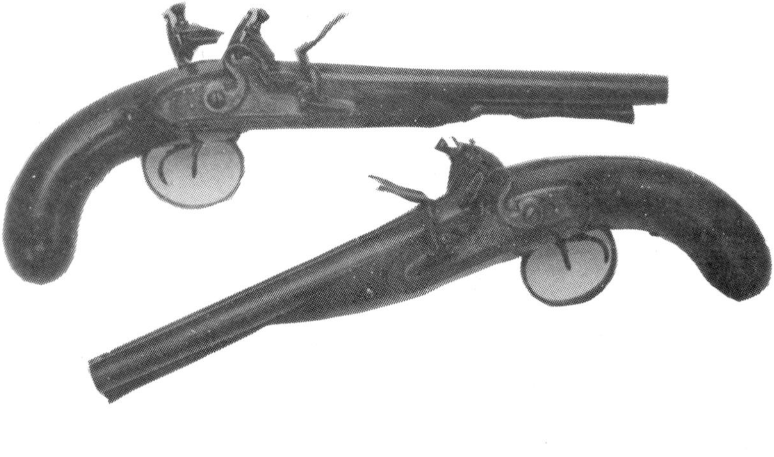

A pair of 40-bore double barrelled flintlock holster pistols by 'Bird & Ashmore', circa 1790, 14½in., browned barrels 9in., engraved 'London' on top ribs. Half-stocked, border engraved locks with roller bearing frizzen springs, pineapple finialled trigger guards and throatpipes. Rounded grips, oval silver escutcheons, horn tipped wooden ramrods with steel worms. $2,130 £900

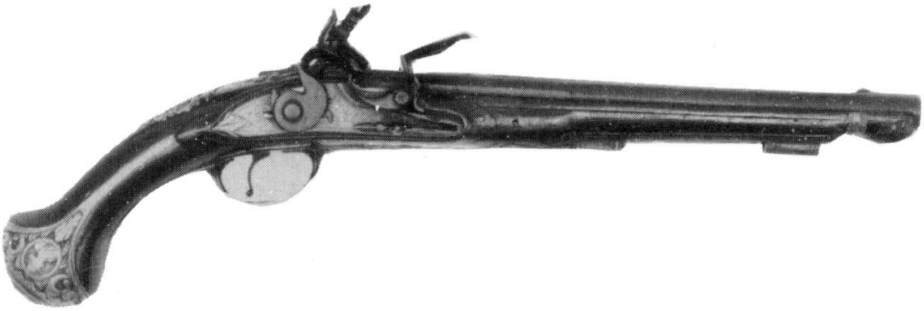

A 16-bore Spanish flintlock holster pistol, circa 1730, by 'Rovira', 19in., barrel 12in., brass inlaid breech band, foliate finialled top sighting rib. Full-stocked, brass lockplate. Horizontally acting scear transversing lockplate, ring top jaw screw. $2,495 £1,150

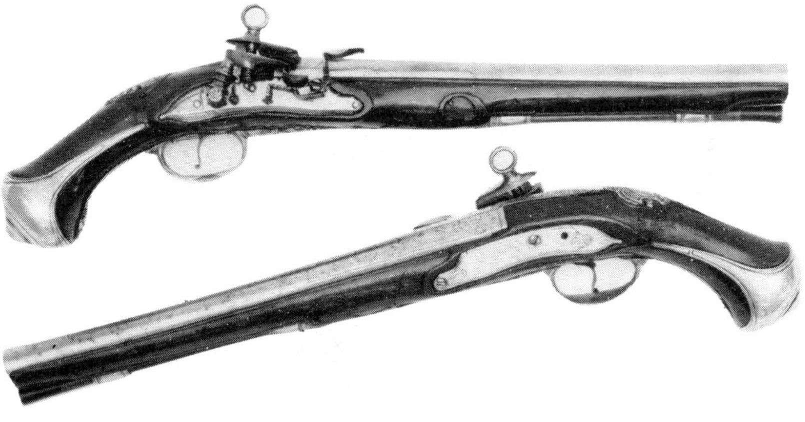

A pair of 18-bore Portuguese silver mounted flintlock holster pistols, 18½in., barrels 12in., with chiselled top ribs and facetted breeches. Full-stocked, stepped cocks with ring top jaw screws and hinged half cock safety catches automatically removed at full cock. Striated unbridled frizzens, frizzen springs under pans. Border engraved silver furniture, longspur buttcaps with stepped bosses, foliate finialled trigger guards. $2,392 £1,150

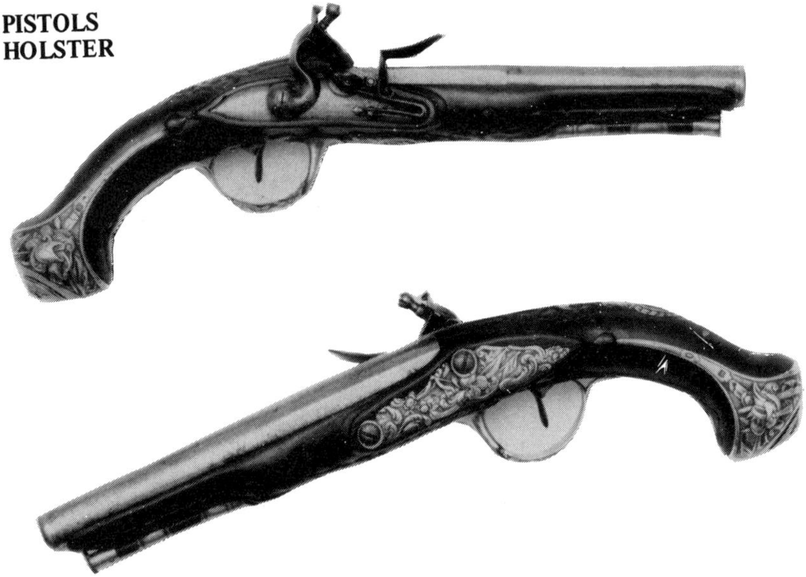

A pair of French 22-bore hallmarked silver mounted flintlock holster pistols by 'Cassaignard of Nantes', circa 1790, 13½in., stepped barrels 7¾in., with swollen muzzles. Full-stocked, rounded line engraved locks, bridled frizzens. Hallmarked silver furniture chiselled in relief against a punctuate ground, foliate and floral finialled trigger guards. Contained in a wooden case. $2,604 £1,200

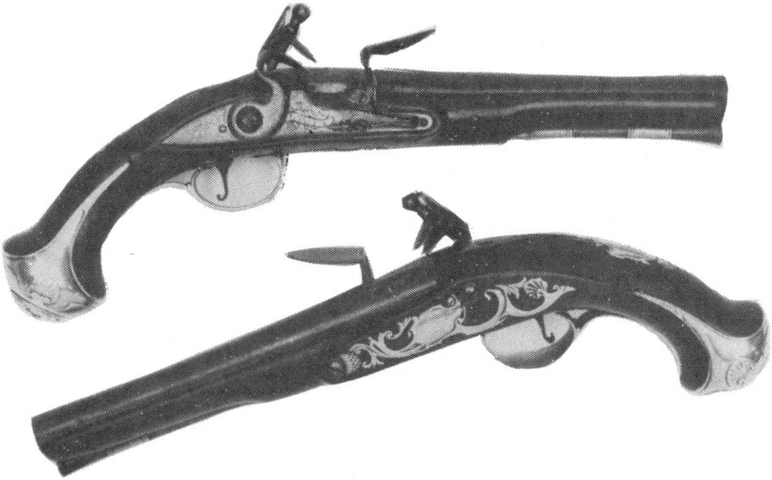

A pair of 18-bore silver mounted flintlock holster pistols by 'Griffin', circa 1751, 13¼in., swamped barrels 8in., London proved with Foreigner's marks, engraved 'Bond Street, London' within teardrops, foliate engraved breeches. Full-stocked in well figured walnut. Hallmarked silver furniture. $3,630 £1,650

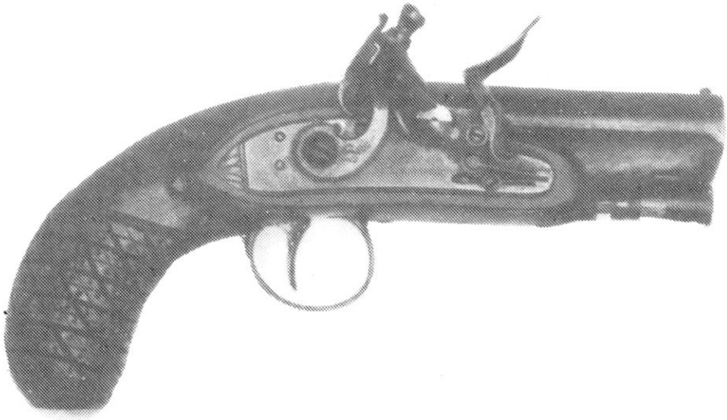

A 50-bore flintlock overcoat pistol by 'McDermot of Dublin', 7¼in., twist barrel 3¼in., engraved 'Dublin' within sighting channel, silver lined vent. Full-stocked, stepped lock, roller bearing frizzen spring. French style cock, pineapple finialled blued steel trigger guard. $682 £310

A pair of 58-bore Queen Anne style boxlock flintlock cannon barrelled overcoat pistols by 'T. Archer', circa 1780, 7¼in., turn-off barrels 2¼in., London proved with maker's mark 'T.A.' beneath crown. Throathole cocks, sliding trigger guard safety catches, frizzen springs sunk in breech tops. $770 £370

A pair of 50-bore cannon barrelled flintlock overcoat pistols by 'T. Henshaw', circa 1750, 7¼in., turn-off barrels 2in., London proved, maker's mark crowned 'T.H.', muzzles cut frizzen spring finials, unbridled frizzens. Half-stocked, slightly rounded locks, treffid finialled trigger guards with flowers on bows. Swollen chunky bulbous grips. $924 £420

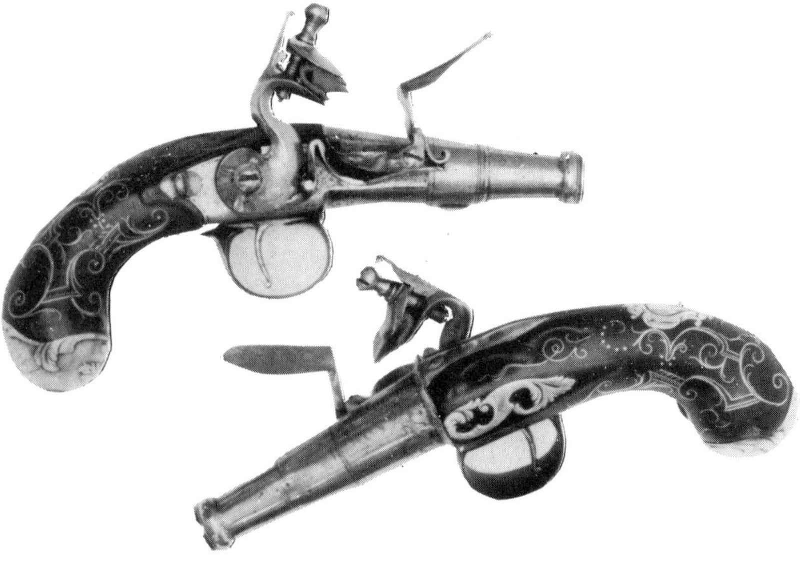

A pair of 42-bore boxlock side cock silver mounted Queen Anne style cannon barrel overcoat pistols by 'H. Delany', circa 1730, 6¾in., turn-off chunky barrels 2in., London proved with maker's mark 'H.D.', foliate engraved breeches. Sliding safety catches behind cocks, trigger guards engraved with military trophies. Rounded walnut butts inlaid with scrolling silver wire and pellets. $1,227 £590

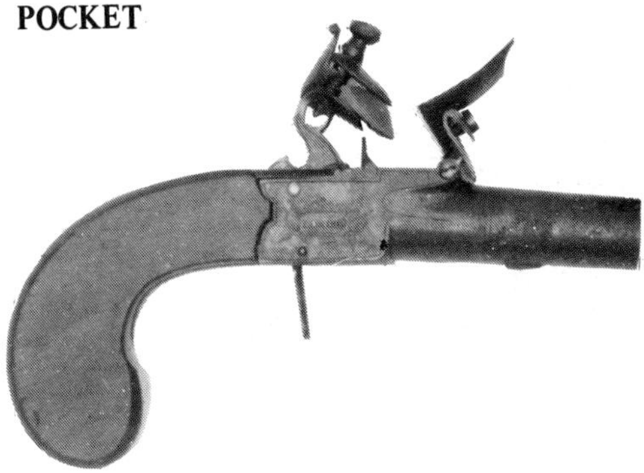

An 18th century boxlock flintlock pocket pistol by 'Twigg', 5¾in., round turn-off barrel 1½in., London proved, slab walnut grip, square action body with folding trigger, throathole cock and teardrop frizzen. $218 £105

A boxlock flintlock pocket pistol by 'Weston Brighton', 6in., turn-off round barrel 1½in., Birmingham proved, plain slab walnut grip, thumb top safety blocking hammer. $264 £120

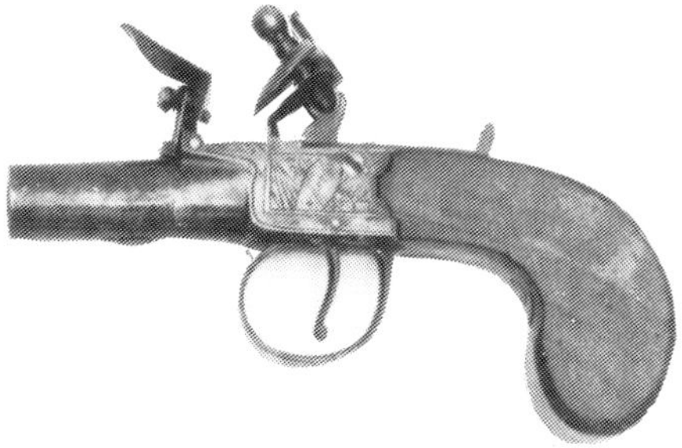

A boxlock flintlock cannon barrelled pocket pistol by 'A. Weston Lewes', 7¾in., turn-off barrel with baluster turned muzzle, 2½in., numbered 3, London proved, plain slab walnut grip. $308 £140

A 50-bore double barrelled French boxlock flintlock pocket pistol, 8½in., barrels 3½in., sliding safety catch to cocks, raised fences. Chequered walnut stock, steel ramrod. $365 £155

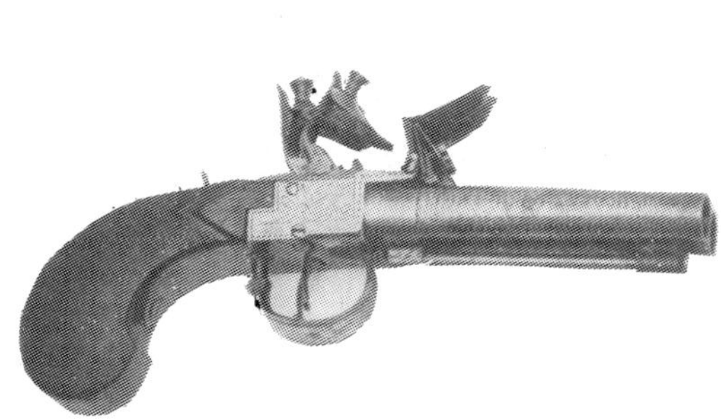

An all steel Segallas type boxlock flintlock pocket pistol, circa 1780, 6in., half octagonal cannon barrel 2½in. Border engraved overall with flowers on frame. Frizzen spring sunk in breech top, sliding trigger guard. $458 £220

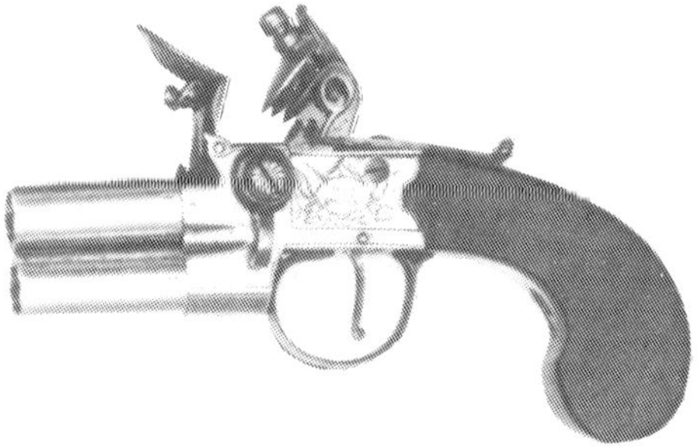

A small brass framed and double barrelled boxlock flintlock tap action pocket pistol by 'Rea & Son', circa 1800, 5in., turn-off barrels 1¼in., single Tower proof. Sliding top thumb safety catch locking frizzen to fence. Slab walnut butt. $638 £290

A 46-bore boxlock flintlock cannon barrelled pocket pistol by 'Griffin of London', circa 1765, 6in., turned reinforced turn-off cannon barrel 1¾in., with swollen muzzle dog tooth border engraved breech. London proved. Frizzen spring inlaid in breech top. Short slab walnut grip. $651 £300

A pair of 48-bore Belgian boxlock flintlock pocket pistols, 7¼in., turn-off barrels 2¼in., Liege proved. Frames engraved with foliate sprigs. Sliding top thumb safety catches locking frizzens to fences. Slightly swollen chequered grips. $651 £300

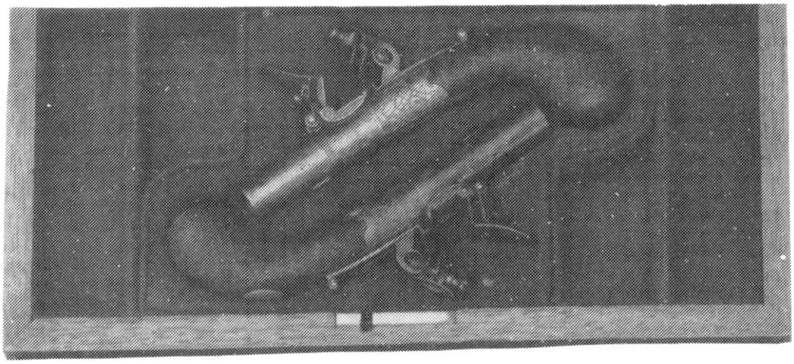

A small pair of flintlock boxlock pocket pistols by 'Staudenmayer', circa 1820, 4½in., turn-off barrels 1¼in., London proofs stamped over Birmingham proofs. Round frames engraved with trophies and 'Staudenmayer London'. Ring neck cocks, sliding top safety catehes locking twin roller bearing frizzen to fences, raised pans, concealed triggers. Rounded chequered walnut butt. Contained in a green beize lined mahogany box. $682 £310

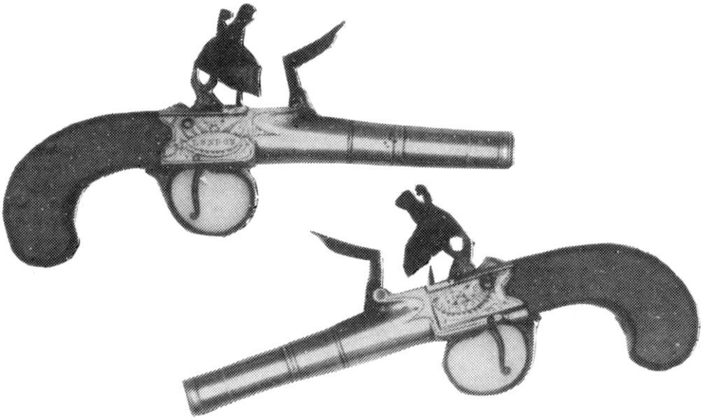

A pair of brass framed and barrelled boxlock flintlock cannon barrelled pocket pistols by 'Bumford, London', circa 1775, 6½in., turn-off barrels 2in., Tower proved. Dog tooth engraved frames. Frizzen springs sunk in breech tops, ring neck cocks, sliding trigger guards and safety guards. Slab walnut butts. $836 £380

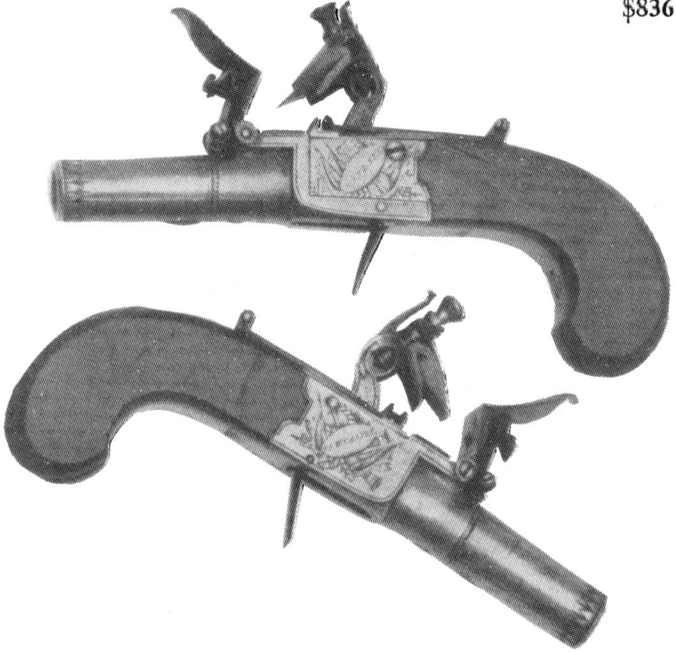

A pair of flintlock boxlock muff pistols by 'Gardner of Newcastle', circa 1800, 5in., turn-off barrels 1¼in., foliate engraved muzzles, Birmingham proved. Sliding top thumb safety catches, through throathole cocks locking twin roller bearing teardrop frizzens to fences. Raised pans, concealed triggers. $811 £390

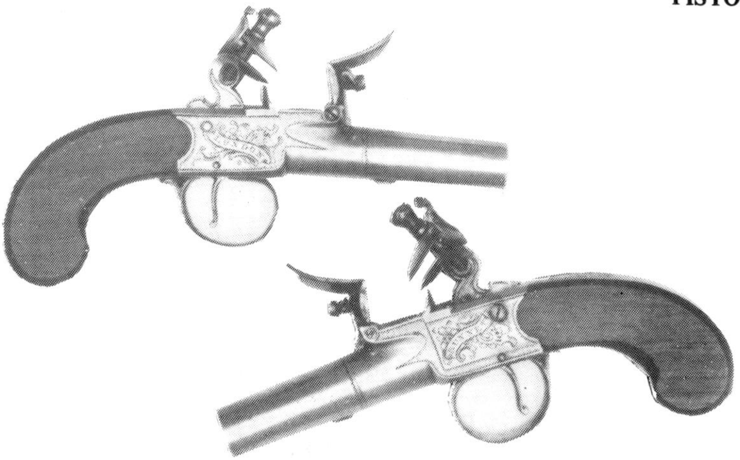

A pair of brass barrelled brass framed boxlock flintlock pocket pistols by 'Bunney of London', 6¼in., turn-off barrels 1¾in., Tower proved. Dog tooth border engraved frames with 'Bunney London' within banners upon flowers and rocaille. Throathole cocks, sliding trigger guards, safety catches. Slab walnut butts. $1,100 £500

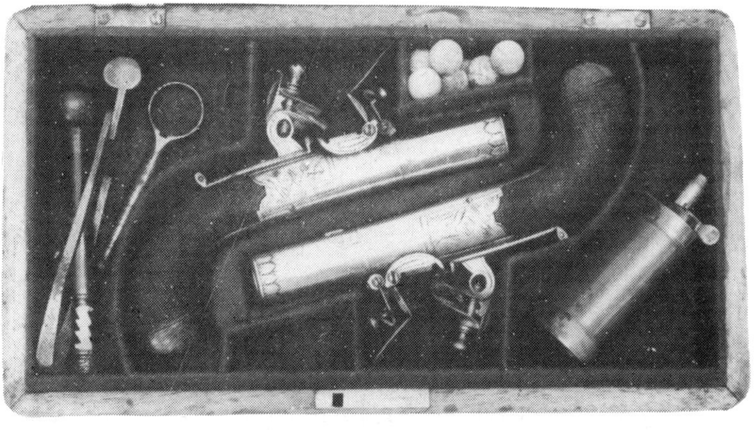

A pair of brass framed brass barrelled boxlock flintlock pocket pistols by 'Twigg', 6in., turn-off barrels 1½in., Birmingham proved, frond engraved muzzles. Frames engraved 'Twigg, London' with Britannia shield centred military trophies, concealed triggers. Sliding top thumb safety catches through throathole cocks locking twin friction roller bearing teardrop frizzens to fences, raised pans. Rounded chequered walnut butts with chamfered silver escutcheons. In a green beize lined wooden case. $1,210 £550

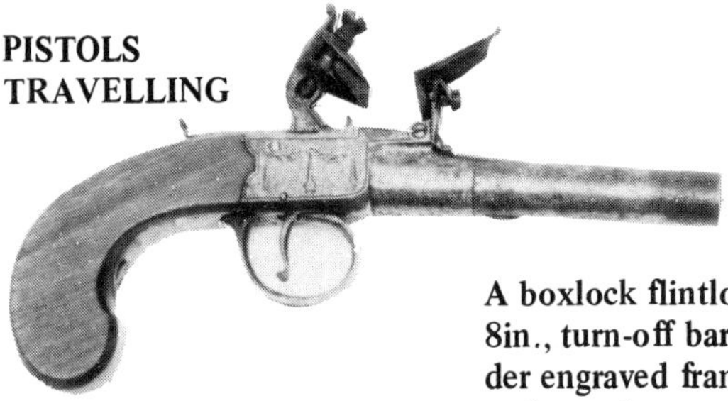

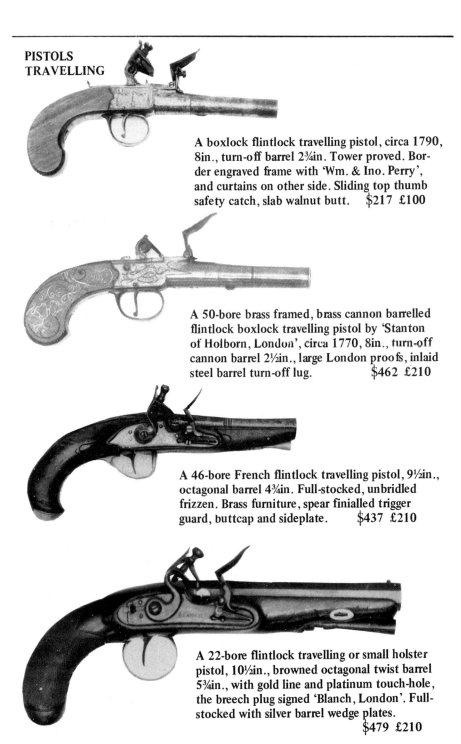

A boxlock flintlock travelling pistol, circa 1790, 8in., turn-off barrel 2¾in. Tower proved. Border engraved frame with 'Wm. & Ino. Perry', and curtains on other side. Sliding top thumb safety catch, slab walnut butt. $217 £100

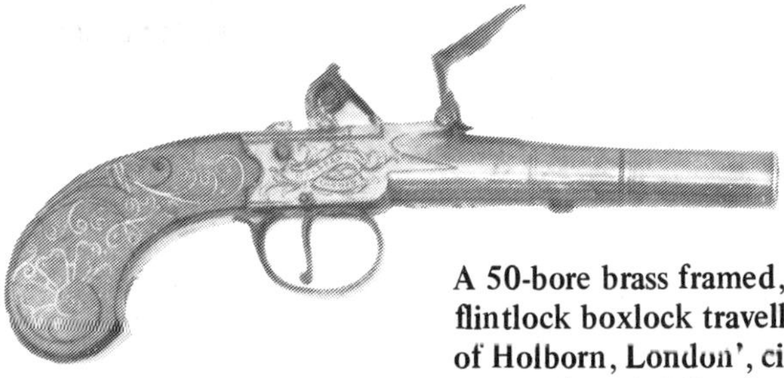

A 50-bore brass framed, brass cannon barrelled flintlock boxlock travelling pistol by 'Stanton of Holborn, London', circa 1770, 8in., turn-off cannon barrel 2½in., large London proofs, inlaid steel barrel turn-off lug. $462 £210

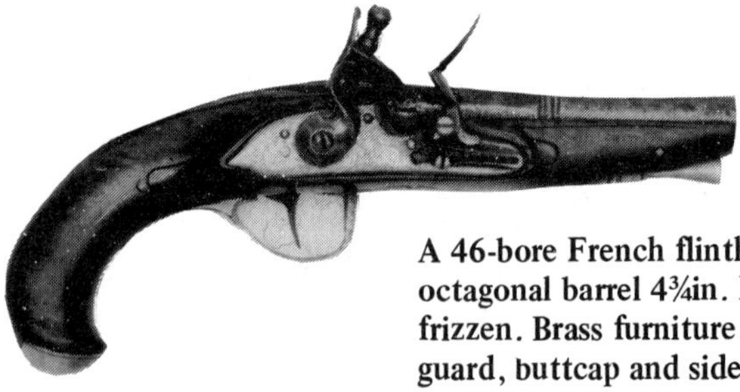

A 46-bore French flintlock travelling pistol, 9½in., octagonal barrel 4¾in. Full-stocked, unbridled frizzen. Brass furniture, spear finialled trigger guard, buttcap and sideplate. $437 £210

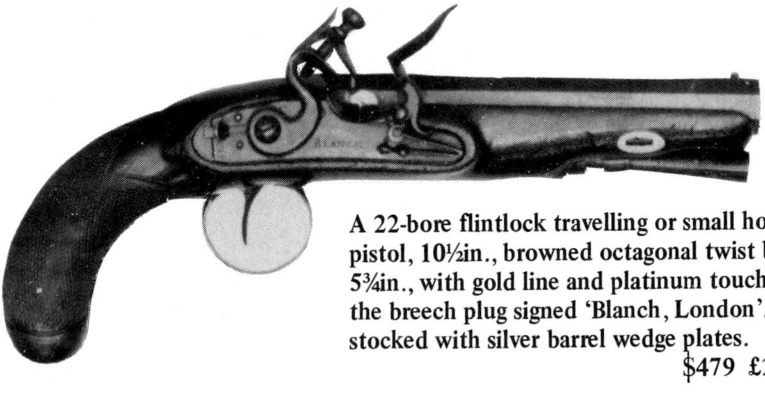

A 22-bore flintlock travelling or small holster pistol, 10½in., browned octagonal twist barrel 5¾in., with gold line and platinum touch-hole, the breech plug signed 'Blanch, London'. Full-stocked with silver barrel wedge plates. $479 £210

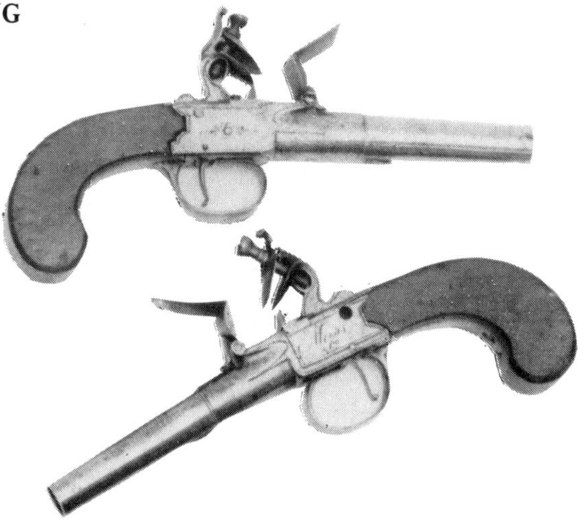

A pair of 50-bore boxlock flintlock travelling pistols by 'Mewis & Co.', circa 1775, 7¾in., turn-off barrels, 2½in., London proved. Dog tooth border to engraved breeches and frames with 'Mewis & Co.' in script. Flower head engraved sliding trigger guard safeties, frizzen springs sunk in breech tops. Throathole cocks and teardrop frizzens. Slab walnut butts. $500 £230

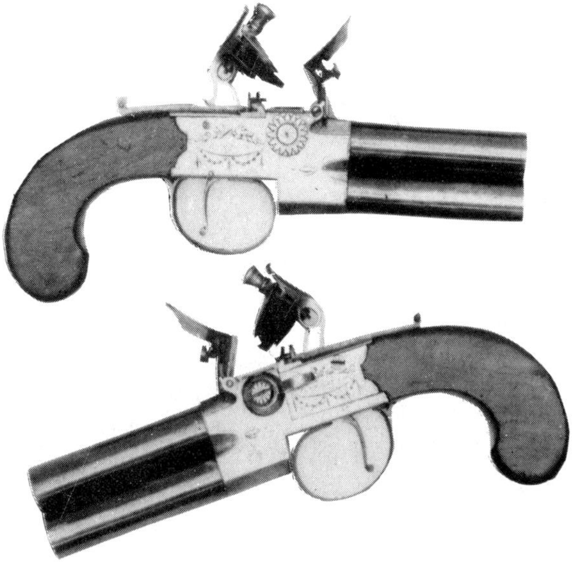

A pair of 55-bore flintlock boxlock double barrelled tap action over and under travelling pistols by 'Bingham of London', 7½in., turn-off barrels 2¾in., London proved. Trophy and swag engraved frames with 'Bingham, London' within ovals. Sliding top thumb safety catches through throathole cocks locking teardrop frizzens. Slab walnut butts. $1,031 £475

A pair of double barrelled boxlock flintlock tap action travelling pistols by 'Golding', circa 1780, 8in., turn-off rifled barrels 2¾in., London proved. Foliate, floral and border engraved frames with 'Golding' within banners. Bead engraved taps, throathole cocks, variable tension sprung teardrop frizzens, floral engraved trigger guard bows. Slab walnut grips. $1,193 £550

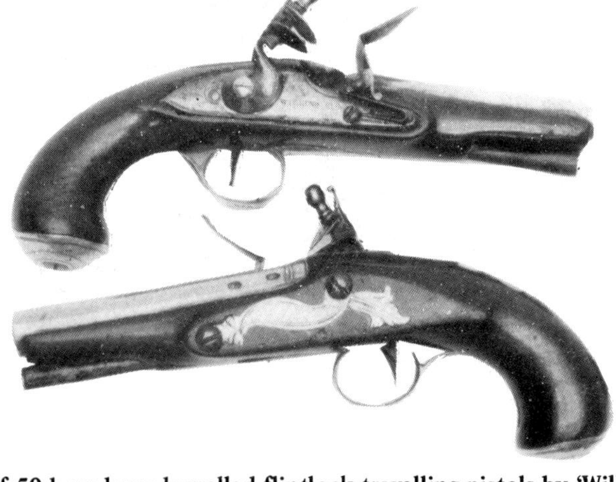

A pair of 50-bore brass barrelled flintlock travelling pistols by 'Wilkins of Eton', circa 1770, 8in., barrels 4¼in., London proved, engraved 'Eton' within foliate frames on barrel tops. Full-stocked, unbridled frizzens. Brass furniture, foliate finialled buttcaps, sideplates and escutcheons. Brass tipped wooden ramrods. $1,302 £600

A Belgian 70-bore four-barrelled boxlock tap action flintlock travelling pistol, 8¼in., turn-off rifled barrels 3in. Liege proved. Border engraved frame with foliate sprigs. Sliding top thumb safety catch locking frizzen to fences. Flattened walnut butt. $1,519 £700

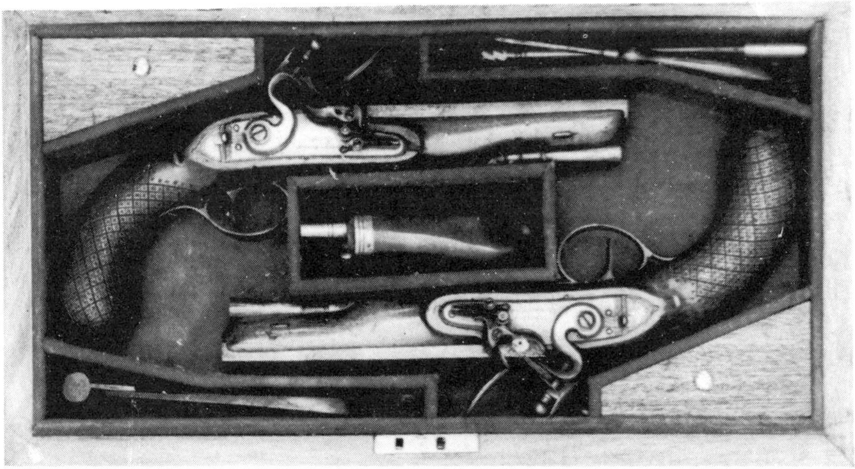

A pair of 22-bore flintlock travelling pistols by 'John Richards', circa 1800, 11in., octagonal barrels 6in., London proved, engraved 'Strand, London', gold lined vents. Full-stocked, stepped bolted locks foliate engraved with 'John Richards', roller bearing frizzen springs. Pineapple finialled trigger guards. Rounded chequered butts, oval silver escutcheons, steel ramrods, one with worm tip. $1,596 £700

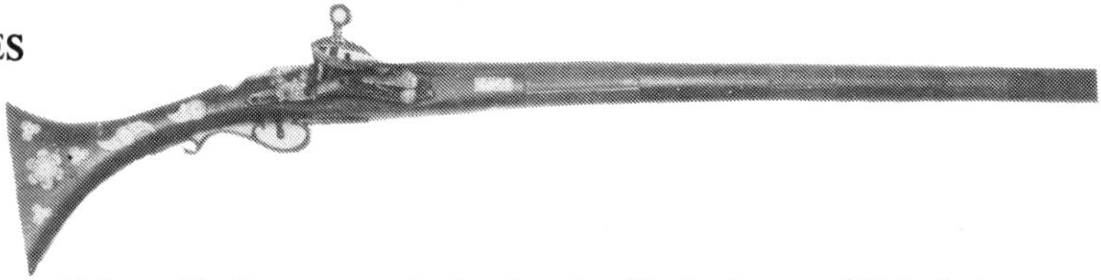

A 10-bore Mediterranean Arab miquelet flintlock gun of Kabyle type, 60½in., heavy barrel 46½in., inlaid in brass overall in Moorish geometric design, swollen fluted muzzle. Full-stocked, brass covered foliate chiselled lock with dog catch, broad striated frizzen. Heavy steel ramrod, fishtail butt, engraved bone inlay, large brass capucines. $429 £165

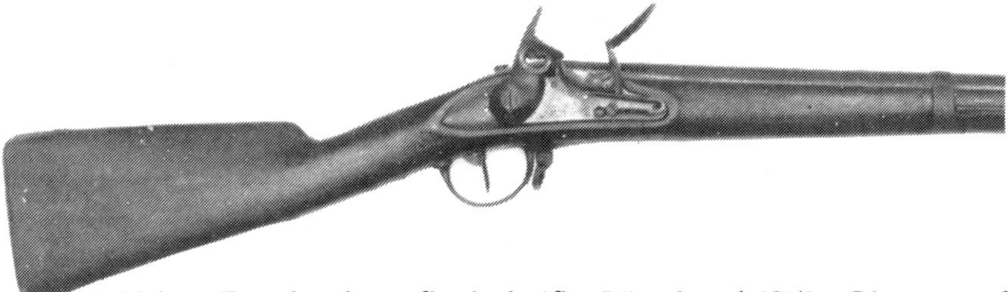

A 13-bore French military flintlock rifle, 56in., barrel 40½in., Liege proved. Full-stocked, regulation lock with brass pan, plate engraved 'Mfre Rle de Tulle'. Regulation iron mounts, three spring retained barrel bands, two sling swivels, steel ramrod. Stock carved with cheekpiece. $484 £220

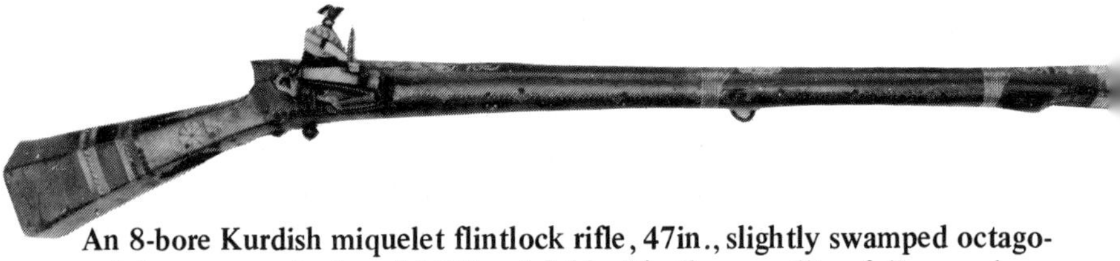

An 8-bore Kurdish miquelet flintlock rifle, 47in., slightly swamped octagonal damascus twist barrel 32½in., inlaid with silver scrolling foliage and bands at breech, muzzle and top flat. Full-stocked, lock inlaid with geometric and foliate engraved silver, large striated frizzen, bridled cock. Square sectioned butt inlaid with bone bands. $803 £370

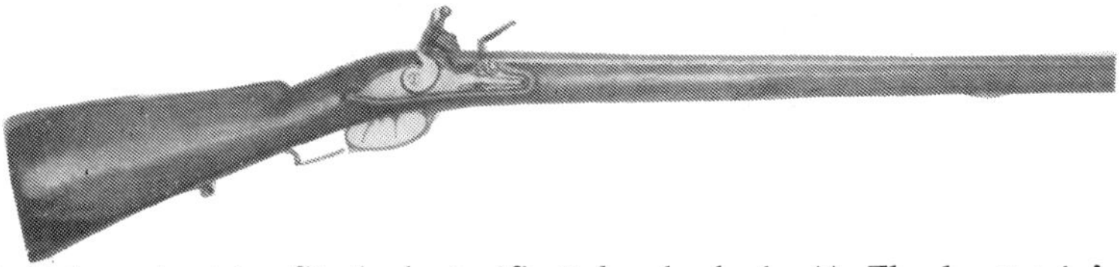

A 42-bore Austrian flintlock air rifle Bolzenbushe by 'A. Ehrnbrettstein', circa 1780, 47½in., octagonal barrel 32in. Full-stocked, flintlock lock, double set triggers. Engraved brass furniture. Diana on trigger guard, stag centred trophy on buttcap. Buttcap with hinge to reveal pump screw. Carved cheekpiece, horn forecap and horn tipped wooden ramrod.
$3,120 £1,200

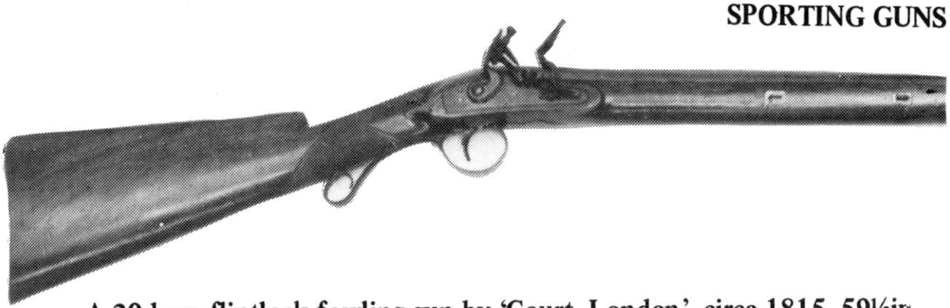

A 20-bore flintlock fowling gun by 'Court, London', circa 1815, 59½in., part round, part octagonal barrel 43¼in., Birmingham proved, chequered walnut half stock with iron furniture, including longspurred buttcap, scrolled trigger guard with pineapple finial, blank silver wrist escutcheon and four silver cross key escutcheons, break-off twist barrel with under rib supporting two ramrod pipes. $1,056 £480

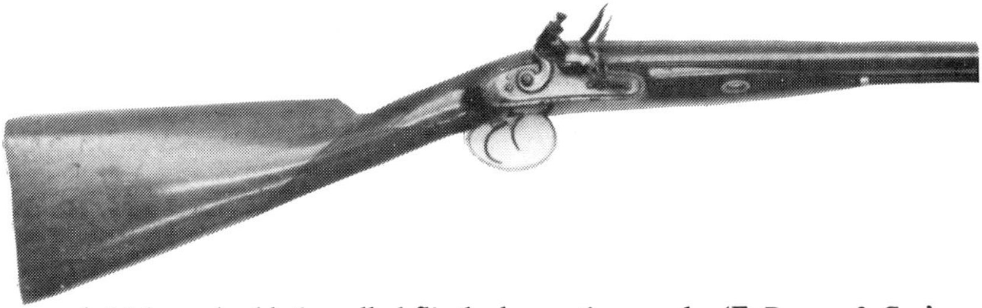

A 16-bore double barrelled flintlock sporting gun by 'F. Barnes & Co.', circa 1810, 47in., twist barrels 30in., London proved. Top rib engraved 'F. Barnes & Co., London', gold line inlaid at foliate engraved breech. Half-stocked, foliate engraved locks with rounded tails. Pigeon-breasted cocks, rainproof pans, silver lined vents, roller bearing frizzens. Foliate engraved white metal furniture, pineapple finialled trigger guard and throatpipe. $2,750 £1,250

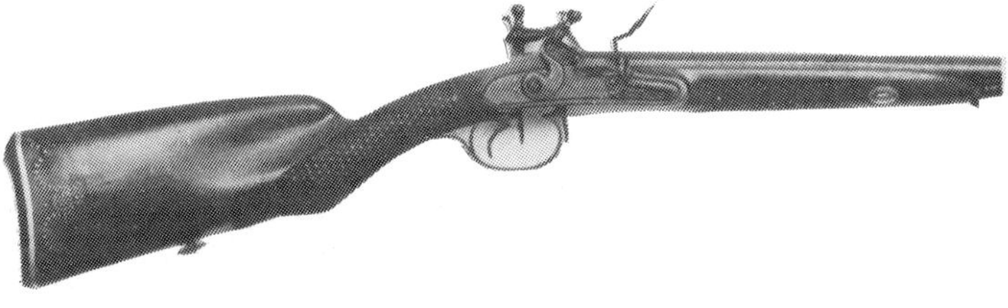

A Belgian 24-bore double barrelled flintlock sporting gun by 'J. B. Heuseux', 49in., browned twist barrels 32½in. Half-stocked, bevelled lockplates, roller bearing frizzen springs, bridled frizzens, scrolled fence tops. Unusual silver mounted horn furniture, horn trigger guard with silver border en suite with buttcap and throatpipe. French walnut stock. Brass tipped wooden ramrod. $4,680 £1,800

SPORTING RIFLE

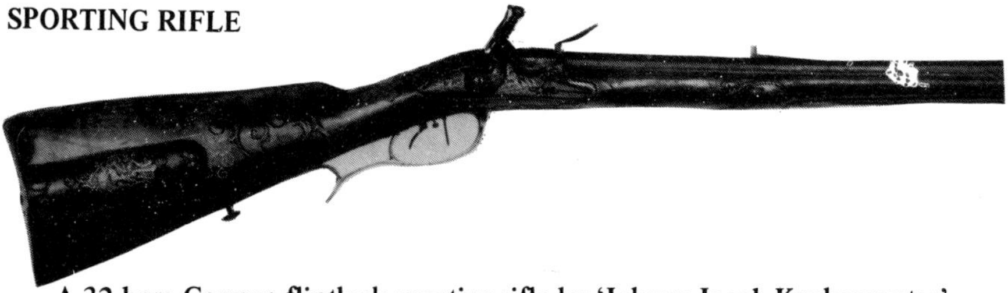

A 32-bore German flintlock sporting rifle by 'Johann Jacob Kuchenreuter', circa 1780, 46½in., octagonal barrel 31¼in., applied gilt portrait bust at breech, fixed sight. Full-stocked, detented lock engraved and chiselled in low relief with two sportsmen and dogs chasing deer, foliate engraved cock and frizzen. Adjustable double set triggers. Chiselled and engraved silvered furniture. Horn forecap and horn tipped wooden ramrod. $7,378 £3,400

WHEELOCKS

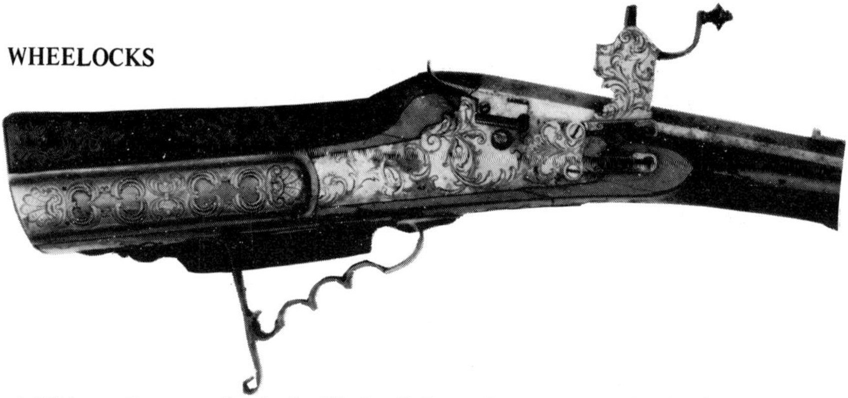

A 38-bore German wheelock rifle by 'Johann Justus Ludvig Pauli of Nushart', circa 1730, 43½in., heavy octagonal rifled barrel 31in., engraved muzzle, foliate finialled foresight, breech inlaid with brass maker's mark of swan and 'I.P.'. Full-stocked, well foliate engraved lock, cock and cock bridle. Concealed wheel, engraved thumb guard, baluster turned cockspur. Double set triggers with micro-adjustable hair trigger. Brass furniture, shaped finger rests to scrolled trigger guard. $3,255 £1,500

A 28-bore early 17th century Continental, probably Swiss, wheelock holster pistol, 24in., half octagonal barrel 15¾in., foliate and floral engraved octagonal section, turned muzzle. Full-stocked, foliate engraved lock borders, external wheel with bird-shaped bridle, bridle cock, sliding pan cover. Foliate and floral engraved trigger guard and ramrod pipe. Steel tipped ramrod. $6,510 £3,000

MILITARIA

ALARM GUNS

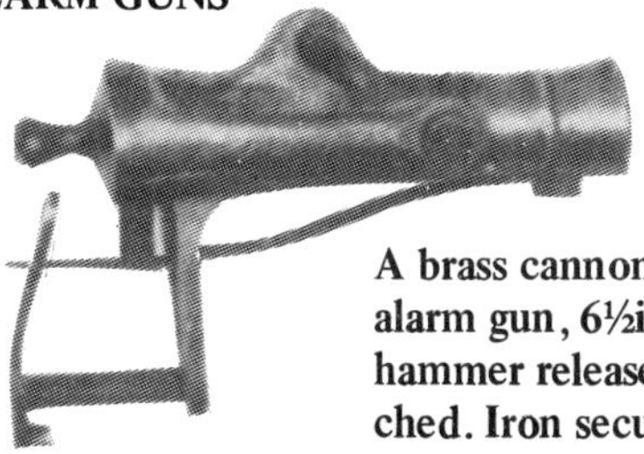

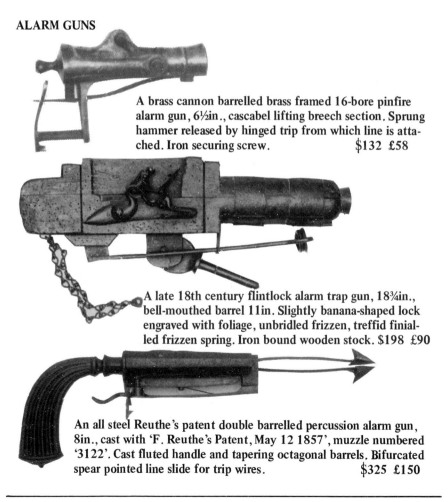

A brass cannon barrelled brass framed 16-bore pinfire alarm gun, 6½in., cascabel lifting breech section. Sprung hammer released by hinged trip from which line is attached. Iron securing screw. $132 £58

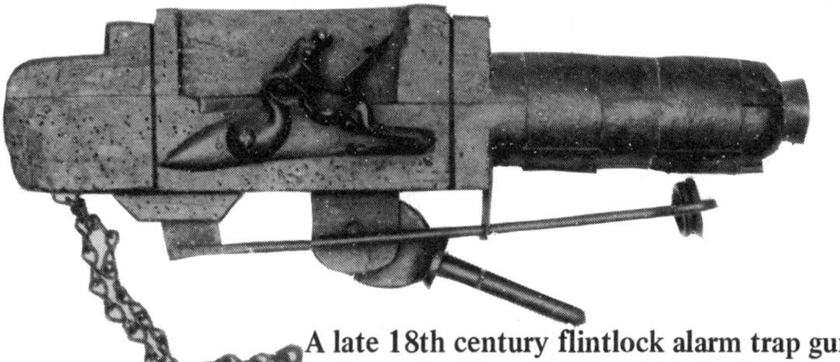

A late 18th century flintlock alarm trap gun, 18¾in., bell-mouthed barrel 11in. Slightly banana-shaped lock engraved with foliage, unbridled frizzen, treffid finialled frizzen spring. Iron bound wooden stock. $198 £90

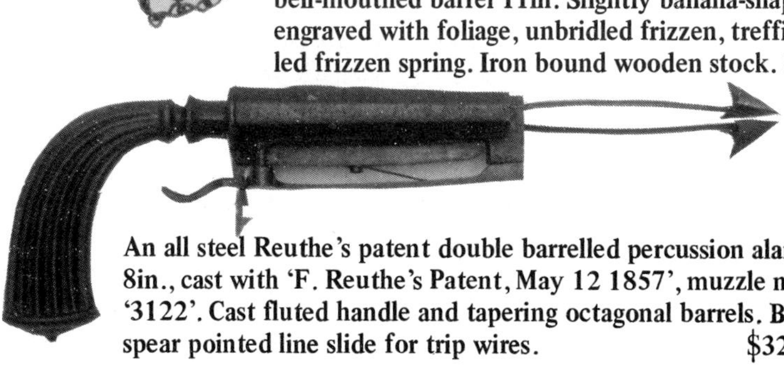

An all steel Reuthe's patent double barrelled percussion alarm gun, 8in., cast with 'F. Reuthe's Patent, May 12 1857', muzzle numbered '3122'. Cast fluted handle and tapering octagonal barrels. Bifurcated spear pointed line slide for trip wires. $325 £150

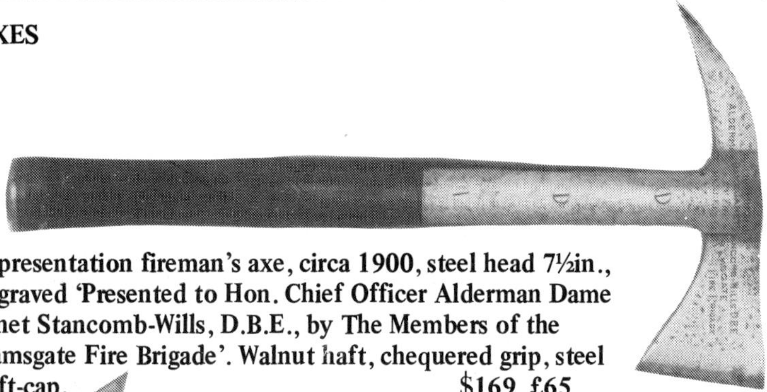

A presentation fireman's axe, circa 1900, steel head 7½in., engraved 'Presented to Hon. Chief Officer Alderman Dame Janet Stancomb-Wills, D.B.E., by The Members of the Ramsgate Fire Brigade'. Walnut haft, chequered grip, steel haft-cap. $169 £65

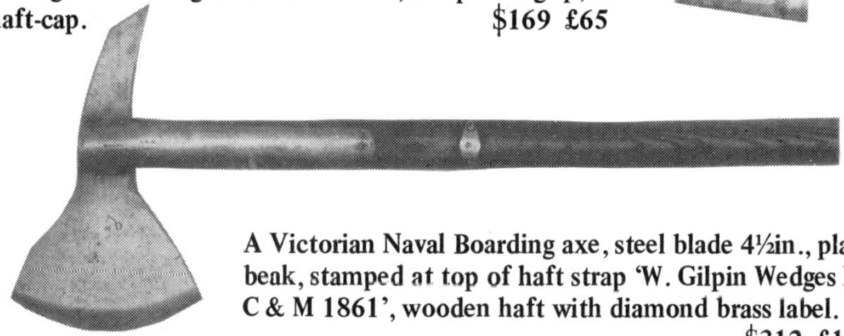

A Victorian Naval Boarding axe, steel blade 4½in., plain beak, stamped at top of haft strap 'W. Gilpin Wedges Mills C & M 1861', wooden haft with diamond brass label. $312 £120

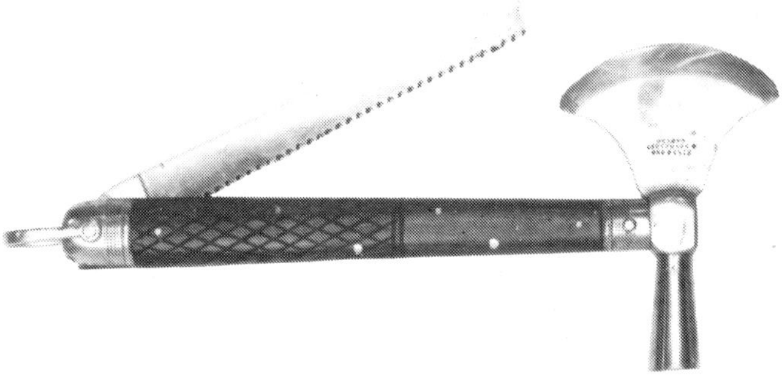

A late Victorian explorer's axe, polished steel crescent head 4in., stamped 'Hill & Son, 4 Haymarket, London' with integral hammer back. Two-piece partly chequered rosewood grips. $275 £125

An old Indian steel axe, crescent shaped blade 3in., smaller etched and silver damascened blade to rear of blade, mounted on an iron haft terminating in steel spike, length overall 25¼in. $130 £55

An officer's gilt 1861 pattern shako badge of The 29th Foot. $46 £20

A silvered plaid brooch of The Black Watch, by Anderson of Edinburgh. $48 £22

An other rank's pre-1881 Glengarry badge of The 6th Foot. $57 £25

An other rank's pre-1881 Glengarry badge of The 3rd Foot. $68 £30

An other rank's pre-1881 Glengarry badge of The 40th Foot. $76 £34

An officer's shako plate of The Royal Military College (prior to 1878), in silver and enamel. $80 £35

A post-1881 officer's gilt and silvered Glengarry badge of The Wiltshire Regt. $94 £36

A post-1902 officer's gilt, silvered and enamel grenade cap badge of The Royal Fusiliers. $79 £36

A Victorian other rank's helmet plate of H.M. Reserve Regt. of Dragoon Guards. $94 £36

An officer's silvered and enamel forage cap badge of The Guards Machine Gun Regt. $98 £38

An Imperial Russian Crimean period other rank's brass helmet plate of The 15th Regt., the double headed eagle surmounting scroll. $98 £38

A Victorian officer cadet's helmet plate of The Royal Military College. $88 £40

An other rank's pre-1881 Glengarry badge of The 8th Foot. $91 £40

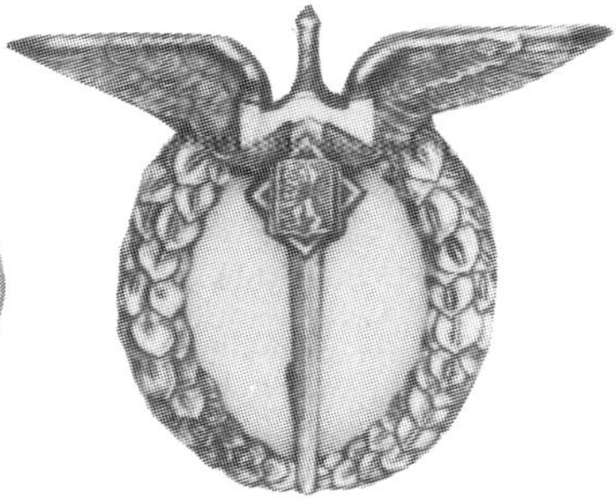

A World War II Free Czech Air Force pilot's badge, in silver, gilt wings to down-pointing sword. $104 £40

An officer's pre-1881 Glengarry badge of The 30th Foot. $91 £40

An officer's pre-1881 Glengarry badge of The 34th Foot. $100 £44

An Imperial Russian Crimean War period other rank's brass helmet plate of The 26th Regt., height 6½in. $120 £50

A Victorian officer's white metal Maltese cross helmet plate of the 2nd Somersetshire Rifle Vols. $115 £50

An 1844 pattern officer's silvered shako badge of The 3rd Royal Lancaster Militia. $125 £55

A pre-1881 officer's gilt and silvered waist belt clasp of The 2nd Somerset Militia. $119 £55

A Victorian officer's gilt, silvered and enamel helmet plate of the R.M.L.I. $132 £60

An officer's 1869 pattern shako badge of The 57th (West Middlesex) Regt. $130 £60

An other rank's pre-1881 Glengarry badge of The 42nd Foot. $137 £60

An officer's gilt 1869 pattern shako badge of The 29th Foot. $137 £60

An officer's silver bonnet badge of The Gordon Highlanders. $140 £60

A good post-1902 officer's gilt, silvered and enamel helmet plate of The Life Guards. $150 £65

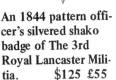

A post-1902 officer's silvered shoulder belt badge of The 4th Bn. The Wiltshire Regt. $169 £65

A Victorian officer's white metal pouch-belt badge of The 5th Punjab Infantry.
$141 £65

A bronze and enamel cap badge of The Household Brigade Officer Cadet Bn. $182 £70

An Indian Army officer's gilt silvered and enamel grenade badge of The Prince of Wales' Own Grenadiers. $154 £70

A Victorian officer's silvered shoulder belt badge of The 2nd Wiltshire Rifle Volunteers. $182 £70

A Victorian officer's silvered helmet plate of The Cambridge University Rifles. $163 £74

A Victorian officer's helmet plate of The Royal Irish Regt.
$165 £75

A Victorian officer's silvered helmet plate of The 1st Glamorgan Rifle Vol. Corps. $156 £75

A Victorian officer's helmet plate of The Gloucestershire Regt.
$165 £75

A silver plaid brooch mounted with a large citrine, hallmarked Edinburgh 1919.
$190 £80

A heavy quality pre-1881 officer's silver glengarry badge of The 93rd(Sutherland Highlanders). $190 £80

An officer's silvered plaid brooch of The 6th V.B. The Gordon Highlanders. $208 £80

A post-1902 officer's helmet plate of The Royal W. Surrey Regt. $190 £80

An officer's silvered helmet plate, circa 1880, of The 2nd Somerset Light Infantry Militia. $190 £80

A post-1902 officer's helmet plate of Alexandria Princess of Wales' Own (Yorkshire) Regt. $190 £80

A post-1902 officer's helmet plate of The Royal West Kent Regt. $190 £80

A Victorian officer's silvered and gilt helmet plate of The 6th Vol. Bn. The Liverpool Regt. $180 £82

An officer's gilt and silvered cap badge of The Public Works Pioneer Bn., The Middlesex Regt. $187 £85

An officer's gilt and silvered 1878 pattern helmet plate of The 6th Foot (185). $200 £85

A pre-1871 officer's silvered gilt and enamel Glengarry badge of The 1st (The Royal) Regt. $195 £90

A Victorian officer's heavy silver Glengarry badge of The Gordon Highlanders, hallmarked London 1895. $234 £90

An officer's gilt silvered and enamel 1866 pattern shako badge of The Royal Marines Light Infantry. $235 £100

A Victorian officer's helmet plate of H.M. Reserve Regt. of Dragoon Guards. $260 £100

An officer's silver plaid brooch of The Cameron Highlanders, hallmarked Edinburgh 1898. $260 £100

An officer's 1878 pattern helmet plate of The 105th (Madras Light Infantry) Regt. $239 £105

A good quality officer's silver plaid brooch of The Gordon Highlanders, hall marked Edinburgh 1926, by T. K. Ebbutt. $240 £105

An officer's helmet plate from a Guard Schutzen shako, plated with enamelled centre. $260 £110

A Victorian officer's gilt and silvered cap badge of The Black Watch. $286 £110

A Victorian officer's silvered helmet plate of The 2nd Vol. Bn.
$260 £110

A Victorian officer's silvered shoulder belt badge of The 2nd V.B. The Wiltshire Regt.
$312 £120

A post-1902 officer's helmet plate of The West Riding Regt.
$312 £120

A post-1902 officer's helmet plate of The Buffs. $312 £120

A Georgian officer's copper gilt helmet plate of The East Regiment of Militia, probably for Regency shako
$275 £125

An officer's white metal 1855 (French) pattern shako badge of The 1st Warwick Militia.
$295 £125

An 1812 pattern gilt universal shako badge, 'GR' cypher device.
$338 £130

A heavy silver plaid brooch of The Argyll and Sutherland Highlanders, hallmarked Edinburgh 1896.
$305 £130

An officer's gilt helmet plate, pre-1902, of The Essex Regt.
$305 £130

A Victorian officer's helmet plate of The 1st Royal Jersey Light Infantry Militia.
$338 £130

A Victorian officer's 1834 pattern gilt helmet plate of The 3rd (Prince of Wales') Dragoon Guards. $282 £130

An other rank's brass 1839 pattern shako badge of The Royal Marines. $320 £135

An officer's gilt silvered and enamel 1879 pattern grenade badge of The Royal Marine Artillery. $330 £140

An officer's hallmarked silver and enamel forage cap badge of The Guards Machine Gun Regt., hallmarked Birmingham 1916.
$364 £140

An 1878-81 pattern officer's helmet plate of The Oxfordshire Militia.
$320 £145

A Victorian officer's gilt silvered and enamelled helmet plate of The Royal Marines Light Infantry.
$355 £150

A post-1908 officer's gilt and silvered helmet plate of The 5th Bn. Somerset Light Infantry.
$380 £160

A Victorian officer's silver plaid brooch of The Highland Light Infantry, hallmarked Birmingham 1898. $358 £165

An officer's gilt 1844 (Albert) pattern shako badge of The 6th Foot. $470 £195

An officer's gilt helmet plate, pre 1902, of The Cameron Highlanders. $456 £210

An officer's gilt and silvered 1845 pattern shako badge of The Royal Marines. $545 £230

An officer's gilt helmet plate of The 80th (Staffordshire) Regt. of Foot, 1878 pattern. $545 £230

An officer's gilt 1816 pattern shako plate of The Royal Marine Artillery. $665 £280

A Bandmaster's badge. Royal Marine Light Infantry, Portsmouth Division, 1876-78. $710 £300

An 1818 pattern officer's gilt helmet plate of The 1st or The King's Dragoon Guards. $572 £275

A Georgian other rank's 1768 pattern mitre cap plate, formed from two thin plates lapped together. $1,193 £550

A Dutch brass mitre cap plate, probably of a grenadier of The Hollandse Garde at The Hague, circa 1750. $1,682 £775

A heavy mid 18th century German Cavalry trooper's breastplate, deep musket ball proof mark, numbered '3', also stamped 'Braun', lugs for belt and shoulder scales. $207 £90

A mid 16th century German or Swiss puffed breastplate, chest embossed with three radial bands. Separate arm cusps and integral and raised neck band pierced for attachment of lining. $356 £155

A German breastplate of bulbous form, circa 1540, distinct medial ridge, slender waist, turned over thickly roped top and separate arm cusps. Two-piece skirt plates. $380 £165

A pair of French 2nd Empire Cuirassier trooper's breast and backplates, the heavy breastplate with brass lugs and studs, engraved inside 'Manufre Rle de Klingenthal Obre 1828. 2T. 1. Lrs. No. 3283'. $391 £180

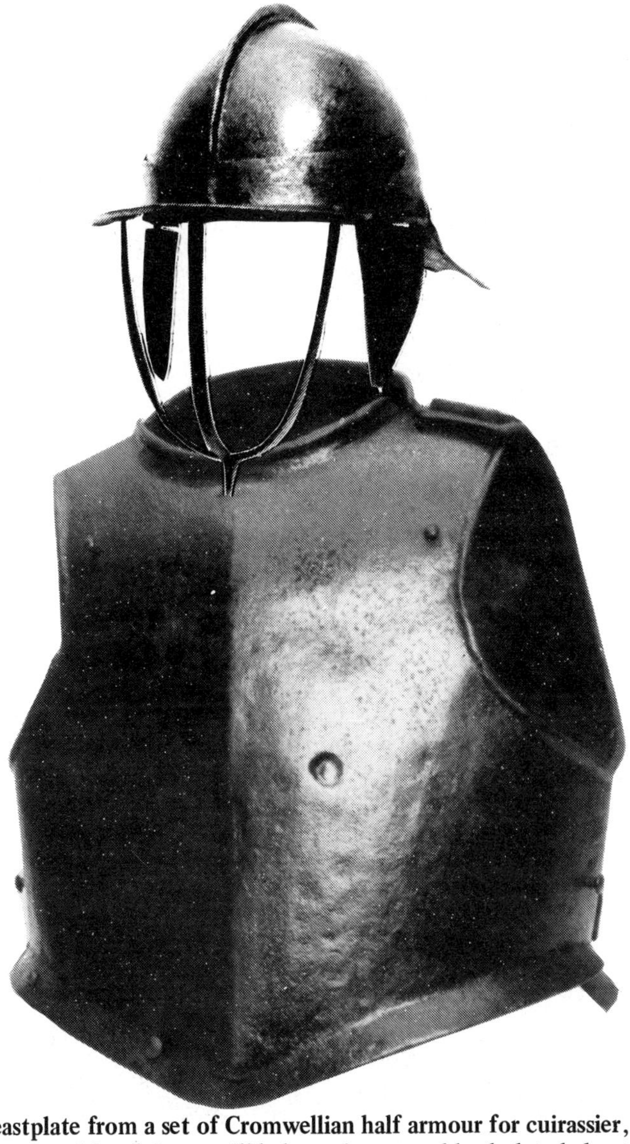

A breastplate from a set of Cromwellian half armour for cuirassier, circa 1640, comprising 'lobster tail' helmet, breast and backplate helmet or 'pot' with two-piece skull pronounced combe, triple bar faceguard on hinged peak. Original ear flaps with rivetted borders. Stepped neckpiece with rivetted turned over border and contemporary repair. Heavy gauge breastplate, musket ball tested, distinct medial ridge. Turned over arm cusps and throat struck with rivet heads for securing shoulder straps and waist strap. Backplate with fine engraved turned over borders. $750 £330

A well made modern model of a brass barrelled field cannon, on four wheeled wooden carriage with steel mounts, barrel 11in., steel sheet shod wheels, brake shoe, elevating screw, overall length 16½in., height 7¼in. $69 £30

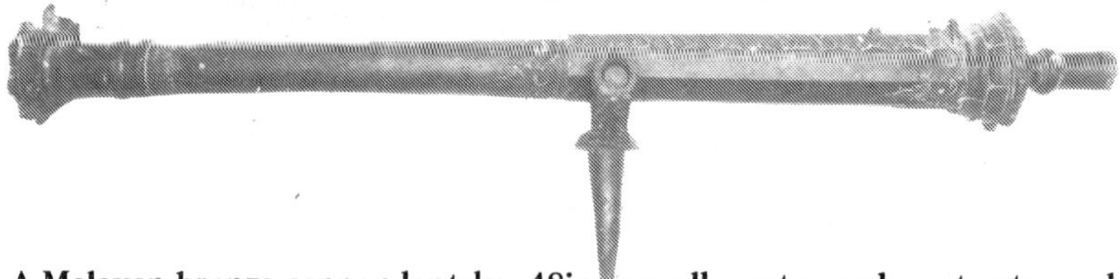

A Malayan bronze cannon lantaka, 48in. overall, part round, part octagonal form with cast swollen muzzle, cast foliate decoration, integral sights, large breech of artichoke form, cylindrical cascabel and swivel support. $484 £200

A model of a British 1816 Mk II field gun, 13in. overall, barrel 6½in., to brass breech-loading breech with interrupted thread locking lever, recoil action to barrel. Brass elevating gear, twin sets on brakes. Composition wheels, steel shod. Protective shield with hinged top and leather accessory boxes. $702 £270

A Victorian scale model of a coastal defence gun, cast iron barrel 32in., with small reinforces, swollen muzzle, integral trunnions and cascabel. On its stepped wooden carriage, with capstan screw elevator and brass rollers to front. Barrel only illustrated. $707 £310

A German cast bronze cannon barrel, 17¾in. overall, turned ribbed reinforces, swollen muzzle chiselled with foliate bands, integral trunnions, chiselled dolphin loops, breech chiselled with crowned crest of half eagle with bar. On stepped wooden carriage with iron trunnion loops. $713 £310

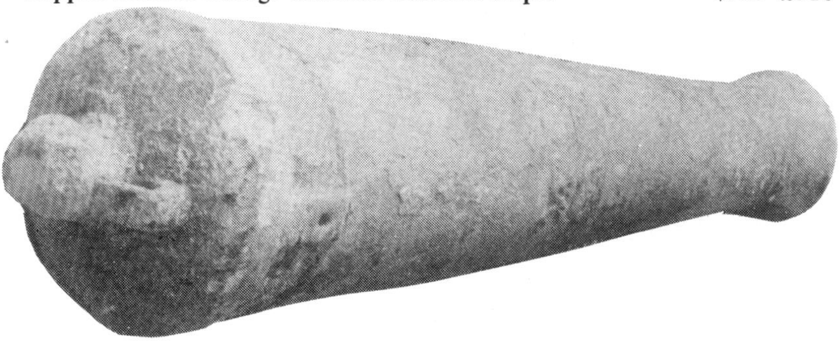

A Georgian six pounder cast iron cannon barrel, 78in., bore 4in. Cast with raised crowned 'GR',cypher, cascabel with integral lifting loop, integral trunnions. $805 £350

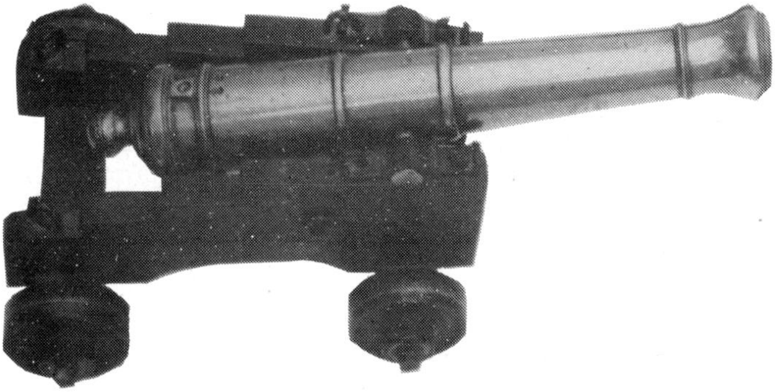

An early 19th century brass signal cannon, reinforced barrel 18in., London proved, integral trunnions and cascabel, swollen muzzle. On its stepped wooden carriage with four bronze wheels and iron fittings. $805 £350

A cast bronze Malayan swivel cannon, lantaka, with octagonal breech and decorated with traditional patterns, overall 34½in. $884 £425

An early 19th century bronze barrelled Naval style cannon, barrel 26in., with four bands, the bore size approximately 1¾in., on its stepped wooden carriage with bronze mounts, wooden wheels and two blocks, overall height 17½in. $1,628 £750

A Georgian Naval cannon 46in. overall with 3in. bore and probably throwing 9lb. shot, three-stage barrel with simple vent, 15in. across trunnions. On a later wheeled wooden carriage with elevating block. $1,736 £800

A Georgian cast iron 'nine-pounder' cannon barrel, 98in. overall, cast with integral raised crowned 'GR' cypher (illustrated). Integral trunnions and cascabel. Swollen muzzle, 4in. (9lb.) bore. $2,470 £950

CAP DISPENSERS

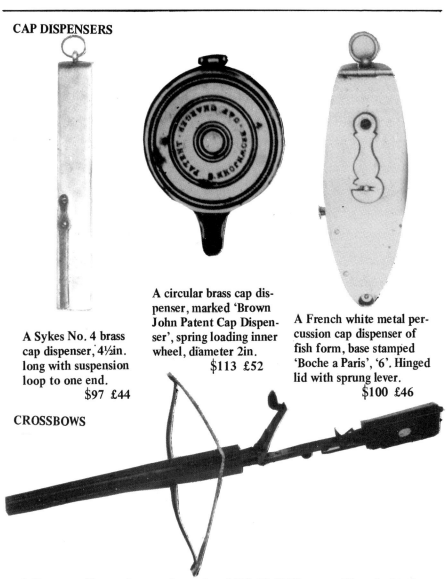

A Sykes No. 4 brass cap dispenser, 4½in. long with suspension loop to one end.
$97 £44

A circular brass cap dispenser, marked 'Brown John Patent Cap Dispenser', spring loading inner wheel, diameter 2in.
$113 £52

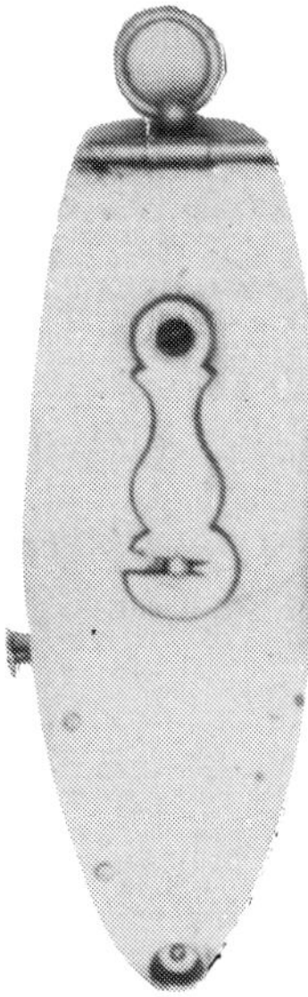

A French white metal percussion cap dispenser of fish form, base stamped 'Boche a Paris', '6'. Hinged lid with sprung lever.
$100 £46

CROSSBOWS

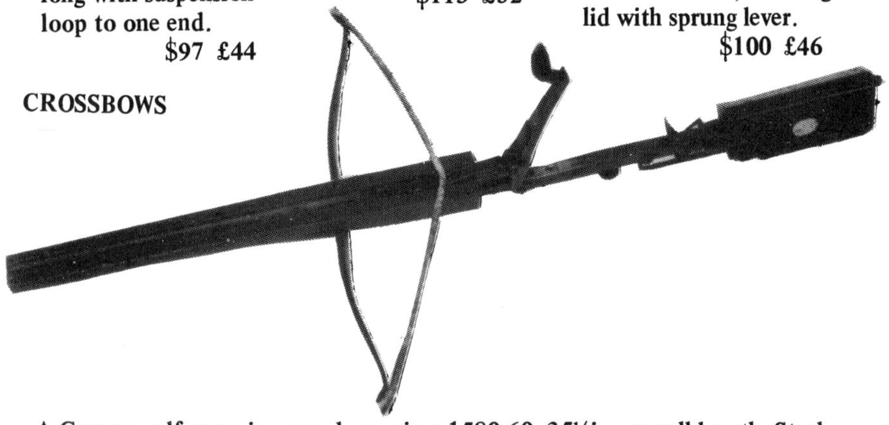

A German self spanning crossbow, circa 1580-60, 35½in. overall length. Steel bow with rounded terminals, 17in. span. Well formed loading lever for spanning, deeply struck with maker's mark of bird in relief beneath initials 'H.S.B.' within squared shield (Stockel f.3133), hemespherical cocking terminal. Set trigger cocked by pressing button beneath frame. Flip-up rearsight, self setting nut. Sprung retaining catch for loading lever. Baluster trigger guard. Carved fruitwood butt, scroll carved cheekpiece inlaid with oval ivory plaque, iron ball finial. Fruitwood bolt, stock, carved channel with inlaid horn fore-tip. Original fibre wood bow-string. $2,052 £900

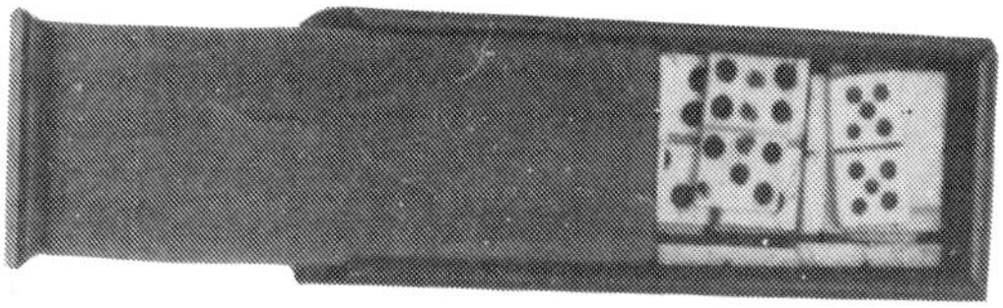

A miniature French Napoleonic prisoner-of-war bone domino set (incomplete 28 dominoes only) in later rectangular wooden box with slide-in lid, 2½ x ¾ x ½in., another similar set (incomplete 32 dominoes) and a small copper box of prisoner-of-war origin the lid engraved 'E' and containing four carved bone dice. $88 £40

A French Napoleonic prisoner-of-war bone domino set of 19 dominoes (incomplete), contained in wooden box in the shape of a shoe, with carved bone sliding lid pierced for cribbage, length 7¼in. $114 £55

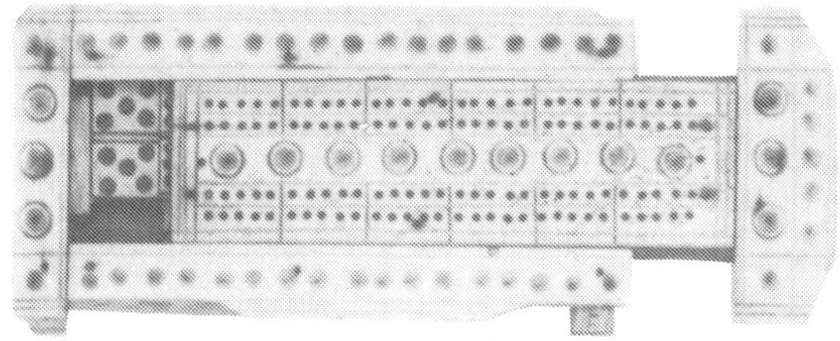

A French Napoleonic prisoner-of-war bone domino set (incomplete 21 dominoes only) in their bone rectangular box on four feet, incised with small, circular and large semi-circular patterns, the sliding lid pierced with holes for cribbage or scoring, 5 x 2½ x 1¾in. $132 £60

A French Napoleonic prisoner-of-war carved bone domino set (complete), contained in rectangular bone box, the sliding lid with pierced panels for scoring, single geometric pattern decoration, 4½ x 1¼ x 1¼in. $143 £65

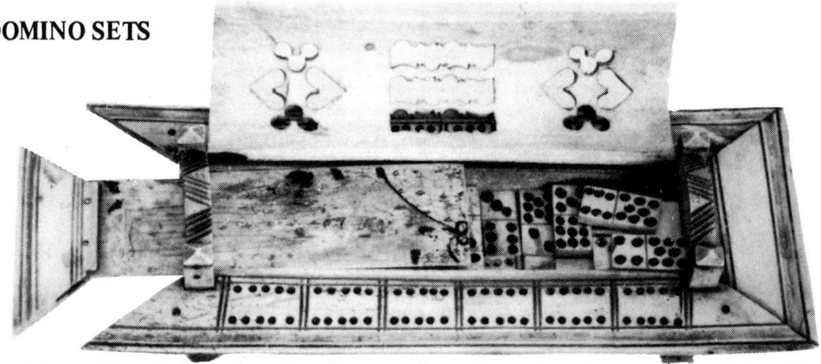

A large French Napoleonic prisoner-of-war bone domino set, containing 55 dominoes (probably not complete), in their rectangular carved bone box, 9½ x 4 x 2in. $156 £75

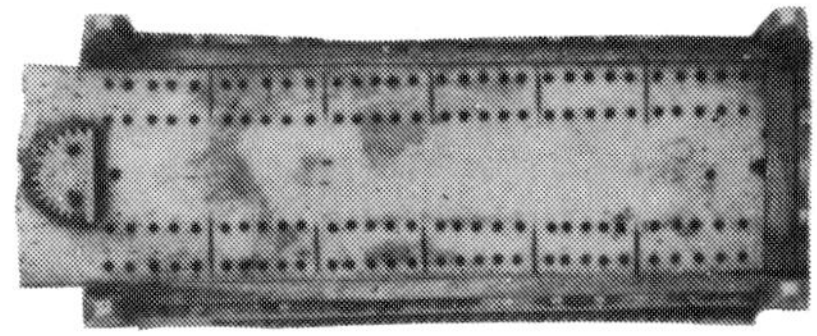

A French Napoleonic prisoner-of-war bone domino set (complete), in its rectangular bone box of 'bed' form, with two pillar mounts at each end, with slide-in lid pierced for cribbage or scoring, 5¼ x 1¾ x 2in. $176 £80

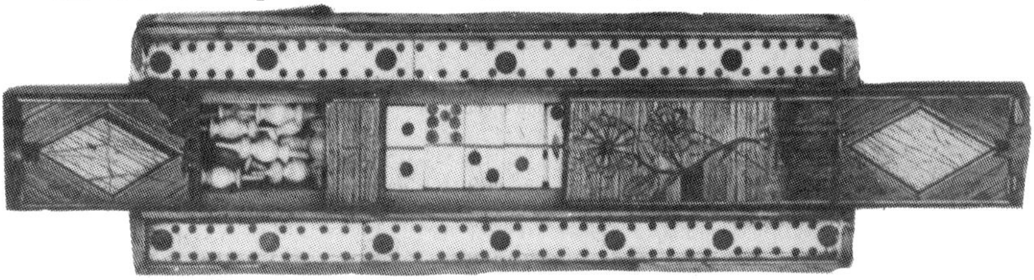

A French Napoleonic prisoner-of-war bone carved domino set (complete, a few contemporary replacements), contained in its rectangular wooden box, sliding lid with floral device, 8¾ x 3 x 1½in. $176 £80

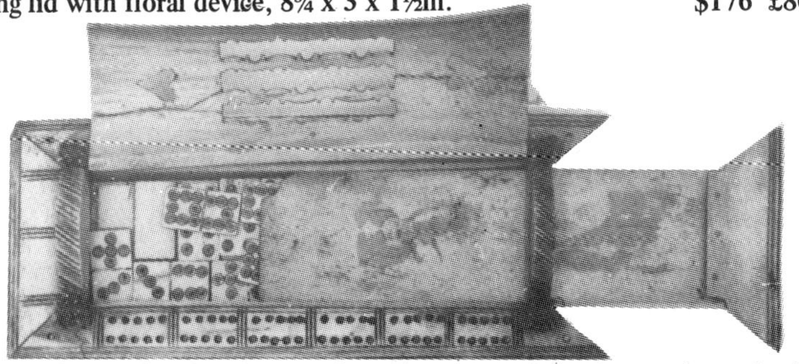

A French Napoleonic prisoner-of-war bone carved domino set (complete), in its carved bone rectangular box, the edges pierced with holes for scoring, slide-in bone lid, domed detachable lid, 8 x 3¾ x 3in. $221 £85

A French Napoleonic prisoner-of-war bone carved domino set, 50 dominoes in all, contained in rectangular bone box, sliding lid and sides decorated with geometric patterns, wooden base, 4½ x 11½ x 1in. $228 £105

A good French Napoleonic P.O.W. Bone Domino Set (complete, a few bone dominoes contemporary replacements), in their rectangular bone box with slide lid and incised top edges, decorated overall with incised geometric patterns, 5½in. X 1¾in. X 1¾in. $239 £115

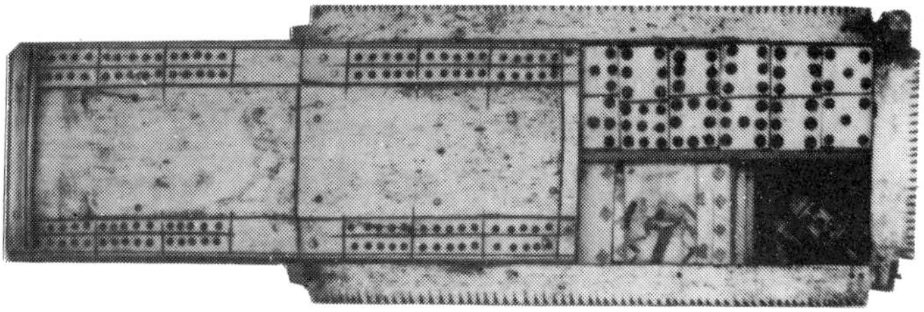

A French Napoleonic prisoner-of-war carved bone combined domino and card set (cards and dominoes complete), the thin bone cards hand-painted, size of cards approximately 1¼ x ¾in., 8 x 3¾ x 3in. $390 £150

A French Napoleonic prisoner-of-war bone combined domino and playing card set, the dominoes complete, the thin bone cards hand-painted, 3¼ x 1¼in., contained in rectangular bone double compartment box, 6½ x 3 x 1½in.
$364 £175

A painted military wooden side-drum of The West Yorkshire Regiment, by Potter, battle honours to Suvla and regimental badge. $341 £155

A heavy bronze bust of Prince Arthur of Connaught, 14in., signed 'H. Hampton 1921', on wooden pedestal. $156 £60

A Nazi bronze bust head of Hitler, signed 'Ferdinand Liebermann', on square marble base, height overall 16½in. $1,122 £510

A pair of Victorian model suits of armour, fully articulated with wooden figures inside the breastplates, tassets and close helmets etched with foliate patterns, height 26in., on wooden plinths. $597 £275

A Nazi D.A.F. district banner, large laid-on D.A.F. emblem on red panel with silver tassel fringes to edges, the top left-hand corner with laid-on rectangular cloth panel of brown, bordered with blue, worked with the District 'Langwedel' in white thread, 42 x 54in., plated hanging rings, mounted on a wooden haft surmounted with restored brass D.A.F. emblem, overall length 8ft.6in. $242 £110

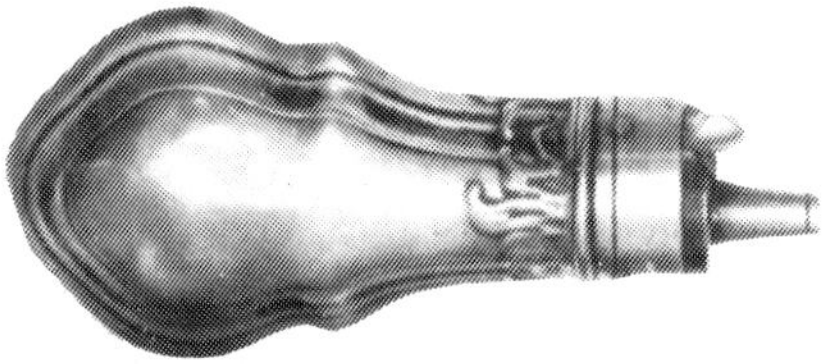

A small copper bodied pistol sized common topped powder flask, body with ribbed edge and floral embossed neck, brass charger unit. $31 £14

A steel bodied, patent topped gun sized powder flask, plain, brass adjustable charger stamped 'Hawksley', the body with white metal band covering seam. $39 £18

A copper bodied common topped gun sized powder flask, plain, adjustable brass charger. $43 £20

A Colonial carved nut powder flask, the surface well carved with crossed Union Jacks, pewter charger nozzle, overall 6½in. $46 £20

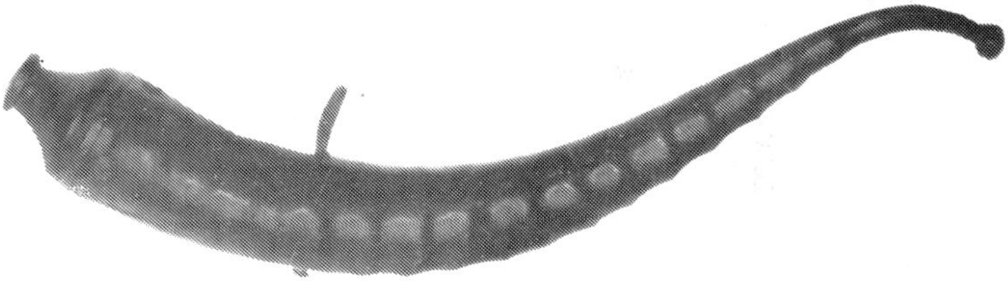

An 18th century Indian flintlock black buck horn priming flask, 11in. overall and of recurved form tapering to a bulbous finial, the horn charger secured to body by means of four horn dowels and of turned ovoid shape, old iron suspension ring at centre of gravity. $57 £26

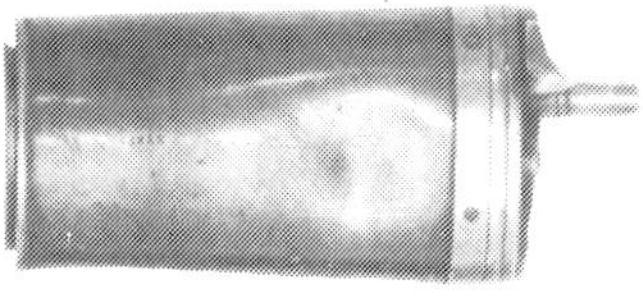

A copper bodied common topped three-way pistol powder flask, ovoid plain body with screw lidded base trap, the top mounts with unadjustable charger. $57 £26

A leather bodied brass patent topped shot-bag, suitable for cased percussion sporting gun. Sykes patent charger unit with spring retained spoon charger. $57 £26

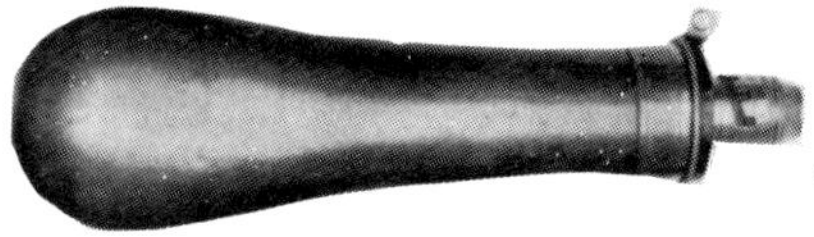

A copper bodied patent topped gun sized powder flask, plain, adjustable charger unit stamped 'Bartram & Co.'. $61 £28

A flattened, curved, translucent Continental powder horn, plain gilt brass patent charger, 8½in. $61 £28

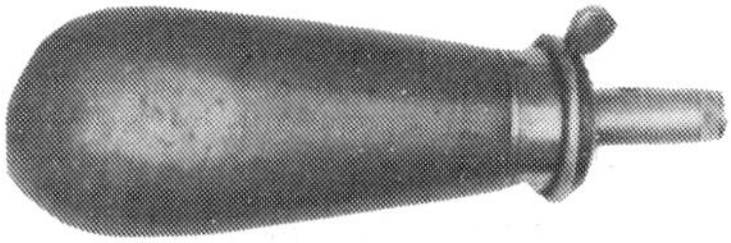

A copper bodied patent topped pistol size powder flask, plain bag-shaped body, adjustable brass charger unit stamped 'Sykes Patent'. $84 £38

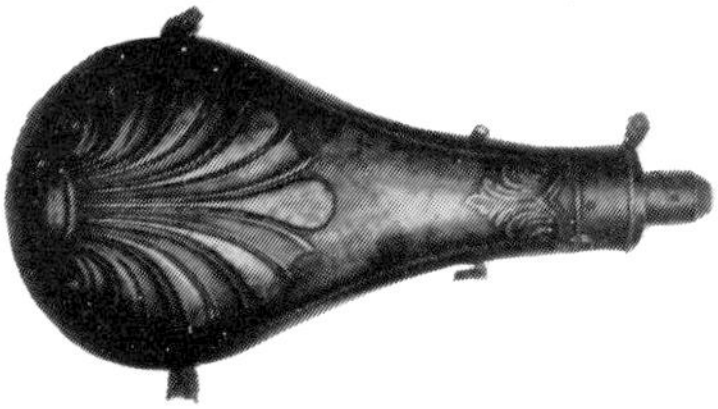

A large shell embossed copper powder flask, 10in., brass top stamped 'G. & J. W. Hawksley Sheffield', charger graduated from 2¼ to 3 drams. $91 £42

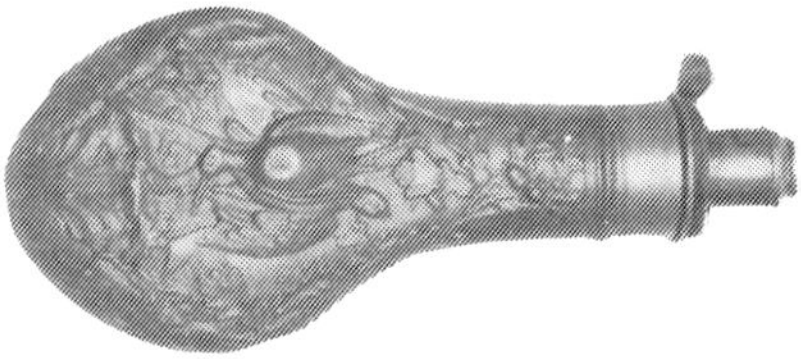

A copper bodied patent topped gun sized powder flask by Hawksley, adjustable brass charger unit with external spring (replaced). $97 £44

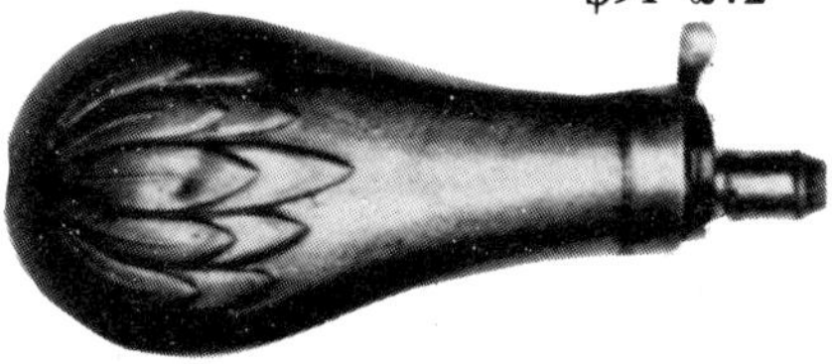

A copper bodied common topped pistol powder flask, Shell & Bush, adjustable charger unit stamped 'Dixon & Sons'. $100 £44

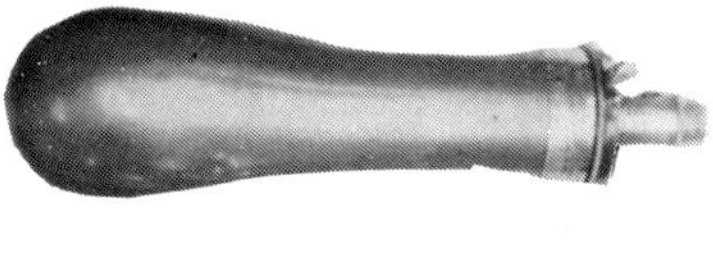

A copper bodied patent topped rifle or large pistol sized powder flask, the adjustable brass charger unit stamped 'Sykes Patent'. $95 £44

A late 18th century Artillery gunner's priming horn flask, turned brass nozzle, with spring lever operated cut-off, round base plate, 6½in. $100 £45

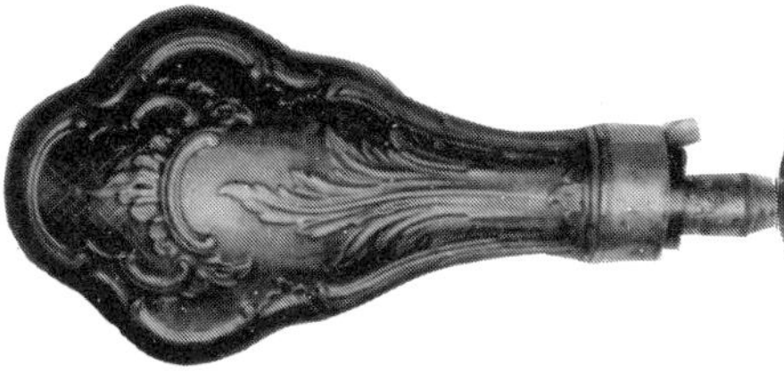

A copper bodied common topped gun sized powder flask, brass adjustable charger unit stamped 'G. & J. W. Hawksley', the body of modified violin shape. $108 £50

An old horn bodied gun sized powder flask, the body with old painted picture of sea captain titled 'Capt'n Porter'. $108 £50

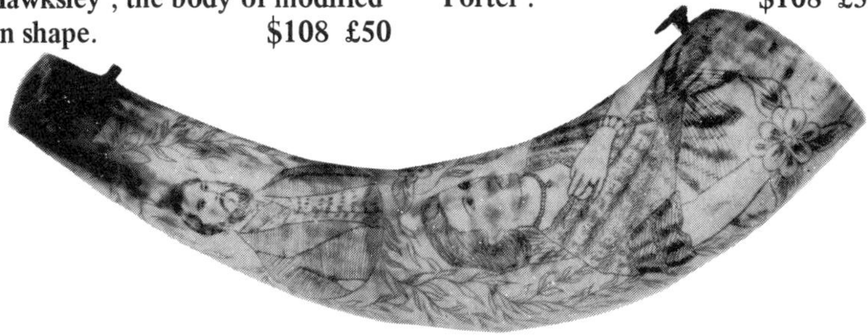

A 19th century powder horn carved with Victorian Colonial lady and gentleman, amid foliage, 12in. $104 £50

A horn bodied, patent topped, Continental gun sized powder flask, brass charger unit, the body ribbed with brass strap. $108 £50

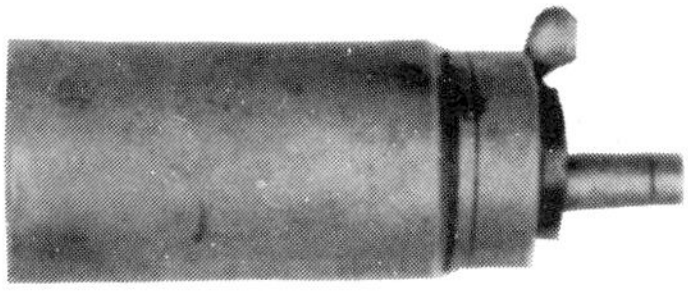

A plain brass bodied common topped pistol powder flask, of the type cased with U.S. pepperbox revolvers, unadjustable charger unit, plain cylindrical body. $108 £50

A three-way pistol powder flask, plain brass fixed common charger unit, the base fitted with two compartments with hinged lids. $114 £50

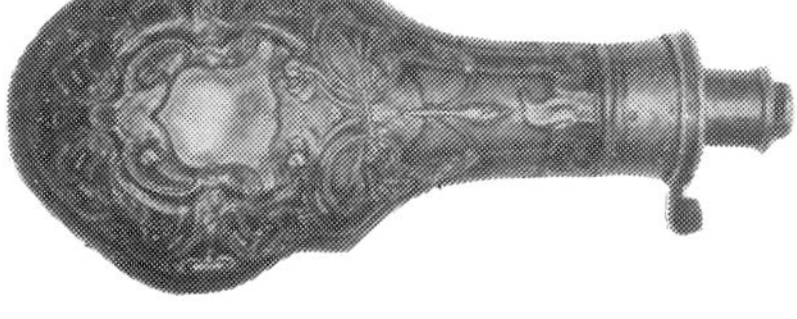

A copper bodied, brass patent topped gun sized powder flask. Adjustable charger unit stamped 'Hawksley', embossed waisted body. $118 £54

A copper bodied common topped gun sized powder flask, brass adjustable charger unit stamped 'Batty', the body fitted with two suspension rings. $119 £55

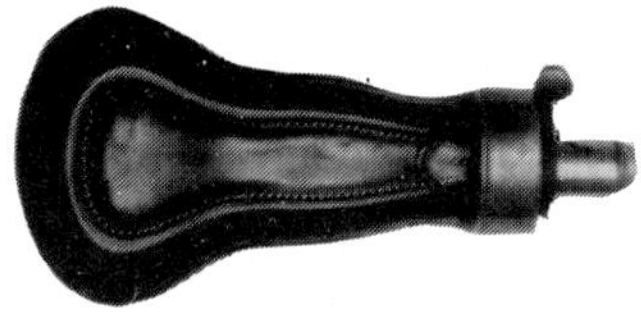

A copper bodied brass common topped powder flask, unmarked adjustable charger. $119 £55

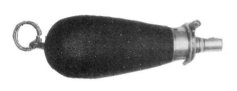

A leather covered, patent topped pistol powder flask, white metal adjustable charger stamped 'Sykes Patent'. $132 £60

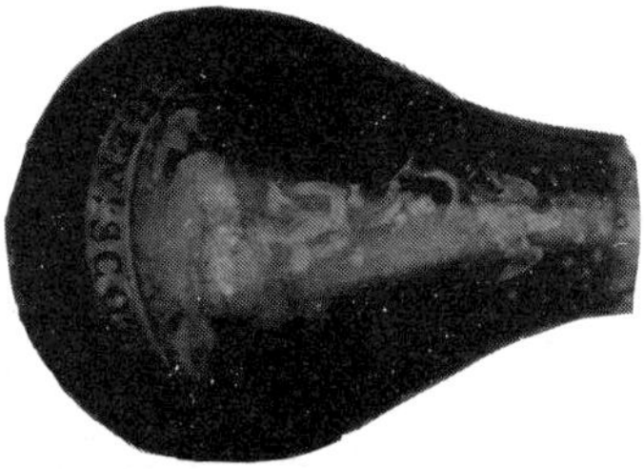

An old horn bodied powder flask, painted with mounted general titled 'Genl. Scott' and surmounted by U.S. Eagle and 21 stars. $130 £60

A composite copper bodied gun sized powder flask with Hawksley's patent visible charger unit, charge sizes 2 to 3 drams. $130 £60

A copper bodied brass common topped gun sized powder flask, plain charger graduated in grains to 55, the brass base mount with sliding covered trap for caps. $130 £60

A copper powder flask, 'fluted', gilt charger unit. $130 £60

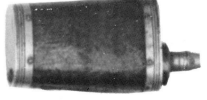

A small brass red leather covered three-way flask, 3¼in. overall, common top, hinged ball cover and cap or flint compartment lid. $132 £60

A copper bodied patent topped gun sized powder flask, Dog & Hunter, brass adjustable charger unit stamped 'Dixon & Sons Sheffield'. $129 £62

A copper bodied, patent topped French gun sized powder flask, the body embossed '6 Onces T.N.N. a Paris'. $163 £75

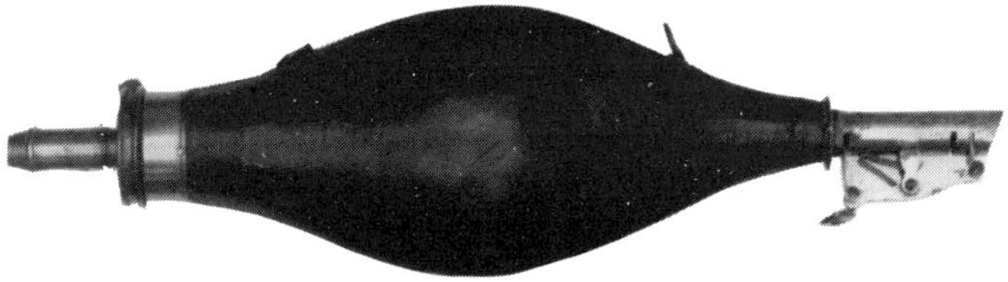

A leather covered double ended sporting gun powder and shot flask combination, brass patent topped charger unit to powder flask, adjustable spout, the shot cut-off stamped 'AM-Flack & Cap Co', the body with two suspension rings. $163 £75

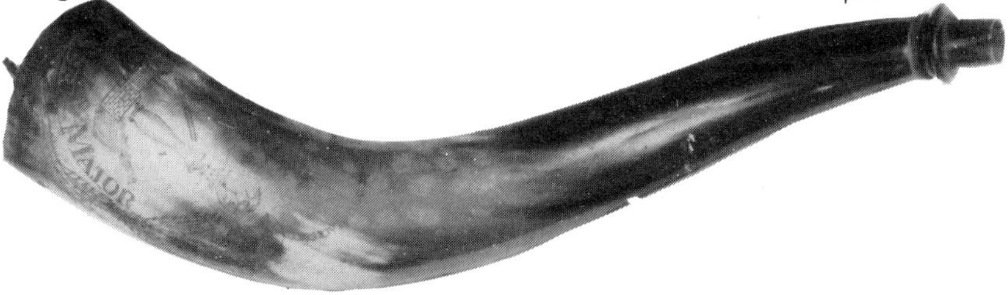

An early 19th century cowhorn powder horn, with contemporary engraving of three-masted man-of-war, thistles, motto 'Nemo Me Impune Lacessit' and 'Alexr. Johnston, Serj Major F.M.', wooden base, 19in. $174 £80

An old Scottish flattened powder horn, engraved with Celtic scrolls and shield with letters 'T.R.' and dated '1690', 10in. wooden base plate. $184 £85

A copper bodied, common topped pistol powder flask for the Robbins & Lawrence pepperbox revolver, brass unadjustable charger unit. $184 £85

A Bohemian carved stag horn powder flask, 9in. overall. Steel top with sprung lever charger and suspension ring. $434 £200

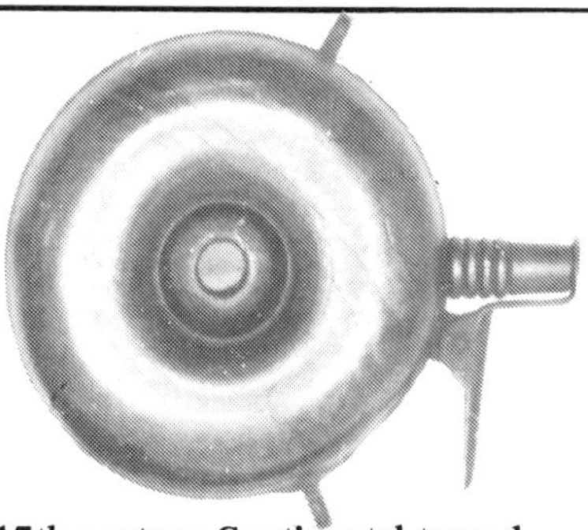

A 17th century Continental turned wooden priming flask, 3in. diam., turned wooden nozzle, sprung brass charger lever, two iron hanging rings. $440 £200

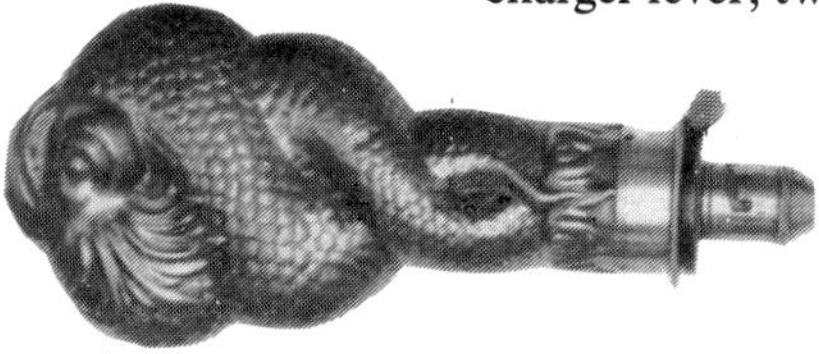

A copper bodied gun sized patent topped powder flask, 'Entwined Dolphin', brass charger unit stamped 'Bartram & Co., Nimrod', graduated charger spout. $553 £255

An engraved powder horn of the period of the war of 1812, brass base plate with ring, brass band mount, oval brass plaque, 22in. $564 £260

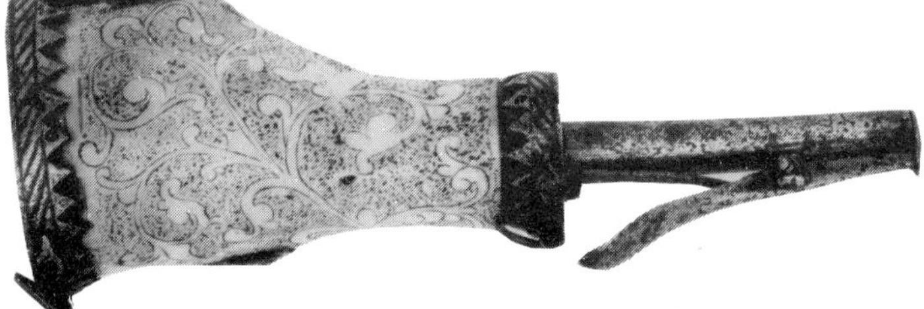

A steel mounted engraved bone powder flask, circa 1600, overall height 9½in., the body of one-piece polished bone engraved with well designed foliate pattern, iron charger and base plate, sprung nozzle, two suspension rings. $651 £300

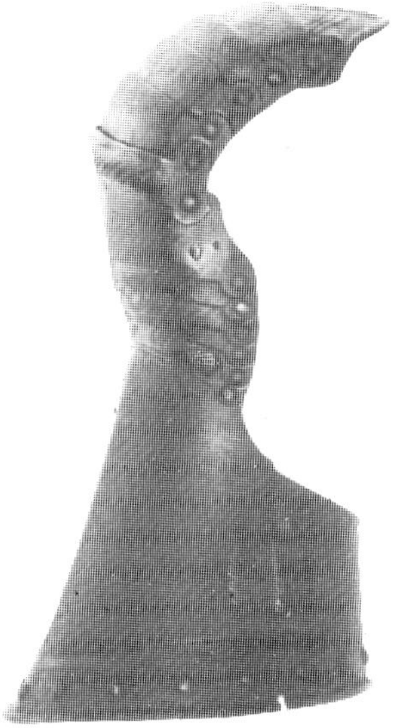

A German articulated mitten gauntlet, circa 1525, 12in., roped, embossed studded border to cuff, decorated iron hinge, twelve plate articulations. $304 £140

A South German or N. Italian articulated gauntlet, circa 1510, 10in., roped, embossed brass studded border to cuff. Brass studded nine plate articulated back of hand. $304 £140

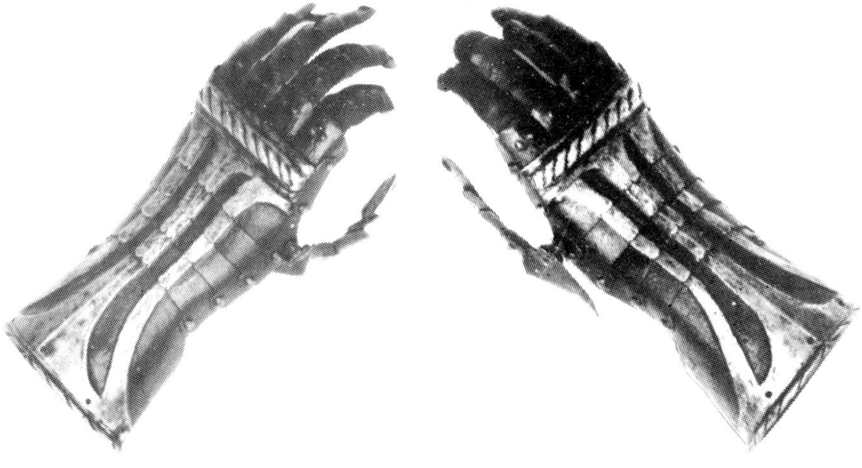

A pair of German articulated gauntlets, circa 1580, from a 'black and white' suit of armour, roped cuffs, four-plate articulated backs of hand with three raised white bands and scalloped edges. $686 £330

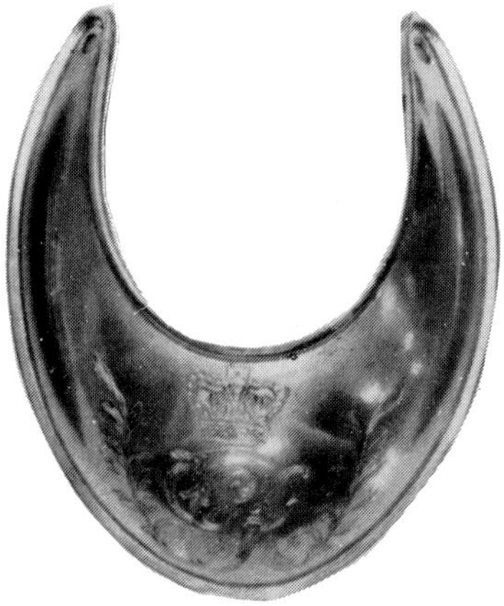

A Georgian officer's 'Universal' pattern copper gilt gorget, engraved with Royal 'GR' cypher within wreath. $125 £60

A Georgian officer's 'Universal' pattern copper gilt gorget. $182 £70

A Nazi political leader's gorget, bronzed finish, large Nazi Eagle, oak leaf borders, with hanging chains of square links of alternating Nazi Eagles and Swastikas, the gorget lugs stamped 'RZM M.1/14' and 'M.1/17'. $174 £80

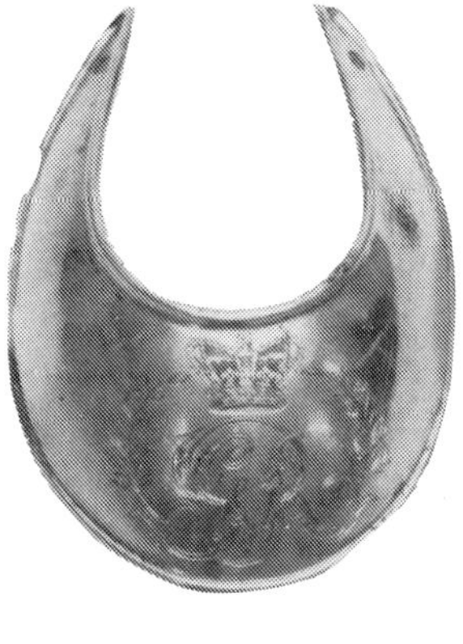

A Georgian officer's gilt 'Universal' pattern gorget, engraved with crown and 'GR' within wreath. $215 £90

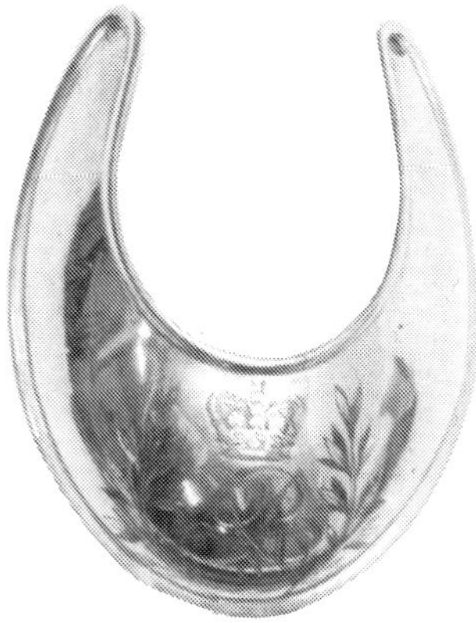

An officer's gorget of the British Auxiliary Legion in Spain, circa 1835, engraved with crown over 'IR2' (Queen Isabella II) within wreath. Together with buff leather shoulder belt and plate. $319 £145

A Georgian officer's copper gilt gorget, circa 1780, wide neck pattern, the ends with embossed decoration, engraved with 'GR' and pre-1801 Royal Arms. $330 £150

A Georgian officer's copper gilt gorget of The Royal Marines, engraved with 1801-16 Royal Arms above fouled anchor in shield within wreath. $416 £160

GORGETS

A Georgian officer's silver gorget of The Staffordshire Militia, heavily embossed design of escutcheon bearing castle, lion and two knots, surmounted by crown with wreath and rays, engraved G111R. $590 £250

A Georgian officer's copper gilt gorget of The 1st Regt. (probably Royal Scots), engraved with pre-1801 Royal Arms. $615 £260

HAMMERS

An Indian war hammer, iron head with long beak, 7in., decorated overall with silver inlaid patterns, on leather bound haft with iron grip decorated en suite with the head, length 26in. $161 £70

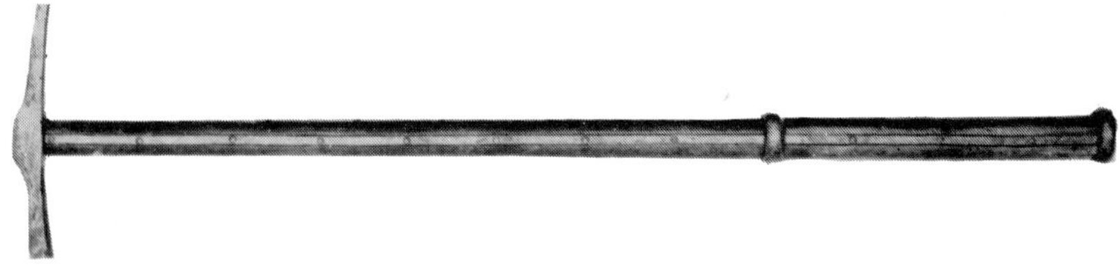

A 16th century mid-European war hammer, iron head, with long beak, 10½in., the head struck with clover type mark, wooden haft with iron straps running for entire length, two iron bands, overall 29in. $434 £200

A Swiss Infantry shako, black felt body, leather top, peaks and head-band bearing white metal numeral '34', small orange and white ball tuft, maker's name 'Henri Tanner, Bienne' and dated 1914. $114 £55

A Victorian Indian officer's tropical helmet, white cloth, silk puggaree with gilt tassel fringe at left, gilt edge binding and gilt embroidery to rounded front and back peaks, gilt rosette on top, white leather backed chin-chain. $156 £60

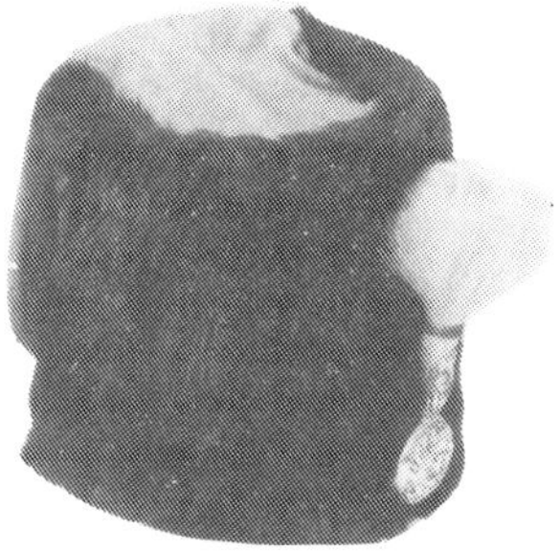

A Victorian Volunteer Artillery other rank's busby, scarlet bag, white metal general pattern grenade holder and white horsehair plume, chin-strap. $169 £65

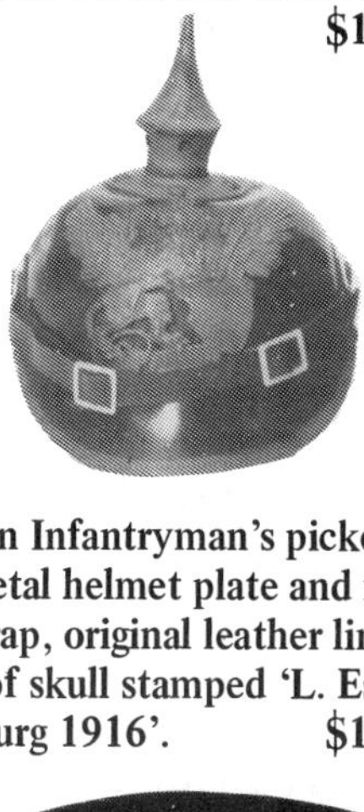

A Baden Infantryman's pickelhaube, grey metal helmet plate and mounts, chin-strap, original leather lining, the inside of skull stamped 'L. Estelmann Strassburg 1916'. $154 £70

A Bavarian Engineer officer's pickel-haube, plated helmet plate, fluted spike and mounts, lion mask chinscale sidemounts, original silk lining. Bavarian metal cockade to left side of lion mask. $165 £75

An officer's 1869 pattern shako of The Dorset Militia, silver lace trimmings, silvered badge, mounts and velvet backed chinchain. $175 £80

A Victorian cadet's grey cloth spiked helmet, white metal badge bearing 'A.C.F.' within wreath, mounts and fawn leather back chinchain. $200 £85

A post-1902 officer's blue cloth spiked helmet of The Royal Berkshire Regt., gilt mounts, badge and velvet backed chinchain. $200 £85

A cabasset, circa 1600, formed in one-piece, pear-stalk finial to crown. $206 £95

A black felt helmet of The Ashford Kent Volunteer Fire Brigade, circa 1840, raised crest, black patent leather band, broad rim. $247 £95

A Victorian officer's blue cloth spiked helmet of The 1st Volunteer Bn. Royal Lancaster Regt., silvered badge and mounts. $225 £95

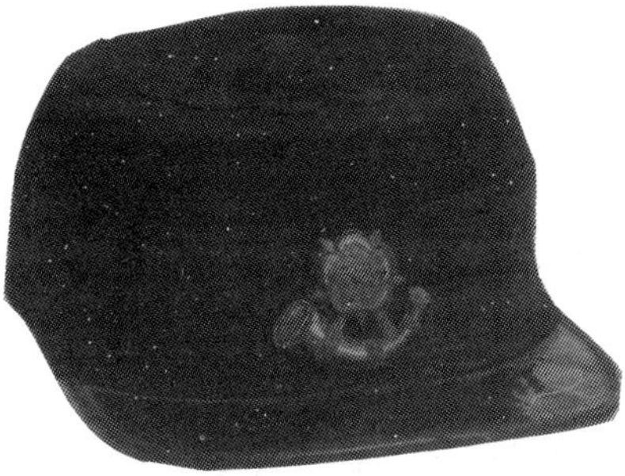

An officer's 1855 pattern peaked patrol cap of The 16th (Harrogate) West Yorks. Rifle Vols. (The Claro Rifles), blue cloth, black lace headband. $208 £100

A Prussian other rank's pickelhaube of the Eisenbahn (Railways) Regt. No. 3, German silver helmet plate and mounts, leather, brass mounted chin-strap. $235 £100

A Bavarian infantryman's ersatz (Pressed Felt) pickelhaube, gilt lacquered helmet plate and mounts, both cockades, leather chin-strap and lining. $235 £100

A Victorian other rank's cloth spiked helmet of The 1st Vol. Bn. Yorkshire Regt., white metal badge, mounts and leather backed chinchain. $225 £105

A Victorian officer's shako of The Cameronians, darkened white metal badge and mounts, black plume in holder. $273 £105

A Victorian officer's blue cloth ball topped helmet of The Artillery Volunteers, silvered badge, top mount and ball, velvet backed chinchain and ear rosettes. $230 £110

A Victorian officer's blue cloth spiked helmet of The 1st Vol. Bn. West Yorks. Regt., silvered mounts, badge and chinchain. $230 £110

An 1862 pattern Swiss Infantry shako, black beaver with leather top, peak and head band with white metal No. '115' in front surmounted by tin, red, white and blue rosette, with plated loop to top, white 'shaving brush' plume. $229 £110

A Victorian officer's green cloth spiked helmet of The Duke of Cornwall's Light Infantry, gilt mounts, badge and velvet backed chinchain. $229 £115

A Baden Infantryman's pickelhaube, brass helmet plate and mounts, both cockades, leather chin-strap and lining, inside of skull with traces of maker's stamp and dated '1916'. $264 £120

A Victorian Royal Artillery officer's blue cloth ball topped helmet, gilt mounts, badge and velvet backed chinchain. $274 £120

An Indo-Persian 'demon mask' helmet kula khud, two curved horns to crown, with small spear blade spike and sliding nasal bar, camail of split links.

$270 £125

A Prussian erstaz (Pressed Felt) Jager Rifleman's shako, grey metal helmet plate, leather chin-strap, one cockade front central, cloth cockade, leather lining. $275 £125

A post-1902 Highland Light Infantry officer's shako, with green ball tuft, in a tin case. $325 £125

A Prussian Jager Zu Pferd other rank's steel helmet, grey painted eagle helmet plate and mounts, both cockades, leather chin-strap, leather lining, studded 'lobster-tail' neckguard. $325 £125

A cabaset formed from one piece, circa 1600, turned over brims, pierced for ornament rivets (now missing), pear stalk finial to medial ridge. $310 £130

An officer's blue cloth spiked helmet of The 1st Vol. Bn. The Leicestershire Regt., silvered mounts, including velvet backed chinchain, silvered and gilt badge. $280 £130

A Victorian officer's blue cloth ball topped helmet of The 2nd W. Yorks Artillery Vols., silvered badge, mounts and velvet backed chinchain. $338 £130

A cabasset formed from one-piece, circa 1600, pear-stalk finial to medial ridge, turned over brims, pierced for ornamental rivets. $310 £130

A post-1902 officer's blue cloth spiked helmet of The Royal Warwickshire Regt., gilt mounts and velvet backed chinchain. $310 £130

A post-1902 officer's blue cloth spiked helmet of Alexandra Princess of Wales' Own (Yorkshire) Regt., gilt mounts and fawn leather backed chinchain. $310 £130

A Victorian officer's blue cloth spiked helmet of The East Kent Regt. (The Buffs), gilt helmet plate and mounts, including velvet backed chinchain. $338 £130

A Victorian officer's green cloth spiked helmet of The 24th Middlesex Rifle Vols, darkened WM badge, beaded link chinchain. $330 £130

A Victorian officer's green cloth spiked helmet of The 5th (The Haytor) Vol. Bn. The Devonshire Regt., silvered mounts, badge and velvet backed chin-chain. $280 £135

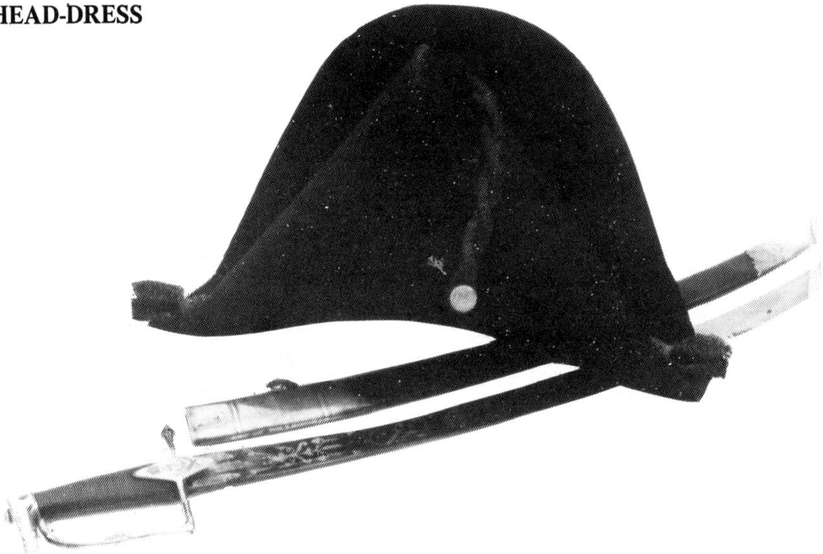

An 1827 pattern Naval officer's cocked hat of black beaver, fan 10in., front 8½in., edge bound with black 1¼in leaf pattern silk braid, black rosette with single gilt bullion twisted loop and button bearing crowned fouled anchor. $319 £140

Also a Georgian Naval officer's sword, circa 1812, curved blade, 28½in., diamond shaped langets, flattened knucklebow, boat-shaped pommel, in its leather scabbard with three copper mounts. $1,482 £650

A Victorian officer cadet's blue cloth spiked helmet of The Royal Military College, gilt and enamel badge, gilt mounts and chinchain. $364 £140

A Victorian officer's blue cloth spiked helmet of The 1st Vol. Bn. The South Lancashire Regt., silvered and gilt badge, silvered mounts and velvet backed chinchain, in its tin box. $300 £145

A Victorian officer's blue cloth helmet of The 1st Vol. Bn. The Welsh Regt., silvered badge, mounts and velvet backed chinchains. $330 £150

A mid 17th century Cromwellian helmet, fluted skull, adjustable nasal bar, iron studded decoration, ear flaps, four lames neckguard. $325 £150

A fireman's brass plated helmet of a Devon Fire Brigade, raised comb embossed with dragons, white metal chinchains, leather lining. $442 £170

An officer's green cloth spiked helmet of The 5th West York Militia, early type with rounded front and rear peaks, silvered badge, mounts and velvet backed chinchain. $442 £170

A Victorian officer's green cloth helmet of The Oxfordshire Light Infantry, gilt and silvered badge, gilt mounts and velvet backed chinchain. $385 £175

An Indo-Persian helmet, kula khud, skull intricately pierced overall with arabesque and geometric designs, adjustable nasal bar, twin plume holders and top spike. $415 £175

An Imperial German Infantry N.C.O's. pickelhaube of The 89th Mecklenburg Grenadiers, helmet plate of Mecklenburg-Schwerin, plated helmet plate, mounts and chinscales. $410 £180

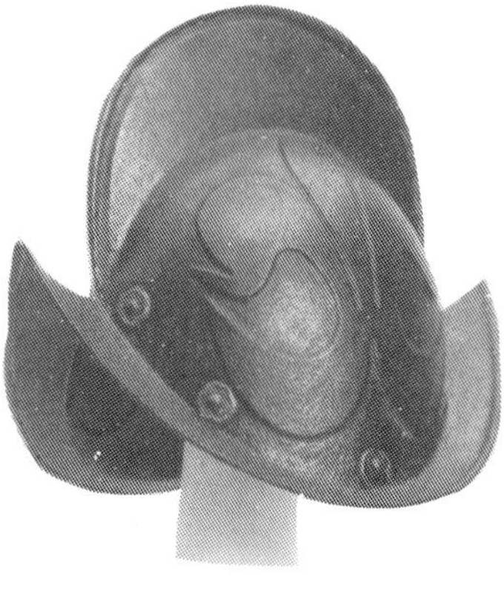

A 17th century German 'Town Guard' morion, roped comb and rim, the sides embossed with fleur-de-lys, brass rosettes. $410 £180

A mid 19th century Bavarian raupenhelm of black leather, black wool comb, leather chin-strap issuing from brass lion's head bosses, metal Bavarian cockade to left of skull, brass helmet plate with crown above 'M' (Maximillian II) on star background, leather lining, neckguard dated '1854'. $407 £185

An Indo-Persian 'demon mask' kula khud, double horned, central spike, two plume holders, stylised face, camail of split links. $418 £190

A post-1902 trooper's lance cap of The 16th Lancers, complete with black horse-hair plume, holder and leather backed chinchain, date inside '1903'.
$410 £190

An 1855 pattern officer's shako of The 87th Prince of Wales' Own Irish Fusiliers, gilt grenade badge.
$450 £200

A Victorian officer's 1855 pattern shako of The 82nd (Prince of Wales' Volunteers) Regt. of Foot, complete with gilt badge, red and white tufted ball plume and leather chin-strap.
$450 £200

A Victorian officer's green cloth spiked helmet of The 1st Cumberland Rifle Vol. Corps., early style with rounded front and back peaks, silvered badge, mounts and chinchain.
$450 £200

An officer's busby of The Queen's Own Oxfordshire Hussars, crimson bag, silver trim and cockade, set of cap lines, beaded link chinchain with crimson backing, with its white over crimson feather plume, in its' tin case.

$440 £200

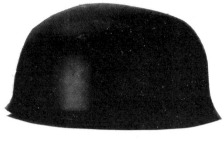

An old leather helmet of similar appearance to a Cromwellian 'lobster-tail' helmet, the domed skull formed in two halves with covered seam, pointed peak and large neckguard to below shoulder level. $445 £205

A Nazi paratrooper's helmet, shield state colours and Luftwaffe Eagle transfer badges, leather lining stamped 'Kopfweite Gr 59 Stahlhaube Nr 71' and traces of maker 'Karl Holst, Berlin'. $460 £210

A pressed red felt Norwich Union Fire Chief's helmet, applied cast gilt mounts, including comb ornament and laurel band. Silver bullion trimmed brim, brass rosettes with fabric liner. $546 £210

A Victorian officer's green cloth spiked helmet of The 1st (East) Regt., The Royal Guernsey Light Infantry early type with rounded back and front peaks. $462 £210

A Victorian officer's helmet of The Fife Mounted Rifles, leather skull, white metal and brass 'star' mounts, and badge with motto scroll and 'FMR', white horse-hair plume, velvet backed chinchain. $545 £230

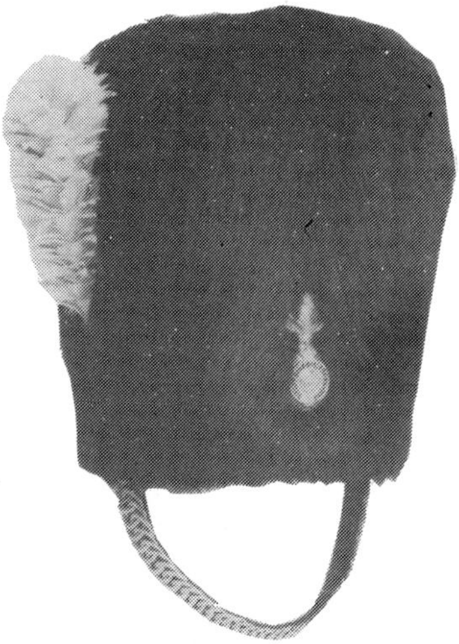

A post-1902 officer's bearskin of The Royal Fusiliers, gilt, silvered and enamel grenade badge, velvet backed chinchain. $570 £240

A post-1902 officer's black cocked hat of The Royal Company of Archers, bearing bullion embroidered badge and gilt wire tassels, complete with green cock's feather plume; also a fine pair of gilt bullion and green cloth full dress epaulettes, bearing woven gilt thistles and bullion badge, the title 'Royal Scotch Archers, King's Bodyguard'. Both in their tin cases. $542 £250

An N.C.O's. white metal helmet of The Montgomeryshire Imperial Yeomanry, complete with crimson leather backed chinchain, white horse-hair plume with gilt rosette. $550 £250

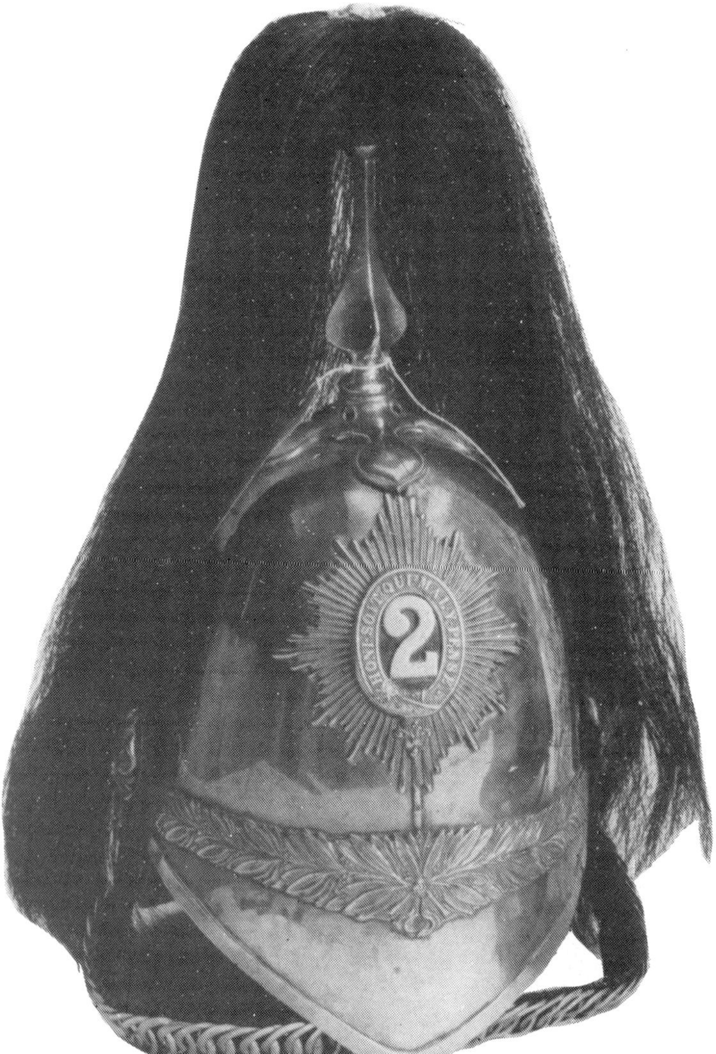

An other rank's brass 1871 pattern helmet of The 2nd Dragoon Guards (Queen's Bays), with its black horse-hair plume and leather backed chinchain. $550 £250

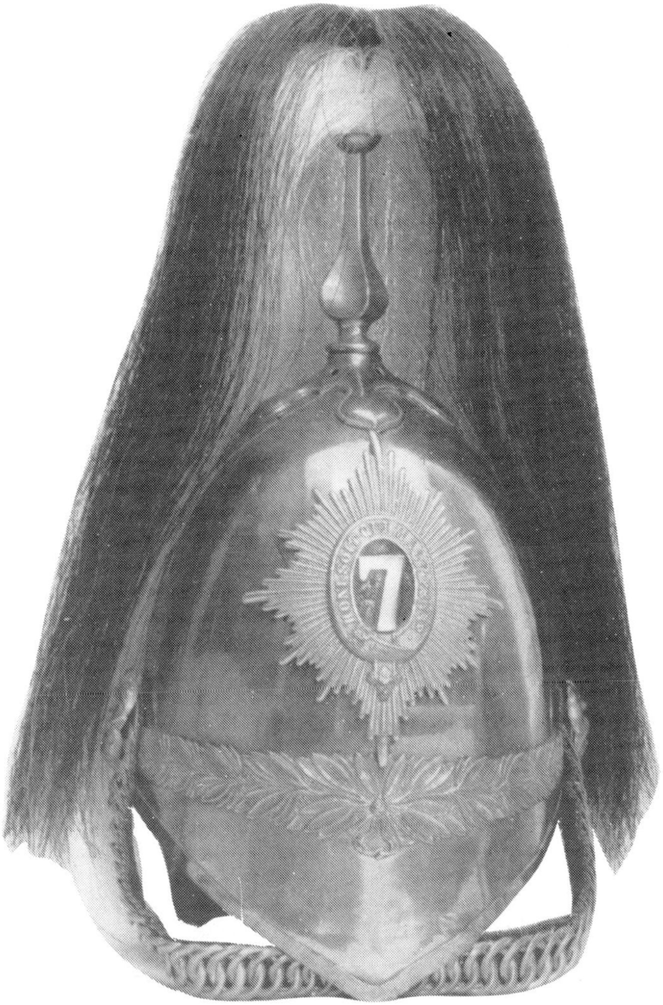

An other rank's brass 1871 pattern helmet of The 7th Dragoon Guards, white metal and brass badge, leather backed graduated link chinchain, black and white horse-hair plume with brass rosette. $595 £260

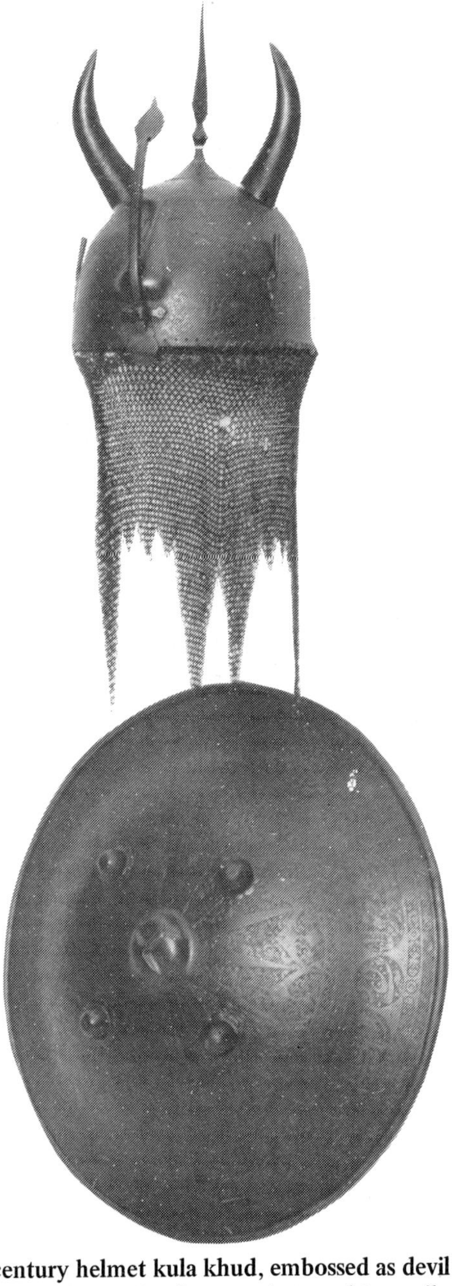

An Indian 19th century helmet kula khud, embossed as devil's mask, with twin horns, fixed nasal bar, twin plume sockets and top spike. Mail camail. Including a matching shield dhal. $700 £270

An Imperial Austrian Dragoon trooper's helmet, black painted metal skull with gilt Imperial double-headed Eagle helmet plate, gilt high comb and leather lining. $640 £280

A Victorian officer's Albert pattern helmet of The Suffolk Yeomanry Cavalry, gilt skull and mounts, white horse-hair plume with rosette. $600 £290

An other rank's helmet of The 5th Dragoon Guards, complete with white over red horse-hair plume with rosette and leather backed chinchain. $806 £310

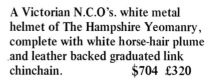

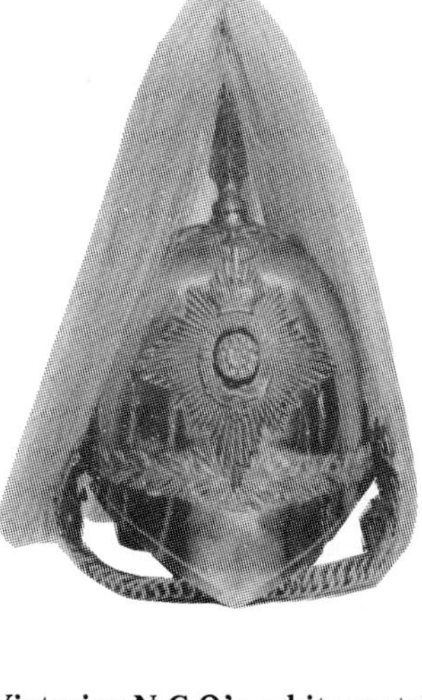

A Victorian N.C.O's. white metal helmet of The Hampshire Yeomanry, complete with white horse-hair plume and leather backed graduated link chinchain. $704 £320

A Victorian officer's helmet of The Lothian and Berwickshire Yeomanry Cavalry, silvered skull with gilt mounts and badge, white horse-hair plume with an incorrect chinchain. $752 £330

A rare Prussian Colonial officer's pickelhaube of the East Asia Brigade of Infantry, C.1900-14, gilt spike, helmet plate and chinscales, grey felt covering to leather skull. $785 £330

The Naval cocked hat, epaulettes and belt, with sword slings, of Admiral of The Fleet J. D. Kelly G.C.V.O., G.C.B. (1871-1936). Gilt lace trim to hat with bullion wire festoon and post-1902 button. Full dress gilt bullion epaulettes bearing silvered 'George V' and 'Edward VIII' crowned cyphers, gilt wire tassels. Also a full dress braided waistbelt. $760 £350

A Victorian officer's helmet of The 4th (Royal Irish) Dragoon Guards, gilt, silvered and enamel badge, chin-chain, white horse-hair plume in ball holder, gilt rosette, in its tin case. $730 £350

An officer's Albert pattern helmet, circa 1860, of The Queen's Own Royal Yeomanry (Staffordshire), black japanned skull, gilt and silvered badge, silvered mounts, velvet backed chinchain, black horse-hair plume. $868 £400

A Victorian officer's white metal helmet of The Fife Light Horse, silvered and gilt badge and motto scroll, leather backed chinchain, white horse-hair plume. $902 £410

A Prussian other rank's late 19th century mitre cap of The 1st Guard Regiment of Foot, scrolled motto 'Semper Talis'. $890 £410

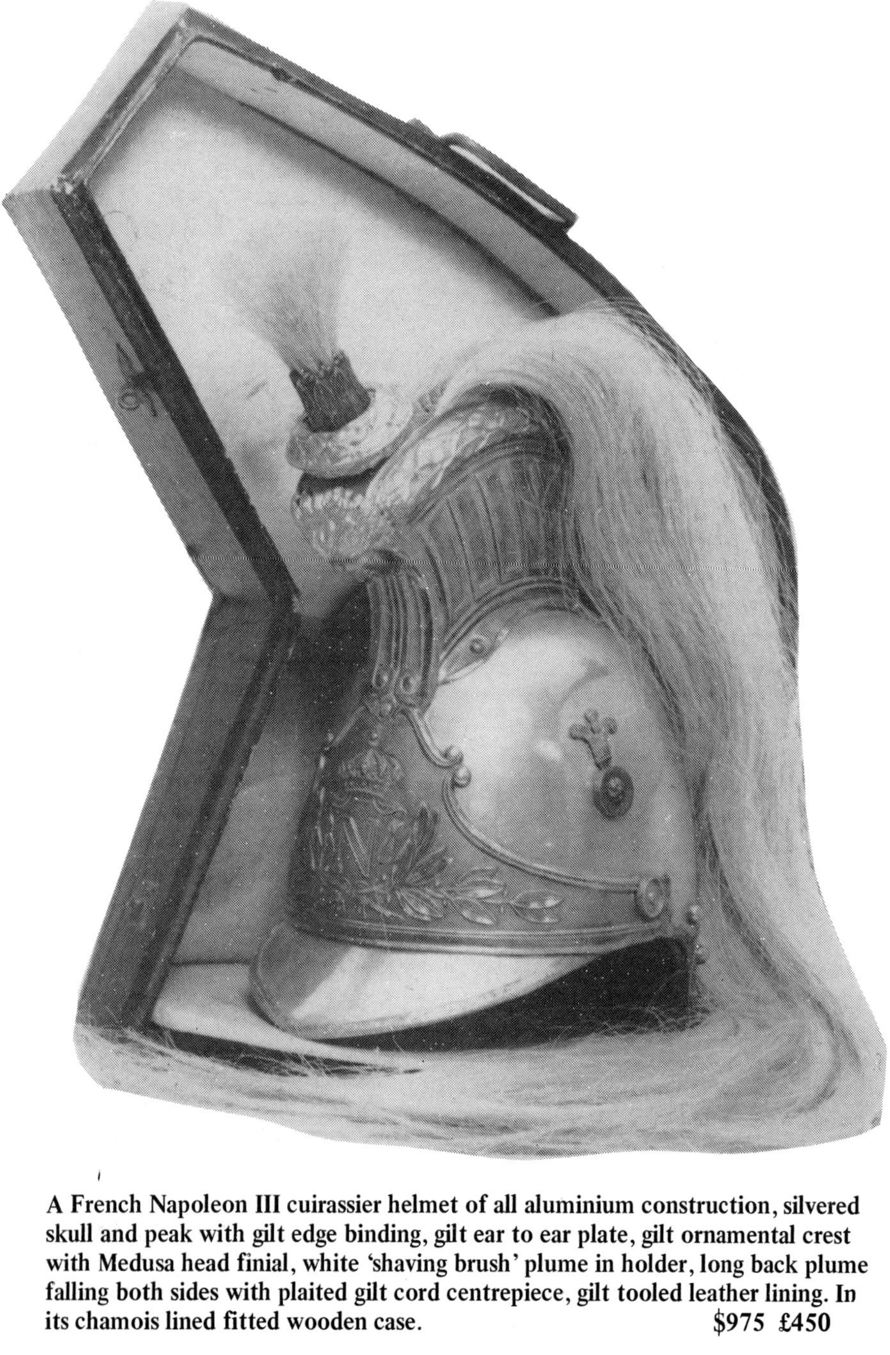

A French Napoleon III cuirassier helmet of all aluminium construction, silvered skull and peak with gilt edge binding, gilt ear to ear plate, gilt ornamental crest with Medusa head finial, white 'shaving brush' plume in holder, long back plume falling both sides with plaited gilt cord centrepiece, gilt tooled leather lining. In its chamois lined fitted wooden case. $975 £450

An Imperial German officer's shako of The Guard Jager Bn., plated Guard star helmet plate, with gilt motto, enamelled wreath and Eagle centre, Prussian National cockade, gilt chinscales, original silk lining. $1,100 £500

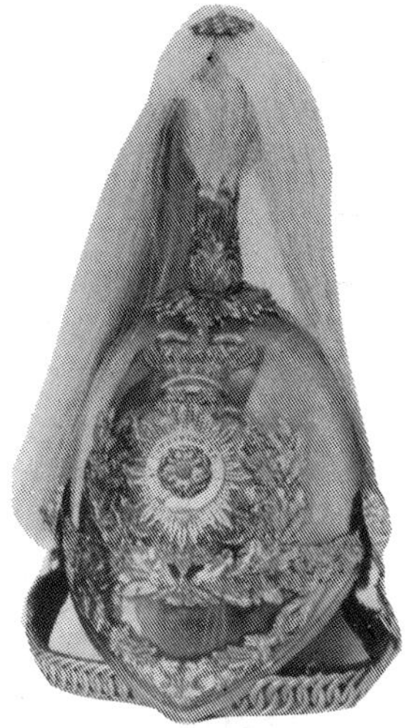

A Victorian officer's Albert pattern helmet of The 2nd West Yorkshire Yeomanry, silvered skull, gilt mounts and wreath, gilt and silvered badge, velvet backed chinchain, white horsehair plume with rosette. $1,300 £500

An officer's helmet of The Queen's Own Regt., Worcestershire Yeomanry, the pattern adopted in 1850, leather skull with plated mounts including peak binding. $1,085 £500

A Prussian Garde cuirassier steel helmet, German silver Garde star with black enamelled Eagle and wreath, two large cockades, plain metal, leather backed chinscales, with brass terminals. $1,365 £525

An officer's Albert pattern helmet of The Duke of Lancaster's Own Yeomanry, circa 1863, black japanned skull, fine gilt badge of crowned escutcheon bearing three lions, within wreath, gilt mounts including crimson leather backed chin-chain, silk lining, black horse-hair plume, with gilt rosette. $1,250 £575

A Victorian officer's 1871 pattern helmet of The Duke of Lancaster's Own Yeomanry, silvered skull with gilt wreath, badge of crowned escutcheon bearing three lions, plume mount, red leather backed chinchain and ear rosettes, white horse-hair plume with white metal rose finial. $1,300 £600

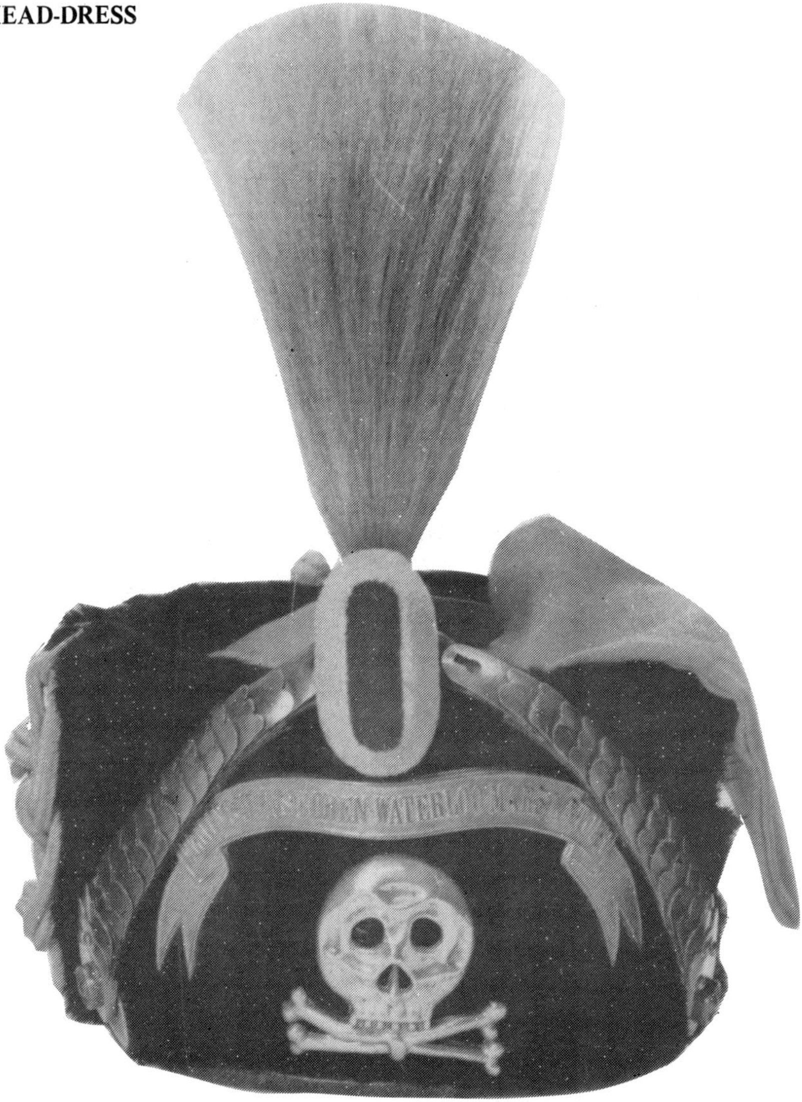

An Imperial German other rank's Hussar's sealskin busby of The 17th (Brunswick) Hussars, scarlet bag, white metal skull and crossbones badge with gilt brass scroll above with Battle Honours 'Peninsula, Sicilien, Waterloo, Mars La Tour', brass chinscales, Prussian State cockade, white horse-hair parade plume, yellow looped cords to crown, original leather lining. $1,465 £675

An officer's lance cap of The 12th (Prince of Wales' Royal) Lancers, circa 1857, black patent leather skull and peak with gilt (rubbed) lace and embroidery, scarlet cloth top measuring 7½in. square, with gilt cord trimmings, good gilt and silvered badge incorporating Battle Honours for 'Egypt, Peninsula, Waterloo and Sevastopol', slide behind boss for plume entering through the top, velvet backed gilt chinchain and lion head bosses. $1,820 £700

An officer's 1871 pattern helmet of The 6th Dragoon Guards (Carabiniers), gilt skull with gilt mounts, leather backed chinchain and ear rosettes, silvered and gilt badge, white horse-hair plume with gilt rose finial. $1,520 £700

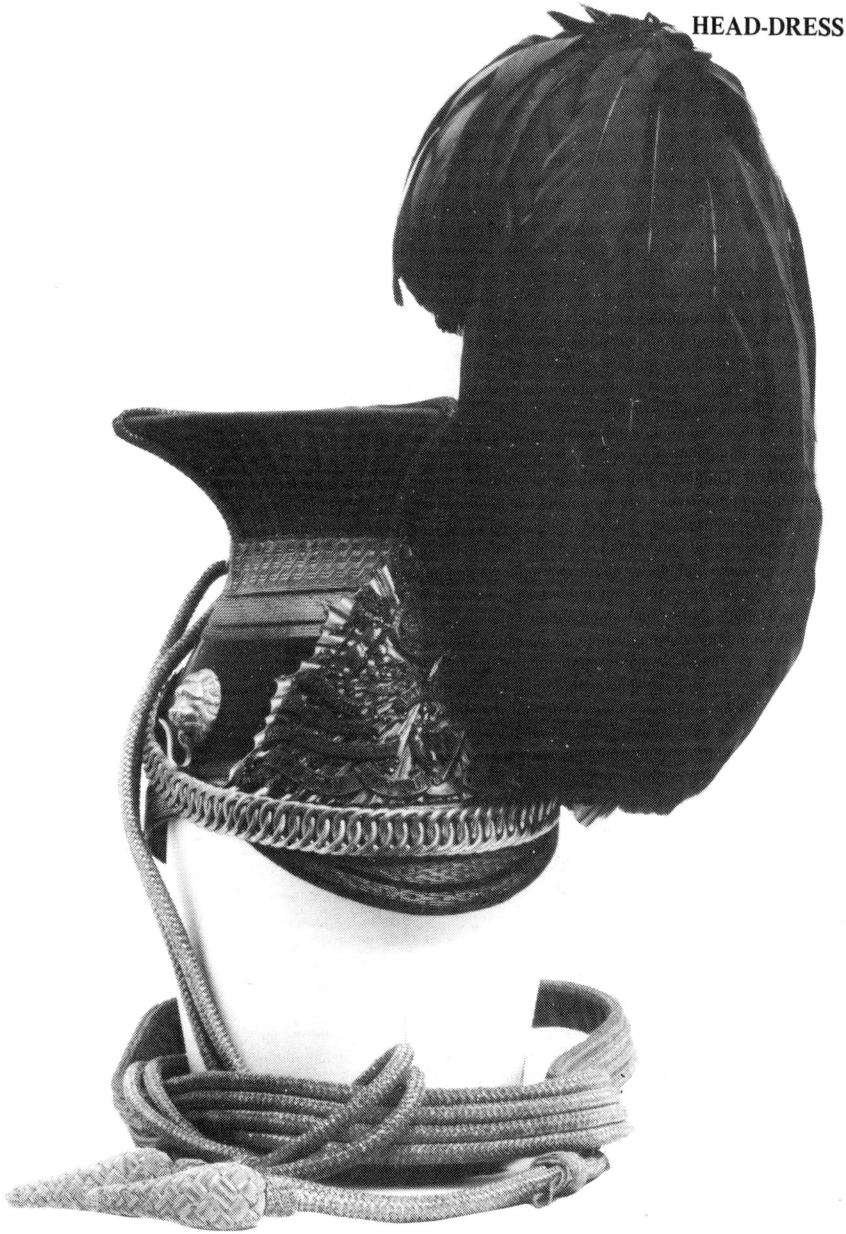

A post-1902 officer's lance cap of The 5th (Royal Irish) Lancers, patent leather skull and peak with gilt embroidery and lace, scarlet cloth top with gilt cord trimmings, gilt and silvered plate with Battle Honours to 'South Africa 1899-1902', gilt chinchain and lion head mounts, green cock's feather plume in gilt holder.

$1,520 £700

A 17th century English funerary helmet with original painted wooden crest, two-piece skull from a close helmet with engraved border lines, the rest assembled for funerary use included securing spike, close gorget, bevor and visor. Wooden crest in the form of a lion's paw holding broken lance upon roped base. $1,630 £750

A late Georgian officer's Regency shaped shako of The Royal Midlothian Yeomanry Cavalry, black beaver on felt body with leather peak and top, and soft turn-down neck-flap, band of 2in. silver lace around the top and ½in. lace loop to front with silver embroidered rosette and central silvered button (detached) bearing crown within 'R.M.L.C.', velvet backed, silver plated copper chinscales with quatrefoil ear bosses. $1,950 £900

An officer's 1871 pattern helmet of The 3rd (Prince of Wales') Dragoon Guards, gilt skull with gilt mounts, red leather backed chinchain and ear rosettes, good silvered, gilt and enamelled badge, black over red horse-hair plume with gilt rose finial, officer's name in ink on lining 'Davies'. $1,950 £900

An officer's Light Dragoon pattern helmet, circa 1820, of The 1st Regiment, Suffolk Yeomanry Cavalry, leather skull and peak with silver plated mounts including high ornamental crest with Medusa head finial, star badge bearing 'GR' within garter and motto, also silver plated peak binding and velvet backed scalloped chinscales with quatrefoil ear bosses. Black pleated silk turban with chains and rear rosette bearing silver bullion tassel.

$3,690 £1,700

HELMET PLATE CENTRES

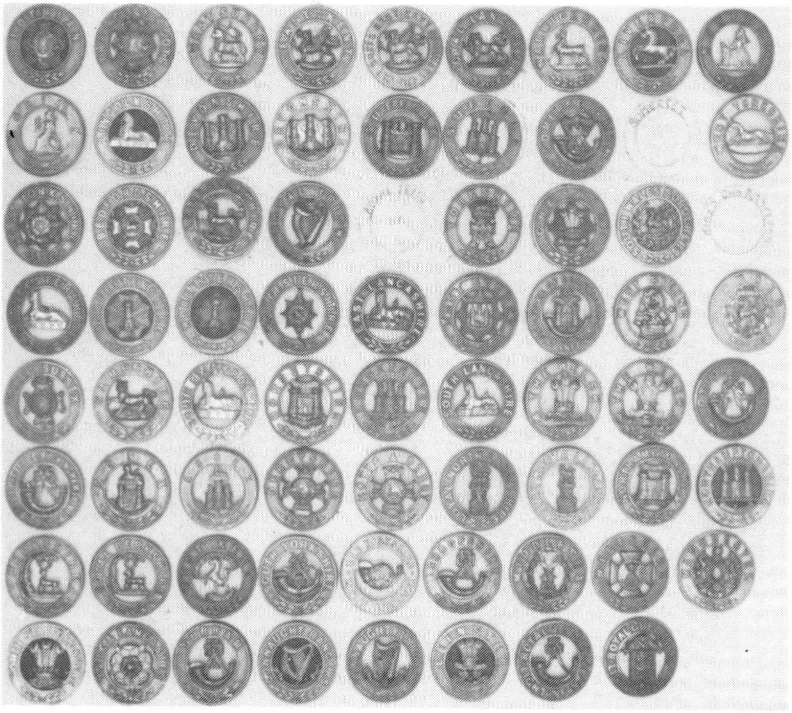

A collection of helmet plate centres, 1881-1914, an almost complete collection of 71, mounted on a card, with a Victorian and a post-1902 helmet plate, includes the three varieties Royal Scots and Worcester, and two varieties Buffs, Norfolk, Devon, Border, Suffolk, E. Yorks, Dorset, Welsh, Oxford, Essex, Derby, L. N. Lancs, Northants, Berks, Connaught (missing are Somerset, post-1902 R. Irish and King's Own Borderers). $1,144 £440

A carved wood painted Malayan kris stand, in the form of a standing grotesque demon, with hand extended to support kris, on carved integral base, overall height 15½in. $110 £50

A carved wood painted Malayan kris stand, in the form of a grotesque standing figure, on round base, height 22in. $159 £70

A carved wood painted Malayan kris stand, in the form of a kneeling demon, on base, height 14½in. $166 £80

A painted wooden Malayan kris stand, in the form of a trunked, seated demon, with winged head-dress, height 16in. $176 £80

A painted, carved wood Malayan kris stand in the form of a standing dancer wearing demon mask, on rounded base, overall height 22in. $194 £85

A carved wood, painted Malayan kris stand, in the form of a standing grotesque demon, on base, height 21in. $177 £85

A carved wood, painted Malayan kris stand for two kris, in the form of a grotesque female elephant headed demon, seated on throne, with double arms, height 20in. $226 £104

A large carved, painted, wooden Malayan kris stand in the form of a grotesque squatting demon, height 21in. $228 £105

Anglo-Boer medal 1899-1902 (Burger F. J. A. Bester). $105 £45

Canada General Service: 1 bar Fenian Raid 1866 (Cpl. E. H. Moran, 22nd Oxford R). $166 £80

China 1857, 2 bars Taku Forts 1860, Pekin 1860 (Sapper John Williams, 23rd C. Royal Engineers). $175 £80

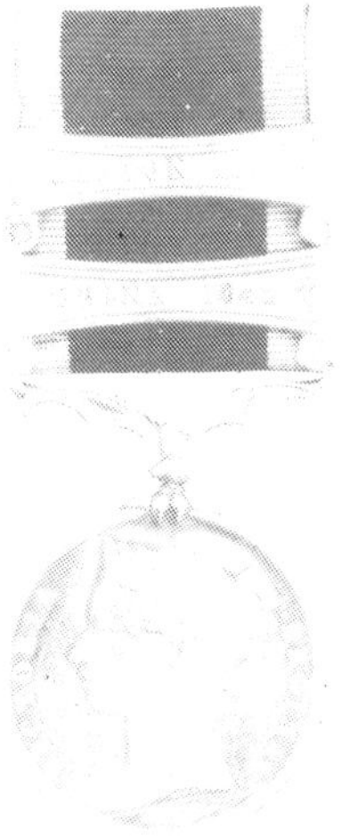

China 1857, 2 bars China 1842, Canton 1857, un-named as issued to the Navy, together with vendor's typewritten list of possible recipients. $198 £90

New Zealand 1864-1866 (3212 Gunr. Robt. Darling C. Batty. 4th Brigade R.A.). $215 £90

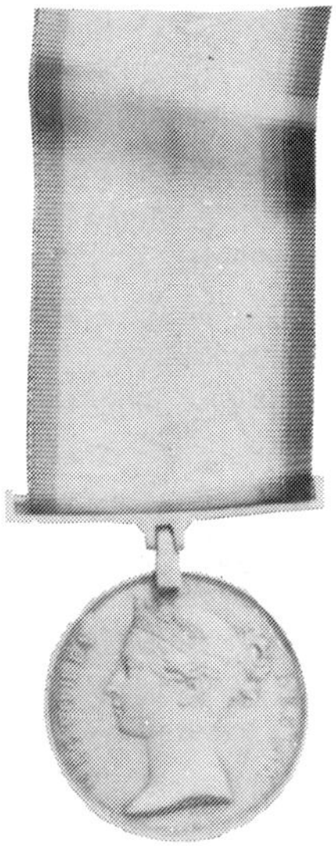

Hyderabad 1843, un-named as issued. $195 £90

C.B.E. neck badge, Military 1st type. $209 £95

Indian Mutiny 1857, 1 bar Lucknow (J. Gribble, 1st Bn., 20th Regt.). $273 £105

Four: I.S.G. 1854, 1 bar Hazara 1891 (IS Cavalry Jodhpore). I.G.S. 1895, 1 bar Punjab Front 1897-98 (Comdr. 2nd Regt. Jodhpore IS Lancers). 1914 star, Victory (Col. Rao Bahadur Thakur Dhonkal-Singh, Jodhpore IS Lancers). Together with relevant miniatures. $220 £100

Egypt: 2 bars Gemaizah 1888, Toski 1889. $242 £105

I.G.S. 1854, 3 bars Burma 1889-92, Chin-Lushai 1889-90, Burma 1887-89 (3209 Sepoy Manbir Thapa, 42nd Bl. Inf.) $264 £120

B.S.A. Co for Rhodesia 1896, no bar. (Trooper Standing, B.S.A. Police). $280 £125

New Zealand 1863 to 1866 (455 John Fraser 43rd Light Infantry) together with photo-copies of recipients medical papers. $286 £130

Gwalior Campaign 1843, star for Punniar, with brass hook and split ring suspension to (Private Peter Walters, H.M. 40th Regt.) $270 £130

M.G.S. 1793, 1 bar St. Sebastian (Francis Berrell, 59th Foot). $351 £135

Four: Crimea, 1 bar Seb (engraved). Indian Mutiny 1857, 1 bar Lucknow impressed (both 2nd Bn. Rifle Bgde). L.S. and G.C., Turkish Crimea (British issue) to Pte. Mears, School of Musketry. $319 £140

D.S.O. George V (named on cross terminals 'E. Surrey Regt. Lt. Col. A. P. White, 29th Sept. 1918, Att'd. 1/5 S. Staff Regt'). $325 £150

Pair: Afghanistan 1878, 2 bars Ahmed Khel, Kandahar, Kabul to Kandahar Star, (1st only named, Pte. W. Barrett, 2/60th Foot). $325 £150

Indian Mutiny 1857, 2 bars Rel. of Lucknow, Lucknow (B. Parker, 1st Bn., 5th Fusiliers). $336 £155

Order of British India in gold and dark blue enamel, diam. 1½in. $325 £155

Sutlej for Aliwal 1846, 1 bar Sobraon (Lieut. J. S. Warren, 73rd Regt. N.I.). Together with recipient's details. $350 £160

Sutlej for Moodkee 1845, 2 bars: Feroz, Sobraon (engraved W. Bryan, 9th Regt.) $350 £160

Three: Maharajpoor star, with non-original split ring mounts (un-named); I.G.S. 1854, 1 bar Pegu; Indian Mutiny, no bar (impressed Cpl. Patk. Clarke, 80th Regt.), with photocopy of service record. $369 £170

Canadian General Service Medal, 2 bars Fenian Raid 1866, Red River 1870, an un-named example. $407 £185

Egypt 1882, 4 bars Tel-El-Kebir, Suakin 1884, El-Teb-Tamaai, The Nile 1884-85. (Pte. F. Webb, 1st Berks. Regt.). $401 £185

B.S.A. Co. medal for Rhodesia 1896, 1 bar Mashonaland 1897. (Tpr. J. Miles, Gwelo Vol.) $435 £200

Pair: China 1900, 1 bar Rel. of Pekin, Edward VII Coronation 1902, together with miniature including C.B.E. and B.W.M., in a fitted leatherette case. $500 £230

Sutlej for Moodkee 1845, with 3 bars: Feroz, Aliwal, Sobraon (impressed William Smith, 50th Foot). $510 £235

D.S.O. George V in gilt and enamels. $553 £255

Five: D.F.C. (1945), 1939-45 star, Air Crew Europe, with 1 bar France and Germany, Defence and War, together with D.F.C. miniature and navigator's cloth badge. All un-named but with service details of Flt. Lt. V. W. Davies, D.F.C., R.A.F.V.R. $550 £250

M.G.S. 1793, 1 bar Vimiera (John Brotherton, 6th Foot). He was one of two soldiers of the 6th Foot to receive Vimiera as a single bar. $676 £260

N.G.S. 1793, 1 bar Java (Charles Easter). $629 £290

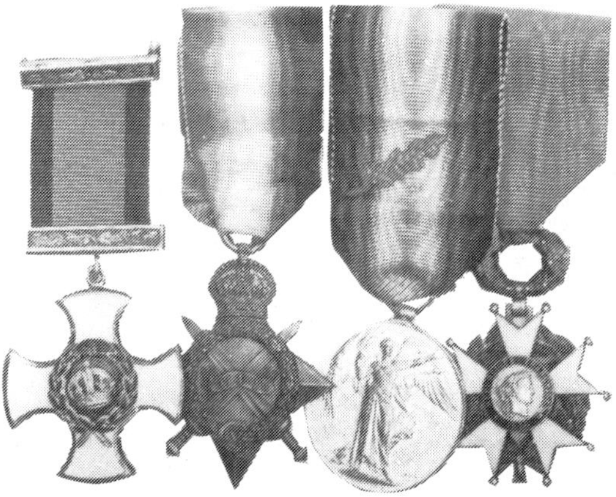

Four: D.S.O. George V, 1914-15 star, Victory with oakleaf; France: Legion of Honour Chevalier's badge (Eng. Lt. Cdr. T. G. Coomber, R.N.). D.S.O. central roundel loose, Legion of Honour chipped, miniature with central roundels detached, one missing. Together with full set of miniatures, shipping certificates, documents etc., silver napkin ring and newspaper cuttings. $685 £290

Four: East and West Africa, 1 bar 1898 (H.M.S. Heron), A.G.S. 1902, 1 bar Somaliland 1908-10, N.G.S. 1915, 1 bar Persian Gulf 1909-1914, Naval L.S. and G.C. (Ed. VII). (G. Mott, C.P.O., H.M.S. Hyacinth). $730 £320

M.G.S. 1793, 10 bars, F.D., C.R., Bad, Sal, Vitt, Pyr, Niv, Nive, Orthes, Toulouse (Robert Beatty, 88th Foot).
$760 £350

Pair: Punjab 1849, 2 bars Chilianwala, Goojerat, I.G.S. 1854, 1 bar North-West Frontier. (Lt. Col. G. B. Tremenheere, Bengal Engrs.). Together with recipients service details. In velvet lined, leatherette case. $825 £380

Waterloo 1815, (Lieut. Thomas Gordon, 1st Batt. 92nd Highlanders), with straight bar suspender. $868 £400

Pair: M.G.S. 1793, 6 bars, Alb, Sal, Vitt, St. Seb, Niv, Nive. (2nd Lt. Bn., K.G.L.) Hanoverian Waterloo.
$868 £400

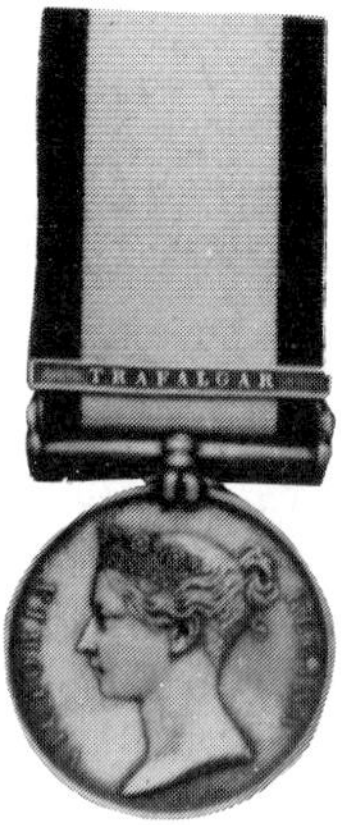

N.G.S. 1793, 1 bar Trafalgar (James Brown). $1,085 £500

K.C.B. Military, neck badge and breast star in gilt and enamels, in case of issue. $1,085 £500

Eight: C.B.E. (military) neck badge, in case, A.F.C. George V, 1914-15 star (Manchester Regt.), B.W.M. Victory (R.A.F.), Khedives Sudan 1910 no bar, (R.F.C.), Greece: Order of the Redeemer badge, Iraq: King Feisel War Medal. $1,368 £600

Seven: I.G.S. 1854, 1 bar Chin Lushai 1889-90, I.G.S. 1895, 3 bars Tirah 1897-98, Samana 1897, Punj. Front 1897-98, China 1900, N.G.S. 1915, 1 bar Persian Gulf 1909-14, B.W.M., Victory, Serbia Order of St. Sava, 5th Class (Col. F. A. Smith, late Hony. Brig. Gen. Indian Army). N.G.S. as Lt. Col., 2nd Rajputs, H.M.S. Pelorus. $1,474 £670

N. G. S. 1793, 1 bar Trafalgar, (John Hodges) good, very fine, Roll confirms as Pte R.M., HMS Swiftsure. $1,519 £700

An original oak framed cartridge display board, showing 168 Eley Kynoch brass cartridges, all identified on a printed background. $1,585 £670

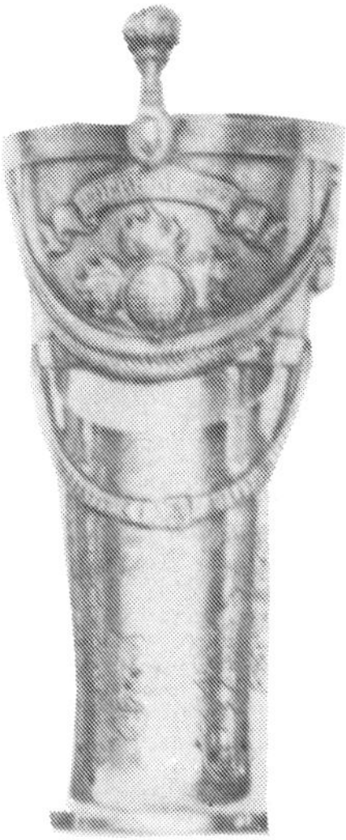

An Imperial German silver presentation schnapps beaker, surmounted by a shako with 'Colberg 1807' battle honour, height 5½in., the base with '800', silver hallmark. $200 £95

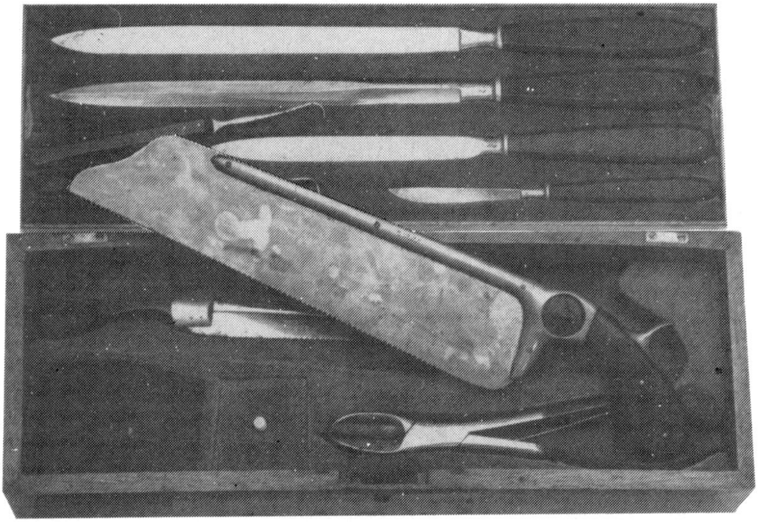

A late 19th century American surgeon's kit by 'Kolbe of Philadelphia', comprising four graduated scalpels with chequered ebony handles, two ebony handled hooks, brass mounted ebony handled saw stamped 'Kolbe Phila', pistol handled white metal mounted saw and pincers. In their red velvet lined brass mounted oak case with lift-out tray. $760 £330

A Victorian regimental mess toast rack of German silver, in the form of fourteen piled Snider Rifles, rifle length 4½in., wreath handle, length 6½in., height overall 5½in. $338 £130

A shakudo nanako tsuba of mokko form, 6¾cm., chiselled with an Oni mischievously aggravating a Portugese trader. Gold lined rim. $315 £145

A pair of 18th century bullion embroidered holsters for a pair of flintlock holster pistols, 16in. overall. $230 £100

A Victorian silver plated presentation twin-handled military cup, height of cup (with figure) 15½in. $250 £115

A pair of oil paintings of Lord Cochrane, the first showing him in full-dress uniform, circa 1850, wearing blue sash, epaulettes and Order star, seated, half-length, full face, the second showing him in civilian dress, in similar pose, both 8½ X 10½in., painted on panels, in moulded gilt frames. $615 £260

A leather bound folio size volume, being the Visitors Book of Gauleiter Dr. Friedrich Rainer. $572 £260

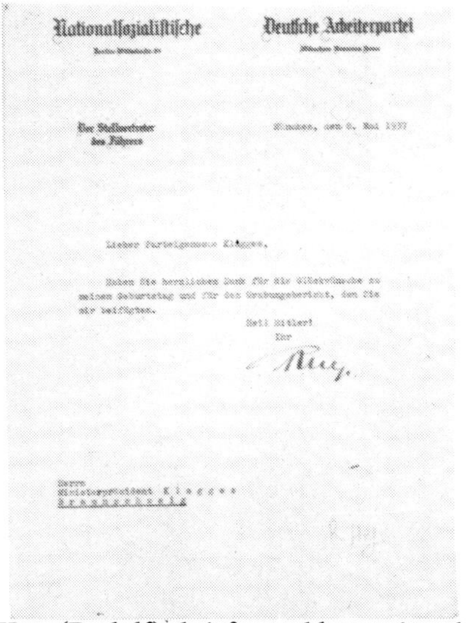

Nationalsozialistische Deutsche Arbeiterpartei

Der Stellvertreter des Führers

Lieber Parteigenosse Klagges,

Heil Hitler!
Ihr

Hess (Rudolf): brief typed letter signed in ink 'R. Hess' to Ministerprasident Klagges, Braunschweig, thanking him for birthday wishes, Munich, 8 May 1937. $88 £40

A Georgian other rank's painted linen marching pack of The 10th Regt., North British Militia, two inner buttoned compartments, 'GR' cypher 'Linens 103' stamp inside, complete with all buff leather straps and buckles. $520 £200

A French Napoleonic prisoner-of-war straw marquetry decorated wooden box, the front with two drawers and two false drawers, 11 x 7 x 3½in. $130 £50

A French Napoleonic prisoner-of-war carved bone religious shrine, surmounted by orb and cross, wooden back containing figure in carved bone of Christ on the cross, double hinged doors, on rectangular base, height 4½in. $182 £70

A unique sealed pattern 'Badge, black silk embroidery, for Colour Serjeants, Rifle Brigade', mounted on original card, five wax seals on reverse, dated 1.9.1877. $73 £28

A mid 18th century brass oblong tobacco box commemorating the Victories of Prussia's Frederick the Great, length 6¼in. $506 £230

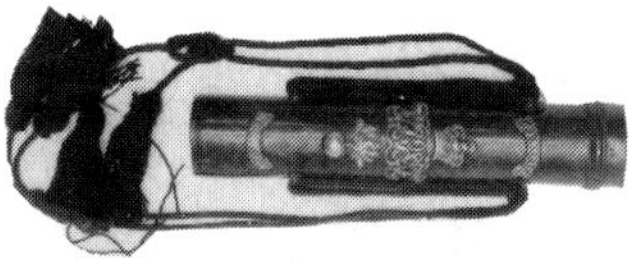

A Victorian bandsman's fife case of the Grenadier Guards, brass half cylindrical case 17½in., with silvered scrolls top and bottom, complete with its green cords and tassels. $271 £125

An Indo-Persian bull-headed all-steel mace 29in. overall, the haft unscrewing to reveal slender 18½in. blade. $260 £100

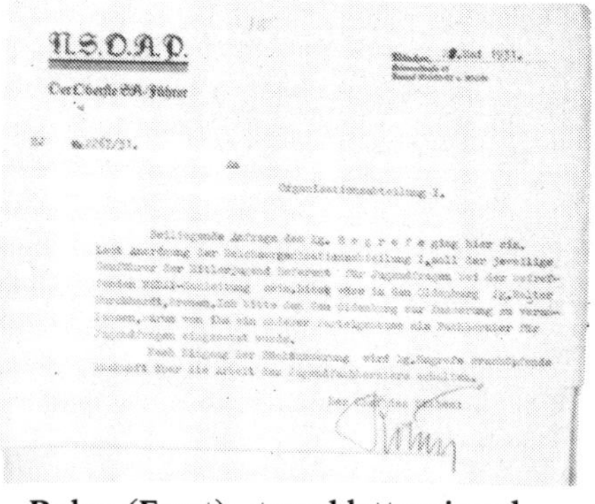

N.S.D.A.P.

Der Oberste SA-Führer

Rohm (Ernst): typed letter signed 'Rohm' in violet crayon, to 'Organistion-sabteilung I', half page, 4to, Munich 28 May 1931. $850 £390

An 18th century bronze stirrup, possibly Tibetan, plain foot rest base, the sides of openwork design, with fleur-de-lys motif, roped support issuing from monsters' heads, 8in. $35 £16

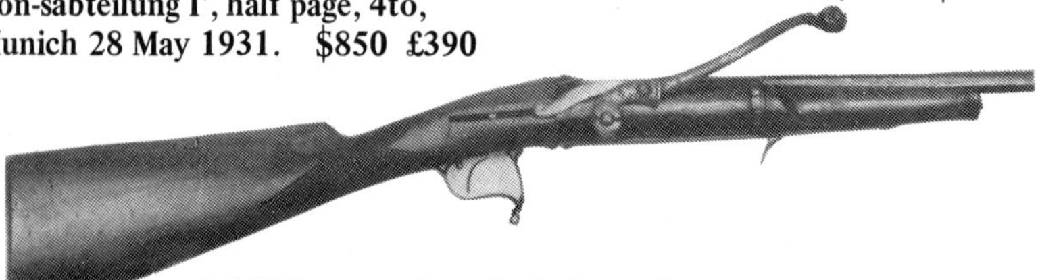

A 100-bore crank cocked air gun by 'A. V. Lebeda of Prague', 38½in., tip-down barrel 18½in. Half-stocked, sidelever cocking crank, set trigger, carved cheekpiece and chequered small of stock. $1,560 £600

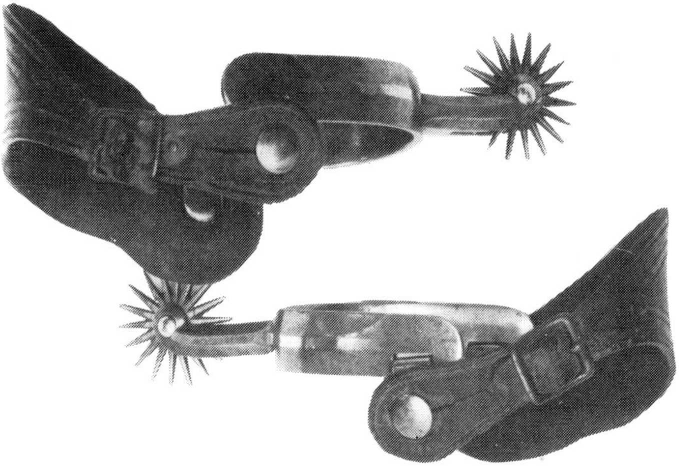

A pair of American cowboy spurs, well made of steel, the sides inlaid with silver and gold lines, silver and gold rivet heads to 18 point rowels. Original leather straps. $215 £90

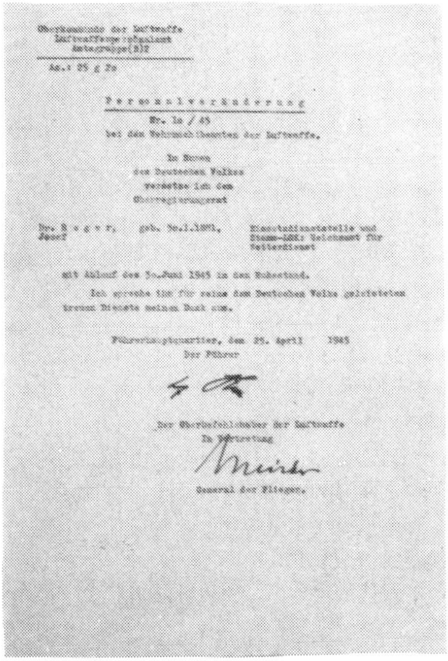

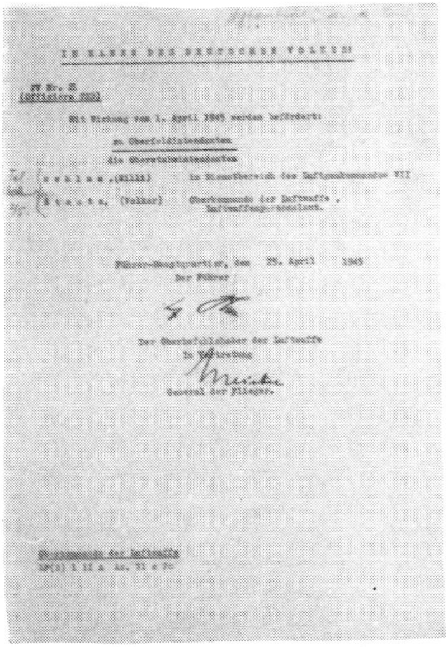

Hitler (Adolf): Two rare late typed documents signed, both dated 25th April 1945: the first a 'Change of Personal Status' of Dr. Jeger Josef, of the Dept. of Meteorology, retiring him with effect from 30th June 1945, as 'Higher Civil Servant' of the 'Oberkommando der Luftwaffe'; and another document, similar promoting to 'Oberfeldintendant' 2 Luftwaffe other ranks with effect from 1st April 1945. $660 £300

A copper Tibetan ceremonial horn, the mouthpiece in the form of a monster's head, overall 16in. $187 £85

A French Napoleonic prisoner-of-war carved bone automata figure of a woman spinning, overall height 4¼in., and another, similar contemporary figure, 3¾in. $264 £120

An original German silver Garde-Du-Corps/Garde Cuirassier helmet parade eagle on oval base, height 7in. $2,080 £800

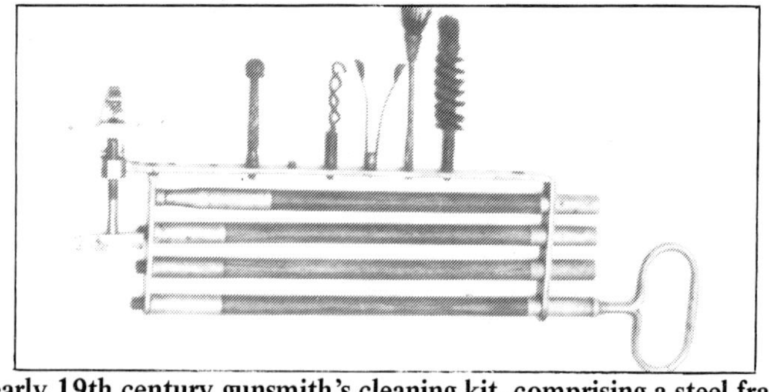

An early 19th century gunsmith's cleaning kit, comprising a steel frame 9½ x 3¼in., four brass mounted hickory cleaning rod sections, one with brass handle. Steel frame contains ball puller, worm, jag, bore brush, breech brush and mainspring cramp with turnscrew doubling as hammer. $70 £32

Ten mounted troopers of The 12th Lancers, movable arms, steel lances, and one mounted officer with sword at the ready, by 'Johilco', in their original painted colours. $76 £35

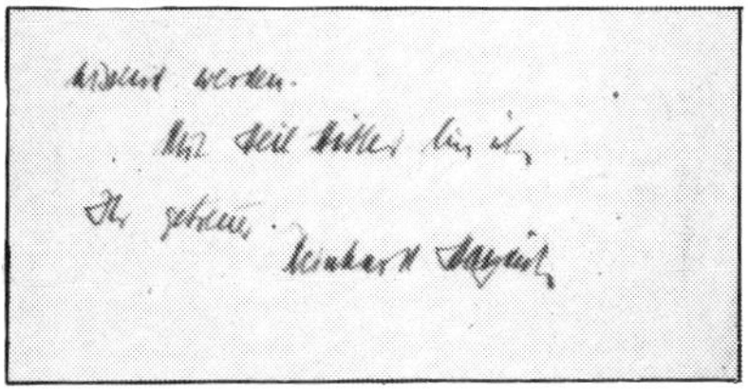

Heydrich (Reinhard), rare autograph letter signed in ink 'Reinhard Heydrich', to a colonel, sending 'sincere birthday wishes', dated 10/12/34. $594 £270

An old Herzegovenian Eastern European iron axe head, inlaid in silver, 5¼in. $242 £110

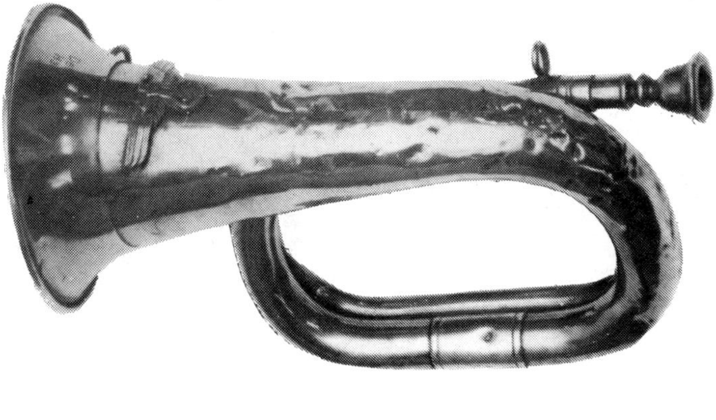

A Nazi bugle, of brass, with white metal mounted mouthpiece and bands, and mounted with coppered Nazi Eagle, mouthpiece engraved 'Detmering Hamburg', 10½in. $115 £50

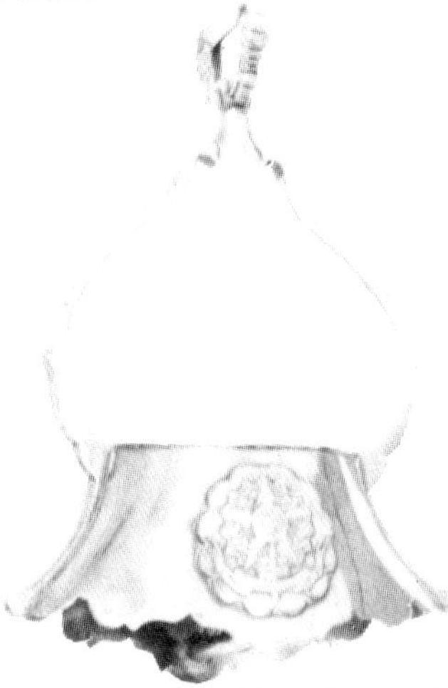

An ornate stirrup of South American silver, with arms of Brazil on sides, with pierced footplate, height 7in., weight approx. 12oz. Together with a pair of silver saddle mounts. $69 £32

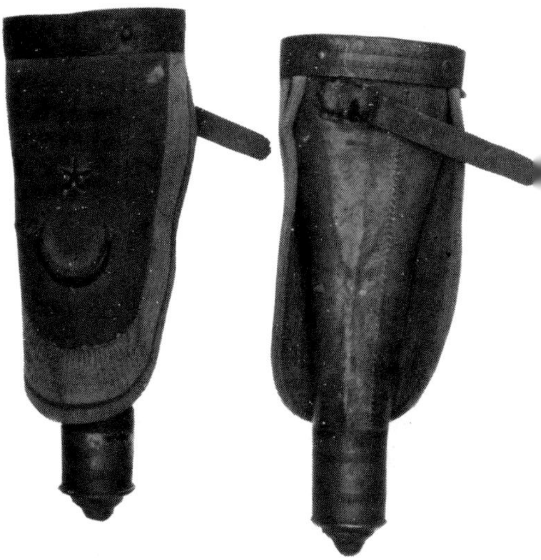

A pair of Turkish 19th century Military pistol saddle holsters, 13½in. overall, leather covered. Large brass mouths and terminals. $135 £65

A French Napoleonic prisoner-of-war straw marquetry covered wooden box, with slide-in drawer, two rectangular side compartments with hinged lids. $130 £50

A Victorian leopard skin of The 15th Hussars, red cloth with leopard skin surrounding bullion wove crown above crossed standards. $143 £65

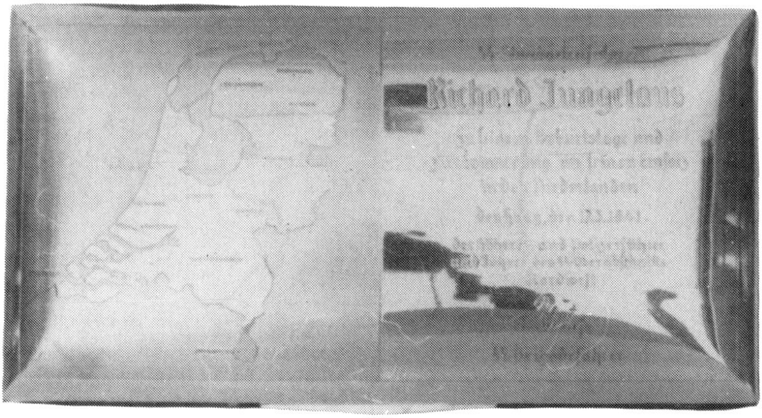

A Nazi presentation silver cigarette box, presented to an S.S. officer, half the lid engraved with a map of Holland, the other half with engraved Presentation inscription: 'S.S. Standartenfuhrer Richard Jungclaus Zu Seinem Geburtstage und Zur Erinnerung an Seinen Einsatz in den Niederladen den Haag, den 17.3.1941. Der Hohere S.S. und Polizeifuhrer und Fuhrer des S.S. Oberabschnitts Nordwest'. Wooden lining and two inner compartments, leather covered base, $10\frac{1}{4}$ x $5\frac{1}{2}$ x 2in. A written history of the box is included with the lot. **$704 £320**

A Nazi Visitor's Book from The Panzertruppen-Schule Wunsdorf (commencing 1.9.1940), the book with hundreds of ink signatures of visitors to the school and with watercolour scenes decorating the various evening and other functions above the visitors' signatures. The fly-leaf also with an inscription 'This Visitor's Book was Found in the Officer's Mess at 'Belsen', April '45.' **$1,122 £510**

An oval Meissen (Dresden) Red Dragon Japanese pattern porcelain dish, in 18th century style, taken from Hitler's private dinner service at Berchtesgaden, the base with blue crossed swords mark and pattern numbers, gilt pie-crust rim, painted with dragons, birds, etc., 9¾ x 12½ x 2½in. Sold with the lot were two letters plus a certificate. $660 £300

A cased set of Military surgeon's instruments by 'Down Bros. – opposite Guy's Hospital', containing many instruments and with two lift-out trays (one missing), plan and list of instruments inside of lid, contained in brass bound wooden case, inner measurements 16½ x 5¼ x 2½in. $391 £180

A Victorian officer's full dress embroidered sabretache of The 10th (Prince of Wales' Own) Hussars, early type measuring 13¾ x 11¾in. $273 £105

A Victorian officer's full dress embroidered sabretache of The 19th (Princess of Wales' Own) Hussars, name inside 'G. Woodmass'. $260 £120

A Victorian officer's full dress embroidered sabretache of The Loyal Suffolk Hussars, scarlet cloth with regimental gilt lace border. $458 £210

A Victorian Yeomanry officer's full dress embroidered sabretache, early pattern, measuring 14 x 12in., blue cloth, silver lace border, with its foul weather cover. $502 £220

A sabretache of The 11th (Prince Albert's Own) Hussars, crimson cloth, gilt lace border, embroidered Guelphic crown. $520 £240

A William IV Yeomanry officer's full dress embroidered sabretache, crimson velvet with broad silver oak leaf lace border. $564 £260

A Victorian officer's full dress embroidered sabretache of The Middlesex Yeomanry, size 12 x 10in., dark blue velvet edged with 1¾in. gilt lace with blue central stripe. $650 £300

A Victorian officer's full dress embroidered sabretache of The 1st Royal Gloucestershire Yeomanry, blue cloth with broad silver lace on scarlet border, size 15 x 12in., with waistbelt. $651 £300

A Victorian officer's full dress embroidered sabretache of The Middlesex Yeomanry, embroidered motto scroll 'Pro Aris et Focis' within wreath, gilt lace border with black central stripe. **$710 £300**

A Victorian officer's full dress embroidered sabretache of The Queen's Own Royal Glasgow Yeomanry, 13½ x 11½in., with its foul weather cover. **$630 £300**

A Victorian officer's full dress embroidered sabretache of The Yorkshire Hussars, early pattern, 13 x 11½in., silver lace border, scarlet cloth, with its foul weather cover. **$910 £350**

A Victorian officer's full dress embroidered sabretache of The Queen's Own Royal Glasgow Yeomanry Cavalry, 13½ x 10½in., with its foul weather cover. **$781 £360**

A Victorian officer's shabraque of The Royal Horse Guards, scarlet cloth with double gilt lace stripe border, embroidered devices in all four corners of Crown over battle honour scrolls to Tel-el-Kebir over Garter Star.
$434 £200

A Victorian officer's shabraque of The 2nd Life Guards, circa 1895, blue cloth with broad gilt lace on scarlet cloth border, embroidered devices in all four corners consisting of Royal Crest above Garter Star surrounded by battle honour scrolls to South Africa 1899-1900, together with its white lambskin roll.
$450 £210

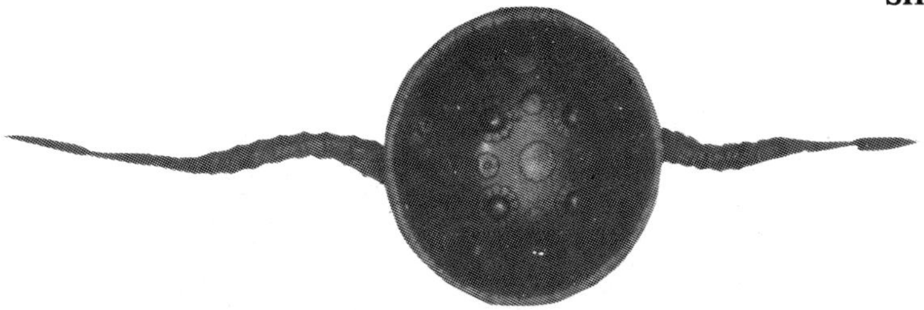

An Indian parrying shield Madu, steel shield 10in., with applied scalloped brass rim, crescents, four central bosses and flower heads. Twin gayals horn parrying bars with steel tips and end cups. $207 £90

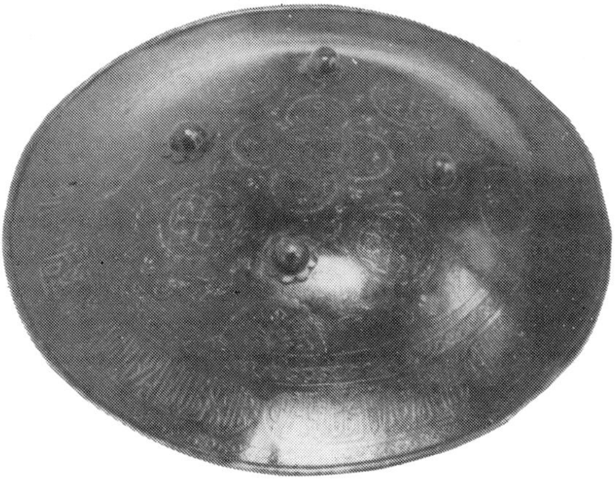

A 19th century Indian shield dhal, 18½in., with four central bosses, reinforced edge and fabric grip. Together with a steel helmet kula khud. $462 £210

An Indian 19th century shield dhal, 18in. diameter, embossed with sun's head centre, four applied bosses, chiselled with radial design of floral patterns and script. Together with a helmet kula khud. $700 £270

SHOULDER BELT PLATES

A Georgian other rank's oval brass shoulder belt plate, circa 1805, engraved with crown over monogram 'L.V.'. $66 £30

An officer's rectangular shoulder belt plate, plain burnished brass (originally gilt) plate, crowned white metal stringed French bugle surrounding florid figure '2'. $76 £35

A Georgian officer's silver plated oval shoulder belt plate of The Macroom Infantry, engraved with crowned Irish harp and title scrolls top and bottom. $121 £55

A Georgian officer's shoulder belt plate of The Stamford Local Militia, silver hallmarked 1809, rectangular plate with copper (originally gilt). $230 £100

A Georgian officer's rectangular silver and gilt shoulder belt plate of The 54th (West Norfolk) Regt., hallmarked 1815. $260 £100

An officer's gilt and silvered shoulder belt plate of The 76th Regt., the elephant over 'LXXVI' within a crowned wreath with battle honours. $208 £100

An 1881-1902 officer's gilt shoulder belt plate of The Queen's Own Cameron Highlanders. $312 £120

An officer's gilt shoulder belt plate, circa 1854, of The Royal Marines Light Infantry. $285 £120

A Georgian officer's oval silver plated copper shoulder belt plate of The Cader Idris Volunteers, engraved with title and Prince of Wales' feathers. $325 £125

A pre-1881 officer's gilt and silvered shoulder belt plate of The 72nd (Duke of Albany's Own Highlanders). $325 £125

An 1881-1902 officer's gilt and silvered shoulder belt plate of The Royal Scots Fusiliers. $338 £130

A post-1881 officer's shoulder belt plate of The Seaforth Highlanders. $338 £130

A pre-1881 officer's gilt shoulder belt plate of The 79th (Cameron Highlanders) Regt. $330 £130

A good officer's 1830-55 gilt shoulder belt plate of the 44th (E Essex) Regt (Parkyn 363). $330 £140

A Georgian or Victorian officer's shoulder belt plate of The 96th Regt. (raised in 1824), frosted gilt rectangular plate with bevelled edge. $333 £16(

An officer's gilt and silvered shoulder belt plate of The 78th Highland Regt. (or Ross-shire Buffs). $475 £200

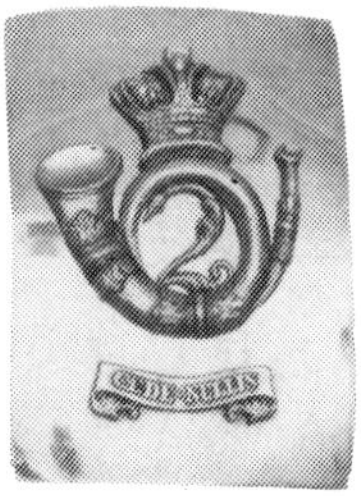

A Victorian officer's rectangular gilt shoulder belt plate, probably 2nd Madras Light Infantry. $450 £205

An officer's gilt and silvered shoulder belt plate of The Highland Light Infantry. $590 £250

A Victorian Gentlemen at Arms full dress embroidered pouch, blue velvet, gilt lace border, embroidered Guelphic crown over 'VR'. $58 £25

A Victorian officer's full dress pouch of The Army Veterinary Dept. $105 £45

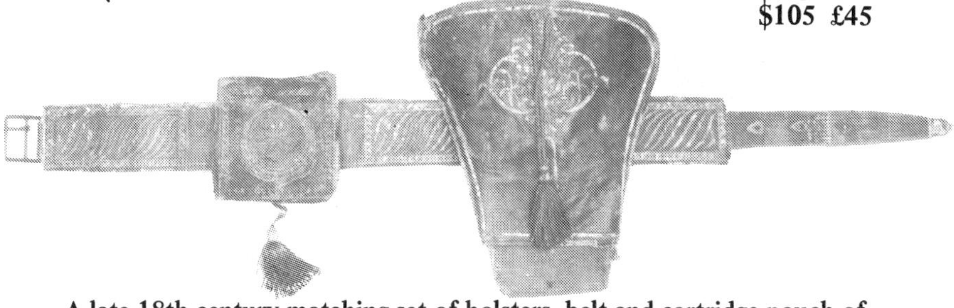

A late 18th century matching set of holsters, belt and cartridge pouch of silver bullion embroidered green Morocco leather. Green Morocco open top, holsters with red Morocco interior, silver bullion borders with central geometric motif, bullion tassel and fabric shoulder sling. $143 £65

An Imperial German (Bavarian) officer's pouch, solid gilt mounts and flap with beaded and roped border and central crown, leather covered pouch with tin liner. $150 £70

An early Victorian Light Dragoon officer's silver flapped pouch, hallmarked Birmingham 1840, flap with engraved border, gilt 'V.R.' cypher, silver mounts.
$217 £100

A post-1902 Indian Army officer's silver shoulder belt pouch of The 29th Deccan Horse, the silver flap of Victorian silver (hallmarked B'ham 1890), engraved around edges with foliate scrolls, the swivels hallmarked Birmingham 1889, gilt badge with crown above crossed lances. Morocco covered pouch with bullion stripes.
$338 £130

A Victorian Yeomanry officer's full dress shoulder belt and pouch, scarlet with silver lace, flap embroidered with crown over 'L.Y.C.', probably Leicester.
$299 £130

A Victorian officer's silver flapped pouch of The Leicester Yeomanry (Prince Albert's Own), hallmarked Birmingham 1886, flap with engraved border, gilt crowned 'L.Y.C.' and title scroll.
$377 £145

An officer's full dress pouch of The 1st Bombay Cavalry, blue velvet with gilt embroidered crown over 'BC' monogram, '1' and battle honour scrolls, within wreath, gilt mounts. $330 £150

A Victorian officer's full dress shoulder belt and pouch of The 6th Dragoon Guards, regimental lace belt with silver mounted (hallmarked Birmingham 1874), silver flapped pouch. $356 £155

A Victorian officer's silver flapped pouch of The 2nd W. York Yeomanry, hallmarked Birmingham 1863, flap with engraved border, gilt 'VR' cypher and title scroll. $403 £155

A Victorian officer's special pattern pouch of The 9th (Queen's Royal) Lancers, scarlet pouch, solid gilt flap with crowned 'AR' cypher within oak leaf border in high relief. $429 £165

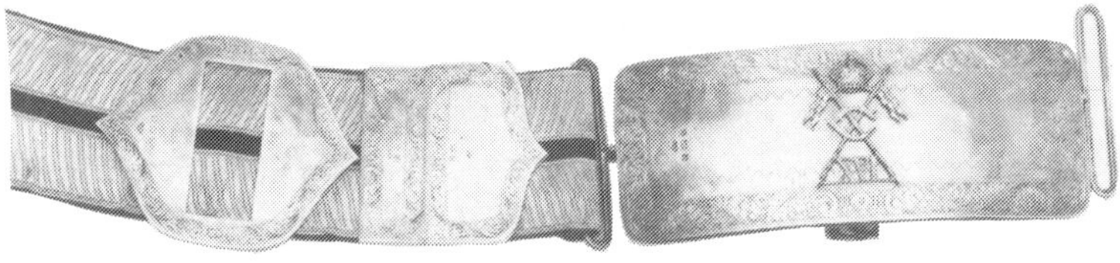

A post-1902 officer's full dress shoulder belt and pouch of The Indian 16th Cavalry, gilt lace belt with blue stripe, on blue morocco, engraved silver mounts, prickers, buckle, tip and slide, hallmarked B'ham 1906, silver flapped pouch with engraved border and gilt badge of crowned crossed lances with 'C' and 'XVI', hallmarked B'ham 1908. $450 £205

SPORRANS

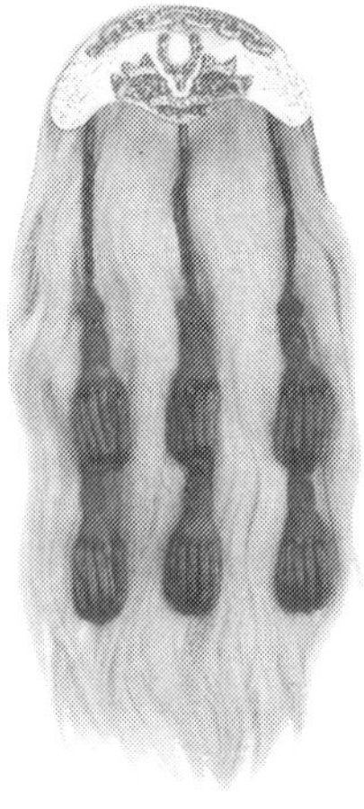

An officer's full dress sporran of The Seaforth Highlanders, engraved brass cantle with silvered badge and battle honour scrolls, six gilt and crimson cords and bullion tassels on white goatskin, crimson leather pouch, in its tin case. $676 £260

A Victorian officer's full dress badger sporran of The Argyll & Sutherland Highlanders, six white hair tassels with gilt metal conical mounts decorated with thistles, suspended from bullion loops, badger head with glass eyes, red morocco leather chamois lined purse, with patent leather hanging strap. $271 £125

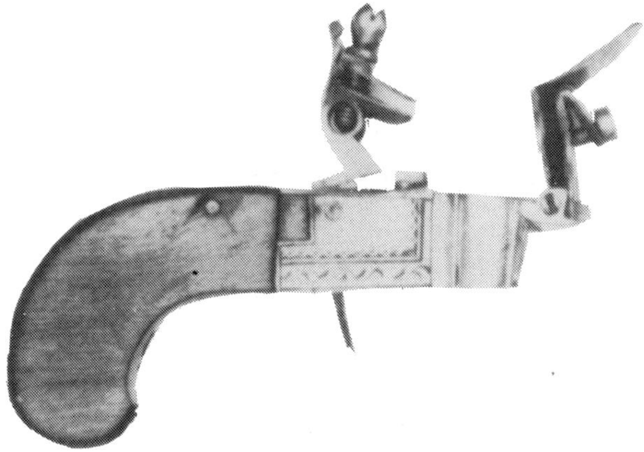

A Belgian or French boxlock flintlock tinderlighter, 4in., polished steel frame engraved with foliage and geometric borders. Cylindrical tinder box, variable tension sprung frizzen, throathole cock. Slab walnut butt.
$250 £115

A mid 18th century all-steel Continental flintlock tinderlighter, 7¾in., squared tinderbox, frame with hinged door for tinder and flints. External action, integral steel grip with ball finial. Staple shaped support stand.
$326 £130

An early 19th century coatee of The Royal Company of Archers, hard unlined tartan cloth, green velvet collar, five sequin and coloured silk loops, buttons, and tassels to chest, similar loops, buttons, and tassels to skirts, two loops and buttons to cuffs. $143 £65

A post-1902 court dress of The Royal Company of Archers, green coatee with dark green velvet facings, slashed cuffs, heavy gilt thistle pattern embroidery, five gilt buttons, matching overalls, white leather shoulder belt with gilt and silvered shoulder belt plate, crimson waist sash and tassels. $198 £90

An early 18th century Indian Maharatta Cavalry trooper's body armour cuirass, composed of ten rectangular chainmail linked body plates with reinforcing scalloped borders. Front plates with six foliate finialled securing loops. Two chainmail linked shoulder plates. The links are hot riveted. $220 £100

The uniform of Air Vice-Marshal J. T. Babington, CBE., DSO., comprising: full dress tunic with gilt lace and embroidery to collar, embroidered shoulder tabs and pilot's wings; matching overalls; Wolseley pattern tropical helmet, R.A.F. blue feather plume in gilt holder, with its tin case; gilt sword belt and clasp; mess jacket, waistcoat and trousers; two pairs white linen trousers; two white linen waistcoats; pair of greatcoat shoulder tabs.

$330 £150

An officer's pre-1848 coatee of The 2nd (Queen's Royal) Regt. of Foot, scarlet with blue facings, padded gilt lace loops to collar, slashed cuffs and slashed skirts, heavy embroidered regimental skirt badges, gilt buttons, with its gilt epaulettes, plain strap, crescents, 3in. slender bullion tassels.
$435 £200

An officer's uniform of The Royal Company of Archers, The King's Bodyguard of Scotland, comprising: a green frock coat, matching shoulder belt sash; pair of matching overalls, black leather waist belt and a Kilmarnock bonnet.
With this uniform a dress sword, also the matching sidearm of Roman form.
$521 £240

A Coldstream Guards officer's full dress uniform, comprising: bearskin with red feather plume and leather backed taper chinchain; tunic, blue facings, slashed cuffs and skirts, gilt embroidery and buttons; pair of overalls with 2in. scarlet stripe; items named 'Lt. G. C. L. Atkinson, 1921'. $858 £330

A Lt.-Colonel's complete full dress uniform of The 10th (Prince of Wales' Own) Hussars, comprising: tunic with gilt frogging and lace; busby with scarlet bag, red velvet backed chinchain, white feather plume in holder; patent leather pouch and belt; scarlet pantaloons; pair of boots; pair of gilt spurs in their velvet lined case. $1,300 £550

An officer's full dress uniform of The Gordon Highlanders, to the rank of 2nd Lieutenant, comprising: Highland feather bonnet, diced wool band five tails, silvered badge, in its tin case with name on lid; full dress doublet; tartan kilt; tartan plaid; gilt lace waist belt and clasp; white goatskin sporran etc.
$1,375 £625

A Colonel's complete uniform of The Princess of Wales' Own Yorkshire Hussars, comprising: busby, with silver braided scarlet bag; jacket and pelisse, each with heavy silver cord frogging; shoulder belt and pouch, silver lace on red cloth. Items named to Col. C. W. E. Duncombe. $2,340 £900

An officer's complete full dress uniform of The Black Watch (Royal Highlanders), circa 1931, belonging to Lieut. G. P. Campbell-Preston who became Lt. Col. during World War II, comprising: ostrich feather bonnet; scarlet doublet with gilt trimmings; white goat hair sporran; regimental dirk; broadsword; silver plaid brooch, hallmarked Edinburgh 1883; buff leather shoulder sword belt with gilt and silvered shoulder belt plate. $2,275 £1,050

A Lieutenant's uniform of The Royal Horse Guards (The Blues), circa 1902, comprising: helmet, silvered skull, gilt mounts; plated cuirass; shoulder cords and aiguilette; gilt lace shoulder belt with crimson cord, black leather pouch with gilt badge; pair of white buckskin breeches etc. $3,360 £1,550

A Georgian gnarled walking stick concealing a dagger blade within body, length overall 33in., the hilt latching to stick by means of spring catch released by pressing small knot on handle, single edged fullered blade 10½in. $62 £30

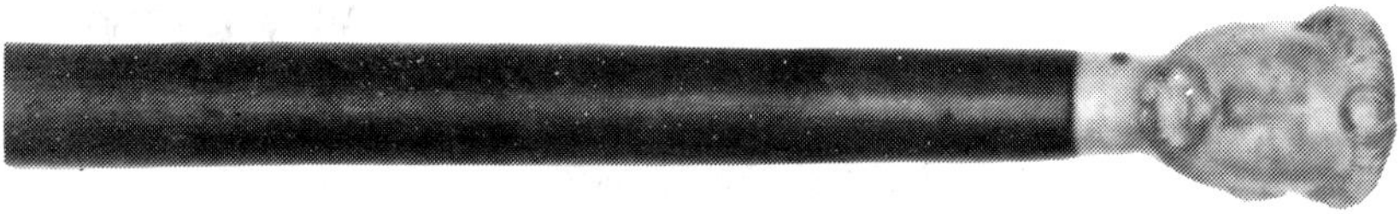

A walking stick, the top mounted with Goa carved 18th century ivory head of a man with beard and tonsure, head 2¼in., overall 36in. $78 £36

A malacca walking stick, the curved grip of whale-bone section with sailor's knot, brass ferrule, 34in. $83 £40

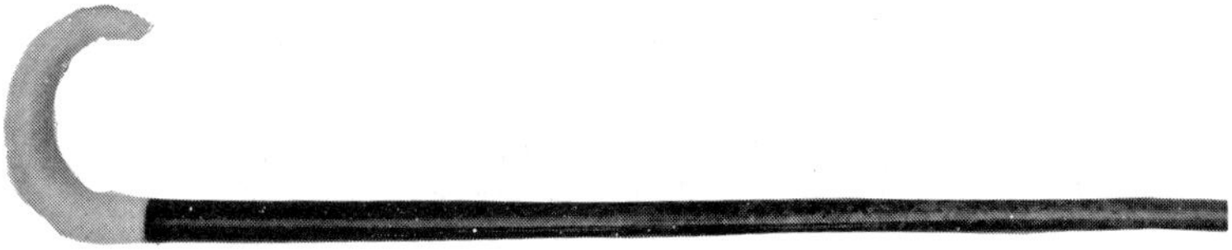

A mottled walking stick with fine ivory crook-shape hilt, horn ferrule, 35in. $94 £45

An animated walking stick, 36in., hallmarked silver ferrule (London 1903). Wooden top carved as a bulldog's head, with glass eyes and sprung lower jaw operated with the finger. Ebonised stick. $98 £45

An Austrian cherrywood walking stick, 36in., head carved as a fox's head and painted realistically with glass eyes, stamped 'Bencox'. $108 £50

A Victorian ivory top malacca walking stick the ivory top finely carved with relief stags and hinds in rustic background, the pommel with a lying hound, 34½in. $110 £50

A walking stick made from whalebone, Balleen pommel 37½in., brass ferrule. $114 £55

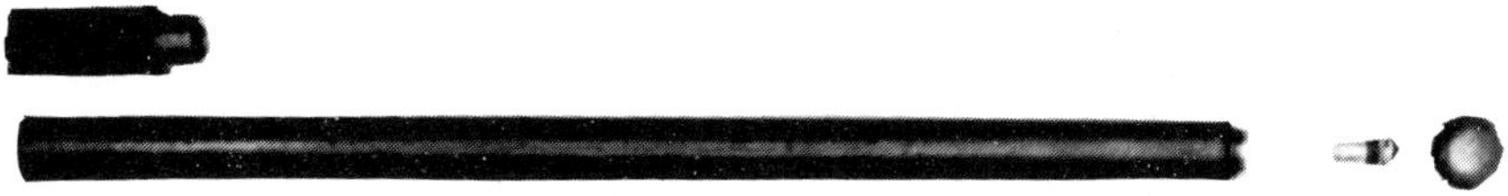

A Victorian malacca Toper's stick, containing, in screw-off sections, long glass phial flask and drinking glass, overall 35in. $130 £60

A Victorian artist's walking cane, 35in., unscrews in four sections with silvered copper fittings to reveal glass lined ink well, pen, pencil and ruling sections. $148 £65

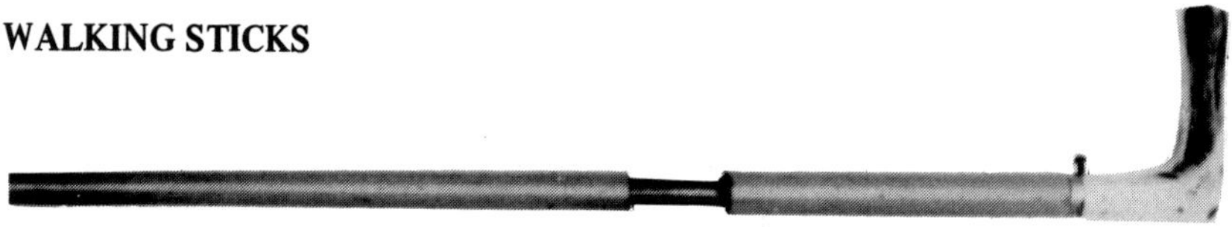

An S.S. 7mm. Continental walking stick shotgun, 35¼in., barrel 26¼in., white metal ferrule stamped 'Dumonthier B.S.G.D.G.', cane covered barrel, stag horn handle with button trigger, breech is opened by twisting grip and pulling. $152 £70

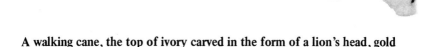

A walking cane, the top of ivory carved in the form of a lion's head, gold band at base, the tip of horn of bullet form, 35in. $198 £90

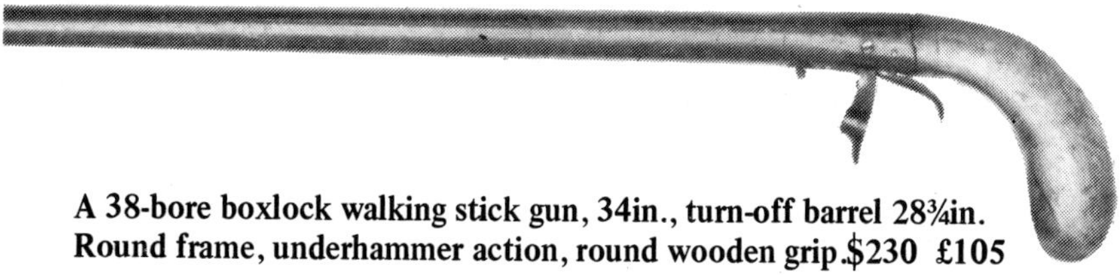

A 38-bore boxlock walking stick gun, 34in., turn-off barrel 28¾in. Round frame, underhammer action, round wooden grip. $230 £105

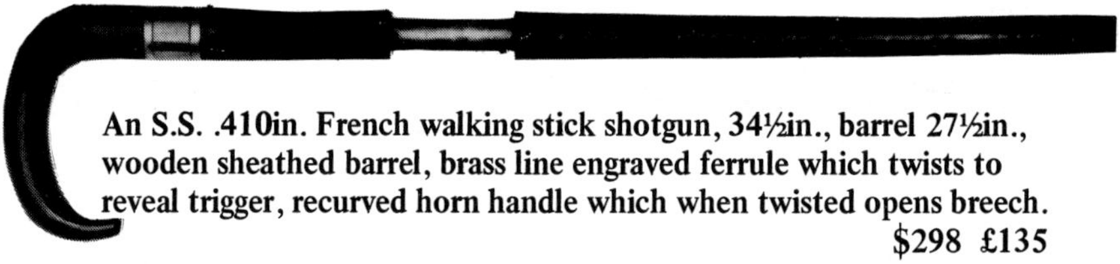

An S.S. .410in. French walking stick shotgun, 34½in., barrel 27½in., wooden sheathed barrel, brass line engraved ferrule which twists to reveal trigger, recurved horn handle which when twisted opens breech. $298 £135

An unusual S.S. 9mm. French walking stick combination shotgun and sword stick, 36in., barrel 30¼in., the top ferrule stamped 'Manufacture Francais d'Armes et Cycles de Saint-Etienne' and 'Canne Etoile cal 9mm.'. $385 £175

PERCUSSION & CARTRIDGE WEAPONS

BLUNDERBUSS

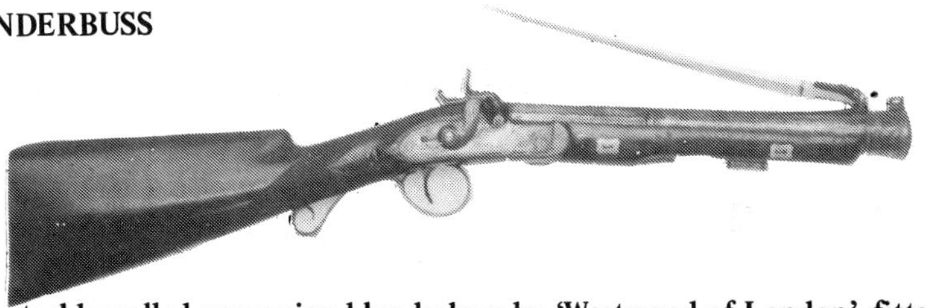

A steel barrelled percussion blunderbuss by 'Westwood of London', fitted with spring bayonet, circa 1835, 30in., half octagonal swollen barrel 14in. Birmingham proved, top thumb sliding catch releases friction roller bearing sprung triangular sectioned bayonet. Full-stocked, foliate engraved bolted lock and dolphin hammer with 'Westwood'. $790 £360

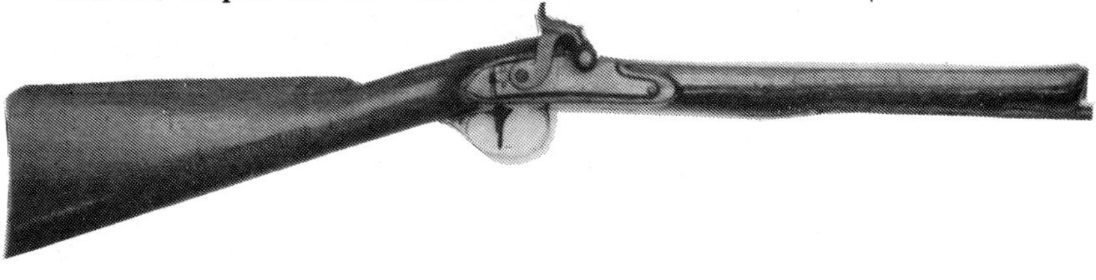

A brass barrelled percussion blunderbuss by 'Sanders', converted from flintlock by breech drum method, 29in., flared barrel 13½in., London proved. Full-stocked, stepped bolted lock, brass mounts of military style. $855 £360

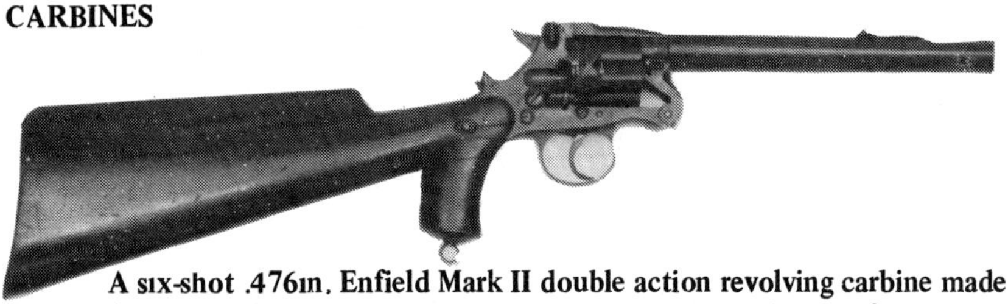

A six-shot .476in. Enfield Mark II double action revolving carbine made from a regulation service revolver, 41in., round barrel 25in., frame stamped with crowned 'VR', 'Enfield' and dated '1882', walnut pistol grip stock with steel buttplate and pin action cap with fitted lanyard ring.
$273 £105

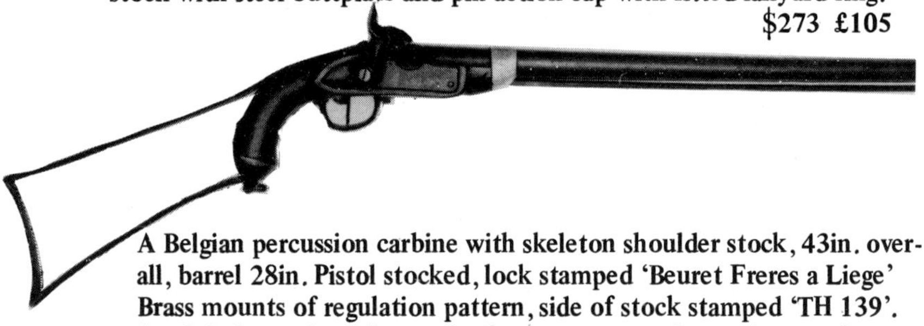

A Belgian percussion carbine with skeleton shoulder stock, 43in. overall, barrel 28in. Pistol stocked, lock stamped 'Beuret Freres a Liege' Brass mounts of regulation pattern, side of stock stamped 'TH 139'. Steel skeleton shoulder stock of contemporary domestic manufacture.
$285 £125

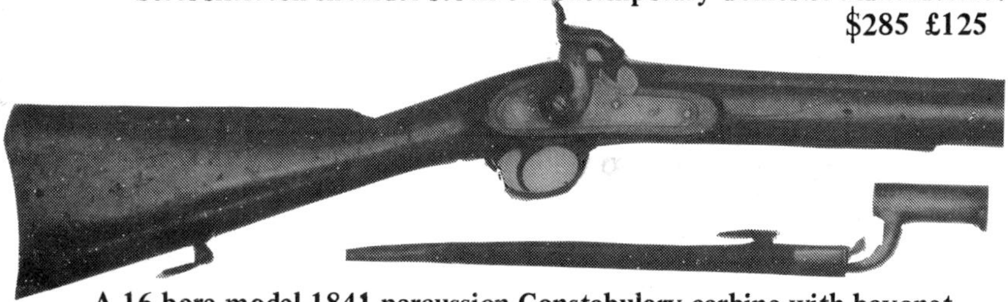

A 16-bore model 1841 percussion Constabulary carbine with bayonet, dated 1847, 42½in., barrel 26½in., Tower proved. Full-stocked, regulation brass mounts, steel sling swivels (one broken) and ramrod, trigger guard stamped 'Scott'. Triangular socket bayonet by 'S. Hill', 13in., spring catch for securing brass mounted leather sheath. $325 £125

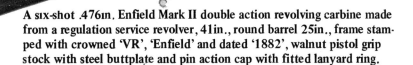

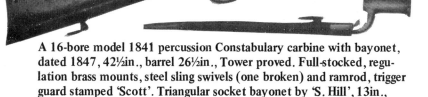

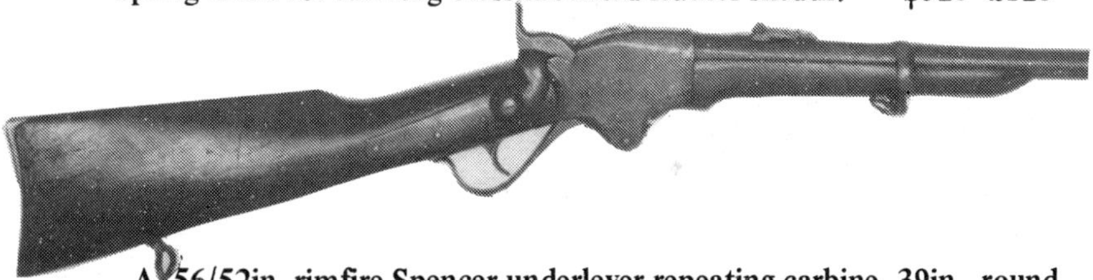

A .56/52in. rimfire Spencer underlever repeating carbine, 39in., round barrel 22in., regulation walnut stock with steel mounts including saddle ring, plain fore-end secured by single barrel band, blade foresight ladder rear to 800 yards, back-action sidelock, complete with sling swivels.
$390 £150

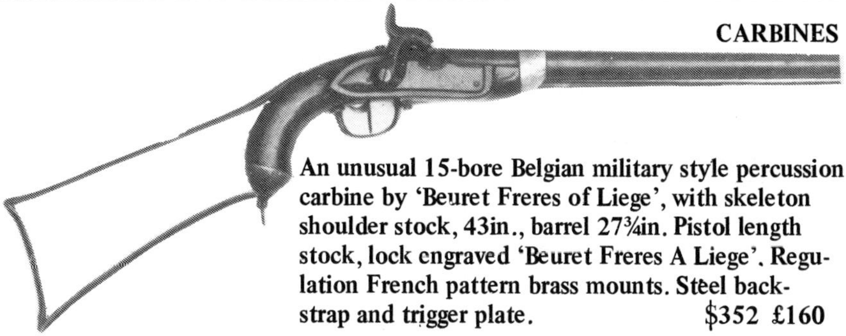

An unusual 15-bore Belgian military style percussion carbine by 'Beuret Freres of Liege', with skeleton shoulder stock, 43in., barrel 27¾in. Pistol length stock, lock engraved 'Beuret Freres A Liege'. Regulation French pattern brass mounts. Steel backstrap and trigger plate. $352 £160

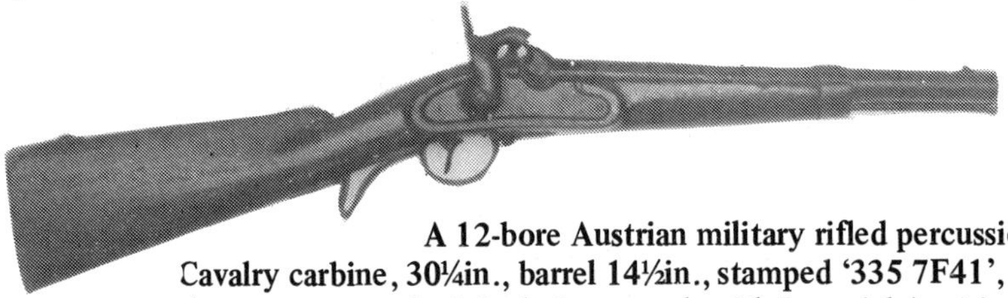

A 12-bore Austrian military rifled percussion Cavalry carbine, 30¼in., barrel 14½in., stamped '335 7F41', threequarter-stocked, lockplate struck with Imperial Austrian Eagle on tail. Regulation steel mounts, carved cheekpiece, steel saddle bar with lanyard ring, steel ramrod. $385 £175

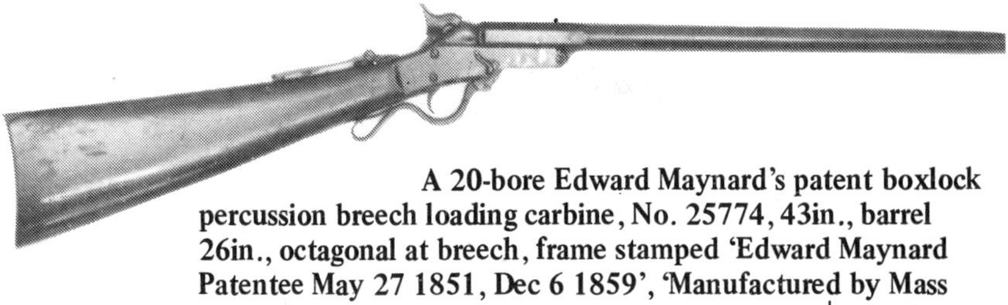

A 20-bore Edward Maynard's patent boxlock percussion breech loading carbine, No. 25774, 43in., barrel 26in., octagonal at breech, frame stamped 'Edward Maynard Patentee May 27 1851, Dec 6 1859', 'Manufactured by Mass Arms Co, Chicopee Falls'. $407 £185

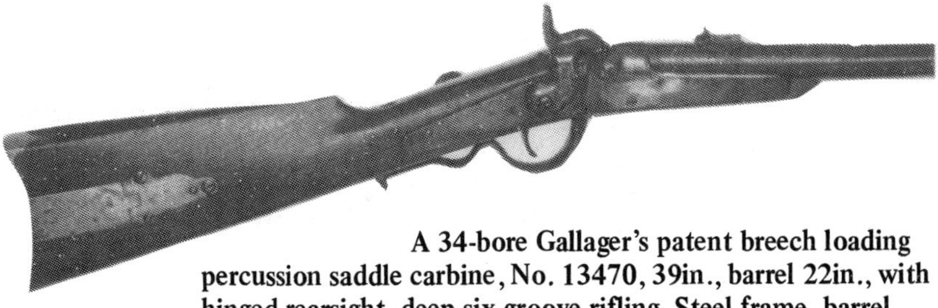

A 34-bore Gallager's patent breech loading percussion saddle carbine, No. 13470, 39in., barrel 22in., with hinged rearsight, deep six-groove rifling. Steel frame, barrel released, slides forward and tips down using trigger guard as lever. Back-action lock stamped 'Gallager's Patent, July 17th 1860', 'Manufactured by Richardson & Overman, Philada'. $494 £190

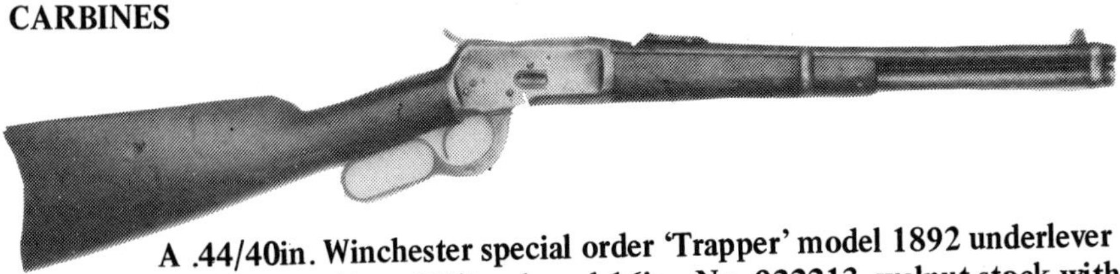

A .44/40in. Winchester special order 'Trapper' model 1892 underlever repeating carbine, 33½in., barrel 16in., No. 922213, walnut stock with steel buttplate, shorter than standard walnut fore-end and secured by single band, full length tube magazine, blade foresight, tangent rear action with saddle ring to left side. $495 £210

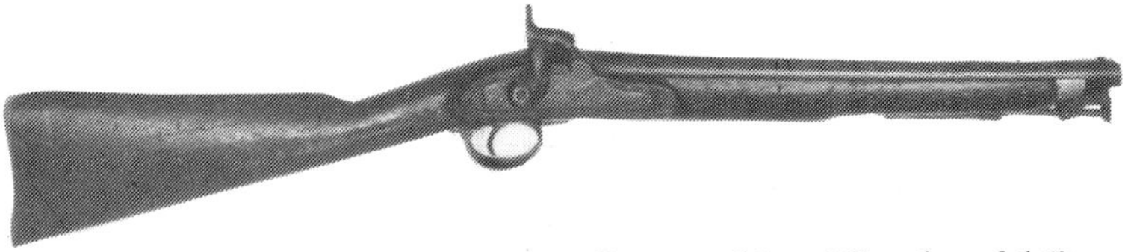

A 16-bore 1847 pattern percussion Paget carbine, 32in., barrel 16in., Tower proved. Full-stocked, stepped lock, border engraved with 'Tower' and crowned 'GR'. Regulation brass mounts, swivel ramrod. Stock struck with Enfield storekeeper's mark for 1848. Buttcap tang engraved 'R.C.H. 380'. $559 £215

A 16-bore Enfield pattern 1857 Native Mounted Police carbine, 37in., barrel 21in., struck with Birmingham proofs, regulation brass mounted walnut full-stock with 'E.I.G. Bombay Arsenal' mark and 'WD Birmingham 1887' storekeeper's stamp.Steel barrel bands, brass capped fore-end with captive rammer, barleycorn fore-sight, fixed rear. $535 £225

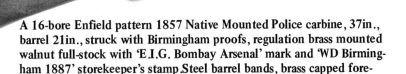

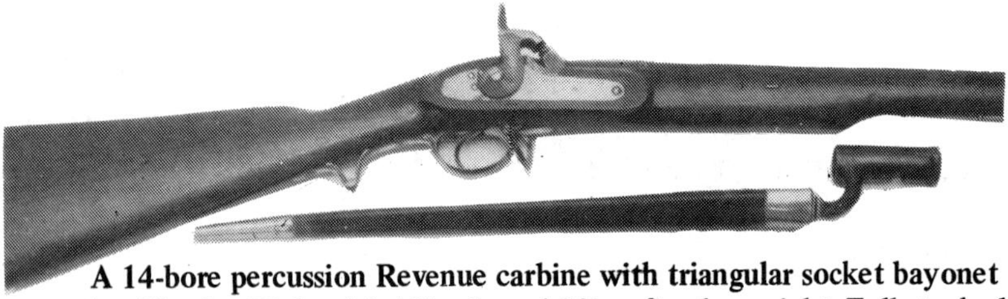

A 14-bore percussion Revenue carbine with triangular socket bayonet by 'Westley Richards', 46in., barrel 30in., fixed rearsight. Full-stocked, military style lock. Triangular socket bayonet 17in. numbered to gun retained by spring catch, with its brass mounted scabbard. Regulation brass mounts, scrolled trigger guard, steel sling swivels and ramrod. $540 £245

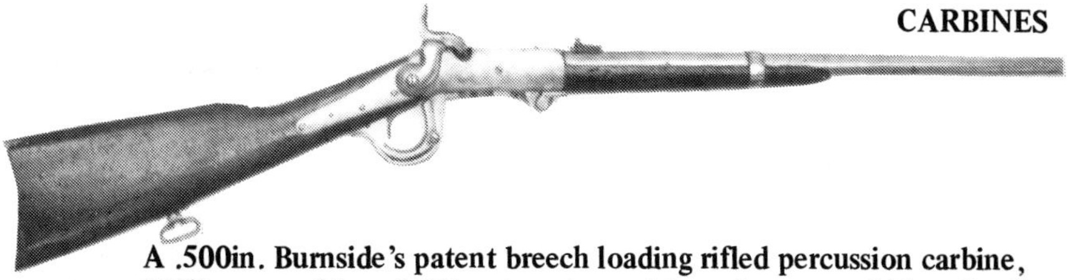

A .500in. Burnside's patent breech loading rifled percussion carbine, 39½in., round barrel 21in., to octagonal breech, stamped 'Cast Steel'. Flip-up fixed rearsight to 500 yards. Half-stocked, back-action lock. Steel saddle bar and lanyard ring. Sprung double trigger guard released hinged breech for loading. $550 £250

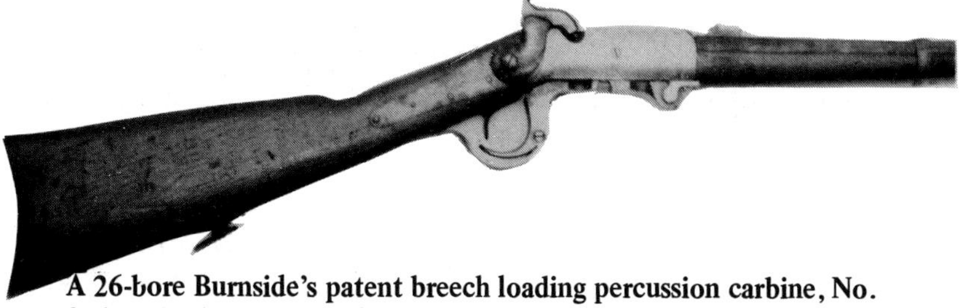

A 26-bore Burnside's patent breech loading percussion carbine, No. 35451, 39½in., round rifled barrel 21in., stamped 'Cast Steel'. Fixed foresight, twin flip-up rearsight with fixed graduations of 100, 300 and 500 yards. Half-stocked, with spring retained steel barrel band. Tip-down breech secured by double sprung trigger guard lever, steel saddle bar and lanyard ring on breech side. Back-action lock, steel buttcap. $564 £260

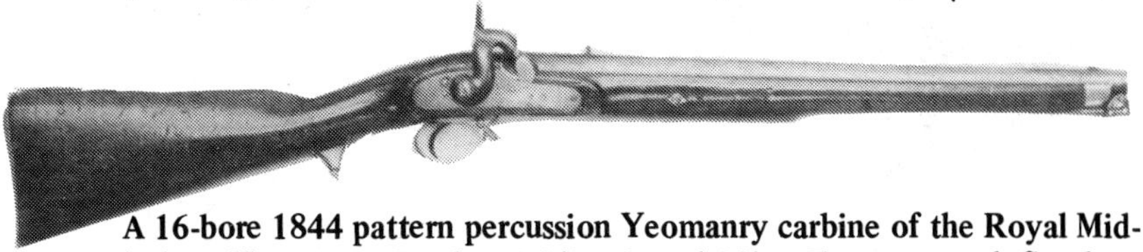

A 16-bore 1844 pattern percussion Yeomanry carbine of the Royal Midlothian Yeomanry Cavalry, 36½in., barrel 20in., Tower proved, fixed rearsight. Full-stocked, regulation brass mounts, trigger guard with finger scroll. Steel swivel ramrod, saddle bar with lanyard ring and lanyard loop on trigger guard. $640 £270

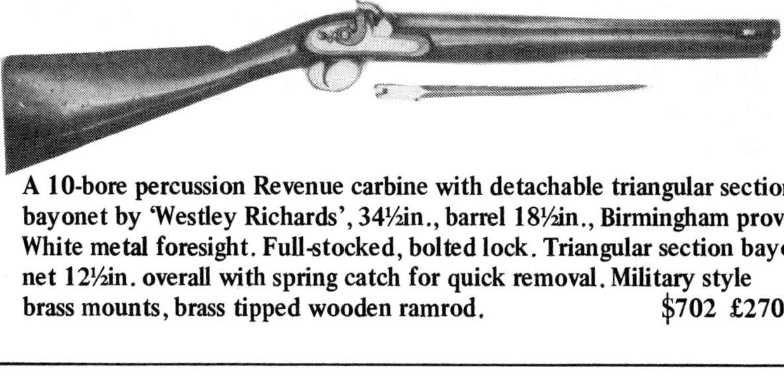

A 10-bore percussion Revenue carbine with detachable triangular section bayonet by 'Westley Richards', 34½in., barrel 18½in., Birmingham proved. White metal foresight. Full-stocked, bolted lock. Triangular section bayonet 12½in. overall with spring catch for quick removal. Military style brass mounts, brass tipped wooden ramrod. $702 £270

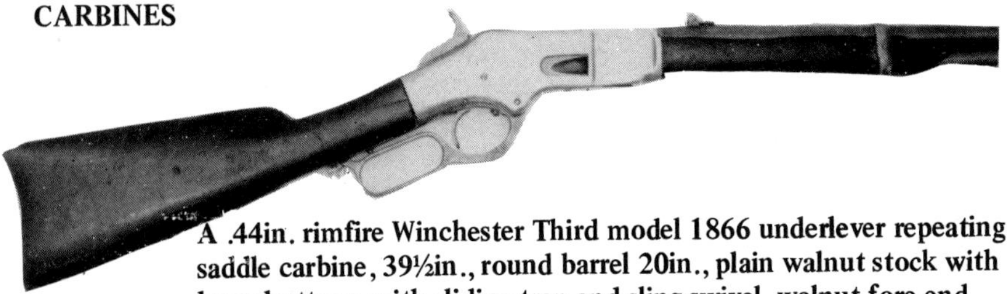

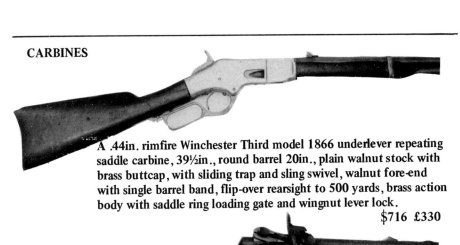

A .44in. rimfire Winchester Third model 1866 underlever repeating saddle carbine, 39½in., round barrel 20in., plain walnut stock with brass buttcap, with sliding trap and sling swivel, walnut fore-end with single barrel band, flip-over rearsight to 500 yards, brass action body with saddle ring loading gate and wingnut lever lock.

$716 £330

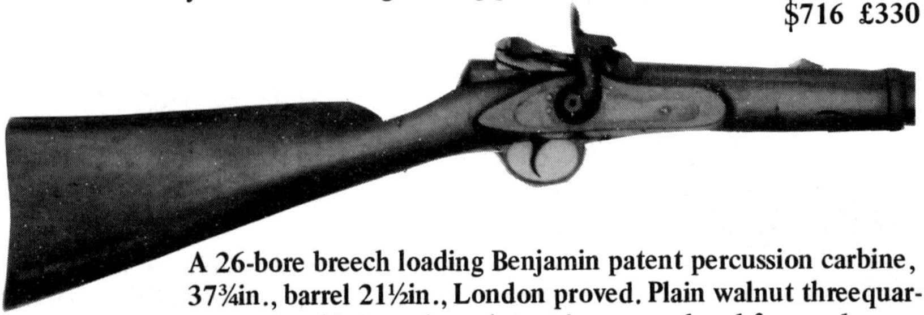

A 26-bore breech loading Benjamin patent percussion carbine, 37¾in., barrel 21½in., London proved. Plain walnut threequarter-stock with brass buttplate, trigger guard and fore-end cap, barrel with two bands, barleycorn foresight and two folding leaf rearsights to 300 yards. $770 £355

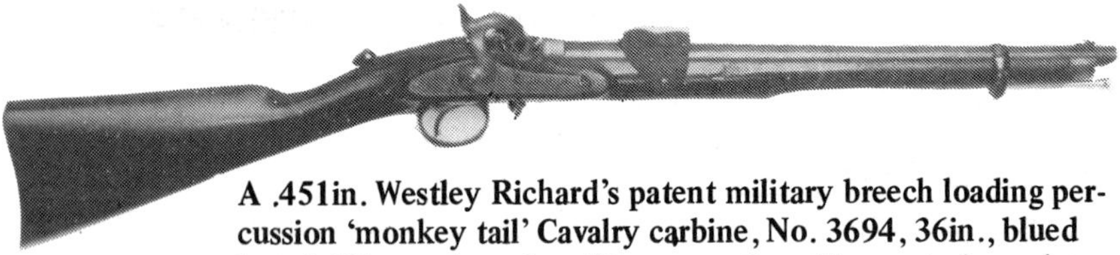

A .451in. Westley Richard's patent military breech loading percussion 'monkey tail' Cavalry carbine, No. 3694, 36in., blued barrel 18in., to breech, military proofs and inspector's marks, ramp ladder rearsight to 800 yards with original leather cover.

$1,185 £500

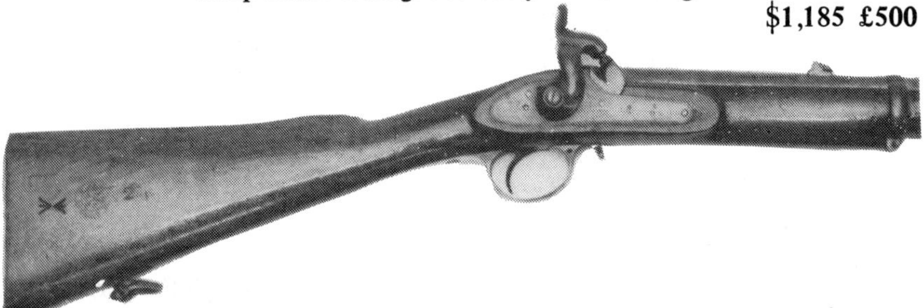

A .577in. Enfield First model 1853 Artillery carbine with long bayonet bar to barrel, 40¼in., barrel 24in., Tower proved. Walnut threequarter-stock with crisp Pimlico storekeeper's stamp with dated 1862, brass buttplate engraved 'V HA 52', brass trigger guard with loop for nipple protector (missing), two iron barrel bands and sling swivels. $1,144 £550

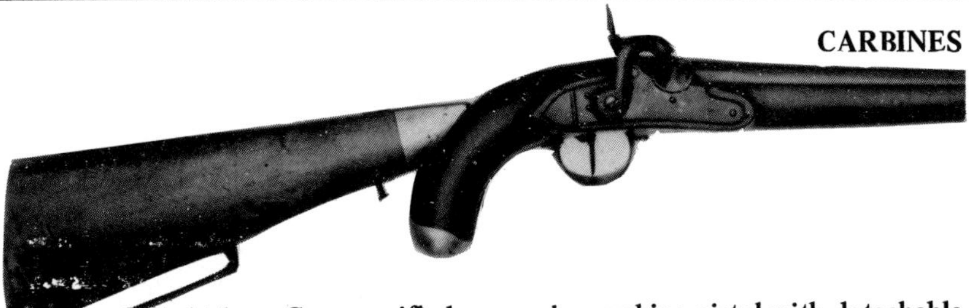

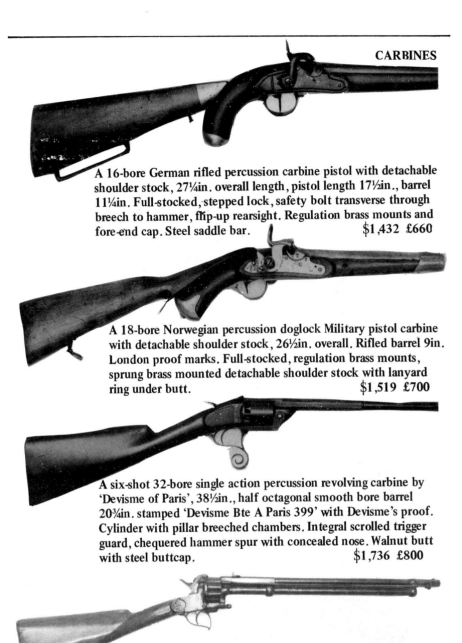

A 16-bore German rifled percussion carbine pistol with detachable shoulder stock, 27¼in. overall length, pistol length 17½in., barrel 11¼in. Full-stocked, stepped lock, safety bolt transverse through breech to hammer, flip-up rearsight. Regulation brass mounts and fore-end cap. Steel saddle bar. $1,432 £660

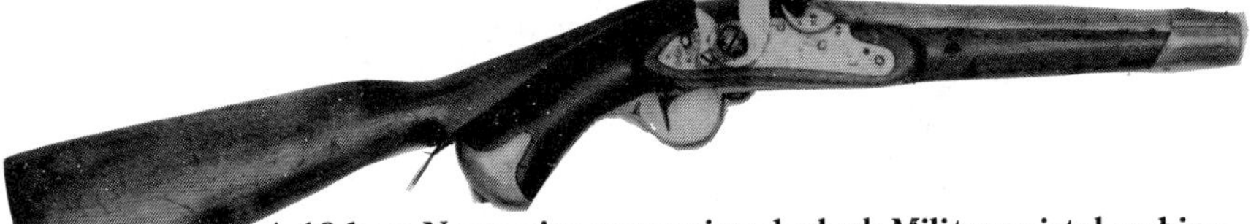

A 18-bore Norwegian percussion doglock Military pistol carbine with detachable shoulder stock, 26½in. overall. Rifled barrel 9in. London proof marks. Full-stocked, regulation brass mounts, sprung brass mounted detachable shoulder stock with lanyard ring under butt. $1,519 £700

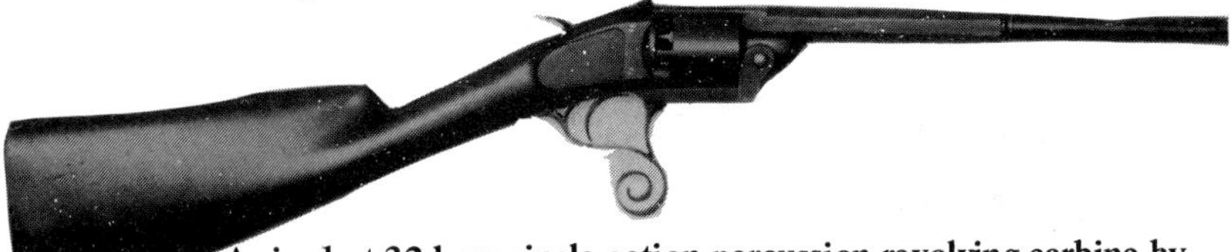

A six-shot 32-bore single action percussion revolving carbine by 'Devisme of Paris', 38½in., half octagonal smooth bore barrel 20¾in. stamped 'Devisme Bte A Paris 399' with Devisme's proof. Cylinder with pillar breeched chambers. Integral scrolled trigger guard, chequered hammer spur with concealed nose. Walnut butt with steel buttcap. $1,736 £800

A ten-shot 12mm/28-bore Le Mat single action pinfire percussion revolving carbine, 37¼in., part round, part octagonal 12mm. barrel 20in., the 28-bore smooth bored barrel 19in., chequered walnut stock with steel longspur buttplate and sling swivel, plain action body, gate loading, bead foresight, single folding leaf rearsight, fully church steeple fluted cylinder. $1,925 £875

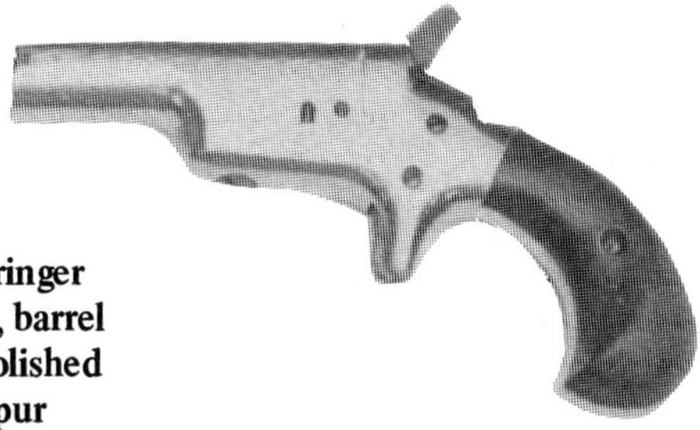

An S.S. .41in. rimfire Colt No. 3 derringer pistol, 5½in., barrel 2½in., No. 5095, barrel stamped 'Colt' and frame '41 Cal', polished rosewood grips to bird's head butt, spur trigger, side swing barrel for loading and ejection. $105 £45

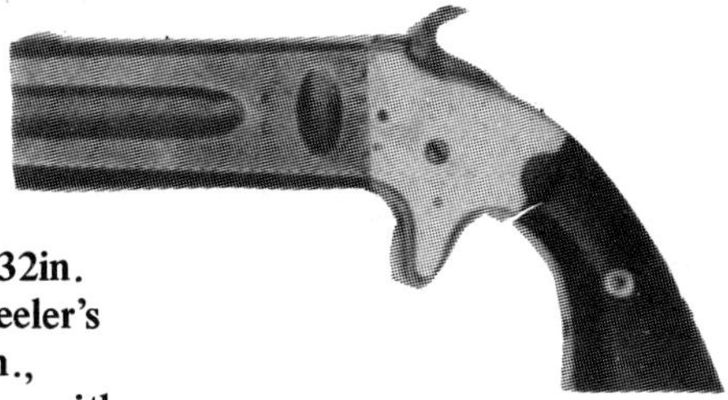

An over and under double barrelled .32in. rimfire 22in. American Arms Co. Wheeler's patent turnover derringer pistol, 5¾in., barrels 3in., nickel plated bronze frame with polished rosewood grips to angular butt, spur trigger. $187 £85

A four-shot .32in. rimfire Remington-Elliot ring trigger double action derringer, 5in., barrel group 3¼in., barrel rib stamped 'Elliot's Patent' with date to Oct 1, 1861, moulded hard rubber grips to angular butt, tip-up barrel for loading, rotating firing pin. $271 £125

An .41in. back-action percussion derringer, 4¼in., rifled barrel 1¾in., stamped 'J. Derringer Philadela' on breech. Full-stocked, foliate engraved lock, white metal furniture, pineapple finialled trigger guard, shield shaped escutcheon. $529 £230

A thirty-shot .303in. Bren Mark II light machine gun by 'Inglis', fully sectioned to show operation of moving parts, 46in., barrel 25in., No. 6T 9594, walnut stock and pistol grip sectioned to show operation of recoil and sear springs, the action body, gas port and piston housing similarly cut away, off-set blade foresight and folding tangent rearsight. $479 £210

MUSKETS

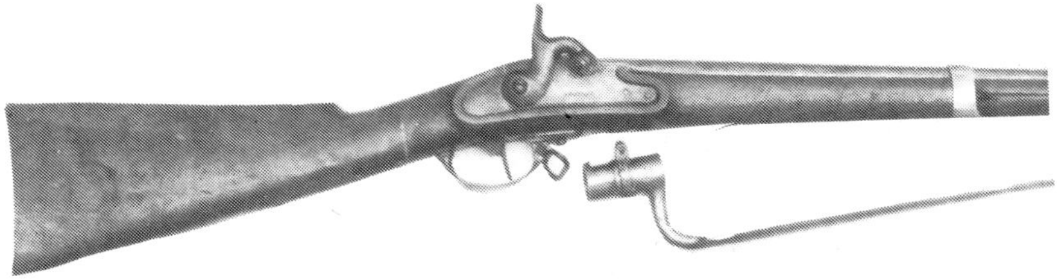

A 14-bore German Military percussion musket, 57½in., barrel 41in., stamped 'Mergentheim'. Full-stocked, lock stamped 'Haffner'. Regulation brass mounts, steel sling swivels, three sprung barrel bands, steel ramrod and triangular socket bayonet. $330 £150

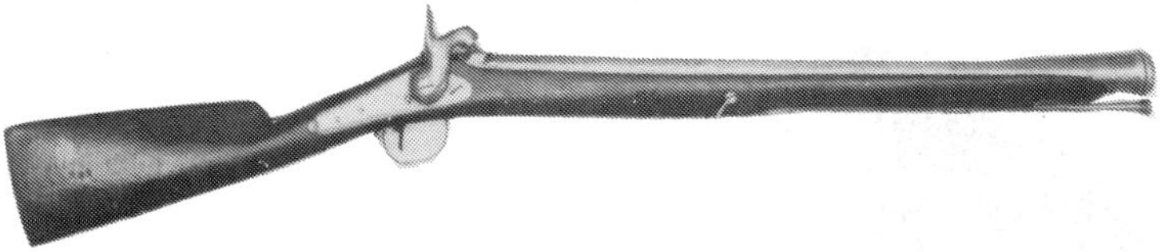

A Belgian back-action Military percussion musketoon, made for the Turkish or Egyptian Army, 39in., half octagonal swamped barrel 23½in. Fullstocked, lock of French military pattern struck with Arabic inscription. Regulation brass mounts, steel sling swivels and ramrod. $676 £260

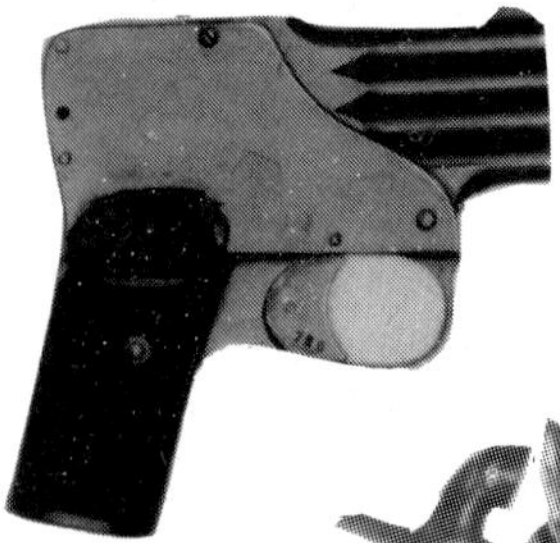

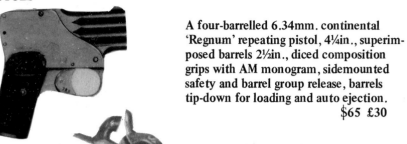

A four-barrelled 6.34mm. continental 'Regnum' repeating pistol, 4¼in., superimposed barrels 2½in., diced composition grips with AM monogram, sidemounted safety and barrel group release, barrels tip-down for loading and auto ejection. $65 £30

A double barrelled 12mm. Spanish pinfire pistol, 8¾in., blued side by side barrels 5½in., inlaid with silver, 'FA De Jose Ao Arizmendi Eibar' amid geometric designs, ebony grip with carved foliate panels and steel cap and lanyard ring, folding triggers, dolphin hammers, tip-up barrels for loading. $171 £75

A .44in. American underhammer boxlock percussion rifled 'Bootleg Pistol', 10¼in., half octagonal, half round rifled barrel 6in., stamped 'Cast Steel'. Foliate engraved steel top-strap. Inlaid white metal sidenail plates and trigger plate with spiked finial. One-piece chequered grip and back-strap. $195 £90

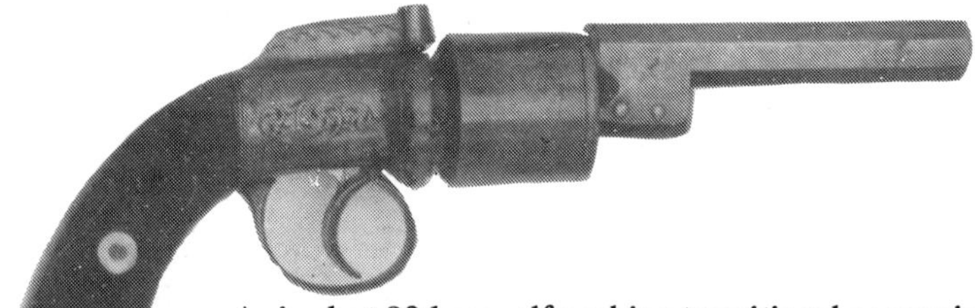

A six-shot 80-bore self-cocking transitional percussion revolving pistol, 10in., octagonal barrel 4in., London proved. Engraved 'Reilly, 205 New Oxford Street, London', foliate and border engraved round frame with integral nipple shield. Frond tip engraved bar hammer pierced for sighting. Two-piece chequered walnut grips. $286 £130

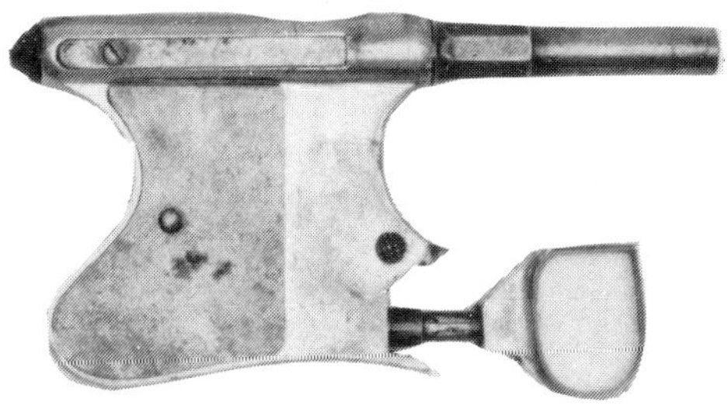

A .32in. Tribuzio squeezer magazine pistol, 5¼in., barrel octagonal at breech 2¾in., brass frame with steel sideplate and magazine cover. 'D' shaped finger ring for middle finger which when squeezed chambers a cartridge, cocks the action and fires. Upon release the breech block retracts ejecting spent cartridge case. $322 £155

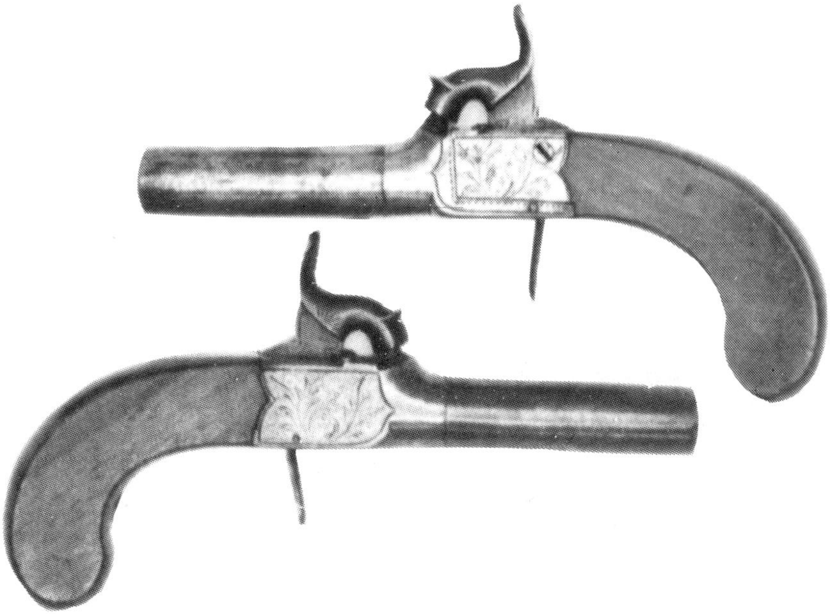

A pair of boxlock percussion pistols by 'Smith, London', 6¾in., turn-off barrels 2½in., plain slab walnut butts with inlet white metal wrist escutcheon, folding triggers, border and scroll engraved frames. Birmingham proved. $385 £175

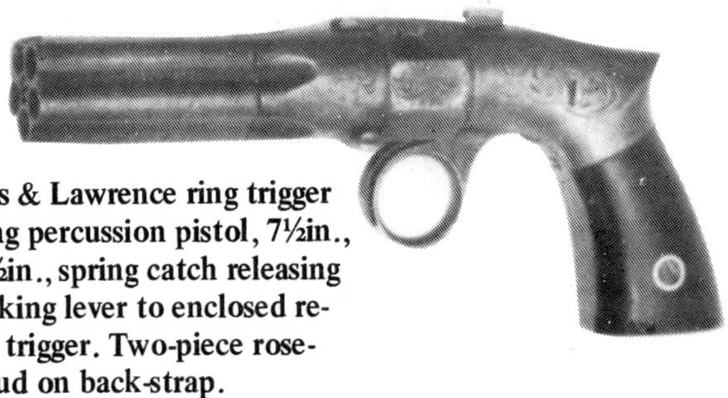

A five-shot .32in. Robbins & Lawrence ring trigger self-cocking breech loading percussion pistol, 7½in., turn-off fluted barrels, 2½in., spring catch releasing tip-down breech, ring cocking lever to enclosed revolving hammer, separate trigger. Two-piece rosewood grips with safety stud on back-strap. $396 £180

A pair of .31in. boxlock underhammer rifled percussion 'bootleg' pistols, 10½in., turn-off heavy octagonal barrels 6in., engraved 'Cocksedge, Hadleigh', Birmingham proved, foliate engraved frames, slab walnut butts with vacant oval white metal escutcheons. $520 £200

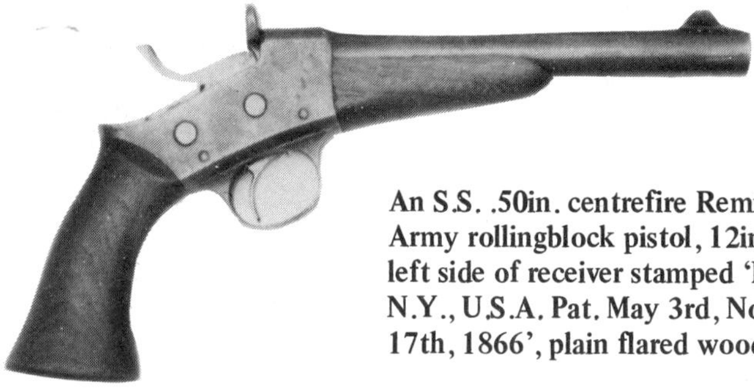

An S.S. .50in. centrefire Remington model 1871 Army rollingblock pistol, 12in., round barrel 8in., left side of receiver stamped 'Remington's, Ilion. N.Y., U.S.A. Pat. May 3rd, Nov 15th 1864, April 17th, 1866', plain flared wooden grip. $532 £245

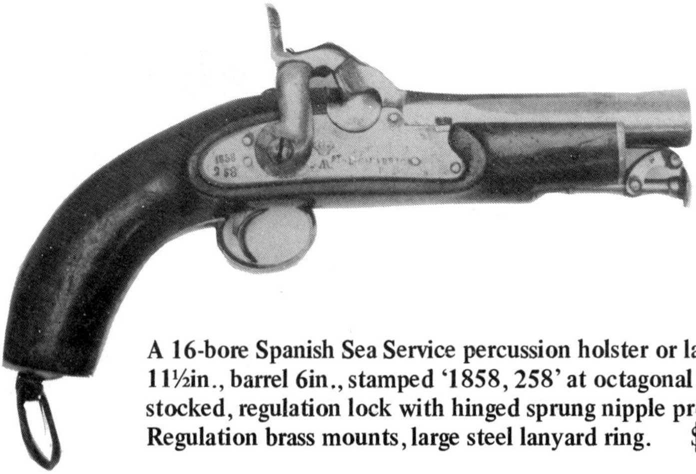

A 16-bore Spanish Sea Service percussion holster or lanyard pistol, 11½in., barrel 6in., stamped '1858, 258' at octagonal breech. Full-stocked, regulation lock with hinged sprung nipple protector. Regulation brass mounts, large steel lanyard ring. $651 £300

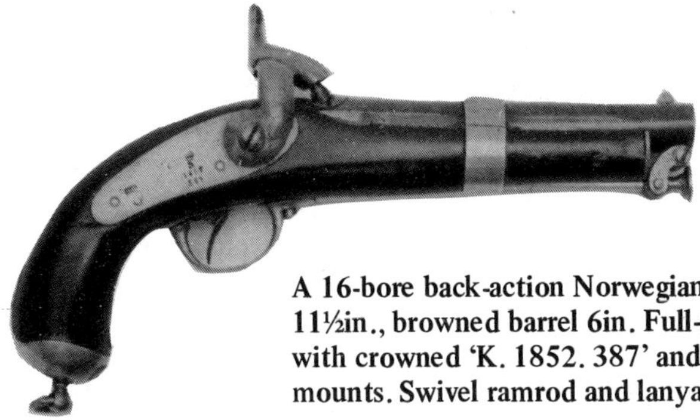

A 16-bore back-action Norwegian Naval percussion pistol, 11½in., browned barrel 6in. Full-stocked, lock stamped with crowned 'K. 1852. 387' and 'O.G.'. Regulation brass mounts. Swivel ramrod and lanyard ring. $673 £310

An H. Colleye's patent Belgian four-shot .36in. rising magazine self-cocking percussion pistol , No. 1443, 10in., octagonal damascus twist rifled barrel 3¾in. Slightly rounded foliate engraved frame, en suite with Liege proved square section re-loadable magazine, numbered to pistol. Ring trigger, two-piece chequered walnut grips. $866 £380

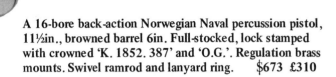

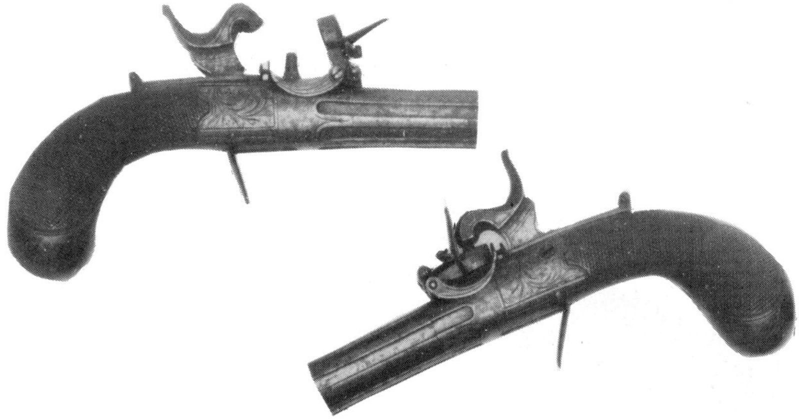

A pair of 48-bore boxlock percussion 'top hat' pistols by 'Mace of Reading', 6in., boldly fluted turn-off barrels, 1¾in., Birmingham proved. Foliate engraved rounded frames. Sliding top thumb safety catch locking tension sprung cap retainers to fences. Cap retainers with twin roller bearing springs. Concealed triggers. Rounded chequered walnut butts with oval silver escutcheons. $988 £475

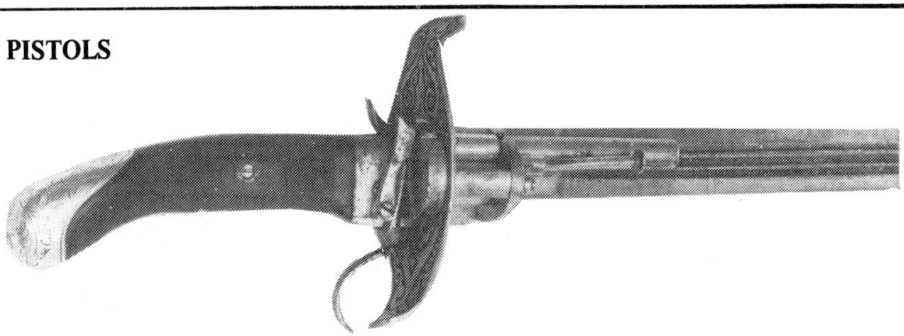

A six-shot 7mm. pinfire Le Faucheux single action hanger pistol, 27in. overall, barrel 3¼in., well chequered ebony grips to hilt with engraved rounded slightly down-turned pommel, multi-fullered double edged spear pointed blade 19½in., mounted slightly to the left side of grip. The revolver, to the right of the blade and mounted through the guard is of the gate loading rod ejection variety. The guard, pistol and hilt mounts all silver plated. $1,300 £500

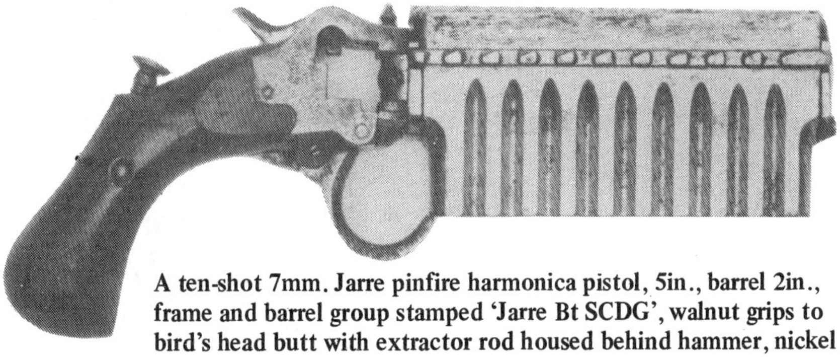

A ten-shot 7mm. Jarre pinfire harmonica pistol, 5in., barrel 2in., frame and barrel group stamped 'Jarre Bt SCDG', walnut grips to bird's head butt with extractor rod housed behind hammer, nickel plated frame with guardless heavily curved trigger, small hammer and turned bead foresight mounted on frame just ahead of hammer. $1,302 £600

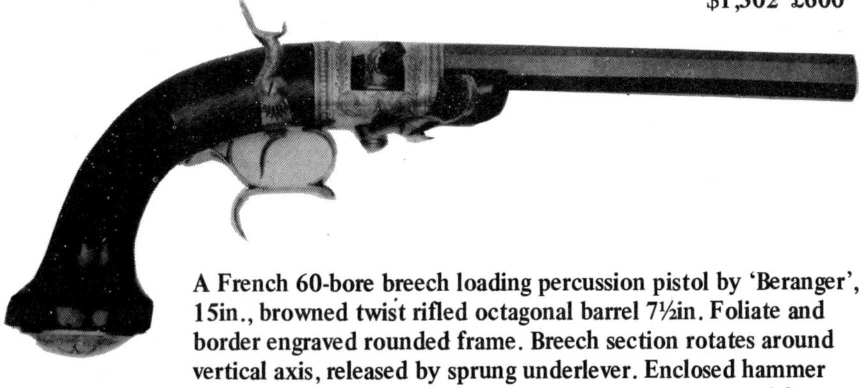

A French 60-bore breech loading percussion pistol by 'Beranger', 15in., browned twist rifled octagonal barrel 7½in. Foliate and border engraved rounded frame. Breech section rotates around vertical axis, released by sprung underlever. Enclosed hammer cocked by engraved external lever. Foliate engraved steel furniture, scrolled trigger guard. Chequered walnut grip. $1,302 £600

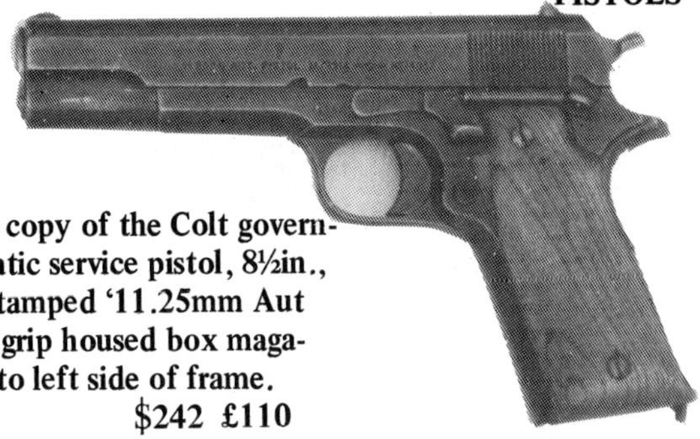

A seven-shot .45in. Norwegian copy of the Colt government model 1911 semi automatic service pistol, 8½in., barrel 5in., dated 1927, slide stamped '11.25mm Aut Pistol M/1914', wooden grips, grip housed box magazine and safety, thumb safety to left side of frame. $242 £110

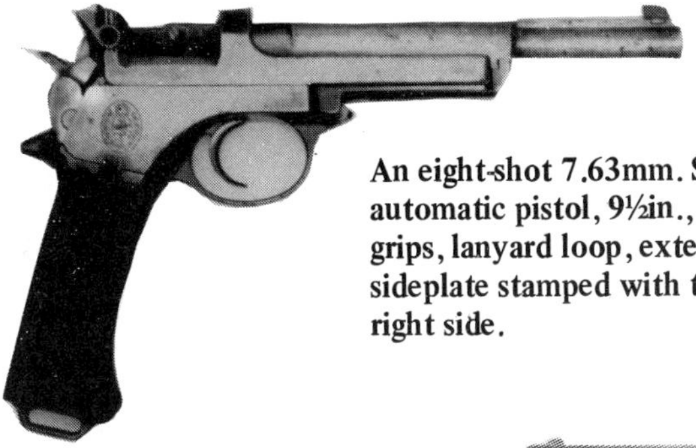

An eight-shot 7.63mm. Steyr Mannlicher 1905 semi automatic pistol, 9½in., barrel 6¼in., ribbed wooden grips, lanyard loop, external hammer, the removeable sideplate stamped with the Argentinian crest to the right side. $282 £130

A seven-shot .45in. ACP Colt model 1905 Military semi automatic pistol, 8¼in., barrel 5in., No. 6034, slide stamped with maker's name and address, patent dates to Dec 19th, 1905 and 'Automatic Colt Calibre 45 Rimless Smokeless', chequered walnut grips, two-point barrel suspension, slide hole open to left side. $355 £150

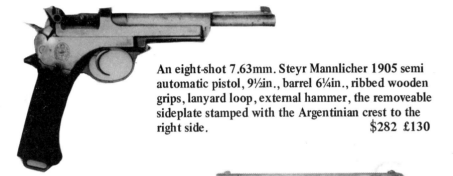

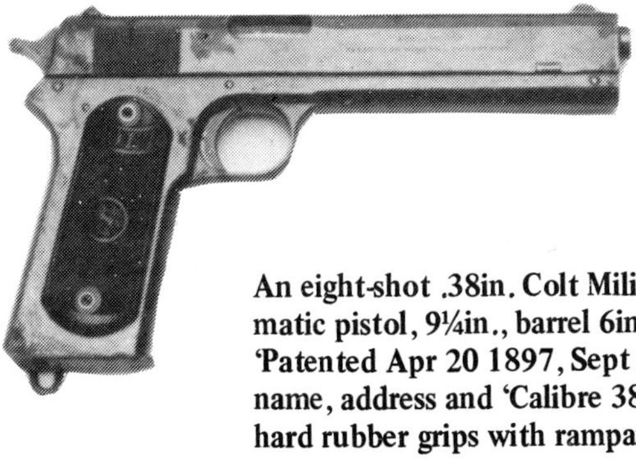

An eight-shot .38in. Colt Military model of 1902, semi-automatic pistol, 9¼in., barrel 6in., No. 37455, slide stamped 'Patented Apr 20 1897, Sept 9 1902', together with maker's name, address and 'Calibre 38 Rimless Smokeless', moulded hard rubber grips with rampant Colt monogram. $365 £155

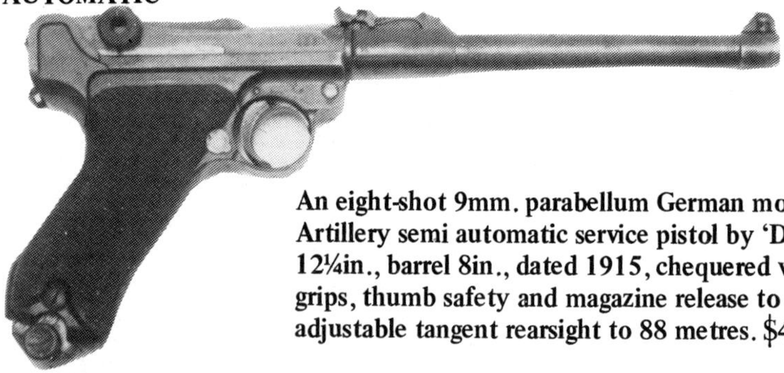

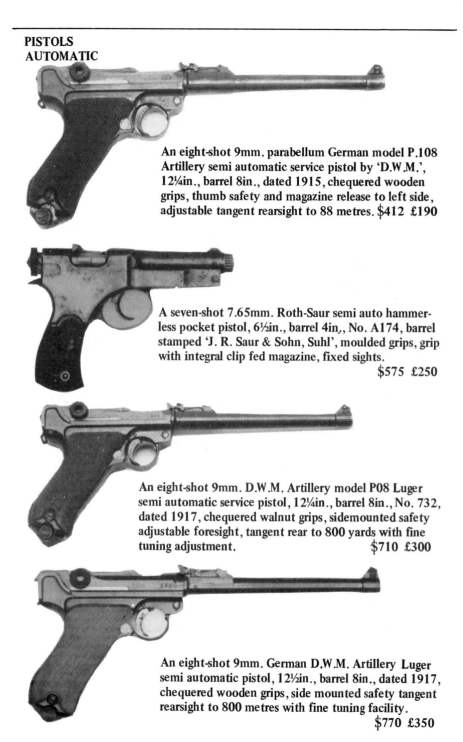

An eight-shot 9mm. parabellum German model P.108 Artillery semi automatic service pistol by 'D.W.M.', 12¼in., barrel 8in., dated 1915, chequered wooden grips, thumb safety and magazine release to left side, adjustable tangent rearsight to 88 metres. $412 £190

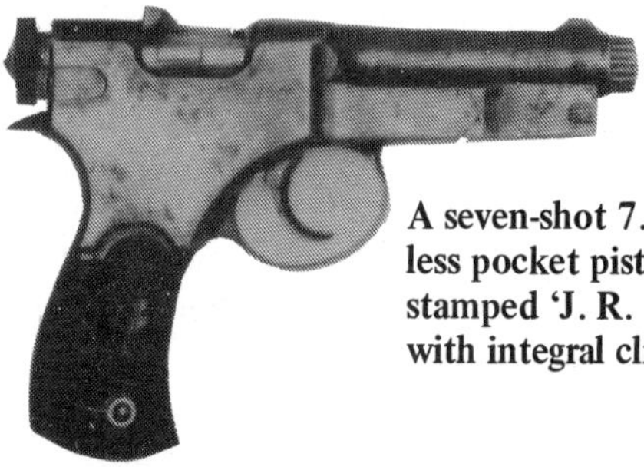

A seven-shot 7.65mm. Roth-Saur semi auto hammerless pocket pistol, 6½in., barrel 4in., No. A174, barrel stamped 'J. R. Saur & Sohn, Suhl', moulded grips, grip with integral clip fed magazine, fixed sights.
$575 £250

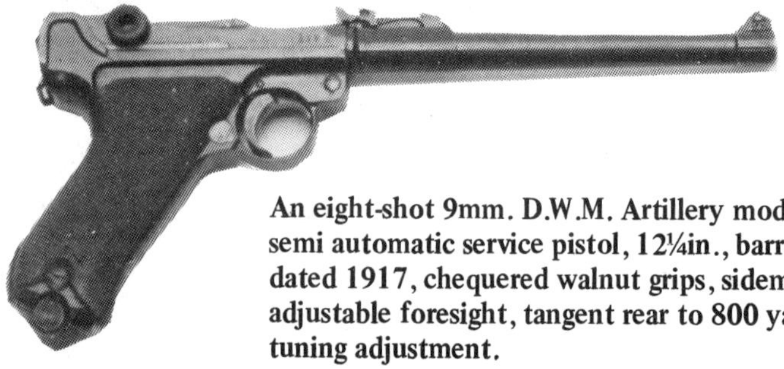

An eight-shot 9mm. D.W.M. Artillery model P08 Luger semi automatic service pistol, 12¼in., barrel 8in., No. 732, dated 1917, chequered walnut grips, sidemounted safety adjustable foresight, tangent rear to 800 yards with fine tuning adjustment. $710 £300

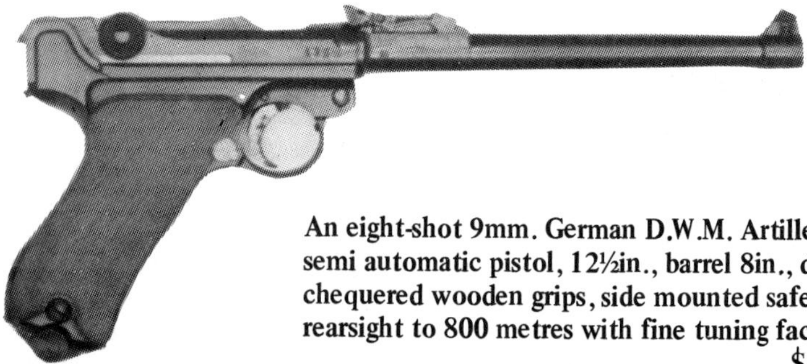

An eight-shot 9mm. German D.W.M. Artillery Luger semi automatic pistol, 12½in., barrel 8in., dated 1917, chequered wooden grips, side mounted safety tangent rearsight to 800 metres with fine tuning facility.
$770 £350

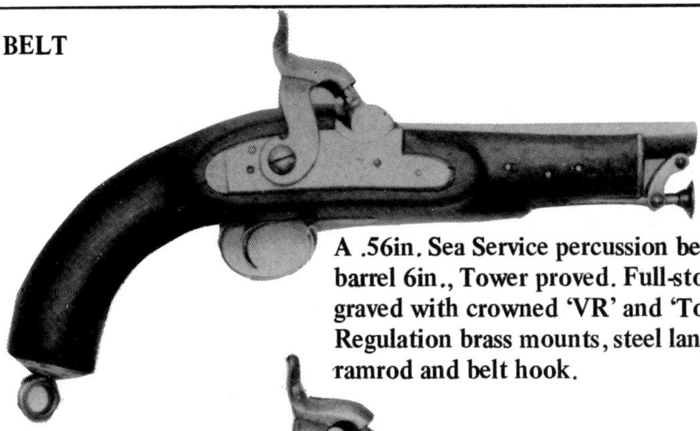

A .56in. Sea Service percussion belt pistol, 11½in., barrel 6in., Tower proved. Full-stocked, lock engraved with crowned 'VR' and 'Tower' on tail. Regulation brass mounts, steel lanyard ring, swivel ramrod and belt hook. $271 £125

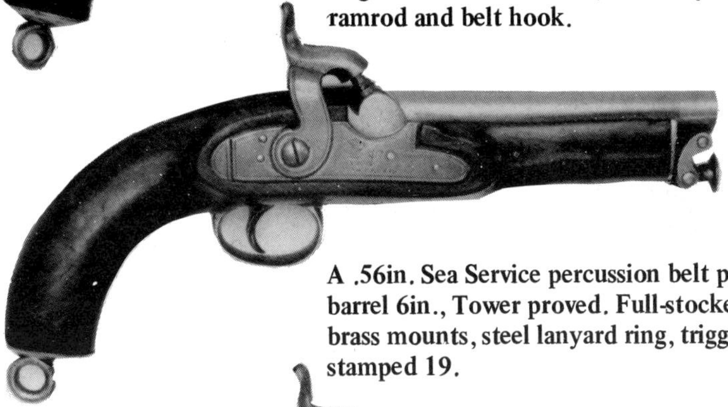

A .56in. Sea Service percussion belt pistol, 11½in., barrel 6in., Tower proved. Full-stocked, regulation brass mounts, steel lanyard ring, trigger guard bow stamped 19. $282 £130

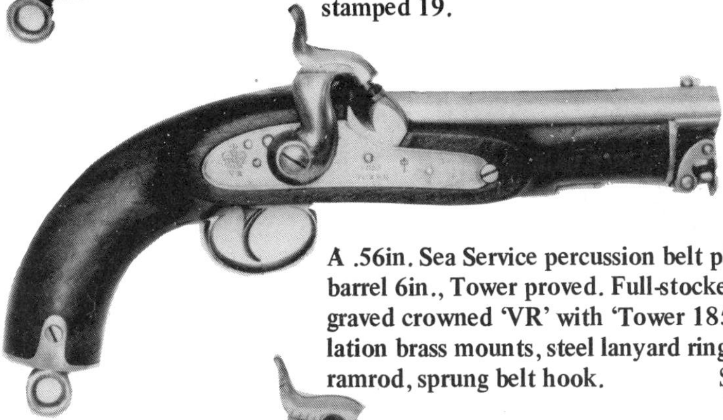

A .56in. Sea Service percussion belt pistol, 11½in., barrel 6in., Tower proved. Full-stocked, lock engraved crowned 'VR' with 'Tower 1855'. Regulation brass mounts, steel lanyard ring, swivel ramrod, sprung belt hook. $325 £150

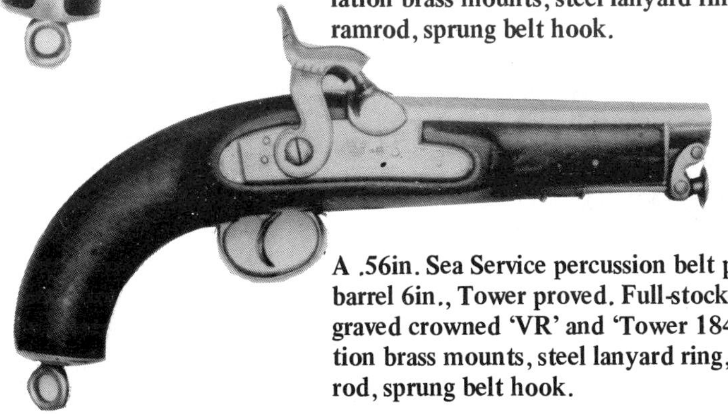

A .56in. Sea Service percussion belt pistol, 11½in., barrel 6in., Tower proved. Full-stocked, lock engraved crowned 'VR' and 'Tower 1846'. Regulation brass mounts, steel lanyard ring, swivel ramrod, sprung belt hook. $369 £170

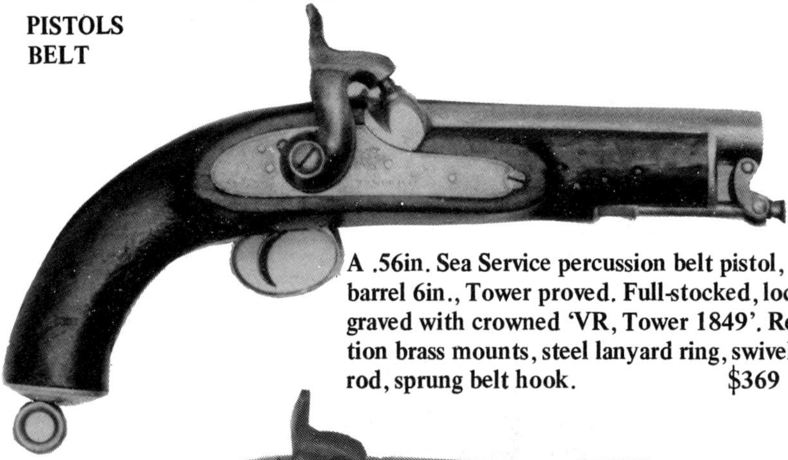

A .56in. Sea Service percussion belt pistol, 11½in., barrel 6in., Tower proved. Full-stocked, lock engraved with crowned 'VR, Tower 1849'. Regulation brass mounts, steel lanyard ring, swivel ramrod, sprung belt hook. $369 £170

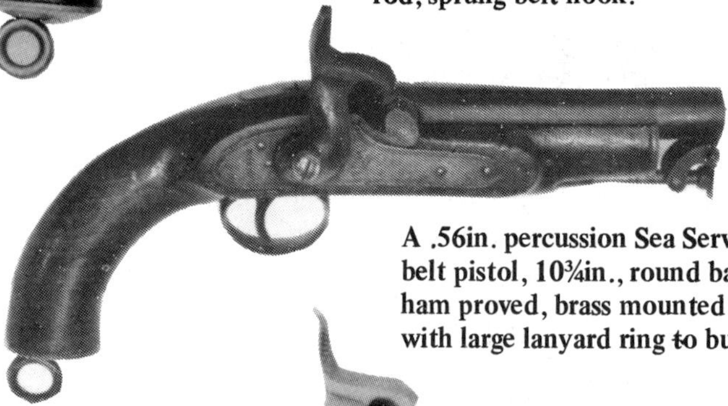

A .56in. percussion Sea Service type percussion belt pistol, 10¾in., round barrel 5¾in., Birmingham proved, brass mounted walnut full-stock, with large lanyard ring to buttcap. $396 £180

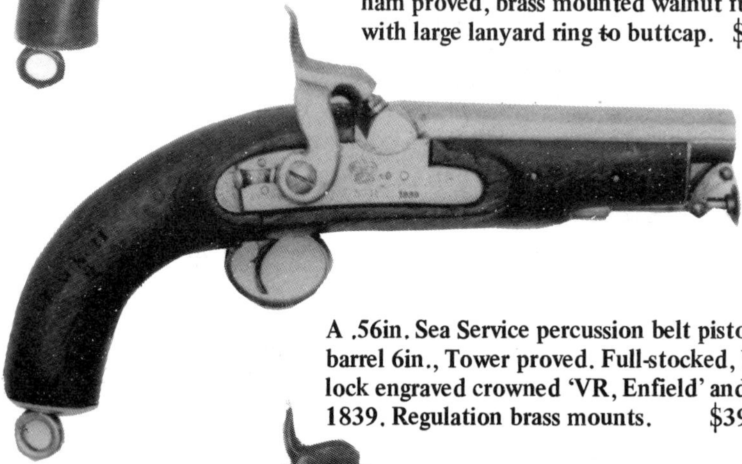

A .56in. Sea Service percussion belt pistol, 11½in., barrel 6in., Tower proved. Full-stocked, bolted lock engraved crowned 'VR, Enfield' and stamped 1839. Regulation brass mounts. $391 £180

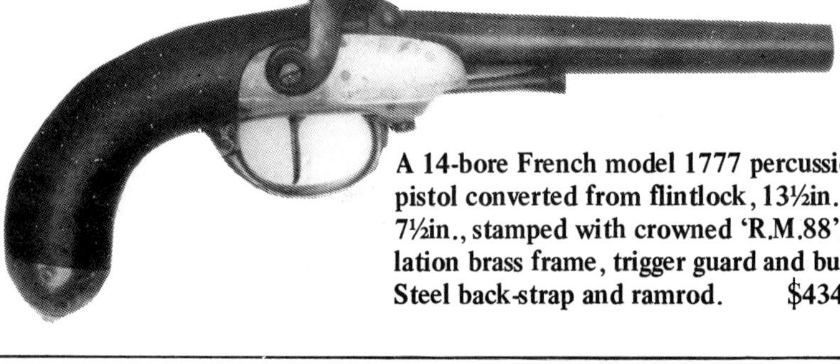

A 14-bore French model 1777 percussion belt pistol converted from flintlock, 13½in., barrel 7½in., stamped with crowned 'R.M.88'. Regulation brass frame, trigger guard and buttcap. Steel back-strap and ramrod. $434 £200

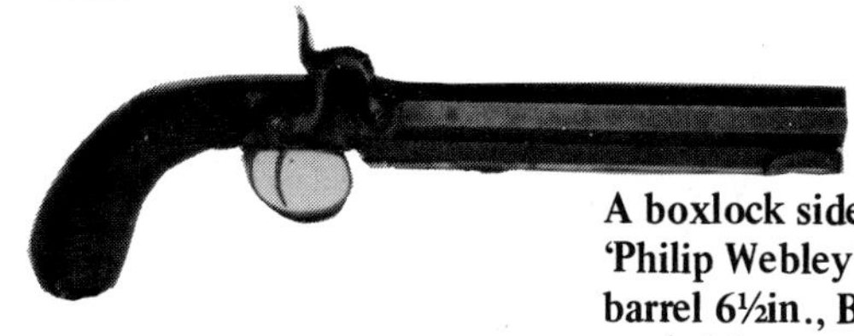

A boxlock sidehammer percussion belt pistol by 'Philip Webley', 11in., deeply rifled octagonal barrel 6½in., Birmingham proved. Foliate engraved frame and dolphin hammer. Swivel ramrod on lower rib. $478 £230

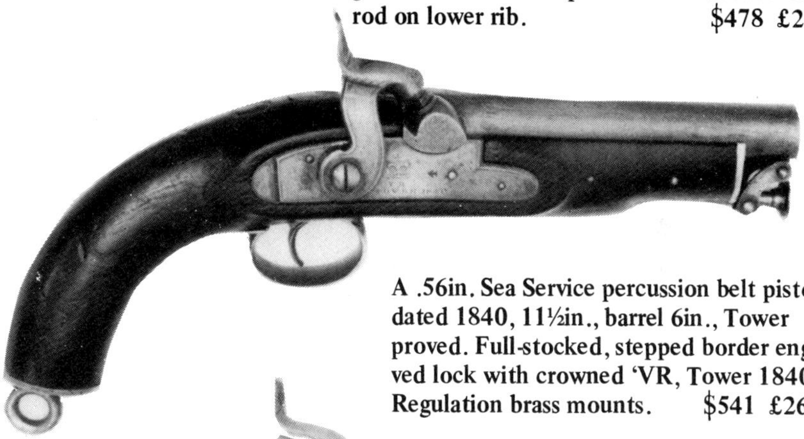

A .56in. Sea Service percussion belt pistol, dated 1840, 11½in., barrel 6in., Tower proved. Full-stocked, stepped border engraved lock with crowned 'VR, Tower 1840'. Regulation brass mounts. $541 £260

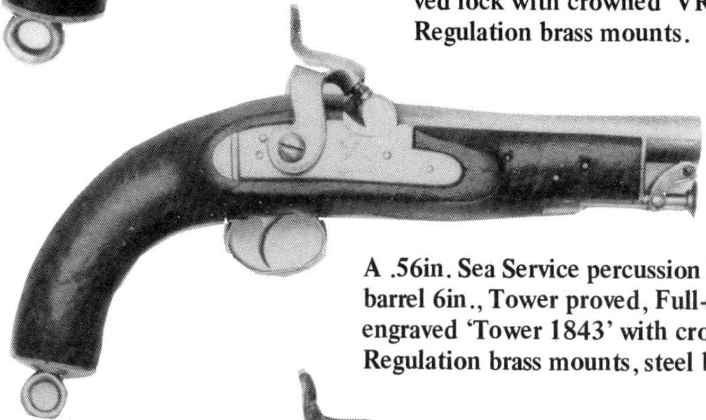

A .56in. Sea Service percussion belt pistol, 11in., barrel 6in., Tower proved, Full-stocked, lock engraved 'Tower 1843' with crowned 'VR'. Regulation brass mounts, steel belt hook. $608 £280

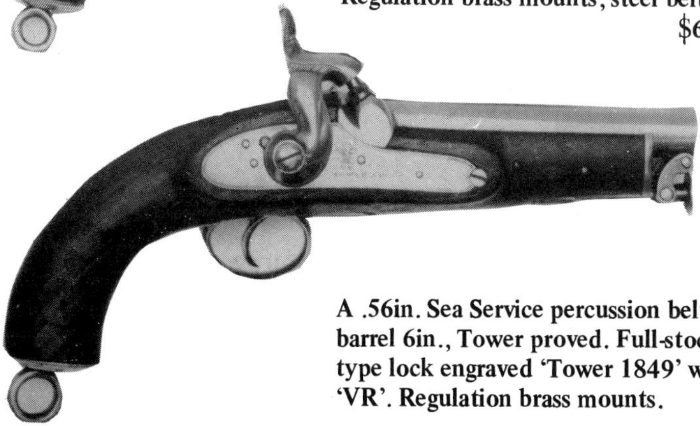

A .56in. Sea Service percussion belt pistol, 11in., barrel 6in., Tower proved. Full-stocked, Enfield type lock engraved 'Tower 1849' with crowned 'VR'. Regulation brass mounts. $608 £280

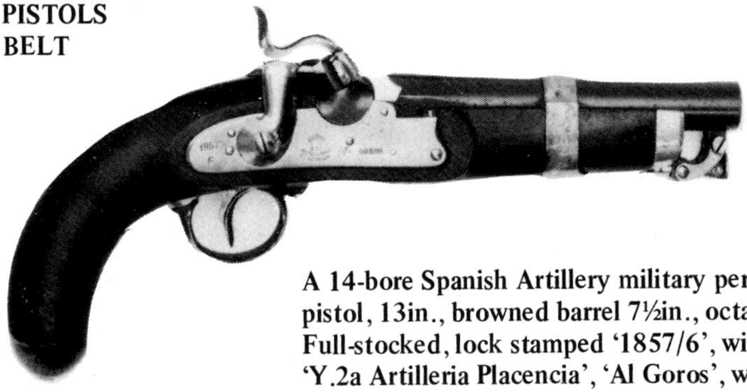

A 14-bore Spanish Artillery military percussion belt pistol, 13in., browned barrel 7½in., octagonal breech. Full-stocked, lock stamped '1857/6', with crowned 'Y.2a Artilleria Placencia', 'Al Goros', with spring hinged nipple safety catch. Regulation brass mounts. $825 £380

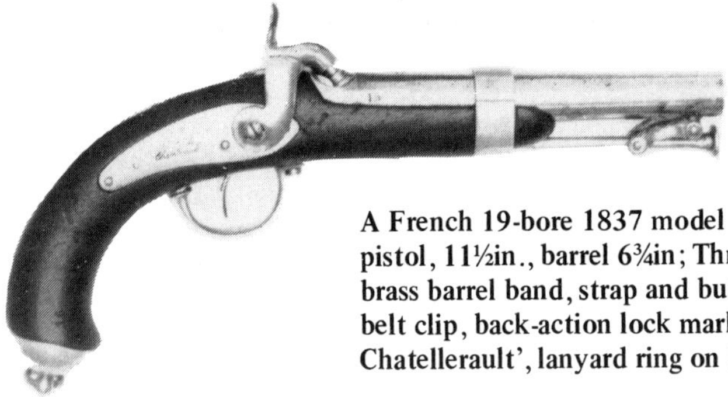

A French 19-bore 1837 model Naval percussion belt pistol, 11½in., barrel 6¾in; Threequarter-stocked, brass barrel band, strap and buttcap, swivel ramrod, belt clip, back-action lock marked 'Mre Rle De Chatellerault', lanyard ring on butt. $980 £430

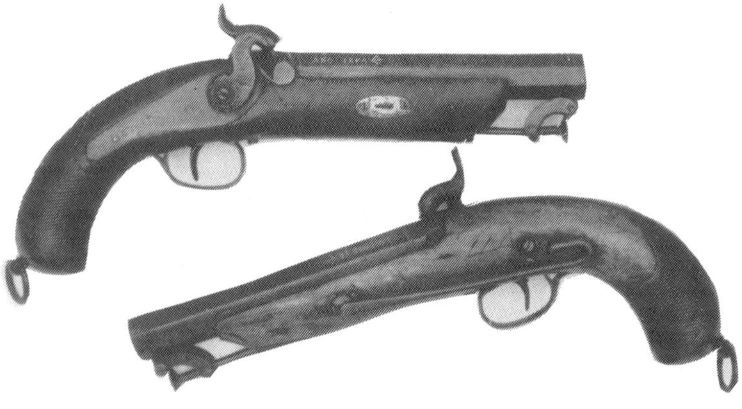

A brace of 12-bore back-action Spanish percussion belt pistols by 'Gastelu of Eibar', dated 1866, 11½in., octagonal barrels 6in., silver inlaid 'En Eibar Por Gastelu Ano 1866' with sprigs and twin silver breech lines. Full-stocked, foliate engraved locks and steel furniture. Steel back-straps integral with butt-caps, steel lanyard rings. $990 £450

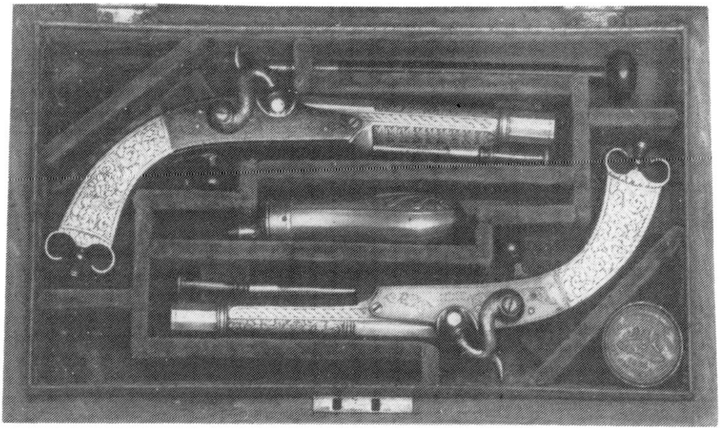

A pair of 54-bore all-metal Scottish percussion belt pistols, by 'J. D. Dougall of Glasgow', 10in., white metal octagonal barrels 6in., foliate engraved breeches, stocks with ram's horn butts. Sprung steel belt hooks, steel ramrod. Contained in a maroon velvet lined and fitted mahogany case. $1,650 £750

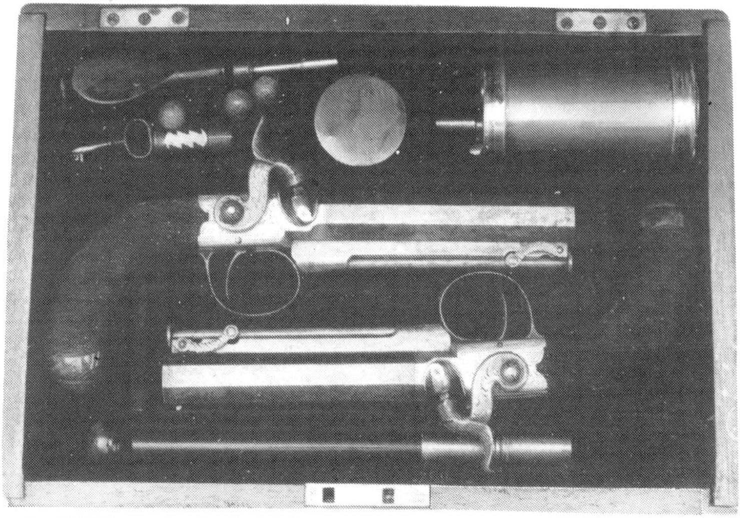

A pair of 32-bore boxlock sidehammer percussion belt pistols, 8¾in., octagonal barrels 4in., Birmingham proved, foliate engraved muzzles, swivel ramrods on lower ribs, engraved 'Egg London' on top flats. Foliate engraved brass frames, sprung belt hooks on left hand of frames, dolphin hammers, rounded chequered grips with white metal escutcheons and buttplates. Contained in a later velvet lined fitted polished mahogany case. $1,953 £900

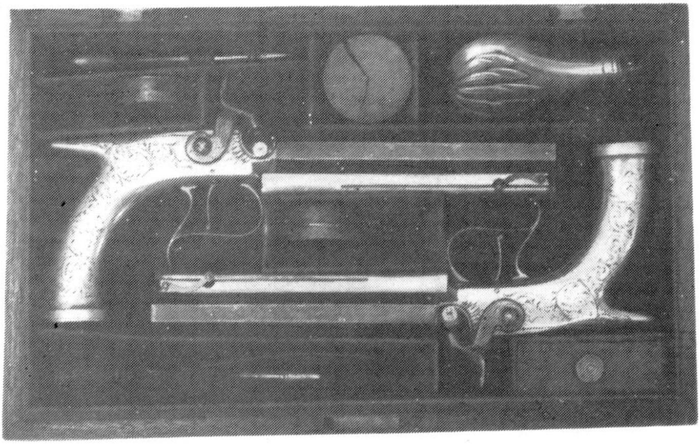

A pair of 44-bore boxlock sidehammer all-metal percussion belt pistols, 9¼in., octagonal twist barrels 5¼in., Birmingham proved, engraved 'Manton Patent, London', foliate engraved muzzles. White metal stocks foliate engraved overall, saw-handled grips, spurred white metal trigger guards, sprung steel belt hooks, swivel ramrods. Contained in their maroon beize lined fitted mahogany case. $2,340 £900

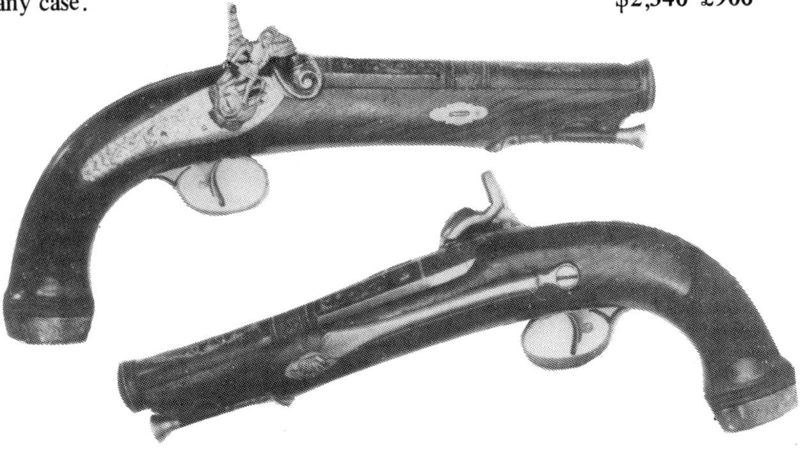

A pair of Spanish back-action percussion belt pistols, circa 1835, 12½in., half octagonal browned barrels 7in., with four gold maker's poincons, crowned 'Potche EP' and three flowers. Finely silver inlaid with scrolling foliate and 'Canon de Cintas', gilt filled foliate engraved breeches, gilt filled foliate chiselled steps. Full-stocked, hammers pierced and chiselled as Roman warriors standing on military trophies, striking nipples with shields. Foliate engraved steel furniture with a little gold infill. $2,730 £1,050

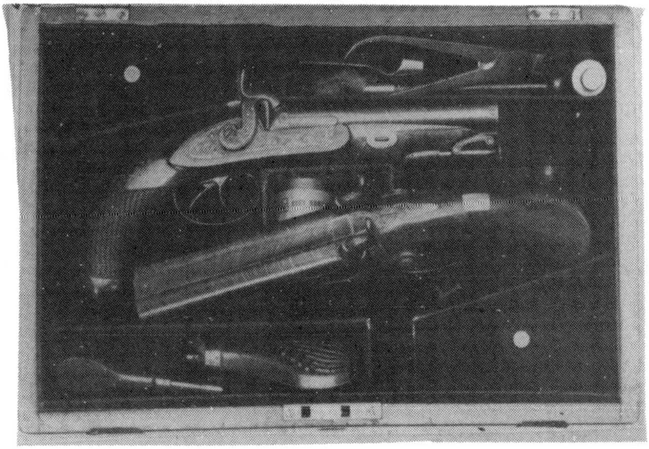

A pair of 28-bore double barrelled percussion belt pistols by 'Stevens', 11in., browned damascus twist barrels 5¾in., engraved 'Stevens London' on top ribs. Foliate engraved case coloured hardened breeches and locks with dolphin hammers. Foliate finialled blued steel trigger guards, swivel ramrods, rounded chequered grips. White metal barrel wedge plates and escutcheons. Polished walnut stocks. $3920 £1750

BLUNDERBUSS

A pair of French boxlock percussion blunderbuss pistols, 7¾in., turn-off half octagonal barrels 3in. with flared muzzles. Foliate engraved frames, top-straps and steel trigger guards. Rounded walnut grips inlaid with scrolling white metal wire, carved buttcaps inlaid with vacant shield shaped white metal escutcheons. $650 £250

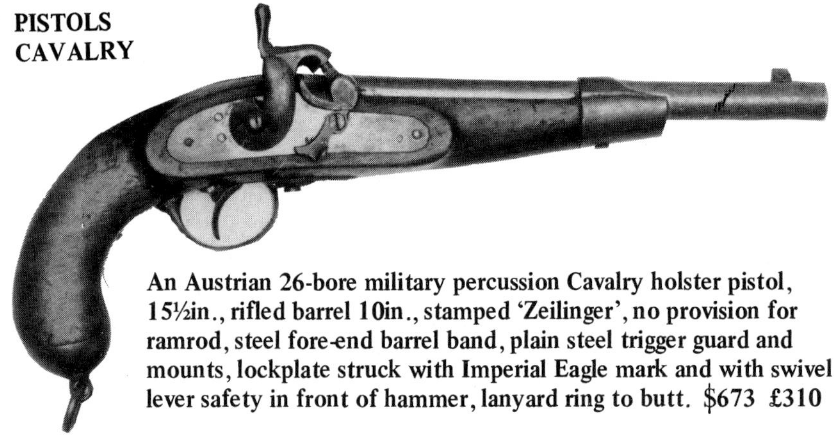

An Austrian 26-bore military percussion Cavalry holster pistol, 15½in., rifled barrel 10in., stamped 'Zeilinger', no provision for ramrod, steel fore-end barrel band, plain steel trigger guard and mounts, lockplate struck with Imperial Eagle mark and with swivel lever safety in front of hammer, lanyard ring to butt. $673 £310

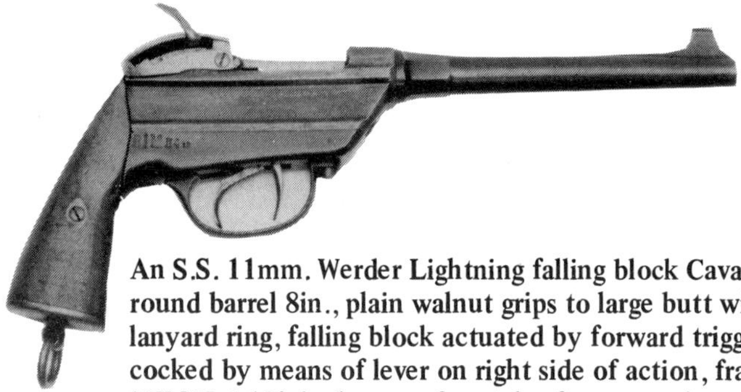

An S.S. 11mm. Werder Lightning falling block Cavalry pistol, 14¼in., round barrel 8in., plain walnut grips to large butt with steel cap, lanyard ring, falling block actuated by forward trigger, mechanism cocked by means of lever on right side of action, frame stamped 'BIM II 4 18', barleycorn foresight, frame notch rear. $868 £400

DUELLING

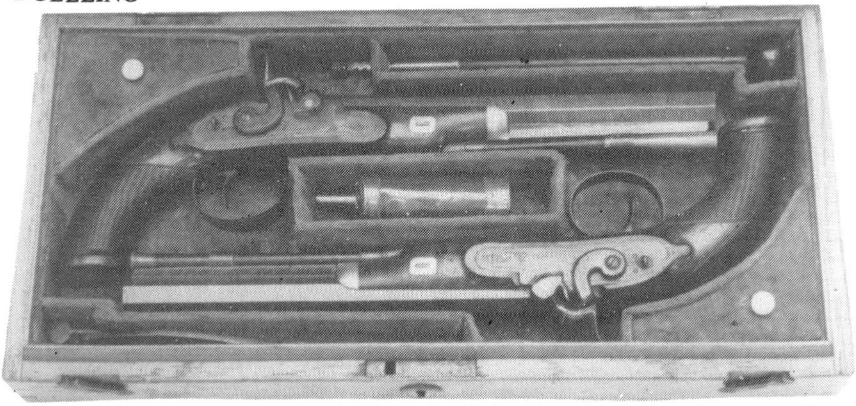

A pair of 30-bore percussion duelling pistols by 'Brander & Potts', converted from flintlock, 15½in., heavy browned octagonal twist barrels 10in., engraved 'Brander & Potts London', silver foresights, half-stocked, set triggers, detented actions. Contained in a velvet lined fitted oak case. $2,130 £900

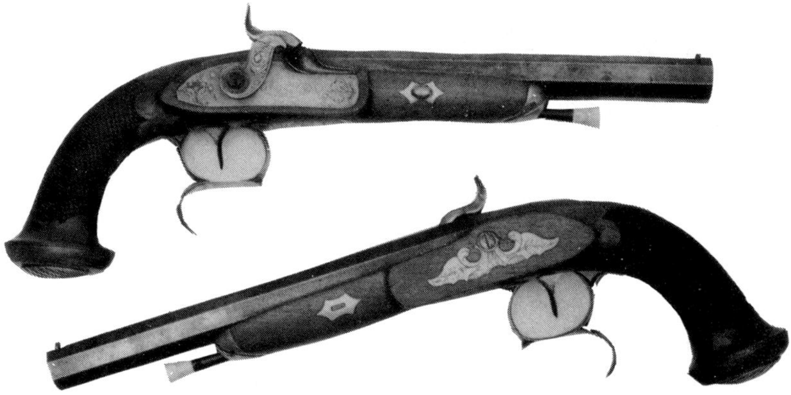

A pair of 32-bore French rifled percussion duelling pistols by 'Martiny of Marseille', 15¾in., octagonal heavy rifled barrels 8¾in., numbered 1 and 2 in gold. Half-stocked, locks silver inlaid 'Martiny a Marseille' and engraved with cornucopia and foliage. Engraved white metal furniture, spurred trigger guards, foliate trigger guard finials. Hinged cap traps in butts with fluted lids, ivory tipped whalebone ramrods with steel tips. Scale carved grips. $2,170 £1,000

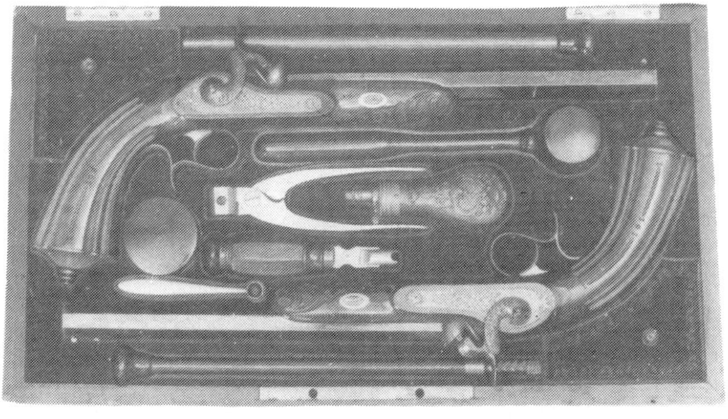

A pair of 46-bore French percussion duelling pistols by 'Verney of Lyon', 16in., blued octagonal barrels 10in., engraved 'Verney Jeune Suce. de Gobert a Lyon', deep fourteen-groove rifling. Half-stocked in finely figured French walnut. Foliate engraved stepped detented locks, en suite with scrolling foliage on steel furniture. Case hardened dull steel furniture, spurred trigger guards, facetted buttcaps with turned bosses. Contained in their maroon velvet close fitted rosewood veneered case. $5,200 £2,000

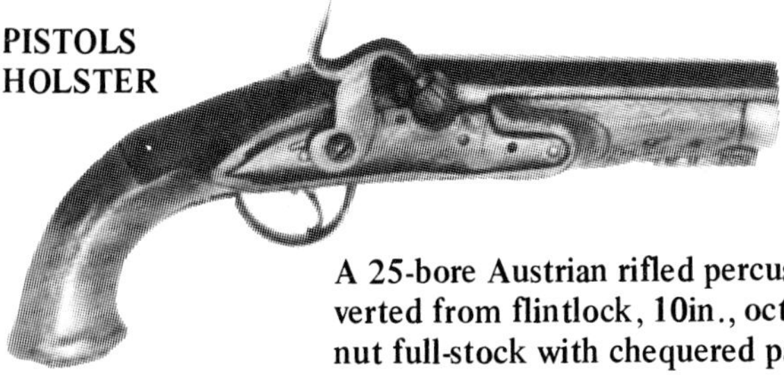

A 25-bore Austrian rifled percussion holster pistol converted from flintlock, 10in., octagonal barrel 5in., walnut full-stock with chequered panel behind barrel tang, horn capped fore-end, iron trigger guard and brass baluster ramrod thimble. $143 £65

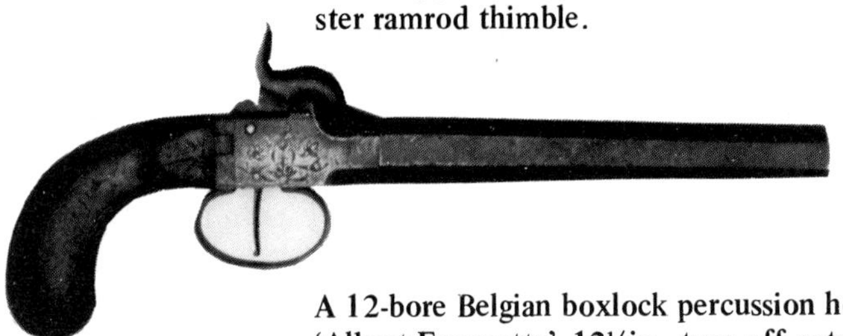

A 12-bore Belgian boxlock percussion holster pistol, by 'Albert Francotte', 12½in., turn-off octagonal barrel 6¾in., frame engraved with foliate and floral tributes, urn and fruit. Swollen walnut grip. $141 £65

A 32-bore Belgian boxlock percussion brass framed and barrelled holster pistol, fitted with spring bayonet, possibly made for a Naval officer, 9in., octagonal barrel 4½in. Liege proved. Roller bearing spring bayonet 4in., released by sliding trigger guard. Slab walnut butt with later brass gripstrap. $217 £100

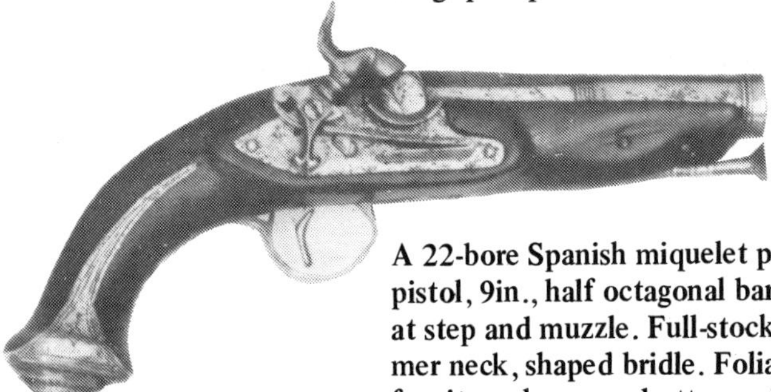

A 22-bore Spanish miquelet percussion holster pistol, 9in., half octagonal barrel 4½in., turned at step and muzzle. Full-stocked, stepped hammer neck, shaped bridle. Foliate engraved brass furniture, longspur buttcap with stepped swollen boss. Large sideplate. $338 £130

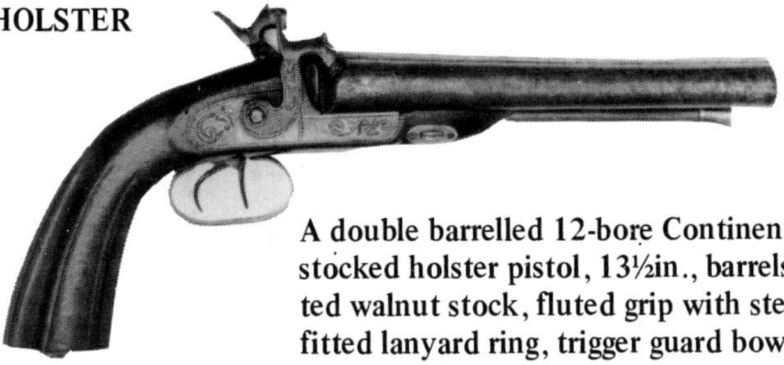

A double barrelled 12-bore Continental percussion half-stocked holster pistol, 13½in., barrels 8in., iron mounted walnut stock, fluted grip with steel buttcap with fitted lanyard ring, trigger guard bow, white metal cross bolt escutcheons. $291 £140

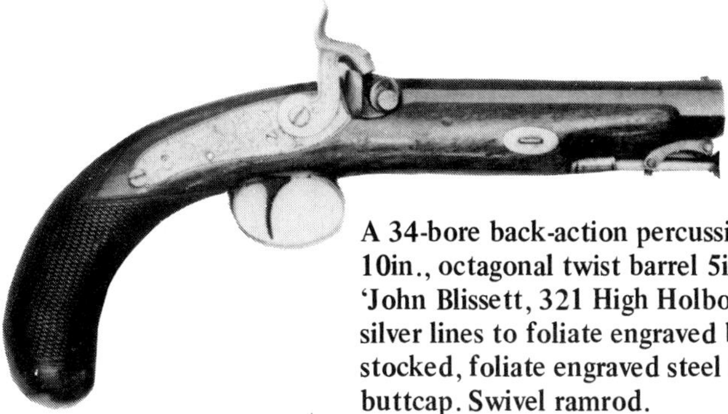

A 34-bore back-action percussion holster pistol, 10in., octagonal twist barrel 5in., engraved 'John Blissett, 321 High Holborn, London', twist silver lines to foliate engraved breech. Full-stocked, foliate engraved steel trigger guard and buttcap. Swivel ramrod. $304 £140

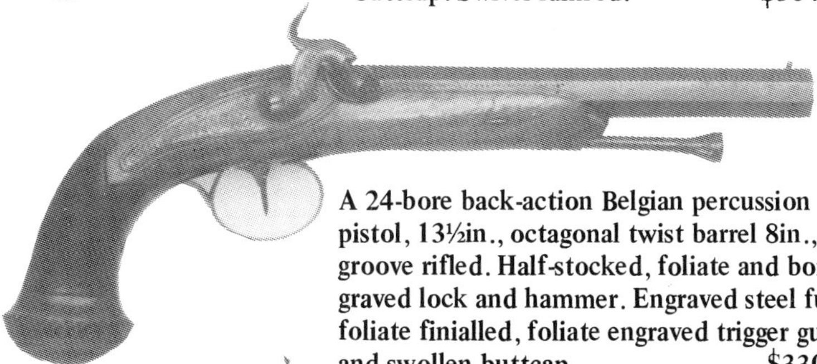

A 24-bore back-action Belgian percussion holster pistol, 13½in., octagonal twist barrel 8in., hair-groove rifled. Half-stocked, foliate and border engraved lock and hammer. Engraved steel furniture, foliate finialled, foliate engraved trigger guard bow and swollen buttcap. $330 £150

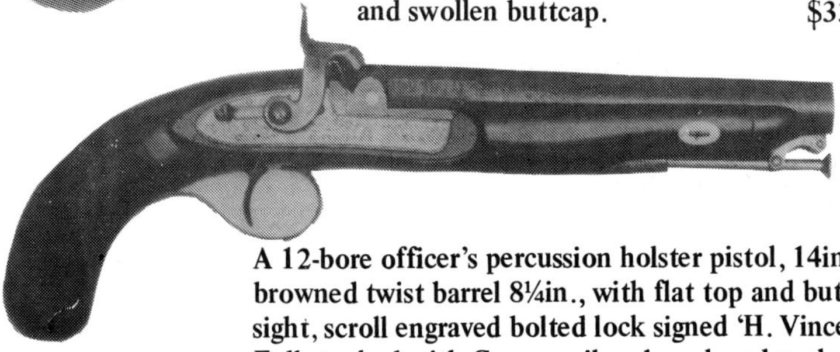

A 12-bore officer's percussion holster pistol, 14in., round browned twist barrel 8¼in., with flat top and button foresight, scroll engraved bolted lock signed 'H. Vincent & Son'. Full-stocked with German silver barrel wedge plates and rectangular escutcheon, rounded chequered butt.
$390 £170

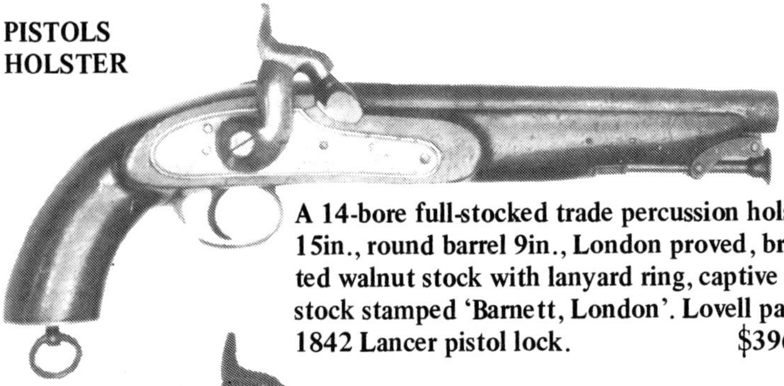

A 14-bore full-stocked trade percussion holster pistol, 15in., round barrel 9in., London proved, brass mounted walnut stock with lanyard ring, captive rammer, stock stamped 'Barnett, London'. Lovell pattern 1842 Lancer pistol lock. $396 £180

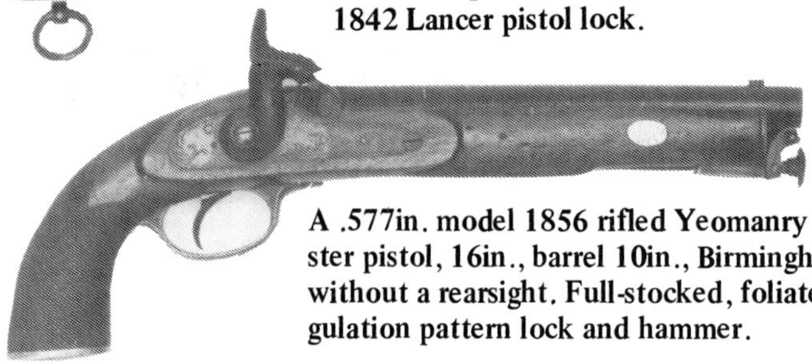

A .577in. model 1856 rifled Yeomanry percussion holster pistol, 16in., barrel 10in., Birmingham proved, without a rearsight. Full-stocked, foliate engraved regulation pattern lock and hammer. $494 £190

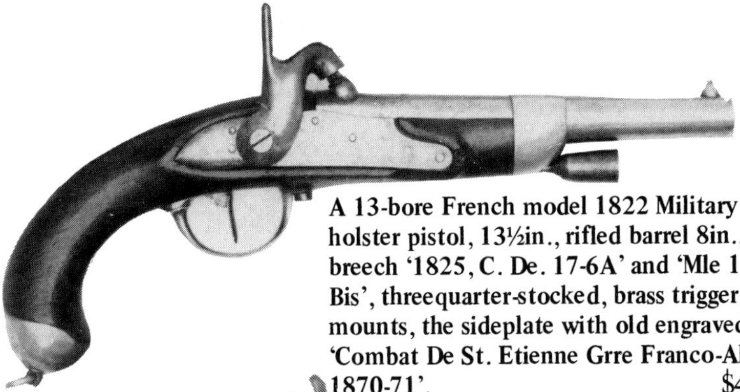

A 13-bore French model 1822 Military percussion holster pistol, 13½in., rifled barrel 8in., dated at breech '1825, C. De. 17-6A' and 'Mle 1822 T. Bis', threequarter-stocked, brass trigger guard and mounts, the sideplate with old engraved inscription 'Combat De St. Etienne Grre Franco-Allemande 1870-71'. $456 £200

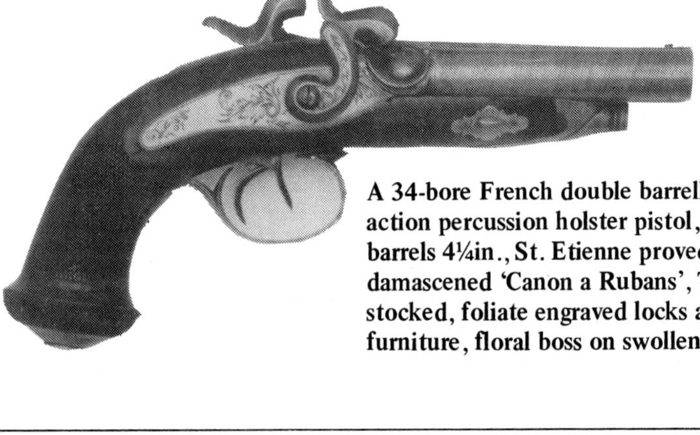

A 34-bore French double barrelled back-action percussion holster pistol, 9in., twist barrels 4¼in., St. Etienne proved, gold damascened 'Canon a Rubans', Threequarter-stocked, foliate engraved locks and steel furniture, floral boss on swollen buttcap. $562 £260

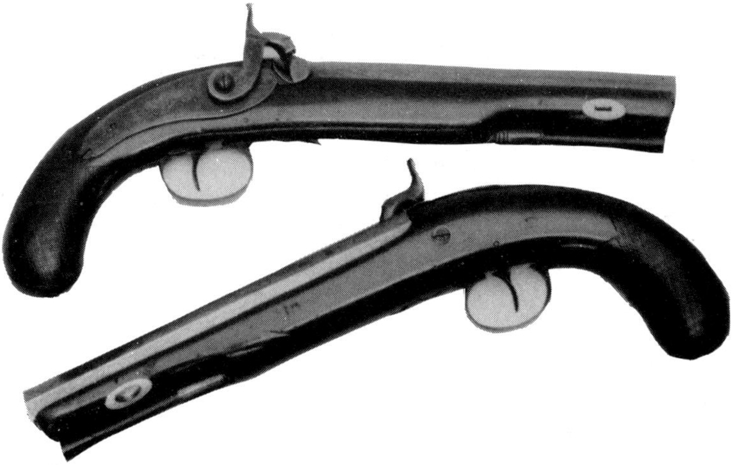

A pair of 34-bore back-action percussion holster pistols, 13in., octagonal barrels 8in., Birmingham proved, engraved 'Fishenden Tunbridge'. Full-stocked, foliate engraved locks, hammers and pineapple finialled trigger guards, white metal barrel wedge plates and diamond shaped escutcheons. $542 £260

A pair of 14-bore Spanish back-action threequarter-stocked percussion holster pistols, 11in., browned octagonal barrels 6¼in. inlaid in silver 'Fabricado Por Ciriaco Villar En Eibar Ano 1858', chequered walnut stocks with flared grips terminating in steel caps with fitted lanyard rings, border and scroll foliate engraved iron trigger guards, brass fore-end cross key escutcheons. $710 £300

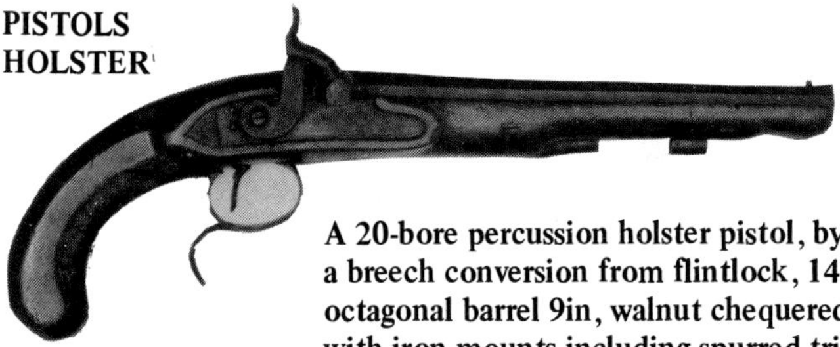

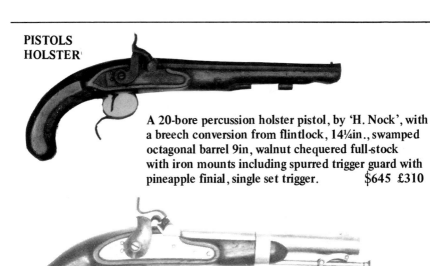

A 20-bore percussion holster pistol, by 'H. Nock', with a breech conversion from flintlock, 14¼in., swamped octagonal barrel 9in, walnut chequered full-stock with iron mounts including spurred trigger guard with pineapple finial, single set trigger. $645 £310

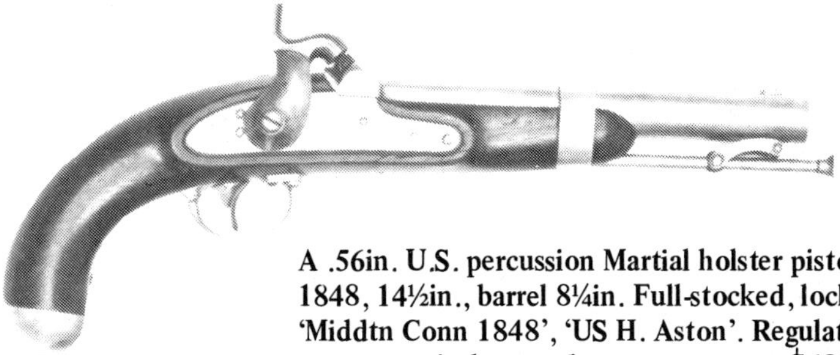

A .56in. U.S. percussion Martial holster pistol, dated 1848, 14½in., barrel 8¼in. Full-stocked, lock stamped 'Middtn Conn 1848', 'US H. Aston'. Regulation brass mounts, swivel ramrod. $682 £310

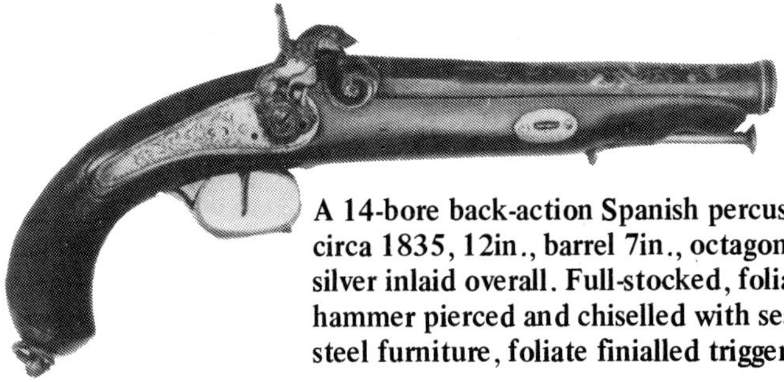

A 14-bore back-action Spanish percussion holster pistol, circa 1835, 12in., barrel 7in., octagonal at breech, well silver inlaid overall. Full-stocked, foliate engraved lock, hammer pierced and chiselled with seated lion. Engraved steel furniture, foliate finialled trigger guard. $858 £330

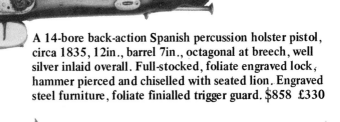

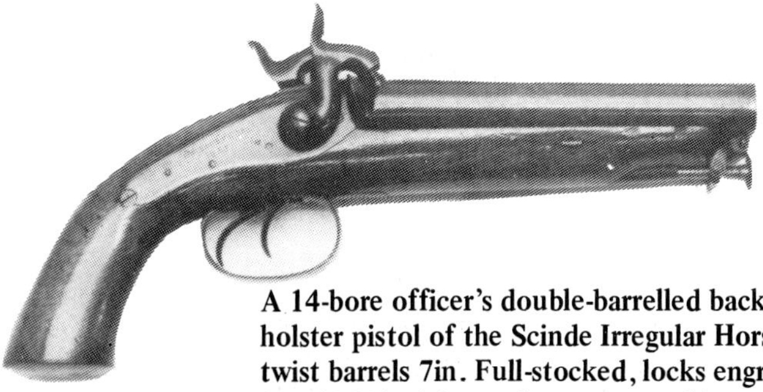

A 14-bore officer's double-barrelled back-action percussion holster pistol of the Scinde Irregular Horse, 13½in., browned twist barrels 7in. Full-stocked, locks engraved 'Swinburne & Son 1853', plain steel mounts, oval buttplate, swivel ramrod. $830 £350

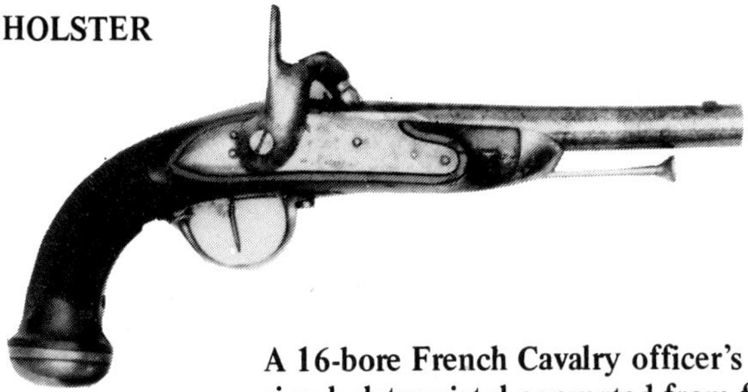

A 16-bore French Cavalry officer's pattern 1816 percussion holster pistol converted from flintlock, 13½in., round barrel 7¾in., dated 1821, chequered brass mounted walnut half-stock, plain lock engraved 'Mre Rle de Mutzig'. $781 £360

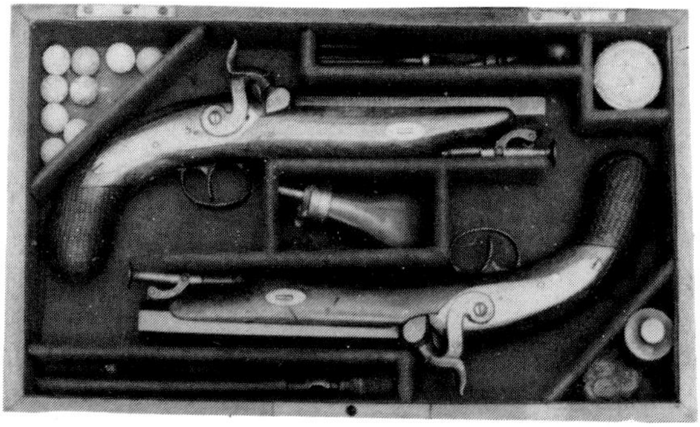

A pair of 16-bore back-action percussion holster pistols, by 'Hollis & Sheath', 11in., octagonal browned twist barrels 6in., engraved 'London' with twin white metal breech lines. Full-stocked, foliate engraved locks and dolphin hammers. Foliate engraved steel trigger guards, swivel ramrod. In a green beize lined fitted brass bound rosewood veneered case. $825 £380

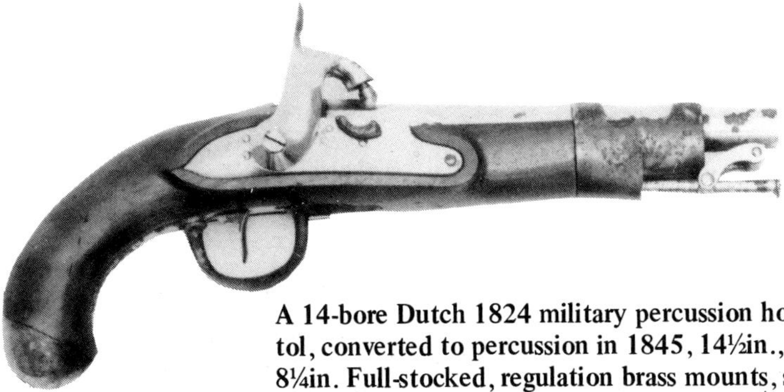

A 14-bore Dutch 1824 military percussion holster pistol, converted to percussion in 1845, 14½in., barrel 8¼in. Full-stocked, regulation brass mounts, steel trigger plate, back-strap and swivel ramrod. $933 £430

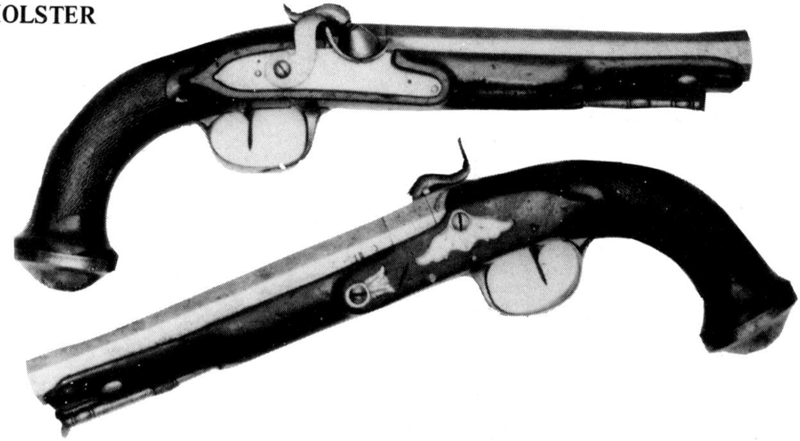

A pair of 14-bore French officer's rifled percussion holster pistols, 13¾in., swamped micro-groove rifled octagonal barrels 8in., St. Etienne proved. Full-stocked, plain locks well converted from flintlock with nipple shields. Engraved steel furniture, urn and pineapple finialled trigger guards with two different scenes of towns. Bat's wing and pineapple shaped sideplates, bulbous star engraved buttcaps. Chequered walnut grips, silver escutcheons.
$976 £450

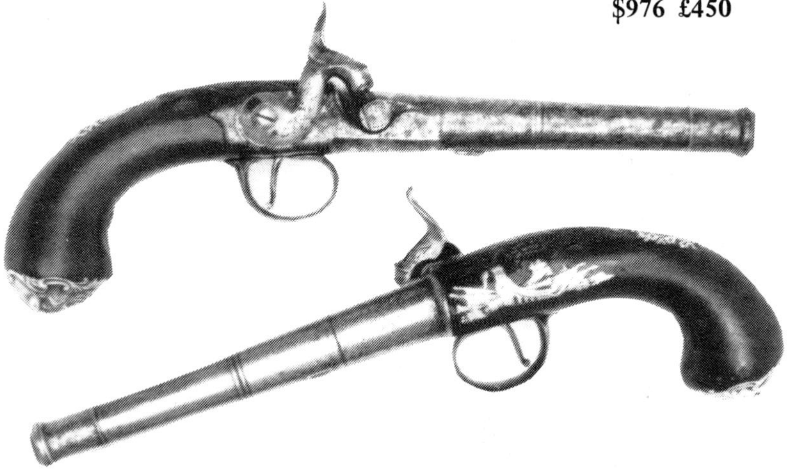

A pair of 22-bore boxlock sidehammer cannon barrelled silver mounted Queen Anne style percussion holster pistols, by 'Collumbell, circa 1765, 12in., turn-off barrels 5in., London proved. Dog tooth border engraved frames and dolphin hammers, drum conversions from flintlock. Sliding trigger guard safeties. Rounded walnut butt hallmarked silver grotesque mask buttcaps. Stock carved around barrel tangs with a trophy of arms apron in low relief. $1,430 £650

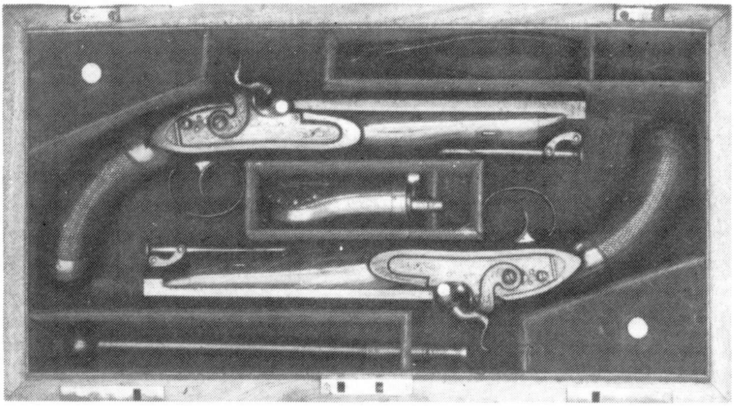

A pair of 16-bore percussion holster pistols by 'Hamburger & Co., London', well converted from flintlock with new breech sections and re-worked locks, 13½in., octagonal browned twist barrels 8in., engraved 'London', platinum breech lines and safety plugs. Foliate engraved dolphin hammers and stepped bolted locks. Full-stocked, foliate engraved blued steel pineapple finialled trigger guards, swivel ramrods, horn forecaps, silver barrel wedge plates and vacant escutcheons.
$1,650 £750

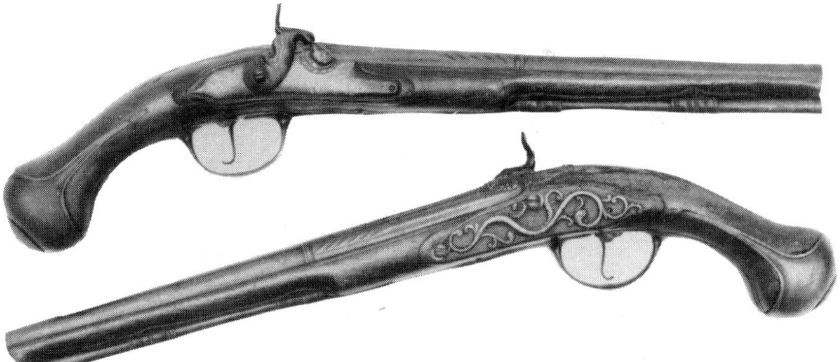

A pair of Italian percussion holster pistols, circa 1700, converted from flintlock, 19in., half fluted barrels 12¼in., deeply engraved within top flutes 'X Lazarino X Cominazzo X', breeches deeply chiselled with large grotesque human masks within foliate borders. Full-stocked, round banana shaped locks with lipped edges. Steel furniture, carved foliate finialled trigger guards with swollen bows.
$1,736 £800

PISTOLS
HOLSTER

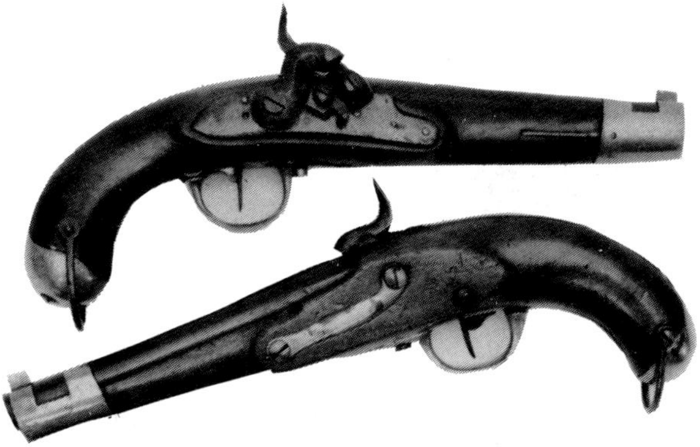

A brace of 12-bore rifled Austrian percussion holster pistols, converted from flintlock, 14¼in., barrels 8in., plain brass mounted walnut full-stocks, the butts pierced with lanyard loops attached, the brass fore-end cap combination barrel band, with blade foresight, barrel tang rear, plain lockplates engraved 'Pistol A. Schmalkalden' and fitted with rotating hammer block safety.
$2,061 £950

KNUCKLEDUSTER

A four-shot boxlock percussion all-steel knuckleduster pistol by 'W. & J. Rigby', circa 1840, 5¼in., turn-off barrels 1¼in., numbered to breeches 5-8, revolving plate on hammer nose manually selects nipple and barrel to be fired. $615 £260

A five-shot .31in. ring trigger self-cocking Robbins & Lawrence percussion pepperbox pistol, 8in., rifled barrels 2¼in., unscrewing from breech section for loading. Breech hinges down for capping, released by top thumb catch. $374 £170

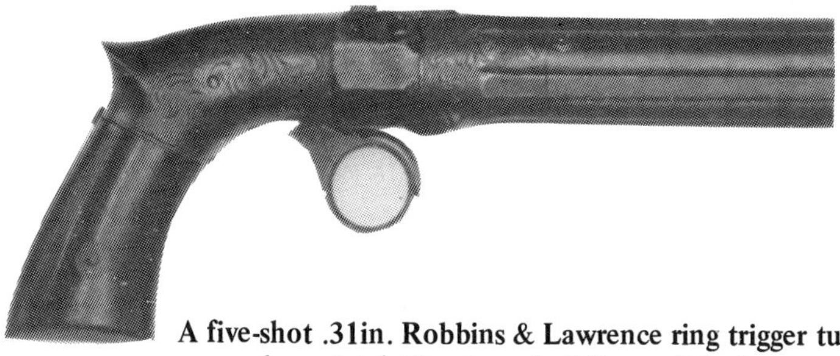

A five-shot .31in. Robbins & Lawrence ring trigger turn-off barrel pepperbox pistol, 9in., barrels 4½in., polished rosewood grips, semi saw-handled grip, ring trigger with auxiliary trigger lever, rotating striker, tip-down barrels for capping. $546 £210

A five-shot .31in. Robbins & Lawrence self-cocking ring trigger breech loading percussion pepperbox pistol, 9¼in., fluted rifled barrel section 4½in., rifled section 3¼in. unscrews for loading. Tip-down breech for capping. Octagonal breech, scroll engraved round frame, ring cocking lever, separate trigger. $542 £250

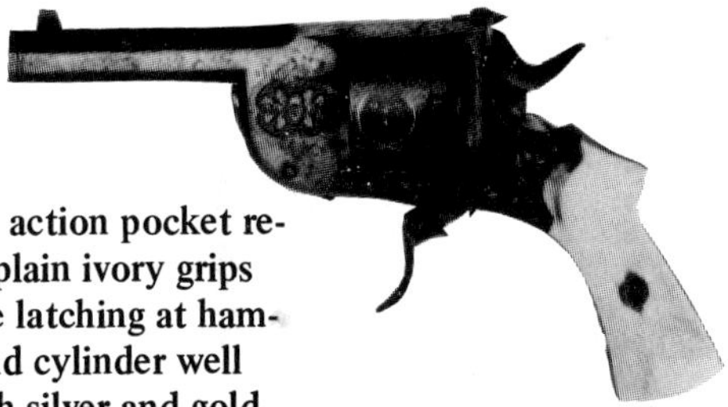

A six-shot .32in. Continental double action pocket revolver, 7in., octagonal barrel 3½in., plain ivory grips to butt, folding trigger, hinged frame latching at hammer bolster, the frame, barrel, lug and cylinder well scroll foliate engraved and inlaid with silver and gold lines and dots. $113 £52

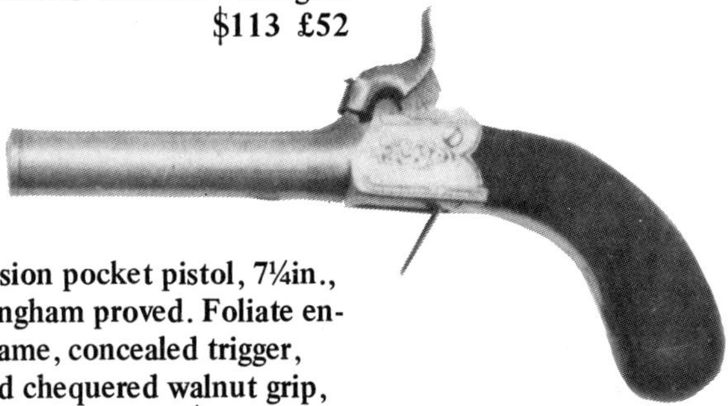

A 48-bore boxlock percussion pocket pistol, 7¼in., turn-off barrel 3in., Birmingham proved. Foliate engraved colour hardened frame, concealed trigger, dolphin hammer. Rounded chequered walnut grip, white metal escutcheon. $174 £80

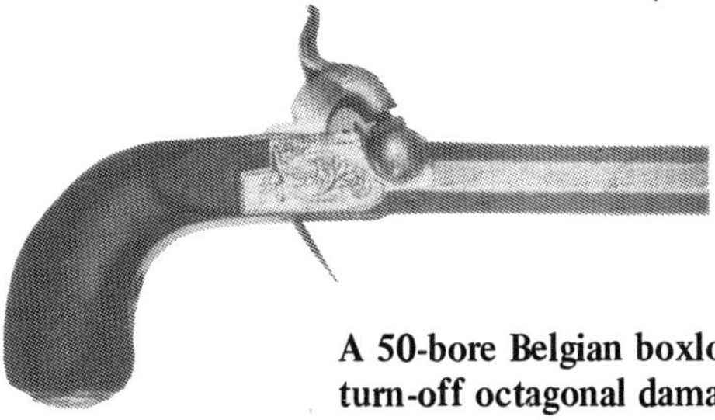

A 50-bore Belgian boxlock percussion pocket pistol, 7in., turn-off octagonal damascus twist rifled barrel 2¾in., Liege proved. Foliate engraved frame, hammer off-set for sighting, concealed foliate engraved trigger. Rounded ebony butt with vacant diamond shaped white metal escutcheon and hinged white metal cap box buttcap. $220 £100

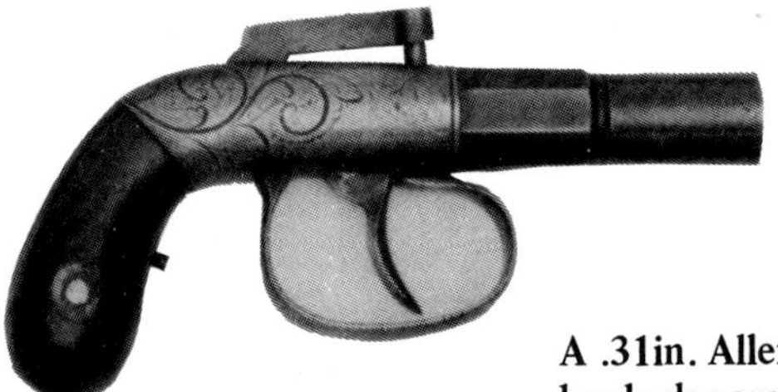

A .31in. Allen's patent self-cocking bar hammer boxlock percussion pocket pistol, 4¾in., turn-off half octagonal barrel 2in. Foliate engraved round steel frame. Two-piece bag-shaped wooden grips. $208 £100

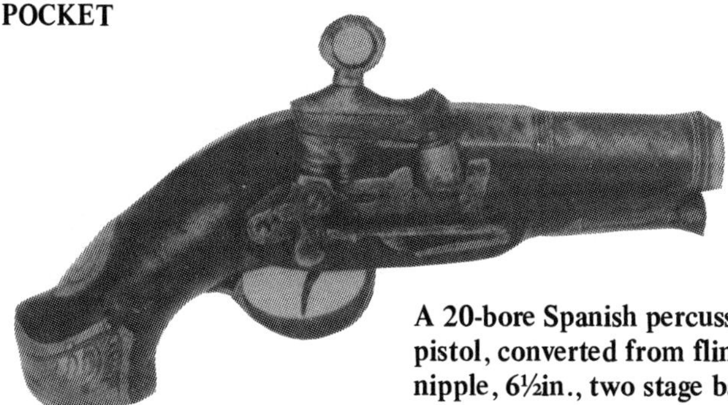

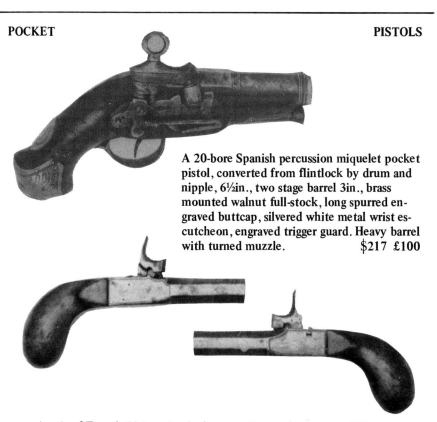

A 20-bore Spanish percussion miquelet pocket pistol, converted from flintlock by drum and nipple, 6½in., two stage barrel 3in., brass mounted walnut full-stock, long spurred engraved buttcap, silvered white metal wrist escutcheon, engraved trigger guard. Heavy barrel with turned muzzle. $217 £100

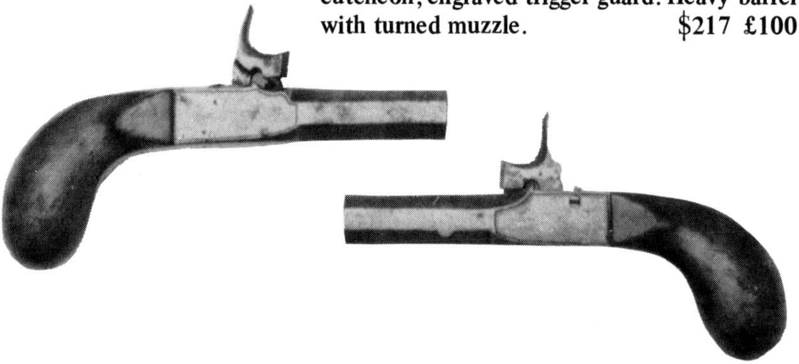

A pair of French 50-bore boxlock percussion pocket pistols, 5½in., turn-off octagonal barrels 2in. Border engraved frames, hammers off-set for sighting, low fences. Concealed triggers, rounded walnut butts. $250 £115

A 50-bore ivory stocked Belgian sidehammer boxlock percussion pocket pistol, 7in., turn-off four blade curly damascus bound barrel 2¾in., Liege proved, finely polished ivory bag grip with tears projecting back from action body. $253 £115

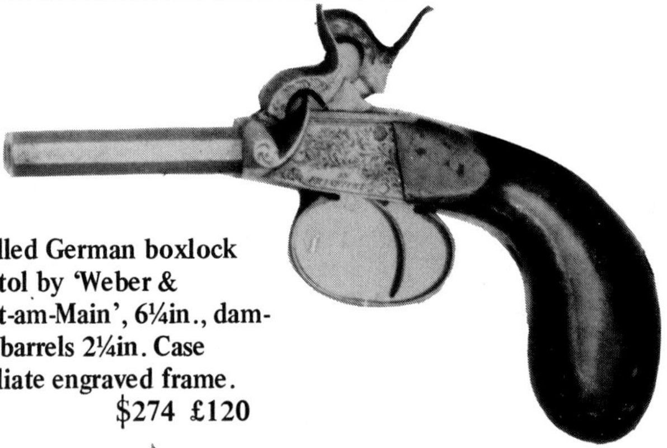

A .25in. double barrelled German boxlock percussion pocket pistol by 'Weber & Schultheis of Franfurt-am-Main', 6¼in., damascus twist octagonal barrels 2¼in. Case coloured hardened foliate engraved frame.
$274 £120

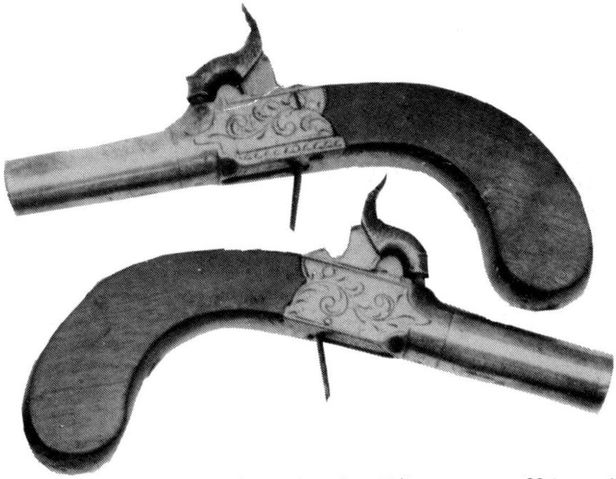

A pair of boxlock percussion pocket pistols, 6¼in., turn-off barrels 2in., Birmingham proved. Foliate engraved frames with retailer's name 'Hast of Colchester' on top plates. Concealed triggers, dolphin hammers, slab wooden butts, oval white metal escutcheons. $274 £120

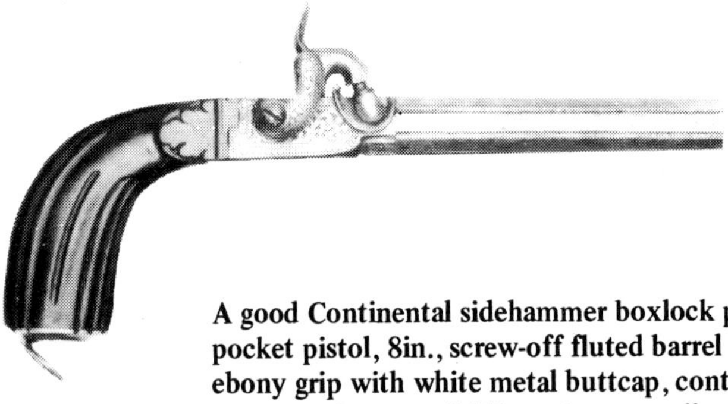

A good Continental sidehammer boxlock percussion pocket pistol, 8in., screw-off fluted barrel 3¾in., fluted ebony grip with white metal buttcap, containing compartment for caps, folding trigger, scroll engraved frame and hammer, the top plate inlaid in gold with initials 'J.K.', fine twist sighted barrel with Belgian proof.
$270 £120

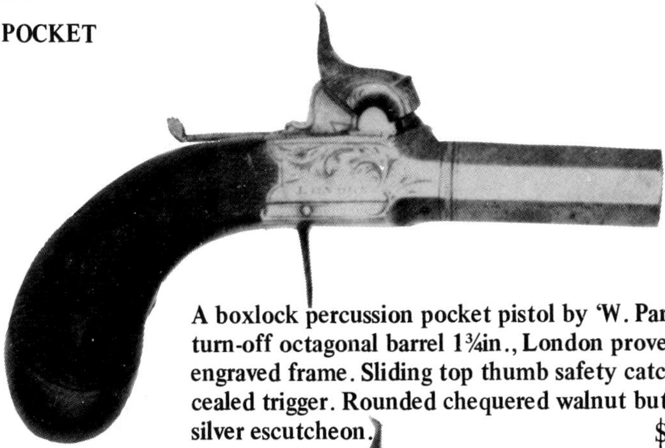

A boxlock percussion pocket pistol by 'W. Parker', 5¼in., turn-off octagonal barrel 1¾in., London proved. Foliate engraved frame. Sliding top thumb safety catch, concealed trigger. Rounded chequered walnut butt with oval silver escutcheon. $271 £125

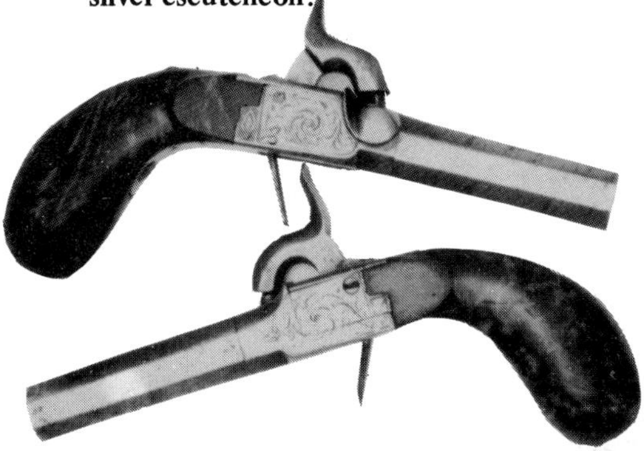

A pair of Belgian boxlock percussion pocket pistols, 6in., turn-off octagonal twist barrels 2¼in., Liege proved. Foliate engraved frames, folding triggers, hammers off-set for sighting. Rounded burr walnut butts with shield-shaped white metal escutcheons. $336 £155

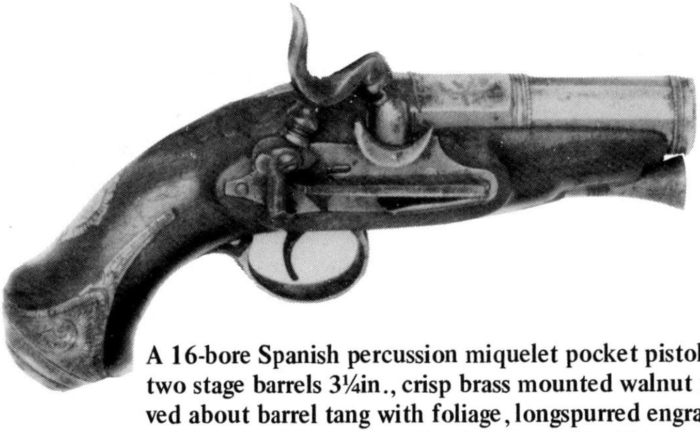

A 16-bore Spanish percussion miquelet pocket pistol, 6½in., heavy two stage barrels 3¼in., crisp brass mounted walnut full-stock carved about barrel tang with foliage, longspurred engraved brass buttcap, engraved trigger guard and ramrod thimble. $358 £165

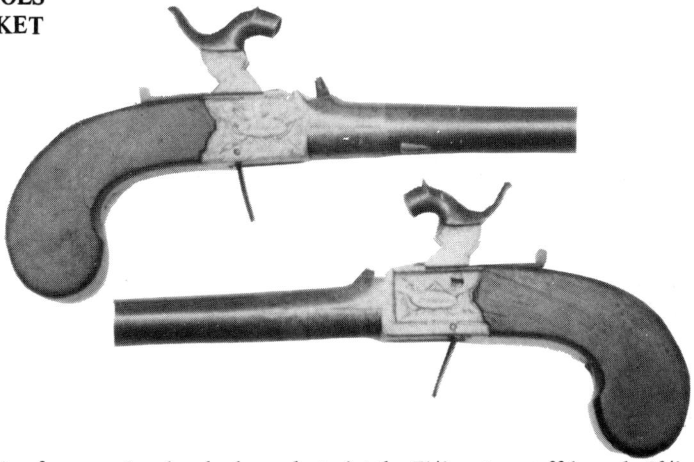

A pair of percussion boxlock pocket pistols, 7½in., turn-off barrels 2¾in., with rifling and slotted for barrel key, by 'Dawes London', sideplates engraved with military trophies, London proofs and with fleur-de-lys stamp, sliding bar top safeties, plain slab sided wooden butts, folding triggers. $391 £180

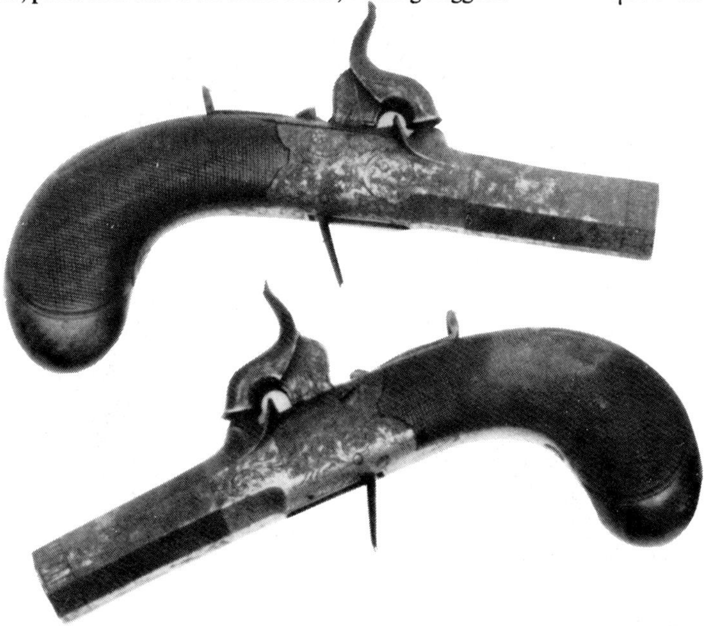

A pair of boxlock percussion pocket pistols by 'Bulman of Newcastle', 6in., turn-off octagonal barrels 1¾in., fern tip engraved muzzles. Foliate engraved slightly rounded frames. Sliding top thumb safety catches to dolphin hammers. Concealed triggers. Rounded chequered walnut butts with silver escutcheon (one missing). $547 £240

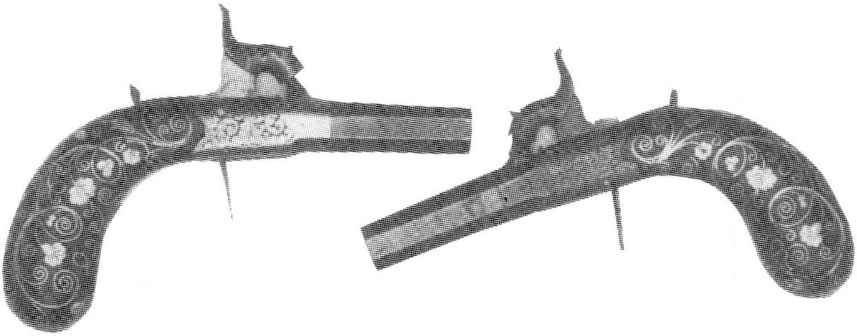

A pair of boxlock percussion pocket pistols, 5¼in., turn-off octagonal barrels 1½in., London proved, foliate engraved frames, sliding top thumb safety catches to dolphin hammers. Concealed triggers. Rounded walnut butts.

$671 £258

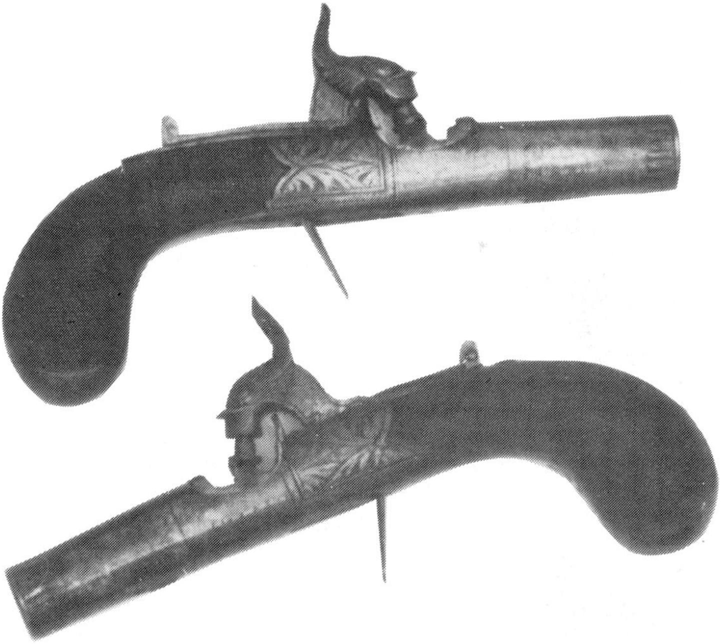

A pair of boxlock percussion pocket pistols by 'Jacques', with top-hat retaining mechanism removed and chiselled dolphin hammers replaced contemporarily, 6½in., turn-off barrels 1¾in., Birmingham proved. Concealed triggers. Sliding top thumb safety catches. Rounded chequered walnut butts.

$616 £280

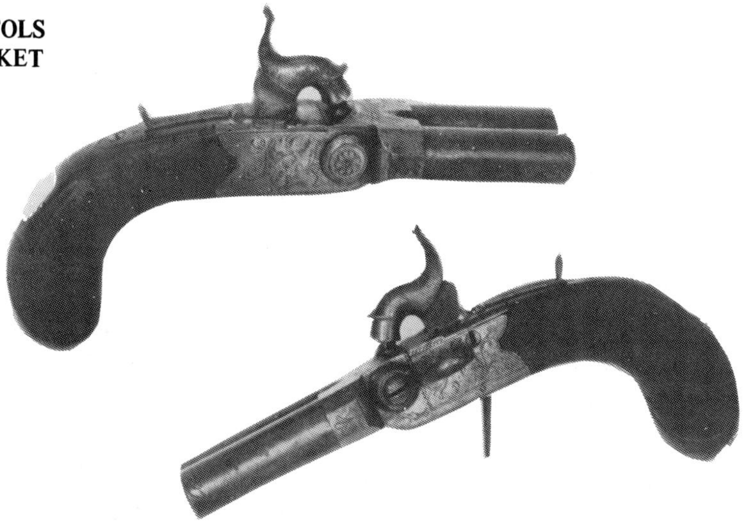

A pair of boxlock percussion double barrelled tap action side-by-side pocket pistols, 6¼in., turn-off barrels 1¾in., Birmingham proved, foliate engraved muzzles. Foliate and dog tooth engraved frames with 'D. Egg London', concealed triggers, sliding top thumb safety catches to dolphin hammers. Rounded chequered walnut grips with silver escutcheons. $868 £400

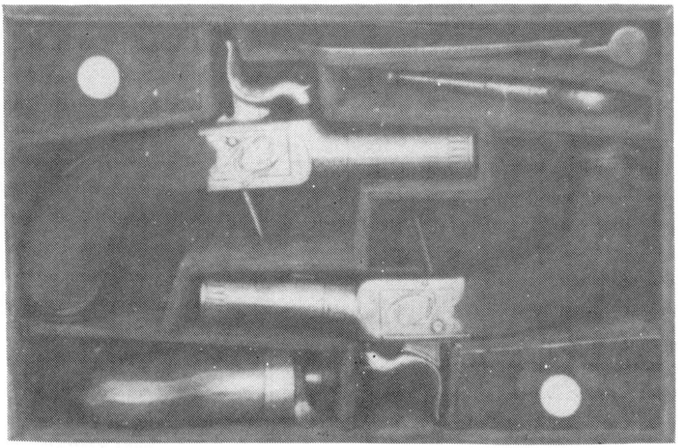

A pair of 60-bore boxlock percussion pocket pistols, 5½in., turn-off barrels 1½in., frond engraved muzzles, London proved. Foliate and serpent engraved frames with 'Egg, London' engraved vertically. Dolphin hammers, concealed triggers. Chequered rounded walnut grips with vacant silver escutcheons. Contained in their velvet lined fitted brass bound mahogany case.$1,155 £525

A 28-bore Belgian rifled percussion target pistol, 16in., octagonal damascus barrel 10¾in., walnut half-stock with fluted steel capped grip, engraved spurred trigger guard with single set trigger. $716 £330

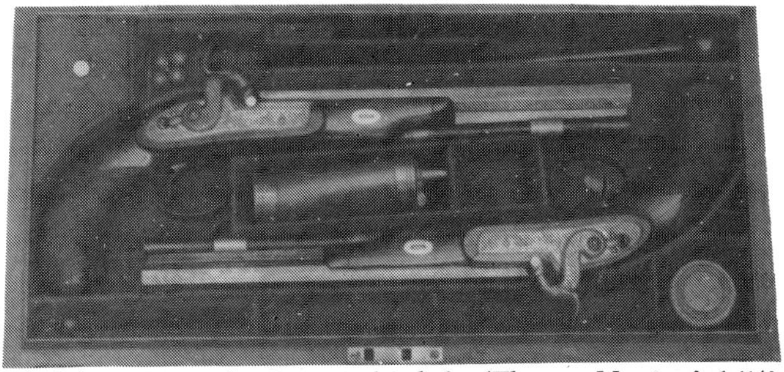

A pair of 38-bore percussion target pistols by 'Thomas Manton', 14½in., octagonal twist barrels 9½in., engraved 'Thomas Manton, 144 Long Acre London'. Half-stocked, bolted detented locks, capstan screw set triggers. Steel furniture. $2,472 £1,600

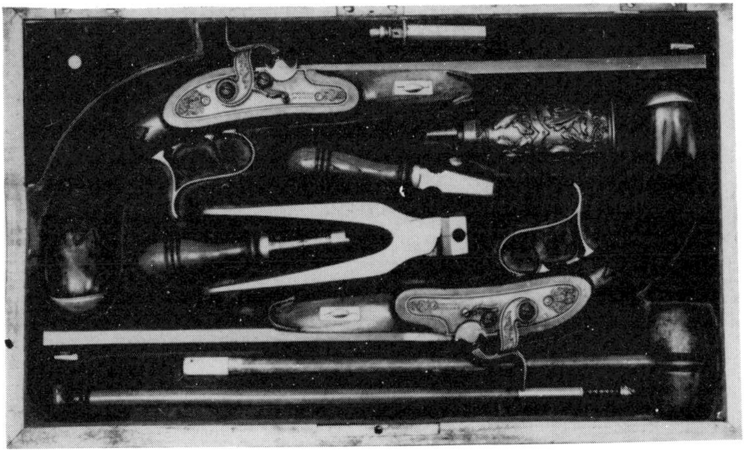

A pair of 55-bore German percussion target pistols by 'F. Weiland of Cassel', 15½in., slender swamped browned octagonal deeply rifled barrels, 10in., large blade white metal foresights. Foliate engraved colour hardened breeches with screw adjustable rearsights. Half-stocked, hinged safety catches to dolphin hammers. Micro-adjustable double set triggers. $4,340 £2,000

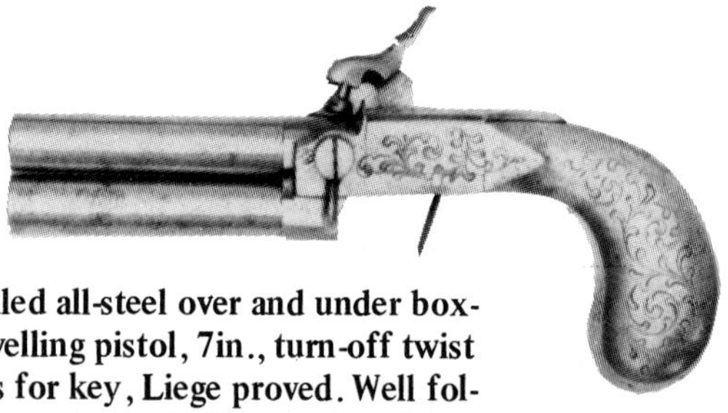

A Belgian 70-bore double barrelled all-steel over and under boxlock sidehammer tap action travelling pistol, 7in., turn-off twist barrels 2¾in., slotted at muzzles for key, Liege proved. Well foliate engraved squared steel frame and rounded integral steel butt. Swivel tap with arched lever, concealed trigger. $130 £60

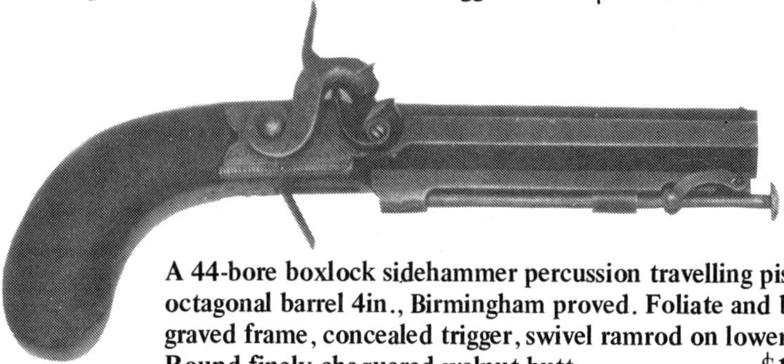

A 44-bore boxlock sidehammer percussion travelling pistol, 9in., octagonal barrel 4in., Birmingham proved. Foliate and border engraved frame, concealed trigger, swivel ramrod on lower rib. Round finely chequered walnut butt. $176 £80

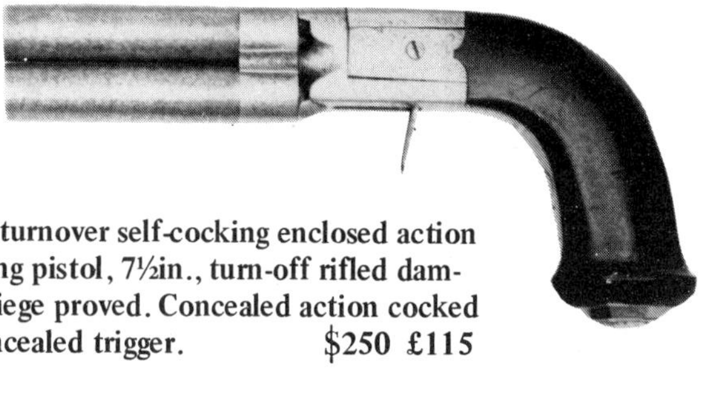

A Belgian double barrelled turnover self-cocking enclosed action boxlock percussion travelling pistol, 7½in., turn-off rifled damascus twist barrels 2¾in., Liege proved. Concealed action cocked by turning barrels over, concealed trigger. $250 £115

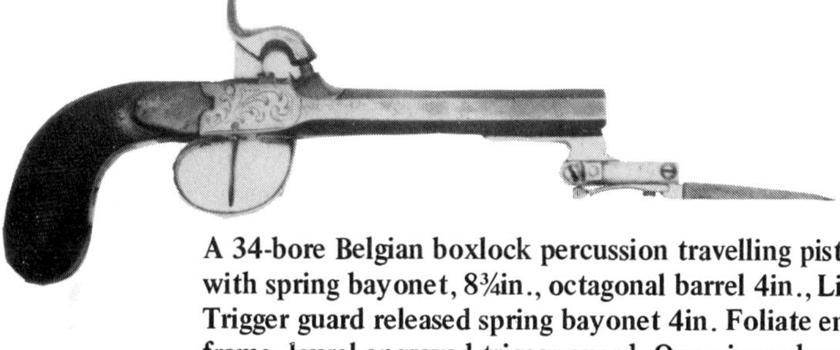

A 34-bore Belgian boxlock percussion travelling pistol fitted with spring bayonet, 8¾in., octagonal barrel 4in., Liege proved. Trigger guard released spring bayonet 4in. Foliate engraved frame, laurel engraved trigger guard. One-piece chequered wooden grip. $304 £140

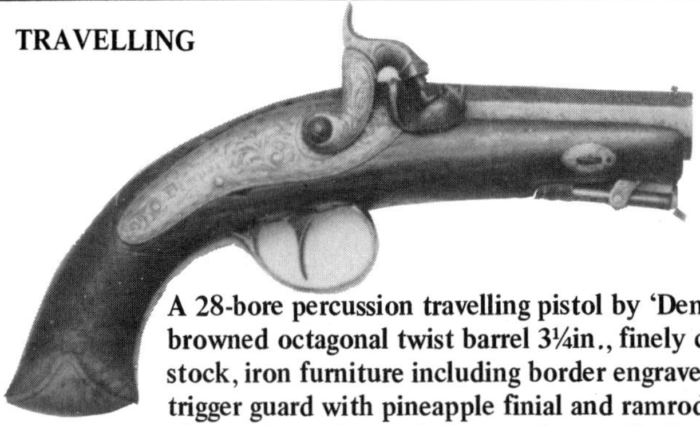

A 28-bore percussion travelling pistol by 'Dempsey of Dublin', 8in., browned octagonal twist barrel 3¼in., finely chequered walnut full-stock, iron furniture including border engraved cap to fish-tail butt, trigger guard with pineapple finial and ramrod throat pipe, blank silver wrist and cross bolt escutcheons, finely scroll engraved.
$369 £170

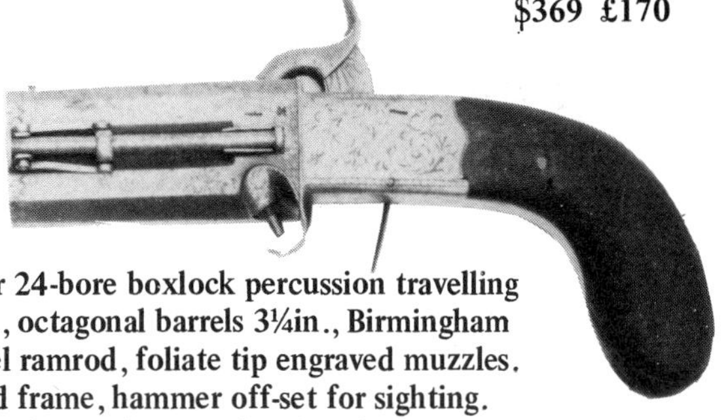

A double barrelled turnover 24-bore boxlock percussion travelling pistol by 'Cashmore', 7½in., octagonal barrels 3¼in., Birmingham proved, side mounted swivel ramrod, foliate tip engraved muzzles. Foliate and border engraved frame, hammer off-set for sighting. Concealed trigger. Rounded, finely chequered walnut butt.
$388 £170

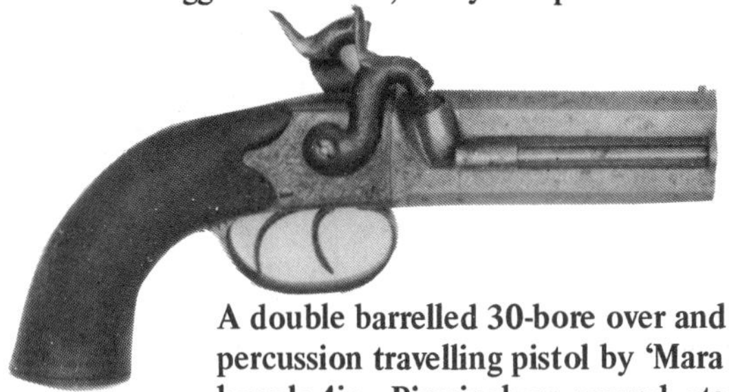

A double barrelled 30-bore over and under boxlock sidehammer percussion travelling pistol by 'Mara of Limerick', 9in., octagonal barrels 4in., Birmingham proved, steel rammer on barrel side. Chequered rounded butt, engraved hinged steel cap trap.
$532 £245

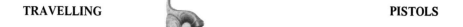

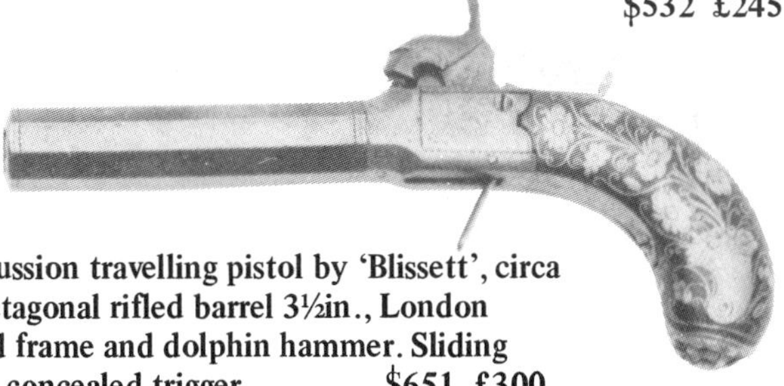

A 50-bore boxlock percussion travelling pistol by 'Blissett', circa 1840, 7½in., turn-off octagonal rifled barrel 3½in., London proved. Foliate engraved frame and dolphin hammer. Sliding top thumb safety catch, concealed trigger. $651 £300

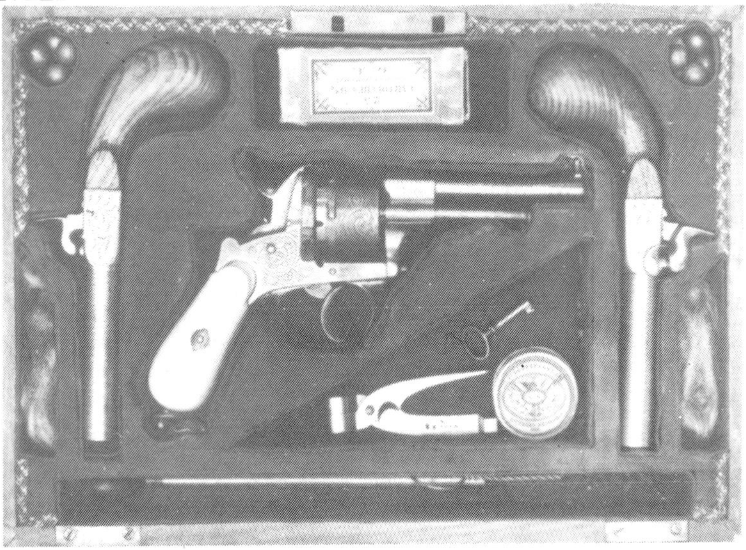

A cased pair of boxlock percussion pistols and Lefaucheux pinfire revolver, boxlock percussion travelling pistols, 7in. overall, turn-off rifled damascus twist barrels 3in., Foliate engraved frames and concealed triggers, hammers off-set for sighting, Lefaucheux six-shot 9mm. double action pinfire revolver 8in., barrel 4in. Contained in their applewood case. $880 £400

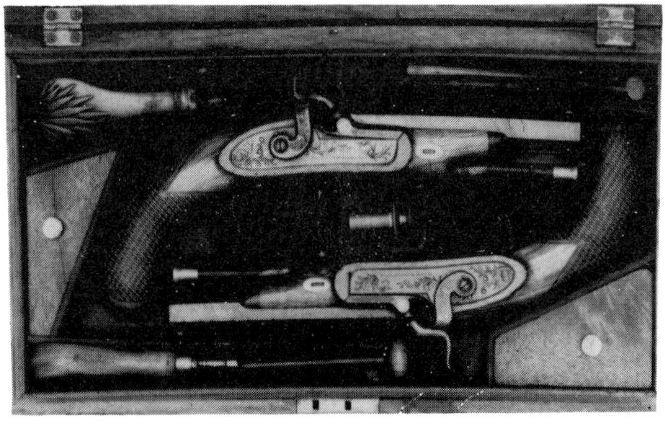

A pair of 38-bore percussion travelling pistols by 'Robert Wheeler', 11½in., octagonal browned twist barrels 6in., Birmingham proved, chequered walnut half-stocks with vacant silver wrist and cross bolt escutcheons, steel large bow trigger guards. Contained in their green beize lined and fitted mahogany case. $2,062 £950

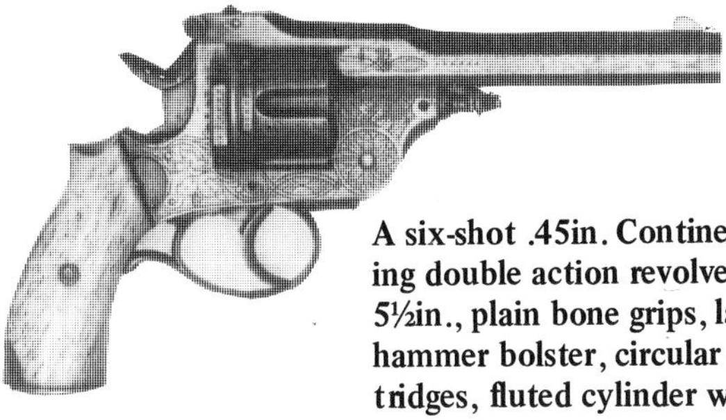

A six-shot .45in. Continental Warnant type self-extracting double action revolver, 10¼in., octagonal barrel 5½in., plain bone grips, large hinged frame latching at hammer bolster, circular extractor ring drilled for cartridges, fluted cylinder with raised cylinder stops.
$70 £32

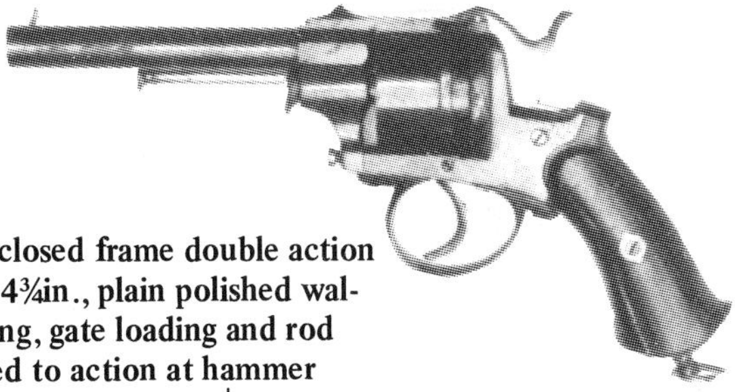

A six-shot 9mm. Continental closed frame double action pinfire revolver, 9½in., barrel 4¾in., plain polished walnut grip with fitted lanyard ring, gate loading and rod ejection, jointed frame screwed to action at hammer bolster and forward of trigger guard. $99 £45

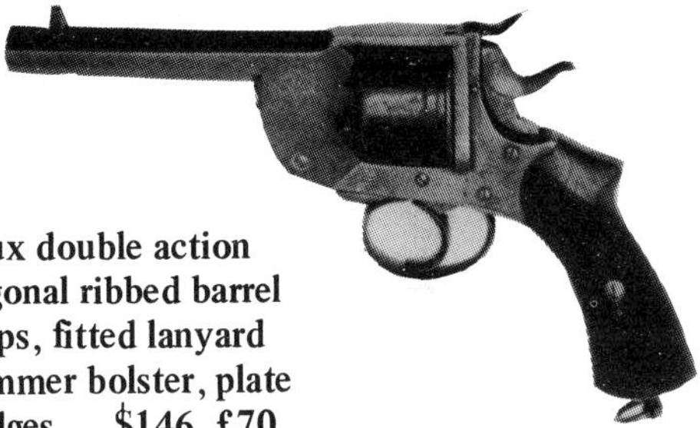

A six-shot .450in. centrefire Le Vaux double action self-extracting revolver, 10in., octagonal ribbed barrel 5½in., finely chequered wooden grips, fitted lanyard ring, tip-down barrel latching at hammer bolster, plate at rear of cylinder drilled for cartridges. $146 £70

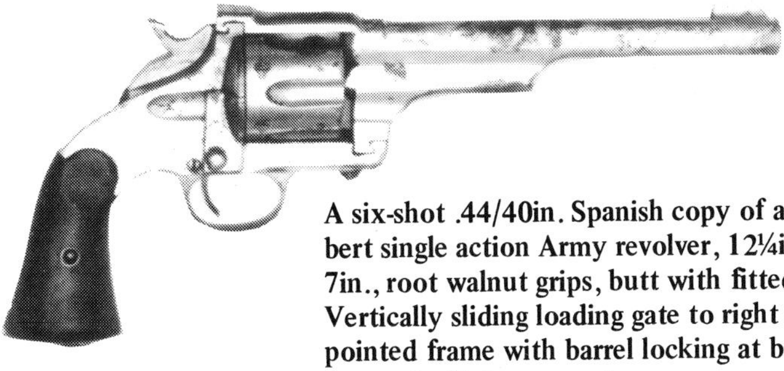

A six-shot .44/40in. Spanish copy of a Mervin & Hulbert single action Army revolver, 12¼in., round barrel 7in., root walnut grips, butt with fitted lanyard ring. Vertically sliding loading gate to right side of frame, pointed frame with barrel locking at bottom strap and forward of trigger guard. $176 £80

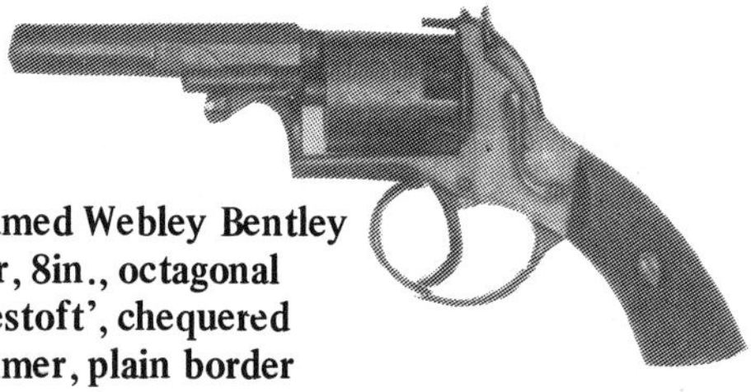

A five-shot 80-bore English open-framed Webley Bentley type self-cocking percussion revolver, 8in., octagonal barrel 3½in., engraved 'Thirtle Lowestoft', chequered walnut grips, sidemounted lever rammer, plain border engraved action body with spring hammer safety to left side, the hammer with small cocking spur to right side, plain cylinder. $187 £85

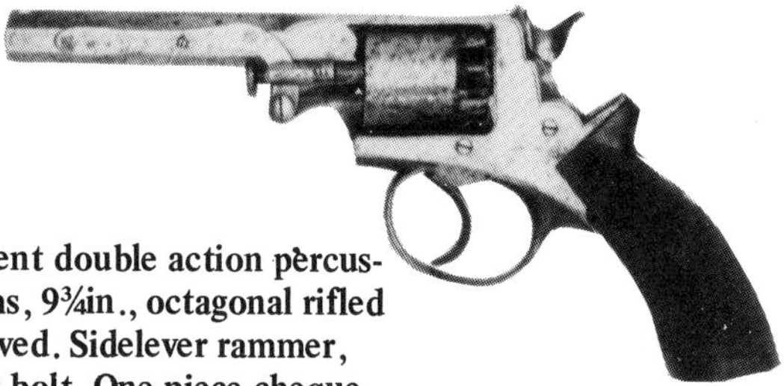

A five-shot .38in. Adams' patent double action percussion revolver by Robert Adams, 9¾in., octagonal rifled barrel 4½in., Birmingham proved. Sidelever rammer, sliding cylinder safety locking bolt. One-piece chequered walnut grip, steel buttcap. $184 £85

A five-shot 85-bore self-cocking open-frame percussion revolver, 10in., octagonal barrel 4¾in., Birmingham proved. Sidelever rammer, sprung hammer safety catch, removable sideplate. Steel frame strap, two-piece chequered walnut grips. $194 £85

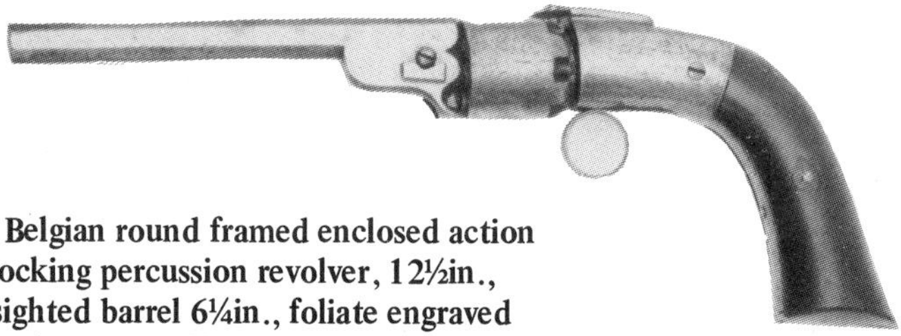

A six-shot .32in. Belgian round framed enclosed action ring trigger self-cocking percussion revolver, 12½in., octagonal rifled sighted barrel 6¼in., foliate engraved Liege proved cylinder. Unusually shaped steel grip strap foliate engraved. Two-piece walnut grips.
$217 £100

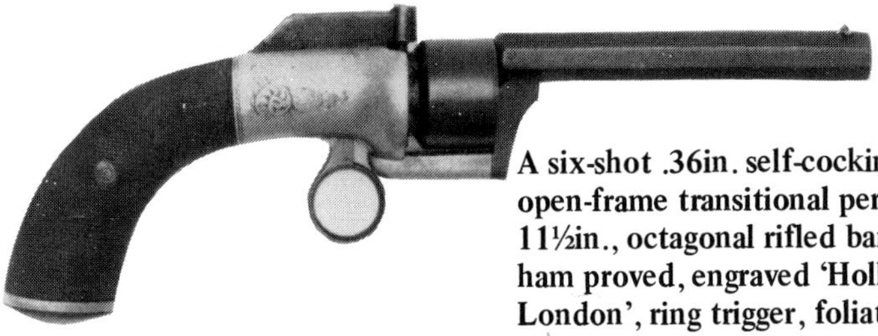

A six-shot .36in. self-cocking white metal open-frame transitional percussion revolver, 11½in., octagonal rifled barrel 5in. Birmingham proved, engraved 'Hollis & Sheath, London', ring trigger, foliate engraved round frame and grip strap. Steel hinged cap trap in butt, two-piece chequered walnut grips.

$228 £100

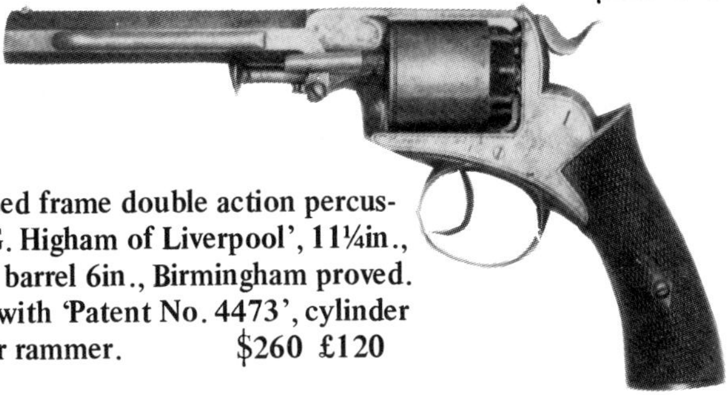

A five-shot 54-bore closed frame double action percussion revolver by 'E. & G. Higham of Liverpool', 11¼in., rifled sighted octagonal barrel 6in., Birmingham proved. Border engraved frame with 'Patent No. 4473', cylinder numbered 1-5. Sidelever rammer. $260 £120

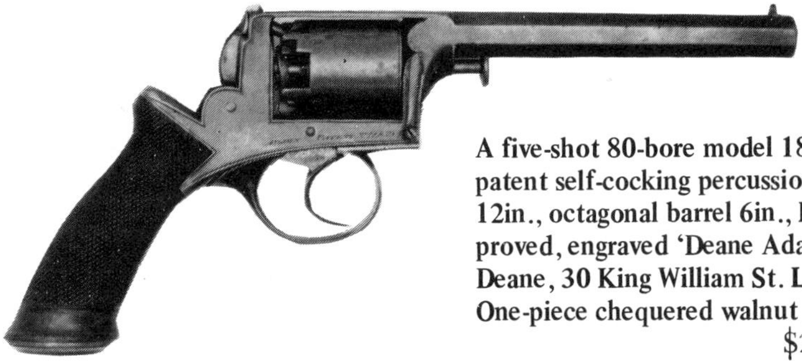

A five-shot 80-bore model 1851 Adams' patent self-cocking percussion revolver, 12in., octagonal barrel 6in., London proved, engraved 'Deane Adams & Deane, 30 King William St. London'. One-piece chequered walnut grip.

$296 £130

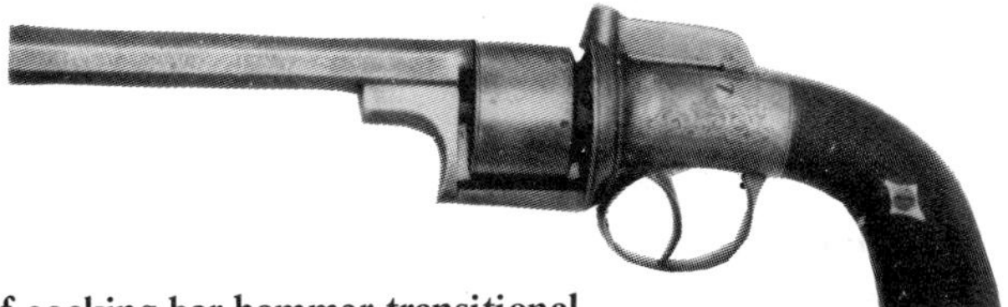

A six-shot 90-bore self-cocking bar hammer transitional revolver, 11in., octagonal barrel 5in., Birmingham proved, the barrel engraved 'Improved Revolver', chequered walnut grip, rounded scroll engraved action body, plain cylinder. $304 £140

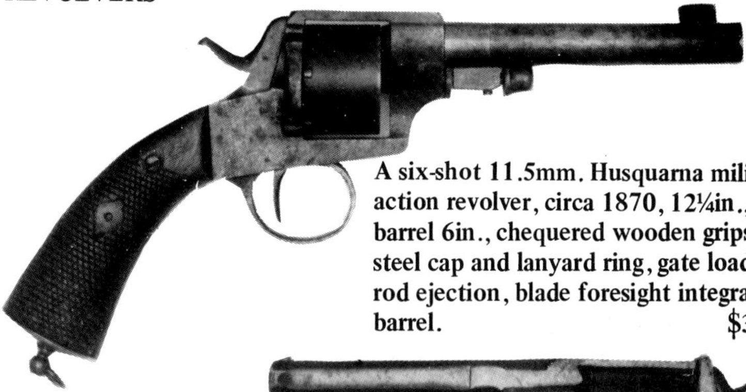

A six-shot 11.5mm. Husquarna military single action revolver, circa 1870, 12¼in., round barrel 6in., chequered wooden grips with steel cap and lanyard ring, gate loading and rod ejection, blade foresight integral with barrel. $315 £145

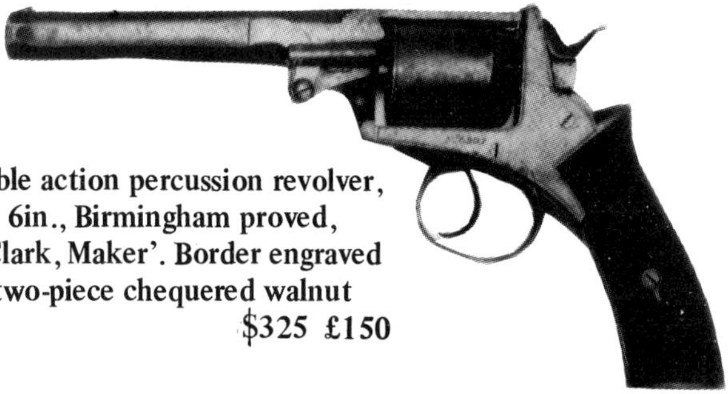

A five-shot 60-bore double action percussion revolver, 11½in., octagonal barrel 6in., Birmingham proved, top strap engraved 'W. Clark, Maker'. Border engraved frame with 'No. 6207', two-piece chequered walnut grips, sidelever rammer. $325 £150

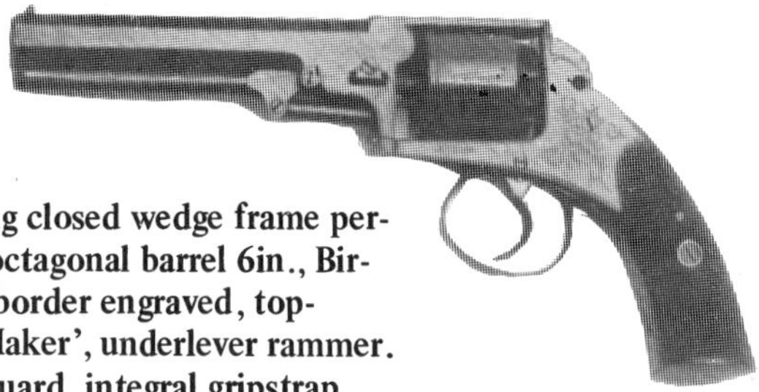

A five-shot 54-bore self-cocking closed wedge frame percussion revolver, 11in., rifled octagonal barrel 6in., Birmingham proved. Foliate and border engraved, topstrap engraved 'T.J. Bradney Maker', underlever rammer. Foliate engraved steel trigger guard, integral gripstrap. $355 £150

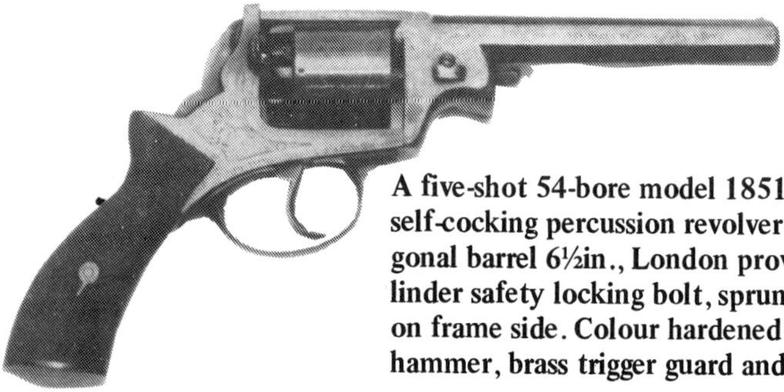

A five-shot 54-bore model 1851 Adam's patent self-cocking percussion revolver, 12½in., octagonal barrel 6½in., London proved. Sliding cylinder safety locking bolt, sprung hammer safety on frame side. Colour hardened cylinder, polished hammer, brass trigger guard and buttplate. $355 £150

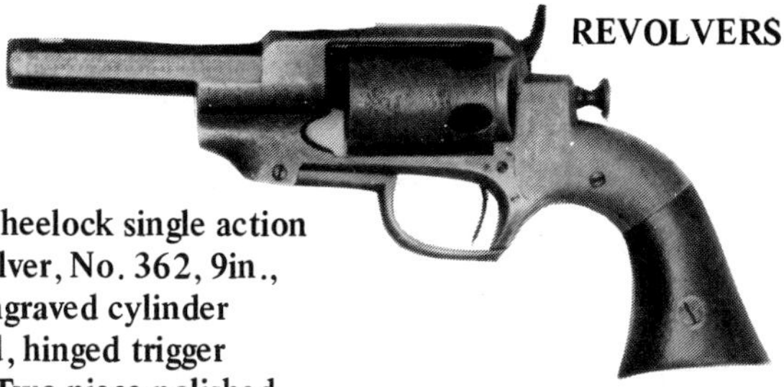

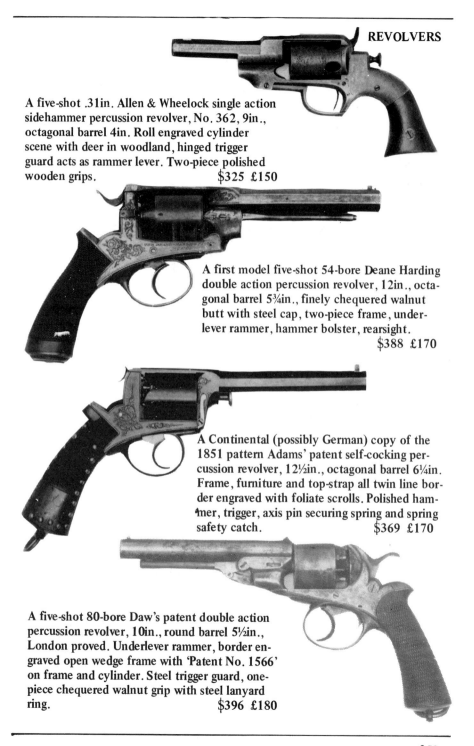

A five-shot .31in. Allen & Wheelock single action sidehammer percussion revolver, No. 362, 9in., octagonal barrel 4in. Roll engraved cylinder scene with deer in woodland, hinged trigger guard acts as rammer lever. Two-piece polished wooden grips. $325 £150

A first model five-shot 54-bore Deane Harding double action percussion revolver, 12in., octagonal barrel 5¾in., finely chequered walnut butt with steel cap, two-piece frame, underlever rammer, hammer bolster, rearsight. $388 £170

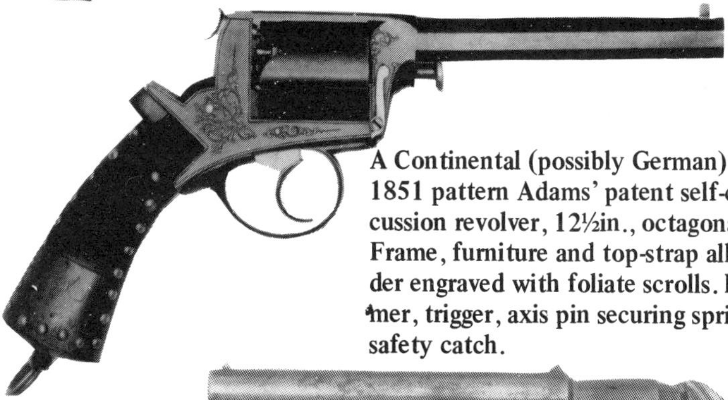

A Continental (possibly German) copy of the 1851 pattern Adams' patent self-cocking percussion revolver, 12½in., octagonal barrel 6¼in. Frame, furniture and top-strap all twin line border engraved with foliate scrolls. Polished hammer, trigger, axis pin securing spring and spring safety catch. $369 £170

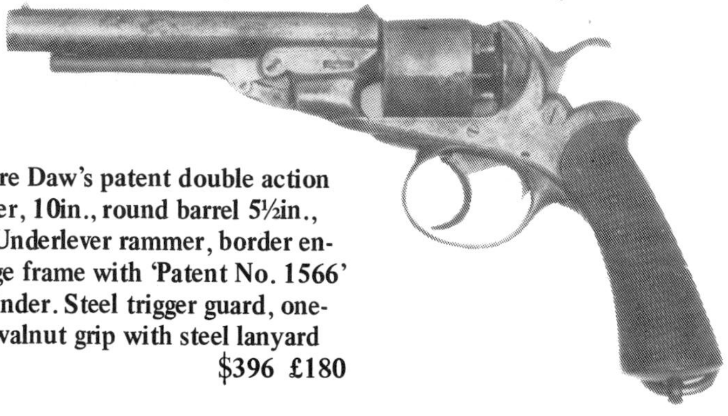

A five-shot 80-bore Daw's patent double action percussion revolver, 10in., round barrel 5½in., London proved. Underlever rammer, border engraved open wedge frame with 'Patent No. 1566' on frame and cylinder. Steel trigger guard, one-piece chequered walnut grip with steel lanyard ring. $396 £180

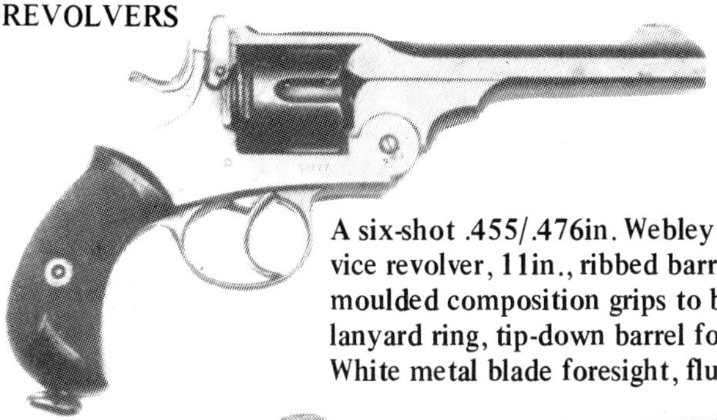

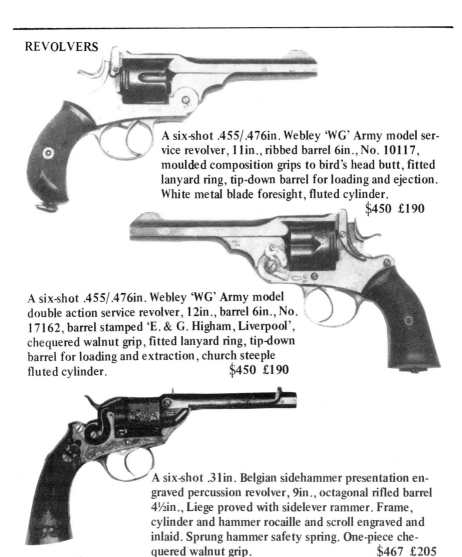

A six-shot .455/.476in. Webley 'WG' Army model service revolver, 11in., ribbed barrel 6in., No. 10117, moulded composition grips to bird's head butt, fitted lanyard ring, tip-down barrel for loading and ejection. White metal blade foresight, fluted cylinder.
$450 £190

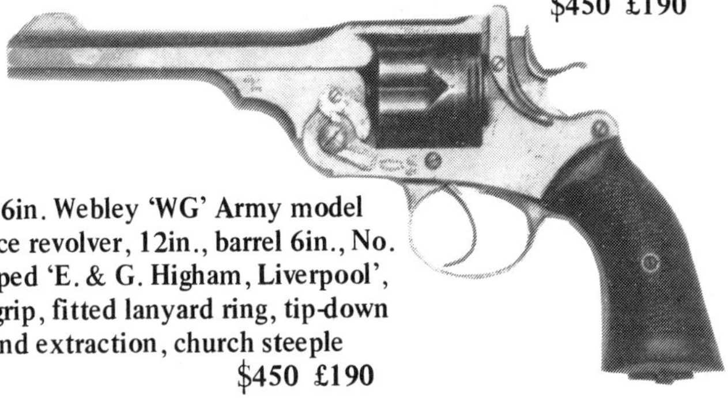

A six-shot .455/.476in. Webley 'WG' Army model double action service revolver, 12in., barrel 6in., No. 17162, barrel stamped 'E. & G. Higham, Liverpool', chequered walnut grip, fitted lanyard ring, tip-down barrel for loading and extraction, church steeple fluted cylinder. $450 £190

A six-shot .31in. Belgian sidehammer presentation engraved percussion revolver, 9in., octagonal rifled barrel 4½in., Liege proved with sidelever rammer. Frame, cylinder and hammer rocaille and scroll engraved and inlaid. Sprung hammer safety spring. One-piece chequered walnut grip. $467 £205

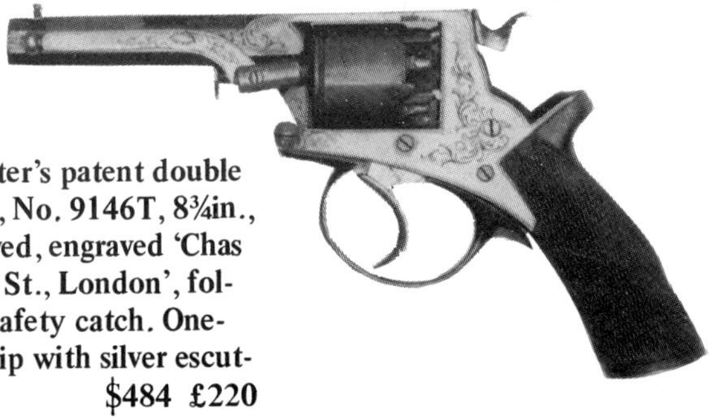

A five-shot 120-bore Tranter's patent double action percussion revolver, No. 9146T, 8¾in., barrel 3¾in., London proved, engraved 'Chas Lancaster, 151 New Bond St., London', foliate engraved frame with safety catch. One-piece chequered walnut grip with silver escutcheon. $484 £220

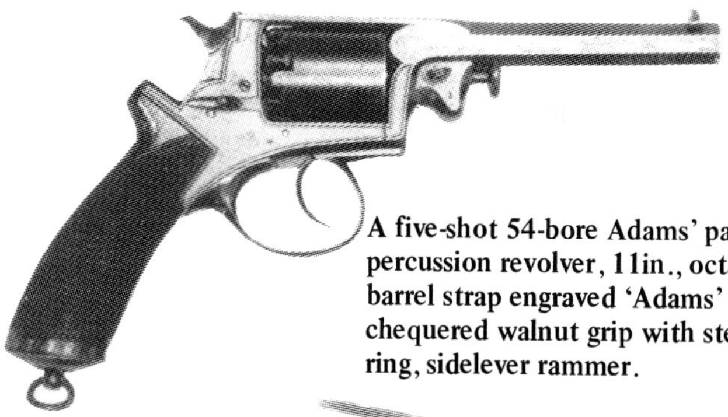

A five-shot 54-bore Adams' patent double action percussion revolver, 11in., octagonal barrel 5½in., barrel strap engraved 'Adams' Patent London', chequered walnut grip with steel cap and lanyard ring, sidelever rammer. $478 £230

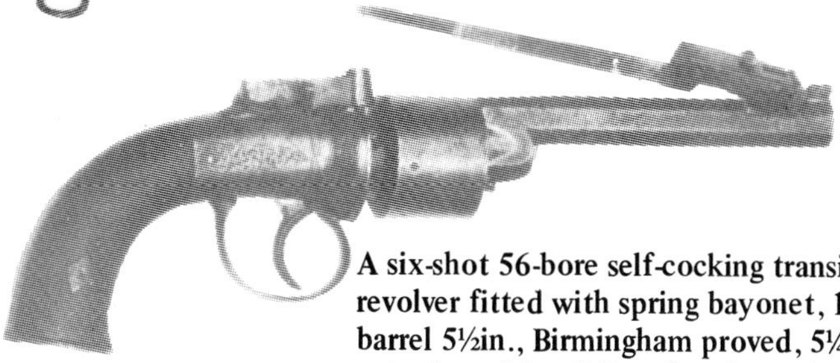

A six-shot 56-bore self-cocking transitional percussion revolver fitted with spring bayonet, 12in., octagonal barrel 5½in., Birmingham proved, 5¼in. spring bayonet released by sliding thumb catch. Two-piece chequered walnut grips. $528 £240

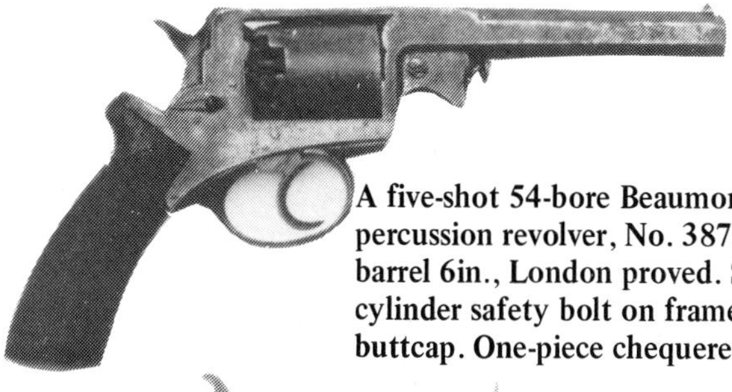

A five-shot 54-bore Beaumont Adams double action percussion revolver, No. 38719, 12in., rifled octagonal barrel 6in., London proved. Sidelever rammer, sliding cylinder safety bolt on frame, steel trigger guard and buttcap. One-piece chequered walnut grip. $575 £250

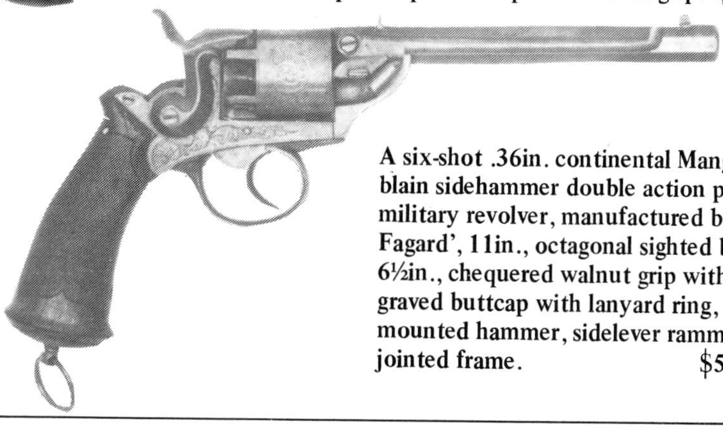

A six-shot .36in. continental Mangeot-Comblain sidehammer double action percussion military revolver, manufactured by 'P. J. Fagard', 11in., octagonal sighted barrel 6½in., chequered walnut grip with scroll engraved buttcap with lanyard ring, side-mounted hammer, sidelever rammer and jointed frame. $550 £250

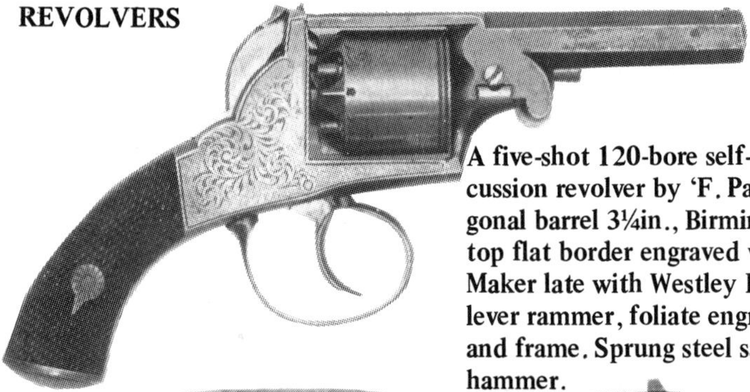

A five-shot 120-bore self-cocking percussion revolver by 'F. Parry', 8in., octagonal barrel 3¼in., Birmingham proved, top flat border engraved with 'F. Parry, Maker late with Westley Richards'. Side-lever rammer, foliate engraved cylinder and frame. Sprung steel safety catch to hammer. $550 £250

A six-shot .44in. Starr Arms Co. double action percussion revolver, No. 1947, 11½in., round barrel 6in., underlever rammer. steel trigger guard, sliding catch on trigger alters action. One-piece walnut grip. $586 £270

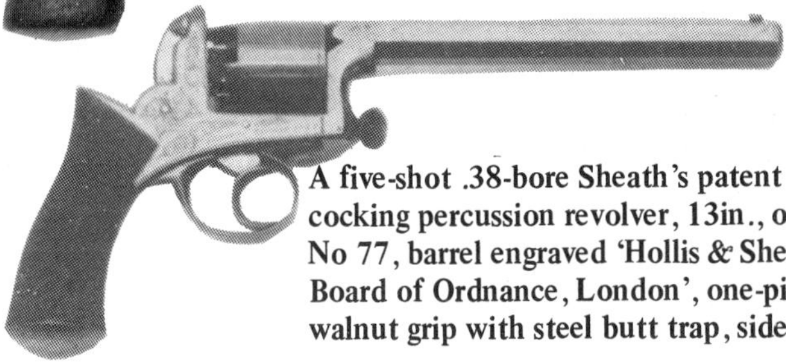

A five-shot .38-bore Sheath's patent open-framed self-cocking percussion revolver, 13in., octagonal barrel 8in., No 77, barrel engraved 'Hollis & Sheath, Makers to H.M.H. Board of Ordnance, London', one-piece finely chequered walnut grip with steel butt trap, sidemounted safety. $640 £270

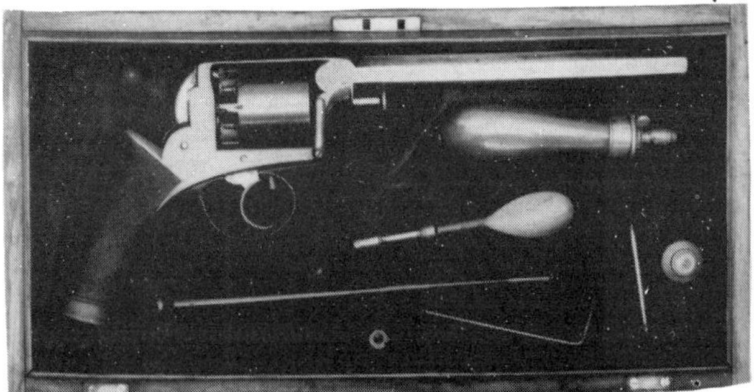

A five-shot 38-bore Deane Adams & Deane, model 1851, self-cocking percussion revolver, 14in., octagonal barrel 8in., London proved, chequered walnut grip with steel buttplate containing cap trap. Contained in its green beize lined and fitted oak case. $586 £270

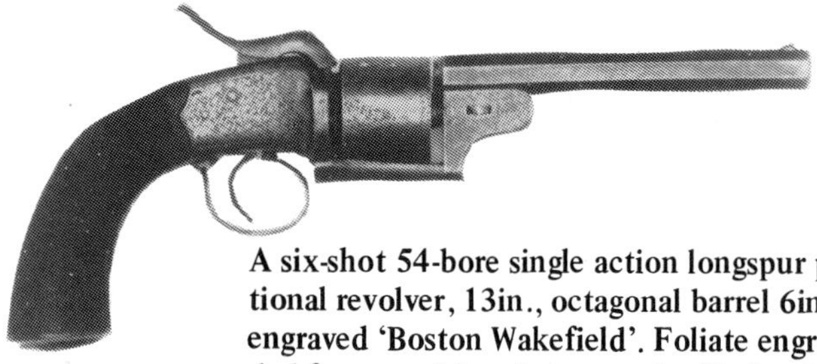

A six-shot 54-bore single action longspur percussion transitional revolver, 13in., octagonal barrel 6in., London proved, engraved 'Boston Wakefield'. Foliate engraved slightly rounded frame and London proved cylinder. Longspur dolphin hammer. Finely chequered rounded walnut grip. $741 £285

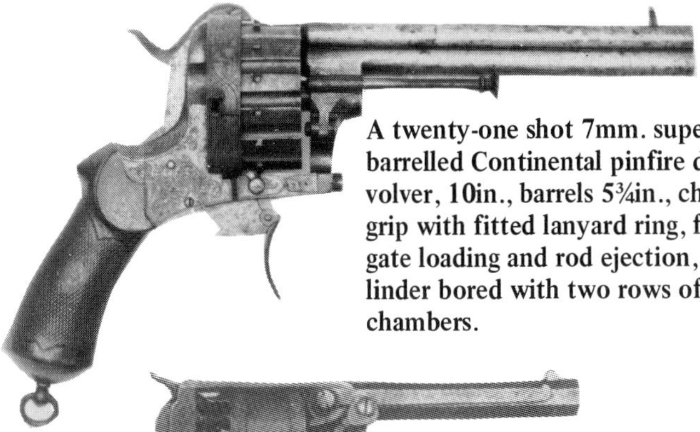

A twenty-one shot 7mm. superposed double barrelled Continental pinfire double action revolver, 10in., barrels 5¾in., chequered walnut grip with fitted lanyard ring, folding trigger, gate loading and rod ejection, fully fluted cylinder bored with two rows of concentric chambers. $684 £300

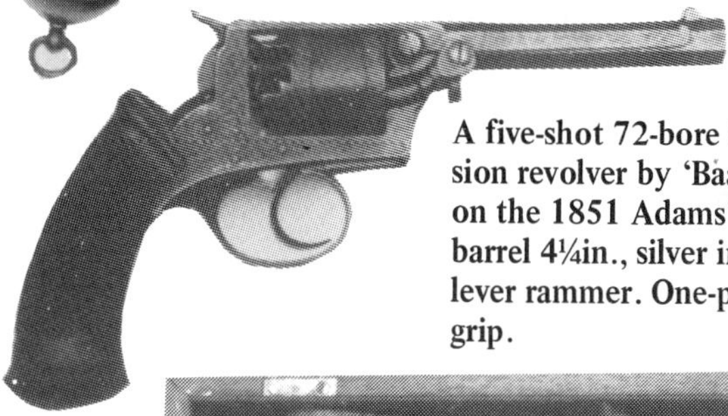

A five-shot 72-bore German self-cocking percussion revolver by 'Baader of Munich', modelled on the 1851 Adams' Patent, 9½in., octagonal barrel 4¼in., silver inlaid on top strap, side-lever rammer. One-piece chequered wooden grip. $713 £310

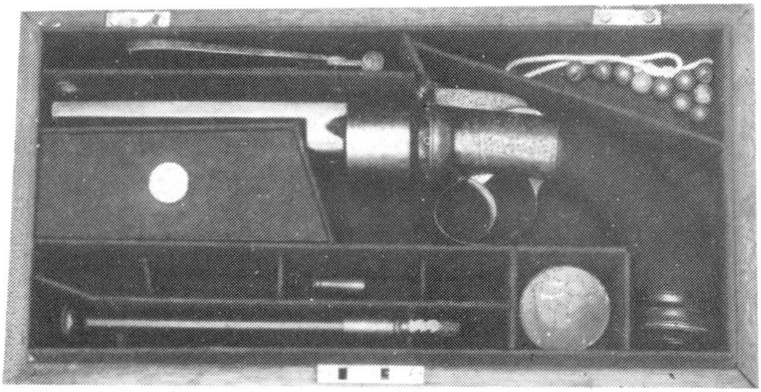

A six-shot 60-bore bar hammer transitional percussion revolver, 12in., octagonal barrel 5½in., Birmingham proved, finely chequered walnut grip with steel buttcap and cap trap and silver escutcheon. Contained in its green beize lined and fitted mahogany case. $682 £310

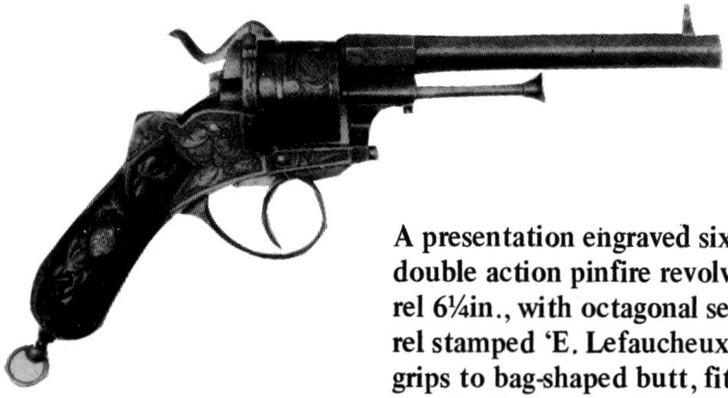

A presentation engraved six-shot 12mm. Belgian double action pinfire revolver, 11in., round barrel 6¼in., with octagonal section at breech, barrel stamped 'E. Lefaucheux Iner Brevete', ebony grips to bag-shaped butt, fitted lanyard ring, gate loading and rod ejection. $673 £310

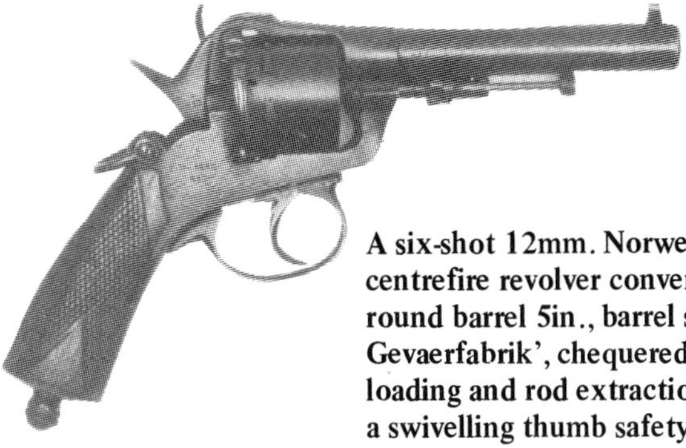

A six-shot 12mm. Norwegian double action military centrefire revolver converted from pinfire, 10in., round barrel 5in., barrel stamped 'Kronborg Gevaerfabrik', chequered one-piece walnut grip, gate loading and rod extraction, the left side fitted with a swivelling thumb safety which blocks the hammer. $858 £330

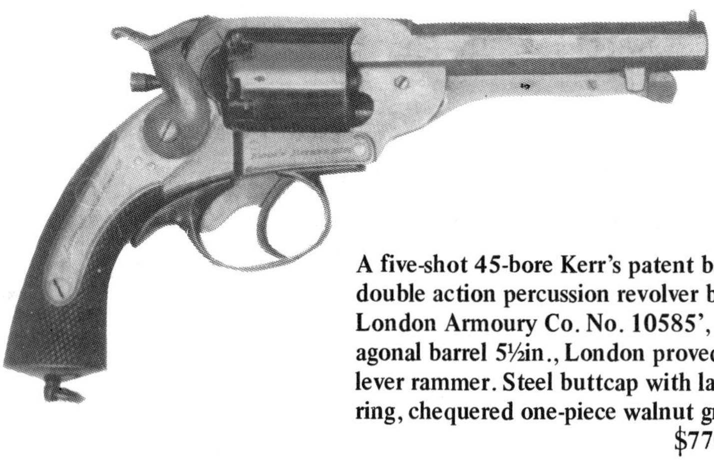

A five-shot 45-bore Kerr's patent back-action double action percussion revolver by 'The London Armoury Co. No. 10585', 11in., octagonal barrel 5½in., London proved. Underlever rammer. Steel buttcap with lanyard ring, chequered one-piece walnut grip. $770 £350

A five-shot 60-bore Tranter second model double trigger, self-cocking percussion revolver 11½in., octagonal barrel 6¼in., the barrel engraved 'Wood, Worcester', finely chequered walnut grip with steel cap, scroll engraved frame with spring hammer safety to left side. Contained in its green beize lined and fitted mahogany box. $760 £350

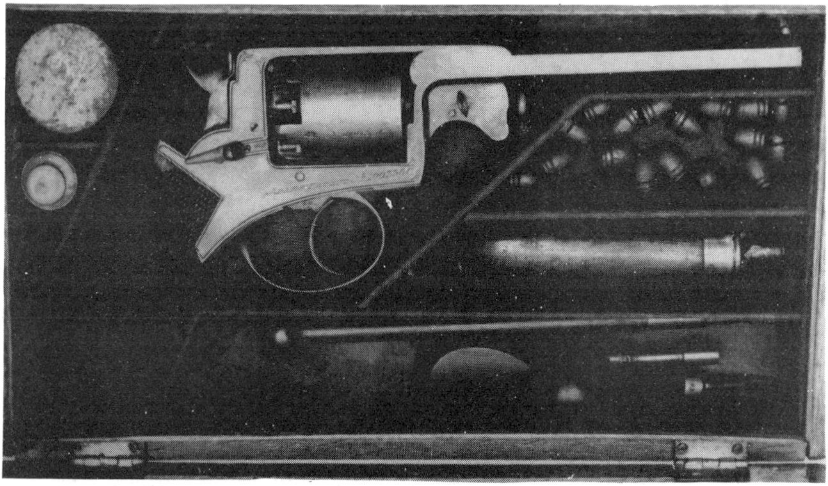

A five-shot 54-bore Beaumont Adams double action percussion revolver, No. 100336 C, 12in., octagonal barrel 6in., London proved, One-piece chequered walnut grip. Contained in its green beize lined fitted oak case, containing Bartram copper flask, ebony handle nipple key and turnscrew, oil bottle, cap tin and cleaning rod. $798 £350

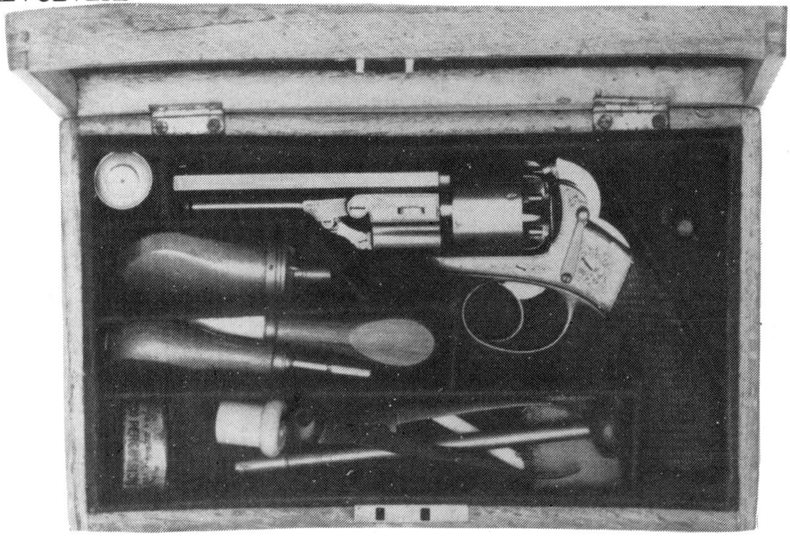

A six-shot 85-bore self-cocking open frame percussion revolver by 'Witton & Daw', 9in., octagonal barrel 4¾in., London proved. Foliate engraved frame, hinged engraved cap trap in one-piece chequered walnut grip. In its blue velvet lined fitted oak case containing copper flask, oil bottle, ball mould, turnscrew, nipple key, cleaning rod and cap tin. $897 £390

A five-shot 80-bore Tranter second model double trigger self-cocking percussion revolver, 10in., octagonal barrel 5in., No. 3106T. London proved, finely chequered walnut grip with steel buttplate, border and foliate scroll engraved action body with hammer spring safety to left side and cylinder pin spring lock to right side, plain border engraved cylinder, sighted barrel, early pattern detachable rammer which fits over pin on left side of frame. Contained in a red beize lined and fitted mahogany case. $880 £400

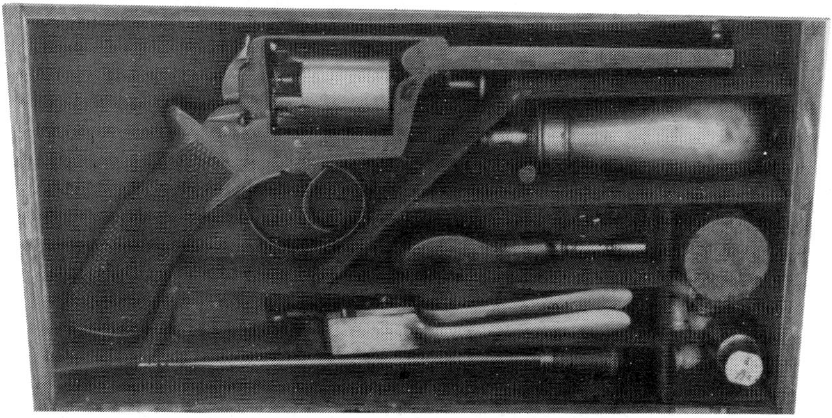

A 54-bore Deane Adams & Deane pattern 1851 self-cocking percussion revolver, 11in., octagonal barrel 6in., London proved, chequered walnut grip, spring hammer safety and cylinder bolt, blade foresight top-strap rear, the left side fitted with Rigby's patent lever rammer, which folds along pistol grip. Contained in its green beize lined and fitted oak case, with brass lid escutcheon and trade label of Deane Adams & Deane. $853 £410

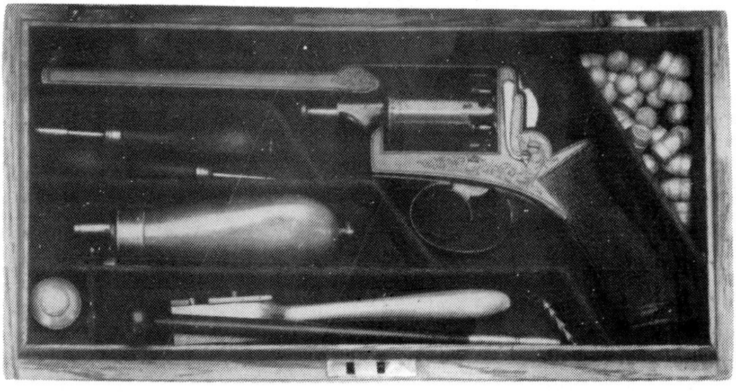

A five-shot 54-bore model 1851 Adam's self-cocking percussion revolver, No. 13052R, 12½in., octagonal barrel 6½in., London proved, engraved 'Deane, Adams & Deane, 30 King William Street, London Bridge' on top flat, line engraved barrel and frame. Foliate engraved frame, shell engraved hinged cap trap, one-piece chequered walnut grip. In its green beize lined fitted oak case, containing copper powder flask, brass twin cavity bullet mould, cleaning rod, nipple key, turnscrew and oil bottle. $989 £430

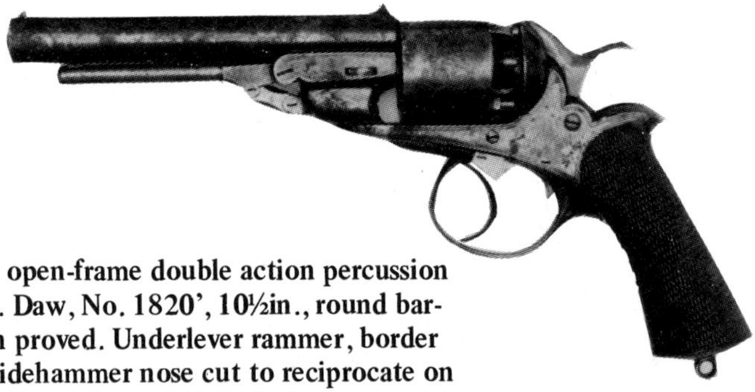

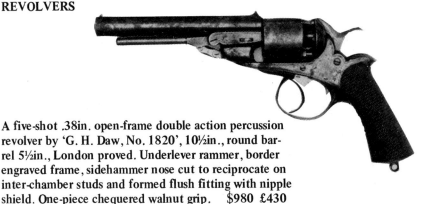

A five-shot .38in. open-frame double action percussion revolver by 'G. H. Daw, No. 1820', 10½in., round barrel 5½in., London proved. Underlever rammer, border engraved frame, sidehammer nose cut to reciprocate on inter-chamber studs and formed flush fitting with nipple shield. One-piece chequered walnut grip. $980 £430

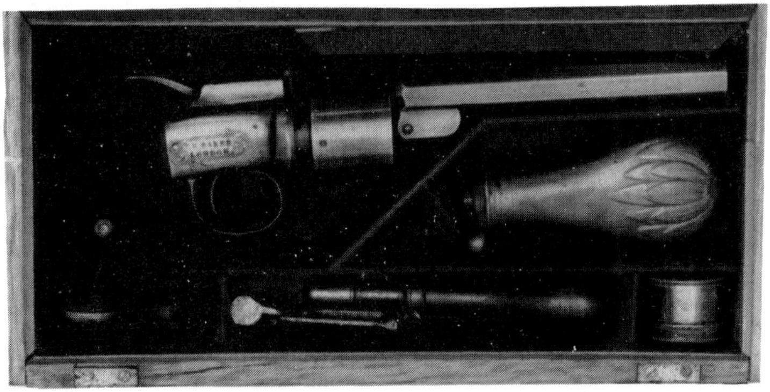

A six-shot 54-bore single action longspur Baker's patent percussion transitional revolver, 11½in., octagonal rifled barrel 5½in., Birmingham proved. Back-strap stamped 'No. 1635', hammer stamped 'Baker's Patent'. Sliding safety bolt on frame side, two-piece chequered walnut grips. Contained in its green beize lined fitted oak case. $955 £440

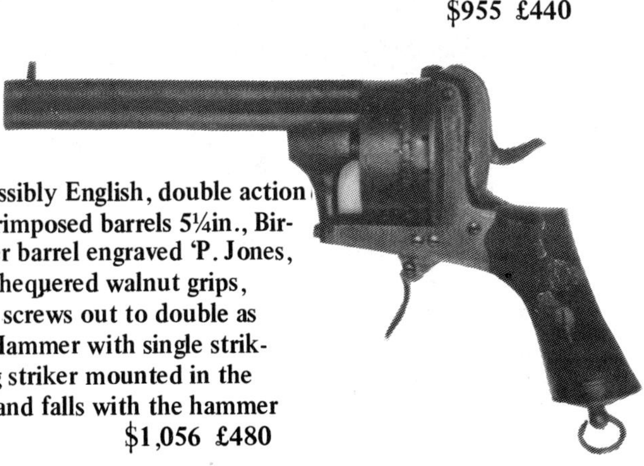

An eighteen-shot 7mm. possibly English, double action pinfire revolver, 9in., superimposed barrels 5¼in., Birmingham proved, the upper barrel engraved 'P. Jones, 6 Chapel St., Liverpool'. Chequered walnut grips, lanyard ring to butt which screws out to double as ejector rod, gate loading. Hammer with single striking nose acting on a sliding striker mounted in the standing breech, this rises and falls with the hammer firing the cartridges. $1,056 £480

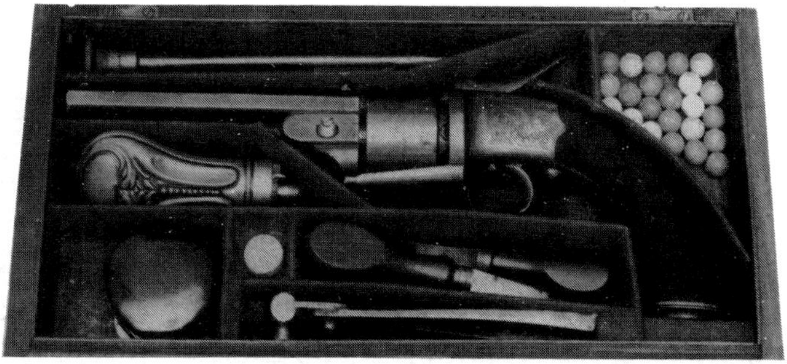

A six-shot 44-bore Webley style longspur single action reciprocating percussion transitional revolver by 'Parker Field & Sons', 13in., octagonal barrel 5¾in., London proved, finely chequered walnut grip with butt trap, well scroll engraved action body. Contained in its green beize lined and fitted mahogany case.

$1,082 £520

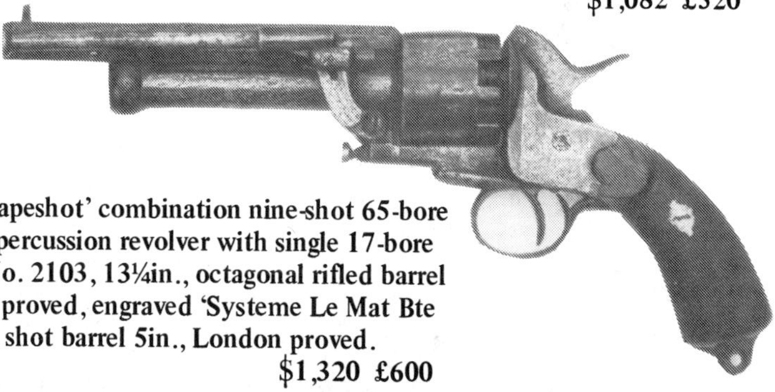

A Le Mat 'Grapeshot' combination nine-shot 65-bore single action percussion revolver with single 17-bore shot barrel, No. 2103, 13¼in., octagonal rifled barrel 7in., London proved, engraved 'Systeme Le Mat Bte s.g.d.g. Paris', shot barrel 5in., London proved.

$1,320 £600

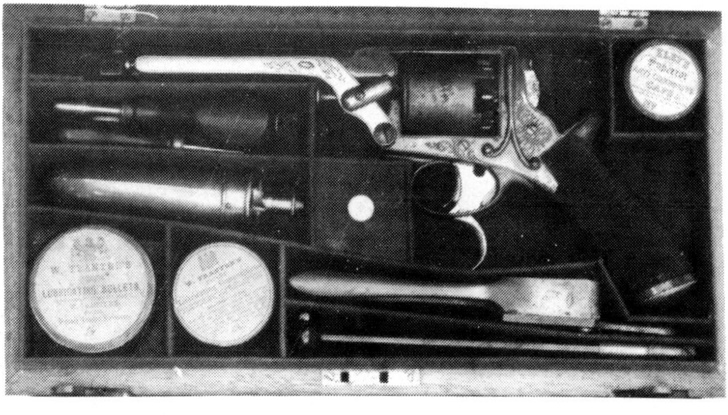

A five-shot 54-bore double trigger Tranter's patent percussion revolver, 12in., octagonal barrel 6in., Birmingham proved. Foliate engraved frame with 'No. 16263T'. Engraved steel buttcap to chequered one-piece walnut grip with silver escutcheon. Contained in its green beize lined fitted mahogany case.

$1,452 £660

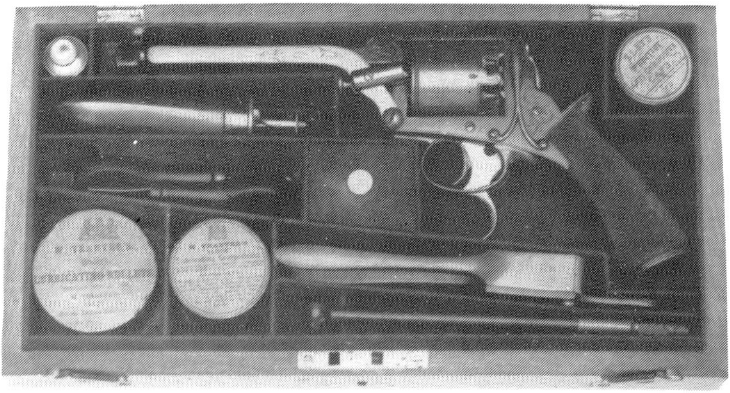

A five-shot 54-bore double trigger Tranter's patent percussion revolver, No. 7071, 11¾in., octagonal barrel 6in., London proved. Foliate engraved frame, sidelever rammer, rounded chequered one-piece walnut grip, case hardened foliate engraved buttcap. Contained in its polished mahogany green beize lined fitted case with all original accessories. $1,485 £675

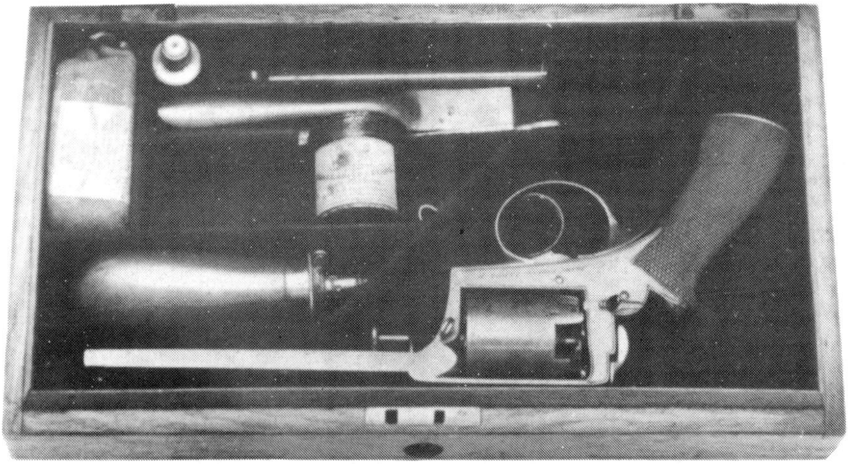

A five-shot 54-bore model 1851 Adams' patent self-cocking percussion revolver, 12½in., octagonal barrel 6½in., London proved, engraved 'Deane Adams and Deane London' on top-strap and 'Lt. Colonel A. Lake' in script on barrel side. Sliding cylinder safety locking bolt. Brass trigger guard and buttplate, one-piece chequered wooden grip. Contained in its loose fitting beize lined oak case with double cavity bronze bullet mould. $1,775 £750

A two-barrelled twenty-shot 7mm. Continental double action pinfire revolver, 9in., round superimposed barrels 4¾in., No. 450, the barrel engraved 'E. Lefaucheux Bte a Paris', plain wooden grips with fitted lanyard ring, folding trigger, gate loading and rod ejection. $2,145 £975

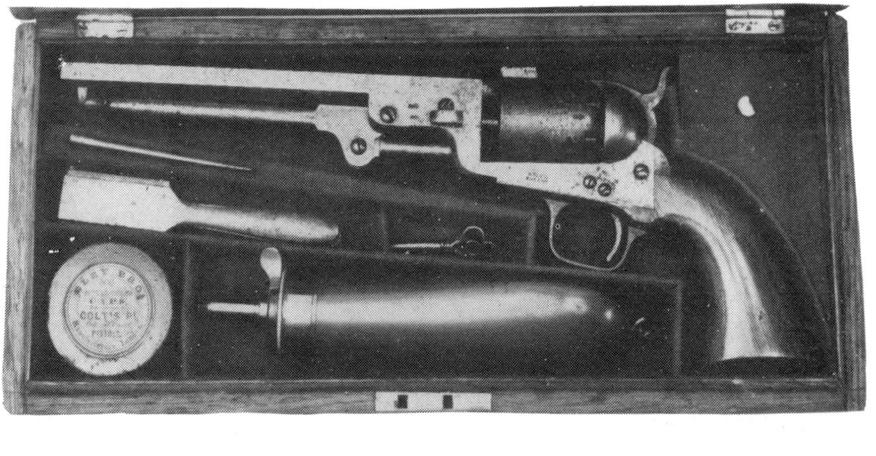

A six-shot .36in. Colt London, Navy single action percussion revolver, No. 27966, 13in., octagonal barrel 7½in., London proved. Underlever rammer. Steel trigger guard and gripstrap. One-piece polished wooden grip. Contained in its green beize lined fitted oak case. $2,170 £1,000

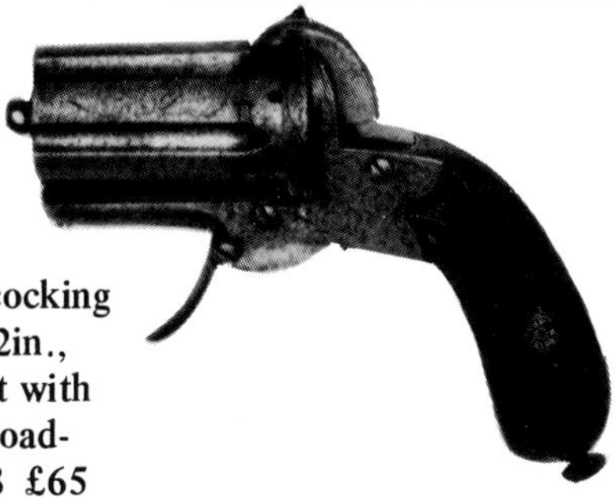

A six-shot 7mm. Continental pinfire self-cocking pepperbox revolver, 4½in., fluted barrels 2in., chequered walnut grips to bag-shaped butt with screw in ejector rod, folding trigger, gate loading. $148 £65

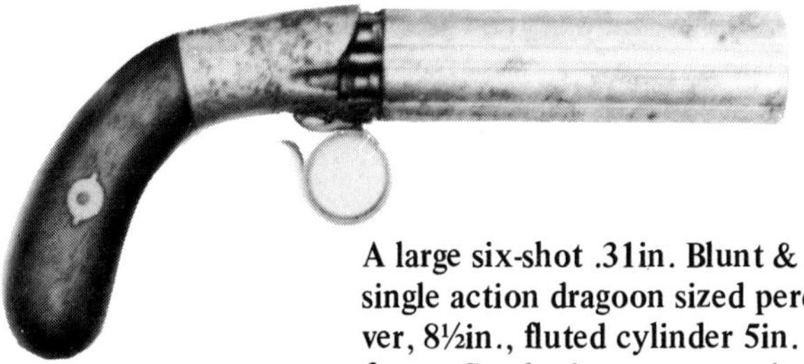

A large six-shot .31in. Blunt & Syms patent ring trigger single action dragoon sized percussion pepperbox revolver, 8½in., fluted cylinder 5in. Foliate engraved round frame. Steel gripstrap, two-piece rounded bag-shaped walnut grips. $174 £80

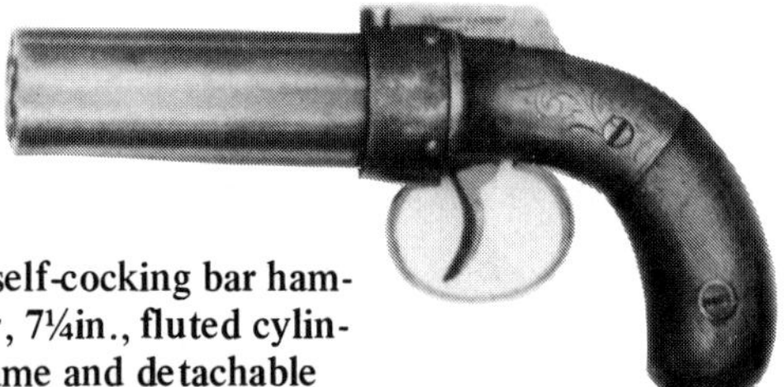

A six-shot .32in. Allen & Thurber self-cocking bar hammer percussion pepperbox revolver, 7¼in., fluted cylinder 4in. Foliate engraved round frame and detachable nipple shield. Steel trigger guard and engraved gripstrap. Two-piece bag-shaped walnut grips. $174 £80

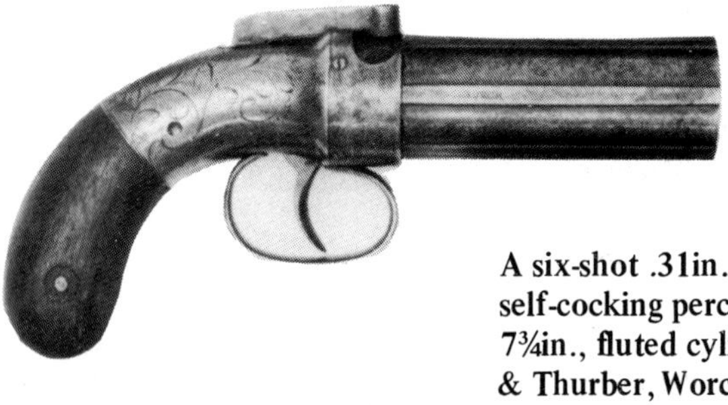

A six-shot .31in. American Allen & Thurber self-cocking percussion pepperbox revolver, 7¾in., fluted cylinder 3½in., stamped 'Allen & Thurber, Worcester, Patented 1852, Cast Steel'. Foliate scroll engraved round frame and nipple shield. $206 £95

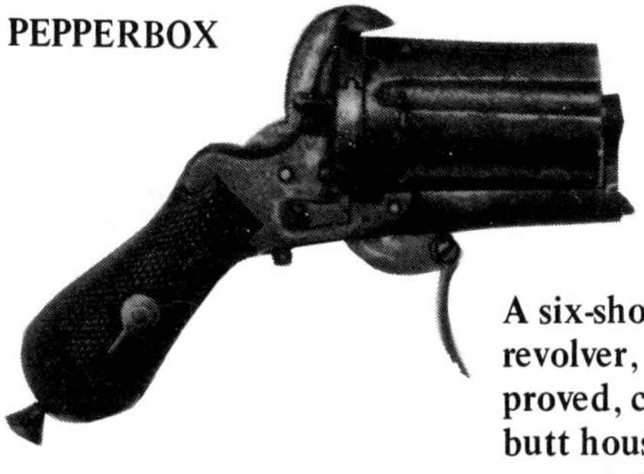

A six-shot 7mm. pinfire self-cocking pepperbox revolver, 5in., barrel group 1¾in., Birmingham proved, chequered walnut grips to bag-shaped butt housing screw in ejector rod, folding trigger, gate loading, long fluted cylinder supported from bottom strap. $185 £100

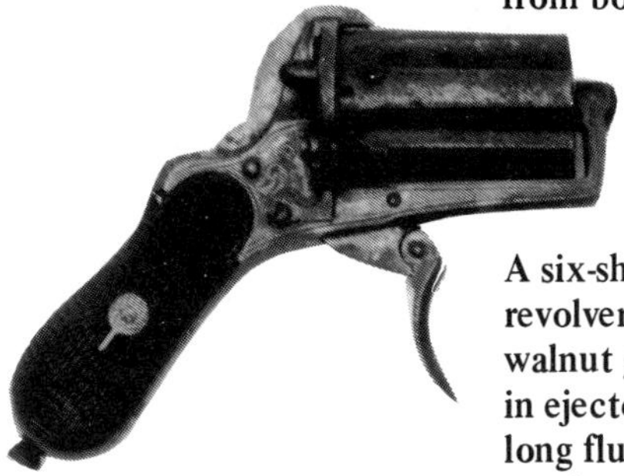

A six-shot 7mm. pinfire self-cocking pepperbox revolver, 5in., barrel group 1¾in., chequered walnut grips to bag-shaped butt housing screw in ejector rod, folding trigger, gate loading, long fluted cylinder. The frame with some border and scroll engraving. $217 £100

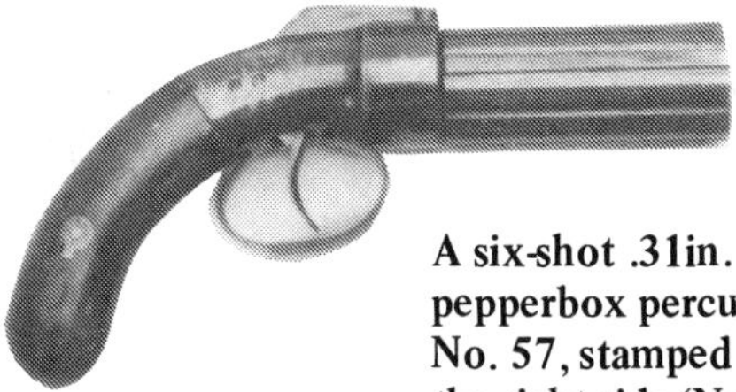

A six-shot .31in. Marston self-cocking bar hammer pepperbox percussion revolver, 8in., fluted barrels 3¼in., No. 57, stamped on top hammer 'W. W. Marston', on the right side 'New York' and the left 'Patented 1849'. Two-piece walnut grips to bag-shaped butt, round action body, riveted nipple shield. $245 £105

A six-shot .31in. Allen & Thurber top snap percussion pepperbox revolver, 7¼in., fluted cylinder 4in. Round frame foliate engraved, two-piece bag-shaped wooden grips. $240 £110

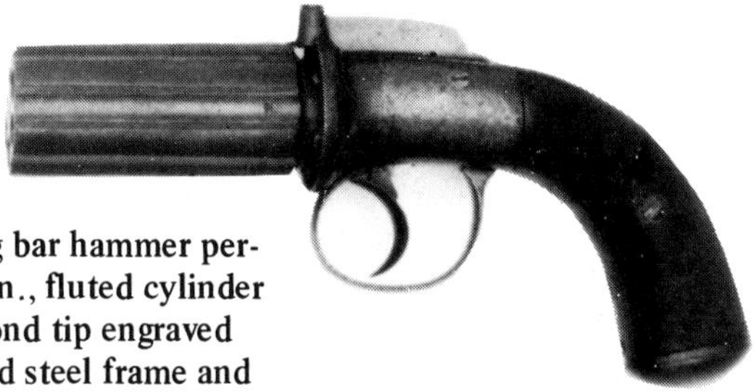

A six-shot 90-bore self-cocking bar hammer percussion pepperbox revolver, 8in., fluted cylinder 3½in., Birmingham proved, frond tip engraved muzzles, round foliate engraved steel frame and stepped flared nipple shield $250 £115

A six-shot .31in. Manhattan self-cocking bar hammer percussion pepperbox revolver, 7in., semi fluted barrels, 3½in., barrel signed 'Manhattan FA Mfg Co, New York, Cast Steel' between flutes. Plain polished walnut grips, rounded scroll foliate engraved action body, plain unsigned hammer and detachable nipple flash shield. $299 £115

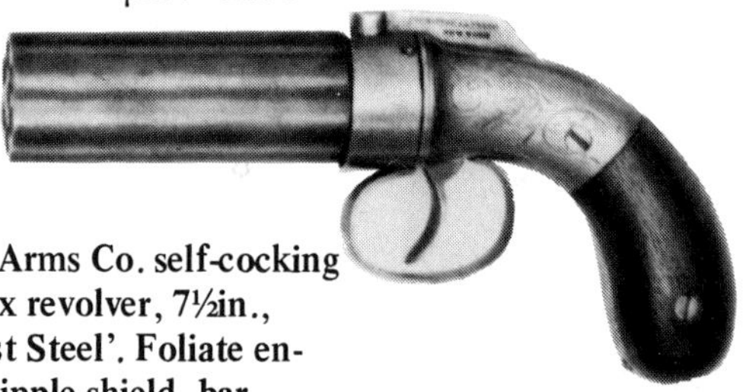

A six-shot .31in. Manhattan Fire Arms Co. self-cocking bar hammer percussion pepperbox revolver, 7½in., fluted cylinder 4in., stamped 'Cast Steel'. Foliate engraved round frame, detachable nipple shield, bar hammer stamped 'Manhattan FA Mfg Co, New York', Steel gripstrap, two-piece bag-shaped walnut grips. $260 £120

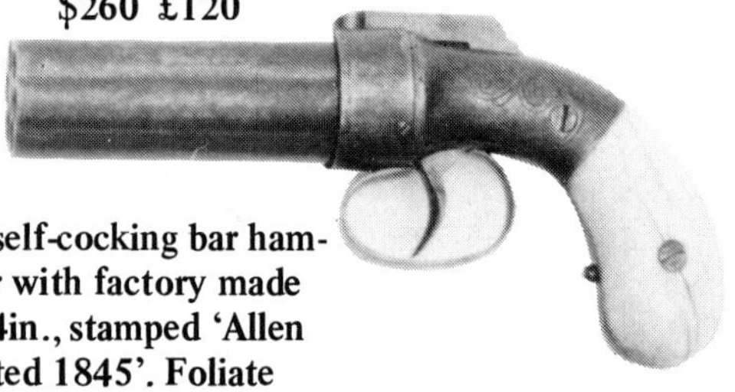

A six-shot .32in. Allen & Thurber self-cocking bar hammer percussion pepperbox revolver with factory made ivory grips, 7½in., fluted cylinder 4in., stamped 'Allen & Thurber & Co, Worcester, Patented 1845'. Foliate engraved round frame and detachable nipple shield, engraved steel gripstrap, original two-piece bag-shaped ivory grips. $260 £120

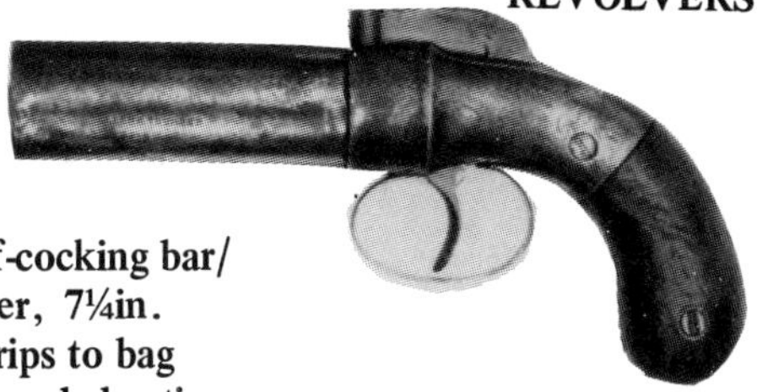

A six-shot .31in. Allen & Thurber self-cocking bar/hammer percussion pepperbox revolver, 7¼in. barrels 3½in., No 300, plain walnut grips to bag shaped butt, scroll foliate engraved rounded action body, non integral nipple shield, semi fluted barrels stamped: 'Allen & Thurber, Worcester'. $274 £120

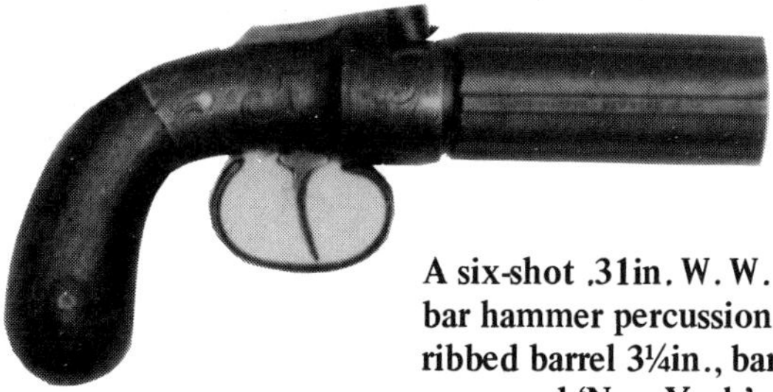

A six-shot .31in. W. W. Marston & Knox self-cocking bar hammer percussion pepperbox revolver, 7½in., ribbed barrel 3¼in., barrel stamped with maker's name and 'New York', wooden grips, rounded action body with some scroll engraving. $260 £120

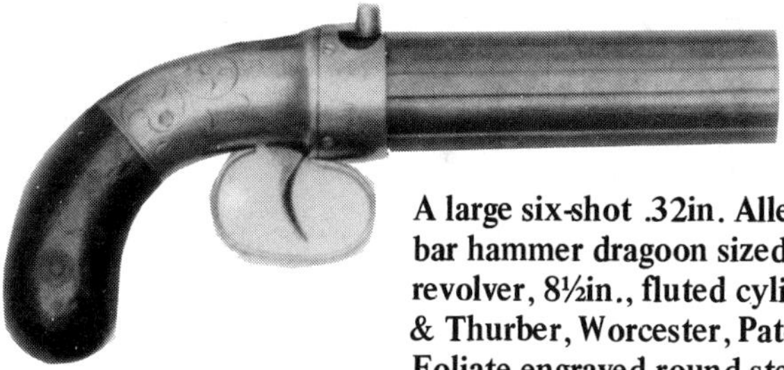

A large six-shot .32in. Allen & Thurber self-cocking bar hammer dragoon sized percussion pepperbox revolver, 8½in., fluted cylinder 5in., stamped 'Allen & Thurber, Worcester, Patented 1837, Cast Steel'. Foliate engraved round steel frame and detachable nipple shield. Steel trigger guard and gripstrap. Two-piece bag-shaped walnut grips. $271 £125

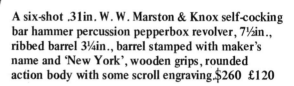

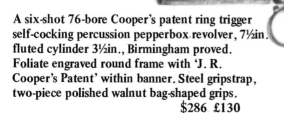

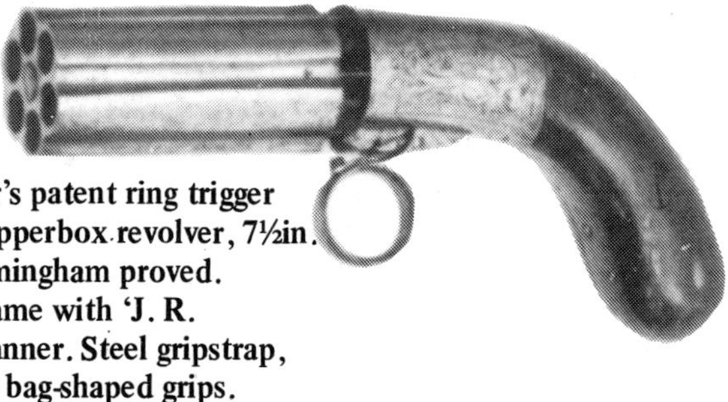

A six-shot 76-bore Cooper's patent ring trigger self-cocking percussion pepperbox revolver, 7½in. fluted cylinder 3½in., Birmingham proved. Foliate engraved round frame with 'J. R. Cooper's Patent' within banner. Steel gripstrap, two-piece polished walnut bag-shaped grips. $286 £130

REVOLVERS
PEPPERBOX

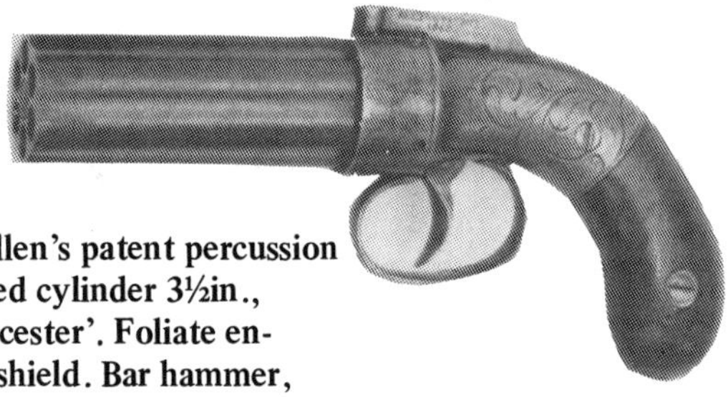

A six-shot .31in. self-cocking Allen's patent percussion pepperbox revolver, 7¼in., fluted cylinder 3½in., stamped 'Allen & Thurber, Worcester'. Foliate engraved round frame and nipple shield. Bar hammer, engraved gripstrap and plain trigger guard, two-piece bag-shaped walnut grips. $308 £140

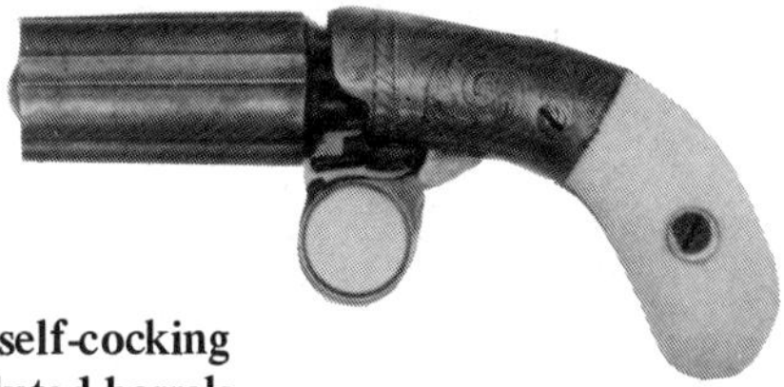

A five-shot .28in. American ring trigger self-cocking percussion pepperbox revolver, 5½in., fluted barrels 2½in. Round frame foliate engraved, steel gripstrap and two-piece bag-shaped ivory grips. $325 £150

A six-shot .40in. Cooper's patent self-cocking ring trigger percussion pepperbox revolver, 7¾in., fluted cylinder 3¼in., Birmingham proved. Foliate and border engraved round frame with 'J. R. Cooper's Patent' within banner. Ring trigger, sliding top thumb safety catch. Two-piece bag-shaped chequered walnut grips. $365 £160

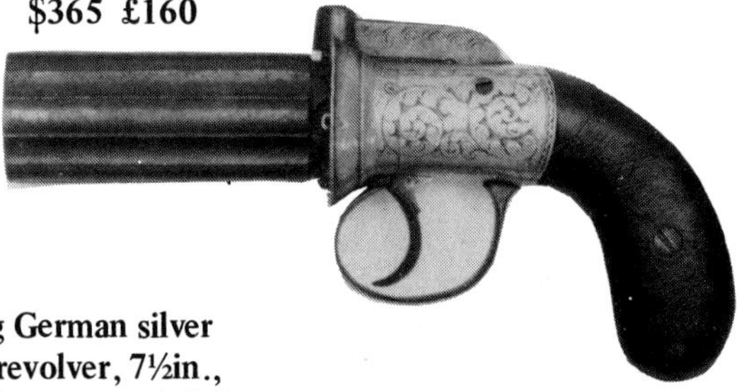

A six-shot 70-bore self-cocking German silver framed percussion pepperbox revolver, 7½in., fluted cylinder 3¼in., Birmingham proved, foliate engraved muzzle. Two-piece bag-shaped chequered walnut grips. $369 £170

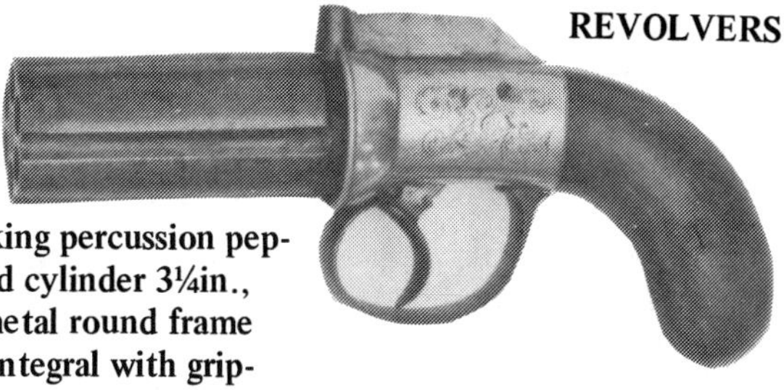

A six-shot 120-bore self-cocking percussion pepperbox revolver, 7½in., fluted cylinder 3¼in., Birmingham proved, white metal round frame foliate and border engraved integral with gripstrap. Foliate engraved trigger guard, bar hammer, two-piece bag-shaped walnut grips.
$385 £175

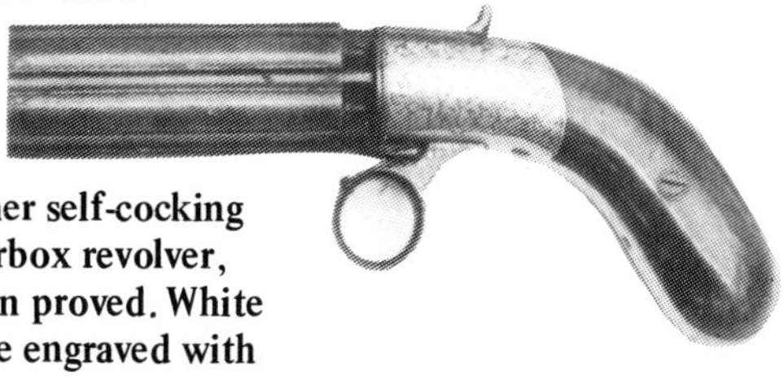

A six-shot ring trigger underhammer self-cocking Cooper's patent percussion pepperbox revolver, 8¼in., fluted cylinder 4in., London proved. White metal frame and back-strap, foliate engraved with retailer's name 'H. Allport-Cork' and 'J. R. Cooper's Patent', sliding steel cylinder locking catch on top of frame. $450 £190

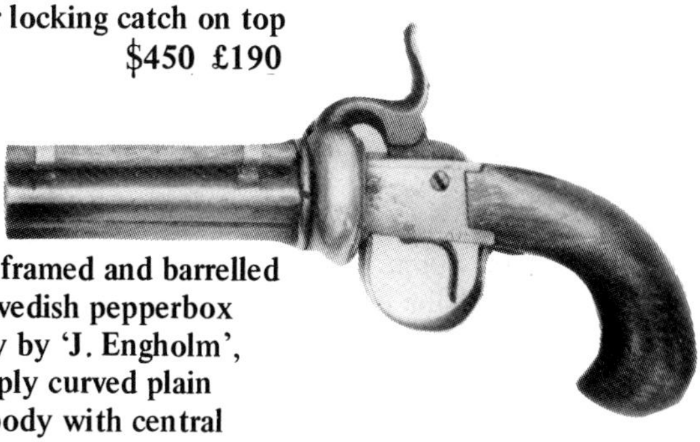

A four-barrelled .31in. brass framed and barrelled single action hand rotated Swedish pepperbox percussion revolver, probably by 'J. Engholm', 8in., square barrels 4in. Sharply curved plain wooden grip, square action body with central boxlock hammer, domed nipple shield.
$434 £200

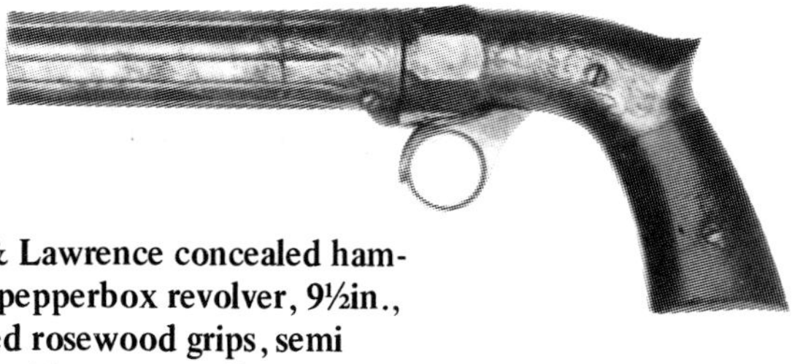

A five-shot .31in. Robbins & Lawrence concealed hammer, ring trigger percussion pepperbox revolver, 9½in., ribbed barrels 4½in., polished rosewood grips, semi saw-handled rounded frame with some scroll engraved decoration, ring trigger, enclosed action vented for cap flash. $462 £210

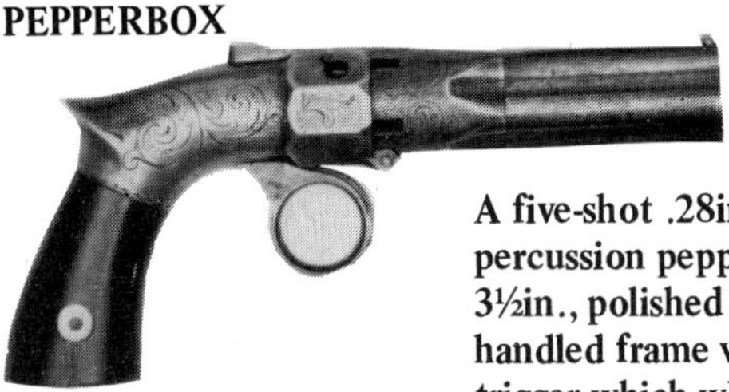

A five-shot .28in. Robbins & Lawrence self-cocking percussion pepperbox revolver, 7½in., fluted barrels 3½in., polished rosewood grip, rounded semi saw-handled frame with some scroll engraving, ring trigger which when pulled cocks and rotates an internal striker which fires barrels. $477 £220

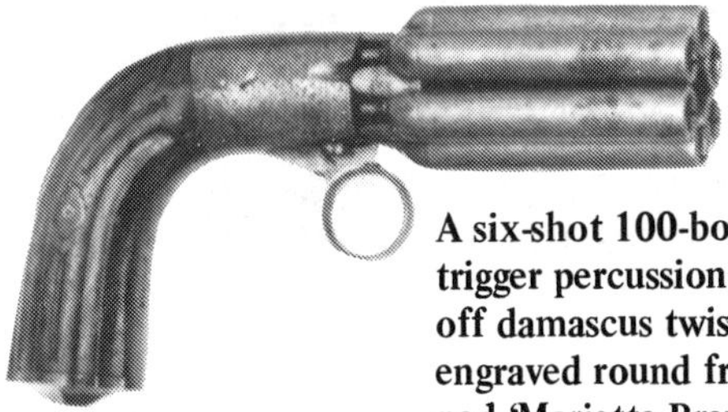

A six-shot 100-bore Mariette patent self-cocking ring trigger percussion pepperbox revolver, 7¾in., turn-off damascus twist barrel 2¾in., Liege proved. Foliate engraved round frame. Lower grip frame strap stamped 'Mariette Brevete'. Fluted two-piece walnut grips. $484 £220

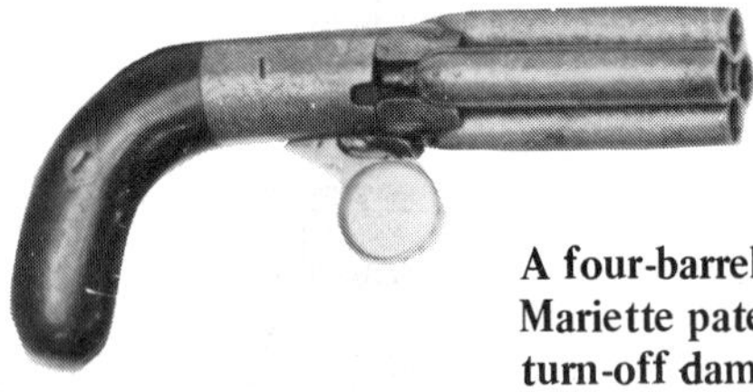

A four-barrelled 90-bore ring trigger self-cocking Mariette patent percussion pepperbox revolver, 7in., turn-off damascus barrels 2½in., Liege proved. Foliate engraved round frame, two-piece bag-shaped ebonised grips. $542 £250

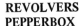

An eight-shot self-cocking ring trigger Mariette percussion pepperbox revolver, 7½in., turn-off damascus twist barrels 3in., Liege proved. Scroll engraved round frame inlaid with silver and gold scrolls. Gripstrap stamped 'Mariette Brevete'. Two-piece bag-shaped ivory grips. $998 £460

A six-shot 120-bore ring trigger self-cocking percussion pepperbox revolver, 7in., fluted cylinder 3in., Birmingham proved, with foliate engraved muzzles. White metal round frame, scroll foliate and border engraved with 'F. Barnes & Co. London' within banners, two-piece bag-shaped polished walnut grips. Contained in its brass bound velvet lined fitted mahogany case. $1,090 £460

An eighteen-shot, eighteen-barrelled ring trigger Mariette's Patent Belgian percussion pepperbox revolver, 8½in., turn-off damascus barrels 3¼in., the outer ring of barrels numbered 1-12, Liege proved. Central button unscrews and can be reversed and rescrewed to reveal a 3in. shallow diamond section knife blade. Foliate engraved round frame and gripstraps, two-piece fluted ebony grips. $7,812 £3,600

REVOLVERS
POCKET

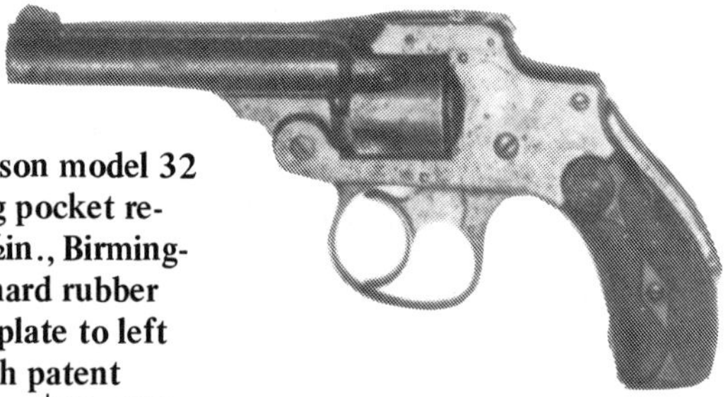

A five-shot .32in. Smith & Wesson model 32 safety, first model, self-cocking pocket revolver, 7¼in., rubbed barrel 3½in., Birmingham proved, chequered black hard rubber grips, grip safety, irregular sideplate to left side, fluted cylinder, barrel with patent dates to August 4, 1885. $88 £40

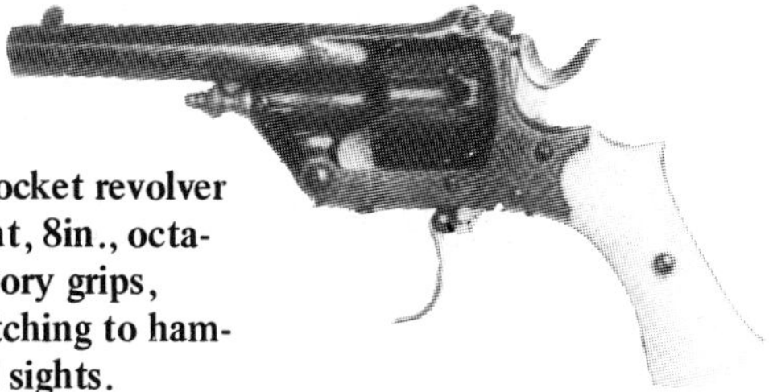

A six-shot .320in. hinged frame pocket revolver made under C. G. Bonehill's patent, 8in., octagonal barrel 4in., plain polished ivory grips, folding trigger, tip-down barrel latching to hammer holster, fluted cylinder, fixed sights. $130 £55

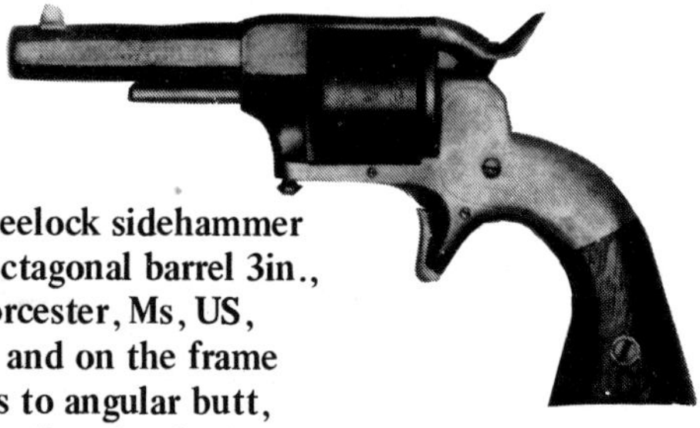

A six-shot .32in. rimfire Allen & Wheelock sidehammer single action pocket revolver, 7in., octagonal barrel 3in., barrel struck 'Allen & Wheelock, Worcester, Ms, US, Allen's Patent, Sept 7, Nov 9, 1858' and on the frame 'July 3 1860', polished wooden grips to angular butt, spur trigger, sidemounted hammer, unfluted cylinder. $137 £60

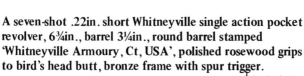

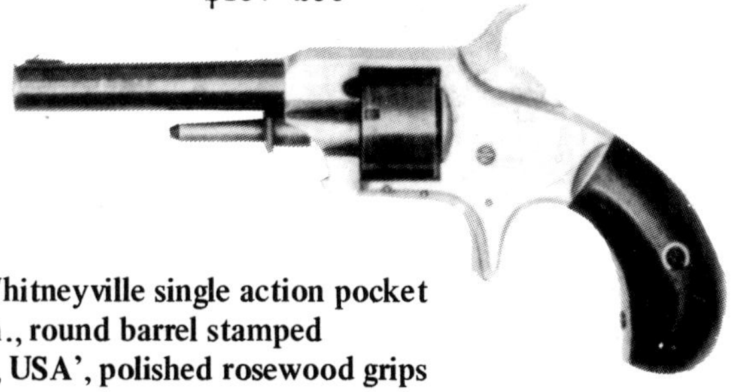

A seven-shot .22in. short Whitneyville single action pocket revolver, 6¾in., barrel 3¼in., round barrel stamped 'Whitneyville Armoury, Ct, USA', polished rosewood grips to bird's head butt, bronze frame with spur trigger. $141 £65

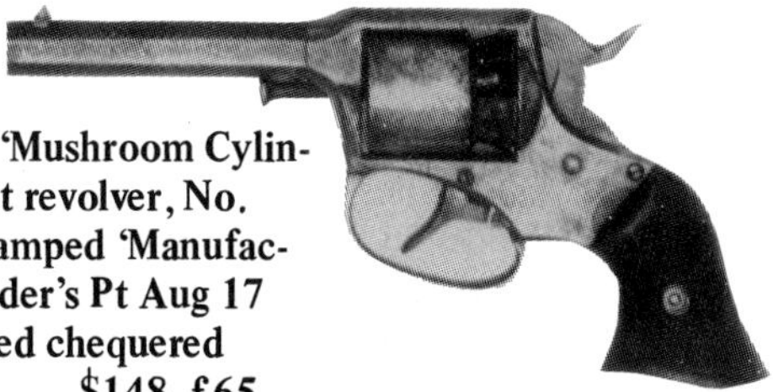

A five-shot .32in. Remington-Rider 'Mushroom Cylinder' double action percussion pocket revolver, No. 226, 6½in., octagonal barrel 3in., stamped 'Manufactured by Remington, Ilion, N.Y., Rider's Pt Aug 17 1858, May 3 1859'. Two-piece shaped chequered grips. $148 £65

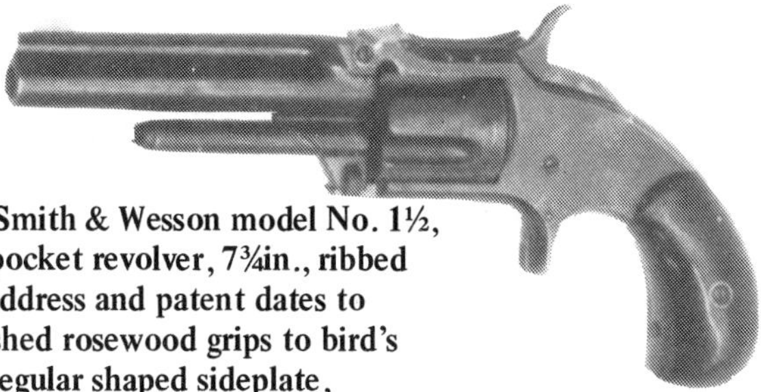

A five-shot .32in. rimfire Smith & Wesson model No. 1½, New Model single action pocket revolver, 7¾in., ribbed barrel 3½in., barrel with address and patent dates to Nov 21, 1865, finely polished rosewood grips to bird's head butt, spur trigger, irregular shaped sideplate, fluted cylinder. $154 £70

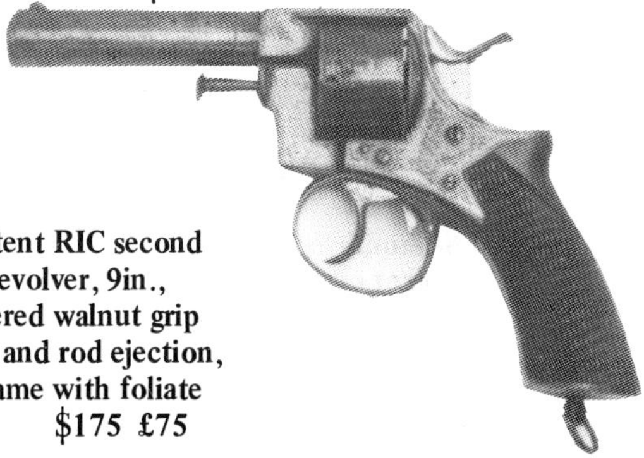

A six-shot .450in. Webley's patent RIC second pattern double action pocket revolver, 9in., barrel 4½in., No. 7194, chequered walnut grip with lanyard ring, gate loading and rod ejection, double border line engraved frame with foliate scrolls about screws. $175 £75

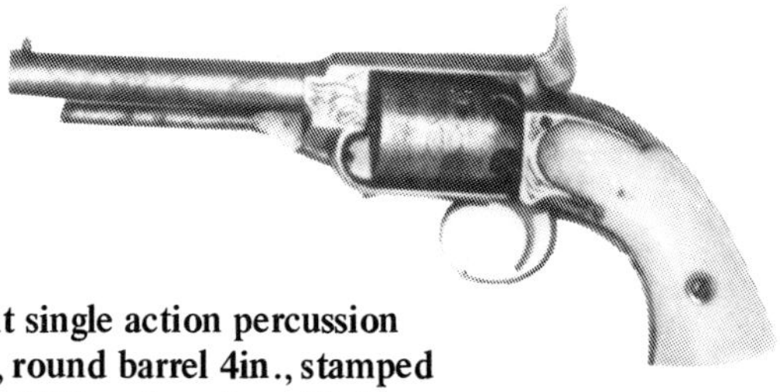

A six-shot .28in. Warner's patent single action percussion pocket revolver, No. 5881, 8in., round barrel 4in., stamped 'James Warner, Springfield, Mass US' on top-strap. Underlever rammer, foliate engraved frame and steel gripstrap, two-piece ivory grips. $187 £85

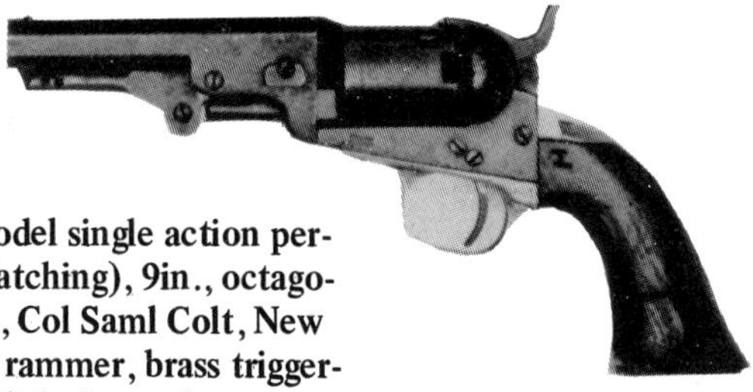

A five-shot .31in. Colt pocket model single action percussion revolver, No. 277360 (matching), 9in., octagonal barrel 4in., stamped 'Address, Col Saml Colt, New York, U.S. America'. Underlever rammer, brass triggerguard and gripstrap, one-piece polished wooden grip. $206 £95

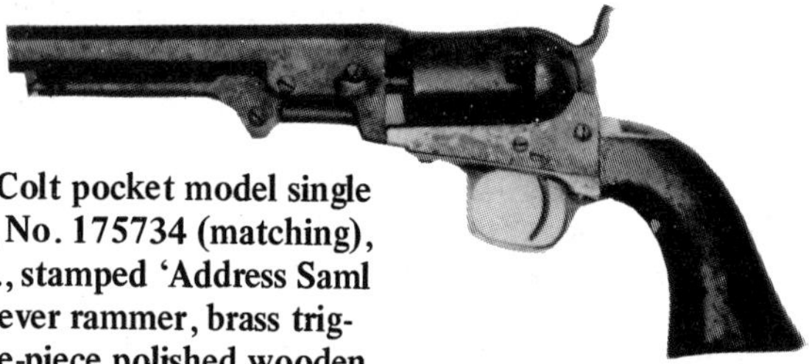

A six-shot .31in. Hartford Colt pocket model single action percussion revolver, No. 175734 (matching), 10in., octagonal barrel 5in., stamped 'Address Saml Colt, Hartford, Ct'. Underlever rammer, brass trigger guard and gripstrap, one-piece polished wooden grip. $217 £100

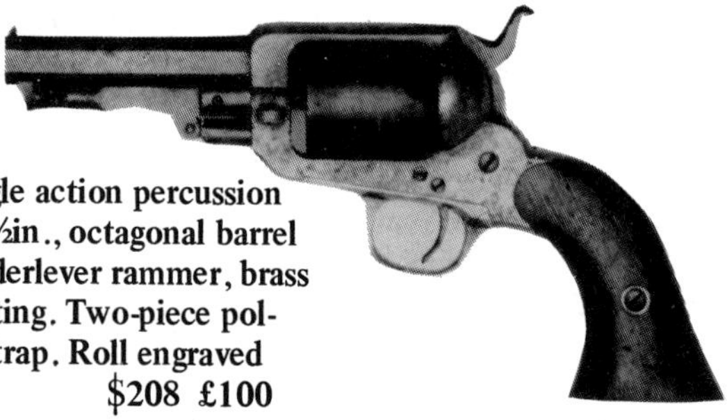

A five-shot .31in. Whitney single action percussion pocket revolver, No. 19725, 8½in., octagonal barrel 3½in., stamped 'N.Haven'. Underlever rammer, brass trigger guard, top channel sighting. Two-piece polished wooden grips, steel gripstrap. Roll engraved cylinder. $208 £100

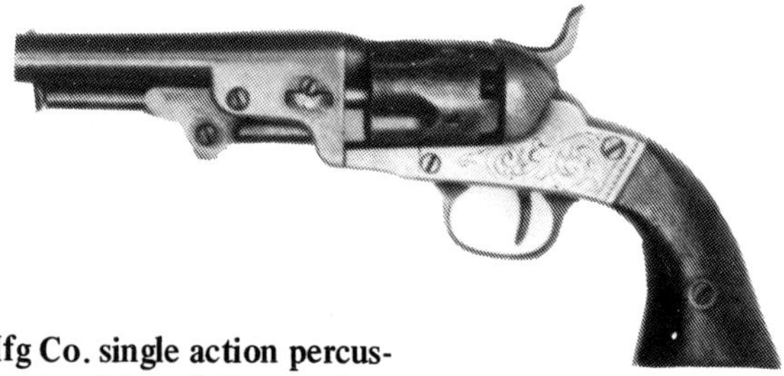

A five-shot .31in. Bacon Mfg Co. single action percussion pocket revolver, 8½in., round barrel 4in., underlever rammer, fluted cylinder, foliate engraved frame, two-piece polished wooden grips. $220 £100

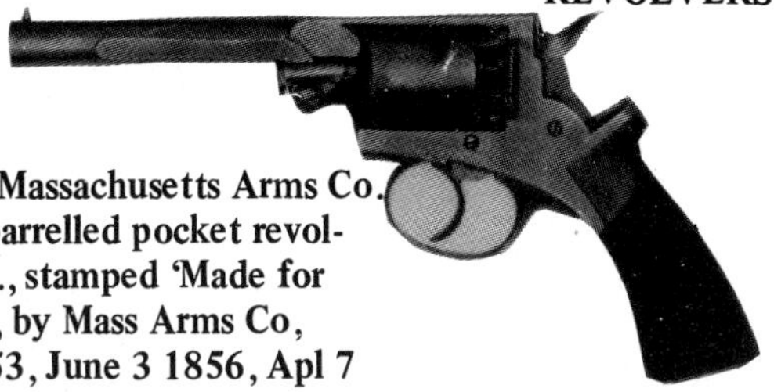

A five-shot .31in. Adams' patent Massachusetts Arms Co. double action percussion round barrelled pocket revolver, No. 2287, round barrel 4¼in., stamped 'Made for Adams Revolving Arms Co. N.Y., by Mass Arms Co, Chicopee Falls, Patent May 8 1853, June 3 1856, Apl 7 1857' on top-strap. Side lever rammer, sliding side safety bolt on frame locking cylinder. $271 £125

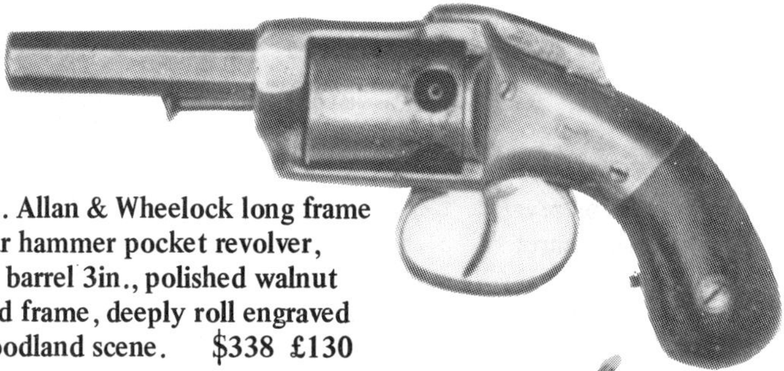

A five-shot .34in. Allan & Wheelock long frame double action bar hammer pocket revolver, 7½in., octagonal barrel 3in., polished walnut grips, plain closed frame, deeply roll engraved cylinder with woodland scene. $338 £130

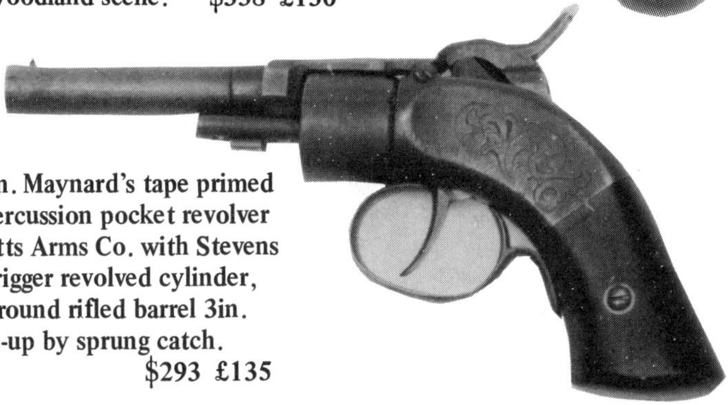

A six-shot .31in. Maynard's tape primed single action percussion pocket revolver by Massachusetts Arms Co. with Stevens 1853 patent, trigger revolved cylinder, No. 861, 7in., round rifled barrel 3in. released for tip-up by sprung catch. $293 £135

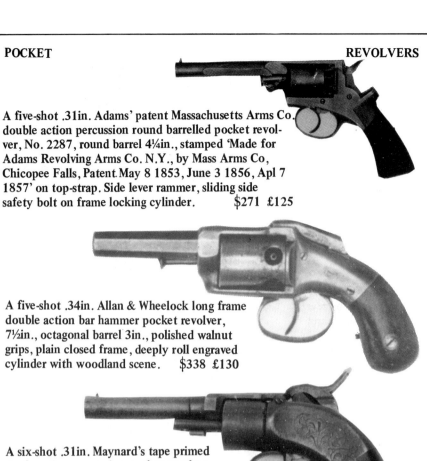

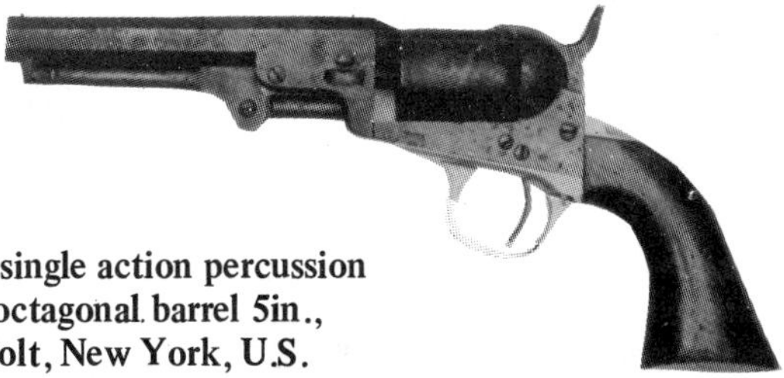

A six-shot .31in. Colt pocket single action percussion revolver, No. 214795, 10in., octagonal barrel 5in., stamped 'Address Col Saml Colt, New York, U.S. America'. Underlever rammer, roll engraved cylinder with stagecoach scene. Brass trigger guard and grip-strap. One-piece polished wooden grip. $304 £140

REVOLVERS
POCKET

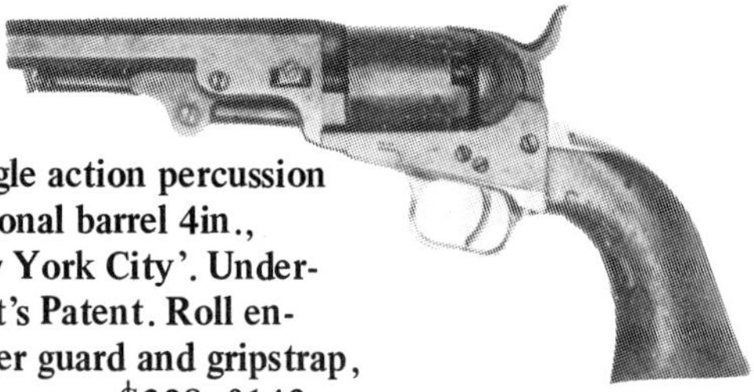

A five-shot .31in. Colt pocket single action percussion revolver, No. 27628, 8½in., octagonal barrel 4in., stamped 'Address Saml Colt, New York City'. Under-lever rammer, frame stamped Colt's Patent. Roll engraved cylinder, plated brass trigger guard and gripstrap, one-piece polished wooden grip. $308 £140

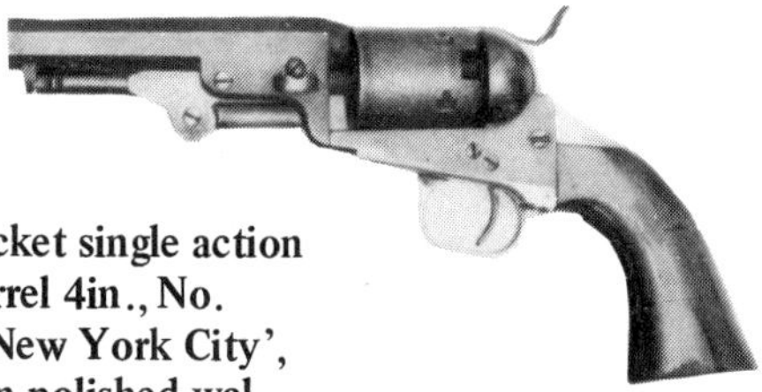

A five-shot .31in. Colt model 1849 pocket single action percussion revolver, 9in., octagonal barrel 4in., No. 109722, barrel with two line address 'New York City', brass trigger guard and back-strap, plain polished walnut grip, underlever rammer. $347 £160

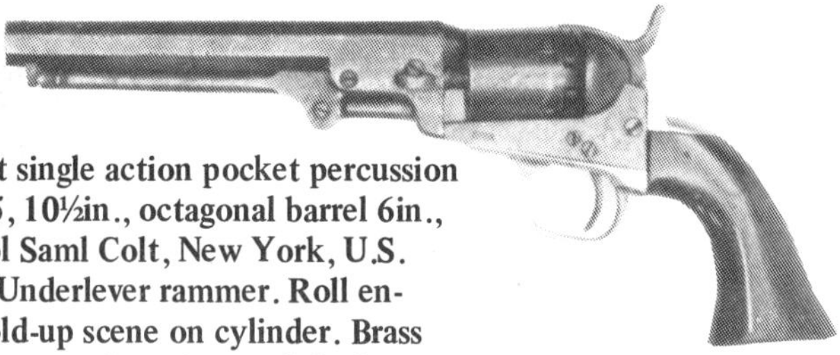

A six-shot .31in. Colt single action pocket percussion revolver, No. 231475, 10½in., octagonal barrel 6in., stamped 'Address Col Saml Colt, New York, U.S. America' (one line). Underlever rammer. Roll engraved stagecoach hold-up scene on cylinder. Brass trigger guard and gripstrap. One-piece polished wooden grip. $363 £165

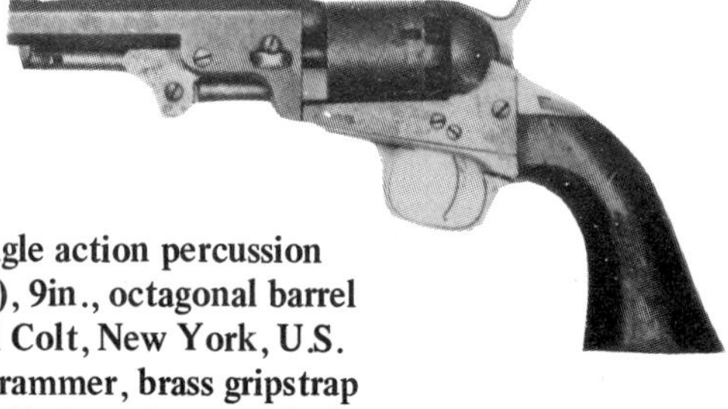

A six-shot .31in. Colt pocket single action percussion revolver, No. 258742 (matching), 9in., octagonal barrel 4in., stamped 'Address Col Saml Colt, New York, U.S. America' (one line). Underlever rammer, brass gripstrap and trigger guard stamped '31 Cal'. One-piece polished wooden grip. $391 £180

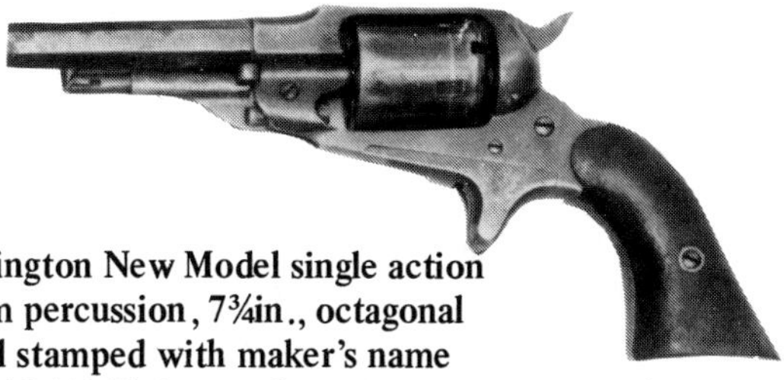

A five-shot .32in. rimfire Remington New Model single action pocket revolver converted from percussion, 7¾in., octagonal barrel 3½in., No. 21879, barrel stamped with maker's name and patent dates to 'March 17 1863'. Plain wooden grips, spur trigger, underlever rammer. $391 £180

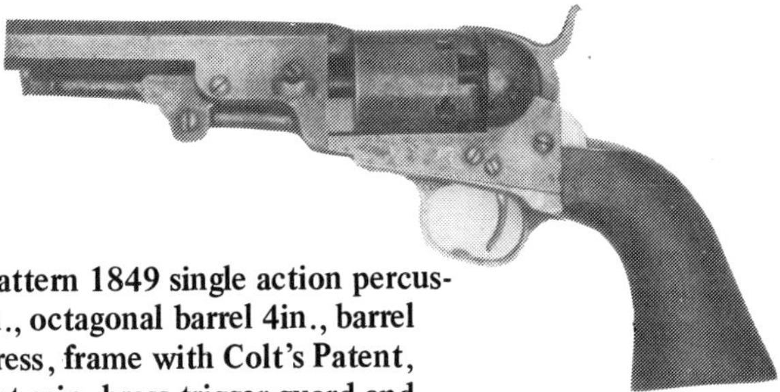

A five-shot .31in. Colt pattern 1849 single action percussion pocket revolver, 9in., octagonal barrel 4in., barrel with two line Colt's address, frame with Colt's Patent, one-piece polished walnut grip, brass trigger guard and back-strap, underlever rammer. $407 £185

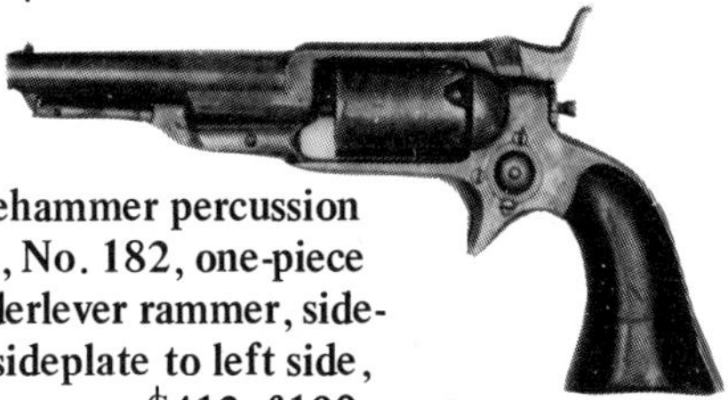

A five-shot .28in. Colt Root's patent sidehammer percussion pocket revolver, 8in., round barrel 3½in., No. 182, one-piece polished rosewood grip, spur trigger, underlever rammer, sidehammer to right side of frame, circular sideplate to left side, unfluted cylinder with screw at rear. $412 £190

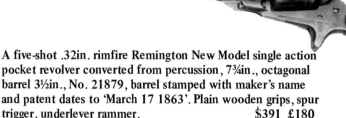

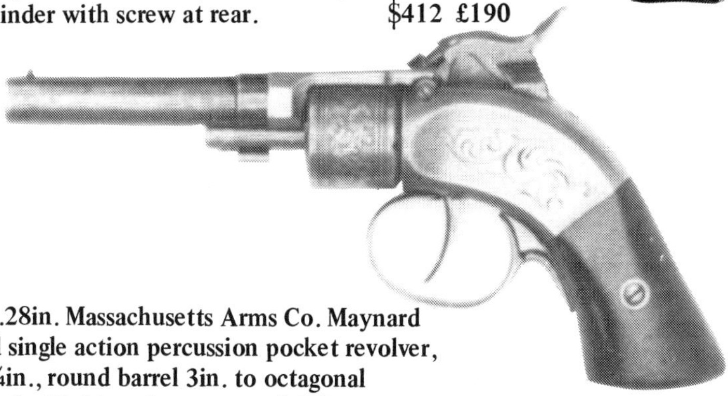

A five-shot .28in. Massachusetts Arms Co. Maynard tape primed single action percussion pocket revolver, No. 310, 7¼in., round barrel 3in. to octagonal breech. Barrel with hinged sprung catch lifts to remove cylinder. Trigger revolves cylinder only. $546 £210

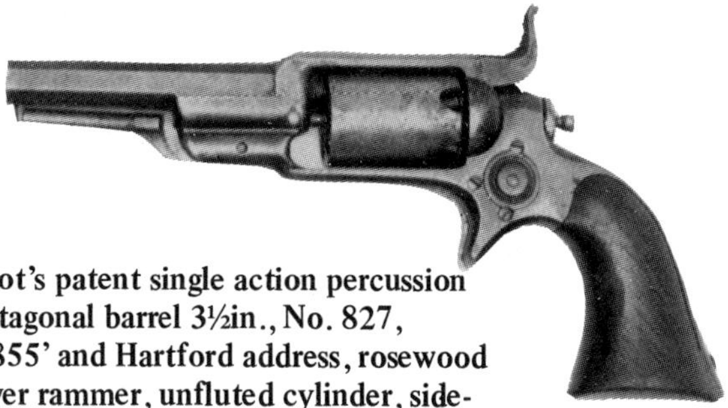

A five-shot .28in. Colt Root's patent single action percussion pocket revolver, 7½in., octagonal barrel 3½in., No. 827, barrel with model date '1855' and Hartford address, rosewood grip, spur trigger, underlever rammer, unfluted cylinder, side-mounted top-strap rear sight. $524 £230

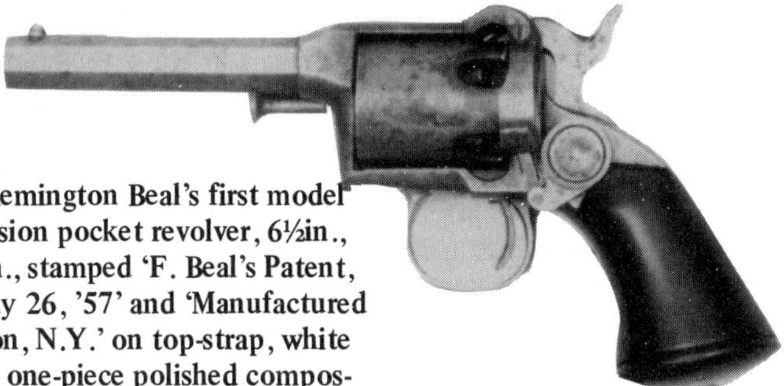

A five-shot .31in. Remington Beal's first model single action percussion pocket revolver, 6½in., octagonal barrel 3in., stamped 'F. Beal's Patent, June 24 '56 and May 26, '57' and 'Manufactured by Remingtons, Ilion, N.Y.' on top-strap, white metal trigger guard, one-piece polished composition grip. $651 £300

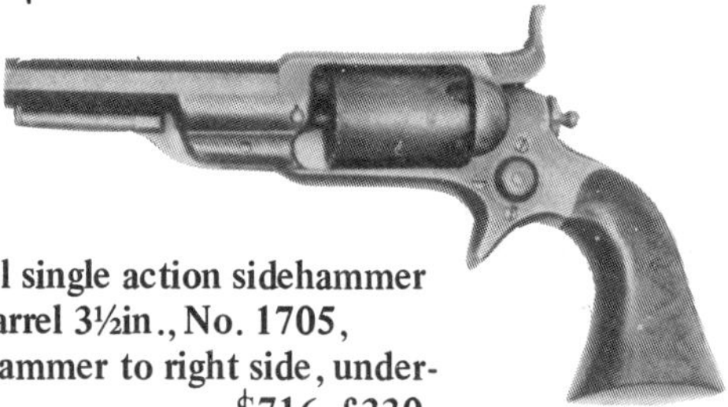

A five-shot .28in. Colt Root's model single action sidehammer pocket revolver, 7¾in., octagonal barrel 3½in., No. 1705, polished walnut grip, spur trigger, hammer to right side, underlever rammer. $716 £330

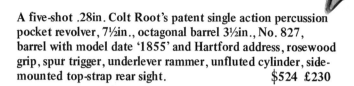

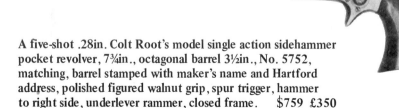

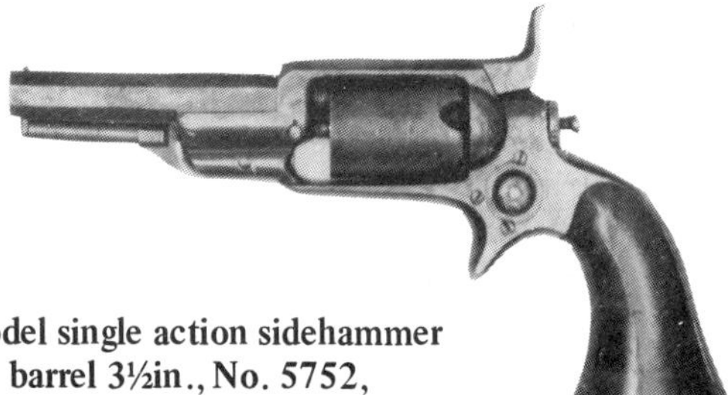

A five-shot .28in. Colt Root's model single action sidehammer pocket revolver, 7¾in., octagonal barrel 3½in., No. 5752, matching, barrel stamped with maker's name and Hartford address, polished figured walnut grip, spur trigger, hammer to right side, underlever rammer, closed frame. $759 £350

POCKET

A six-shot .31in. Wesson & Leavitt single action percussion pocket revolver, manufactured by the Massachusetts Arms Co., 9¼in., round blued barrel with octagonal rear 3¼in., No. 77, top-strap stamped 'Mass Arms Co. Chicopee Falls', lock 'Wesson's & Leavitt's Patent', cylinder rear 'Leavitt's Patent April 29, 1837', polished walnut grips, silver plated brass trigger guard and back-strap. $922 £425

POLICE

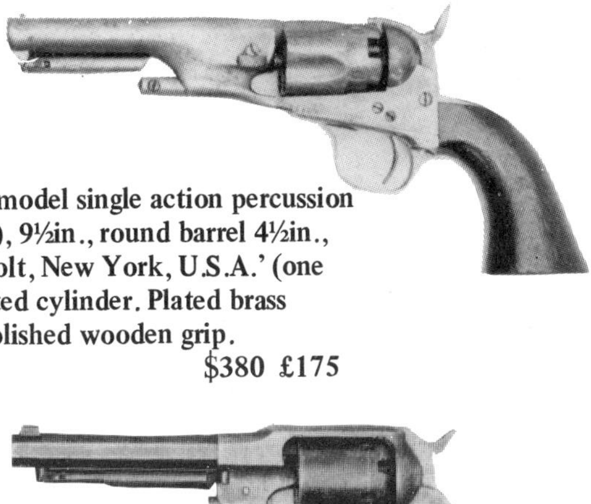

A five-shot .36in. Colt Police model single action percussion revolver, No. 2907 (matching), 9½in., round barrel 4½in., stamped 'Address Col Saml Colt, New York, U.S.A.' (one line). Underlever rammer, fluted cylinder. Plated brass trigger guard and one-piece polished wooden grip.
$380 £175

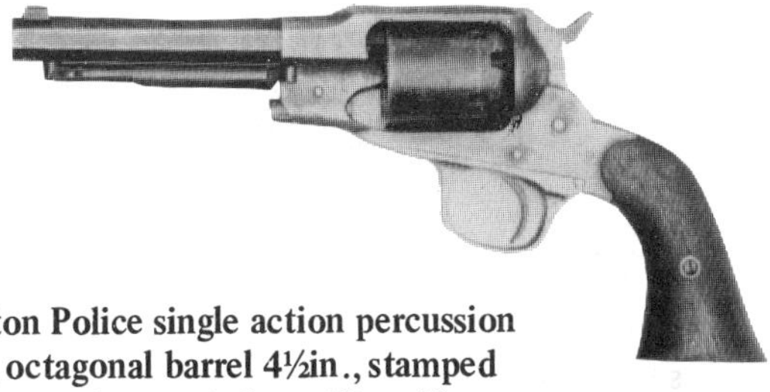

A five-shot .36in. Remington Police single action percussion revolver, No. 5871, 9¼in., octagonal barrel 4½in., stamped 'Patented Sept 14 1858, E. Remington & Sons, Ilion, New York, U.S.'. Underlever rammer, plated brass trigger guard. Steel frame and gripstrap. Two-piece polished walnut grips.
$391 £180

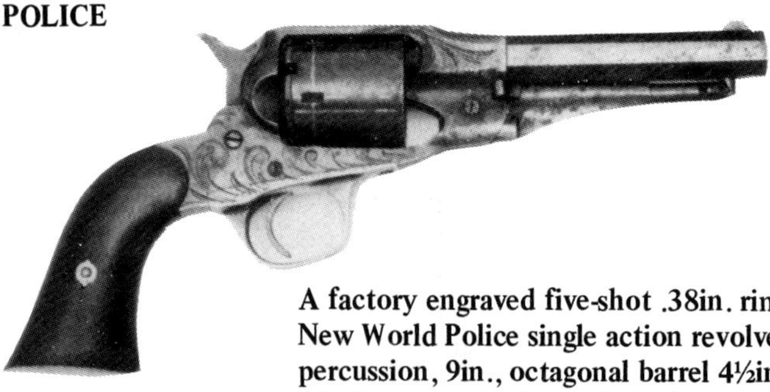

A factory engraved five-shot .38in. rimfire Remington New World Police single action revolver, converted from percussion, 9in., octagonal barrel 4½in., No. 095, polished rosewood grips to butt, brass trigger guard, underlever rammer, the frame with scroll engraving and some border engraving to back-strap and cylinder top-strap. $608 £280

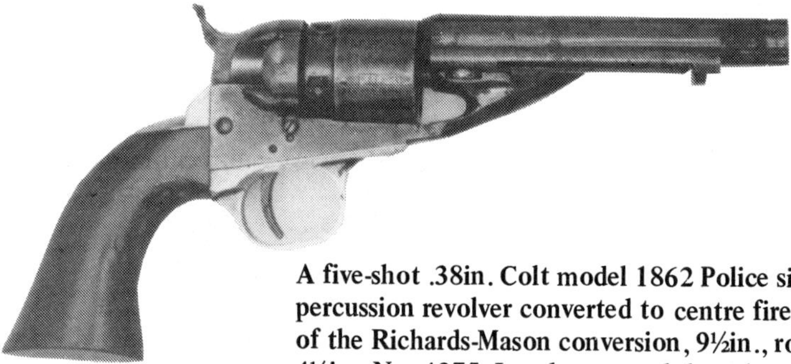

A five-shot .38in. Colt model 1862 Police single action percussion revolver converted to centre fire by means of the Richards-Mason conversion, 9½in., round barrel 4½in., No. 4975, London proved, barrel stamped 'Address Col Saml Colt, New York, U.S. America'. One-piece polished walnut grip, brass trigger guard and back-strap, gate loading and rod ejection. $682 £310

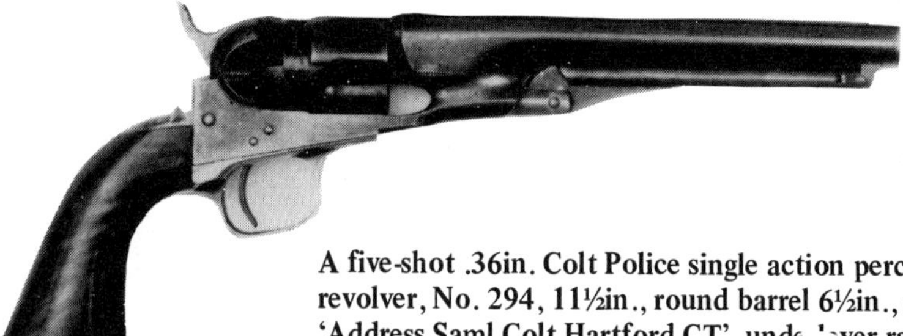

A five-shot .36in. Colt Police single action percussion revolver, No. 294, 11½in., round barrel 6½in., stamped 'Address Saml Colt Hartford CT', under-lever rammer. Fluted cylinder, frame stamped 'Colt's Patent'. Plated steel trigger guard and gripstrap, one-piece polished wooden grip. $1,573 £725

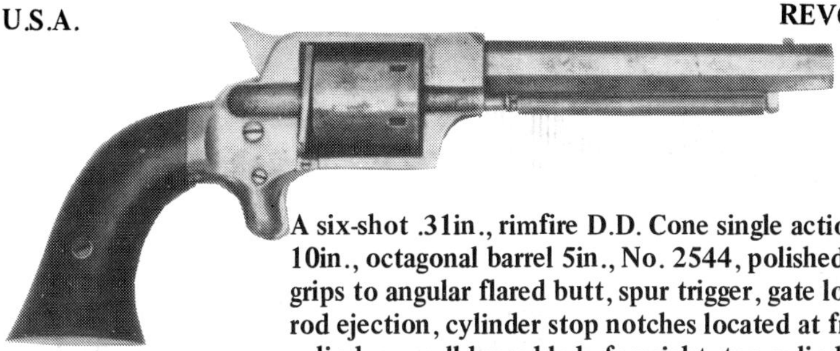

A six-shot .31in., rimfire D.D. Cone single action revolver, 10in., octagonal barrel 5in., No. 2544, polished rosewood grips to angular flared butt, spur trigger, gate loading and rod ejection, cylinder stop notches located at front of cylinder, small brass blade foresight, top cylinder strap rear. $44 £20

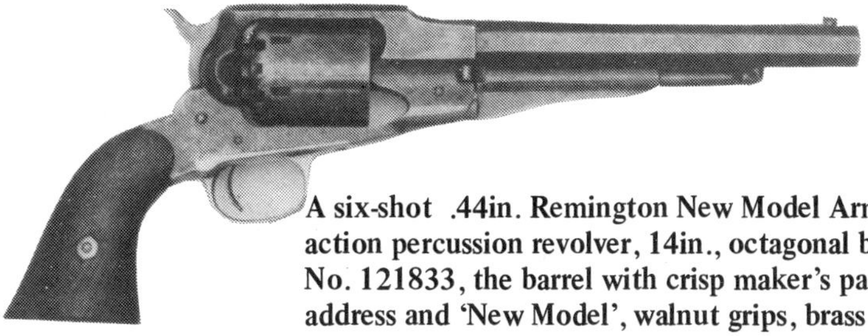

A six-shot .44in. Remington New Model Army single action percussion revolver, 14in., octagonal barrel 8in., No. 121833, the barrel with crisp maker's patent dates, address and 'New Model', walnut grips, brass trigger guard, underlever rammer, bead foresight top-strap groove rear. $176 £80

A five-shot .31in. Cooper's patent double action percussion revolver, No. 3754 (matching), 9in., octagonal barrel 4in., stamped 'Cooper Fire Arms Mfg Co, Frankford, Phila, Pat Jan 7 1851, Apr 25 1854, Sep 4 1860, Sep 1 1863, Sep 22 1863'. Underlever rammer, brass trigger guard and grip-strap. One-piece polished wooden grip. $228 £105

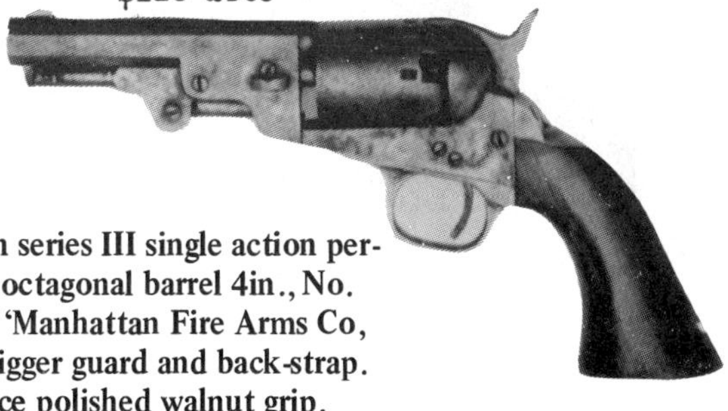

A five-shot .36in. Manhattan series III single action percussion Navy revolver, 9in., octagonal barrel 4in., No. 23874, barrel stamped with 'Manhattan Fire Arms Co, Newark, NJ', plated brass trigger guard and back-strap. Underlever rammer, one-piece polished walnut grip. $229 £110

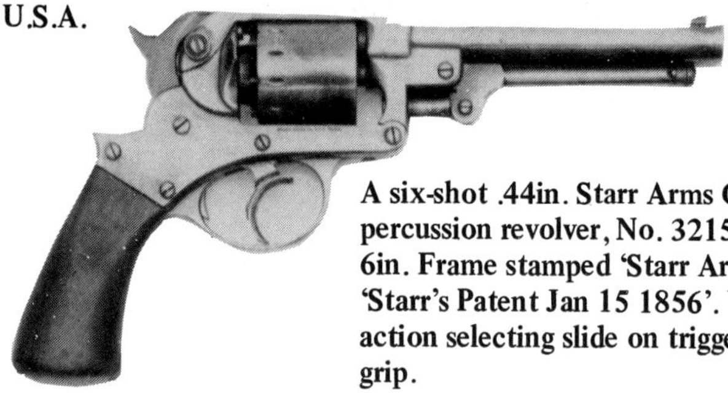

A six-shot .44in. Starr Arms Co. double action Army percussion revolver, No. 3215, 11½in., round barrel 6in. Frame stamped 'Starr Arms Co, New York', 'Starr's Patent Jan 15 1856'. Underlever rammer, action selecting slide on trigger. One-piece walnut grip. $271 £125

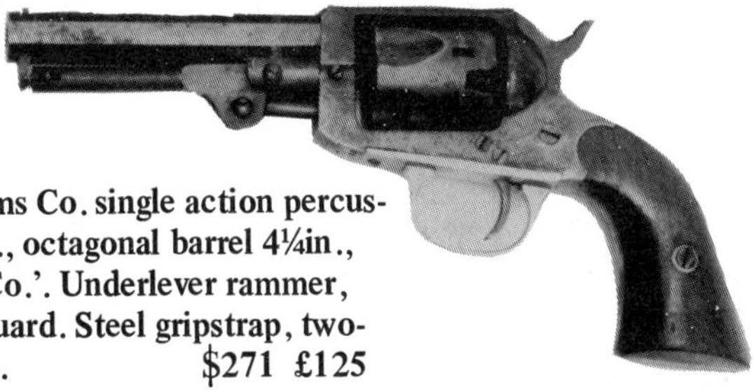

A five-shot .31in. Union Arms Co. single action percussion revolver, No. 7810, 9in., octagonal barrel 4¼in., stamped 'The Union Arms Co.'. Underlever rammer, closed frame, brass trigger guard. Steel gripstrap, two-piece polished wooden grips. $271 £125

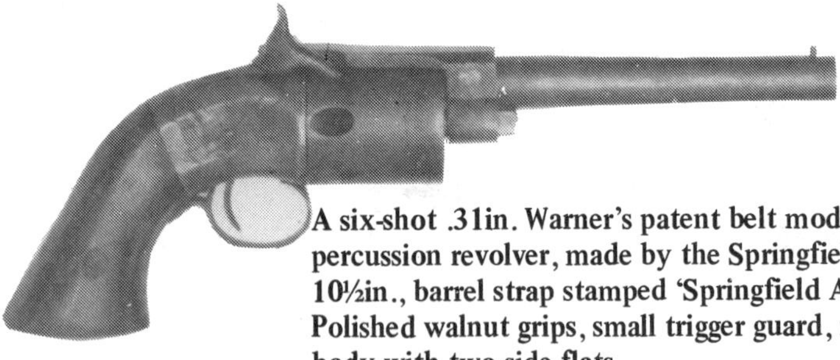

A six-shot .31in. Warner's patent belt model single action percussion revolver, made by the Springfield Arms Co., 10½in., barrel strap stamped 'Springfield Arms Co.' Polished walnut grips, small trigger guard, rounded action body with two side flats. $281 £135

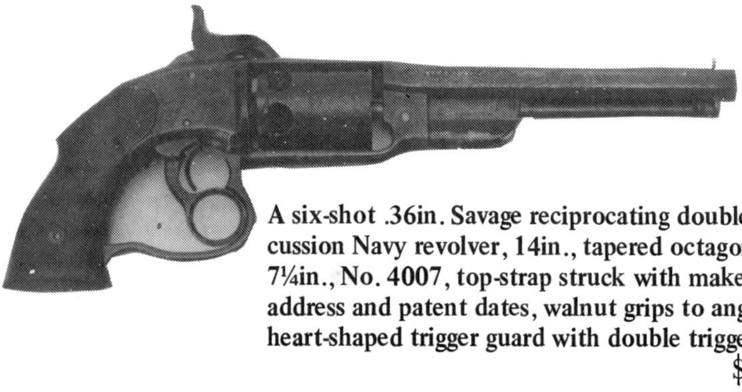

A six-shot .36in. Savage reciprocating double trigger percussion Navy revolver, 14in., tapered octagonal barrel 7¼in., No. 4007, top-strap struck with maker's name, address and patent dates, walnut grips to angular butt, heart-shaped trigger guard with double triggers. $330 £150

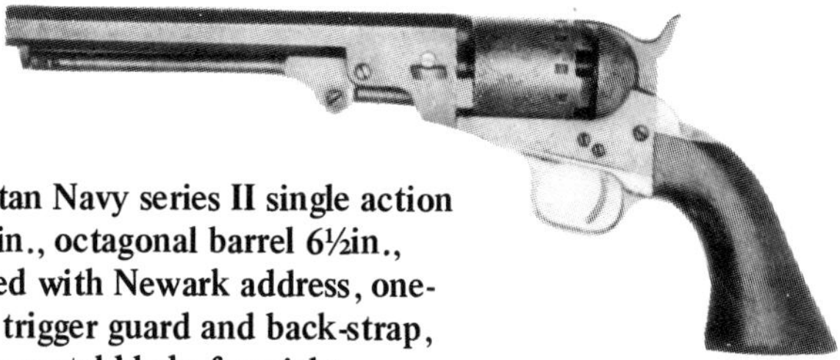

A six-shot .36in. Manhattan Navy series II single action percussion revolver, 11½in., octagonal barrel 6½in., No. 21623, barrel stamped with Newark address, one-piece wooden grip, brass trigger guard and back-strap, underlever rammer, white metal blade foresight.
$333 £160

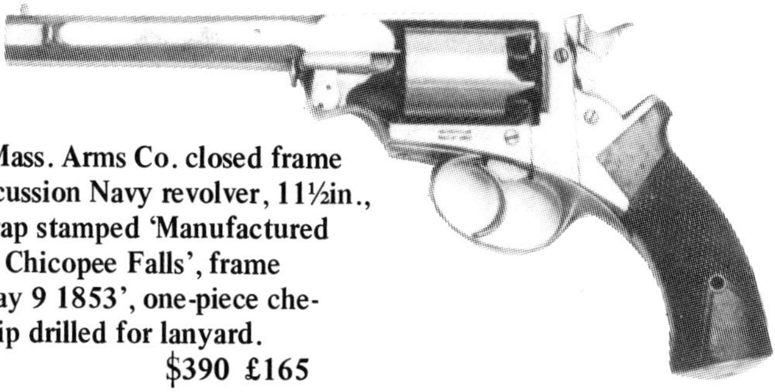

A six-shot .36in. Mass. Arms Co. closed frame double action percussion Navy revolver, 11½in., barrel 6in., top-strap stamped 'Manufactured by Mass Arms Co, Chicopee Falls', frame 'Adams Patent, May 9 1853', one-piece chequered wooden grip drilled for lanyard.
$390 £165

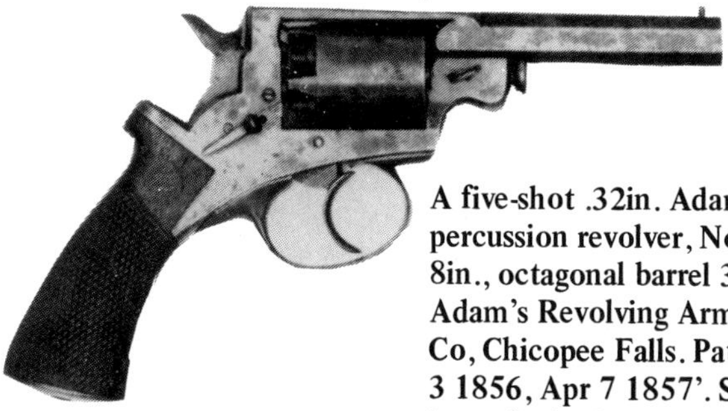

A five-shot .32in. Adam's patent double action percussion revolver, No. 729, by Mass Arms Co., 8in., octagonal barrel 3¼in., stamped 'Made for Adam's Revolving Arms Co. N.Y. by Mass Arms Co, Chicopee Falls. Patented May 3 1853, June 3 1856, Apr 7 1857'. Sidelever rammer and sliding cylinder locking safety bolt. $410 £180

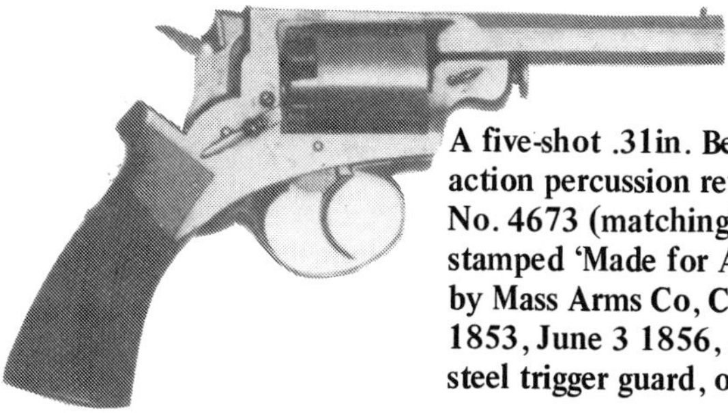

A five-shot .31in. Beaumont Adams patent double action percussion revolver made by Mass Arms Co., No. 4673 (matching), 8in., octagonal barrel 3¼in., stamped 'Made for Adams Revolving Arms Co, N.Y. by Mass Arms Co, Chicopee Falls, Patent May 3 1853, June 3 1856, Apl 7 1857'. Sidelever rammer, steel trigger guard, one-piece chequered walnut grip.
$468 £180

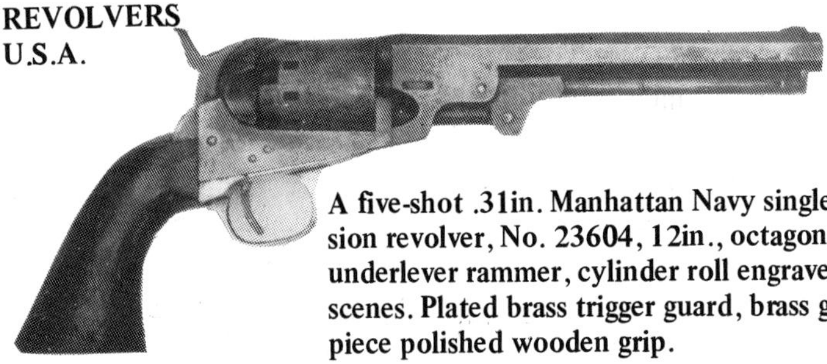

A five-shot .31in. Manhattan Navy single action percussion revolver, No. 23604, 12in., octagonal barrel 6½in., underlever rammer, cylinder roll engraved with vignette scenes. Plated brass trigger guard, brass gripstrap, one-piece polished wooden grip. $429 £195

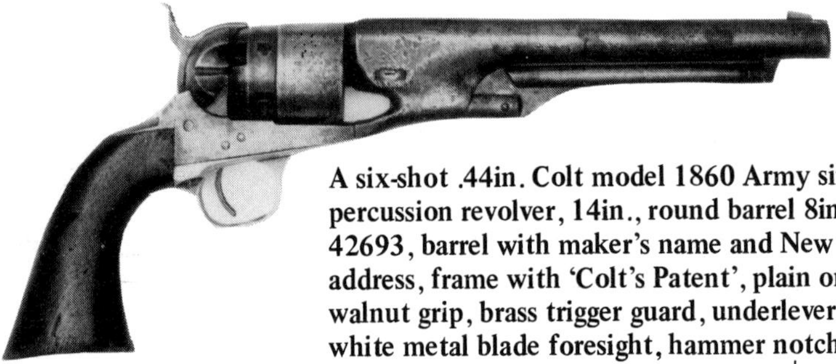

A six-shot .44in. Colt model 1860 Army single action percussion revolver, 14in., round barrel 8in., No. 42693, barrel with maker's name and New York address, frame with 'Colt's Patent', plain one-piece walnut grip, brass trigger guard, underlever rammer, white metal blade foresight, hammer notch rear. $434 £200

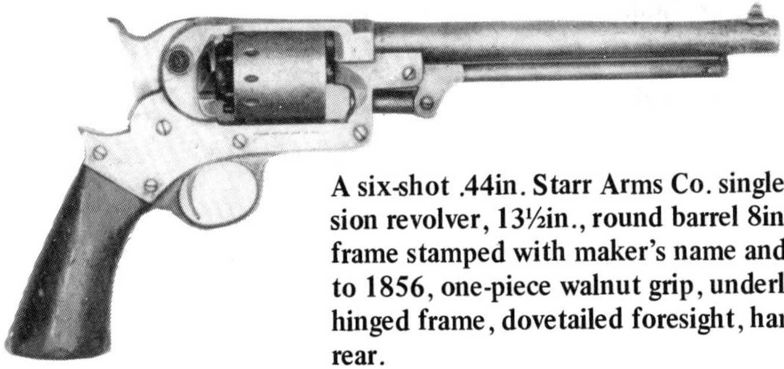

A six-shot .44in. Starr Arms Co. single action percussion revolver, 13½in., round barrel 8in., No. 37381, frame stamped with maker's name and patent dates to 1856, one-piece walnut grip, underlever rammer, hinged frame, dovetailed foresight, hammer notch rear. $416 £200

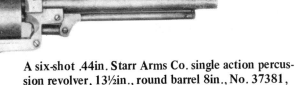

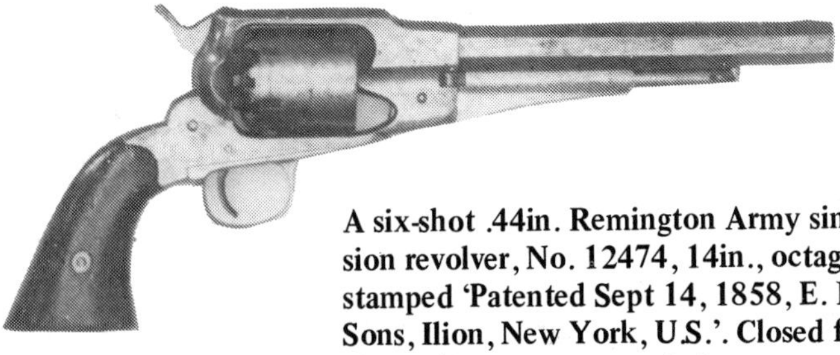

A six-shot .44in. Remington Army single action percussion revolver, No. 12474, 14in., octagonal barrel 8in., stamped 'Patented Sept 14, 1858, E. Remington & Sons, Ilion, New York, U.S.'. Closed frame, sighting channel in top-strap, underlever rammer, brass trigger guard. $520 £200

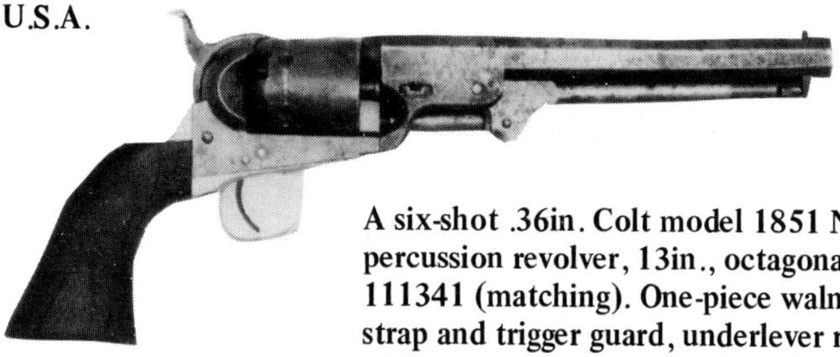

A six-shot .36in. Colt model 1851 Navy single action percussion revolver, 13in., octagonal barrel 7½in., No. 111341 (matching). One-piece walnut grip, brass back-strap and trigger guard, underlever rammer, cylinder with traces of roll engraved naval scene. $434 £200

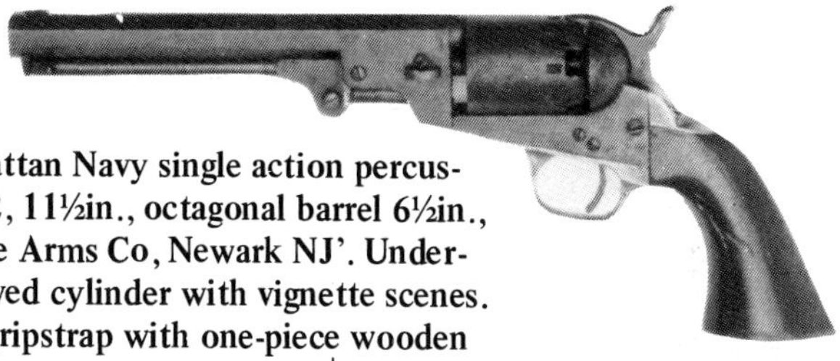

A five-shot .36in. Manhattan Navy single action percussion revolver, No. 26022, 11½in., octagonal barrel 6½in., stamped 'Manhattan Fire Arms Co, Newark NJ'. Underlever rammer, roll engraved cylinder with vignette scenes. Brass trigger guard and gripstrap with one-piece wooden grip. $416 £200

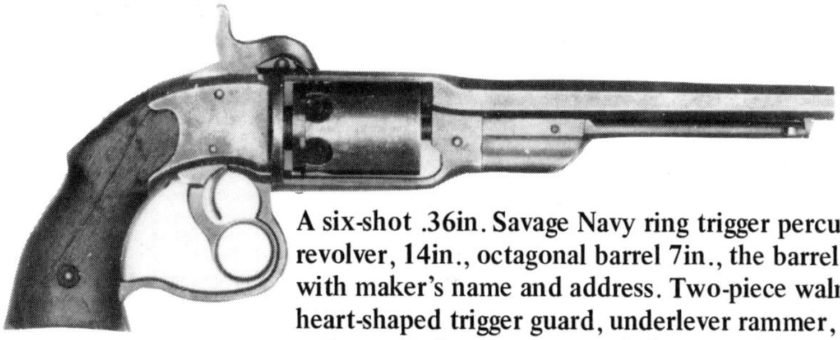

A six-shot .36in. Savage Navy ring trigger percussion revolver, 14in., octagonal barrel 7in., the barrel stamped with maker's name and address. Two-piece walnut grips, heart-shaped trigger guard, underlever rammer, reciprocating cylinder, hammer angled to one side to allow sighting. $458 £220

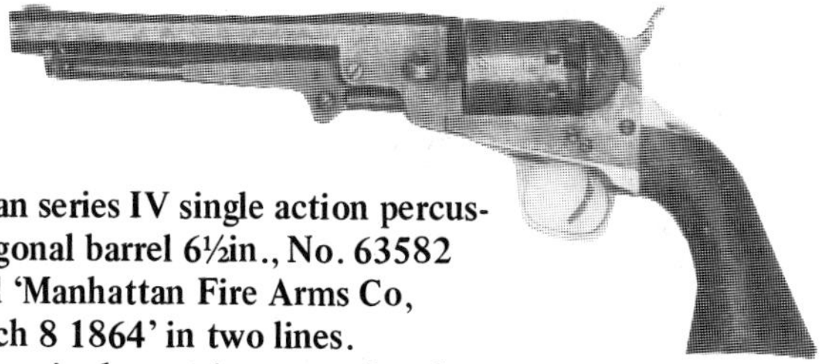

A five-shot .36in. Manhattan series IV single action percussion revolver, 11½in., octagonal barrel 6½in., No. 63582 (matching), barrel stamped 'Manhattan Fire Arms Co, Newark, NJ. Patented March 8 1864' in two lines. Polished 'Slim Jim' wooden grip, brass trigger guard and back-strap, square shanked underlever rammer. $572 £220

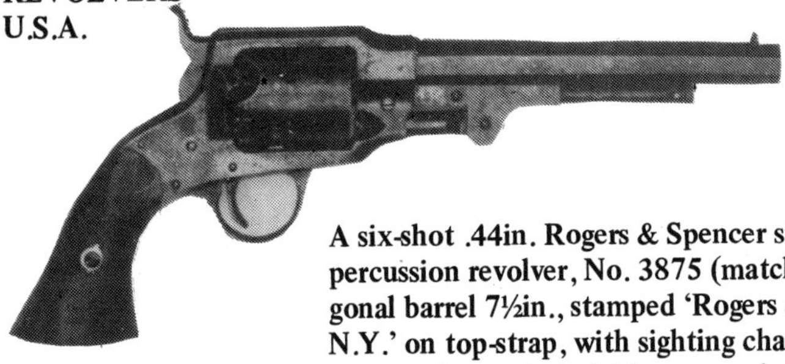

A six-shot .44in. Rogers & Spencer single action Army percussion revolver, No. 3875 (matching), 13½in., octagonal barrel 7½in., stamped 'Rogers & Spencer, Utica, N.Y.' on top-strap, with sighting channel. Underlever rammer, integral steel trigger guard and gripstrap, two-piece wooden grips. $572 £220

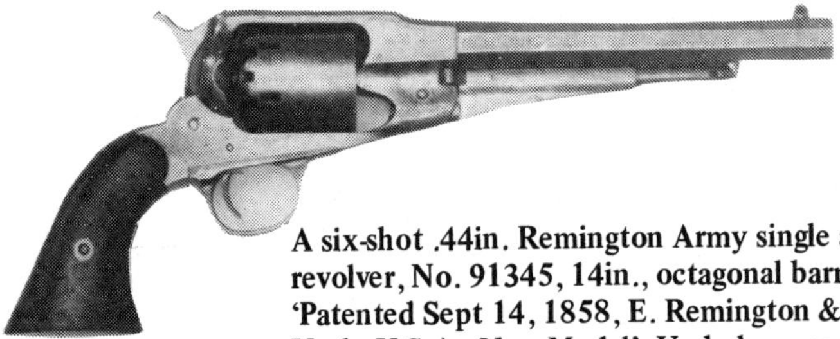

A six-shot .44in. Remington Army single action percussion revolver, No. 91345, 14in., octagonal barrel 8in., stamped 'Patented Sept 14, 1858, E. Remington & Sons, Ilion, New York, U.S.A., New Model'. Underlever rammer, brass trigger guard, two-piece wooden grips. $598 £230

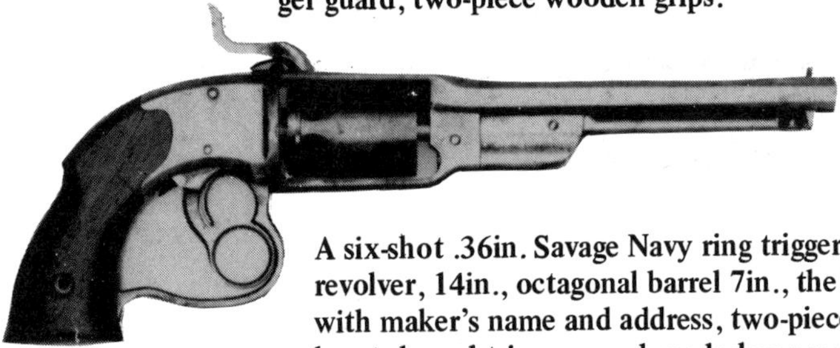

A six-shot .36in. Savage Navy ring trigger percussion revolver, 14in., octagonal barrel 7in., the barrel stamped with maker's name and address, two-piece walnut grips, heart-shaped trigger guard, underlever rammer, reciprocating cylinder, hammer angled to one side to allow sighting. $500 £240

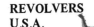

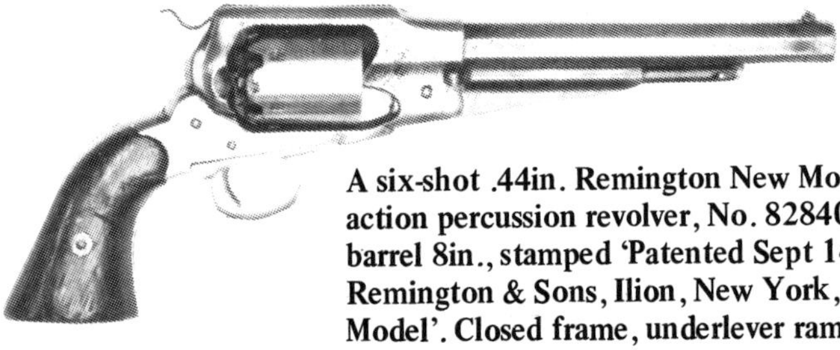

A six-shot .44in. Remington New Model Army single action percussion revolver, No. 82840, 14in., octagonal barrel 8in., stamped 'Patented Sept 14, 1858, E. Remington & Sons, Ilion, New York, U.S.A., New Model'. Closed frame, underlever rammer, brass trigger guard, steel gripstrap, two-piece wooden grips. $528 £240

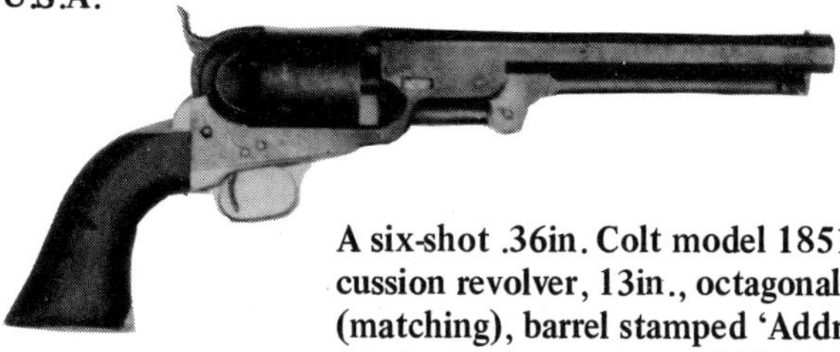

A six-shot .36in. Colt model 1851 Navy single action percussion revolver, 13in., octagonal barrel 7½in., No. 57223 (matching), barrel stamped 'Address Saml Colt, New York City' with frame stamped 'Colt's Patent', one-piece walnut grip, brass trigger guard and back-strap. $499 £240

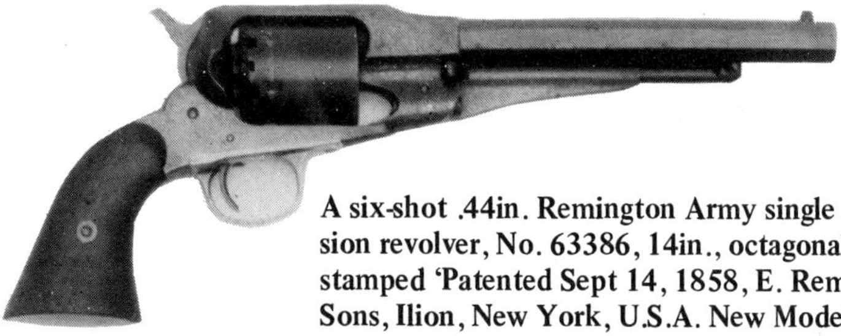

A six-shot .44in. Remington Army single action percussion revolver, No. 63386, 14in., octagonal barrel 8in., stamped 'Patented Sept 14, 1858, E. Remington & Sons, Ilion, New York, U.S.A. New Model'. Underlever rammer, brass trigger guard, steel frame and gripstrap. Two-piece walnut grips. $542 £250

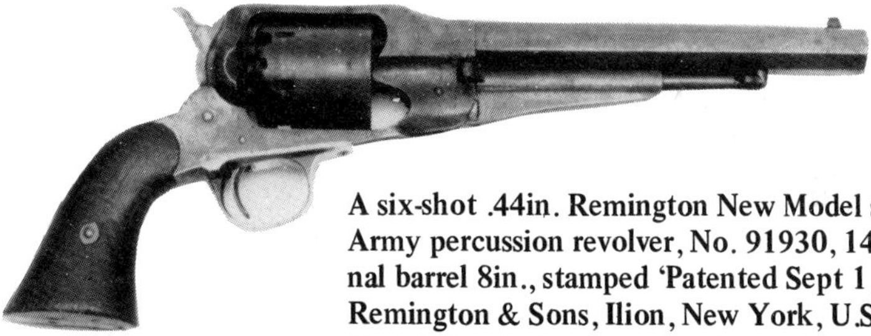

A six-shot .44in. Remington New Model single action Army percussion revolver, No. 91930, 14in., octagonal barrel 8in., stamped 'Patented Sept 1, 1858, E. Remington & Sons, Ilion, New York, U.S.A. New Model'. Underlever rammer, brass trigger guard, two-piece wooden grips. $564 £260

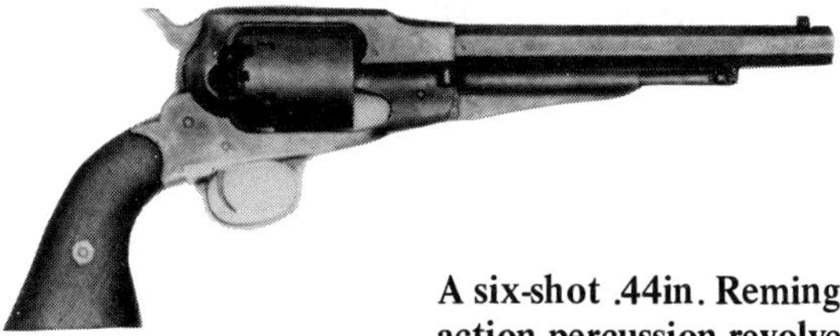

A six-shot .44in. Remington New Model Army single action percussion revolver, 14in., octagonal barrel 8in., No. 122978, plain walnut grips, brass trigger guard, underlever rammer, plain cylinder, top-strap groove rearsight. $593 £260

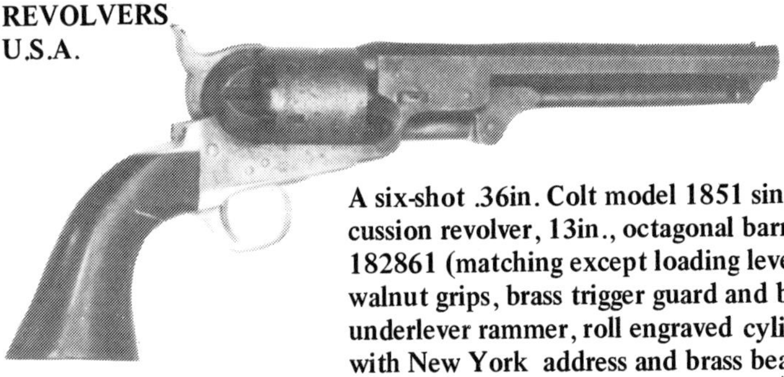

A six-shot .36in. Colt model 1851 single action percussion revolver, 13in., octagonal barrel 7½in., No. 182861 (matching except loading lever), polished walnut grips, brass trigger guard and back-strap, underlever rammer, roll engraved cylinder, barrel with New York address and brass bead foresight.
$572 £260

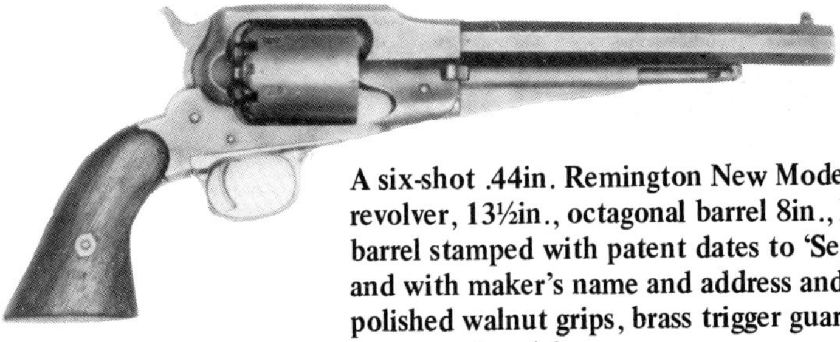

A six-shot .44in. Remington New Model percussion revolver, 13½in., octagonal barrel 8in., No. 103445, barrel stamped with patent dates to 'Sept 14 1858' and with maker's name and address and 'New Model', polished walnut grips, brass trigger guard, underlever rammer, closed frame. $562 £270

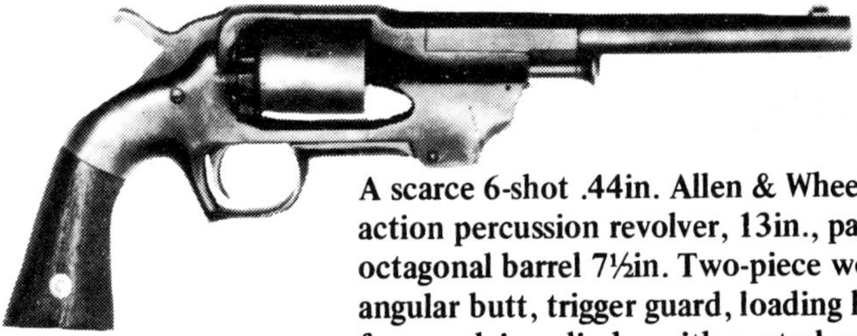

A scarce 6-shot .44in. Allen & Wheelock Army single action percussion revolver, 13in., part round, part octagonal barrel 7½in. Two-piece wooden grip to angular butt, trigger guard, loading lever, closed frame, plain cylinder with central row of stop notches, under barrel mounted cylinder pin, brass foresight hammer notch rear. $590 £275

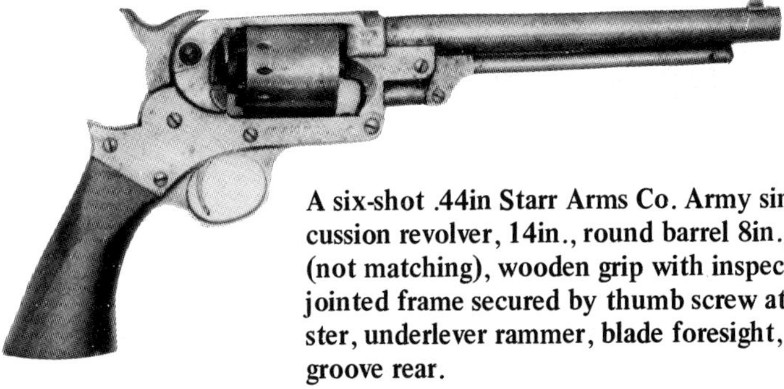

A six-shot .44in Starr Arms Co. Army single action percussion revolver, 14in., round barrel 8in., No. 28543 (not matching), wooden grip with inspector's stamp, jointed frame secured by thumb screw at hammer bolster, underlever rammer, blade foresight, hammer groove rear. $597 £275

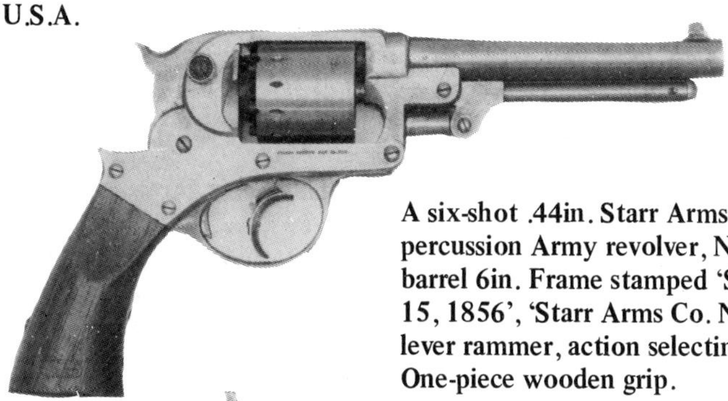

A six-shot .44in. Starr Arms Co. double action percussion Army revolver, No. 15841, 12in., barrel 6in. Frame stamped 'Starr's Patent, Jan 15, 1856', 'Starr Arms Co. New York'. Underlever rammer, action selecting slide on trigger. One-piece wooden grip. $651 £300

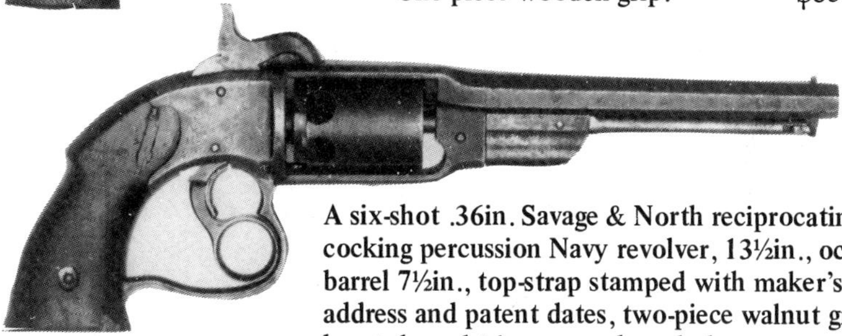

A six-shot .36in. Savage & North reciprocating self-cocking percussion Navy revolver, 13½in., octagonal barrel 7½in., top-strap stamped with maker's name, address and patent dates, two-piece walnut grips, heart-shaped trigger guard, underlever rammer, brass bead foresight. $624 £300

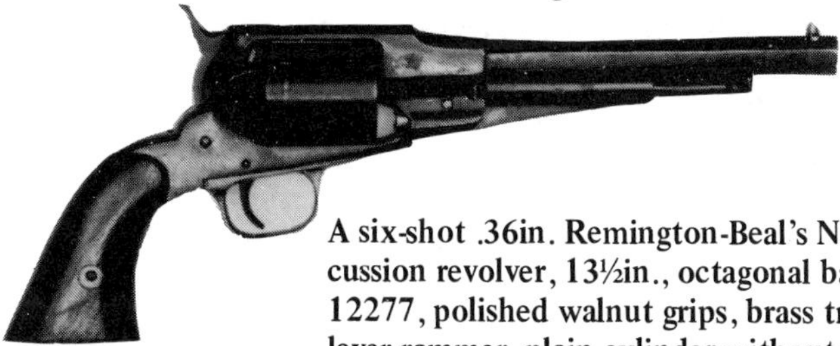

A six-shot .36in. Remington-Beal's Navy single action percussion revolver, 13½in., octagonal barrel 7½in., No. 12277, polished walnut grips, brass trigger guard, underlever rammer, plain cylinder without intermediate hammer notches, white metal cone foresight, top-strap groove rear. $651 £300

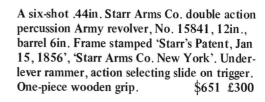

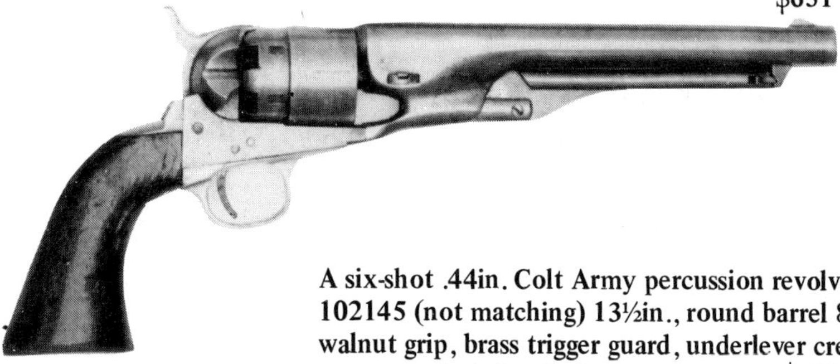

A six-shot .44in. Colt Army percussion revolver, No. 102145 (not matching) 13½in., round barrel 8in., walnut grip, brass trigger guard, underlever creeping rammer, rebated cylinder. $651 £300

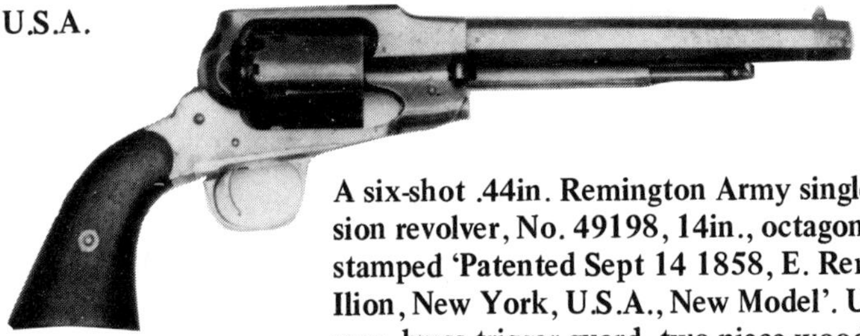

A six-shot .44in. Remington Army single action percussion revolver, No. 49198, 14in., octagonal barrel 8in., stamped 'Patented Sept 14 1858, E. Remington & Sons, Ilion, New York, U.S.A., New Model'. Underlever rammer, brass trigger guard, two-piece wooden grips.
$673 £310

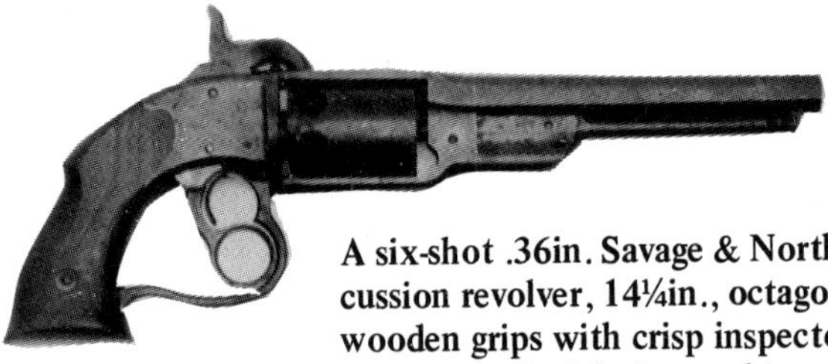

A six-shot .36in. Savage & North Navy double action percussion revolver, 14¼in., octagonal barrel 7in., No. 10475, wooden grips with crisp inspector's stamp, heart-shaped trigger guard with ring cocking trigger, reciprocating cylinder, underlever rammer. $798 £350

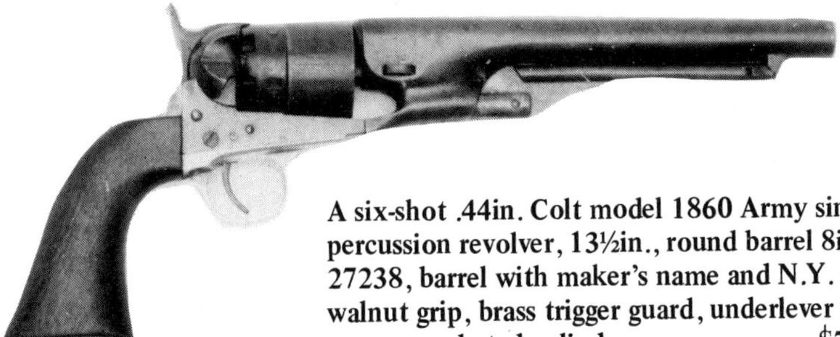

A six-shot .44in. Colt model 1860 Army single action percussion revolver, 13½in., round barrel 8in., No. 27238, barrel with maker's name and N.Y. address, walnut grip, brass trigger guard, underlever creeping rammer, rebated cylinder. $759 £350

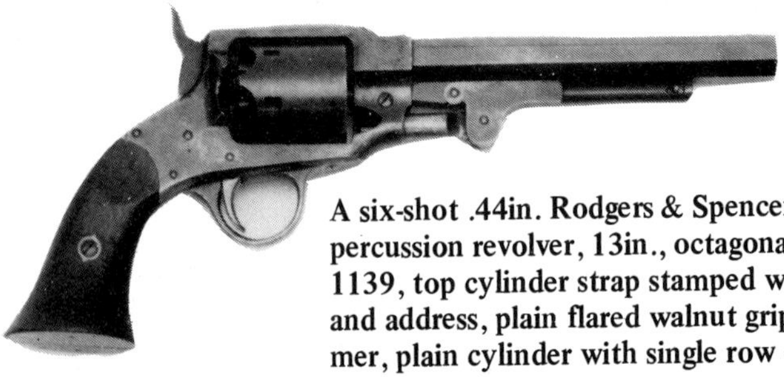

A six-shot .44in. Rodgers & Spencer Army single action percussion revolver, 13in., octagonal barrel 7½in., No. 1139, top cylinder strap stamped with maker's name and address, plain flared walnut grips, underlever rammer, plain cylinder with single row of stop notches.
$760 £350

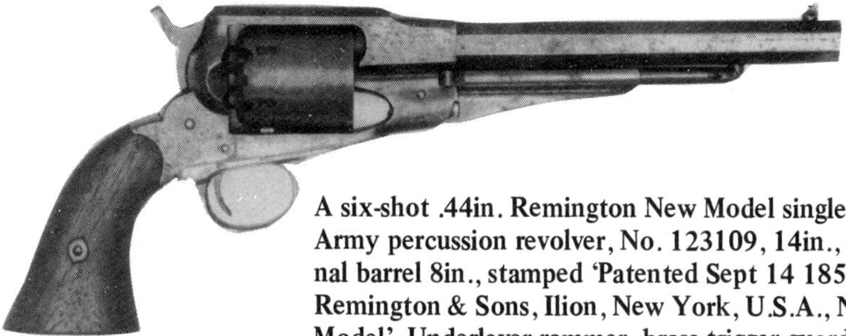

A six-shot .44in. Remington New Model single action Army percussion revolver, No. 123109, 14in., octagonal barrel 8in., stamped 'Patented Sept 14 1858, E. Remington & Sons, Ilion, New York, U.S.A., New Model'. Underlever rammer, brass trigger guard, two-piece wooden grips. $760 £350

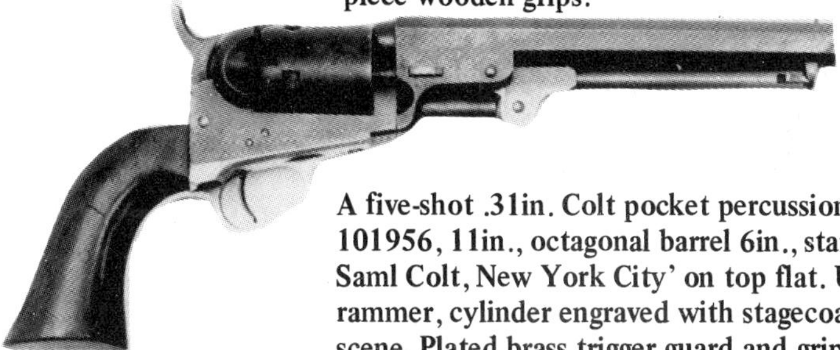

A five-shot .31in. Colt pocket percussion revolver, No. 101956, 11in., octagonal barrel 6in., stamped 'Address Saml Colt, New York City' on top flat. Underlever rammer, cylinder engraved with stagecoach hold-up scene. Plated brass trigger guard and gripstrap. One-piece polished wooden grips. $955 £440

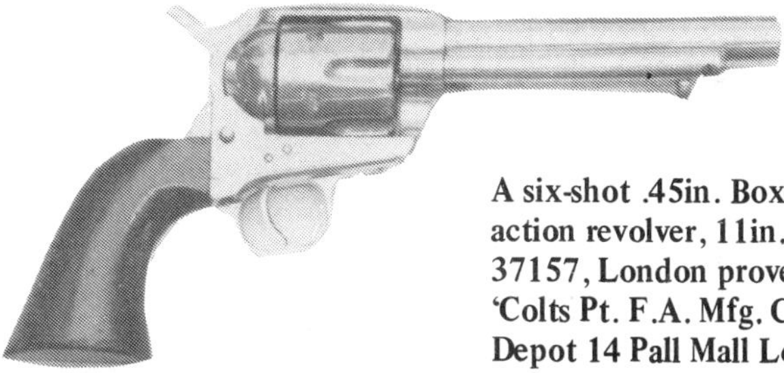

A six-shot .45in. Boxer Colt model 'P' single action revolver, 11in., barrel 5½in., No. 37157, London proved and barrel stamped 'Colts Pt. F.A. Mfg. Co. Hartford CT. U.S.A. Depot 14 Pall Mall London'. One-piece polished walnut grips. $1,300 £550

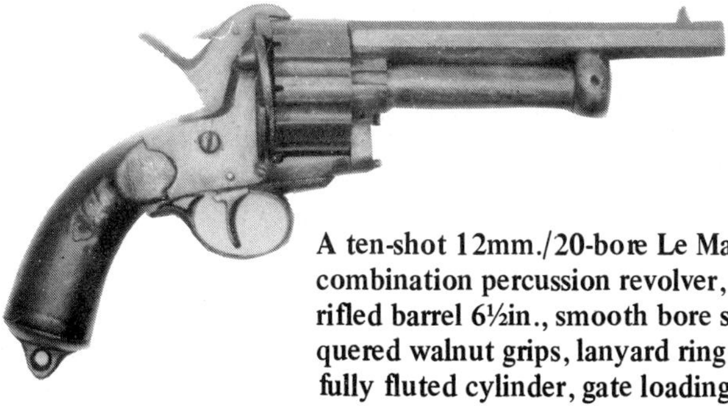

A ten-shot 12mm./20-bore Le Mat single action pinfire combination percussion revolver, 12½in., octagonal rifled barrel 6½in., smooth bore shot barrel 6in., chequered walnut grips, lanyard ring, plain action body, fully fluted cylinder, gate loading. $1,302 £600

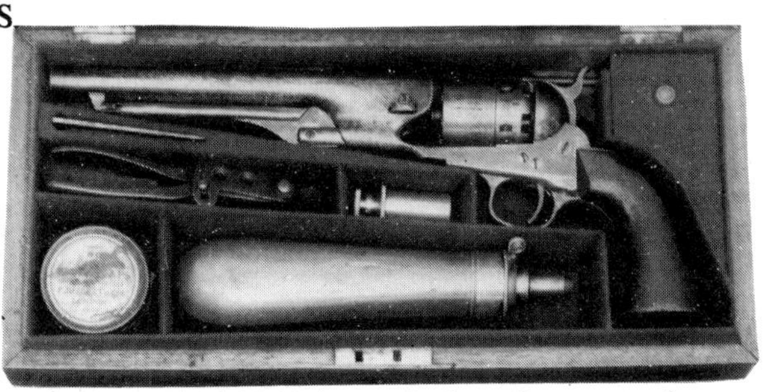

A six-shot .44in. Colt model 1860 Army single action percussion revolver, 13½in., barrel 8in., No. 95003L (matching), barrel with one line New York address, polished walnut grips, brass trigger guard, underlever creeping rammer, the rebated cylinder and barrel with London Black Powder proof marks. Contained in its green beize lined and fitted mahogany case. $1,519 £700

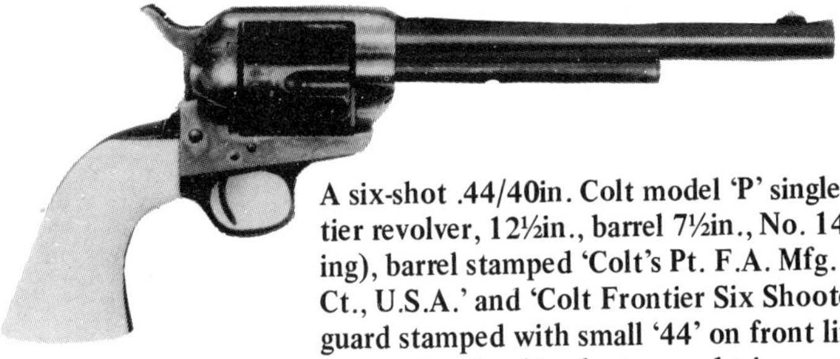

A six-shot .44/40in. Colt model 'P' single action Frontier revolver, 12½in., barrel 7½in., No. 140452 (matching), barrel stamped 'Colt's Pt. F.A. Mfg. Co., Hartford Ct., U.S.A.' and 'Colt Frontier Six Shooter', the trigger guard stamped with small '44' on front limb. One-piece ivory grip, blued back-strap and trigger guard. $2,007 £925

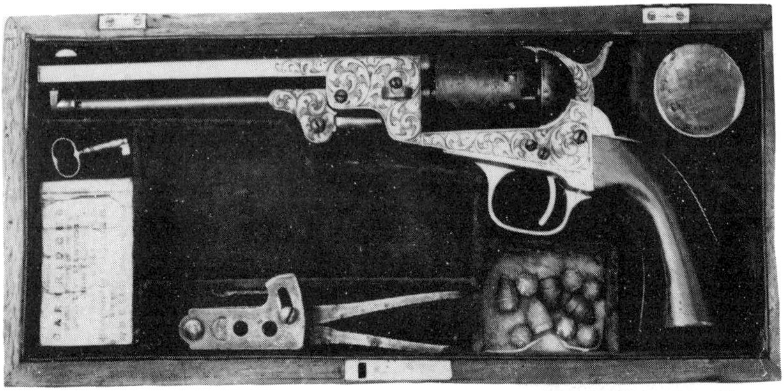

A five-shot .36in. Manhattan Fire Arms Co., presentation single action Navy percussion revolver, No. 26588, 11½in., octagonal barrel 6½in., profusely foliate engraved against a punched ground en suite with frame and wolf head hammer. Cylinder roll engraved with vignette scenes of American history. Underlever rammer, plated brass trigger guard and gripstrap, one-piece polished wooden grip. Contained in its red velvet lined fitted case. $2,170 £1,000

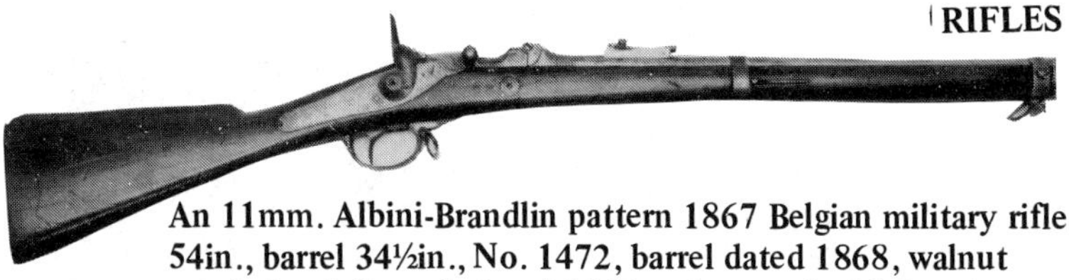

An 11mm. Albini-Brandlin pattern 1867 Belgian military rifle, 54in., barrel 34½in., No. 1472, barrel dated 1868, walnut regulation full-stock dated 1867 on butt and with iron butt-plate, trigger guard and barrel bands, plain back-action lock and trapdoor type breech locked by means of hammer extension. $208 £100

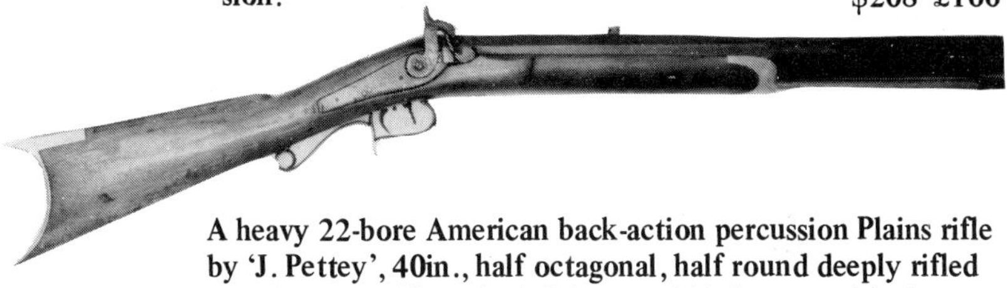

A heavy 22-bore American back-action percussion Plains rifle by 'J. Pettey', 40in., half octagonal, half round deeply rifled barrel 24in. Half-stocked, foliate and bird engraved lock. Brass furniture, adjustable double set triggers. Scrolled brass trigger guard, hooked buttcap, long barrel tang spur. $217 £100

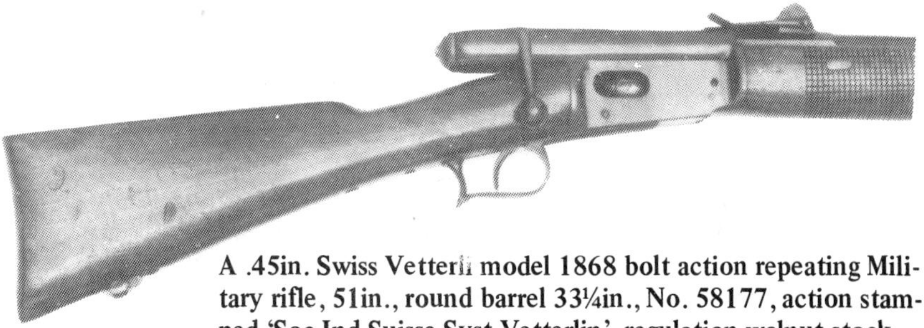

A .45in. Swiss Vetterli model 1868 bolt action repeating Military rifle, 51in., round barrel 33¼in., No. 58177, action stamped 'Soc Ind Suisse Syst Vetterlin', regulation walnut stock with sling swivel steel buttcaps and spurred trigger guard, full length steel mounted fore-end with chequered panel. $253 £115

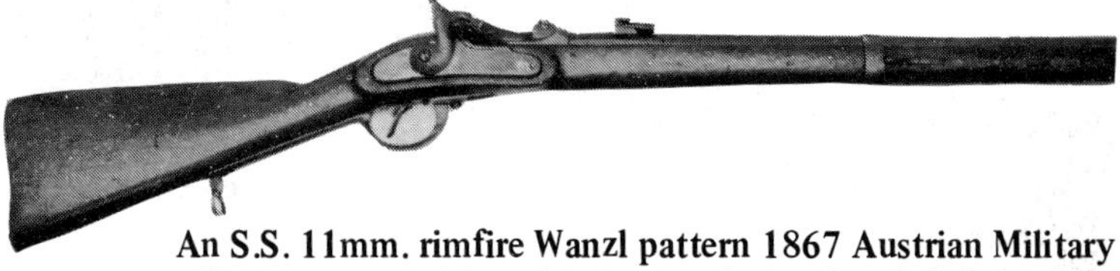

An S.S. 11mm. rimfire Wanzl pattern 1867 Austrian Military rifle, 53in., round barrel 35in., regulation beech full-stock with iron buttplate, trigger guard, barrel bands and sideplate, round barrel with barleycorn foresight and tangent rear. $260 £125

A .577in. model 1858 two-band Navy percussion rifle, 49in., barrel 33in., made under Belgian contract, Liege proved with government inspector's marks. Ladder rearsight to 950 yards by 'Deane Adams & Deane'. Full-stocked, regulation brass mounts. $380 £160

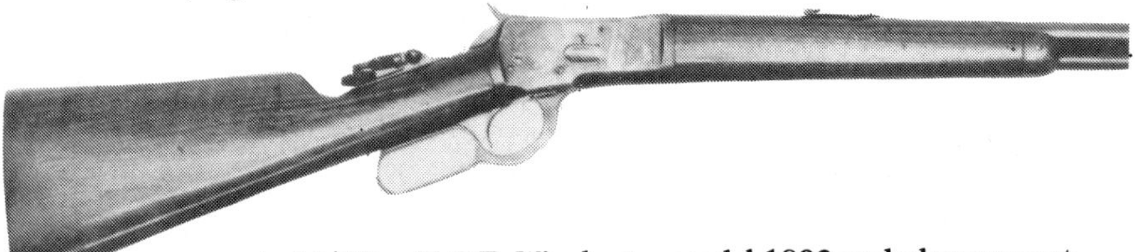

A .25/30in. W.C.F. Winchester model 1892 underlever repeating rifle, 41½in., barrel 24¼in., No. 400399, London proof, barrel with patent dates to 1884, walnut shotgun style stock with chequered steel buttplate. $410 £180

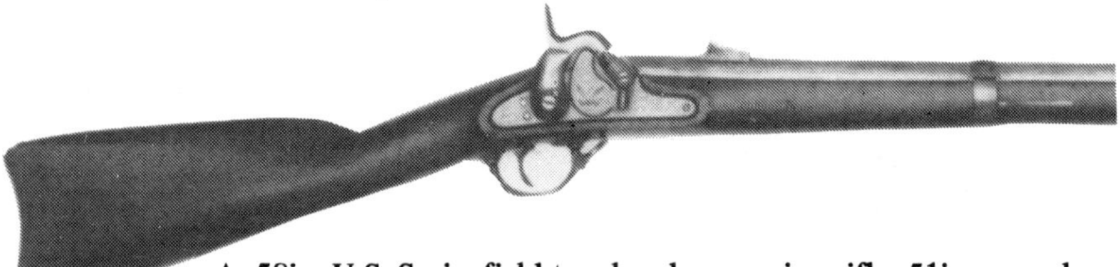

A .58in. U.S. Springfield two-band percussion rifle, 51in., round barrel 35in., dated 1858, regulation walnut full-stock with two iron mounts, including sling swivels, barrel with barleycorn foresight and two folding leaf rear, the lock dated 1860, incorporating Maynard's Patent tape primer. $412 £190

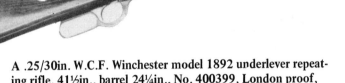

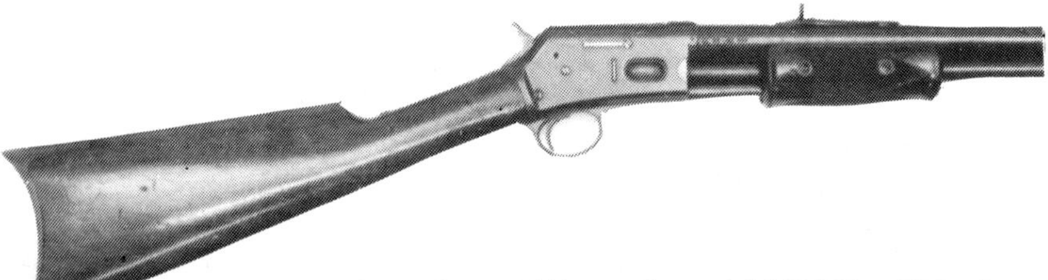

A fifteen-shot .44/40in. Colt model 1885 New Lightning pump action magazine rifle, 43in., round barrel 26in., No. 40515, barrel stamped with maker's name, address and patent dates to 'Feb. 22, 1887' also '44 Cal', walnut stock with heavy crescent buttplate. $462 £210

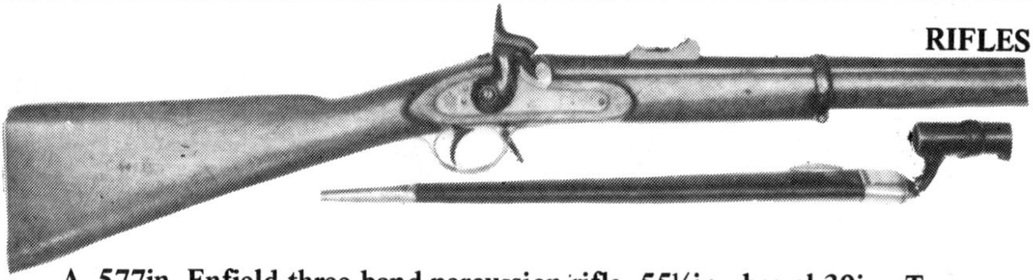

A .577in. Enfield three-band percussion rifle, 55½in., barrel 39in., Tower proved, ladder rearsight to 800 yards. Full-stocked, lock stamped with crowned 'VR' and '1859 Tower'. Regulation brass mounts. Stock struck with Pimlico Storekeeper's mark, dated 1860. Steel sling swivels. Together with its triangular socket bayonet. $462 £210

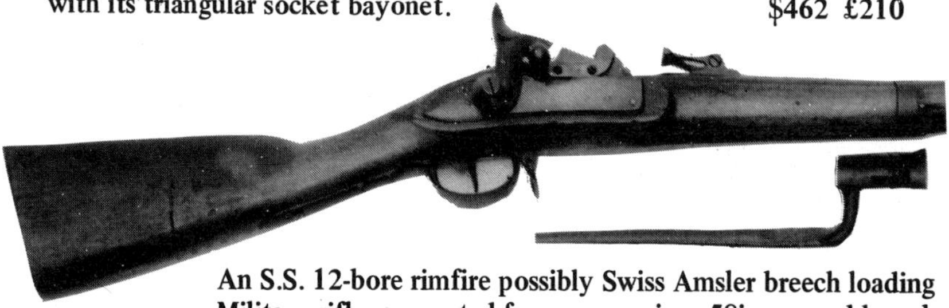

An S.S. 12-bore rimfire possibly Swiss Amsler breech loading Military rifle, converted from percussion, 58in., round barrel 40½in., No. 6997, regulation walnut full-stock with steel mounts, including buttcap, trigger guard, three barrel bands and sling swivels. Together with its triangular socket bayonet. $499 £230

A .36in. Edward Maynard's patent breech loading percussion marksman's rifle, No. 6408, 43in., heavy round rifled barrel 26in., with twin flip-up rearsights and twin flip-up foresights. Adjustable peephole ladder rearsight spring mounted on top-strap. $521 £240

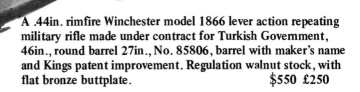

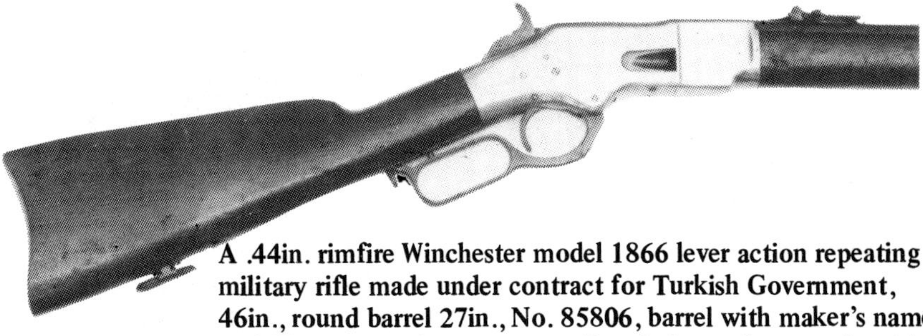

A .44in. rimfire Winchester model 1866 lever action repeating military rifle made under contract for Turkish Government, 46in., round barrel 27in., No. 85806, barrel with maker's name and Kings patent improvement. Regulation walnut stock, with flat bronze buttplate. $550 £250

A 32-bore Japanese percussion gun, signed Shige, lock made in imitation of a Jenks 'mule-ear', presumably soon after the visit of Captain Perry, 47½in., octagonal barrel 35¾in., integral block sights and swollen muzzle. Full-stocked in magnolia wood. Back-action percussion lock. Paddle-shaped butt, brass trigger and plate. $542 £250

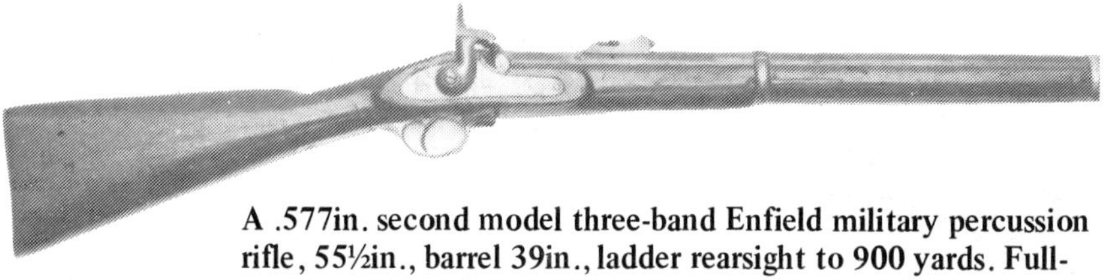

A .577in. second model three-band Enfield military percussion rifle, 55½in., barrel 39in., ladder rearsight to 900 yards. Full-stocked, Enfield lock, regulation brass mounts, buttcap tang. Steel barrel bands, retained by springs, steel sling swivels and ramrod. $615 £260

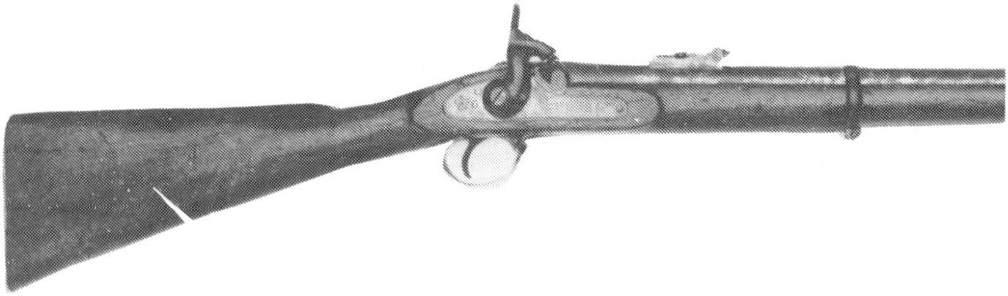

A .577in., 3rd model 1853 Enfield military percussion rifle, 55½in., barrel 39in., struck with bore size 25 and Birmingham proof marks, regulation walnut full-stock, brass buttplate and trigger guard with sling swivel, screw barrel bands, barleycorn foresight, ladder tangent rear to 900 yards. $621 £270

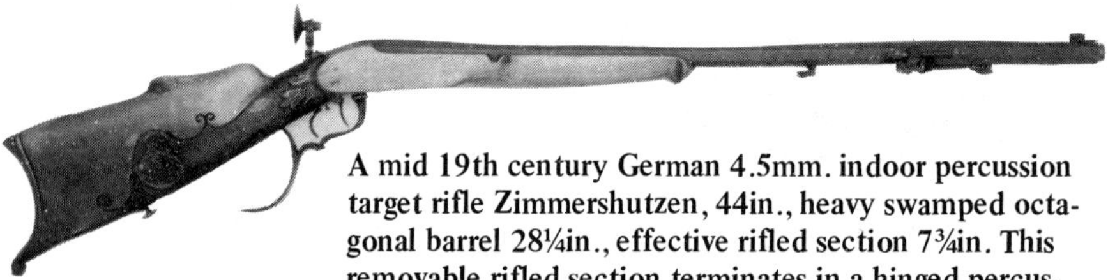

A mid 19th century German 4.5mm. indoor percussion target rifle Zimmershutzen, 44in., heavy swamped octagonal barrel 28¼in., effective rifled section 7¾in. This removable rifled section terminates in a hinged percussion nipple, the base of which accepts a fixed load of powder. $597 £275

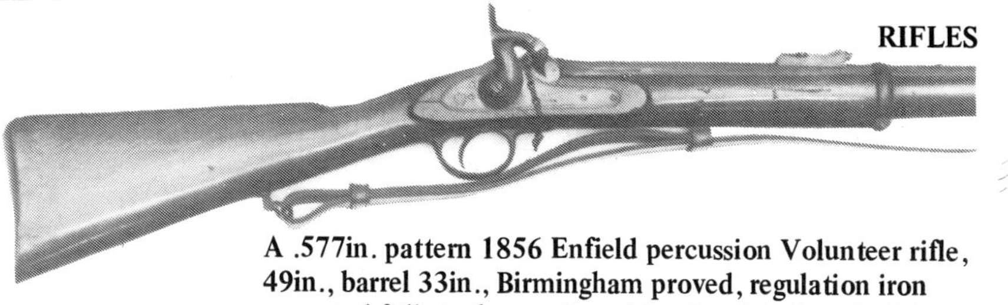

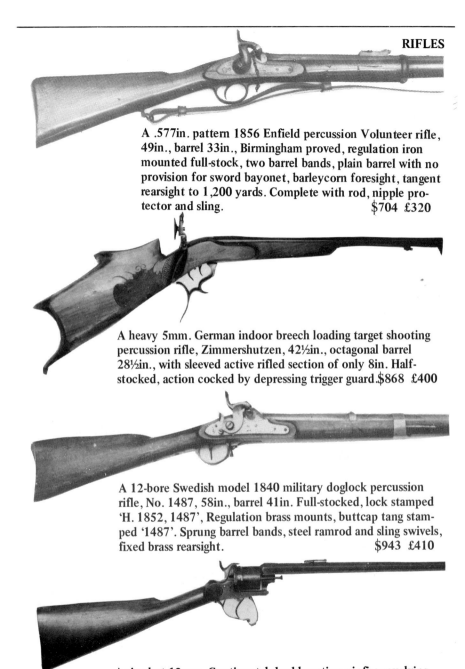

A .577in. pattern 1856 Enfield percussion Volunteer rifle, 49in., barrel 33in., Birmingham proved, regulation iron mounted full-stock, two barrel bands, plain barrel with no provision for sword bayonet, barleycorn foresight, tangent rearsight to 1,200 yards. Complete with rod, nipple protector and sling. $704 £320

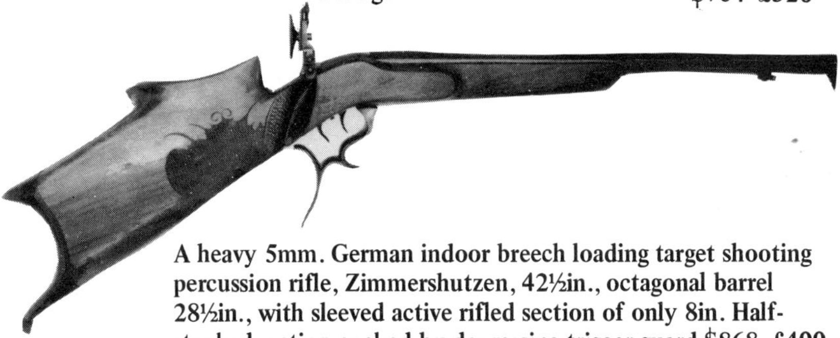

A heavy 5mm. German indoor breech loading target shooting percussion rifle, Zimmershutzen, 42½in., octagonal barrel 28½in., with sleeved active rifled section of only 8in. Half-stocked, action cocked by depressing trigger guard. $868 £400

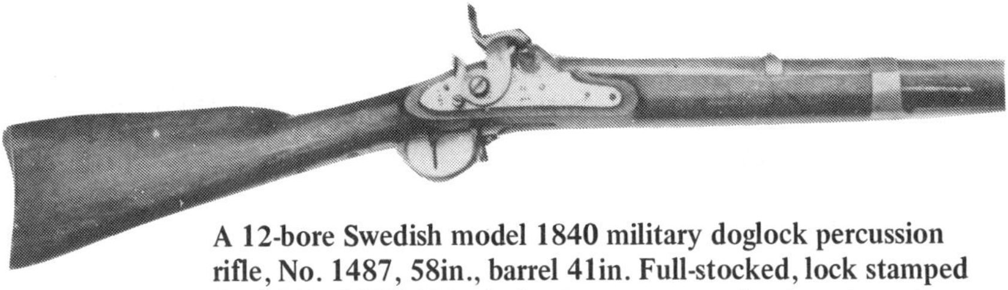

A 12-bore Swedish model 1840 military doglock percussion rifle, No. 1487, 58in., barrel 41in. Full-stocked, lock stamped 'H. 1852, 1487', Regulation brass mounts, buttcap tang stamped '1487'. Sprung barrel bands, steel ramrod and sling swivels, fixed brass rearsight. $943 £410

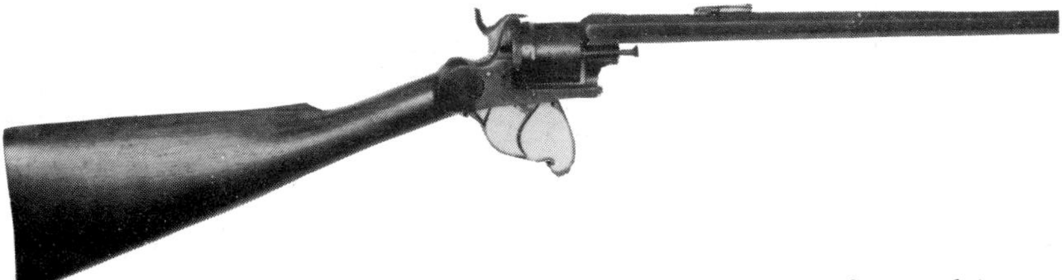

A six-shot 12mm. Continental double action pinfire revolving rifle, 41in., octagonal barrel 24¾in., Belgian proof marks. Walnut stock with steel buttplate and long wrist straps, scrolled trigger guard, gate loading and rod ejection. $976 £450

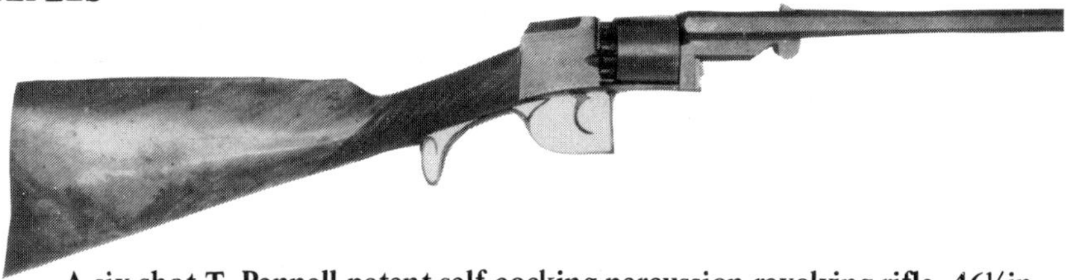

A six-shot T. Pennell patent self-cocking percussion revolving rifle, 46¼in., octagonal twist barrel 28¼in., Birmingham proved, barrel flat engraved 'F. Barnes & Co, London', chequered walnut stock, longspurred buttplate. Barrel with bead foresight and fixed and single folding leaf rear. $976 £450

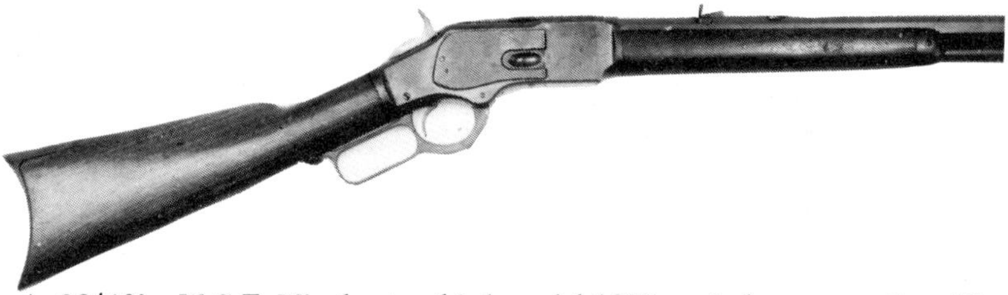

A .38/40in. W.C.F. Winchester third model 1873 underlever repeating rifle, 43¼in., octagonal barrel 24¼in., No. 262928B, polished walnut stock with heavy crescent buttplate complete with trap containing four-piece jointed cleaning rod, full length tube magazine under barrel. $976 £450

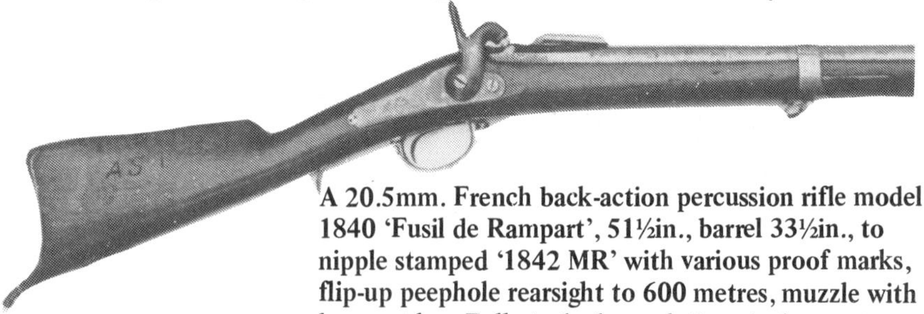

A 20.5mm. French back-action percussion rifle model 1840 'Fusil de Rampart', 51½in., barrel 33½in., to nipple stamped '1842 MR' with various proof marks, flip-up peephole rearsight to 600 metres, muzzle with bayonet lug. Full-stocked, regulation steel mounts. $1,150 £500

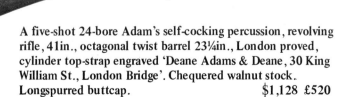

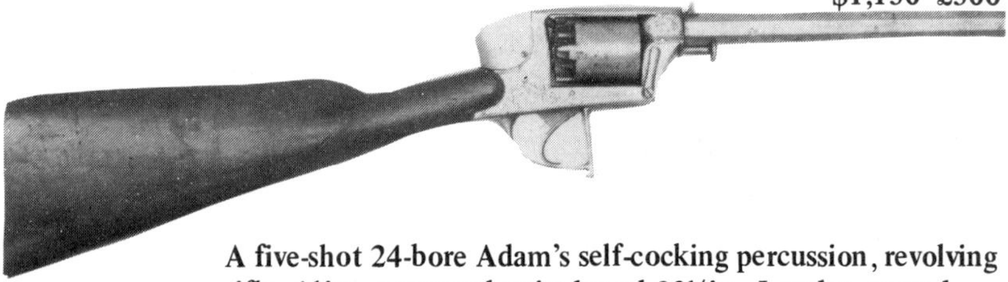

A five-shot 24-bore Adam's self-cocking percussion, revolving rifle, 41in., octagonal twist barrel 23¼in., London proved, cylinder top-strap engraved 'Deane Adams & Deane, 30 King William St., London Bridge'. Chequered walnut stock. Longspurred buttcap. $1,128 £520

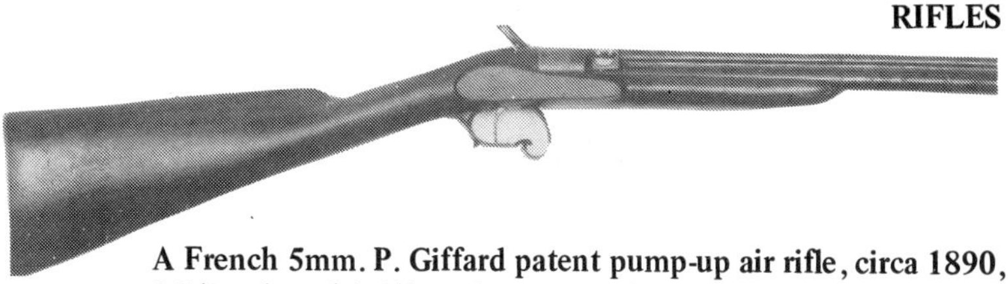

A French 5mm. P. Giffard patent pump-up air rifle, circa 1890, 36½in., barrel 19½in., above pump joined vertically by ribs. Boxlock action, exposed hammer spur. Steel furniture, walnut half-stock. $1,365 £525

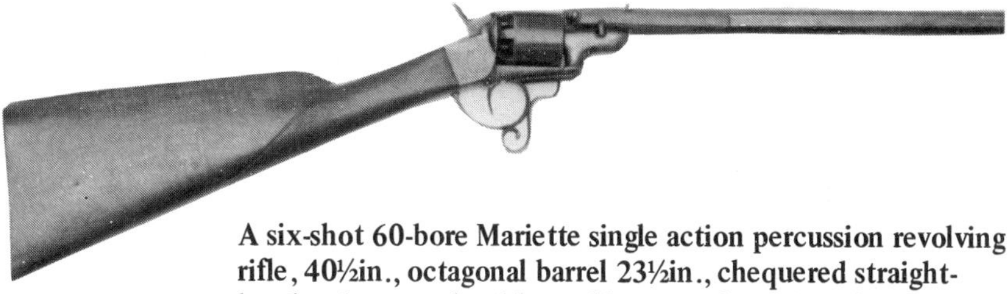

A six-shot 60-bore Mariette single action percussion revolving rifle, 40½in., octagonal barrel 23½in., chequered straight-hand walnut stock with steel longspur buttplate, border and scroll engraved action body top and bottom wrist straps. $1,302 £600

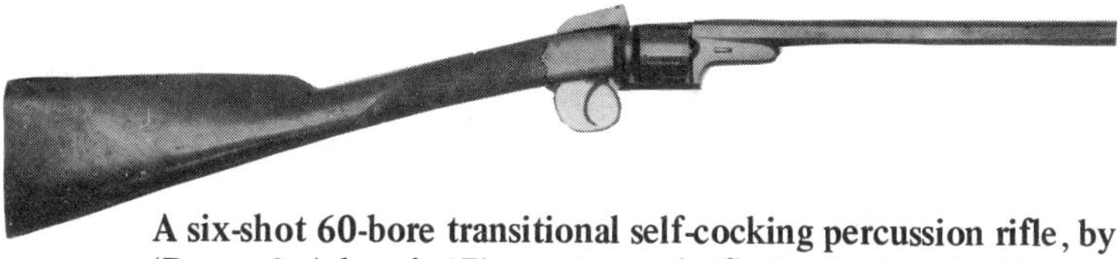

A six-shot 60-bore transitional self-cocking percussion rifle, by 'Deane & Adams', 47in., octagonal rifled twist barrel 27in., finely grained polished chequered walnut stock with border and scroll foliate engraved long tanged steel buttcap. $1,352 £650

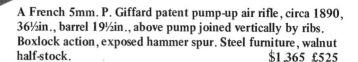

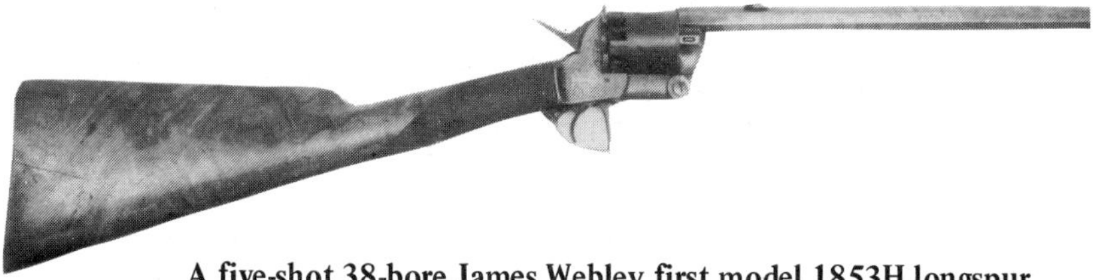

A five-shot 38-bore James Webley first model 1853H longspur single action revolving percussion rifle, 45½in., octagonal twist barrel 27¾in., Birmingham proved, top-strap engraved 'By Her Majesty's Royal Letters Patent', removable sideplate. $1,519 £700

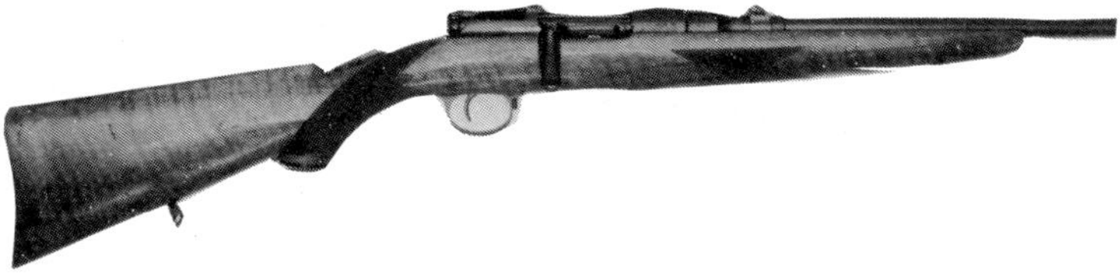

A five-shot 9.5mm. Mannlicher Schoenauer model 1910 take-down bolt action magazine sporting rifle, 45in., barrel 24in., No. 9893, figured walnut stock with cheekpiece, butt trap for jointed clearing rod and two cartridges, chequered pistol grip. $166 £80

A 12-bore double barrelled percussion sporting gun by 'William Moore & Co., London', circa 1835, 47in., twist barrels 30½in., half-stocked, border engraved steel furniture, long trigger guard and throatpipe finial. $338 £130

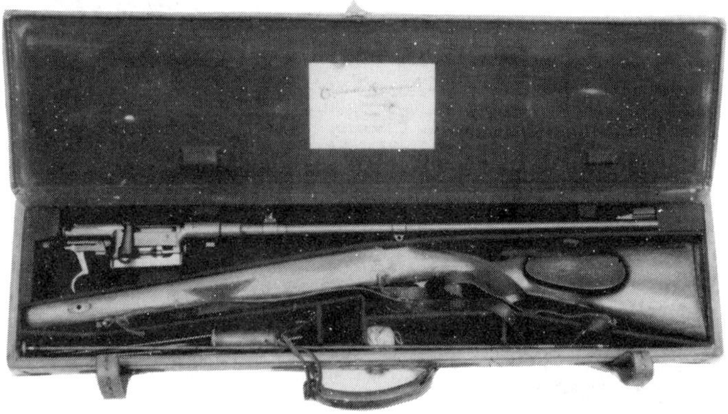

A five-shot 6.5mm. Mannlicher Schoenauer model 1903 bolt action repeating take-down sporting rifle, 43¾in., barrel 22½in., No. 20257, walnut chequered semi pistol grip stock with cheekpiece, butt trap and sling swivels, hooded foresight and single folding leaf rearsight. Contained in its green beize lined and fitted canvas covered motor case. $331 £145

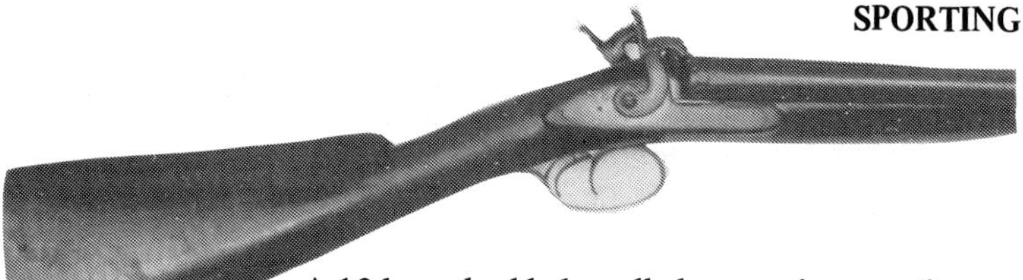

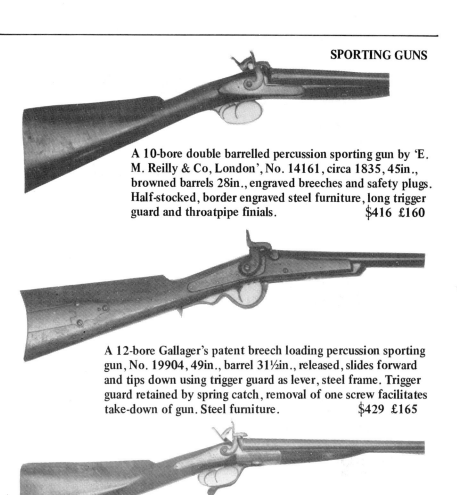

A 10-bore double barrelled percussion sporting gun by 'E. M. Reilly & Co, London', No. 14161, circa 1835, 45in., browned barrels 28in., engraved breeches and safety plugs. Half-stocked, border engraved steel furniture, long trigger guard and throatpipe finials. $416 £160

A 12-bore Gallager's patent breech loading percussion sporting gun, No. 19904, 49in., barrel 31½in., released, slides forward and tips down using trigger guard as lever, steel frame. Trigger guard retained by spring catch, removal of one screw facilitates take-down of gun. Steel furniture. $429 £165

A double barrelled 20-bore pinfire underlever opening hammer sporting gun, by 'W. Watson & Son', 43½in., browned twist barrels 28in., No. 5549, figured chequered walnut straight hand stock with steel buttplate and blank white metal escutcheon. $418 £190

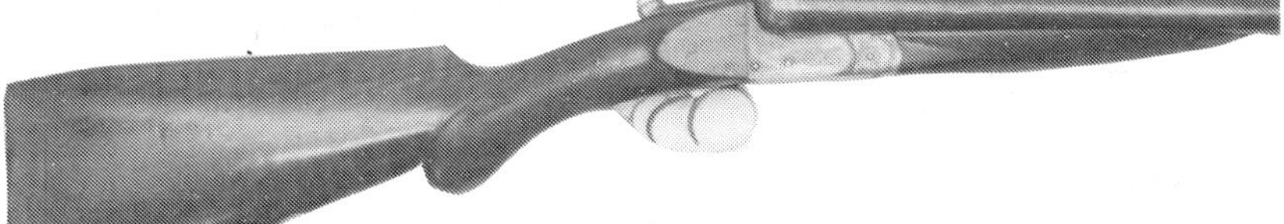

A double barrelled 12-bore x 2½in., top lever opening boxlock hammerless non-ejector sporting gun, by 'W. & C. Scott & Son', 47in., barrels 30in., No. 78728. Chequered semi pistol grip walnut stock with short butt extension. $450 £205

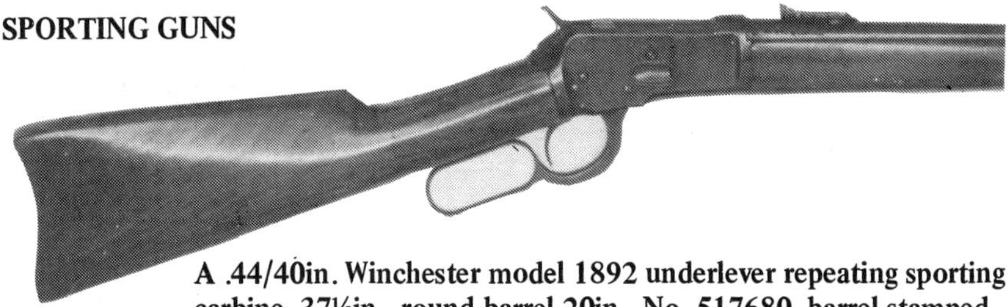

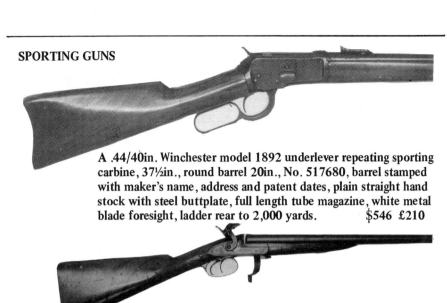

A .44/40in. Winchester model 1892 underlever repeating sporting carbine, 37½in., round barrel 20in., No. 517680, barrel stamped with maker's name, address and patent dates, plain straight hand stock with steel buttplate, full length tube magazine, white metal blade foresight, ladder rear to 2,000 yards. $546 £210

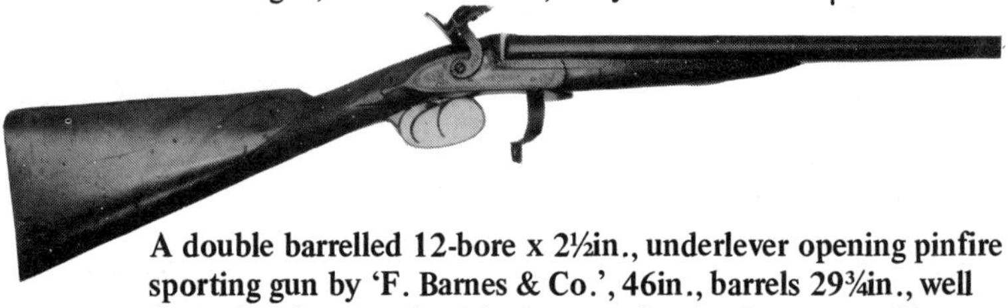

A double barrelled 12-bore x 2½in., underlever opening pinfire sporting gun by 'F. Barnes & Co.', 46in., barrels 29¾in., well figured walnut stock with chequered wrist, longspurred butt-plate and blank escutcheon, chequered fore-end. $477 £215

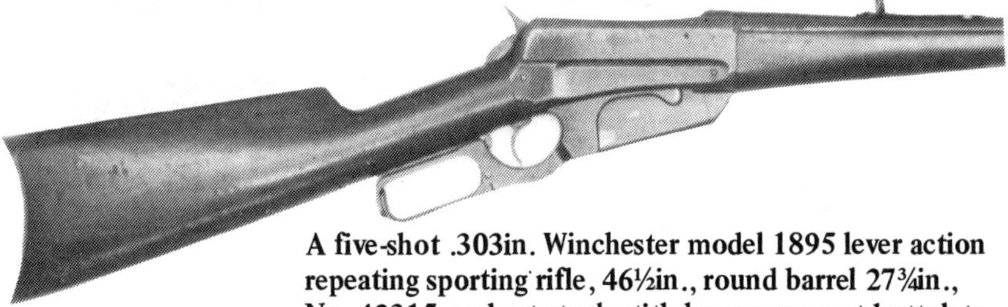

A five-shot .303in. Winchester model 1895 lever action repeating sporting rifle, 46½in., round barrel 27¾in., No. 42315, walnut stock with heavy crescent buttplate, plain walnut fore-end with small horn inlay at tip, heavy action with box magazine. $484 £220

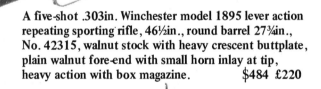

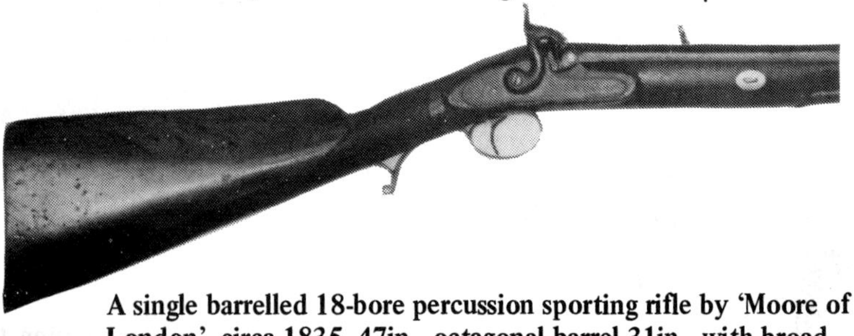

A single barrelled 18-bore percussion sporting rifle by 'Moore of London', circa 1835, 47in., octagonal barrel 31in., with broad four groove rifling. Half-stocked, lock engraved 'Moore', steel furniture, pineapple finialled trigger guard with star burst engraved finger scroll. $585 £225

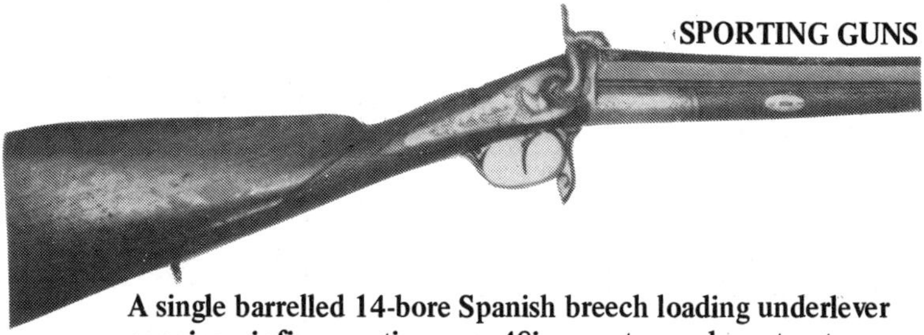

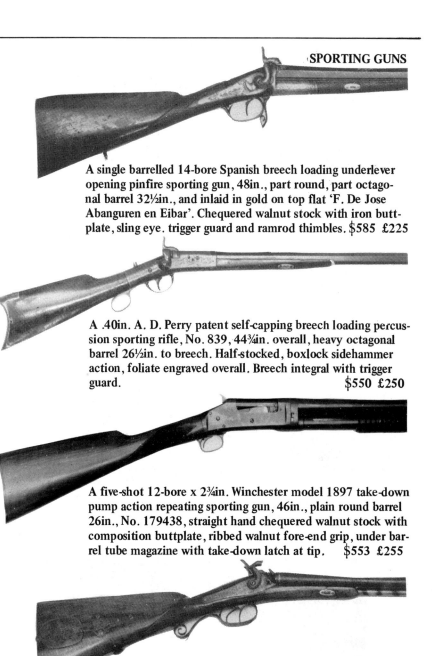

A single barrelled 14-bore Spanish breech loading underlever opening pinfire sporting gun, 48in., part round, part octagonal barrel 32½in., and inlaid in gold on top flat 'F. De Jose Abanguren en Eibar'. Chequered walnut stock with iron buttplate, sling eye. trigger guard and ramrod thimbles. $585 £225

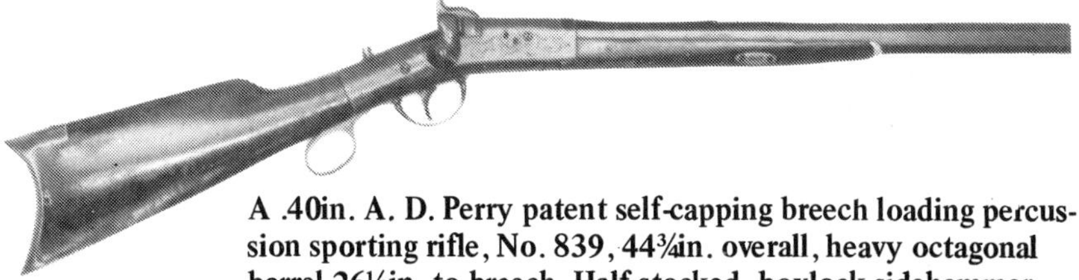

A .40in. A. D. Perry patent self-capping breech loading percussion sporting rifle, No. 839, 44¾in. overall, heavy octagonal barrel 26½in. to breech. Half-stocked, boxlock sidehammer action, foliate engraved overall. Breech integral with trigger guard. $550 £250

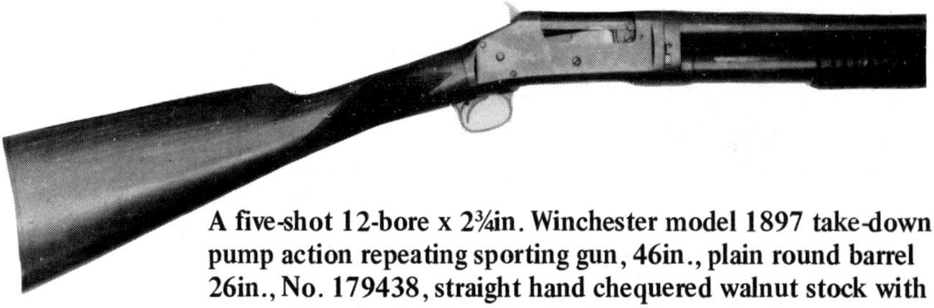

A five-shot 12-bore x 2¾in. Winchester model 1897 take-down pump action repeating sporting gun, 46in., plain round barrel 26in., No. 179438, straight hand chequered walnut stock with composition buttplate, ribbed walnut fore-end grip, under barrel tube magazine with take-down latch at tip. $553 £255

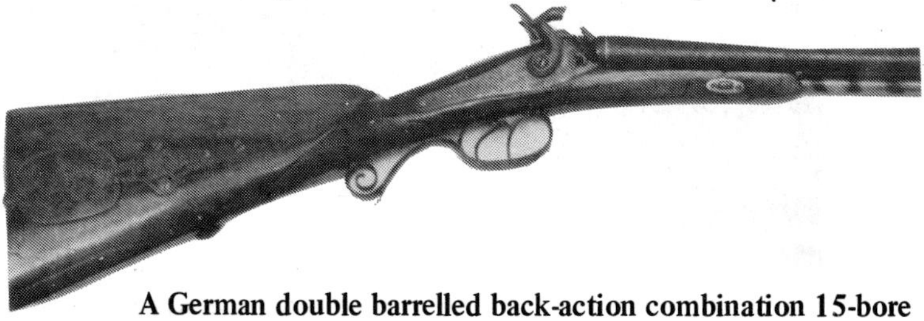

A German double barrelled back-action combination 15-bore percussion sporting gun and 18-bore percussion sporting rifle by 'Christoph Funk of Suhl', No. 13253, 43in., barrels 26in. to twin silver inlaid breech lines. Half-stocked. $1,040 £400

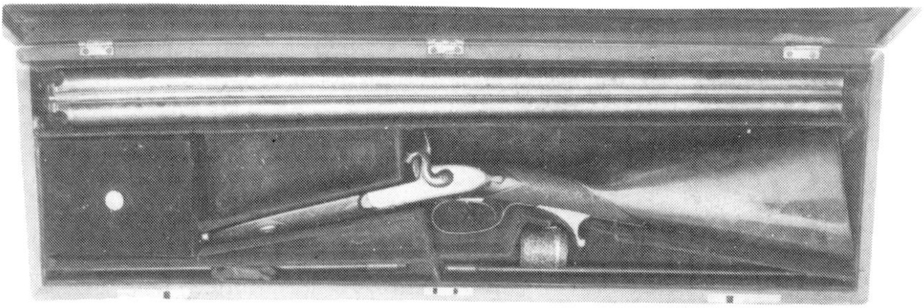

An 8-bore double barrelled percussion sporting gun by 'Charles Lancaster', No. 2095, 47¾in., twist barrels 30¾in. Half-stocked, foliate engraved steel furniture. In its brass bound blue velvet lined mahogany case. $995 £420

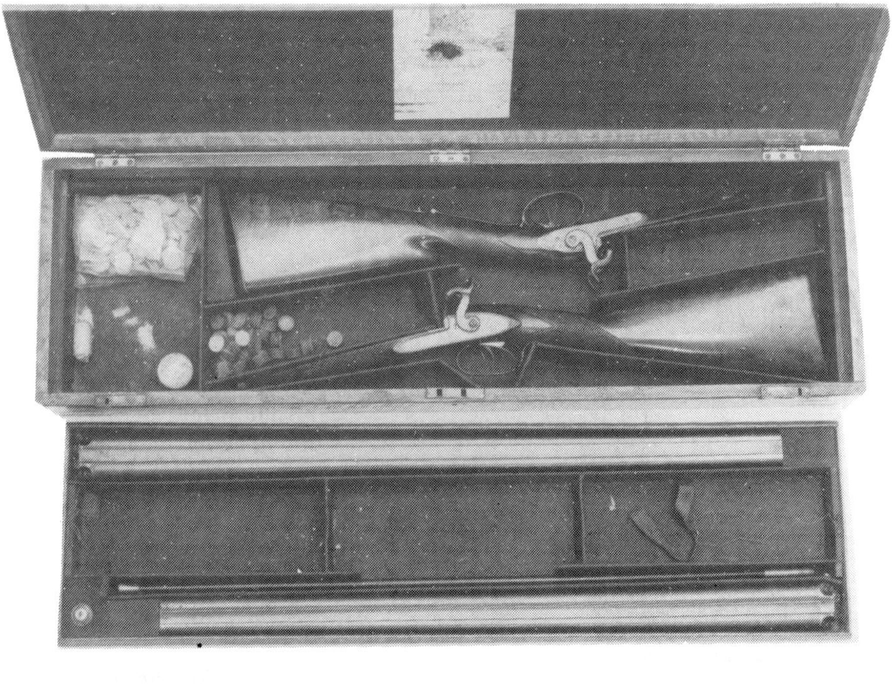

A composed pair of double barrelled 12-bore percussion sporting guns by 'Westley Richards', gun No. 3722, 44½in., browned twist barrels. Gun No. 7745, 46½in., browned twist barrels 26½in., contained in their two-tier brass bound fitted oak case. $1,040 £440

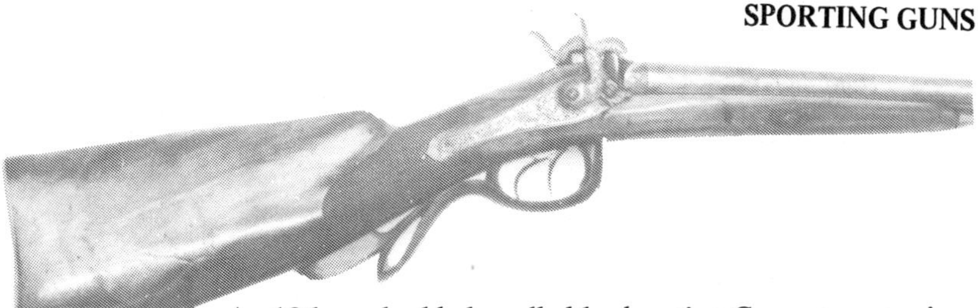

An 18-bore double barrelled back-action German percussion sporting gun by 'E. M. Sick of Gunzburg', circa 1850, 48in., twist barrels 32in. Half-stocked, steel buttcap tang, trigger guard and throatpipe finials. Hinged safety catches at front of locks. $990 £450

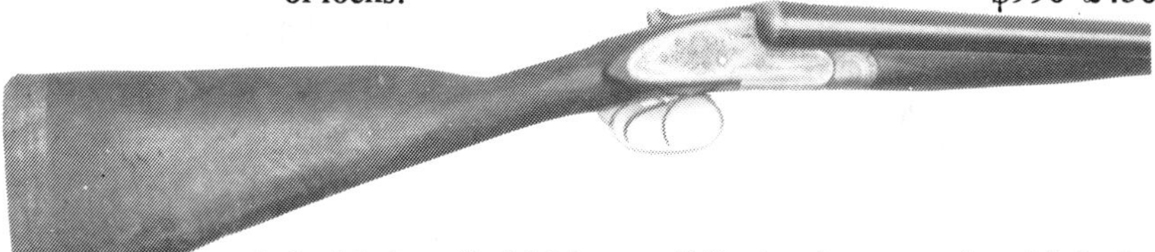

A double barrelled 12-bore x 2½in. top lever opening side-lock ejector sporting gun made for the London Sporting Park Ltd., 45¾in., barrels 28in., No. B92, finely figured chequered walnut stock with engraved gold escutcheon and butt extension. $1,100 £500

A double barrelled 12-bore x 2¾in. top lever opening boxlock ejector sporting gun by 'E. J. Churchill Ltd.', 45in., barrels 28in., No. 7006, chequered straight hand walnut stock and Anson fore-end, narrow elevated matted barrel rib, auto safety. $1,193 £550

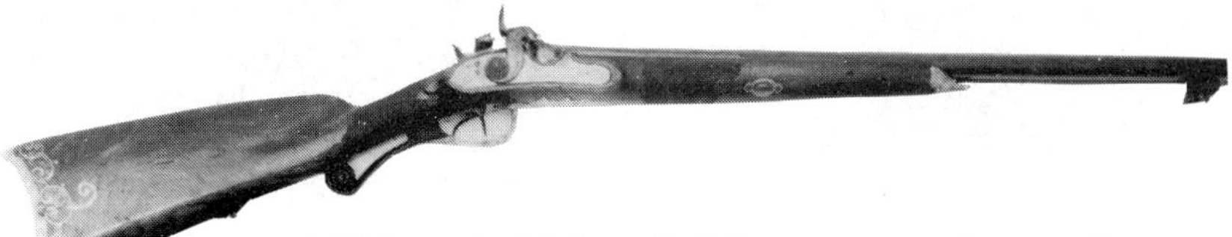

A 22-bore double barrelled German percussion sporting gun by 'G. Sturm & Sohn of Solingen', circa 1790, probably converted from flintlock, 50in., browned barrels 33½in., gold inlaid 'Fabrik in Suhl' with gold foliage, silver foresight. Half-stocked, German silver furniture. $1,248 £575

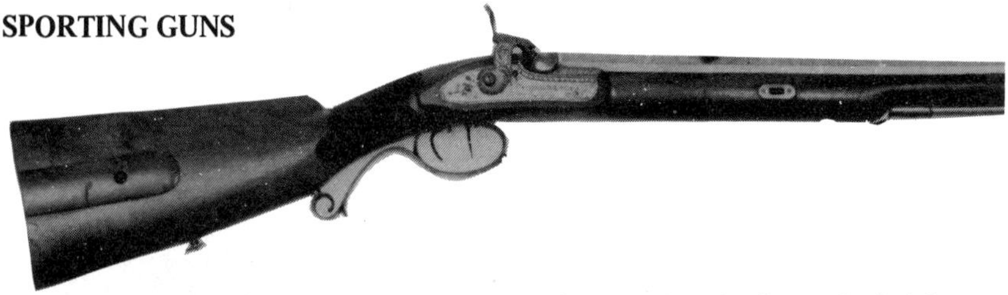

A 25-bore German percussion sporting rifle by 'Ulbrich of Dresden', 46in., heavy octagonal deeply rifled barrel 30in., twin gold lines inlaid at foliate engraved breech, fixed sights, engraved muzzle. Full-stocked, gold safety plug, dolphin hammer. Micro-adjustable double set triggers. $1,356 £625

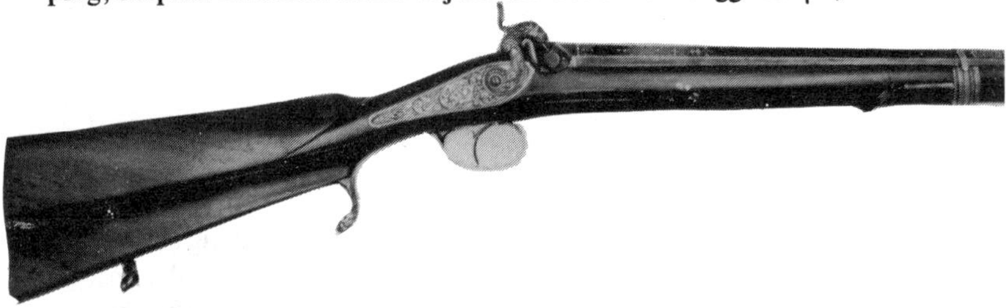

A 14-bore Spanish percussion sporting gun, 50¼in., part octagonal, part round browned twist barrel 35in., inlaid 'Leandro Candano' in gold amid scrolls and geometric designs, plain walnut Madrid style stock with steel half buttplate, polished steel trigger with heavy finger spur. $1,232 £750

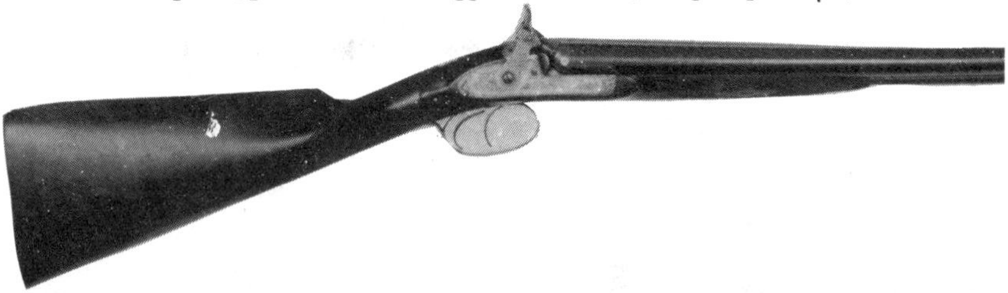

A double barrelled 12-bore percussion sporting gun by 'W. & C. Scott', No. 7390, 46½in., browned twist damascus barrels 30in. Half-stocked, foliate engraved locks with 'W. & C. Scott & Son', detachable hammer noses. Foliate engraved silver breech reinforce plates. Contained in its green beize lined fitted brass bound mahogany case. $1,627 £750

A 16-bore double barrelled Lefaucheux patent breech loading back-action percussion sporting gun by 'N. M. Lesoinne et Pirlot of Liege' 47½in., browned twist barrels 31½in., gold inlaid on top rib 'Invon Lefaucheux Bte A Paris'. Underlever opening drops barrels down for loading. Dolphin hammers and steel furniture. $1,976 £760

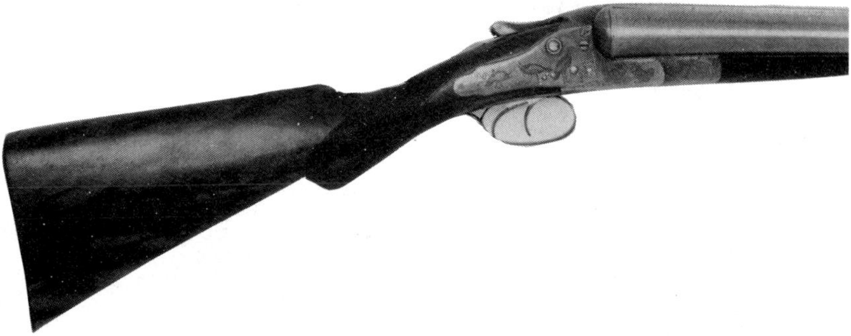

A double barrelled 10-bore x 2¾in. top lever opening, sidelock, non-ejector sporting gun by 'W. & C. Scott & Son', 46¾in., three blade damascus barrels 30 3/16in., No. 33618, recent London Nitro proof. Chequered semi pistol grip walnut stock with horn buttplate and blank gold shield escutcheon at wrist. The browned barrels with elevated rib terminating in doll's head extension to provide third action bite, auto safety, back-action side locks. $1,899 £875

INDEX